*This Dictionary Belongs To*

_Paolo_

We want to thank the individuals who made contributions to this dictionary by sending in their suggestions and comments. They made this edition better than the last one.

Darian Afkhami, M. Ansari, Dr. Richard Barshinger, John Beiter, Gael E. Bohannon, Caroline Brost, Dahmen Brown, David Carr, Nick Cowie, Laurie David, Stanley Dixon, Sergey M. Szekunov, Ph.D., Evan Eckersley, Phil Ferrara, Ryan Fiorillo, Mary Gallagher, Ali Gelineau, Stella Guenther, Chris Hope, Elizabeth Jewell, Arman Kandarian, Timothy Knigth, Ruth Kent, Mary Lavarnway, Ann Macaluso, Kaitlin MacAulay, Phyllis Makinster, Richard McArthur, Larry Margolis, Claude and Isaac Mertzenich, Colista Moore, Joan Morgan, Constance Mote, Mark Nabb, Wanda Parker, Judith Pendleton, Lianna Prill, Sasha Sagan, Storrs Warinner, Turdie Weiden, Don White, Dorothy Willard and Betty Williford, Cynthia Xia.

We are grateful for your ideas and contributions. Please write to us, to let us know what you would like to see in the next edition of the dictionary.

www.TheDictionaryProject.com

Cover designed by Jason Fletcher

*We want to thank NASA for providing the image of the earth on the cover.*

# A STUDENT'S DICTIONARY
## & Gazetteer, 11th edition

# Table of Contents

ABCDEFGHIJKLMNOPQRSTUVWXYZ

It is truly amazing that out of twenty-six letters there can be thousands of combinations of letters to make up the words in our vocabulary.

This little dictionary touches on between 32,000 and 33,000 of the most commonly used words.

Words have power and can govern our lives. Whether talking to a friend or a family member, making a speech, or in the world of business, it is to your advantage to have a storehouse of words to convey your thoughts to whoever is listening. It builds strong self-confidence.

As you carry this book with you through your school years and use it, your vocabulary will grow along with you. New technical words and phrases will be abreast of the times, but the basics will live on to be uttered by you and upcoming generations.

This dictionary is given to you with best wishes for a word-endowed future.

Colista Moore
Rogue River, OR

Aa Bb Cc Dd Ee Ff Gg Hh Ii Jj Kk
Ll Mm Nn Oo Pp Qq Rr Ss Tt Uu
Vv Ww Xx Yy Zz

# NINE PARTS OF SPEECH

Three little words you often see,
Are Articles – *a, an,* and *the.*
A Noun's the name of anything,
As *school*, or *garden*, *hoop,* or *swing*.
Adjectives tell the kind of Noun,
As *great, small, pretty, white,* or *brown*.
Instead of Nouns the Pronouns stand-
*Her* head, *his* face, *your* arm, *my* hand.
Verbs tell of something to be done –
To *read*, *count*, *sing, laugh, jump*, or *run*.
How things are done, the Adverbs tell,
As *slowly, quickly, ill,* or *well*.
Conjunctions join the words together
As man *and* woman, wind *or* weather.
The Preposition stands before
A noun, as *in*, or *through* a door.
The Interjection shows surprise,
As *oh!* How pretty – *ah*! How wise.
The whole are called Nine Parts of Speech,
Which reading, writing, speaking teach.

*Dr. Chase , 1867*

# Punctuation

*Punctuation marks and pauses are used to separate written or printed information into sentences and parts of sentences to assist the reader in understanding the meaning of the writer.*

A **Period** (.) is placed at the end of a sentence; as,
> *I admit I made a mistake.*
> Or is used after an abbreviation; as
> *Dr. Johnson      Jan. 1, 2004*

A **question mark** (?) indicates a question; as
> *What is your opinion?*

An **Exclamation Point** (!) denotes humor or strong feeling; as,
> *Facing it—always facing it – that's the way to get through it.*
> *Face it!* Joseph Conrad, 1924

The **Comma** (,), **Semicolon** (;), and **Colon** (:) mark grammatical division in a sentence; as,
> *There are three genders: feminine, masculine, and neuter; in language they are referred to as she, he, and it, respectively.*

A **comma** is used to list items in a series. The **colon** may separate two clauses when the second explains the first, and is also used before an explanatory list.The **semicolon** is used to separate two independent clauses when there is no conjunction.  Sometimes it is called a weak period.

A **Hyphen** (-) is used between syllables in a word divided at the end of a line; as,
> *knowl-edge      pow-er*
> And between the parts of a compound word, as
> *self-improvement    absent-minded*

4

The **Dash** (--) is used where there is a sudden break or pause in a sentence; as,

*Individual commitment to a group effort-- that is what makes a team work, a company work, a society work, a civilization work.*
Vince Lombardi, 1970


**Quotation marks** (" ") denote the words of another; as

*"My name is Margalo," said the little bird softly in a musical voice. "I come from fields once tall with wheat, from pastures deep in fern and thistle; I come from vales of meadow-sweet, and I love to whistle."* Stuart Little, E.B. White, 1985


An **apostrophe** (') denotes that a letter or letters are left out; as,

*I'd be better off if I had gone to school longer, and so will you.*
Joe Louis

And is also used to show ownership; as

*There are spaces between our fingers so that another person's fingers can fill them in.* Anonymous


## *Pronunciation Key*

| | | | | | | | |
|---|---|---|---|---|---|---|---|
| a̧, | for | ŏ, | as in | want | y̆, | for ĭ, as in | chlorophyll |
| ê, | " | â, | " | tear | e, | " k, " | character |
| ȩ, | " | ā, | " | eight | ç, | " s, " | city |
| ï, | " | ê, | " | police | çh, | " sh, " | chivalry |
| ĩ, | " | ẽ, | " | sir | eh, | " k, " | chorus |
| ô, | " | ŭ, | " | ton | ġ, | " j, " | general |
| o̧, | " | ōō, | " | do | n̞, | " ng, " | sang |
| o̧, | " | ŏŏ, | " | book | s̞, | " z, " | hands |
| ô̧. | ". | a̧, | " | pork | s, | " sh, " | sure |
| õ, | " | û, | " | worm | x, | " g̃z, " | example |
| u, | " | ŏŏ, | " | pull | gh, | " f, " | laugh |
| u̧, | " | ōō, | " | rule | ph, | " f, " | phone |
| y̆, | " | ĭ, | " | try | qu, | " k. " | plaque |
| | | | | **qu, for kw, as in** | | quiet | |

5

# Guide to the Dictionary

| | |
|---|---|
| **entry word** | **re-spect** [rĭ-spĕkt′] *noun*, 1) an aspect 2) consideration for someone, *verb*, 3) to have a good opinion of someone, to look up to, to hold in esteem |
| **spelling** | **cour-te-ous** [kûr′tē-əs] *adjective*, showing good manners, polite |
| **meaning** | **com-pas-sion** [kəm-păsh′ən] *noun*, kindness, tenderness, pity, sympathy for suffering |
| **more than one meaning** | **char-ac-ter** [kăr′ək-tər] *noun* 1) the moral makeup of a person 2) a person in a book or movie or play 3) a symbol, sign, or written letter used in a language |
| **part of speech** | **hon-or** [ŏn′ər] *noun*, 1) fame or a rank of high esteem, *verb*, 2) to hold in high respect 3) to keep an agreement |
| **no plural** | **cour-age** [kûr′ĭj] *noun*, *no plural*, the strength to face danger when overwhelmed by fear |
| **guide words** | **persevere**          **phrase** |
| | **per-se-vere** [pûr′sə-vîr′] *verb*, to work to accomplish a goal despite difficulty |
| | **per-sist** [pər-sĭst′] *verb*, to keep doing something, to persevere |
| | **phrase** [frāz] *noun*, 1) a part of a sentence 2) an expression, a saying, *verb*, 3) to express in words or a particular way |
| **syllabic pronunciation** | **in-teg-ri-ty** [ĭn-tĕg′rĭ-tē] *noun*, honesty, uprighteousness |
| **phonetic spelling** | **in-spire** [ĭn-spīr′] *verb*, to stimulate to think and to act, to influence |

6

a [ā] *article*, used to indicate one before a noun

**a-ba-cus** [ăb′ə-kəs] *noun*, a frame holding parallel rods with beads, used for doing arithmetic

**ab-a-lo-ne** [ăb′ə-lō′nē] *noun*, a shell sea mollusk animal whose shell is lined with mother-of-pearl

**a-ban-don** [ə-băn′dən] *verb*, to leave or give up completely, to walk away from

**a-bate** [ə-bāt′] *verb*, to gradually become less in amount or degree

**ab-bre-vi-ate** [ə-brē′vē-āt′] *verb*, to shorten, to cut down, to contract

**ab-di-cation** [ăb′dĭ-kā-shŭn] *noun*, a surrender, abandonment

**ab-do-men** [ăb′də-mən] *noun*, the digestive system in the body, belly

**ab-duct** [ăb-dŭkt′] *verb*, to kidnap

**ab-er-ra-tion** [ăb′ə-rā′shən] *noun*, a departure from what is right, correct or natural

**a-bet** [ə-bĕt′] *verb*, to encourage or assist, especially in wrongdoing

**ab-hor** [ăb-hôr′] *verb*, to withdraw in disgust or horror

**a-bide** [ə-bīd′] *verb,* 1) to put up with, tolerate 2) to wait patiently for 3) to withstand

**a-bil-i-ty** [ə-bĭl′ĭ-tē] *noun*, 1) capability, power or knowledge 2) skill, expertise

**a-ble** [ā′bəl] *adjective*, having the strength or knowledge to do something

**ab-nor-mal** [ăb-nôr′məl] *adjective*, irregular, unusual, peculiar

**a-board** [ə-bôrd′] *preposition*, on, in, upon (a ship)

**a-bode** [ə-bōd′] *noun*, home; a place of residence; a habitation

**a-bol-ish** [ə-bŏl′ĭsh] *verb*, to do away with entirely

**ab-o-li-tion** [ăb′ə-lĭsh′ən] *noun*, complete destruction

**a-bom-i-na-ble** [ə-bŏm′ə-nə-bəl] *adjective*, detestable, odious

**ab-o-rig-i-ne** [ăb′ə-rĭj′ə-nē] *noun*, a primitive native

**a-bor-tive** [ə-bôr′tĭv] *adjective*, unsuccessful, fruitless, unfinished

**a-bound** [ə-bound′] *verb*, to overflow, to prevail, to exist in large numbers

**a-bout** [ə-bout′] *adverb*, 1) concerning 2) approximately 3) here or there, everywhere

**a-bove** [ə-bŭv′] *adverb*, 1) at a higher level, *preposition*, 2) over, in a higher place

**a-bra-sion** [ə-brā′zhən] *noun*, a wearing away or rubbing that causes scratches

**a-bridge** [ə-brĭj′] *verb*, to shorten by using fewer words

**a-bridg-ment** [ə-brĭj′mənt] *noun*, abbreviation, shortening

**a-broad** [ə-brôd′] *adverb*, in a foreign country, overseas

**ab-rupt** [ə-brŭpt′] *adjective*, happening without warning, suddenly

**ab-scess** [ăb′sĕs′] *noun*, an accumulation of pus due to an infection from bacteria

7

**ab-sence** [ăb′səns] *noun*, 1)the state of being away from someplace or someone 2) lack

**ab-sent** [ăb′sənt] *adjective*, missing, not present, unavailable

**ab-sent-mind-ed** [ăb′səntmīn′dĭd] *adjective*, forgetful, not paying attention

**ab-so-lute** [ăb′sə-lōōt′] *adjective*, complete, perfect, total

**ab-solve** [əb-zŏlv′, -sŏlv′] *verb*, to pardon, to forgive

**ab-sorb** [əb-sôrb′, -zôrb′] *verb*, 1) to soak up a fluid or moisture 2) to hold someone's attention 3) to dissolve a debt completely and accept the loss 4) to assimilate information

**ab-sorb-ent** [əb-sôr′bənt] *adjective*, absorbing moisture, fluid or light rays

**ab-stain** [ăb-stān′] *verb*, to deliberately avoid doing something

**ab-sti-nence** [ăb′stə-nəns] *noun*, the act of depriving oneself of some indulgence, voluntary denial

**ab-stract** [ăb-străkt′] *adjective*, difficult to describe or qualify

**ab-surd** [əb-sûrd′, -zûrd′] *adjective*, outrageous, silly, untrue

**ab-surd-i-ty** [əb-sûrd′ĭt ē] *noun*, that which is ridiculous or unreasonable

**a-bun-dance** [ə-bŭn′dəns] *noun*, large quantity, plenty

**a-bun-dant** [ə-bŭn′dənt] *adjective*, plentiful, more than enough

**a-buse** [ə-byōō′s] *noun*, 1) hurtful treatment, *verb*[ə-byōōz′], 2) to hurt someone or something intentionally

**a-bu-sive** [ə-byōō′sĭv, -zĭv] *adjective*, using insulting words or bad treatment

**a-but** [ə-bŭt′] *verb*, to border upon, to be next to or touching

**a-bys-mal** [ə-bĭz′məl] *adjective*, 1) immeasurably bad 2) bottomless

**a-byss** [ə-bĭs′] *noun*, a very deep crack in the earth, a bottomless gulf, a deep chasm

**ac-a-dem-ic** [ăk′ə-dĕm′ĭk] *adjective*, 1) of or relating to an education in the arts 2) having no practical importance

**a-cad-e-my** [ə-kăd′ə-mē] *noun*, a school offering specialized training and education

**ac-cel-er-a-tion** [ăk-sĕl′ə-rā′shən] *noun*, an increase in the speed of something

**ac-cent** [ăk′sĕnt′] *noun*, 1) the sound and tone of a foreign language, *verb*, 2) to emphasize a sound or letter when pronouncing a word 3) to emphasize something

**ac-cept** [ăk-sĕpt′] *verb*, 1) to agree with 2) to receive

**ac-cep-tance** [ăk-sĕp′təns] *noun*, the act of receiving something graciously

**ac-cess** [ăk′sĕs] *noun*, a way to get to a person, place, or thing

**ac-ces-si-ble** [ăk-sĕs′ə-bəl] *adjective*, easy to reach or use, approachable

**ac-ces-so-ry** [ăk-sĕs′ə-rē] *noun*, 1) an accomplice, connected as a subordinate 2) an article or decoration worn to complete an outfit, such as a belt, scarf, hat, etc.

**ac-ci-dent** [ăk′sĭ-dənt] *noun*, 1) an incident involving bodily injury or death 2) a mistake

**ac-claim** [ə-klām′] *verb*, to applaud, to announce with great approval

**ac-cli-mate** [ə-klī′mĭt] *verb*, to change or adjust to a different temperature or environment

**ac-com-mo-date** [ə-kŏm′ə-dāt′] *verb* 1) to adapt or make fit 2) to do a favor 3) to provide lodging

**ac-com-mo-da-tion** [ə-kŏm′ə-dā′shən] *noun*, an adaptation, an adjustment made to assist someone

**ac-com-pa-ny** [ə-kŭm′pə-nē] *verb*, to go with, to join

**ac-com-plice** [ə-kŏm′plĭs] *noun*, someone who goes along with something, usually something wrong

**ac-com-plish** [ə-kŏm′plĭsh] *verb*, to finish, to complete a task or reach a goal

**ac-com-plish-ment** [ə-kŏm′plĭsh-mənt] *noun*, something done, a goal that has been reached, a finished task

**ac-cord** [ə-kôrd′] *noun*, 1) mutual agreement, *verb*, 2) to be in harmony, to conform

**ac-cor-di-on** [ə-kôr′dē-ən] *noun*, a musical instrument that is played by fingering a keyboard on one side and squeezing bellows in and out on the other side

**ac-cost** [ə-kôst′] *verb*, to approach abruptly and speak to first

**ac-count** [ə-kount′] *noun*, 1) an explanation, a statement of money or inventory, *verb*, 2) to give a reason, to explain

**ac-crue** [ə-krōō′] *verb*, to be added on to, to increase

**ac-cu-mu-late** [ə-kyōōm′yə-lāt′] *verb*, to collect, to amass

**ac-cu-mu-la-tion** [ə-kyōōm′yə-lā′shən] *noun*, gathering a quantity of something

**ac-cu-ra-cy** [ăk′yər-ə-sē] *noun*, exactness, correctness, precision

**ac-cu-rate** [ăk′yər-ĭt] *adjective*, having no mistakes

**ac-cu-sa-tion** [ăk′yōō-zā′shən] *noun*, a claim that someone has done something wrong

**ac-cuse** [ə-kyōōz′] *verb*, to say someone has committed an offense or crime

**ac-cus-tom** [ə-kŭs′təm] *verb*, to become familiar with something through use or habit

**ace** [ās] *noun*, 1) a playing card 2) a fighter pilot who was shot down

**ache** [āk] *noun*, 1) a painful or sore spot, *verb*, 2) to hurt, to feel pain

**a-chieve** [ə-chēv′] *verb*, to do what one sets out to do

**a-chieve-ment** [ə-chēv′mənt] *noun*, something that a person has done to reach a goal

**ac-id** [ăs′ĭd] *noun*, a chemical substance soluble in water, sour in taste, that reddens litmus paper

**ac-knowl-edge** [ăk-nŏl′ĭj] *verb*, 1) to look at someone and speak to him or her 2) to admit the truth

**ac-knowl-edg-ment** [ăk-nŏl′ĭj-mənt] *noun*, 1) admission, recognition of an achievement 2) an expression of thanks

**a-corn** [ā′kôrn′, ā′kərn] *noun*, the seed of an oak tree

**a-cous-tic** [ə-kōō'stĭk] *adjective*, of or relating to the ability to carry a sound without distortion

**ac-quaint** [ə-kwānt'] *verb*, to cause to know or be aware of someone or something

**ac-quaint-ance** [ə-kwān'təns] *noun*, a person with whom one is familiar

**ac-qui-esce** [ăk'wē-ĕs'] *verb*, to submit, to consent, to agree

**ac-quire** [ə-kwīr'] *verb*, to get or to buy, to gain possession of

**ac-qui-si-tion** [ăk'wĭ-zĭsh'ən] *noun*, something gained or acquired

**ac-quit** [ə-kwĭt'] *verb*, to render a verdict that an accused person is not guilty of a crime, to exonerate

**ac-quit-tal** [ə-kwĭt'l] *noun*, a setting free from a charge, a finding of "not guilty"

**a-cre** [ā'kər] *noun*, a plot of land measuring 43,560 square feet

**ac-ri-mo-ny** [ăk'rə-mō'nē] *noun*, bitterness or caustic temper or speech, bad feelings

**ac-ro-bat** [ăk'rə-băt'] *noun*, a person skilled in tumbling or in using gymnastics equipment

**ac-ro-nym** [ăk'rə-nĭm'] *noun*, a word formed from the initial letters of a series of words, e.g. AIDS: *Acquired Immune Deficiency Syndrome*

**a-cross** [ə-krôs', ə-krŏs'] *adverb*, 1) from one side of a place to the other, *preposition*, 2) on the opposite side from something

**act** [ăkt] *noun*, 1) something that has been done, a deed 2) a part of a play containing different scenes, *verb*, 3) to pretend to be something or someone 4) to behave 5) to carry out, to perform

**ac-tion** [ăk'shən] *noun*, 1) something done 2) the process of doing

**ac-tive** [ăk'tĭv] *adjective*, 1) always busy doing something 2) taking part

**ac-tiv-i-ty** [ăk-tĭv'ĭ-tē] *noun*, state of action, energy, a task

**ac-tor** [ăk'tər] *noun*, a male or female performer in a play, a film or television program

**ac-tu-al** [ăk'chōō-əl] *adjective*, real, existing in fact

**ac-tu-al-ly** [ăk'chōō-əl-ē] *adverb*, really, truly, in reality

**a-cu-i-ty** [ə-kyōō'ĭ-tē] *noun*, keenness, as of thought and vision

**a-cute** [ə-kyōōt'] *adjective*, 1) sharp, pointed, keen, sensitive 2) describing an angle formed by intersecting lines that is less than 90 degrees

**A.D.** abbreviation for the Latin words **Anno Domini**, the time after the birth of Christ

**ad-age** [ăd'ĭj] *noun*, a proverb or a saying with a moral message

**ad-a-mant** [ăd'ə-mənt] *adjective*, inflexible, unyielding

**a-dapt** [ə-dăpt'] *verb*, to change to fit the environment

**ad-ap-ta-tion** [ăd'ăp-tā'shən] *noun*, a change to improve the way things work

**add** [ăd] *verb*, 1) to put together with something else 2) to count

**ad-der** [ăd'ər] *noun*, a snake with a poisonous bite, a viper

**ad-dict** [ə-dĭkt′] *noun*, someone who has a strong habit or a physical despondency, as for drugs

**ad-dic-tion** [ə-dĭk′shən] *noun*, a dependency, such as a physical craving for a drug

**ad-di-tion** [ə-dĭsh′ən] *noun*, 1) the act of putting or joining things together 2) an annexation

**ad-di-tion-al** [ə-dĭsh′ən-əl] *adjective*, added on, extra

**ad-dress** [ə-drĕs′] *noun*, 1) the location of something, usually the street number, city, and state, *verb*, 2) to speak or write to someone 3) to direct in writing, as in a letter 4) to speak to an audience, as in a speech

**a-dept** [ə-dĕpt′] *adjective*, proficient, expert, highly skilled

**ad-e-quate** [ăd′ĭ-kwĭt] *adjective*, just enough, sufficient, all right

**ad-here** [ăd-hîr′] *verb*, to hold, to be attached, to stick to

**ad-her-ent** [ăd-hîr′ənt] *adjective*, 1) sticking securely, *noun*, 2) a supporter or follower

**ad-he-sive** [ăd-hē′sĭv, -zĭv] *noun*, a sticky substance that holds things in place

**a-dieu** [ə-dyoo′, ə-doo′] *noun and interjection*, farewell, goodbye

**ad in-fi-ni-tum** [ăd ĭn′fə-nī′təm] *adverb*, to infinity, endlessly

**ad-ja-cent** [ə-jā′sənt] *adjective*, next to, lying near or touching

**ad-jec-tive** [ăj′ĭk-tĭv] *noun*, a word that describes a person, place or thing

**ad-join** [ə-join′] *verb*, to be next to and connected to something

**ad-journ** [ə-jûrn′] *verb*, to put off a meeting until later, to postpone

**ad-just** [ə-jŭst′] *verb*, to reposition or reset something

**ad-just-a-ble** [ə-jŭst′ə-bəl] *adjective*, capable of being arranged or altered

**ad-just-ment** [ə-jŭst′mənt] *noun*, a minor modification or change

**ad lib** [ăd lĭb′] *verb*, to make up words or actions at the moment, not before

**ad-min-is-ter** [ăd-mĭn′ĭ-stər] *verb*, 1) to look after or tend 2) to distribute, to disperse 3) to manage, to run

**ad-min-is-tra-tion** [ăd-mĭn′ĭ-strā′shən] *noun*, those who are empowered to make decisions, management

**ad-min-is-tra-tor** [ăd-mĭn′ĭ-strā′tər] *noun*, a person authorized to carry out certain duties

**ad-mi-ra-ble** [ăd′mər-ə-bəl] *adjective*, excellent, deserving the highest praise

**ad-mi-ral** [ăd′mər-əl] *noun*, the highest ranking officer in the navy

**ad-mi-ra-tion** [ăd′mə-rā′shən] *noun*, appreciation, esteem

**ad-mire** [ăd-mīr′] *verb*, 1) to look up to someone, to revere 2) to look at with pleasure

**ad-mis-si-ble** [ăd-mĭs′ə-bəl] *adjective*, that may be allowed

**ad-mis-sion** [ăd-mĭsh′ən] *noun*, 1) access, admittance 2) acknowledgment, confession

**ad-mit** [ăd-mĭt′] *verb*, 1) to allow someone to enter 2) to acknowledge as true

**a-do** [ədōō]*noun*, fuss, excitment

**a-do-be** [ə-dō′bē] *noun*, 1) a type of clay or the sun-dried bricks made from it, 2) a home made with baked mud, usually in the Southwest

**ad-o-les-cent** [ăd′l-ĕs′ənt] *noun*, a teenager

**a-dopt** [ə-dŏpt′] *verb*, 1) to use someone else's idea 2) to make someone a member of your family, legally

**a-dore** [ə-dôr′, ə-dōr′] *verb*, to like or love very much

**a-dorn** [ə-dôrn′] *verb*, to decorate, to add beauty, to embellish

**a-drift** [ə-drĭft′] *adverb*, out in water or space without means of control, drifting

**a-dult** [ə-dŭlt′] *noun*, a grown person or animal

**ad-vance** [ăd-văns′] *adjective*, 1) ahead of time, done beforehand, *noun*, 2) a positive change, progress *verb*, 3) to move forward

**ad-van-tage** [ăd-văn′tĭj] *noun*, something that helps a person

**ad-van-ta-geous** [ăd′văn-tā′jəs,] *adjective*, profitable, useful, beneficial, favorable

**ad-vent** [ăd′vĕnt′] *noun*, the arrival of someone or something

**ad-ven-ture** [ăd-vĕn′chər] *noun*, 1) a bold or hazardous undertaking, 2) an exciting or extraordinary experience

**ad-verb** [ăd′vûrb] *noun*, a word that tells how, when, or where something is done

**ad-ver-sar-y** [ăd′vər-sĕr′ē] *noun*, a rival, foe, or opponent

**ad-verse** [ăd-vûrs′] *adjective*, opposed, hostile

**ad-ver-si-ty** [ăd-vûr′sĭ-tē] *noun*, hard times, trouble

**ad-ver-tise** [ăd′vər-tīz′] *verb*, 1) to announce publicly 2) to try to sell something by promoting it

**ad-ver-tise-ment** [ăd′vər-tīz′mənt] *noun*, a notice or short film about something that is for sale

**ad-vice** [ăd-vīs′] *noun*, counsel, opinion given for acceptable conduct, guidance

**ad-vis-a-ble** [ăd-vī′zə-bəl] *adjective*, proper, recommended, prudent

**ad-vise** [ăd-vīz′] *verb*, to suggest to someone what to do, to inform, to recommend, to counsel

**ad-vis-er** [ăd-vī′zər] *noun*, one who advises, one who gives counsel or information

**ad-vo-cate** [ăd′və-k t′] *noun*, 1) one who pleads the cause of another or himself, [ăd′və-kāt′] *verb*, 2) to defend, to urge, to support, to endorse

**aer-i-al** [âr′ē-əl] *adjective*, pertaining to or inhabiting the air

**aer-o-bic** [â-rō′bĭk] *adjective*, requiring the presence of free oxygen to live

**aer-o-dy-nam-ics** [âr′ō-dī-năm′ĭks] *noun*, the science of the movement of flying bodies in air

**aer-o-sol** [âr′ə-sôl′] *noun*, a gaseous suspension of fine particles, a mist

**aer-o-space** [âr′ō-spās′] *adjective*, having to do with the atmosphere and space

**aes-thet-ic** [ĕs-thĕt′ĭk] *adjective*, relating to beauty or the arts

**af-fair** [ə-fâr′] *noun*, matter, concern, business of any kind

**af-fect** [ə-fĕkt′] *verb*, 1) to act upon to bring about a change 2) to move the feelings of someone 3) to pretend to do something

**af-fec-ta-tion** [ăf′ĕk-tā′shən] *noun*, insincerity, pretense

**af-fec-tion** [ə-fĕk′shən] *noun*, tenderness, warmth, love, devotion, kindness

**af-fec-tion-ate** [ə-fĕk′shə-nĭt] *adjective*, feeling or showing love

**af-fec-tion-ate-ly** [ə-fĕk′shə-nĭt-lē] *adverb*, showing love and care

**af-fi-da-vit** [ăf′ĭ-dā′vĭt] *noun*, a written declaration, an oath

**af-fil-i-ate** [ə-fĭl′ē-āt′] *verb*, to closely connect or associate with someone or groups of people

**af-fil-i-a-tion** [ə-fĭl-ē-ā′shən] *noun*, an association, a connection

**af-fin-i-ty** [ə-fĭn′ĭ-tē] *noun*, a feeling of attraction to a person or thing

**af-firm** [ə-fûrm′] *verb*, to approve, to confirm, to endorse

**af-fir-ma-tion** [ăf′ər-mā′shən] *noun*, a solemn pledge

**af-firm-a-tive** [ə-fûr′mə-tĭv] *adjective*, 1) being positive and helpful, *noun*, 2) a word or phrase expressing a positive reply

**af-flict** [ə-flĭkt′] *verb*, to hurt, to torment, to cause pain

**af-flic-tion** [ə-flĭk′shən] *noun*, state or cause of distress, pain or misery

**af-flu-ence** [ăf′lōō-əns] *noun*, an abundant supply, wealth

**af-ford** [ə-fôrd′] *verb*, to have enough money to buy something

**a-float** [ə-flōt′] *adjective*, on or above the water, buoyant

**a-fraid** [ə-frād′] *adjective*, scared

**Af-ri-ca** [ăf′rĭ-kə] *noun*, one of the seven continents, surrounded by the Atlantic and Indian Oceans, containing 12.7% of the world's population

**af-ter** [ăf′tər] *adverb*, 1) following, next, *preposition*, 2) behind

**af-ter-math** [ăf′tər-măth′] *noun*, the end result, outcome, consequence

**af-ter-noon** [ăf′tər-nōōn′] *noun*, time between noon and evening

**af-ter-ward** [ăf′tər-wərd] *adverb*, later

**a-gain** [ə-gĕn′] *adverb*, once more

**a-gainst** [ə-gĕnst′] *preposition*, 1) in opposition to 2) in contact with, touching 3) in the other direction, opposite

**age** [āj] *noun*, 1) the amount of time something has lived 2) a particular period of time, *verb*, 3) to grow or cause to become old

**aged** [ā′jĭd] *adjective*, old

**a-gen-cy** [ā′jən-sē] *noun*, an organization designed to distribute funds and services to people

**a-gen-da** [ə-jĕn′də] *noun*, a list of items that need attention

**a-gent** [ā′jənt] *noun*, 1) a person who represents a group 2) a force of change

**ag-gran-dize** [ə-grăn′dīz′] *verb*, to make greater in power, rank or riches

**ag-gra-vate** [ăg′rə-vāt′] *verb*, to make worse, to annoy

**ag-gre-gate** [ăg′rĭ-gĭt] *noun*, the sum
total of a group of things

**ag-gres-sion** [ə-grĕsh′ən] *noun*,
anger in an attack

**ag-gres-sive** [ə-grĕs′ĭv] *adjective*,
forceful, likely to attack

**ag-ile** [ăj′əl, -īl′] *adjective*, swift,
nimble, able to move easily

**ag-i-tate** [ăj′ĭ-tāt′] *verb*, to shake up

**ag-i-ta-tion** [ăj′ĭ-tā′shən] *noun*,
confusion, frenzy, excitement

**ag-nos-tic** [ăg-nŏs′tĭk] *noun*, a
person who believes that the
human mind cannot comprehend
the beginning of the universe or
the existence of God

**a-go** [ə-gō′] *adverb*, in the past

**ag-o-ny** [ăg′ə-nē] *noun*, very bad
physical or emotional pain

**a-gree-a-ble** [ə-grē′ə-bəl] *adjective*,
easy to get along with

**a-gree-ment** [ə-grē′mənt] *noun*, a
mutual understanding

**ag-ri-cul-ture** [ăg′rĭ-kŭl′chər] *noun*,
the science and art of cultivating
soil and growing crops

**a-head** [ə-hĕd′] *adverb*, 1) in front,
preceding 2) into the future

**aid** [ād] *noun*, 1) a form of help
2) assistance, support, *verb*, 3) to
help or assist

**aide** [ād] *noun*, an assistant, a helper

**ail-ment** [āl′mənt] *noun*, a sickness,

**aim** [ām] *noun*, 1) target, direction
2) intention, purpose, goal, *verb*,
3) to point toward a target when
ready to throw something, fire
something, or take a picture

**air** [âr] *noun* 1) the mixture of gases
surrounding the earth 2) an
appearance or atmosphere, *verb*,
3) to refresh or ventilate

**air-borne** [âr′bôrn′] *adjective*,
carried by or through the air

**air-craft** [âr′krăft′] *noun*, a machine
capable of flying

**air force** [âr′fôrs′] *noun*, a group of
soldiers trained to fight and destroy
using aircraft

**air-plane** [âr′plān′] *noun*, a flying
machine used to transport people
or cargo moving through the air
by means of motor driven
propellers or engines and kept
aloft by the upward thrust of the
air on its fixed wings

**air pol-lu-tion** [âr - pə-lōō′shən]
*noun*, particles that contaminate the
air and make it unsafe to breathe

**air-port** [âr′pôrt′] *noun*, a place
where aircraft land and take off

**aisle** [īl] *noun*, the passageway
between seats in a bus,
auditorium, church, etc., or
between shelves in a store

**a-jar** [ə-jär′] *adjective and adverb*,
slightly open

**Al-a-bama** [ăl′ə-băm′ə] *noun*, one of
the southern United States the
capital is Montgomery. The state
flower for **Alabama** is the
camellia and the motto is "We
dare to defend our rights."

**a-lac-ri-ty** [ə-lăk′rĭ-tē] *noun*,
1) cheerful willingness or
readiness 2) speed

**a-larm** [ə-lärm′] *noun*, 1) a feeling of
fear or danger 2) a programmed
sound to awaken persons from
sleep or warn of danger, *verb*, 3) to
worry or frighten

**a-las** [ə-lăs′] *interjection*, an expression of pity or concern

**Alas-ka** [ə-lăs′kə] *noun*, one of the 50 United States located in the North, the capital city is Juneau. The state flower of **Alaska** is the forget me-not, and the motto is "North to the Future."

**al-ba-tross** [ăl′bə-trôs′] *noun*, a large bird with long narrow wings found near the ocean, especially in the South Seas

**al-bi-no** [ăl-bī′nō] *noun*, a person or animal lacking pigmentation, and therefore extraordinarily pale

**al-bum** [ăl′bəm] *noun*, 1) a book that holds a collection of pictures, stamps or autographs 2) a collection of recordings

**al-che-my** [ăl′kə-mē] *noun*, medieval chemistry that attempted to turn ordinary things into gold

**al-co-hol** [ăl′kə-hôl′] *noun*, 1) an intoxicating beverage, such as wine, beer or liquor, the result of fermentation 2) an organic compound used as an antiseptic

**al-co-hol-ic** [ăl′kə-hô′lĭk] *adjective*, 1) containing alcohol as an ingredient, *noun*, 2) a person with the disease of alcoholism

**al-der-man** [ôl′dər-mən] *noun*, a member of a city council

**a-lert** [ə-lûrt′] *adjective*, 1) awake and ready to act, *noun*, 2) a warning of danger

**al-fal-fa** [ăl-făl′fə] *noun*, a plant in the pea family

**al-ga** [ăl′gə] *noun*, *plural*, **algae**, an organism, often one-celled, that continuously divides itself, with no root or stem that lives in water

**al–ge–bra** [ăl′jə-brə] *noun*, a branch of mathematics in which the expressions of quantity are in symbols that express general relationships

**a–li–as** [ā′lē-əs] *noun*, an assumed name, a fake name

**al-i-bi** [ăl′ə-bī′] *noun*, the plea of having been elsewhere at the time a crime was committed

**al-ien** [ā′lē-ən] *adjective*, 1) strange, wholly different in nature, *noun*, 2) a person from another country

**al-ien-ate** [āl′yə-nāt′] *verb*, to separate, to make hostile

**a-light** [ə-līt′] *verb*, to come from, to get off

**a-lign-ment** [ə-līn′mənt] *noun*, 1) arrangement in a line 2) the condition of cooperation

**a-like** [ə-līk′] *adjective*, 1) similar, *adverb*, 2) in the same manner

**al-i-men-ta-ry** [ăl′ə-měn′tə-rē] *adjective*, supplying nourishment

**al-i-mo-ny** [ăl′ə-mō′nē] *noun*, an allowance given to a spouse for his or her support after a divorce

**a-live** [ə-līv′] *adjective*, 1) living, not dead 2) active, moving

**al-ka-li** [ăl′kə-lī′] *noun*, any soluble substance having marked basic qualities as a mineral salt or mixture of salts that can neutralize acids and turns litmus blue

**all** [ôl] *adjective*, 1) the whole of, any, *adverb*, 2) completely, totally, *pronoun*, 3) everyone, the whole thing

**al-le-ga-tion** [ăl′ĭ-gā′shən] *noun*, the statement of something that is to be proved, an accusation

**al-lege** [ə-lĕj′] *verb*, to urge as a reason, to assert, to suggest

**al-le-giance** [ə-lē′jəns] *noun*, strong support of something, an obligation to a government or ruler, loyal support

**al-le-go-ry** [ăl′ĭ-gôr′ē] *noun*, a story with a moral in which characters are used as symbols, a fable

**al-ler-gy** [ăl′ər-jē] *noun*, an abnormal reaction to substances in the environment such as pollen, dust or insect bites

**al-le-vi-ate** [ə-lē′vē-āt′] *verb*, to lighten or lessen pressure

**al-ley** [ăl′ē] *noun*, a very narrow road between buildings

**al-li-ance** [ə-lī′əns] *noun*, a partnership based on trust, common objectives, etc.

**al-li-ga-tor** [ăl′ĭ-gā′tər] *noun*, a large reptile that lives near water and is a carnivore

**al-lit-er-a-tion** [ə-lĭt′ə-rā′shən] *noun*, repetition of the beginning sound, e.g., *Peter Piper picked a peck of pickled peppers*

**al-lo-cate** [ăl′ə-kāt′] *verb*, to set something aside for a special use

**al-lot** [ə-lŏt′] *verb*, to divide something and then to give someone his or her portion

**al-lot-ment** [ə-lŏt′mənt] *noun*, the portion given to each

**al-low** [ə-lou′] *verb*, to permit someone to do something

**al-low-ance** [ə-lou′əns] *noun*, a definite sum granted, an abatement or deduction

**al-loy** [ăl′oi′] *noun*, a substance composed of two or more metals mixed together

**al-lude** [ə-lōōd′] *verb*, to hint or suggest indirectly

**al-lu-sion** [ə-lōō′zhən] *noun*, an indirect reference, knowledge of something not actually mentioned

**al-ly** [ə-lī′] *noun*, 1) someone who helps you fight against someone else, a person or group who has the same purpose or cause, *verb*, 2) to unite, to join

**al-ma ma-ter** [ăl′mə mä′tər] *noun*, a school from which a person has graduated

**al-ma-nac** [ôl′mə-năk′] *noun*, a book containing a calendar and certain statistics

**al-might-y** [ôl-mī′tē] *adjective*, having very great power

**al-mond** [ä′mənd] *noun*, a nut-like kernel of the fruit of the almond tree

**al-most** [ôl′mōst′] *adverb*, nearly, not quite

**alms** [ämz] *noun*, *plural*, money or items given to charity

**a-lo-ha** [ə-lō-ha′] *noun and interjection*, Hawaiian word used for greeting or parting

**a-lone** [ə-lōn′] *adjective and adverb* without others, singular

**a-long** [ə-lông′] *adverb*, 1) following the length of something from end to end 2) moving forward 3) as a companion, *preposition*, 4) over, through, by the course of

**a-loof** [ə-l ōof] *adjective*, 1) reserved in social relationships, *adverb* 2) away in place or time

**a-loud** [ə-loud′] *adverb*, in a clear voice that can be easily heard

**al-pha-bet** [ăl′fə-bĕt′] *noun*, the letters of a language arranged in customary order

**al-pha-bet-i-cal** [ăl′fə-bĕt′ĭ-kəl] *adjective*, arranged in the same order as the letters of the alphabet

**al-read-y** [ôl-rĕd′ē] *adverb*, even now, before a certain time

**al-so** [ôl′sō] *adverb*, in addition, too

**al-tar** [ôl′tər] *noun*, a table in a holy place where religious rites are performed

**al-ter** [ôl′tər] *verb*, to change

**al-ter-a-tion** [ôl′tə-rā′shən] *noun*, a change or an adjustment

**al-ter-nate** [ôl′tər-nāt′] *verb*, to take turns, to switch off

**al-ter-na-tive** [ôl-tûr′nə-tĭv] *adjective*, 1) other, *noun*, 2) something you can choose

**al-though** [ôl-thō′] *conjunction*, supposing that, notwithstanding

**al-ti-tude** [ăl′tĭ-tōōd′] *noun*, extent upward, the height of something measured in relation to a reference level, such as sea level

**al-to** [ăl′tō] *noun*, a singing voice between tenor and soprano

**al-to-geth-er** [ôl′tə-gĕth′ər] *adverb*, wholly, completely, including everyone, united

**al-tru-is-tic** [ăl′trōō-ĭs′tĭk] *adjective*, unselfish, concerned about others

**al-u-mi-num** [ə-lōō′mə-nəm] *noun*, a very soft silver metal made chiefly of bauxite ore

**al-ways** [ôl′wāz] *adverb*, at all times, forever

**am** [ăm] *verb*, the part of the verb **be** used with **I**

**a.m.** in the morning, the hours between midnight and noon, from the Latin ante meridiem "before midday"

**a-mass** [ə-măs′] *verb*, to collect, to accumulate

**am-a-teur** [ăm′ə-tûr′] *adjective*, 1) for enjoyment rather than money, not professional, *noun*, 2) someone who is not paid for doing something but does it for pleasure

**a-maze** [ə-māz′] *verb*, to surprise or bewilder

**a-maze-ment** [ə-māz′mənt] *noun*, a state of surprise, awe, wonder

**am-a-zon** [ăm′ə-zŏn′] *noun*, a mythical female warrior

**am-bas-sa-dor** [ăm-băs′ə-dər] *noun*, an appointed official who represents his or her country in another country

**am-ber** [ăm′bər] *noun*, the fossilized sap from a pine tree

**am-bi-dex-trous** [ăm′bĭ-dĕk′strəs] *adjective*, capable of using either hand with equal ease

**am-bi-ence** [ăm′bē-əns] *noun*, the environment, the atmosphere in a room or building

**am-big-u-ous** [ăm-bĭg′yōō-əs] *adjective*, capable of more than one interpretation, unclear

**am-bi-tion** [ăm-bĭsh′ən] *noun*, a strong desire to achieve

**am-bi-tious** [ăm-bĭsh′əs] *adjective*, wanting to have power, driven to achieve

**am-biv-a-lent** [ăm-bĭv′ə-lənt] *adjective,* having conflicting emotional attitudes

**am-bul-ance** [ăm′byə-ləns] *noun,* a vehicle equipped to carry the injured or sick

**am-bush** [ăm′bŏŏsh] *noun,* a surprise attack

**a-mel-io-rate** [ə-mēl′yə-rāt′] *verb,* to improve a deplorable condition

**A-men** [ā-měn′, ä-měn′] *interjection,* an expression of approval, to say I agree

**a-mend** [ə-měnd′] *verb,* to correct, to change generally for the better

**a-mend-ment** [ə-měnd′mənt] *noun,* a change made in a bill or motion

**a-men-i-ty** [ə-měn′ĭ-tē] *noun,* a courtesy, a thoughtful action of consideration, a convenience

**A-mer-i-ca** [ə-měr′ĭ-kə] *noun,* a country in North America with a democratic form of government

**A-mer-i-can In-di-an** [ə-měr′ĭ-kən ĭn′dē-ən] *noun,* the people whose ancestors lived in North America for thousands of years

**am-e-thyst** [ăm′ə-thĭst] *noun,* a purple or bluish-violet stone

**a-mi-a-ble** [ā′mē-ə-bəl] *adjective,* friendly, easy to get along with

**a-mid** [ə-mĭd′] *preposition,* among, surrounded by

**am-mo-nia** [ə-mōn′yə] *noun,* a colorless compound of hydrogen and nitrogen

**am-mu-ni-tion** [ăm′yə-nĭsh′ən] *noun,* rockets, bombs and bullets used in loading or charging guns and rifles

**am-ne-sia** [ăm-nē′zhə] *noun,* loss of memory

**am-nes-ty** [ăm′nĭ-stē] *noun,* a pardon that absolves or discounts past offe

**a-mong** [ə-mŭng′] *preposition,* between, surrounded by

**a-mount** [ə-mount′] *noun,* 1) a sum, the total number 2) quantity, mass, *verb,* 3) to add up

**am-phib-i-an** [ăm-fĭb′ē-ən] *noun,* 1) a cold-blooded animal living both on land and in the water 2) an airplane designed to take off on the water or on land

**am-phib-i-ous** [ăm-fĭb′ē-əs] *adjective,* able to live or operate on land or in water

**am-phi-the-a-ter** [ăm′fə-thē′ə-tər] *noun,* a theater with seats all around the stage or arena

**am-ple** [ăm′pəl] *adjective,* abundant, plentiful, more than enough

**am-pli-fy** [ăm′plə-fī′] *verb,* to increase in size, to make louder

**am-pu-tate** [ăm′pyŏŏ-tāt′] *verb,* to cut off

**am-u-let** [ăm′yə-lĭt] *noun,* a good luck charm, a talisman

**a-muse** [ə-myōōz′] *verb,* to entertain or delight, to make someone smile

**a-muse-ment** [ə-myōōz′mənt] *noun,* entertainment, a distraction

**an** [ən; ăn when stressed] *article,* used instead of a in front of a vowel

**an-aer-o-bic** [ăn′ə-rō′bĭk] *adjective,* able to live only in the absence of free oxygen

**a-nal-o-gous** [ə-năl′ə-gəs] *adjective,* similar, comparable, resembling

**a-nal-o-gy** [ə-năl′ə-jē] *noun*, an explanation based on resemblances between different objects or cases

**a-nal-y-sis** [ə-năl′ĭ-sĭs] *noun*, a thorough examination

**an-a-lyze** [ăn′ə-līz′] *verb*, to examine critically elements or constituent parts

**an-ar-chist** [ăn′ər-kĭst] *noun*, a person who rebels against the established order or laws

**an-ar-chy** [ăn′ər-kē] *noun*, a lawless condition of society, chaos

**a-nat-o-my** [ə-năt′ə-mē] *noun*, the study of the structure of people, animals or plants

**an-ces-tor** [ăn′sĕs′tər] *noun*, a person from whom one is descended

**an-ces-try** [ăn′sĕs′trē] *noun*, family members or ethnic descent

**an-chor** [ăng′kər] *noun*, 1) a heavy piece of metal on the end of a rope or chain lowered into the water to keep a boat from drifting, *verb*, 2) to secure or fasten firmly, to fix in place

**an-cient** [ān′shənt] *adjective*, belonging to a remote period of time, very old

**and** [ənd, ən; ănd when stressed] *conjunction*, a word that adds or joins other words

**an-ec-dote** [ăn′ĭk-dōt′] *noun*, a short story or fact of an interesting nature

**a-ne-mi-a** [ə-nē′mē-ə] *noun*, a condition marked by a low red blood cell count

**an-e-mom-e-ter** [ăn′ə-mŏm′ĭ-tər] *noun*, an instrument to measure the force or speed of wind

**an-es-the-sia** [ăn′ĭs-thē′zhə] *noun*, the loss of sensation or consciousness, especially when caused by anesthetic

**an-es-thet-ic** [ăn′ĭs-thĕt′ĭk] *noun*, a substance that causes loss of sensation or consciousness

**an-gel** [ān′jəl] *noun*, 1) a messenger of God 2) a kind, loveable person

**an-ger** [ăng′gər] *noun*, feelings of hostility and hurt, a desire to fight or argue

**an-gle** [ăng′gəl] *noun*, 1) the shape made when two lines or planes intersect 2) a point of view, *verb*, 3) to fish with a hook and line

**an-gry** [ăng′grē] *adjective*, feeling extreme emotion due to hurt feelings, hostile

**an-guish** [ăng′gwĭsh] *noun*, extreme pain either of body or mind, acute suffering, deep sadness

**an-i-mal** [ăn′ə-məl] *noun*, a living creature that is not a plant

**an-i-mate** [ăn′ə-māt′] *verb*, to inspire with energy, to enliven

**an-i-mos-i-ty** [ăn′ə-mŏs′ĭ-tē] *noun*, a feeling of hatred leading to opposition, hostility

**an-kle** [ăng′kəl] *noun*, the joint connecting the foot to the leg

**an-nals** [ăn′əlz] *noun*, records, history, chronicles, accounts

**an-neal** [ə-nēl′] *verb*, to subject to high heat, with subsequent cooling, for the purpose of softening thoroughly and making less brittle

**an-nex** [ə-nĕks′] *noun*, 1) a building added onto a larger building, *verb*, 2) to add on, to attach a smaller thing to something larger

**an-nex-a-tion** [ăn′ĭk-sā′shən] *noun*, the territory or thing that has been added

**an-ni-hi-late** [ə-nī′ə-lāt′] *verb*, to reduce to nothing, to destroy entirely, to obliterate

**an-ni-ver-sa-ry** [ăn′ə-vûr′sə-rē] *noun*, a day celebrated each year to remember something important from the past

**an-no-tate** [ăn′ō-tāt′] *verb*, to write comments or explanatory notes

**an-nounce** [ə-nouns′] *verb*, to give notice of the arrival of something, to proclaim, to declare

**an-nounce-ment** [ə-nouns′mənt] *noun*, 1) act of making something publicly known 2) a printed notice

**an-noy** [ə-noi′] *verb*, to disturb or irritate, to bother

**an-noy-ance** [ə-noi′əns] *noun*, anything that irritates

**an-nu-al** [ăn′yo͞o-əl] *adjective*, 1) occurring once a year, *noun*, 2) a plant that lives for one year

**a-noint** [ə-noint′] *verb*, to baptize, to purify, to sprinkle with oil or holy water

**a-nom-a-ly** [ə-nŏm′ə-lē] *noun*, an irregularity, a deviation from the normal, one of a kind

**a-non-y-mous** [ə-nŏn′ə-məs] *adjective*, of unknown name

**an-o-rex-i-a** [ăn′ə-rĕk′sē-ə] *noun*, a lack of appetite and inability or refusal to consume food

**an-oth-er** [ə-nŭth′ər] *adjective, and pronoun*, 1) an additional, one more 2) someone else

**an-swer** [ăn′sər] *noun*, 1) a reply to a question, *verb*, 2) to make a response, to reply

**ant** [ănt] *noun*, a small insect that lives in colonies, known for its social order and industry

**an-tag-o-nist** [ăn-tăg′ə-nĭst] *noun*, one who opposes with active resistance, an opponent

**Ant-arc-ti-ca** [ănt-ärk′tĭ-kə] *noun*, one of the seven continents in the world, the area containing the South Pole

**an-te-ced-ent** [ăn′tĭ-sēd′nt] *adjective*, going before, preceding

**an-te-lope** [ăn′tl-ōp′] *noun*, a wild animal, similar to a deer, which runs fast and usually has antlers

**an-ten-na** [ăn-tĕn′ə] *noun, plural*, **antennae**, 1) the sensory organ of an insect or crustacean 2) wire supported in the air for directly transmitting and receiving electromagnetic waves

**an-them** [ăn′thəm] *noun*, a song or hymn of praise

**an-thro-po-log-ist** [ăn′thrə-pŏl′ə-jĭst] *noun*, a student of the history and science of mankind

**an-thro-po-mor-phic** [ăn′thrə-pə-môr′-fĭk] *adjective*, having human form or characteristics

**an-ti-bi-ot-ic** [ăn′tĭ-bī-ŏt′ĭk] *noun*, a substance such as penicillin, effective in fighting destructive microorganisms and used for treatment of diseases

**an-tic-i-pate** [ăn-tĭs′ə-pāt′] *verb*, to look forward to

**an-ti-dote** [ăn′tĭ-dōt′] *noun*, 1) a remedy to counteract poison 2) anything that counteracts evil

**an-tip-a-thy** [ăn-tĭp′ə-thē] *noun*, a strong dislike, a natural aversion

**an-ti-quat-ed** [ăn′tĭ-kwā′tĭd] *adjective*, old-fashioned, obsolete

**an-tique** [ăn-tēk′] *adjective*, 1) old-fashioned, from another time, *noun*, 2) something made long ago and valued for its age

**an-ti-sep-tic** [ăn′tĭ-sĕp′tĭk] *adjective*, 1) clean, sterile, *noun*, 2) a substance that tends to prevent harmful effects of bacteria growth

**an-tith-e-sis** [ăn-tĭth′ĭ-sĭs] *noun*, the exact opposite

**ant-ler** [ănt′lər] *noun*, one of a pair of branched horns on the head of a deer

**an-to-nym** [ăn′tə-nĭm′] *noun*, a word that has the opposite meaning to another

**anx-i-e-ty** [ăng-zī′ĭ-tē] *noun*, uneasiness of mind, concern about future events

**anx-ious** [ăngk′shəs] *adjective*, worried, concerned, nervous

**any** [ĕn′ē] *adjective*, 1) some, an uncertain number, quantity, volume or degree 2) every 3) one

**an-y-bod-y** [ĕn′ē-bŏd′ē] *pronoun*, any person

**an-y-one** [ĕn′ē-wŭn′] *pronoun*, anybody

**an-y-thing** [ĕn′ē-thĭng′] *noun*, something

**an-y-way** [ĕn′ē-wā′] *adverb*, 1) no matter what happens, in any case, 2) haphazardly, in any fashion

**an-y-where** [ĕn′ē-hwâr′] *adverb*, in, at, or to any place

**a-part** [ə-pärt′] *adverb*, separately in place or time

**a-part-ment** [ə-pärt′mənt] *noun*, rooms or a part of a building where someone lives

**ap-a-thy** [ăp′ə-thē] *noun*, lack of interest or concern

**ape** [āp] *noun*, 1) a large mammal similar to a monkey without a tail, for example, a gorilla, chimpanzee, etc., *verb*, 2) to copy, to imitate

**aph-o-rism** [ăf′ə-rĭz′əm] *noun*, a statement of truth, an adage

**a-poc-a-lyp-tic** [ə-pŏk′ə-lĭp′tĭk] *adjective*, prophetic, pertaining to revelations about the end of the world

**a-pol-ogize** [ə-pŏl′ə-jīz′] *verb*, to say you're sorry for what you have done, to express regret

**a-pol-o-gy** [ə-pŏl′ə-jē] *noun*, an explanation by way of asking for forgiveness

**a-pos-tle** [ə-pŏs′əl] *noun*, any person zealously advocating a cause

**a-pos-tro-phe** [ə-pŏs′trə-fē] *noun*, a mark (′) used to indicate an omission of a letter, i.e. *I'll*, or letters, or to denote the possessive case i.e. *Kara's*

**ap-o-thegm** [ăp′ə-thĕm′] *noun*, a pithy, compact saying, a proverb

**a-poth-e-o-sis** [ə-pŏth′ē-ō′sĭs] *noun*, deification, glorification, making into a god

**ap-pall** [ə-pôl'] *verb,* to fill with horror or dismay, to shock

**ap-pa-rat-us** [ăp'ə-rā'təs] *noun,* equipment, a collection or set of implements for a specific purpose

**ap-par-el** [ə-păr'əl] *noun,* clothing, garments

**ap-par-ent** [ə-păr'ənt] *adjective,* capable of seeming or appearing to be evident, easily understood

**ap-par-ent-ly** [ə-păr'ənt] *adverb,* clearly, evidently, obviously

**ap-pa-ri-tion** [ăp'ə-rĭsh'ən] *noun,* a ghost, a phantom

**ap-peal** [ə-pēl'] *noun,* 1) the proceeding by which a case is brought to a superior court for reexamination or review 2) a request, *verb,* 3) to plead, to ask urgently 4) to seem attractive

**ap-pear** [ə-pîr'] *verb,* 1) to come into view unexpectedly 2) to seem to be

**ap-pear-ance** [ə-pîr'əns] *noun,* 1) the act of appearing or becoming visible 2) the way something or someone looks

**ap-pease** [ə-pēz'] *verb,* to satisfy or often by granting demands

**ap-pel-lant** [ə-pĕl'ənt] *noun,* one who asks for a judicial decree

**ap-pel-la-tion** [ăp'ə-lā'shən] *noun,* a name or title

**ap-pen-di-ci-tis** [ə-pĕn'dĭ-sī'tĭs] *noun,* inflammation of the appendix

**ap-pen-dix** [ə-pĕn'dĭks] *noun,* 1) information added to a section at the end of a book 2) a small tube-like part growing out from the intestine

**ap-pe-tite** [ăp'ĭ-tīt'] *noun,* craving, the desire for food

**ap-plaud** [ə-plôd'] *verb,* to show approval especially by clapping hands together in praise

**ap-plause** [ə-plôz'] *noun,* praise for someone, usually expressed by clapping hands

**ap-ple** [ăp'əl] *noun,* the firm-fleshed, round, juicy fruit of an apple tree

**ap-pli-ance** [ə-plī'əns] *noun,* an apparatus or device, a machine

**ap-pli-ca-ble** [ăp'lĭ-kə-bəl] *adjective,* relevant, appropriate

**ap-plic-ant** [ăp'lĭ-kənt] *noun,* one who makes a request, a petitioner

**ap-pli-ca-tion** [ăp'lĭ-kā'shən] *noun,* 1) work or effort 2) a use 3) a form used to make a request

**ap-pli-que** [ăp'lĭ-kā'] *noun,* ornamental patterns put on textiles

**ap-ply** [ə-plī'] *verb,* 1) to seek or ask 2) to put on 3) to pertain to

**ap-point** [ə-point'] *verb,* to choose for a job

**ap-point-ment** [ə-point'mənt] *noun,* 1) a meeting, a date, a rendezvous 2) a selection, a nomination

**ap-prais-al** [ə-prā'zəl] *noun,* value or worth, assessment

**ap-praise** [ə-prāz'] *verb,* to evaluate something to establish its worth

**ap-pre-ci-ate** [ə-prē'shē-āt'] *verb,* 1) to recognize the value of something, 2) to increase in value

**ap-pre-ci-a-tion** [ə-prē'shē-ā'shən] *noun,* grateful recognition

**ap-pre-hend** [ăp'rĭ-hĕnd'] *verb,* 1) to arrest a criminal 2) to anticipate

with anxiety, dread, or, fear
3)to understand

**ap-pre-hen-sion** [ăp′rĭ-hĕn′shən]
*noun*, 1) the ability to understand
2) fear, anxiety, dread

**ap-pren-tice** [ə-prĕn′tĭs] *noun*, a
novice or learner who works with
a master to learn a skill

**ap-prise** [ə-prīz′] *verb*, to give notice
to, to inform

**ap-proach** [ə-prōch′] *noun*, 1) a way
of dealing with something, 2) the
way that leads to a place, *verb*,
3) to move toward

**ap-proach-able** [ə-prō′chə-bəl]
*adjective*, friendly, nice, easy to
talk to

**ap-pro-pri-ate** [ə-prō′prē-ĭt]
*adjective*, 1) suitable, proper, [ə-
prō′prē-āt]*verb*, 2) to allocate, to
set aside for a purpose

**ap-pro-pri-a-tion** [ə-prō′prē-ā′shən]
*noun*, a setting apart for a
particular purpose

**ap-prov-al** [ə-prōō′vəl] *noun*,
1) praise 2) the go-ahead or okay
to proceed, permission

**ap-prove** [ə-prōōv′] *verb*, to say that
something is favorable

**ap-prox-i-mate** [ə-prŏk′sə-mĭt]
*adjective*, 1) almost accurate or
exact, near, [ə-prŏk′sə-māt]*verb*,
2) to estimate or guess

**ap-prox-i-mate-ly** [ə-prŏk′sə-mĭt-lē]
*adverb*, closely, nearly

**ap-pur-te-nance** [ə-pûr′tn-əns]
*noun*, something connected but
not as important, accessory

**A-pril** [ā′prəl] *noun*, the fourth
month of the year, having 30 days

**a-pron** [ā′prən] *noun*, a cover worn
over the front of one's clothing to
protect it

**ap-ro-pos** [ăp′rə-pō′] *adjective*,
appropriate, pertinent

**apt** [ăpt] *adjective*, 1) suited to,
fitting, 2) likely or almost certain

**ap-ti-tude** [ăp′tĭ-tōōd′] *noun*, natural
ability, fitness, talent

**a-quar-i-um** [ə-kwâr′ē-əm] *noun*, a
container, usually with glass sides,
to keep animals or plants in water

**a-quat-ic** [ə-kwăt′ĭk] *adjective*,
occurring on or in the water

**aq-ue-duct** [ăk′wĭ-dŭkt′] *noun*, a
passage used to bring water from
a distant source

**aq-ui-fer** [ăk′wə-fər] *noun*, an
underground geologic formation
in which the cracks in rock, sand,
soil, or gravel are filled with water

**Ar-ab** [ăr′ə-b] a native or inhabitant
of Arabia, 2) any of a Semitic
people originating in Arabia

**Ar-a-bic** [ăr′ə-bĭk] *adjective*,
1) relating to the Arab language and
culture, *noun*, 2) the Semitic
language of the Arabs

**ar-bi-ter** [är′bĭ-tər] *noun*, a judge, an
umpire or referee, a mediator

**ar-bi-trar-y** [är′bĭ-trĕr′ē] *adjective*,
chosen without any qualifications

**ar-bi-tra-tion** [är′bĭ-trā′shən] *noun*,
the hearing and determination of a
matter in dispute by a third party

**ar-bor** [är′bər] *noun*, a place shaded
by trees or shrubs

**arc** [ärk] *noun*, a segment of a circle,
a curve in an arch

**arch** [ärch] *noun*, a curved part of a
structure sometimes supporting.

weight above it, as in bridges, doorways, etc

**ar-chae-ol-o-gist** [är′kē-ŏl′ə-jĭst] *noun*, an expert in the study of past civilizations and ancient cultures, mainly through digging up remains

**ar-chae-ol-o-gy** [är′kē-ŏl′ə-jē] *noun*, the study of ancient things made by man from an earlier civilization

**ar-cha-ic** [är-kā′ĭk] *adjective*, antiquated, ancient, very old

**arch-bish-op** [ärch-bĭsh′əp] *noun*, the chief bishop in the Christian church

**ar-cher-y** [är′chə-rē] *noun*, the practice or art of shooting with a bow and arrow

**ar-chi-pel-a-go** [är′kə-pĕl′ə-gō′] *noun*, a group or chain of islands

**ar-chi-tect** [är′kĭ-tĕkt′] *noun*, one who draws plans and specifications for buildings

**ar-chi-tec-ture** [är′kĭ-tĕk′chər] *noun*, the art and study of building design and structure

**ar-chive** [är′kīv′] *noun*, a place in which public records and historic documents are kept

**arc-tic** [ärk′tĭk, är′tĭk] *adjective*, relating to the area around the North Pole

**ar-dent** [är′dnt] *adjective*, passionate, zealous

**ar-dor** [är′dər] *noun*, passion, zeal, enthusiasm, great excitement

**ar-du-ous** [är′jōō-əs] *adjective*, difficult, attended with great labor or exertion, strenuous

**are** [är] *verb*, the part of the *verb* **is** used with we, you and they

**ar-e-a** [âr′ē-ə] *noun*, 1) a location or vicinity 2) a surface measured by multiplying the width times the length

**a-re-na** [ə-rē′nə] *noun*, a playing field or a stadium surrounded by seats used for sports or entertainment

**aren't** [ärnt, är′ənt] the *contraction,*for the two words **are** and **not**

**ar-gon** [är′gŏn′] *noun*, one of the noble gases, a colorless, odorless, inert gas

**ar-gue** [är′gyōō] *verb*, to fight by using words, to disagree, to debate, to dispute

**ar-gu-ment** [är′gyə-mənt] *noun*, a disagreement, a dispute

**ar-id** [ăr′ĭd] *adjective*, dry, parched, dusty

**a-rise** [ə-rīz′] *verb*, to come up, to issue, to spring forth, to get up

**a-ris-to-crat** [ə-rĭs′tə-krăt′] *noun*, a man or woman of fashion, a member of the nobility

**a-rith-me-tic** [ə-rĭth′mĭ-tĭk] *noun*, the science of numbers

**Ar-i-zo-na** [ăr′ĭ-zō′nə] *noun*, one of the 50 United States, located in the Southwest, the capital is Phoenix. The state flower of **Arizona** is the blossom of the saguaro cactus and the motto is "God enriches."

**ark** [ärk] *noun*, a large flat-bottomed ship

**Ar-kan-sas** [är′kən-sô′] *noun*, a state in the southern part of the United States, the capital is Little Rock. The **Arkansas** state flower is the apple blossom and the motto is "The people rule."

**arm** [ärm] *noun*, 1) the part of the body between the shoulder and the hand, *verb*, 2) to provide with weapons, to prepare for combat

**ar-ma-ments** [är′mə-mənts] *noun*, *plural*, military forces and weapons

**ar-mi-stice** [är′mǐ-stǐs] *noun*, a treaty of peace, a truce

**ar-mor** [är′mər] *noun*, a covering of metal worn by soldiers for protection

**ar-mor-y** [är′mə-rē] *noun*, a military storehouse

**arms** [ärmz] *noun*, *plural*, weapons, such as bombs and guns

**ar-my** [är′mē] *noun*, a large number of soldiers training for war on land, ground troops

**a-ro-ma** [ə-rō′mə] *noun*, smell, scent, fragrance

**a-round** [ə-round′] *adverb*, 1) in a circle, surrounding all sides, 2) nearby 3) approximately, *preposition*, 4) on every side

**a-rouse** [ə-rouz′] *verb*, 1) to awaken, to animate, to coax 2) to excite, to provoke, to stimulate

**ar-raign** [ə-rān′] *verb*, to call to account, to bring into court to answer charges, to accuse publicly

**ar-range** [ə-rānj′] *verb*, to put in proper order or sequence

**ar-range-ment** [ə-rānj′mənt] *noun*, 1) the act of putting in an orderly condition 2) plan

**ar-ray** [ə-rā′] *noun*, 1) a display, an exhibition, *verb*, 2) to arrange in a display, to place, to order

**ar-rest** [ə-rěst′] *noun*, 1) the act of taking someone into custody,

*verb*, 2) to stop the movement or progress of 3) to seize by legal authority and charge with breaking the law

**ar-ri-val** [ə-rī′vəl] *noun*, the moment when a place or object is reached

**ar-rive** [ə-rīv′] *verb*, to reach a destination or a goal

**ar-ro-gance** [ăr′ə-gəns] *noun*, an overbearing sense of self-importance. excessive pride

**ar-ro-gant** [ăr′ə-gənt] *adjective*, having a high opinion of oneself

**ar-row** [ăr′ō] *noun*, 1) a pointed stick that is shot from a bow 2) a mark shaped like an arrow that shows direction

**ar-se-nal** [är′sə-nəl] *noun*, a collection of weapons, a storehouse of ammunition

**ar-son** [är′sən] *noun*, the crime of purposely setting property on fire

**art** [ärt] *noun*, the creation of beautiful or significant things through music, drawing, painting, sculpture, cooking, dancing, etc.

**ar-ter-y** [är′tə-rē] *noun*, the thick blood vessels that carry blood from the heart

**ar-te-sian well** [är-tē′zhən] *noun*, a well that taps ground water that is under pressure and therefore does not require a pump, so called from Artois, France

**ar-thri-tis** [är-thrī′tǐs] *noun*, inflammation of the joints

**ar-ti-cle** [är′tǐ-kəl] *noun*, 1) a particular thing 2) a section, provision, item 3) a brief written composition, as in a newspaper or magazine 4) one of the limiting articles, *a*, *an*, or *the*

# articulate

**ar-tic-u-late** [är-tĭk′yə-lĭt]
*adjective*, 1) effective, distinct,
able to express ideas clearly, [är-
tĭk′yə-lāt] *verb*, 2) to speak
clearly to express an idea

**ar-ti-fact** [är′tə-făkt′] *noun*,
something made by humans
from an earlier civilization

**ar-ti-fice** [är′tə-fĭs] *noun*, skill,
scheme, ability, trick

**ar-ti-fi-cial** [är′tə-fĭsh′əl] *adjective*,
1) made of or contrived by art
2) not natural, not made by
nature, made by humans 3)
assumed, affected

**ar-t-il-ler-y** [är-tĭl′ə-rē] *noun*, the
mounted guns in an army, the
soldiers in charge of such guns

**art-ist** [är′tĭst] *noun*, a person
skilled in the techniques of the
fine arts, such as painting,
dancing, drama, etc.

**as** [ăz] conjunction, 1) when, while
2) because, *preposition*, 3) in
such a way, like

**ascend** [ə-sĕnd′] *verb*, to climb, to
go upward, to rise

**as-cen-sion** [ə-sĕn′shən] *noun*, the
act of going up, a rising

**as-cent** [ə-sĕnt′] *noun*, the act of
climbing up an incline, a slope

**as-cer-tain** [ăs′ər-tān′] *verb*, to
determine, to establish

**as-cet-ic** [ə-sĕt′ĭk] *adjective*, self-
denying, austere, disciplined

**ash** [ăsh] *noun*, 1) the gray powder
residue left after something has
burned 2) a tree of the olive
family, with hard wood

**a-shamed** [ə-shāmd′] *adjective*,
upset because you have done

something that you think is silly,
not good enough or wrong,
embarrassed, feeling inadequate

**a-shore** [ə-shôr′] *adverb*, on to land

**A-sia** [ā′zhə] *noun*, one of the
seven continents in the world,
holding 57% of the population

**a-side** [ə-sīd′] *adverb*, 1) to or
toward one side, away, *noun*,
2) departure from the main topic,
3) a whisper

**ask** [ăsk] *verb*, 1) to pose or speak
a question, to inquire 2) to
request something

**a-skew** [ə-skyo͞o′] *adjective*, out of
line, crooked

**a-sleep** [ə-slēp′] *adjective*,
sleeping, not awake

**as-pect** [ăs′pĕkt] *noun*,
1) appearance, look 2) part, or
point of view

**as-phalt** [ăs′fôlt′] *noun*, a tar like
material mixed with sand or
gravel for highway surfaces or
pavement,

**as-phyx-i-a-tion** [ăs-fĭk′sē-ā′-shən]
*noun*, death by lack of oxygen

**as-pi-ra-tion** [ăs′pə-rā′shən] *noun*,
an ambition, a strong desire

**as-pire** [ə-spīr′] *verb*, to desire, to
strive, to hope for

**as-pi-rin** [ăs′pər-ĭn, -prĭn] *noun*, a
medicine used to relieve pain,
acetylsalicylic acid

**as-sas-si-nate** [ə-săs′ə-nāt′] *verb*,
to murder a public official or
other important person

**as-sault** [ə-sôlt′] *noun*, 1) an attack,
*verb*, 2) to strike, to hit

**as-sem-ble** [ə-sĕm′bəl] *verb*, to
gather or put together

26

**as-sem-bly** [ə-sĕm′blē] *noun*, 1) a
gathering, for educational,
religious, or entertainment
programs of students and
teachers 2) a legal body such as
Congress or a legislature

**as-sert** [ə-sûrt′] *verb*, to declare,
to state forcefully

**as-sess** [ə-sĕs′] *verb*, to evaluate

**as-sess-ment** [ə-sĕs′mənt] *noun*, an
appraisal, an estimation

**as-set** [ăs′ĕt′] *noun*, something of
value or worth

**as-sign** [ə-sīn′] *verb*, 1) to give out
or allot 2) to delegate a task

**as-sign-ment** [ə-sīn′mənt] *noun*,
homework, an obligation, work
given to someone to accomplish

**as-sim-i-late** [ə-sĭm′ə-lāt′] *verb*, to
take in food or knowledge, to
make part of oneself

**as-sist** [ə-sĭst′] *verb*, to aid or help

**as-sis-tance** [ə-sĭs′təns] *noun*, help
or aid given

**as-sis-tant** [ə-sĭs′tənt] *noun*, a
helper, an aide, a subordinate,

**as-so-ci-ate** *noun*, [ə-sō′shē-ĭt]
1) a colleague or co-worker,
[ə-sō′shē-āt′] *verb*, 2) to think of
something in relation with
something else 3) to keep
company, to socialize with
someone

**as-so-ci-a-tion** [ə-sō′sē-ā′shən,]
*noun*, a group of people joined
together for one purpose

**as-sort-ment** [ə-sôrt′mənt] *noun*, a
variety of things

**as-suage** [ə-swāj′] *verb*, to lessen,
to ease, to comfort

**as-sume** [ə-sōōm′] *verb*, to think
something is true without proof

**as-sump-tion** [ə-sŭmp′shən] *noun*,
something taken for granted

**as-sur-ance** [ə-shŏŏr′əns] *noun*, a
promise, a pledge

**as-sure** [ə-shŏŏr′] *verb*, to tell
someone firmly, to promise

**as-ter-isk** [ăs′tə-rĭsk′] *noun*, the
sign *

**as-ter-oid** [ăs′tə-roid′] *noun*, small
planets, most of which are located
between Mars and Jupiter, that
revolve around the sun

**asth-ma** [ăz′mə] *noun*, a
respiratory disorder that causes
difficulty in breathing
accompanied by wheezing

**a-stig-ma-tism** [ə-stĭg′mə-tĭz′əm]
*noun*, an eye defect that prevents
proper focus

**as-ton-ish** [ə-stŏn′ĭsh] *verb*, to
give a feeling of surprise, amaze

**as-ton-ish-ment** [ə-stŏn′ĭsh-mənt]
*noun*, complete surprise,
amazement

**as-tound** [ə-stound′] *verb*, to
amaze, to shock, to surprise

**as-tral** [ăs′trəl] *adjective*, relating
to the stars

**a-stray** [ə-strā′] *adverb*, off course,
in error

**as-trin-gent** [ə-strĭn′jənt] *adjective*,
capable of drawing tissue together

**as-tro-naut** [ăs′trə-nôt′] *noun*, a
person who travels in space

**as-trol-o-gy** [ə-strŏl′ə-jē] *noun*, the
study of the assumed influence
of planets and stars on the course
of human affairs

**as-tron-o-mer** [ə-strŏn′ə-mər] *noun*, a person who studies the stars and the heavens

**as-tro-nom-i-cal** [ăs′trə-nŏm′ĭ-kəl] *adjective*, enormously large or extensive, huge

**as-tron-o-my** [ə-strŏn′ə-mē] *noun*, the study of the sun, moon, stars, and the heavens

**as-tute** [ə-stŌŌt′] *adjective*, having a clever, shrewd, or cunning mind, perceptive, insightful

**a-sy-lum** [ə-sī′ləm] *noun*, protection from persecution

**at** [ăt] *preposition*, 1) showing where 2) showing when 3) showing how much

**ate** [āt] *verb*, the *past tense* of **eat**

**a-the-ism** [ā′thē-ĭz′əm] *noun*, the belief that there is no God

**ath-lete** [ăth′lēt′] *noun*, someone who is good at sports

**ath-let-ic** [ăth-lĕt′ĭk] *adjective*, strong, vigorous, having to do with sports

**at-las** [ăt′ləs] *noun*, a book or section of a book that has maps

**at-mos-phere** [ăt′mə-sfîr′] *noun*, 1) the mass of air surrounding the earth 2) the mood or feeling of a place, a tone conveyed

**at-om** [ăt′əm] *noun*, the smallest particle of an element

**a-tom-ic** [ə-tŏm′ĭk] *adjective*, tiny, infinitesimal, having to do with atoms

**at-om-iz-er** [ăt′ə-mī′zər] *noun*, an instrument for reducing a liquid to a fine spray

**a-tri-um** [ā′trē-əm] *noun*, **atria** or **atriums**, *plural*, 1) one of the chambers of the heart 2) the central court in a Roman building

**a-tro-cious** [ə-trō′shəs] *adjective*, very bad, outrageously cruel

**a-troc-i-ty** [ə-trŏs′ĭ-tē] *noun*, a brutal deed, a cruel act

**a-tro-phy** [ăt′rə-fē] *verb*, to stop the development of an organ, to wither from lack of use

**at-tach** [ə-tăch′] *verb*, 1) to connect something with something else 2) to feel affection toward someone 3) to ascribe

**at-tach-ment** [ə-tăch′mənt] *noun*, 1) an affection, fondness 2) an additional part for a machine

**at-tack** [ə-tăk′] *noun*, 1) fight, an attempt to harm someone, *verb*, 2) to assail, to try to injure someone, to assault

**at-tain** [ə-tān′] *verb*, to succeed in getting something done, to reach a goal

**at-tempt** [ə-tĕmpt′] *noun*, 1) a try, an endeavor, *verb*, 2) to try, to endeavor, to make an effort

**at-tend** [ə-tĕnd′] *verb*, 1) to be present at 2) to take care of 3) to pay attention to

**at-tend-ance** [ə-tĕn′dəns] *noun*, the act of showing up or putting in an appearance, presence

**at-tend-ant** [ə-tĕn′dənt] *noun*, one who accompanies or attends, as a companion, a servant

**at-ten-tion** [ə-tĕn′shən] *noun*, application of the mind to something, concentration

**at-ten-tive** [ə-tĕn′tĭv] *adjective*, careful to notice little things

**at-tic** [ăt′ĭk] *noun*, the top floor of a house, right under the roof

**at-tire** [ə-tīr′] *noun*, anything that dresses or adorns, clothing

**at-ti-tude** [ăt′ĭ-tood′] *noun*, a mood or feeling, a way of thinking

**at-tor-ney** [ə-tûr′nē] *noun*, one legally authorized to act for another, a lawyer

**at-tract** [ə-trăkt′] *verb*, 1) to draw the attention of someone or something 2) to cause someone or something to come near

**at-trac-tion** [ə-trăk′shən] *noun*, 1) the power to bring things together 2) a fascination that holds someone's attention

**at-trac-tive** [ə-trăk′tĭv] *adjective*, pleasing to look at, appealing

**at-trib-ute** *noun*, [ə-trăb′yoot] 1) a distinguishing feature that belongs to someone, [ətrĭb′yoot] *verb*, 2) to explain how one thing is associated with another

**at-tri-tion** [ə-trĭsh′ən] *noun*, a gradual wearing down

**auc-tion** [ôk′shən] *noun*, a public sale at which buyers bid on items to be sold

**auc-tion-eer** [ôk′shə-nîr′] *noun*, one licensed to hold a public sale at which items go to the highest bidder

**au-dac-i-ty** [ô-dăs′ĭ-tē] *noun*, impertinence, boldness, self-assurance, daring

**au-di-ble** [ô′də-bəl] *adjective*, capable of being heard

**au-di-ence** [ô′dē-əns] *noun*, 1) a group gathered to watch or listen to a performance 2) a formal hearing

**au-di-o** [ô′dē-ō′] *adjective*, relating to sound or sound reproduction

**au-dit** [ô′dĭt] *noun*, 1) a special examination of accounting records, *verb*, 2) to examine or investigate, to evaluate

**au-di-tion** [ô-dĭsh′ən] *noun*, a tryout for a performance

**au-di-to-ri-um** [ô′dĭ-tôr′ē-əm] *noun*, an assembly hall with a stage and seats

**au-ger** [ô′gər] *noun*, a tool for making holes, a drill

**aug-ment** [ôg-mĕnt′] *verb*, to make larger, to increase, to add on to

**au-gur** [ô′gər] *verb*, to foretell, to see into the future, to portend, to be an omen

**Au-gust** [ô′gəst] *noun*, the eighth month of the year, having 31 days

**aunt** [ănt, änt] *noun*, the sister of one of your parents or the wife of the brother of one parent

**aus-pices** [ô′spĭ-sēz′] *noun*, *plural*, 1) patronage, protection 2) omens

**aus-pi-cious** [ô-spĭsh′əs] *adjective*, fortunate, showing signs that promise success

**aus-tere** [ô-stîr′] *adjective*, 1) severe or strict in judging, harsh, rough or bitter acting, 2) very plain, simple, bare, ascetic

**Aus-tra-lia** [ô-strāl′yə] *noun*, one of the seven continents in the world, the only continent that is also a country containing .5% of the world's population

**au-then-tic** [ô-thĕn′tĭk] *adjective*, genuine, known to be true

**au-then-ti-cate** [ô-thĕn′tĭ-kāt′] *verb*, to prove genuine

**au-thor** [ô′thər] *noun*, a person who writes books, articles, etc.

**au-thor-i-ta-tive** [ə-thôr′ĭ-tā′tĭv] *adjective*, reliably accurate

**au-thor-i-ty** [ə-thôr′ĭ-tē] *noun*, 1) a person who runs something or controls it 2) command, prestige, influence, control 3) an expert

**au-thor-ize** [ô′thə-rīz′] *verb*, 1) to empower 2) to make legal 3) to give permission to act

**au-to-bi-og-ra-phy** [ô′tō-bī-ŏg′rə-fē] *noun*, a story written about the author's life

**au-to-crat** [ô′tə-krăt′] *noun*, a ruler with supreme power

**au-to-graph** [ô′tə-grăf′] *noun*, a person's signature

**au-to-mat-ic** [ô′tə-măt′ĭk] *adjective*, acting mechanically without human direction

**au-to-mat-i-cal-ly** [ô′tə-măt′ĭk-lē] *adverb*, 1) by a machine 2) without trying or thinking first

**au-tom-a-tion** [ô′tə-mā′shən] *noun*, a machine that imitates the actions of humans, a robot

**au-to-mo-bile** [ô′tə-mō-bēl′] *noun*, a vehicle on wheels, powered by an engine to transport people on roads, a car

**au-ton-o-mous** [ô-tŏn′ə-məs] *adjective*, self-governing, acting independently from government

**au-top-sy** [ô′tŏp′sē] *noun*, the dissection of a dead body to determine the cause of death

**au-tumn** [ô′təm] *noun*, the third season of each year, between summer and winter, September 22-December 21, known as fall

**aux-il-ia-ry** [ôg-zĭl′yə-rē] *adjective*, additional, serving alongside another, supporting

**a-vail-a-ble** [ə-vā′lə-bəl] *adjective*, capable of being used, accessible

**av-a-lanche** [ăv′ə-lănch′] *noun*, a large overwhelming quantity of snow, rocks, or mud that falls from a mountain suddenly, gaining size as it falls

**av-a-rice** [ăv′ə-rĭs] *noun*, greed for money or power

**a-venge** [ə-vĕnj′] *verb*, to punish in kind, to retaliate, to get even

**av-e-nue** [ăv′ə-nōō′] *noun*, a wide road, often with many roads intersecting at right angles

**av-er-age** [ăv′ər-ĭj] *adjective*, 1) ordinary, usual, typical, *noun*, 2) the mean value of a set of numbers, *verb*, 3) to find the mean

**a-ver-sion** [ə-vûr′zhən] *noun*, a dislike, antipathy, opposition

**a-vert** [ə-vûrt′] *verb*, to avoid, to prevent or turn away

**a-vi-a-tion** [ā′vē-ā′shən, ăv′ē-] *noun*, air transportation

**a-vi-a-tor** [ā′vē-ā′tər] *noun*, an airplane or helicopter pilot

**av-id** [ăv′ĭd] *adjective*, eager, enthusiastic, excited

**av-o-ca-tion** [ăv′ō-kā′shən] *noun*, a hobby

**a-void** [ə-void′] *verb*, to stay away from, to evade, to shun

**a-wait** [ə-wāt⁄] *verb*, to expect, to wait, to anticipate

**a-wake** [ə-wāk⁄] *adjective*, not sleeping, alert

**a-ward** [ə-wôrd⁄] *noun*, 1) a prize or an honor to recognize exceptional service, achievement, etc., *verb*, 2) to present a certificate or plaque or trophy in recognition of an honor

**a-ware** [ə-wâr⁄] *adjective*, knowing, conscious, informed

**a-way** [ə-wā⁄] *adverb*, 1) off in a different direction 2) from one's possession

**awe** [ô] *noun*, a solemn wonder

**aw-ful** [ô⁄fəl] *adjective*, very bad, appalling, frightful, horrible

**awk-ward** [ôk⁄wərd] *adjective*, 1) clumsy, ungraceful 2) embarrassing

**awl** [ôl] *noun*, a pointed tool used to make holes in wood or leather

**awn-ing** [ô⁄nĭng] *noun*, a sunshade, a canvas covering for a porch, patio, deck, etc.

**a-wry** [ə-rī⁄] *adjective*, 1) amiss, crooked, wrong, *adverb*, 2) distorted, twisted to one side

**ax or axe** [ăks] *noun*, a tool with a metal blade fixed onto a handle, used for chopping

**ax-i-om** [ăk⁄sē-əm] *noun*, a self-evident truth or principle

**ax-is** [ăk⁄sĭs] *noun*, a real or imaginary line around which something rotates

**ax-le** [ăk⁄səl] *noun*, the rod on which a wheel revolves

# B

**ba-by** [bā⁄bē] *noun*, an infant, a very young child or animal

**bach-e-lor** [băch⁄ə-lər] *noun*, a man who has never been married

**back** [băk] *adverb*, 1) to or in a place where something or someone was before 2) toward the back part, away from the front, *noun*, 3) the part of the body opposite the face, extending from the neck to the hips, *verb*, 4) to move in the opposite direction from 5) to give support to

**back-ground** [băk⁄ground⁄] *noun*, 1) the surroundings behind something 2) past experience, culture

**back-ward** [băk⁄wərd] *adjective*, 1) having the part designed for the back in the front 2) following tradition and resisting progress, *adverb*, 3) in reverse 4) beginning at the end

**ba-con** [bā⁄kən] *noun*, meat from the back and sides of a pig, salted and smoked

**bac-te-ri-um** [băk-tîr⁄ē-əm] *noun*, **bacteria**, *plural*, a single-celled living thing that cannot be seen without a microscope, reproducing rapidly and sometimes causing diseases

**bad** [băd] *adjective*, 1) not good, rotten 2) severe, unpleasant

**badge** [băj] *noun*, a pin or emblem worn to show authority or accomplishment

**baf-fle** [băf⁄əl] *verb*, to mix up, to confuse, to puzzle

# bag

**bag** [băg] *noun*, a container made of paper, cloth, plastic, or leather that has an opening at the top or in the side

**bag-gage** [băg′ĭj] *noun, no plural*, suitcases, bags, or trunks one takes along on a journey

**bail** [bāl] *noun*, 1) a bond or pledge backed with money or property, *verb*, 2) to ladle or empty out

**bail-iff** [bā′lĭf] *noun*, an official who keeps order in the court

**bait** [bāt] *noun*, 1) food used to lure or entice fish or animals, *verb*, 2) to annoy or taunt

**bake** [bāk] *verb*, to cook by dry heat, usually in an oven

**bak-er** [bā′kər] *noun*, someone who makes pastries, cakes and breads for a living

**bak-er-y** [bā′kə-rē] *noun*, a place where pastries, cakes, and breads are made and sold

**bal-ance** [băl′əns] *noun*, 1) steadiness 2) an instrument used to weigh something 3) the difference between the debits and credits of an account, *verb*, 4) to keep oneself steady 5) to make equal and stable, to compensate for

**bal-co-ny** [băl′kə-nē] *noun*, a porch outside of a building and above the first floor

**bald** [bôld] *adjective*, having no hair

**bale** [bāl] *noun*, 1) a large amount of materials bundled tightly together, *verb*, 2) to bundle into a package

**balk** [bôk] *verb*, 1) to hesitate, to refuse to act 2) to hinder

**ball** [bôl] *noun*, 1) a round object used in games or as a toy 2) a large party for dancing

**bal-lad** [băl′əd] *noun*, a poem or song that tells a story

**bal-last** [băl′əst] *noun*, 1) heavy material carried by a ship to balance it 2) crushed stones

**bal-let** [bă-lā′] *noun*, a play without speech in which the story is told through dance

**bal-loon** [bə-lōōn′] *noun*, a rubber bag that expands as it is filled with air or gas

**bal-lot** [băl′ət] *noun*, 1) a printed ticket used in voting to make a choice 2) the whole vote cast

**balm** [bäm] *noun*, 1) something that relieves pain 2) a soothing ointment

**balm-y** [bä′mē] *adjective*, mild, refreshing, soft and warm

**bam-boo** [băm-bōō′] *noun*, a woody grass with hollow stems, abundant in the tropics

**ban** [băn] *noun*, 1) an order that does not allow something, *verb*, 2) to not allow something or to prevent it from taking place

**ba-nal** [bə-năl′, bā′nəl] *adjective*, ordinary, commonplace, trite

**ba-nan-a** [bə-năn′ə] *noun*, a long yellow tropical fruit having a tasty soft pulp

**band** [bănd] *noun*, 1) a group of musicians who get together to play their instruments, usually brass, percussion, and woodwinds 2) a strip of something 3) a group 4) a piece that wraps around something, *verb*, 5) to join together

**band-age** [băn′dĭj] *noun*, 1) a piece of cloth or adhesive strip put over a wound, *verb*, 2) to cover a wound with a cloth or adhesive strip

**ban-dan-na** [băn-dăn′ə] *noun*, a cotton scarf or handkerchief

**ban-dit** [băn′dĭt] *noun*, a robber

**ban-dy** [băn′dē] *verb*, to exchange, to pass to and fro

**bane** [bān] *noun*, the cause of ruin

**bane-ful** [bān′fəl] *adjective*, ruinous, having poisonous qualities, causing misery

**bang** [băng] *noun*, 1) a startling loud sound, *verb*, 2) to produce a loud sound by striking one thing against another

**ban-ish** [băn′ĭsh] *verb*, 1) to send away, to dismiss 2)2 to exile as a form of punishment

**ban-is-ter** [băn′ĭ-stər] *noun*, a railing that guards the edges of stairs to prevent someone from falling

**ban-jo** [băn′jō] *noun*, a stringed musical instrument, like a ukulele or guitar, but with a circular sound box

**bank** [băngk] *noun*, 1) the land along a body of water, the side of a hill 2) a commercial institution where money is kept and loaned

**bank-er** [băng′kər] *noun*, one who conducts the business of a bank

**bank-rupt** [băngk′rŭpt] *adjective*, broke, out of business

**ban-ner** [băn′ər] *noun*, a flag, a cloth bearing an emblem

**ban-quet** [băng′kwĭt] *noun*, a feast or ceremonious dinner

**ban-ter** [băn′tər] *noun*, 1) good-natured ridiculing or teasing 2) to speak or to address in a witty or teasing manner

**bap-tism** [băp′tĭz′əm] *noun*, the ceremony of initiation into Christianity

**bap-tize** [băp-tīz′] *verb*, to sprinkle someone with holy water and bestow a name

**bar** [bär] *noun*, 1) a counter where drinks are sold 2) a long solid object made of wood or metal 3) the legal profession, *verb*, 4) to exclude or block

**barb** [bärb] *noun*, the sharp projections from a fishhook, arrow, etc.

**bar-ber** [bär′bər] *noun*, a person who cuts men's hair

**bare** [bâr] *adjective*, 1) uncovered, naked 2) unadorned, empty

**bare-ly** [bâr′lē] *adverb*, almost, not, hardly, only, scarcely

**bar-gain** [bär′gĭn] *noun*, 1) something bought at a lower price than expected 2) an agreement or compact between two parties, *verb*, 3) to haggle for a lower price

**barge** [bärj] *noun*, a large boat with a flat bottom, used to carry things on a river or a canal

**bar-i-um** [bâr′ē-əm] *noun*, one of the elements of the alkaline earth group

**bark** [bärk] *noun*, 1) the outer covering of a tree trunk and branches 2) a sound made by a dog or a brusque voice, *verb*, 3) to speak like a dog

**bar-ley** [bär′lē] *noun*, one of the cereal grains

**barn** [bärn] *noun*, a farm building where animals and harvested crops are kept

**bar-na-cle** [bär′nə-kəl] *noun*, a marine crustacean that attaches itself to rocks and boats

**ba-rom-e-ter** [bə-rŏm′ĭ-tər] *noun*, a device that measures air pressure in the atmosphere

**bar-on** [băr′ən] *noun*, a nobleman, an aristocrat, a tycoon

**ba-roque** [bə-rōk′] *adjective*, an ornate style of the 17th and 18th centuries

**bar-racks** [băr′əks] *noun*, *plural*, buildings for lodging soldiers

**bar-rage** [bär′ĭj] *noun*, an artillary attack covering a wide area

**bar-rel** [băr′əl] *noun*, 1) a large container shaped like a cylinder 2) the long metal tube forming part of a gun

**bar-ren** [băr′ən] *adjective*, 1) bleak, lacking in good things 2) unable to bear children, unable to support growth

**bar-ri-cade** [băr′ĭ-kād] *noun*, 1) an obstruction or means of defense, a barrier, *verb*, 2) to block, to fortify, to bar

**bar-ri-er** [băr′ē-ər] *noun*, 1) a stumbling block, a deterrent, an obstacle, something blocking the way 2) a fence or wall to mark the limits of a place

**bar-ris-ter** [băr′ĭ-stər] *noun*, in England, a counselor at law, a lawyer

**bar-ter** [bär′tər] *verb*, to trade

**base** [bās] *adjective*, 1) low, menial, inferior, *noun*, 2) the bottom on which something stands 3) an area designated safe, in baseball one of four sandbags

**base-ball** [bās′bôl′] *noun*, a game played with a bat and a ball by two teams with nine players on a side, on a field with four bases at the corners of a diamond

**base-ment** [bās′mənt] *noun*, storage or living space in the foundation of a building

**ba-sic** [bā′sĭk] *adjective*, 1) forming a starting point, fundamental 2) plain, simple

**ba-sin** [bā′sĭn] *noun*, 1) a low, bowl-shaped area, a depression in the land 2) a shallow sink

**ba-sis** [bā′sĭs] *noun*, the starting point or central idea of something, the core

**bask** [băsk] *verb*, to lay in the sun

**bas-ket** [băs′kĭt] *noun*, a container woven from reeds or twigs and used to carry things

**bas-ket-ball** [băs′kĭt-bôl′] *noun*, a game in which two teams of five players each compete to throw a ball through a hoop

**bass** [bās] *adjective*, 1) the lowest range of the male voice, as in sound, [ băs] *noun*, 2) a fresh-water fish

**bas-tion** [băs′chən] *noun*, a fortress, a defense

**bat** [băt] *noun*, 1) a piece of wood used to hit a ball in a game 2) a flying mammal, *verb*, 3) to hit a ball with a piece of wood

**batch** [băch] *noun*, a number of things in a group

**bath** [băth, bäth] *noun*, 1) a container large enough to hold water to wash a body 2) the act of washing one's body

**bathe** [bāth] *verb*, to wash with water, usually a part of a body

**bath-room** [băth′rōōm] *noun*, a room with a toilet and a sink where people wash

**ba-ton** [bə-tŏn] *noun*, a wand, a night-stick, a rod, a stick used for conducting an orchestra

**bat-tal-ion** [bə-tăl′yən] *noun*, a large group of army soldiers ready for battle

**bat-ter** [băt′ər] *noun*, 1) the person holding the bat in baseball 2) a mixture of flour, eggs, and milk, *verb*, 3) to hit repeatedly

**bat-ter-y** [băt′ə-rē] *noun*, an apparatus for storing chemical energy and converting it to electrical power

**bat-tle** [băt′l] *noun*, 1) a fight or skirmish between people or different groups, *verb*, 2) to fight

**bay** [bā] *adjective*, 1) reddish-brown, *noun*, 2) part of a sea that stretches into land 3) a recess in a room 4) a tree or shrub of the laurel family, *verb*, 5) to howl, to bark at

**bay-o-net** [bā′ə-nĭt] *noun*, a blade on the end of a rifle

**ba-zaar** [bə-zär′] *noun*, a marketplace where miscellaneous articles are sold

**B.C.**, signifying a time before the birth of Christ

**be** [bē] *verb*, 1) used to give information about people or things and to join words for people or things to the qualities or position they have 2) the present indicative of verb **be**

| Singular | Plural |
|---|---|
| I **am** | We **are** |

*I **am** proud of you.*
*We **are** happy to see you.*

You **are**      You **are**

*You **are** what you eat.*
*You **are** the students in the class.*

He/she/it **is**      They **are**

*He **is** a gentleman, he **is** kind.*
*They **are** all our friends.*

Past Tense

I **was**      We **were**

*I **was** waiting for you.*
*We **were** hoping you could stay.*

You **were**      You **were**

*You **were** a true friend.*
*You **were** good children.*

He/she it **was**      They **were**

*It **was** time to go.*
*They **were** our heroes.*

**beach** [bēch] *noun*, a shore of sand or pebbles along a lake or ocean

**bea-con** [bē′kən] *noun*, a lantern, a beam of light, a signal

**bead** [bēd] *noun*, a small ball of glass or other material, with a small hole for string or wire to pass through

**beak** [bēk] *noun*, the hard, pointed mouth of a bird

**beak-er** [bē′kər] *noun*, 1) a deep, open-mouthed, thin, glass vessel with a lip 2) a tall wide-mouthed cup

**beam** [bēm] *noun*, 1) a large piece of timber used to brace or support a ceiling 2) a ray, a shaft of light, *verb*, 3) to smile happily 4) to send or transmit, to shine

**bean** [bēn] *noun*, the seed of any bean plant, often used for food

**bear** [bâr] *adjective*, 1) referring to unfavorable market conditions. *noun*, 2) a large, furry mammal with four feet, *verb*, 3) to carry 4) to suffer or endure 5) to produce, to bring forth, to yield 6) to exhibit, to show, to relate

**beard** [bîrd] *noun*, hair on the face below the mouth

**beast** [bēst] *noun*, an animal, especially a savage animal

**beat** [bēt] *noun*, 1) a stroke or movement that is part of a rhythm, *verb*, 2) to pound, to tap 3) to conquer, to defeat

**beau-ti-ful** [byōō'tə-fəl] *adjective*, charming and delightful to the senses, very pretty, lovely

**beau-ty** [byōō'tē] *noun*, qualities pleasing to the eye or ear, charm

**bea-ver** [bē'vər] *noun*, an amphibious rodent with brown fur that builds dams as homes

**be-cause** [bǐ-kôz] *conjunction*, since, for the reason that

**beck-on** [běk'ən] *verb*, to signal, call or summon to come over by motioning silently

**be-come** [bǐ-kǔm'] *verb*, to change or to grow to be, to suit

**bed** [běd] *noun*, 1) a piece of furniture on which someone sleeps 2) the bottom of something 3) a garden plot

**bed-lam** [běd'ləm] *noun*, confusion, noise, uproar

**bed-room** [běd'rōōm] *noun*, the room for sleeping in

**bee** [bē] *noun*, an insect with a stinger and wings that makes honey and carries pollen from flower to flower

**beech** [bēch] *noun*, a family of hardwood trees that includes oak and elm

**beef** [bēf] *noun*, the meat from cattle

**bee-hive** [bē'hīv'] *noun*, a house made for bees to live in

**been** [bǐn] the *past tense* of the *verb* **to be**

**beer** [bîr] *noun*, an alcoholic beverage made of grain and hops

**beet** [bēt] *noun*, a purplish root vegetable, used for dye and eaten like a turnip

**bee-tle** [bēt'l] *noun*, an insect whose outside wings make a hard, protective cover for its body

**be-fore** [bǐ-fôr] *adverb*, 1) happening in advance of, earlier than, *preposition*, 2) in front of, ahead of

**be-fore-hand** [bǐ-fôr'hănd] *adverb*, ahead of, in advance

**beg** [běg] *verb*, to ask as a favor

**be-gan** [bǐ-găn'] *verb*, *past tense* of **begin**

**beg-gar** [běg'ər] *noun*, one who asks for favors or money

**be-gin** [bǐ-gǐn'] *verb*, to start, to commence

**be-gin-ning** [bĭ-gĭn′ĭng] *noun*, the start of something, the origin

**be-guile** [bĭ-gīl′] *verb*, to divert or to entertain, to trick, to charm

**be-gun** [bĭ-gŭn′] *verb, past tense of* **begin**

**be-half** [bĭ-hăf] *noun*, interest, side

**be-have** [bĭ-hāv′] *verb*, to act, to conduct yourself

**be-hav-ior** [bĭ-hāv′yər] *noun*, manner of acting or bearing oneself, conduct

**be-he-moth** [bĭ-hē′məth] *noun*, a huge creature

**be-hind** [bĭ-hīnd′] *adverb*,
1) further away from, late, *preposition*, 2) following, at the back of, remaining after

**be-hoove** [bĭ-hōōv′] *verb*, to be fitting or proper, to require

**be-ing** [bē′ĭng] *noun*, 1) a living thing, *verb*, 2) *present participle of the verb* to **be**

**be-la-bor** [bĭ-lā′bər] *verb*, to repeat over and over

**be-lat-ed** [bĭ-lā′tĭd] *adjective*, too late, delayed, tardy

**be-lea-guered** [bĭ-lē′gərd] *adjective*, in a difficult position, besieged, attacked

**bel-fry** [bĕl′frē] *noun*, a tower where bells hang above a building

**be-lie** [bĭ-lī′] *verb*, to contradict, to give a false impression

**be-lief** [bĭ-lēf′] *noun*, faith, acceptance, conviction

**be-lieve** [bĭ-lēv′] *verb*, 1) to have faith or confidence 2) to think

**be-lit-tle** [bĭ-lĭt′l] *verb*, to tease, to

make fun of

**bell** [bĕl] *noun*, a round, hollow object of metal or glass that sounds when it is struck

**bel-li-cose** [bĕl′ĭ-kōs′] *adjective*, warlike, ready to fight

**bel-lig-er-ent** [bə-lĭj′ər-ənt] *adjective*, hostile, pugnacious, preparing to fight, aggressive

**bel-low** [bĕl′ō] *verb*, to make a loud deep sound like a bull

**bel-lows** [bĕl′ōz] *noun, plural*, a machine that draws air through a valve and expels it through a tube by alternate expansion and contraction, used in an organ or to blow air on a fire

**bel-ly** [bĕl′ē] *noun*, stomach, gut,

**be-long** [bĭ-lông] *verb*, 1) to be a part of, to be a member 2) to own or have possession of

**be-long-ings** [bĭ-lông′ĭngs] *noun*, *plural*, one's personal possessions

**be-lov-ed** [bĭ-lŭv′ĭd] *adjective*, cherished, highly valued, adored

**be-low** [bĭ-lō′] *adverb*, 1) at a lower level, *preposition*, 2) at a lower place or rank

**belt** [bĕlt] *noun*, 1) a band worn around the waist,, often made of cloth or leather 2) a band or strip indicating a region or zone, *verb*, 3) to hit or smack, to clobber 4) to strap, to surround, to attach by wrapping a cord around something

**bench** [bĕnch] *noun*, 1) a long seat often wooden 2) the table at which someone works 3) a judge's seat in court

# bend

**bend** [bĕnd] *noun*, 1) a curve, *verb*,
2) to shape into a curve or make
crooked 3) to stoop

**be-neath** [bĭ-nēth'] *preposition*,
below, under, at a lower level
than

**ben-e-dic-tion** [bĕn'ĭ-dĭk'shən]
*noun*, a blessing

**ben-e-fac-tor** [bĕn'ə-făk'tər] *noun*,
a gift-giver, a patron

**be-nef-i-cent** [bə-nĕf'ĭ-sənt]
*adjective*, performing acts of
kindness and charity, generous

**ben-e-fi-cial** [bĕn'ə-fĭsh'əl]
*adjectiven*, useful, profitable

**ben-e-fi-ci-ar-y** [bĕn'ə-fĭsh'ē-ĕr'ē]
*noun*, one who is going to
receive something valuable

**ben-e-fit** [bĕn'ə-fĭt] *noun*, 1) an
advantage, 2) a fundraiser *verb*,
3) to be helpful, to aid

**be-nev-o-lence** [bə-nĕv'ə-ləns]
*noun*, goodwill or kindness,
charity given, generosity

**be-nev-o-lent** [bə-nĕv'ə-lənt]
*adjective*, generous, kind-hearted

**be-nign** [bĭ-nīn'] *adjective*,
harmless, not cancerous, kind

**bent** [bĕnt] *past tense* of **bend**

**be-quest** [bĭ-kwĕst'] *noun*, the act
of leaving by a written will, a
legacy for the next generation

**be-rate** [bĭ-rāt'] *verb*, to criticize or
scold vigorously

**be-reave-ment** [bĭ-rēv'-mĕnt]
*noun*, the state of being deprived
of something, sorrow, mourning

**be-reft** [bĭ-rĕft'] *adjective*, lacking,
deprived of, doing without

**ber-ry** [bĕ-rē'] *noun*, a small,
round fruit from a bush

**ber-serk** [bər-sûrk] *adjective*,
frenzied with rage, crazy

**be-seech** [bĭ-sēch'] *verb*, to ask or
entreat, to implore, to beg

**be-side** [bĭ-sīd'] *preposition*, next
to, at the side of, adjacent

**be-sides** [bĭ-sīdz'] *adverb*, also, in
addition to, as an extra

**be-siege** [bĭ-sēj'] *verb*, to surround
with armed forces, to harass, to
encircle, to crowd around

**best** [bĕst] *adjective*, finest,
exceeding all others in quality

**be-stow** [bĭ-stō'] *verb*, to give
something, to confer

**bet** [bĕt] *noun*, 1) an agreement to
risk money on the odds of
winning, *verb*, 2) to risk money
on a gamble, to wager

**be-tray** [bĭ-trā'] *verb*, to break a
trust, to reveal a secret

**bet-ter** [bĕt'ər] *adjective*,
1) superior, *adverb*, 2) more,
larger, *verb*, 3) to improve

**bet-ween** [bĭ-twēn'] *adverb*,
1) showing where in relation to
things or places on either side
2) showing when in relation to
events before and after,
*preposition*, 3) showing how
things are joined 4) showing
how things are divided

**bev-er-age** [bĕv'ər-ij] *noun*, a
drink, a liquid refreshment

**bev-y** [bĕv'ē] *noun*, 1) a large
group, 2) a group of birds

**be-ware** [bĭ-wâr']*verb*, to be wary,
to be careful, to be on guard of

**be-wild-er-ed** [bĭ-wĭl'dərd]
*adjective*, confused, puzzled,
perplexed

**be-witch** [bǐ-wǐch′] *verb* to charm, to put under a magic spell

**be-yond** [bē-ŏnd] *preposition*, at a distance farther away, on the other side of, past

**bi-as** [bī′əs] *adjective*, 1) in a slanting manner, obliquely, diagonally, *noun*, 2) inclination, tendency, *verb*, 3) to influence, to show prejudice, to sway

**Bi-ble** [bī′bəl] *noun*, the religious book of the Christian and Jewish faiths

**bib-li-og-ra-phy** [bǐb′lē-ŏg′rə-fē] *noun*, a list of books on any subject usually found at the end of a manuscript

**bick-er** [bǐk′ər] *verb*, to quarrel about petty things

**bi-cy-cle** [bī′sǐk′əl] *noun*, a two wheeled vehicle propelled by pedals

**bid** [bǐd] *noun*, 1) an offer to buy something, *verb*, 2) to offer a price for something 3) to ask, plea 4) to utter a greeting

**bi-en-ni-al** [bī-ĕn′ē-əl] *adjective*, happening every two years

**big** [bǐg] *adjective*, large in size, weight, importance, etc.

**big-ot** [bǐg′ət] *noun*, a person filled with stubborn hatred

**big-ot-ry** [bǐg′ə-trē] *noun*, prejudice, intolerance

**bi-lin-gual** [bī-lǐng′gwəl] *adjective*, capable of speaking two languages

**bill** [bǐl] *noun*, 1) a piece of paper stating what you owe 2) a plan for a new law 3) the beak of a bird, *verb*, 4) to send a list of charges to someone

**bil-liards** [bǐl′yərdz] *noun*, *plural*, a game similar to pool

**bil-lion** [bǐl′yən] *noun*, *adjective*, a thousand million, written 1,000,000,000

**bil-low** [bǐl′ō] *noun*, 1) a wave, a surge of water or smoke, *verb*, 2) to surge, to swell

**bin** [bǐn] *noun*, a large container with a lid, for flour, grain, etc.

**bind** [bīnd] *verb*, 1) to tie with rope or string 2) to constrict 3) to put under an obligation

**bind-er** [bīn′dər] *noun*, that which fastens or binds together, such as a notebook with large rings to hold paper

**binge** [bǐnj] *noun*, a spree, uncontrolled eating

**bin-oc-u-lars** [bə-nŏk′yə-lərz] *noun*, *plural*, a pair of special glasses that make things in the distance look closer

**bi-o-de-grad-a-ble** [bī′ō-dǐ-grā′də-bəl] *adjective*, capable of being broken down by microorganisms into simple, stable compounds such as carbon dioxide and water

**bi-og-ra-phy** [bī-ŏg′rə-fē] *noun*, a written history of a person's life

**bi-ol-o-gy** [bī-ŏl′ə-jē] *noun*, the branch of knowledge that studies all living things

**birch** [bûrch] *noun*, a hardwood tree known for its thin, peeling bark and yellow leaves in the fall

**bird** [bûrd] *noun*, any of a class of warm-blooded, two-legged, egg-laying vertebrates with feathers and wings

**birth** [bûrth] *noun*, the act of being born, the beginning of existence

**birth-day** [bûrth′dā′] *noun*, the day someone is born

**bis-cuit** [bĭs′kĭt] *noun*, a small soft bread

**bish-op** [bĭsh′əp] *noun*, a senior member of the Christian clergy

**bi-son** [bī′sən, -zən] *noun*, a large mammal native to North America and Europe, including the buffalo

**bit** [bĭt] *noun*, 1) a very small amount 2) the metal mouthpiece on a bridle used to control a horse 3) the cutting edge of a tool, *verb*, 4) *past tense* of **bite**

**bite** [bīt] *noun*, 1) a wound made by biting or stinging, *verb*, 2) to seize or cut with teeth

**bit-ter** [bĭt′ər] *adjective*, 1) having a sharp, sour taste 2) grievous, painful 3) piercingly cold

**bi-zarre** [bĭ-zär′] *adjective*, very strange or unusual, weird

**black** [blăk] *adjective*, 1) lacking color or light, the opposite of white, *noun*, 2) a Negro or person of African descent

**black-mail** [blăk′māl′] *noun*, 1) compliance with another person's terms, hush money, *verb*, 2) to threaten to reveal a secret unless money is paid or favors given

**blad-der** [blăd′ər] *noun*, a sack attached to the kidneys to hold urine

**blade** [blād] *noun*, 1) the flat cutting part of anything sharp 2) a long flat leaf of grass, or anything with such a shape

**blame** [blām] *noun*, 1) responsibility for something bad, *verb*, 2) to say that someone is the cause of something unfortunate

**blanch** [blănch] *verb*, 1) to bleach, to whiten, to fade 2) to cook briefly in boiling water

**bland** [blănd] *adjective*, mild, almost tasteless, neutral

**blank** [blăngk] *adjective*, 1) without writing or other marks 2) without expression

**blan-ket** [blăng′kĭt] *noun*, a warm cloth cover used on a bed

**blas-phe-my** [blăs′fə-mē] *noun*, speech or actions that are disrespectful to God or sacred things

**blast** [blăst] *noun*, 1) a strong gust of wind 2) an explosion, *verb*, 3) to launch into space 4) to use explosions to break something apart 4) to make a loud sound

**bla-tant** [blāt′nt] *adjective*, loudly offensive, very obvious

**blaze** [blāz] *noun*, 1) a strong fire, *verb*, 2) to burn, to burst into flame 3) to shine brightly

**blaz-er** [blā′zər] *noun*, a light sports jacket of wool or silk

**bleach** [blēch] *noun*, 1) a substance used to whiten or remove color, *verb*, 2) to make white, to remove color

**bleach-ers** [blē′chərs] *noun*, *plural*, seats for spectators

**bleak** [blēk] *adjective*, cold and unpleasant, empty

**bleed** [blēd] *verb*, 1) to lose blood 2) to become mixed or run (e.g., dyes in wet cloth)

**blem-ish** [blĕm/ĭsh] *noun*, a flaw, an imperfection, a pimple

**blend** [blĕnd] *noun*, 1) a thorough mixture, *verb*, 2) to mix together into one 3) to go together

**bless** [blĕs] *verb*, to make holy, to ask God's favor, to praise

**bless-ing** [blĕs/ĭng] *noun*, 1) words that thank God for His gifts 2) good fortune

**blew** [bloo] *verb*, *past tense* of **blow**

**blight** [blīt] *noun*, 1) a disease on plants that makes the leaves dry up, *verb*, 2) to injure, to damage, to ruin a crop

**blind** [blīnd] *adjective*, 1) unable to see, without the sense of sight 2) concealed, hard to see 3) oblivious, unaware, ignorant, *noun*, 4) a window covering to keep out light, *verb*, 5) to make unable to see

**blink** [blĭngk] *noun*, 1) the quick opening and closing of an eyelid, *verb*, 2) to open and shut the eyes quickly

**bliss** [blĭs] *noun*, complete joy, happiness, or delight

**blis-ter** [blĭs/tər] *noun*, a sack under the skin filled with water or blood, from a burn or rubbing

**bliz-zard** [blĭz/ərd] *noun*, a snow storm with strong winds and cold temperatures

**block** [blŏk] *noun*, 1) a cube, a chunk 2) the area bounded by four city streets 3) something that stands in the way and prevents movement, *verb*, 4) to hinder, clog or jam, to impede, prevent, stop, or obstruct 5) to form, shape, or press

**block-ade** [blŏ/kād] *noun*, the closure of an area , port, etc.

**blond or blonde** [blŏnd] *adjective*, a light hair color the shade of straw or wheat

**blood** [blŭd] *noun*, a red fluid in the veins of people and animals

**blood ves-sel** [blŭd vĕs/əl] *noun*, any of the tubes in the body that carry blood, veins, arteries, capillaries

**bloom** [bloom] *noun*, 1) a flower, *verb*, 2) to have a flower

**blos-som** [blŏs/əm] *noun*, 1) a flower, *verb*, 2) to bloom or open from a bud to come in to a flower

**blot** [blŏt] *noun*, 1) a spot or stain, *verb*, 2) to absorb a liquid with cloth or a sponge to remove it

**blouse** [blous] *noun*, a garment similar to a shirt covering the top of a woman's body, from the neck to the waist

**blow** [blō] *noun*, 1) a sudden strike with a hand or weapon, *verb*, 2) to force air into a current, to expel air from the mouth

**blue** [bloo] *adjective*, 1) having the color of a cloudless sky, 2) unhappy, depressed, *noun*, 3) one of the three primary colors: red, blue, yellow 3) a feeling of unhappiness, sadness

**bluff** [blŭf] *noun*, 1) a high, steep bank, *verb*, 2) to try to trick or fool someone 3) to pretend

**blun-der** [blŭn/dər] *noun*, a stupid mistake, an error

**blunt** [blŭnt] *adjective*, 1) not sharp 2) frank, candid, abrupt, *verb*, 3) to deaden, insensitize, dull

**blur** [blûr] *verb*, to make unreadable or indistinct, to obscure

**blush** [blŭsh] *verb*, to become red in the face from embarrassment

**board** [bôrd] *noun*, 1) a long flat piece of wood 2) a group of directors who act as a body 3) a piece of cardboard or wood on which a game is played, *verb*, 4) to cover with wood 5) to climb onto a vessel or vehicle

**board-er** [bôr′dər] *noun*, a paying guest who receives meals

**boast** [bōst] *verb*, to brag, to praise oneself, to show off

**boat** [bōt] *noun*, a small ship or vessel that floats on water

**bode** [bōd] *verb*, to predict, to portend, to foretell

**bod-y** [bŏd′ē] *noun*, 1) the form of a person or animal or object 2) a group of persons who act as a unit 3) a corpse

**bog** [bôg] *noun*, a swamp, a marsh

**boil** [boil] *noun*, 1) a painful sore under the skin, *verb*, 2) to heat to 212 degrees Fahrenheit 3) to be angered, to be enraged

**bold** [bōld] *adjective*, brave, assertive, forward, fearless

**bolt** [bōlt] *noun*, 1) a metal screw used with a nut to hold something in place, a metal bar 2) a stroke of lightning, a thunderbolt, *verb*, 3) to lock with a bar across a doorway 4) to run quickly from the scene

**bomb** [bŏm] *noun*, 1) a device of explosive materials, *verb*, 2) to bombard with explosives

**bom-bard** [bŏm-bärd] *verb*, to attack repeatedly

**bond** [bŏnd] *noun*, 1) a mutual feeling of trust that joins people together 2) a written promise to pay money, *verb*, 3) to join together, to unite

**bond-age** [bŏn′dĭj] *noun*, confinement, servitude

**bone** [bōn] *noun*, a hard white substance forming the skeleton of an animal

**bon-fire** [bŏn′fīr′] *noun*, a large controlled fire

**bo-nus** [bō′nəs] *noun*, a sum paid in addition to a salary

**book** [bŏŏk] *noun*, 1) sheets of paper bound together for reading or writing, a long work of literature, etc., in electronic form, *verb*, 2) to make reservations for a future date

**book-keep-ing** [bŏŏk′kē′pĭng] *noun*, a systematic record of business transactions

**boo-mer-ang** [bŏŏ′mə-răng′] *noun*, an angular shaped object that returns after it is thrown

**boor** [bŏŏr] *noun*, a rude person, a jerk, a brash individual

**boost** [bŏŏst] *noun*, 1) a lift, a helping hand, *verb*, 2) to support, to encourage

**boot** [bŏŏt] *noun*, 1) a shoe that covers above the ankle, *verb*, 2) to kick 3) to load the operating system on a computer

**booth** [bŏŏth] *noun*, an enclosure, a cubicle, a compartment

**bor-der** [bôr′dər] *noun*, 1) the dividing line between two countries or territories 2) an edge or trim, *verb*, 3) to lie along the edge of a geographic boundary

**bore** [bôr] *noun*, 1) a tiresome person, a nuisance, *verb*, 2) to drill a hole, to penetrate 3) to make someone feel disinterested

**bore-dom** [bôr/dəm] *noun*, dullness, lack of interest

**boring** [bôr/ĭng] *adjective*, not interesting, dull, tedious

**born** [bôrn] *adjective*, having been given life, existing as a result of birth

**bor-ough** [bûr/ō] *noun*, a self-governing incorporated town

**bor-row** [bŏr/ō] *verb*, 1) to use a thing that does not belong to you, then return it 2) to adopt or use as one's own

**bos-om** [bŏŏz/əm] *adjective*, 1)relating to the closeness between friends or family, *noun*, 2) chest area 3) a woman's breast

**boss** [bôs] *noun*, 1) the person in charge, someone in control, the employer, *verb*, 2) to give orders in a domineering way

**bot-a-nist** [bŏt/n-ĭst] *noun*, one who studies plants

**bot-a-ny** [bŏt/n-ē] *noun*, the science of plants

**both** [bōth] *adjective*, *pronoun*, the two together in conjunction

**both-er** [bŏth/ər] *noun*, *no plural*, 1) trouble or difficulty, a nuisance, *verb*, 2) to trouble or annoy, to harass or pester

**bot-tle** [bŏt/l] *noun*, 1) a container with a narrow neck, usually made of glass or plastic, used to hold liquids *verb*, 2) to store in a glass container

**bot-tom** [bŏt/əm] *noun*, 1) the lowest part or end of something 2) the buttocks, seat

**bough** [bou] *noun*, a tree branch

**bouil-lon** [bŏŏl/yŏn′, -yən] *noun*, a broth, consommé

**boul-der** [bōl/dər] *noun*, a very large stone or rock

**bounce** [bouns] *verb*, to spring back from a surface, to jump

**bound** [bound] *adjective*, 1) constrained, restricted, confined 2) going to, destined for, *noun*, 3) a jump, a leap

**bound-a-ry** [boun/də-rē] *noun*, a real or imaginary limit, especially between two properties

**boun-ti-ful** [boun/tə-fəl] *adjective*, generous, plentiful, provided freely, abundant

**bow** [bō] *noun*, 1) a ribbon worn as a hair ornament 2) a piece of wood bent with a string, used to shoot arrows 3) a piece of wood with hairs fastened, to create vibrations when pulled across the strings of an instrument, such as a violin, [bou] 4) the front of a boat, *verb*, 5) to bend the body forward to show respect 6) to submit to another, to consent

**bowl** [bōl] *noun*, a round deep dish

**box** [bŏks] *noun*, 1) a container like a cube, constructed from wood, cardboard, metal, etc. *verb*, 2) to fight with clenched fists

**boy** [boi] *noun*, a male child

**boy-cott** [boi/kŏt′] *noun*, 1) the refusal to purchase the products of an individual, corporation, or nation as a way to bring

43

economic pressure for social or political change, *verb*, 2) to refuse to deal with or trade with, to desert, to abandon

**brace** [brās] *noun*, 1) a support, a vise, 2) two like items, a pair, *verb*, 3) to fortify

**brack-et** [brăk′ĭt] *noun*, 1) a shelf supported against a wall 2) one of the signs [ ] in a sentence that encloses additional information

**brack-ish** [brăk′ĭsh] *adjective*, a mixture of fresh and salt water

**brag** [brăg] *verb*, to praise oneself, to sound conceited, to boast

**braid** [brād] *noun*, 1) a rope, twine, *verb*, 2) to weave hair or rope

**Braille** [brāl] *noun*, a system of writing for people who are blind using raised dots as letters and numbers to be read with the fingertips

**brain** [brān] *noun*, 1) the mass of nerve tissue in the heads of people and animals, the center of the nervous system 2) the intellect, where we get our thoughts and ideas

**brake** [brāk] *noun*, 1) a mechanical device used to stop a bicycle, car, train, etc., *verb*, 2) to stop with the help of a mechanical device

**branch** [brănch] *noun*, 1) a part of a tree that extends from the trunk 2) an office that is located some distance from the headquarters 3) a stream or river that flows into a larger one, *verb*, 4) to move away or divide from the main body into branches

**brand** [brănd] *noun*, 1) a label indicating the name of a product and the manufacturer, *verb*, 2) to make a permanent mark on an animal to identify it

**brass** [brăs] *noun*, 1) a yellow metal that is a copper and zinc alloy 2) musical instruments, such as a trumpet, that are made out of metal and that give a loud sound when blown

**bra-va-do** [brə-vä′dō] *noun*, an air of defiance, fake bravery

**brave** [brāv] *adjective*, willing to make a personal sacrifice

**brav-er-y** [brā′və-rē] *noun*, courage, daring, boldness

**brawl** [brôl] *noun*, 1) a fight, an altercation, a dispute, *verb*, 2) to argue and wrestle or fight

**breach** [brēch] *noun*, the breaking of a contract, a gap in a fence

**bread** [brĕd] *noun*, a food made of flour, water, and yeast that is baked

**breadth** [brĕdth] *noun*, the distance from one side to the other, width

**break** [brāk] *noun*, 1) an opening made when something is torn or broken, 2) a pause, a rest, a time away from school or work, *verb*, 3) to cause to fall apart 4) to violate, to disobey

**break-fast** [brĕk′fəst] *noun*, the first meal of the day, eaten in the morning

**breast** [brĕst] *noun*, 1) one of the two parts on the front of a woman's body that can give milk 2) the top part of the front of the body

**breath** [brĕth] *noun*, air inhaled and exhaled in respiration

**breathe** [brēth] *verb*, to inhale air into the lung and then exhale

**bred** [brĕd] *verb, past tense and past participle* of **breed**

**breed** [brēd] *noun*, 1) a type or group of animals descended from a common ancestor, *verb*, 2) to reproduce, to multiply 3) to train and raise animals

**breed-ing** [brē'dĭng] *noun*, values a person learns, upbringing

**breeze** [brēz] *noun*, a gentle wind

**brev-i-ty** [brĕv'ĭ-tē] *noun*, shortness, ability to say something briefly, succinctly

**brew** [brōō] *verb*, to make drinks such as tea, coffee, or beer

**bribe** [brīb] *noun*, 1) money given to buy cooperation, *verb*, 2) to get someone's cooperation by paying them, to pay off

**brick** [brĭk] *noun*, a block of baked clay used in construction

**brid-al** [brīd'əl] *adjective*, referring to the bride in a wedding

**bride** [brīd] *noun*, a woman about to be married, is in the process of being married, or who has just been married

**bride-groom** [brīd'grōōm] *noun*, a man who is going to be married, is in the process of being married, or has just been married

**bridge** [brĭj] *noun*, 1) an elevated structure such as a viaduct or an overpass that crosses over water or a highway 2) a card game 3) a link, a connection, *verb*, 4) to join, connect, bring together

**bri-dle** [brīd'l] *noun*, 1) a leather band on the head of a horse used

for control, *verb*, 2) to show anger or resentment

**brief** [brēf] *adjective*, 1) for a short period of time, *noun*, 2) a summary of a case for the court, *verb*, 3) to inform

**bri-er** [brī'ər] *noun* prickly vegetation

**bri-gade** [brĭ-gād'] *noun*, a large group of soldiers

**bright** [brīt] *adjective*, 1) giving light 2) shining, not dull 3) smart, intelligent 4) cheerful

**bril-liant** [brĭl'yənt] *adjective*, 1) very bright, glittering, splendid 2) very clever

**brim** [brĭm] *noun*, 1) the edge of a cup, glass, or bowl 2) the part of the hat that is the edge

**bring** [brĭng] *verb*, to carry something or to lead someone

**brink** [brĭngk] *noun*, the edge of a steep slope, the verge

**brisk** [brĭsk] *adjective*, 1) quick and active, energetic 2) curt

**bris-tle** [brĭs'əl] *noun*, 1) a coarse brush, *verb*, 2) to feel irritated or annoyed, to show indignation

**brit-tle** [brĭt'l] *adjective*, hard but easily broken or snapped

**broach** [brōch] *verb*, to bring up, to begin discussion of

**broad** [brôd] *adjective*, 1) wide, extensive 2) tolerant

**broad-cast** [brôd'kăst'] *noun*, 1) a program aired on television or radio, *verb*, 2) to convey a message through radio or television or other electronic media

**broad-en** [brôd'n] *verb*, to expand

**bro-chure** [brō-shoŏr′] *noun*, a pamphlet dealing with a subject of passing interest, a leaflet

**broc-co-li** [brŏk′ə-lē] *noun*, a plant with dense green flowers eaten as a vegetable

**broil** [broil] *verb*, to cook by exposing to direct, intense heat

**broke** [brōk] *adjective*, 1) without money, bankrupt, *verb*, 2) *past tense* of **break**

**bro-ker** [brō′kər] *noun*, an agent who buys and sells for others

**bron-chi-tis** [brŏn-kī′tĭs] *noun*, an inflammation of the lungs that causes chronic coughing

**bronze** [brŏnz] *noun*, a hard metal made by mixing copper and tin

**brooch** [brōch] *noun*, an ornamental dress-clasp, a decorative pin

**brood** [broōd] *noun*, 1) a group of animals born together, or the children of a family, *verb*, 2) to think deeply and sadly about something

**brook** [broŏk] *noun*, 1) a small river or stream, *verb*, 2) to allow

**broom** [broōm] *noun*, a brush with a long handle

**broth** [brôth] *noun*, watery soup, bouillon

**broth-er** [brŭth′ər] *noun*, a boy or man with the same parents as another person

**brought** [brôt/ *verb*, *past tense* of **bring**

**brow** [brou] *noun*, the part of the face between the eyes and the hair, the forehead

**brown** [broun] *adjective*, a dark color like coffee or earth

**browse** [brouz] *verb*, to leaf through, to scan, to pass over

**bruise** [broōz] *noun*, 1) a red or blue mark left on damaged skin caused by blood vessels breaking beneath the skin, *verb*, 2) to injure in such a way that the blood vessels beneath the skin are broken

**brunch** [brŭnch]*noun*, a meal between breakfast and lunch

**bru-nette** [broō-nĕt′] *noun*, a woman with brown hair

**brush** [brŭsh] *noun*, 1) a device with wires or plastic bristles spread from a handle for combing, or cleaning, or painting, *verb*, 2) to clean, straighten, or paint with a brush

**brusque** [brŭsk] *adjective*, rough and short in manner, blunt,

**bru-tal** [broōt′l] *adjective*, fierce, harsh, destructive

**brute** [broōt] *noun*, a cruel person who acts like a wild animal

**bub-ble** [bŭb′əl] *noun*, 1) a sphere containing liquid or gas, *verb*, 2) to boil, to froth

**buck** [bŭk].*noun*, a male deer, goat, or rabbit

**buck-et** [bŭk′ĭt] *noun*, a container, usually with a curved handle to carry something, a pail

**buck-le** [bŭk′əl] *noun*, a device for uniting two loose ends of a belt or to fasten shoes, etc.

**bu-col-ic** [byoō-kŏl′ĭk] *adjective*, rustic, pastoral, in the country

**bud** [bŭd] *noun*, a sprout on a stem that becomes a flower or branch

**Bud-dhism** [boo'dĭz'əm] *noun*, one of the world's major religions, practiced primarily in Asia and taught by monks

**budge** [bŭj] *verb*, to make something heavy move a little

**budg-et** [bŭj'ĭt] *noun*, a plan that indicates how money will be spent

**buf-fa-lo** [bŭf'ə-lō'] *noun*, a large, shaggy, wild ox

**buff-er** [bŭf'ər] *noun*, 1) a solution that neutralizes different substances 2) a person or thing between two opposing forces that softens the impact of their collision, *verb*, 3) to lessen

**buf-fet** [bə-fā'] *noun*, 1) a counter or table for refreshments, [bə-fĭt] *verb*, 2) to batter, to flap, to hit

**buf-foon** [bə-foon'] *noun*, one who clowns around

**bug** [bŭg] *noun*, 1) an insect that drinks juices from plants or animals 2) an error in data, *verb*, 3) to eavesdrop electronically

**bug-gy** [bŭg'ē] *noun*, 1) a hand-pushed carriage for babies 2) a one-horse carriage for two people

**bu-gle** [byoo'gəl] *noun*, a musical instrument, a horn used mainly in the military

**build** [bĭld] *verb*, 1) to create or construct 2) to increase

**build-ing** [bĭl'dĭng] *noun*, a structure with a foundation, roof, and walls

**built** [bĭlt] *verb*, *past tense* of **build**

**bulb** [bŭlb] *noun*, 1) the underground part of a plant formed by thick leaves, which separates and becomes a new plant 2) any object of this shape, such as a light bulb

**bulge** [bŭlj] *noun*, 1) a swelling shape, *verb*, 2) to swell outwards

**bulk-head** [bŭlk'hĕd'] *noun*, a partition separating the compartments of a vessel

**bull** [bool] *adjective*, 1) describing the stock market when prices are going up and the economy is strong, *noun*, 2) male animal of the ox, cow, whale, or other animals

**bull-doz-er** [bool'dō'zər] *noun*, a heavy machine that moves earth

**bul-let** [bool'ĭt] *noun*, a piece of metal fired from a gun

**bul-le-tin** [bool'ĭ-tn] *noun*, an announcement made by an organization, a newsletter

**bul-lion** [bool'yən] *noun*, a block of metal such as gold or silver

**bul-ly** [bool'ē] *noun*, 1) a person who likes to hurt or tease weaker people, *verb*, 2) to intimidate someone, to make someone feel afraid or overpowered

**bul-wark** [bool'wərk] *noun*, protection, a defensive wall

**bum-ble-bee** [bŭm'bəl-bē'] *noun*, a large yellow and black hairy social bee

**bump** [bŭmp] *noun*, 1) a sudden blow 2) a raised round lump due to swelling 3) an elevated place in the road or on a surface, *verb*, 4) to knock against, to strike

**bun** [bŭn] *noun*, 1) a small sweet roll or dinner roll 2) a hairstyle in which the hair is lifted off the neck and wrapped into a circle

**bunch** [bŭnch] *noun*, 1) a cluster of similar things grouped together, *verb*, 2) to gather together in a mass

**bun-dle** [bŭn'dl] *noun*, 1) a group of things tied together to make a package, *verb*, 2) to make into a bunch by tying things together

**bu-oy** [boo'ē] *noun*, an anchored floating device used as a navigation marker

**buoy-ant** [boi'ənt] *adjective*, 1) having the quality of rising or floating in fluid 2) light-hearted

**bur-den** [bûr'dn] *noun*, 1) a heavy thought or object that is carried, *verb*, 2) to load

**bu-reau** [byoor'ō] *noun*, 1) a chest of drawers 2) a satellite office for a news agency

**bu-reauc-ra-cy** [byoo-rŏk'rə-sē] *noun*, a system of government through agencies to which tasks and authority are delegated

**bur-geon** [bûr'jən] *verb*, to grow and develop rapidly

**bur-glar** [bûr'glər] *noun*, one who breaks into other people's property to rob them

**bur-i-al** [bĕr'ē-əl] *noun*, the act of putting a dead body in the ground, internment

**burn** [bûrn] *noun*, 1) a wound caused by fire or heat, or friction, *verb*, 2) to be destroyed by fire, heat or acid

**burnt** [bûrnt] *adjective*, showing damage by fire

**burr** [bûr] *noun*, a round seed covered with spurs or barbs

**bur-ro** [bûr'ō] *noun*, a donkey

**bur-row** [bûr'ō] *noun*, 1) a tunnel or hole dug by an animal as a den, *verb*, 2) to dig or hide in a hole

**burst** [bûrst] *noun*, 1) a sudden action, *verb*, 2) to break due to force from inside, to combust

**bury** [bĕr'ē] *verb*, to dig a hole to conceal something underground, to cover, to conceal

**bus** [bŭs] *noun*, a large vehicle that carries many people to a destination by a road

**bush** [boosh] *noun*, a shrub

**bush-el** [boosh'əl] *noun*, dry measure equal to 64 pints or 32 quarts

**busi-ness** [bĭz'nĭs] *noun*, 1) regular occupation, work, profession 2) something to be transacted 3) affairs involving money

**bust** [bŭst] *noun*, a sculpture of a person from the chest up

**bus-y** [bĭz'ē] *adjective*, 1) having a lot to do, *verb*, to work actively

**but** [bŭt; bət when unstressed] *adverb*, 1) only, merely, *conjunction*, 2) yet, however, *preposition*, 3) except, save 4) other than

**butch-er** [booch'ər] *noun*, a person who cuts meat for sale

**but-ter** [bŭt'ər] *noun*, a substance made from churning cream

**but-ter-fly** [bŭt'ər-flī'] *noun*, an insect with four colorful wings and a slender body

**but-ton** [bŭt'n] *noun*, 1) a variety of forms or materials used to fasten a dress, pants, shirt, etc. 2) a badge, a form of identification, 3) a knob pressed to operate a device, *verb,* 4) to secure with a button or snap

**but-ton-hole** [bŭt/n-hōl/] *noun,* the hole in a piece of clothing that a button goes through in order to fasten two sides together

**but-tress** [bŭt/rĭs] *noun,* a support projecting outwards to strengthen the walls of a building

**buy** [bī] *verb,* to acquire something by giving an accepted price, to purchase with money

**buy-er** [bī/ər] *noun,* a customer, one who makes a purchase

**by** [bī] *adverb,* 1) near, aside, past *preposition,* 2) near, beside 3) through, by way of, via 4) before 5) past

**by-pro-duct** [bī/prŏd/əkt] *noun,* anything produced in the process of making something else

**byte** [bīt] *noun,* 1) a small unit of information 2) a fixed number of bits (usually eight)

# C

**cab** [kăb] *noun,* 1) a vehicle for hire, a taxi 2) the part of a truck or train where the driver sits

**cab-bage** [kăb/ĭj] *noun,* a vegetable with a short stem and thick green or purple overlapping leaves that form a dense head

**cab-in** [kăb/ĭn] *noun,* 1) a small wooden house 2) a room for living quarters on a ship 3) the passenger area on an airplane

**cab-i-net** [kăb/ə-nĭt] *noun,* 1) a cupboard with drawers or

shelves for keeping items 2) a group of people who advise the head of state

**ca-ble** [kā/bəl] *noun,* 1) a strong, large diameter wire or rope 2) a bundle of insulated wires that carry electrical current 3) a system delivering television signals by cable

**ca-boose** [kə-bōos/] *noun,* the last car used on a freight train, containing facilities for the crew

**cache** [kăsh] *noun,* 1) a hiding place for food or treasures, *verb,* 2) to hide or store something

**cack-le** [kăk/əl] *noun,* 1) a loud laugh, *verb,* 2) to laugh loudly to sound like a hen

**ca-coph-o-ny** [kə-kŏf/ə-nē] *noun,* harsh or dissonant noise, a discordant mixture of sounds

**cac-tus** [kăk/təs] *noun, plural,* **cacti or cactuses,** a prickly, succulent plant with thick stems that grows in hot, dry climates

**ca-dav-er** [kə-dăv/ər] *noun,* a dead body

**ca-det** [kə-dĕt/] *noun,* a student at a military school

**caf-e-te-ri-a** [kăf/ĭ-tîr/ē-ə] *noun,* a place to eat where customers select food from a serving line

**caf-feine** [kă-fēn] *noun,* a stimulant found especially in coffee, tea, or some sodas

**cage** [kāj] *noun,* a box-like enclosure with bars in which birds or animals are kept, a pen

**cake** [kāk] *noun,* 1) a sweet, baked food made of flour, fat, and eggs, *verb,* 2) to harden from a wet substance into a solid crust

**ca-lam-i-ty** [kə-lăm′ĭ-tē] *noun*, an unfortunate event, a disaster

**cal-ci-um** [kăl′sē-əm] *noun*, a silver-white, rather soft metal that occurs in bones, shells, etc.

**cal-cu-late** [kăl′kyə-lāt′] *verb*, to find the answer using arithmetic, to plan using reasoning

**cal-cu-la-tion** [kăl′kyə-lā′shən] *noun*, the result of numbers added together, subtracted, etc.

**cal-cu-la-tor** [kăl′kyə-lā′tər] *noun*, a small computer used to perform math problems

**cal-cu-lus** [kăl′kyə-ləs] *noun*,
1) a branch of mathematics that provides a method for describing change 2) a buildup of materials within the body, such as a gallstone

**cal-en-dar** [kăl′ən-dər] *noun*, a table of the days and the months of the year

**calf** [kăf] *noun*, 1) the newborn or young of any large mammal, such as a cow, whale, or elephant 2) part of the leg between the knee and the ankle, the back of the shin

**cal-i-ber** [kăl′ə-bər] *noun*, 1) the diameter of a cylinder or tube 2) a person's degree of ability

**Cal-i-for-nia** [kăl′ĭ-fôr′nyə] *noun*, a state on the Pacific coast of the United States, the capital is Sacramento. The state flower of **California** is the golden poppy and the motto is "Eureka!"

**cal-lis-then-ics** [kăl′ĭs-thĕn′ĭks] *noun*, *plural*, exercise to promote strength and grace

**call** [kôl] *noun*, 1) the act of reaching someone on the telephone or paying a visit 2) a shout or plea, *verb*, 3) to name 4) to shout 5) to ask someone to come 6) to telephone 7) to visit

**cal-lig-ra-phy** [kə-lĭg′rə-fē] *noun*, beautiful writing, the art of hand lettering

**cal-lous** [kăl′əs] *adjective*,
1) lacking feeling, hard-hearted, feeling no pity 2) thick skinned

**cal-lus** [kăl′əs] noun, a hard thickened spot (of skin)

**calm** [käm] *adjective*, quiet, not excited

**cal-o-rie** [kăl′ə-rē] *noun*, a unit used to measure the amount of energy produced

**cam-el** [kăm′əl] *noun*, a large animal with one or two humps on its back, used for transportation

**cam-e-o** [kăm′ē-ō′] *noun*, a piece of jewelry with a stone or shell on which figures are carved

**cam-er-a** [kăm′ər-ə] *noun*, an instrument used to take photographs or film pictures

**cam-ou-flage** [kăm′ə-fläzh] *noun*,
1) special clothing for people or colors in an animal that help them blend into their surroundings, *verb*, 2) an organism's ability to blend in with the environment

**camp** [kămp] *noun*, 1) a place with tents or cabins for temporary shelter, *verb*, 2) to live outdoors and sleep in a tent under the stars, etc.

**cam-paign** [kăm-pān′] *noun*,
1) activities organized to gain or win something, *verb*, 2) to create a connected series of operations to achieve a desired result

**cam-pus** [kăm′pəs] *noun*, the grounds surrounding a college, school, or organization

**can** [kăn] *noun*, 1) a metal container, *verb*, 2) able to, to know how to 3) to preserve food in a can

**ca-nal** [kə-năl′] *noun*, 1) an artificial waterway designed for navigation 2) a duct in the body

**ca-nar-y** [kə-nâr′ē] *noun*, a songbird, usually yellow

**can-cel** [kăn′səl] *verb*, to annul, to revoke, to end or stop

**can-cel-la-tion** [kăn′sə-lā′shən] *noun*, a stop or end to something, withdrawal

**can-cer** [kăn′sər] *noun*, a serious illness in which abnormal cells multiply rapidly

**can-di-date** [kăn′dĭ-dāt′] *noun*, one who is being considered or who applies for a certain job

**can-dle** [kăn′dl] *noun*, a cylinder of wax with a wick embedded in it designed to burn to give off light

**can-dor** [kăn′dər] *noun*, the quality of being fair, unprejudiced, and honest

**cane** [kān] *noun*, 1) a hollow stick made from some plants 2) a stick with a curved handle used for support when walking

**ca-nine** [kā′nīn] *adjective*, relating to dogs

**can-is-ter** [kăn′ĭ-stər] *noun*, a small box or container, often of metal, for holding tea, coffee, etc.

**can-ni-bal** [kăn′ə-bəl] *noun*, a person who eats people or an animal who eats one of its own kind

**can-non** [kăn′ən] *noun*, a mounted gun or piece of artillery

**can-not** [kăn′ŏt] unable to

**ca-noe** [kə-nōō′] *noun*, a narrow light boat tapered at the ends, moved with paddles

**can-o-py** [kăn′ə-pē] *noun*, a covering from the sun, an awning or umbrella

**cant** [kănt] *noun*, 1) empty talk, deceit, 2) jargon, slang, *verb*, 3) to speak insincerely

**can't** [kănt] the *contraction* of the words **can** and **not**

**can-ta-loupe** [kăn′tl-ōp′] *noun*, a variety of muskmelon with an orange-red color fruit

**can-tan-ker-ous** [kăn-tăng′kər-əs] *adjective*, irritable, cross

**can-vas** [kăn′vəs] *noun*, 1) a strong, coarse, water-repellant cloth used to make tents, sails, etc. 2) a piece of heavy cloth, stretched over a frame, on which pictures are painted

**can-vass** [kăn′vəs] *verb*, 1) to examine thoroughly, scrutinize 2) to solicit votes or opinions

**can-yon** [kăn′yən] *noun*, a valley with high, steep sides between hills or mountains

**cap** [kăp] *noun*, 1) a soft hat 2) the covering for a bottle or tube

**ca-pa-ble** [kā'pə-bəl] *noun*, able to do things well, having ability, competent or efficient

**ca-pac-i-ty** [kə-păs'ĭ-tē] *noun*, 1) the maximum amount of liquid a container can hold, 2) the ability or aptitude for a specified task

**cape** [kāp] *noun*, 1) a piece of land that goes out into the sea 2) a coat without sleeves that covers shoulders, arms, and back

**cap-il-lar-y** [kăp'ə-lĕr'ē] *noun*, one of the tiniest blood vessels

**cap-i-tal** [kăp'ĭ-tl] *adjective*, 1) first, chief, 2 punishable by death, *noun*, 3) resources, means or money 4) the city where the rules for a state or county or country are made 5) a letter that begins a sentence or a proper noun

**cap-i-tal-ism** [kăp'ĭ-tl-ĭz'əm] *noun*, an economic system based on profit and private ownership

**cap-i-tal-ize** [kăp'ĭ-tl-īz'] *verb*, 1) to finance or invest in for profit 2) to use a capital letter

**Cap-i-tol** [kăp'ĭ-tl] *noun*, 1) the building in which the Congress of the United States meets to create laws, **capitol** 2) the building in which a state legislature meets to create laws

**ca-price** [kə-prēs'] *noun*, a silly thought, a notion, whimsy

**cap-size** [kăp'sīz'] *verb*, to upset or overturn as of a boat

**cap-sule** [kăp'səl] *noun*, 1) a container with a matching top and bottom that holds medicine 2) a small spacecraft

**cap-tain** [kăp'tən] *noun*, the leader of a team or a company of soldiers, or the commander of a ship or aircraft

**cap-tion** [kăp'shən] *noun*, 1) a short title heading 2) text under an illustration

**cap-tive** [kăp'tĭv] *adjective*, 1) unable to escape, *noun*, 2) a prisoner

**cap-ture** [kăp'chər] *verb*, 1) to seize and hold as a prisoner 2) to take hold of something

**car** [kär] *noun*, an automobile, a form of transportation with four wheels and an engine, usually fueled by gasoline

**ca-rafe** [kə-răf'] *noun*, a glass bottle, a decanter

**car-at** [kăr'ət] *noun*, a unit of weight for precious stones

**car-a-van** [kăr'ə-văn'] *noun*, 1) a group of people traveling together with vehicles or animals 2) a mobile home

**car-bo-hy-drate** [kär'bō-hī'drāt'] *noun*, a class of foods, that supply energy to the body

**car-bon** [kär'bən] *noun*, a nonmetallic element, symbolized as C, the required common substance in organic chemistry

**car-bo-nate** [kär'bə-nāt'] *noun*, a salt of carbonic acid

**car-bon di-ox-ide** [kär'bən dī-ŏk'sīd] *noun*, a colorless, odorless gas that is absorbed by plants

**car-bon mon-ox-ide** [kär'bən mə-nŏk'sīd'] *noun*, a colorless, odorless poisonous gas

**car-cass** [kär′kəs] *noun*, the dead body of an animal or bird

**car-cin-o-gen** [kär-sĭn′ə-jən] *noun*, a substance that causes cancer

**card** [kärd] *noun*, a small, flat piece of thick, stiff paper (e.g., a playing card, a postcard, a greeting or business card)

**car-di-ac** [kär′dē-ăk′] *adjective*, pertaining to the heart, stimulating the heart action

**car-di-gan** [kär′dĭ-gən] *noun*, a sweater that buttons or opens down the front

**car-di-nal** [kär′dn-əl] *adjective*, 1) chief, most important, *noun*, 2) an important leader of the Roman Catholic church, appointed by the pope as one of his advisors 3) a bright red bird common in North America

**care** [kâr] *noun*, 1) thought or interest 2) worry, anxiety, *verb*, 3) to show concern for others 4) to look after someone and tend to his or her needs 5) to show affection or love

**ca-reen** [kə-rēn′] *verb*, to sway or lean over to one side

**ca-reer** [kə-rîr′] *noun*, a profession, a chosen pursuit

**care-ful** [kâr′fəl] *adjective*, cautious, watchful

**care-ful-ly** [kâr′fə-lē] *adverb*, cautiously, with much care

**care-less** [kâr′lĭs] *adjective*, neglectful, reckless

**ca-ress** [kə-rĕs′] *noun*, 1) a tender or loving touch, *verb*, 2) to stroke with affection, to touch in a loving way

**car-et** [kăr′ĭt] *noun*, a mark used by writers to indicate something – like a word – to be inserted

**car-go** [kär′gō] *noun*, the goods or freight carried by a ship, train, plane, or any vehicle

**car-i-bou** [kăr′ə-bōō′] *noun*, a type of reindeer

**car-i-ca-ture** [kăr′ĭ-kə-chŏŏr′] *noun*, a representation of a person or thing in which the peculiarities are exaggerated to produce a ridiculous effect

**car-nage** [kär′nĭj] *noun*, the killing of many people, a massacre

**car-na-tion** [kär-nā′shən] *noun*, a garden flower of the pink family

**car-ni-val** [kär′nə-vəl] *noun*, a festival with parades and dancing, a fair

**car-niv-o-rous** [kär-nĭv′ər-əs] *adjective*, meat-eating

**car-ol** [kăr′əl] *noun*, a song of joy

**ca-rouse** [kə-rouz′] *verb*, to drink and be merry, especially with a group

**carp** [kärp] *noun*, 1) a kind of fish, *verb*, 2) to find fault, to criticize

**car-pen-ter** [kär′pən-tər] *noun*, a builder or repairer of wooden structures or objects

**car-pen-try** [kär′pən-trē] *noun*, the art of making things out of wood

**car-pet** [kär′pĭt] *noun*, a woven or felted floor covering of wool, cotton, or a synthetic, a rug

**car-riage** [kăr′ĭj] *noun*, 1) a wheeled vehicle 2) a manner of bearing or posture

**car-ri-er** [kăr′ē-ər] *noun*, 1) a messenger 2) one engaged in the business of carrying goods for others for hire

**car-rot** [kăr′ət] *noun*, a plant with an edible root of orange color used as a vegetable

**car-ry** [kăr′ē] *verb*, 1) to transport something, to convey, to move, to haul 2) to support a weight

**cart** [kärt] *noun*, a small wagon used to carry goods

**car-ti-lage** [kär′tl-ĭj] *noun*, elastic animal tissue attached to bones near the joints

**car-tog-ra-pher** [kär-tŏg′rə-fûr] *noun*, a maker of maps or charts

**car-ton** [kär′tn] *noun*, a box or container made of cardboard

**car-toon** [kär-tōōn′] *noun*, a comical drawing of a person, event, or place

**car-tridge** [kär′trĭj] *noun*, a case holding something that is dispensed mechanically

**cart-wheel** [kärt′hwēl′] *noun*, a sideways flip that is done by springing the body onto one hand and then the other, followed by the feet

**carve** [kärv] *verb*, 1) to reshape in an artistic or decorative manner by cutting 2) to cut meat for serving

**cas-cade** [kă-skād′] *noun*, a small waterfall, a profusion

**case** [kās] *noun*, 1) a container to hold things 2) a condition, an example of an illness 3) a question of law decided in court 4) something that has happened, an instance

**cash** [kăsh] *noun*, 1) money consisting of dollars or loose change, *verb*, 2) to receive bills and coins in exchange for a check

**cash-ier** [kă-shîr′] *noun*, one who has charge of payments, etc., as at a store

**cas-ket** [kăs′kĭt] *noun*, a coffin

**cas-se-role** [kăs′ə-rōl′] *noun*, a dish consisting of several different foods combined together

**cas-sette** [kə-sĕt′, kă-] *noun*, a magnetic tape used for electronic recording enclosed in a plastic case that can fit directly into a recorder

**cast** [kăst] *noun*, 1) the performers in a play 2) a plaster dressing used to hold surgery in place, *verb*, 3) to direct a glance at someone or something 4) to assign a role in a play 5) to form a shape from clay on a potter's wheel 6) to throw or toss 7) the act of throwing a fishing line 8) to overshadow 9) to register a vote 10) to discard or shed

**caste** [kăst] *noun*, 1) one of the hereditary classes in Hindu society 2) any exclusive social class

**cas-tle** [kăs′əl] *noun*, 1) a fortress or palace usually the residence of nobility 2) a chess piece also known as the rook

**cas-u-al** [kăzh′ōō-əl] *adjective*, 1) not planned or prearranged 2) informal 3) careless

**cas-u-al-ty** [kăzh′ōō-əl-tē] *noun*, one injured or killed, as in a battle

**cat** [kăt] *noun*, a furry animal kept in the house as a pet or to catch mice

**cat-a-combs** [kăt′ə-kōmz′] *noun*, *plural*, a burial ground of underground rooms

**cat-a-log** [kăt′l-ôg′] *noun*, 1) a list of names, titles, or articles arranged in order, *verb*, 2) to list names and objects with a description of each one

**cat-a-lyst** [kăt′l-ĭst] *noun*, an agitator or force of change

**cat-a-pult** [kăt′ə-pŭlt′] noun, 1) a device that uses tension to throw objects, a weapon, *verb*, 2) to hurl or make an object go as far as possible

**cat-a-ract** [kăt′ə-răkt′] *noun*, 1) a great waterfall 2) an eye abnormality, cloudiness on the lens of the eye resulting in blurry vision

**ca-tas-tro-phe** [kə-tăs′trə-fē] *noun*, a sudden calamity, a disaster

**catch** [kăch, kĕch] *noun* 1) something that has been captured 2) the metal clasp that connects a door to a door frame, *verb*, 3) to get hold of something and not let go, to grasp 4) to get someone's attention 5) to trap

**cat-e-chism** [kăt′ĭ-kĭz′əm] *noun*, a set of questions and answers, especially for teaching about religion

**cat-e-go-ry** [kăt′ĭ-gôr′ē] *noun*, division or class to which something belongs

**ca-ter** [kā′tər] *verb*, to provide food or personal attention, to serve up

**ca-ter-pil-lar** [kăt′ər-pĭl′ər] *noun*, the larva of a butterfly

**ca-thar-sis** [kə-thär′sĭs] *noun*, 1) purging or cleansing of any part of the body 2) a release of tension or strong feelings

**ca-the-dral** [kə-thē′drəl] *noun*, a very large church, the main church of a diocese

**Cath-o-lic** [kăth′ə-lĭk] *noun*, a member of the church that recognizes the pope as its leader

**cat-tle** [kăt′l] *noun*, livestock such as cows, bulls, or steer kept for meat, milk, or skins

**cau-cus** [kô′kəs] *noun*, a group of politicians who gather to decide a policy or select a candidate

**caught** [kôt] *verb*, *past tense* of **catch**

**caulk** [kôk] *verb*, to make water-tight, to seal cracks

**cause** [kôz] *noun*, 1) the reason, the thing that made something happen 2) something you believe in strongly enough to take action, *verb*, 3) to bring about, to make something happen

**caus-tic** [kô′stĭk] *adjective*, 1) burning 2) sarcastically biting

**cau-tion** [kô′shən] *noun*, care and watchfulness, a warning

**cau-tious** [kô′shəs] *adjective*, wary, prudent, careful, watchful

**cave** [kāv] *noun*, a hollow place under the ground or in the side of a mountain or rock, sheltered from the elements

**ca-ve-at** [kā′vē-ăt′] *noun*, an indication of limitations

**cav-ern** [kăv′ərn] *noun*, a hollow place in a rock, a cave

**cav-i-ar** [kăv′ē-är′] *noun*, the prepared and salted eggs of the sturgeon or other large fish

**cav-i-ty** [kăv′ĭ-tē] *noun*, 1) a hollow place or a hole 2) a hole in the tooth caused by decay

**cease** [sēs] *verb*, to end, to stop

**cease-less** [sēs′lĭs] *adjective*, without end or interruption

**ce-dar** [sē′dər] *noun*, a large evergreen tree with reddish, fragrant wood

**ceil-ing** [sē′lĭng] *noun*, 1) the covering of a room 2) the top of a space 3) upper limit

**cel-e-brate** [sĕl′ə-brāt′] *verb*, to do certain things because of a special occasion, to rejoice

**cel-e-bra-tion** [sĕl′ə-brā′-shən] *noun*, a festive occasion

**ce-leb-ri-ty** [sə-lĕb′rĭ-tē] *noun*, fame, renown, a famous person

**ce-ler-i-ty** [sə-lĕr′ĭ-tē] *noun*, speed,

**cel-er-y** [sĕl′ə-rē] *noun*, a plant of the parsley family, whose leaf - stalks are eaten raw or cooked

**ce-les-tial** [sə-lĕs′chəl] *adjective*, in the stars, heavenly

**cel-i-ba-cy** [sĕl′ə-bə-sē] *noun*, the state of being unmarried

**cell** [sĕl] *noun*, 1) a small room where a prisoner is kept or where a nun or monk lives 2) a small, microscopic piece of a living organism

**cel-lar** [sĕl′ər] *noun*, a room under a house, partly or completely underground, a basement

**cel-lu-lar** [sĕl′yə-lər] *adjective*, 1) formed of cells 2) relating to a mobile telephone system

**Cel-si-us** [sĕl′sē-əs] *noun*, a scale on which the freezing point is 0

**ce-ment** [sĭ-mĕnt′] *noun*, a substance that consists of burned lime and clay, which is mixed with water and sand to make concrete

**cem-e-ter-y** [sĕm′ĭ-tĕr′ē] *noun*, a burial place, a graveyard

**cen-sor** [sĕn′sər] *noun*, 1) one who filters inappropriate material from books, movies, etc., before they are published or released *verb*, 2) to filter out information considered unsuitable

**cen-sus** [sĕn′səs] *noun*, an official count of a population

**cent** [sĕnt] *noun*, a metal coin equal to one penny or 1/100 of a dollar

**cen-ten-ni-al** [sĕn-tĕn′ē-əl] *adjective*, of or pertaining to a hundredth anniversary

**cen-ter** [sĕn′tər] *noun*, 1) the middle, a point equidistant from all sides 2) a place where people gather 3) a hub of activity

**cen-ti-grade** [sĕn′tĭ-grād′] *noun*, the temperature scale in which 0 degrees is the freezing point and 100 degrees is the boiling point of water

**cen-ti-me-ter** [sĕn′tə-mē′tər] *noun*, a measure of length somewhat less than ½ an inch, a standard unit in the metric system

**cen-tral** [sĕn′trəl] *adjective*, located in the middle

**cen-trif-u-gal** [sĕn-trĭf′yə-gəl] *adjective*, relating to forces caused by rotation directed outward from the center

**cen-trip-e-tal** [sĕn-trĭp′ĭ-tl] *adjective*, directed toward the center

**cen-tu-ry** [sĕn′chə-rē] *noun*, a period of one hundred years

**ce·re·al** [sîr′ē-əl] *noun*, any edible grain, including oats, rye, rice

**cer·e·bel·lum** [sĕr′ə-bĕl′əm] *noun*, the part of the brain related to muscular movements and coordination

**ce·re·bral** [sĕr′ə-brəl] *adjective*, appealing to the intellect and not the emotions

**cer·e·mo·ni·al** [sĕr′ə-mō′nē-əl] *adjective*, following a tradition or certain rituals, formal

**cer·e·mo·ny** [sĕr′ə-mō′nē] *noun*, a special occasion that honors traditions or rituals

**cer·tain** [sûr ′tn] *adjective*, 1) sure 2) unquestionable 3) not named, but thought to be known

**cer·tain·ty** [sûr′tn-tē] *noun*, a state of being sure of something

**cer·tif·i·cate** [sər-tĭf′ĭ-kĭt] *noun*, a document verifying qualification or ability or fact

**cer·ti·fy** [sûr′tə-fī′] *verb*, to authorize the validity of something, to guarantee

**chafe** [chāf] *verb*, 1) to rub together leaving a sore 2) to annoy

**chaff** [chăf] *noun*, 1) a worthless or trivial thing 2) the outer coating of wheat

**cha·grin** [shə-grĭn′] *noun*, a feeling of embarrassment because one has failed, deep disappointment

**chain** [chān] *noun*, 1) links or rings joined together, *verb*, 2) to hold with a chain, to restrain

**chair** [châr] *noun*, furniture with four legs and a back used to seat someone

**chal·ice** [chăl′ĭs] *noun*, a goblet

**chalk** [chôk] *noun*, a soft white limestone substance used to write on a blackboard

**chal·lenge** [chăl′ənj] *noun*, 1) an offer to test ability or skill 2) a formal objection, *verb*, 2) to call or invite to a contest of any kind

**cham·ber** [chām′bər] *noun*, 1) a room 2) a space surrouded by walls 3) a compartment in a firearm that holds the ammunition

**cham·pi·on** [chăm′pē-ən] *noun*, the winner of a competition

**cham·pi·on·ship** [chăm′pē-ən-shĭp′] *noun*, a competition among people or teams to decide who is best

**chance** [chăns] *noun*, 1) luck, fate 2) possibility or probability 3) risk 4) a turn to do something, an opportunity 5) a coincidence

**chan·de·lier** [shăn′də-lîr′] *noun*, a branched lighting fixture that hangs from the ceiling in a frame

**change** [chānj] *noun*, 1) a transformation, the process of becoming different 2) loose coins, *verb*, 3) to make or become different 4) to transform

**change·a·ble** [chānj′jə-bəl] *adjective*, variable, adaptable

**chan·nel** [chăn′əl] *noun*, 1) a narrow stream of flowing water that connects two large bodies of water, *verb*, 2) to make something, such as energy or water, flow in a certain direction

**chant** [chănt] *noun*, 1) words repeated in rhythm, *verb*, 2) to speak in a singing way

**cha-os** [kā'ŏs'] *noun*, disorder, confusion, upheaval

**chap-el** [chăp'əl] *noun*, a small room within a larger building set aside for religious purposes

**chap-er-one** [shăp'ə-rōn'] (also **chaperon**) *noun*, an older person who accompanies as a protector

**chap-lain** [chăp'lĭn] *noun*, a clergyman, minister priest or rabbi serving in a hospital, the armed forces, etc.

**chap-ter** [chăp'tər] *noun*, a division of a book

**char** [chär] *verb*, to burn, to scorch

**char-ac-ter** [kăr'ək-tər] *noun*, 1) the moral makeup of a person 2) a person in a book or movie or play 3) a symbol, sign, or written letter used in a language

**char-ac-ter-is-tic** [kăr'ək-tə-rĭs'tĭk] *noun*, a trait, an attribute

**char-ac-ter-ize** [kăr'ək-tə-rīz'] *verb*, to describe, to indicate details or traits of someone or something

**char-ac-ter-i-za-tion** [kăr'ək-tə-rīz'ā'-shən] *noun*, a description of someone or something

**char-coal** [chär'kōl'] *noun*, a black porous material made by partially burning wood

**charge** [chärj] *noun*, 1) an accusation 2) care or instruction given 3) the cost, expense, *verb*, 4) to request money 5) to accuse someone of doing something wrong 6) to rush or attack 7) to fill with power 8) to control

**char-i-ot** [chăr'ē-ət] *noun*, a horse-drawn cart

**cha-ris-ma** [kə-rĭz'mə] *noun*, attraction, charm, and allure, having a strong effect on others

**char-i-ta-ble** [chăr'ĭ-tə-bəl] *adjective*, 1) giving freely and generously 2) lenient, kind

**char-i-ty** [chăr'ĭ-tē] *noun*, 1) goodness, generosity, and kindness 2) an agency that provides a service to those in need, especially the poor

**charm** [chärm] *noun*, 1) a pleasant, courteous manner 2) a thing like a talisman or a group of words spoken to cause good luck, *verb*, 3) to please someone

**charm-ing** [chär'mĭng] *adjective*, pleasing, beautiful, enchanting

**chart** [chärt] *noun*, 1) a piece of paper or spreadsheet with information on it indicating, patterns, information, or changes, *verb*, 2) to plan a route on a map of the ocean or other large area

**char-ter** [chär'tər] *noun*, 1) a document establishing the creation of an entity 2) a reservation of a vehicle, ship, etc., *verb*, 3) to hire a ship, bus, plane, etc.

**chase** [chās] *noun*, 1) the act of running after someone, *verb*, 2) to follow someone while trying to capture them, to pursue

**chasm** [kăz'əm] *noun*, a deep hole

**chas-sis** [shăs'ē] *noun*, the under part of a car, consisting of the frame with the wheels and machinery

**chaste** [chāst] *adjective*, 1) pure, celibate 2) simple in style

**chat** [chăt] *noun*, 1) a pleasant conversation, *verb*, 2) to make conversation or small talk

**chauf-feur** [shō′fər] *noun*, a person employed as a driver of a private automobile

**chau-vin-ist** [shō′və-nĭst] *noun*, a prejudiced belief in the superiority of your own race, sex, etc.

**cheap** [chēp] *adjective*, low in price, inexpensive, poorly made

**cheat** [chēt] *verb*, to do something that is not honest, to deceive

**check** [chĕk] *noun*, 1) an order for money, *verb*, 2) to make sure everything is in order

**check-ers** [chĕk′ərz] *noun*, *plural*, a board game played by two people, each with twelve pieces

**cheek** [chēk] *noun*, 1) the fleshy skin covering the bone beneath the eye socket on both sides of the face 2) impudent speech

**cheer** [chîr] *noun*, 1) a shout of support 2) gladness, a joyful state of mind, *verb*, 3) to make happy 4) to encourage with shouts

**cheer-ful** [chîr′fəl] *adjective*, smiling and happy

**cheese** [chēz] *noun*, the consolidated curd of milk, used as food

**chef** [shĕf] *noun*, a head cook

**chem-i-cal** [kĕm′ĭ-kəl] *noun*, a substance or mixture of substances used in or produced by changes in atoms or molecules

**chem-ist** [kĕm′ĭst] *noun*, a person who studies matter such as gases, metal, and liquids to see what they do and what they are made of

**chem-is-try** [kĕm′ĭ-strē] *noun*, the study of the composition, properties, and reactions of matter, particularly at the level of atoms and molecules

**cher-ish** [chĕr′ĭsh] *verb*, 1) to love dearly, to adore 2) to cling to an idea or feeling

**cher-ry** [chĕr′ē] *noun*, an edible, fleshy, red fruit containing a pit

**chess** [chĕs] *noun*, a game of skill played on a checkered board by two players each with 16 pieces

**chest** [chĕst] *noun*, 1) the front of the body between the shoulders and the waist 2) a large box made of metal, wood, etc.

**chew** [chōō] *verb*, to grind food between the teeth

**chic** [shēk] *noun*, great artistic cleverness or skill, style

**chick-en** [chĭk′ən] *noun*, fowl kept for eggs or meat

**chide** [chīd] *verb*, to scold

**chief** [chēf] *adjective*, 1) highest in office or rank, *noun* 2) the leader of a group or organization

**chif-fon** [shĭ-fŏn′] *noun*, 1) a soft gauzy silk material used for dresses 2) a light airy dessert made with egg whites

**child** [chīld] *noun*, *plural* **children**, a young person, offspring

**child-ish** [chīl′dĭsh] *adjective*, to be selfish and inconsiderate

**chil-i or chili con carne** [chĭl′ē] *noun*, a dish of tomatoes, meat, and sometimes beans, flavored with hot spices

**chill** [chĭl] *adjective*, 1) cold, frosty, *noun*, 2) coldness, freezing, *verb*, 3) to make or become cold

**chime** [chīm] *verb*, to make a tinkling sound like a bell

**chim-ney** [chĭm′nē] *noun*, a structure by which smoke passes from a building to the outdoors

**chim-pan-zee** [chĭm′păn-zē′] *noun*, an ape native to Africa larger than a monkey, without a tail

**chin** [chĭn] *noun*, the part of the face below the lips

**chi-na** [chī′nə] *noun*, *no plural*, dishes, such as plates, cups, and saucers, made of fine clay or porcelain, used to serve a meal

**chip** [chĭp] *noun*, 1) a small piece of something that has broken off 2) a cracker or a thinly sliced fried food 3) the small silicon object that enables the computer to process information, *verb*, 4) to break off small pieces from the main part

**chip-munk** [chĭp′mŭngk′] *noun*, a tan rodent like a small squirrel with a black stripe from its head to the tip of its tail

**chirp** [chûrp] *noun*, 1) a high pitched sound, *verb*, 2) to warble, to tweet like a bird

**chis-el** [chĭz′əl] *noun*, 1) a metal tool with a cutting edge at the end of a blade, *verb*, 2) to carve a sculpture or use a chisel as a tool 3) to swindle, to cheat

**chiv-al-ry** [shĭv′əl-rē] *noun*, bravery, heroism, courtesy,

**chlo-ride** [klôr′īd] *noun*, a compound of chlorine with another substance

**chlo-rine** [klôr′ēn′] *noun*, a yellow-green gas added to water supplies as a disinfectant

**chlo-ro-form** [klôr′ə-fôrm′] *noun*, a colorless, sweetish liquid used as an anesthetic

**chlo-ro-phyll** [klôr′ə-fĭl] *noun*, a green pigment in plants, essential for photosynthesis

**choc-o-late** [chô′kə-lĭt] *noun*, a candy made from cocoa, the roasted seeds of cacao

**choice** [chois] *adjective*, 1) first rate, *noun*, 2) an act of making a selection or choosing

**choir** [kwīr] *noun*, a band of singers, especially in church

**choke** [chōk] *verb*, 1) to feel suffocated because the throat is obstructed 2) to repress

**chol-er** [kŏl′ər] *noun*, anger

**choose** [chooz] *verb*, to pick or select from a group, to make a choice

**chop** [chŏp] *noun*, 1) a piece of meat near the bone, *verb*, 2) to cut with a sharp blade

**cho-ral** [kôr′əl] *adjective*, for or relating to a chorus

**chord** [kôrd] *noun*, a combination of three or more tones sounded together in harmony

**chore** [chôr] *noun*, a job or distasteful task

**cho-re-og-ra-phy** [kôr′ē-ŏg′rə-fē, kōr′-] *noun*, 1) the plan of the steps and movements in dancing 2) the creation of ballets or dances

**chor-tle** [chôr′tl] *verb*, to make a chuckling or snorting noise

**cho-rus** [kôr′əs] *noun*, 1) a company of singers singing in concert 2) the part of a song that is repeated, the refrain

**chow-der** [chou′dər] *noun*, a thick soup or stew usually featuring fish, corn, etc.

**chris-ten** [krĭs′ən] *verb*, to give a name to someone who is baptized into the Christian faith

**Chris-tian** [krĭs′chən] *noun*, a person who believes in Jesus Christ

**chromosome** [krō′mə-sōm′] *noun*, a thread-like structure in the nucleus of a cell that carries the genes

**chron-ic** [krŏn′ĭk] *adjective*, continuing for a long time, habitual, prolonged

**chron-i-cle** [krŏn′ĭ-kəl] *noun*, 1) a historical register of facts in order of their occurrence, *verb*, 2) to record in a factual and detailed way

**chron-o-log-i-cal** [krŏn′ə-lŏj′ĭ-kəl] *adjective*, documented according to the order of time

**chuck-le** [chŭk′əl] *noun*, 1) a quick laugh or giggle, *verb*, 2) to laugh softly, in a gentle manner

**chunk** [chŭngk] *noun*, a thick piece of something, a block, a slab

**church** [chûrch] *noun*, a building in which Christians meet to worship and pray

**churn** [chûrn] *verb*, to move about with force, to turn violently

**ci-der** [sī′dər] *noun*, a drink made from pressed apples

**ci-gar** [sĭ-gär′] *noun*, tobacco leaves rolled together in paper for smoking

**cig-a-ret-te** [sĭg′ə-rĕt′] *noun*, a cylinder of finely cut tobacco rolled in paper

**cin-der** [sĭn′dərz] *noun*, a hot coal, an ember

**cin-e-ma** [sĭn′ə-mə] *noun*, 1) a building where films are shown 2) the movie business

**cin-na-mon** [sĭn′ə-mən] *noun*, the bark of an East Indian tree, ground into a spice

**cir-cle** [sûr′kəl] *noun*, 1) a closed curve in which all points are equidistant from the center, a ring 2) a group of people

**cir-cuit** [sûr′kĭt] *noun*, the circumference or distance around an area

**cir-cuit-ous** [sər-kyōō′ĭ-təs] *adjective*, roundabout, indirect, meandering, winding

**cir-cu-lar** [sûr′kyə-lər] *adjective*, 1) round, *noun*, 2) a leaflet, a pamphlet, a newsletter

**cir-cu-late** [sûr′kyə-lāt′] *verb*, to move about or around

**cir-cu-la-tion** [sûr′kyə-lā′shən] *noun*, 1) the act of moving around, especially of blood through the body 2) the extent or amount of distribution, dissemination

**cir-cum-fer-ence** [sər-kŭm′fər-əns] *noun*, the distance around a circle or circular figure

**cir-cum-lo-cu-tion** [sûr′kəm-lō-kyōō′shən] *noun*, an indirect or roundabout way of expressing something

**cir-cum-spec-tion** [sûr′kəm-spĕk′shən] *noun*, caution, care, forethought

**cir-cum-stance** [sûr′kəm-stăns′] *noun*, a particular incident, a state of affairs, events

**cir-cum-stan-tial** [sûr′kəm-stăn′shəl] *adjective*, relating to evidence that tends to prove a fact at issue by proving other basic events

**cir-cum-vent** [sûr′kəm-věnt′] *verb*, to find a way around, to evade a difficulty

**cir-cus** [sûr′kəs] *noun*, a traveling show usually performed by clowns and acrobats and tamed animals presented in an arena

**cit-a-del** [sĭt′ə-dəl] *noun*, fortress

**ci-ta-tion** [sī-tā′shən] *noun*, 1) a summons to appear in court, a ticket 2) a quote or reference to a document 3) honorary mention to receive an award or degree for meritorious service

**cite** [sīt] *verb*, 1) to quote or refer to a document 2) to recognize someone for commendable service 3) to write a ticket for violating the law

**cit-i-zen** [sĭt′ĭ-zən] *noun*, a person whose legal home is a certain place or nation

**cit-i-zen-ship** [sĭt′ĭ-zən-shĭp′] *noun*, 1) the fact of being a citizen 2) community participation

**cit-y** [sĭt′ē] *noun*, a large important town, a metropolis

**civ-ic** [sĭv′ĭk] *adjective*, pertaining to a community or city

**civ-il** [sĭv′əl] *adjective*, 1) polite 2) relating to a government employee who is not in the armed forces

**ci-vil-ian** [sĭ-vĭl′yən] *noun*, a person not in the armed forces

**ci-vil-i-ty** [sĭ-vĭl′ĭ-tē] *noun*, good manners, courtesy

**civ-i-li-za-tion** [sĭv′ə-lĭ-zā′shən] *noun*, 1) the condition of being civilized or having culture 2) people sharing their way of life and living in one place at a time, any human society

**civ-i-lize** [sĭv′ə-līz′] *verb*, to reclaim from a savage state

**civ-il war** *noun*, a war fought in a country between two different groups of the same nation

**claim** [klām] *noun*, 1) a statement, an assertion *verb*, 2) to say and demand possession of something by demonstrating ownership

**claim-ant** [klā′mənt] *noun*, a person submitting an application or making a claim

**clair-voy-ant** [klâr-voi′ənt] *adjective*, having foresight

**clam** [klăm] *noun*, a shellfish similar to an oyster

**clam-or** [klăm′ər] *noun*, 1) a loud steady noise, an outcry, *verb*, 2) to make a lot of noise

**clan** [klăn] *noun*, a group of people sharing one ancestor

**clan-des-tine** [klăn-děs′tĭn] *adjective*, secret, concealed

**clang** [klăng] *noun*, the sound of one piece of metal hitting another, a ringing sound

**clap** [klăp] *noun*, 1) a loud noise, as in thunder, *verb*, 2) to make a sound by hitting your hands together, applause

**clar-i-fy** [klăr′ə-fī′] *verb*, to make or become clear, to explain

**clar-i-on** [klăr′ē-ən] *adjective*, shrill, loud and clear

**clar-i-ty** [klăr′ĭ-tē] *adjective*, clearness

**clash** [klăsh] *noun*, 1) a fight or angry dispute 2) the sound of metal on metal, *verb*, 3) to hit or fight 4)of colors, to look awful together 5) to collide noisily

**clasp** [klăsp] *noun*, 1) a fastening, *verb*, 2) to hold tightly

**class** [klăs] *noun*, 1) a group of similar things or people 2) students meeting together for instruction, *verb*, 3) to classify

**clas-sic** [klăs′ĭk] *adjective*, showing excellence, exemplary

**clas-si-cal** [klăs′ĭ-kəl] *adjective*, 1)pertaining to ancient Greeks and Romans 2)excellent in a traditional style, esp. of music

**clas-si-fi-ca-tion** [klăs′ə-fĭ-kā′shən] *noun*, categorizing, grouping

**clas-si-fy** [klăs′ə-fī′] *verb*, to sort, to form into classes or groupings

**clause** [klôz] *noun*, 1) a group of words in a sentence that contains a subject and a verb 2) a single part in a contract, law, or treaty

**claus-tro-pho-bi-a** [klô′strə-fō′bē-ə] *noun*, a fear of being in a close space

**claw** [klô] *noun*, 1) the sharp, hard nails on the foot of an animal or bird, *verb*, 2) to tear or scratch with the hand or nails

**clay** [klā] *noun*, a common earth used for making pottery and bricks when baked

**clean** [klēn] *adjective*, 1) free from dirt, neat, *verb*, 2) to remove dirt and soil or impurities

**clean-li-ness** [klĕn′lē-nĭs] *noun*, the state of being clean, neatness of person, good hygiene

**cleanse** [klĕnz] *verb*, 1) to scrub, to wash, to disinfect 2) to absolve

**clear** [klîr] *adjective*, 1) easily understood 2) transparent 3) distinct or easy to hear, *verb*, 4) to remove items 5) to remove an obstacle, to bring into focus

**clear-ance** [klîr′əns] *noun*, 1) the act of removing whatever may obstruct 2) permission

**clear-ly** [klîr′lē] *adverb*, plainly

**cleave** [klēv] *verb*, 1) to cling, to adhere to 2) to separate or split

**cleft** [klĕft] *noun*, a space or opening made by or as if by splitting, a crack, a fissure

**clem-en-cy** [klĕm′ən-sē] *noun*, mildness, leniency, mercy

**clench** [klĕnch] *verb*, to hold tightly, to grip, to grasp

**cler-gy** [klûr′j*noun*, ministers of the church as a group

**clerk** [klûrk] *noun*, a person who does office work, a salesperson

**cle-ver** [klĕv′ər] *adjective*, quick at learning, smart, good at doing things, resourceful, intelligent

**cli-ché** [klē-shā′] *noun*, a phrase repeated often, e.g. *down and out*

**click** [klĭk] *verb*, 1) to make a small noise like a tick on a clock 2) to press the mouse button once

**cli-ent** [klī′ənt] *noun*, a customer who uses the professional help of another, a patron

**cliff** [klĭf] *noun*, a high, steep wall of rock or bank on a coast

**cli-mate** [klī′mĭt] *noun*, the typical weather or atmosphere of a place year after year

**cli-max** [klī′măks′] *noun*, the crucial point when everything comes together, culmination

**climb** [klīm] *noun*, 1) the distance traveled up a hill or mountain, *verb*, 2) to go up, to ascend

**clime** [klīm] *noun*, region, climate

**cling** [klĭng] *verb*, to hold on tightly, to clutch, to grip

**cling-ing** [klĭng′ĭng] *adjective*, 1) devoted 2) holding fast 3) dependent

**clin-ic** [klĭn′ĭk] *noun*, a place that provides medical treatment

**clin-ic-al** [klĭn′ĭ-kəl] *adjective*, 1) related to observation and treatment of patients 2) scientific and observable

**clip** [klĭp] *noun*, 1) an object used to fasten things 2) a brisk pace, *verb*, 3) to cut or trim

**clique** [klēk] *noun*, a small group with joint interests, an exclusive set of friends, a gang

**cloak** [klōk] *noun*, 1) a loose piece of clothing, usually sleeveless, worn as an outer garment, *verb*, 2) to conceal

**clock** [klŏk] *noun*, an instrument used to measure time

**clog** [klŏg] *noun*, 1) a blockage 2) a thick-soled shoe with an open back, *verb*, 3) to dance in the shoes 4) to hinder or obstruct, to be blocked up

**close** [klōs] *adjective*, 1) near 2) alike, similar, *verb*, 3) to shut out 4) to bring or come to an end

**clos-et** [klŏz′ĭt] *noun*, a small room or space where clothes are hung and items are stored

**clot** [klŏt] *noun*, a thickened mass of blood tissue

**cloth** [klôth] *noun*, a piece of fabric made of natural or synthetic fibers, such as cotton or rayon

**cloth-ing** [klō′thĭng] *noun*, *no plural*, garments, apparel, things worn as clothes, articles of dress

**cloud** [kloud] *noun*, 1) a visible mass of water droplets floating in the sky 2) a mass of dust

**cloud-y** [klou′dē] *adjective*, filled with clouds, overcast

**clown** [kloun] *noun*, a person who has the ability to turn himself or herself into a comical character that brings happiness and joy; especially to children, the sick, and sad

**club** [klŭb] *noun*, 1) a group of people who meet for a common purpose 2) a heavy stick

**clue** [kloo] *noun*, information or evidence that helps you find the answer to a puzzling question

**clum-sy** [klŭm′zē] *adjective*, awkward, unhandy, unwieldy

**clus-ter** [klŭs′tər] *noun*, 1) a clump, a bunch, a small, close group, *verb*, 2) to gather together into a small group

**clutch** [klŭch] *noun*, 1) the part of a machine that connects and disconnects the power from the rest of the machine, *verb*, 2) to hold something tightly, to grip, to cling to

**clut-ter** [klŭt'ər] *noun*, things lying about, a mess

**coach** [kōch] *noun*, 1) one who trains athletes, actors, or singers 2) a part of a train or bus that carries passengers 3) a carriage drawn by horses, *verb*, 4) to assist talented people develop their capability, to train

**co-ag-u-late** [kō-ăg'yə-lāt'] *verb*, to form into a dense mass, solidify from a liquid, to congeal

**coal** [kōl] *noun*, a fossil fuel in solid form that gives off heat when burned

**co-a-lesce** [kō'ə-lĕs'] *verb*, to combine, to fuse, to join together

**co-a-li-tion** [kō'ə-lĭsh'ən] *noun*, a union of people of differing views in a single body or group

**coarse** [kôrs, kōrs] *adjective*, 1) rough in surface or texture 2) crude, ill-mannered

**coast** [kōst] *noun*, 1) the edge of land that touches the ocean, *verb*, 2) to slide or glide

**coat** [kōt] *noun*, a piece of clothing with sleeves, worn over everything else, a jacket

**coax** [kōks] *verb*, to gently persuade

**cob-bler** [kŏb'lər] *noun*, someone who makes and repairs shoes

**cob-web** [kŏb'wĕb'] *noun*, threads woven by a spider in which it catches insects

**co-caine** [kō-kān'] *noun*, a bitter, crystalline alkaloid used as a local anesthetic and illegally as a stimulant

**cock** [kŏk] *noun*, a male bird

**cock-pit** [kŏk'pĭt'] *noun*, the compartment in a vehicle where the driver of a race car or the pilot of an airplane sits

**co-co-nut** [kō'kə-nŭt'] *noun*, the fruit of a variety of palm tree

**co-coon** [kə-kōōn'] *noun*, the silky case insects live in during the pupa stage

**cod** [kŏd] *noun*, *no plural*, a family of sea fish used for food

**cod-dle** [kŏd'l] *verb*, to treat gently, to pamper, to spoil

**code** [kōd] *noun*, 1) a collection of laws 2) a system of symbols given certain meanings

**co-erce** [kō-ûrs'] *verb*, to persuade by force

**co-er-cion** [kō-ûr'zhən] *noun*, persuasion by force or threats, pressuring

**cof-fee** [kô'fē] *noun*, the hot beverage made from the seeds of a coffee plant, a pale brown color

**cof-fin** [kô'fĭn] *noun*, a box in which a dead body is placed

**cog** [kŏg] *noun*, the tooth projecting from a wheel rim or a bar

**cog-ni-zant** [kŏg'nĭ-zənt] *adjective*, conscious, aware, knowledgeable

**co-her-ent** [kō-hîr'ənt] *adjective*, 1) able to be understood 2) forming a connection

**co-he-sion** [kō-hē'zhən] *noun*, the act of sticking together

**coil** [koil] *noun*, 1) a wire in a continuous circling shape, *verb*, 2) to wrap up around in a ring

**coin** [koin] *noun*, 1) a piece of money made of metal, legally authorized by a government 2) a quantity of value, *verb*, 3) to make coins 4) to invent

**co-in-cide** [kō'ĭn-sīd'] *verb*, to occur at the same time, to correspond exactly

**co-in-cid-ence** [kō-ĭn'sĭ-dəns] *noun*, random events that happen at the same time, chance, luck

**col-an-der** [kŭl'ən-dər] *noun*, a bowl-shaped container that is perforated for use as a strainer

**cold** [kōld] *adjective*, 1) feeling no heat, not warm 2) unfriendly, *noun*, 3) a virus with symptoms of a sore throat and runny nose

**col-lab-o-rate** [kə-lăb'ə-rāt'] *verb*, to work together as a group

**col-lab-o-ra-tion** [kə-lăb'ə-rā'shən] *noun*, a project that includes ideas from two or more people working together

**col-lapse** [kə-lăps'] *noun*, 1) any sudden or complete breakdown, *verb*, 2) to break down suddenly 3) to fall down

**col-lar** [kŏl'ər] *noun*, 1) a band worn around the neck of an animal 2) the part of a shirt around the neck

**col-late** [kə-lāt'] *verb*, 1) to examine in order to verify a special authenticity 2) to combine and arrange in order

**col-lat-er-al** [kə-lăt'ər-əl] *adjective*, 1) secondary, *noun*, 2) security in the form of property for repayment of a loan

**col-league** [kŏl'ēg'] *noun*, an associate from work, a friend or a peer, a co-worker

**col-lect** [kə-lĕkt'] *verb*, 1) to accumulate, to compile, to scrape together 2) to gather, to meet, to flock, to convene

**col-lec-tion** [kə-lĕk'shən] *noun*, an accumulation of things of a similar nature

**col-lec-tive** [kə-lĕk'tĭv] *adjective*, gathered, compiled, joint

**col-lege** [kŏl'ĭj] *noun*, a place where people study after high school that gives degrees

**col-lide** [kə-līd'] *verb*, to come together with great force

**col-li-sion** [kə-lĭzh'ən] *noun*, the act of striking or dashing together, a crash

**co-lon** [kō'lən] *noun*, 1) the sign [:] which is used before a listing or examples 2) the part of the large intestine extending to the rectum

**colo-nel** [kûr'nəl] *noun*, the commanding officer of a regiment, below brigadier general

**co-lo-ni-al** [kə-lō'nē-əl] *adjective*, relating to a period in America before independence

**col-o-nist** [kŏl'ə-nĭst] *noun*, someone who settles a territory

**col-o-ni-za-tion** [kŏl'ə-nĭ-zā'shən] *noun*, the act of setting up homes and starting a community in a new place with the purpose of living there a long time

**col-o-ny** [kŏl'ə-nē] *noun*, a country, area, etc. under the jurisdiction of another country and occupied by settlers

**col-or** [kŭl'ər] *noun*, 1) any of the hues of the rainbow, including white, *verb*, 2) to paint, dye, tint, to change the hue 3) to affect

**Col-o-rado** [kŏl′ə-răd′ō] *noun*, one of the United States, the capital city is Denver. The state flower of Colorado is the rocky mountain columbine, and the motto is "Nothing without the divine will."

**co-los-sal** [kə-lŏs′əl] *adjective*, huge, gigantic, immense

**colt** [kōlt] *noun*, a young male horse

**col-umn** [kŏl′əm] *noun*, 1) a supporting pillar 2) a perpendicular set of lines of a text in a book or periodical or newspaper or web page

**col-um-nist** [kŏl′əm-nĭst] *noun*, a writer who is featured regularly in a newspaper, or magazine, or Web site

**co-ma** [kō′mə] *noun*, state of being unresponsive, unconsciousness

**comb** [kōm] *noun*, 1) a piece of plastic, wood, or metal with teeth to smooth and adjust hair, *verb*, 2) to tidy hair with a comb

**com-bat** [kəm-băt′] *noun*, 1) an armed battle, *verb*, 2) to fight

**com-bi-na-tion** [kŏm′bə-nā′shən] *noun*, the act or result of combining, a union, a mixture

**com-bine** [kəm-bīn′] *verb*, to mix together, to blend, to unite

**com-bus-ti-ble** [kəm-bŭs′tə-bəl] *adjective*, apt to catch fire, flammable

**come** [kŭm] *verb*, 1) to arrive, to approach 2) to happen

**com-e-dy** [kŏm′ĭ-dē] *noun*, a funny performance that makes the audience laugh, humor

**come-ly** [kŭm′lē] *adjective*, attractive, beautiful, or handsome

**com-et** [kŏm′ĭt] *noun*, a celestial object of a frozen mass of dust that vaporizes as it nears the sun

**com-fort** [kŭm′fərt] *noun*, 1) consolation in trouble, *verb*, 2) to show kindness to someone, to console

**com-fort-a-ble** [kŭm′fər-tə-bəl] *adjective*, to feel at ease

**com-ic** [kŏm′ĭk] *adjective*, funny, humorous

**com-ma** [kŏm′ə] *noun*, a punctuation mark (,) used to indicate pauses and to separate elements within a sentence

**com-mand** [kə-mănd′] *noun*, 1) an order 2) mastery, rule, *verb*, 3) to be in charge of, to order someone to do something

**com-man-deer** [kŏm′ən-dîr′] *verb*, to take, often for military use

**com-mem-o-rate** [kə-měm′ə-rāt′] *verb*, to honor, to memorialize

**com-mence-ment** [kə-měns′mənt] *noun*, 1) the beginning 2) the ceremony of graduation

**com-mend** [kə-měnd′] *verb*, to praise, to compliment, to support

**com-men-su-rate** [kə-měn′sər-ĭt] *adjective*, equal in extent, in proportion, corresponding

**com-ment** [kŏm′ent] *noun*, 1) a remark or something said, *verb*, 2) to make a remark about something, to express an opinion

**com-merce** [kŏm′ərs] *noun*, business, the buying and selling of goods, all forms of trade

**com-mer-cial** [kə-mûr′shəl] *adjective*,
1) for business purposes, having
profit as an aim, *noun*, 2) an
advertisement on television or radio

**com-mis-er-ate** [kə-mĭz′ə-rāt′]
*verb*, to feel or express sorrow

**com-mis-sion** [kə-mĭsh′ən] *noun*,
1) a committee or board that
studies an issue 2) the
percentage paid to an agent

**com-mit** [kə-mĭt′] *verb*, 1) to
entrust 2) to pledge 3) to act out,
to perform 4) to put into custody

**com-mit-ment** [kə-mĭt′mənt] *noun*, a
pledge, a promise, a responsibility

**com-mit-tee** [kə-mĭt′ē] *noun*, a
group appointed or formed to
consider or accomplish some
matter or business

**com-mod-i-ty** [kə-mŏd′ĭ-tē] *noun*,
an item that can be bought and
sold, merchandise

**com-mon** [kŏm′ən] *adjective*,
1) ordinary, found everywhere,
general 2) joint, shared, *noun*,
3) a public outdoor space

**com-mon-wealth** [kŏm′ən-wĕlth′]
*noun*, 1) a group of independent
states in a country 2) a self-
governed nation or state

**com-mo-tion** [kə-mō′shən] *noun*,
noise, confusion, disruption,

**com-mune** [kŏm′yoōn′] *noun*,
a living arrangement in which
everyone shares possessions,
work, etc.

**com-mu-ni-ca-ble**
[kə-myoō′nĭ-kə-bəl] *adjective*,
contagious, infectious

**com-mu-ni-cate** [kə-myoō′nĭ-kāt′]
*verb*, 1) to give or exchange
information 2) to transmit

**com-mu-ni-ca-tion**
[kə-myoō′nĭ-kā′shən] *noun*,
1) exchange of information
between people 2) that which is
made known 3) transmission

**com-mun-ion** [kə′myoōnyən]
*noun*, 1) the mutual sharing of
feelings and thoughts 2) a
religious fellowship among
members of a church

**com-mu-nism** [kŏm′yə-nĭz′əm]
*noun*, a political system in which
property is owned by the state

**com-mu-nist** [kŏm′yə-nĭst] *noun*, a
person who believes the state
should own all industry and land

**com-mu-ni-ty** [kə-myoō′nĭ-tē]
*noun*, a town, city, suburb, or
other place where people live
and work, a society

**com-mute** [kə-myoōt′] *verb*, 1) to
make a sentence of punishment
less severe 2) to travel, to go back
and forth to work

**com-pact** [kəm-păkt′] *adjective*,
1) taking up a small amount of
space, *noun*, 2) a small case
with makeup and a mirror 3) an
agreement, *verb*, 4) to press
close together

**com-pan-ion** [kəm-păn′yən] *noun*,
a friend or associate, one who
accompanies another

**com-pa-ny** [kŭm′pə-nē] *noun*,
1) an association for business or
social purposes 2) a corporation
or firm 3) guests, visitors 4) a
subdivision of a regiment

**com-pa-ra-ble** [kŏm′pər-ə-bəl]
*adjective*, similar, equivalent

**com-pare** [kəm-pâr′] *verb*, to look
at similarities and differences

**com-par-i-son** [kəm-păr′ĭ-sən] *noun*, an examination of two or more objects with the view to discovering the similarities or differences, contrast

**com-pass** [kŭm′pəs] *noun*, 1) an instrument using a magnetic needle that always points to the north 2) a tool used to draw a circle 3) a range, scope, or limits

**com-pas-sion** [kəm-păsh′ən] *noun*, sympathy for suffering, kindness

**com-pat-i-ble** [kəm-păt′ə-bəl] *adjective*, in harmony with something, well-suited

**com-pel** [kəm-pĕl′] *verb*, 1) to drive or urge with force 2) to coerce

**com-pen-di-um** [kəm-pĕn′dē-əm] *noun*, an abridgement, collection, summary of information

**com-pen-sate** [kŏm′pən-sāt′] *verb*, to make up for something, to make amends, to pay

**com-pen-sa-tion** [kŏm′pən-sā′shən] *noun*, an amount paid to make up for something, payment

**com-pete** [kəm-pēt′] *verb*, to try to win a race, contest, etc.

**com-pe-tent** [kŏm′pĭ-tənt] *adjective*, capable, qualified, adequate, proficient, able

**com-pe-ti-tion** [kŏm′pĭ-tĭsh′ən] *noun*, 1) rivalry, free market conditions 2) a contest to see who performs better, a game

**com-pet-i-tor** [kəm-pĕt′ĭ-tər] *noun*, a rival, one who competes

**com-pile** [kəm-pīl′] *verb*, to gather information

**com-pla-cen-cy** [kəm-plā′sən-sē] *noun*, self-satisfaction, smugness

**com-plac-ent** [kəm-plā′sənt] *adjective*, 1) self-satisfied, smug 2) agreeable, lazy

**com-plain** [kəm-plān′] *verb*, 1) to express unhappiness or dissatisfaction or resentment 2) to make a formal accusation

**com-plaint** [kəm-plānt′] *noun*, 1) a criticism, reproach 2) an illness

**com-ple-ment** [kŏm′plə-mənt] *noun*, that which fills up, completes, or balances

**com-plete** [kəm-plēt′] *adjective*, 1) lacking nothing, full, whole, 2) finished, *verb*, 3) to finish

**com-plex** [kəm-plĕks′] *adjective*, 1) complicated, puzzling 2) consisting of connected parts, *noun*, 3) a group of buildings

**com-plex-ion** [kəm-plĕk′shən] *noun*, 1) the color or hue of the skin of the face 2) general appearance or aspect

**com-pli-ance** [kəm-plī′əns] *noun*, the act of yielding to demand, consent, agreement

**com-plic-ate** [kŏm′plĭ-kāt′] *verb*, to confuse, to perplex, to make more difficult or complex

**com-pli-ment** [kŏm′plə-mənt] *noun*, 1) nice words said about someone, praise, *verb*, 2) to express admiration, to laud

**com-ply** [kəm-plī′] *verb*, to follow, to conform, to go along with an order or a rule

**com-po-nent** [kəm-pō′nənt] *noun*, an essential part, a fundamental piece, a constituent part

**com-port** [kəm-pôrt/] *verb*, formal conduct of oneself, behavior

**com-pose** [kəm-pōz/] *verb*, 1) to write or create music, literature, etc. 2) to blend the ingredients or components of something

**com-pos-ite** [kəm-pŏz/ĭt] *adjective*, 1) made up of separate distinctive parts 2) relating to a combination of the Corinthian and Ionic styles

**com-po-si-tion** [kŏm/pə-zĭsh/ən] *noun*, 1) something written, such as a story or music 2) a creation or formation

**com-post** [kŏm/pōst/] *noun*, the product from the decomposition of organic materials, such as yard waste or dead plants

**com-po-sure** [kəm-pō/zhər] *noun*, a settled state, calmness

**com-pound** [kŏm-pound/] *noun*, 1) a composite, a mixture 2) a fenced-in area with one or more buildings in it, *verb*, 3) to make by mixing together 4) to increase

**com-pre-hend** [kŏm/prĭ-hěnd/] *verb*, to understand

**com-pre-hen-sive** [kŏm/prĭ-hěn/sĭv] *adjective*, thorough, all-inclusive

**com-press** [kŏm/prěs/] *noun*, 1) a bandage, a pad, *verb*, [kŭm/prěs] 2) to pack, to squeeze

**com-prise** [kəm-prīz/] *verb*, to include, consisting of

**com-pro-mise** [kŏm/prə-mīz/] *noun*, 1) the result of adjustments made by concessions to make a mutual agreement, *verb* 2) to adjust by making concessions

**com-pul-sion** [kəm-pŭl/shən] *noun*, an obsession, a fixation

**com-pul-so-ry** [kəm-pŭl/sə-rē] *adjective*, required, mandatory

**com-pute** [kəm-pyōot/] *verb*, to figure mathematically

**com-put-er** [kəm-pyōot/ər] an electronic device for storing and processing data, usually in binary form according to instructions given to it in a variable program

**com-rade** [kŏm/răd/] *noun*, a faithful friend, a colleague

**con-cave** [kŏn-kāv/] *adjective*, sunken, as the inside of a sphere or a spoon

**con-ceal** [kən-sēl/] *verb*, 1) to hide, to keep from sight 2) to disguise

**con-cede** [kən-sēd/] *verb*, to surrender, to grant, to allow

**con-ceit** [kən-sēt/] *noun*, vanity, an exaggerated opinion of oneself

**con-ceive** [kən-sēv/] *verb*, 1) to imagine, to take into one's mind 2) to become pregnant

**con-cen-trate** [kŏn/sən-trāt/] *verb*, 1) to focus all one's thoughts and efforts on 2) to bring or come together in one place to increase the strength of

**con-cen-tra-tion** [kŏn/sən-trā/shən] *noun*, 1) density, consistency 2) close attention, intense thought

**con-cept** [kŏn/sěpt/] *noun*, an abstract idea, a thought

**con-cep-tion** [kən-sěp/shən] *noun*, 1) the act of conceiving life 2) the beginning or understanding of an idea

**con-cern** [kən-sûrn/] *noun*, 1) anxiety 2) something that

involves a person or people,
*verb*, 3) to be about, to interest
4) to trouble or worry

**con-cert** [kŏn′sûrt′] *noun*, 1) music
played for an audience,
[kŏn′sûrt] *verb* 2) to plan or
arrange together

**con-ces-sion** [kən-sĕsh′ən] *noun*,
the act of yielding, a grant

**con-cil-i-ate** [kən-sĭl′ē-āt]*verb*, to
gain goodwill, to placate

**con-cil-i-a-to-ry** [kən-sĭl′ē-ə-tôr′ē]
*adjective*, making less angry or
hostile to overcome animosity

**con-cise** [kən-sīs′] *adjective*, short,
to the point, brief, succinct

**con-clude** [kən-klōōd′] *verb*, 1) to
form an opinion after thinking
about something 2) to finish to
bring or come to an end

**con-clu-sion** [kən-klōō′zhən] *noun*,
1) the end, an outcome 2) a
decision, a judgment

**con-coct** [kən-kŏkt′] *verb*, 1) to
prepare by combining different
ingredients 2) to devise a plan or
scheme, to invent

**con-cor-dant** [kən-kôr′dant]
*adjective*, in agreement,
harmonious

**con-crete** [kŏn-krēt′] *adjective*,
1) not abstract, particular, *noun*,
2) a compound mass of cement,
sand, gravel, and water used for
building

**con-cus-sion** [kən-kŭsh′ən] *noun*, a
head injury that is the result of a
blow or a fall, a shock

**con-demn** [kən-dĕm′] *verb*, 1)to
pronounce sentence against
someone 2) to disapprove of or
censure, to denounce

**con-dem-na-tion**
[kŏn′dĕm-nā′shən] *noun*,
criticism, blame, an objection

**con-den-sa-tion** [kŏn′dĕn-sā′shən]
*noun*, 1) the act, process, or state
of compressing or being
compressed into a smaller
enclosed space 2) the process by
which a substance changes from
its gaseous state to a liquid state
3) the liquid formed by this
process

**con-dense** [kən-dĕns′] *verb*, to
shorten or compress

**con-de-scend** [kŏn′dĭ-sĕnd′] *verb*,
to act superior to someone else

**con-di-ment** [kŏn′də-mənt] *noun*, a
type of relish or seasoning

**con-di-tion** [kən-dĭsh′ən] *noun*,
1) a stipulation or provision
2) the state in which a person or
thing exists, *verb*, 3) to prepare,
to adapt, to train, to influence

**con-di-tion-ing** [kən-dĭsh′ən-ing]
*noun*, preparation, training

**con-dol-ence** [kən-dō′ləns] *noun*,
an offering of sympathy, an
expression of regret

**con-done** [kən-dōn′] *verb*, to
pardon, to forgive, to overlook

**con-du-cive** [kən-dōō′sĭv]
*adjective*, tending to promote,
helpful, beneficial

**con-duct** *noun*, [kən-dŭkt′]
1) behavior, [kən-dŭkt′] *verb*, 2)
to lead or guide 3) to direct

**con-duc-tor** [kən-dŭk′tər] *noun*,
1) someone who sells tickets on
a train 2) something that
transmits energy 3) the leader of
a musical ensemble

**con-duit** [kŏn′dōō-ĭt] *noun*, a channel or passage through which electrical wires run

**cone** [kōn] *noun*, 1) a cylinder that tapers to a point at the end 2) the reproductive structures of the conifer trees, a pine cone 3) a cylindrical wafer on which a scoop of ice cream is placed

**con-fed-er-ate** [kən-fĕd′ər-ĭt] *noun*, 1) an ally, an accomplice **Condederate** 2) someone who fought for the Confederacy during the Civil War

**con-fed-er-a-tion** [kən-fĕd′ə-rā/shən] *noun*, a coalition, a group of people working together, an alliance

**con-fer** [kən-fûr′] *verb*, 1) to give as a gift 2) to meet and discuss

**con-fer-ence** [kŏn′fər-əns] *noun*, a meeting for an exchange of ideas, a conversation with someone to share information

**con-fess** [kən-fĕs′] *verb*, to acknowledge or admit a fault

**con-fes-sion** [kən-fĕsh′ən] *noun*, an admission of guilt or wrongdoing

**con-fet-ti** [kən-fĕt′ē] *noun*, small pieces of colorful paper

**con-fi-dant** [kŏn′fĭ-dănt′] *noun*, one to whom secrets are entrusted, a friend

**con-fide** [kən-fīd′] *verb*, to trust, to disclose a secret, to reveal

**con-fi-dence** [kŏn′fĭ-dəns] *noun*, complete trust, a secret

**con-fi-dent** [kŏn′fĭ-dənt] *adjective*, assured beyond doubt, certain

**con-fi-den-tial** [kŏn′fĭ-dĕn′shəl] *adjective*, secret, private, trusted

**con-fine** [kən-fīn′] *verb*, to restrain within a specific place, to limit

**con-firm** [kən-fûrm′] *verb*, to give proof of something, to ratify

**con-fir-ma-tion** [kŏn′fər-mā′shən] *noun*, 1) proof, collaboration 2) a ceremony recognizing a member of the church

**con-fis-cate** [kŏn′fĭ-skāt′] *verb*, to seize, to take without consent

**con-flict** [kŏn′flĭkt′] *noun*, 1) a fight or argument, a disagreement, *verb*, 2) to disagree or clash

**con-form** [kən-fôrm′] *verb*, to comply, to obey social norms

**con-form-i-ty** [kən-fôr′mĭ-tē] *noun*, harmony, agreement

**con-front** [kən- frŭnt] *verb*, to face boldly or defiantly

**con-fuse** [kən-fyōōz′] *verb*, to mix up in the mind, to perplex

**con-fu-sion** [kən-fyōō′zhən] *noun*, a state of disorder, chaos, bewilderment

**con-geal** [kən-jēl′] *verb*, 1) to change from a fluid state to a solid state 2) to thicken

**con-gen-ial** [kən-jēn′yəl] *adjective*, naturally adapted, pleasant and sympathetic, good-natured

**con-gen-i-tal** [kən-jĕn′ĭ-tl] *adjective*, existing at birth

**con-ges-tion** [kən-jĕs′shən] *noun*, 1) a gathering or accumulation 2) an overcrowded state

**con-glom-er-a-tion** [kən-glŏm′ə-rā/shən] *noun*, material sticking together

**con-grat-u-la-tions** [kən-grăch′ə-lā/shənz] *noun,plural*, expressions of good

wishes for a happy event or
achievement

**con-gre-gate** [kŏng′grĭ-gāt′] *verb*,
to gather together, to assemble

**con-gre-ga-tion** [kŏng′grĭ-gā′shən]
*noun*, a gathering or assembly

**con-gress** [kŏng′grĭs] *noun*, 1) a
meeting of a group of people
**Congress** 2)the legislature of the
United States consisting of the
Senate and the House of
Representatives

**con-gru-ent** [kŏng′grōō-ənt]
*adjective*, in agreement, exactly
alike, matching, equal

**con-jec-ture** [kən-jĕk′chər] *noun*,
theory, an unfounded remark

**con-ju-gate** [kŏn′jə-gāt′] *verb*, to
change the form of a verb
depending on the subject and
the tense, e.g. *I am, you are, he
is, we are, you are, they are*

**con-junc-tion** [kən-jŭngk′shən]
*noun*, a word that joins two other
words or phrases together

**con-jure** [kŏn′jər] *verb*, 1) to seem
to create out of thin air as if by
magic 2) to entreat, to summon

**con-nect** [kə-nĕkt′] *verb*, to join or
bring together, to link, to unite

**Con-nect-i-cut** [kə-nĕt′ĭ-kət] *noun*,
one of the 50 United States, the
capital is Hartford. The state
flower of **Connecticut** is the
mountain laurel, and the motto is
"He who transplanted still
sustains."

**con-nec-tion** [kə-nĕk′shən] *noun*,
the act of joining, a relationship

**con-nive** [kə-nīv′] *verb*, to
cooperate in a crime or fault, to
secretly allow, to deceive

**con-nois-seur** [kŏn′ə-sûr′] *noun*,
one who is an expert judge of art
and style or taste

**con-no-ta-tion** [kŏn′ə-tā′shən]
*noun*, suggested meaning

**con-quer** [kŏng′kər] *verb*,
1) to gain or acquire by force, to
be victorious, to win, to defeat
2) to master, to overcome

**con-quest** [kŏn′kwĕst′] *noun*, a
takeover, a triumph, a victory

**con-science** [kŏn′shəns] *noun*, a
sense of moral goodness

**con-sci-en-tious** [kŏn′shē-ĕn′shəs]
*adjective*, influenced by
conscience, careful, thoughtful

**con-scious** [kŏn′shəs] *adjective*,
aware of, awake, alert

**con-scious-ly** [kŏn′shəs-lē] *adverb*,
after thorough consideration,
with full awareness

**con-se-crate** [kŏn′sĭ-krāt′] *verb*, to
dedicate, to declare sacred

**con-sec-u-tive** [kən-sĕk′yə-tĭv]
*adjective*, one after another

**con-sen-sus** [kən-sĕn′səs] *noun*,
agreement in opinion, custom, or
function, the popular choice

**con-sent** [kən-sĕnt′] *noun*, 1) an
agreement, permission, *verb*,
2) to agree, to comply

**con-se-quence** [kŏn′sĭ-kwĕns′]
*noun*, 1) that which follows as a
result, outcome 2) importance

**con-se-quen-tial**
[kŏn′sĭ-kwĕn′shəl] *adjective*,
significant, very important

**con-ser-va-tion** [kŏn′sûr-vā′shən]
*noun*, the planned management
of natural resources to prevent
loss, destruction, or waste

**con-serv-a-tive** [kən-sûr′və-tĭv]
*adjective*, 1) opposed to change
or innovation 2) traditional
3) a low estimated number

**con-ser-va-tor-y** [kən-sûr′və-tôr′ē]
*noun*, 1) a small greenhouse for
growing plants 2) a college of
music, an academy

**con-serve** [kən-sûrv′] *verb*, to keep
from loss or waste, to preserve

**con-sid-er** [kən-sĭd′ər] *verb*, 1) to
think about carefully, 2) to take
into account 3) to believe

**con-sid-er-a-ble** [kən-sĭd′ər-ə-bəl]
*adjective*, important, great, large

**con-sid-er-ate** [kən-sĭd′ər-ĭt]
*adjective*, caring about a
person's feelings, courteous

**con-sid-er-a-tion**
[kən-sĭd′ə-rā′shən] *noun*,
1) thought and attention
2) a payment

**con-sign** [kən-sīn′] *verb*, 1) to ship
something to an agent in another
place, to deliver 2) to assign

**con-sign-ment** [kən-sīn′mənt]
*noun*, 1) the entrusting of
something to another's care 2) a
quantity of goods for delivery

**con-sist** [kən-sĭst′] *verb*, to be
made of or composed of

**con-sist-ent** [kən-sĭs′tənt]
*adjective*, sticking to the same
principles, the same throughout

**con-so-la-tion** [kŏn′sə-lā′shən]
*noun*, comfort, sympathy

**con-sole** [kən-sōl′] *verb*, to
comfort, to calm, to soothe

**con-sol-i-date** [kən-sŏl′ĭ-dāt′] *verb*,
to unite, to bring together , to
strengthen, to make solid

**con-so-nant** [kŏn′sə-nənt]
*adjective*, 1) in agreement, *noun*,
2) a letter in the alphabet other
than a vowel

**con-spic-u-ous** [kən-spĭk′yōō-əs]
*adjective*, plainly visible,
prominent, attracting attention

**con-spir-a-cy** [kən-spĭr′ə-sē] *noun*,
a combination of people often
for an evil purpose, a secret plan

**con-stant** [kŏn′stənt] *adjective*,
continuous, unceasing, faithful

**con-stel-la-tion** [kŏn′stə-lā′shən]
*noun*, an arrangement of stars
that resembles a figure

**con-sti-tute** [kŏn′stĭ-tōōt′] *verb*, to
make up, to empower

**con-sti-tu-tion** [kŏn′stĭ-tōō′shən]
*noun*, the fundamental law of a
nation, state, or society

**con-sti-tu-tion-al**[kŏn′stĭtōō′shənl]
*adjective*, according to law

**con-strain** [kən-strān′] *verb*, to
force, to restrain unnaturally

**con-struct** [kən-strŭkt′] *verb*, to
build a structure, to erect

**con-struc-tion** [kən-strŭk′shən]
*noun*, 1) something that is built,
a structure 2) the arrangement of
words in parts of a sentence

**con-struc-tive** [kən-strŭk′tĭv]
*adjective*, helpful, useful,
productive, beneficial

**con-strue** [kən-strōō′] *verb*, to
interpret, to try to understand

**con-sult** [kən-sŭlt′] *verb*, to ask for
help looking for more
information, to confer

**con-sult-ant** [kən-sŭl′tənt] *noun*,
an expert hired to study data to
resolve a problem or give advice

**con-sume** [kən-sōōm′] *verb*, 1) to eat 2) to exhaust, to expend 3) to make use of, to apply 4) to destroy

**con-sum-er** [kən-sōō′mər] *noun*, 1)a higher level organism that gets its food from other living things 2) someone who buys products, a customer

**con-sum-mate** [kŏn′sə-māt′] *verb*, to bring to completion, to perfect

**con-sump-tion** [kən-sŭmp′shən] *noun*, 1) the use of goods 2) a disease of the lungs, such as tuberculosis 3) the eating of food

**con-tact** [kŏn′tăkt′] *noun*, 1) a physical touch 2) a connection through writing or speaking, *verb*, 3) to talk or write to, to touch

**con-ta-gi-ous** [kən-tā′jəs] *adjective*, of a disease passed from one person to another by touch or proximity

**con-tain** [kən-tān′] *verb*, 1) to have inside, to hold 2) to include

**con-tain-er** [kən-tā′nər] *noun*, anything that can hold and carry something, eg., a box, jar, basket

**con-tam-i-nant** [kən-tăm′ə-nənt] *noun*, a compound that pollutes, making the original substance impure, a poison, a toxin

**con-tam-i-nate** [kən-tăm′ə-nāt′] *verb*, to soil, to stain or corrupt by contact, to pollute, to infect

**con-tam-i-na-tion** [kən-tăm′ə-nā′shən] *noun*, the act of making a substance impure or unusable

**con-tem-plate** [kŏn′təm-plāt′] *verb*, to consider with continued attention, to think about, to ponder

**con-tem-po-rar-y** [kən-tĕm′pə-rĕr′ē] *adjective*, 1) of the present day, current, *noun*, 2) a person of the same age, a peer

**con-tempt** [kən-tĕmpt′] *noun*, a feeling that someone or something is bad

**con-tempt-i-ble** [kən-tĕmp′tə-bəl] *adjective*, despicable, vile

**con-tent** [kən-tĕnt′] *adjective*, 1) happy, satisfied, [kŏn′-tĕnt] *noun*, 2) that which is inside 3) the subject matter of a book

**con-ten-tion** [kən-tĕn′shən] *noun*, a struggle, an argument, a dispute

**con-ten-tious** [kən-tĕn′shəs] *adjective*, argumentative, quarrelsome, causing disagreement

**con-test** [kŏn′tĕst] *noun*, 1) a game in which there is a winner [kən-tĕst′]*verb*, 2) to disagree, to object to, to challenge

**con-text** [kŏn′tĕkst′] *noun*, the words or actions that provide a necessary link or explanation to the meaning of a word or event

**con-tig-u-ous** [kən-tĭg′yōō-əs] *adjective*, adjoining, touching

**con-ti-nent** [kŏn′tə-nənt] *noun*, a major land area in the world unbroken by major oceans

**con-tin-gent** [kən-tĭn′jənt] *adjective*, conditional, relying on chance or something happening

**con-tin-u-al** [kən-tĭn′yōō-əl] *adjective*, happening repeatedly

**con-tin-ue** [kən-tĭn′yōō] *verb*, 1) to go on, to resume 2) to persevere

**con-tin-u-ous** [kən-tĭn′yōō-əs] *adjective*, uninterrupted

**con-tor-tion** [kən-tôr′shən] *noun*, something bent or twisted out of shape, a distortion

**con-tour** [kŏn′tŏŏr′] *noun*, the outline of a figure, body, hill, coastline, etc.

**con-tra-band** [kŏn′trə-bănd′] *noun*, illegal goods, smuggled materials

**con-tract** [kŏn′trăkt′] *noun*, 1) a written agreement between two or more persons that has the force of law, [kən′-trăkt′] *verb*, 2) to draw closer together 3) to make a binding agreement

**con-trac-tion** [kŏn′trăk′ shən] *noun*, 1) the shortening of a word or group of words by omitting a letter or letters and replacing them with an apostrophe, e.g. *you'll* 2) the act of drawing together like muscles

**con-tra-dict** [kŏn′trə-dĭkt′] *verb*, to say the opposite, to oppose in words, to conflict with

**con-trar-y** [kŏn′trĕr′ē] *adjective,* opposite, perverse, wayward

**con-trast** [kən-trăst′] *noun*, 1) the difference, *verb*, 2) to compare in order to show the differences between two things

**con-trib-ute** [kən-trĭb′yŏŏt] *verb*, to give as part of a group effort, to help in causing

**con-tri-bu-tion** [kŏn′trĭ-byŏŏ′shən] *noun*, an offering, a donation

**con-trite** [kən-trīt′] *adjective*, asking forgiveness, remorseful

**con-trive** [kən-trīv′] *verb*, to invent or make a clever device

**con-trol** [kən-trōl′] *noun*, 1) power, guidance, *verb*, 2) to manage or oversee a situation or machine

**con-tro-ver-sy** [kŏn′trə-vûr′sē] *noun*, a disagreement or debate

**con-tu-sion** [kən-tŏŏ′zhən] *noun*, a wound or bruise that does not break the skin

**con-va-les-cent** [kŏn′və-lĕs′ənt] *adjective*, recovering from sickness

**con-vene** [kən-vēn′] *verb*, to assemble, to call together

**con-ven-ience** [kən-vēn′yəns] *noun*, the state of being easily used or immediately available

**con-ven-ient** [kən-vēn′yənt] *adjective*, adapted to one's comfort or ready use, handy

**con-vent** [kŏn′vənt] *noun*, a home where nuns live

**con-ven-tion** [kən-vĕn′shən] *noun*, 1) an assembly of members of a delegation 2) a practice or custom 3) a formal agreement

**con-ven-tion-al** [kən-vĕn′shə-nəl] *adjective*, contemporary

**con-verge** [kən-vûrj′] *verb*, to come together, to assemble

**con-ver-sant** [kən-vûr′sənt] *adjective*, familiar with

**con-ver-sa-tion** [kŏn′vər-sā′shən] *noun*, an informal discourse, a chat or familiar talk

**con-verse** *noun*, [kən- vûrs′] 1) the contrary or opposite, [kŏn′vûrs′] *verb*, 2) to talk or exchange ideas

**con-ver-sion** [kən-vûr′zhən] *noun*, a change from one thing, state, or religion to another

**con-vert** [kən-vûrt′] *verb*, to change into something else

**con-vex** [kŏn′věks′] *adjective*, curved out like the outside of a sphere or ball or spoon

**con-vey** [kən-vā′] *verb*, 1) to take or transport, to carry 2) to communicate, to pass on, to impart, to give 3) to transmit

**con-vict** [kən-vĭkt′] *noun*, 1) a person who has been judged guilty of a crime, and sentenced *verb*, 2) to decide in court that someone has committed a crime

**con-vic-tion** [kən-vĭk′shən] *noun*, a strong belief, the state of being convinced, complete confidence

**con-vince** [kən-vĭns′] *verb*, to satisfy by proof

**con-vo-lut-ed** [kŏn′və-loo′tĭd] *adjective*, coiled around, intricate, complicated

**con-vul-sions** [kŏn′və-loo′shənz] *noun*, *plural*, strong and uncontrolled involuntary muscle contractions

**cook** [kŏok] *noun*, 1) someone who prepares food to eat, *verb*, 2) to prepare food for eating on the stove or in an oven, to bake

**cool** [kŏol] *adjective*, 1) moderately cold 2) calm, *verb*, 3) to lower temperature 4) to calm down

**coop** [kŏop] *noun*, a pen, a hen-house, a cage for poultry

**co-op-er-ate** [kō-ŏp′ə-rāt′] *verb*, to work together, to collaborate

**co-op-er-a-tion** [kō-ŏp′ə-rā′shən] *noun*, the process of working together toward a common goal

**co-op-er-a-tive** [kō-ŏp′ər-ə-tĭv] *adjective*, willing to join together to help other people

**co-or-di-nate** [kō-ôr′dn-āt′] *verb*, to make the parts of something work together, to harmonize

**co-or-di-na-tion** [kō-ôr′dn-ā′shən] *noun*, 1)the organization of separate elements working together 2) dexterity

**cope** [kōp] *verb*, to deal successfully with something

**cop-per** [kŏp′ər] *noun*, a common metal of a reddish color, a good conductor of heat and electricity

**cop-y** [kŏp′ē] *noun*, 1) an imitation, reproduction, *verb*, 2) to make something that is the same as something else

**cop-y-right** [kŏp′ē-rīt′] *noun*, the exclusive right to publish and sell the matter and form of a literary or artistic work

**cor-al** [kôr′əl] *noun*, 1) a pink reddish color, salmon 2) a stony substance formed from the skeletons of tiny animals that live on reefs in the ocean

**cord** [kôrd] *noun*, thin rope

**cor-dial** [kôr′jəl] *adjective*, sincere, friendly, encouraging, gracious

**core** [kôr] *noun*, 1) the heart, essence 2) the center of focus

**cork** [kôrk] *noun*, a light substance that comes from the outer bark of a tree

**corn** [kôrn] *noun*, 1) a sore that sometimes grows on toes when shoes are tight 2) a grain grown on a stalk as an ear (maize)

**cor-ner** [kôr′nər] *noun*, 1) a nook, a niche 2) where two lines, edges or streets meet, *verb*, 3) to put someone in a place they cannot escape 4) to monopolize

**cor-nu-co-pi-a** [kôr′nə-kō′pē-ə] *noun*, 1) a horn containing an abundantly overflowing supply of food 2) abundance, plenty

**cor-ol-lary** [kôr′ə-lĕr-ē] *noun*, what follows logically, the consequence or effect

**cor-o-na-tion** [kôr′ə-nā′shən] *noun*, a ceremony to crown a king or queen

**cor-po-ra-tion** [kôr′pə-rā′shən] *noun*, a business that operates as a person under the law

**corps** [kôr] *noun*, a troop, a main subdivision of an army

**corpse** [kôrps] *noun*, a dead body

**cor-pu-lent** [kôr′pyə-lənt] *adjective*, very fat

**cor-pus-cle** [kôr′pə-səl] *noun*, a minute particle of matter, a cell, a red or white blood cell

**cor-ral** [kə-răl′] *noun*, a pen for livestock

**cor-rect** [kə-rĕkt′] *adjective*, 1) without error, *verb*, 2) to point out an error 3) to make right

**cor-rec-tion** [kə-rĕk′shən] *noun*, a change or revision, to remove error, to make right

**cor-rel-ate** [kôr′ə-lāt′] *verb*, to be linked to something

**cor-re-la-tion** [kôr′ə-lā′shən] *noun*, a mutual relationship, a connection

**cor-re-spond** [kôr′ĭ-spŏnd′] *verb*, 1) to communicate by writing and receiving letters 2) to fit in with, to match, to agree

**cor-re-spond-ence** [kôr′ĭ-spŏn′dəns] *noun*, an exchange of letters

**cor-ri-dor** [kôr′ĭ-dər] *noun*, a hallway connecting rooms or apartments opening onto it

**cor-rob-o-rate** [kə-rŏb′ə-rāt′] *verb*, to confirm or support with facts,

**cor-ro-sive** [kə-rō′sĭv] *adjective*, 1) eating away gradually by chemicals 2) sarcastic

**cor-ru-gat-ed** [kôr′ə-gā′tĭd] *adjective*, bent into a series of alternate ridges and grooves for added stiffness

**cor-rupt** [kə-rŭpt′] *adjective*, 1) crooked, dishonest, *verb*, 2) to cause to become dishonest

**cor-rup-tion** [kə-rŭp′shən] *noun*, dishonesty, depravity

**cort-ege** [kôr-tĕzh′] *noun*, a funeral procession

**cos-met-ic** [kŏz-mĕt′ĭk] *noun*, a beauty product

**cos-mic** [kŏz′mĭk] *adjective*, universal, vast

**cost** [kôst] *noun*, 1) the price you pay when you buy something, *verb*, 2) to have as a price

**cos-tume** [kŏs′tōōm′] *noun*, clothes worn for a special occasion to represent a particular period in history, traditions of a country, or an assumed character

**cot** [kŏt] *noun*, a lightweight collapsible bed that usually folds up to a smaller size

**cot-tage** [kŏt′ĭj] *noun*, a small country house, a bungalow

**cot-ton** [kŏt′n] *noun*, 1) the white part of the cotton plant used to make cloth 2) the fabric made from this

**couch** [kouch] *noun*, an upholstered piece of furniture that seats several people

**cough** [kôf] *noun*, 1) a hacking sound made when air is expelled from the lungs, *verb*, 2) to make a sharp noise when air comes up from the lungs

**could** [kŏŏd]*verb past tense* of **can**

**could-n't** [kŏŏd′nt] the *contraction* of the words **could** and **not**

**coun-cil** [koun′səl] *noun*, an assembly of men and women convened for consultation

**coun-sel** [koun′səl] *noun*, 1) an attorney, a lawyer 2) an interchange of opinions, advice, *verb*, 3) to advise

**coun-se-lor** [koun′sə-lər] *noun*, someone who helps you make the best choice

**count** [kount] *noun*, 1) the total number added together, *verb*, 2) to add up 3) to recite numbers in the correct order 4) to list

**coun-te-nance** [koun′tə-nəns] *noun*, a facial expression, aspect, appearance, composure

**coun-ter** [koun′tər] *noun*, 1) the table between customers and workers in a business, *verb*, 2) to make an offer against another

**coun-ter-act** [koun′tər-ăkt′] *verb*, to act against, to neutralize, to prevent the effects of

**coun-ter-clock-wise** [koun′tər-klŏk′wīz′] *adjective*, in the opposite direction from the movement of the hands of a clock

**coun-ter-feit** [koun′tər-fĭt′] *noun*, 1) an imitation intended to deceive, *verb*, 2) to imitate or make a copy of

**coun-ter-part** [koun′tər-pärt′] *noun*, a thing that completes another, a mate

**coun-try** [kŭn′trē] *noun*, 1) the land ruled by a government, a nation 2) the land outside of a city, usually farmland or forests

**coun-ty** [koun′tē] *noun*, an administrative division of a state

**coup** [kōō] *noun*, a successful sudden attack to seize power

**coupe** [kōōp] *noun*, a sports car with a sloping back

**cou-ple** [kŭp′əl] *noun*, 1) two people or things that are usually thought of together, a pair, *verb*, 2) to fasten

**cou-pon** [kōō′pŏn′] *noun*, a certificate that gives a discount on a purchase, a rebate

**cour-age** [kûr′ĭj] *noun, no plural*, the strength to face danger when overwhelmed by fear

**cou-ra-geous** [kə-rā′jəs] *adjective*, brave or bold in danger

**cour-i-er** [kŏŏr′ē-ər] *noun*, a messenger who carries documents

**course** [kôrs] *noun*, 1) the path of something, the sequence of events 2) a portion of a meal 3) a series of lessons in a school

**court** [kôrt] *noun*, 1) a place where judges decide how people who break laws should be punished and civil cases heard 2) an open space next to a house in an enclosed area 3) the members of

a royal family 4) a royal palace
*verb*, 5) to date

**cour-te-ous** [kûr′tē-əs] *adjective*,
showing good manners, polite

**cour-te-sy** [kûr′tĭ-sē] *noun*,
politeness, civility, consideration

**court-ship** [kôrt′shĭp′] *noun*, going
steady, a period of dating before
marriage

**cous-in** [kŭz′ĭn] *noun*, the son or
daughter of your uncle or aunt

**cove** [kōv] *noun*, an inlet

**cov-e-nant** [kŭv′ə-nənt] *noun*, 1) a
legal undertaking to do or to
refrain from doing some act or
thing 2) a contract under seal

**cov-er** [kŭv′ər] *noun*, 1) something
that is placed over something to
protect it, *verb*, 2) to protect by
placing a lid, wrapping, etc.,
around or on top of 3) to hide
4) to go over

**co-vert** [kŭv′ərt] *adjective*,
concealed, hidden, or sheltered

**cov-et** [kŭv′ĭt] *verb*, to want to
have a thing belonging to
another person

**cow** [kou] *noun*, a grown female
cattle or certain other large
animals

**cow-ard** [kou′ərd] *noun*, someone
who is easily frightened, a
person who lacks courage

**cow-ard-ice** [kou′ər-dĭs]*noun*, lack
of courage to face danger,
timidity, fearfulness

**cow-ard-ly** [kou′ərd-lē] *adjective*,
timid, afraid, scared, fearful

**cow-boy** [kou′boi′] *noun*, a man
who rides a horse and looks after
livestock on a ranch

**cow-er** [kou′ər] *verb*, to shrink
from as if from fear, to tremble

**coy-o-te** [kī-ō′tē] *noun*, a North
American, wolflike dog

**co-zy** [kō′zē] *adjective*, snug, warm

**crab** [krăb] *noun*, a sea animal with
eight legs, a pair of pincers and a
hard shell that lives in a hole

**crack** [krăk] *noun*, 1) a line
showing where something is
broken, a crevice 2) a sharp
noise, such as a gunshot or
thunder, *verb*, 3) to break while
separating

**cra-dle** [krād′l] *noun*, 1) a small
bed for an infant 2) the holder
for a telephone, *verb*, 3) to rock
or shelter an infant or comfort a
crying baby

**craft** [krăft] *noun*, 1) something
made by hand to be used as a
decoration 2) a boat or plane 3)
guile, slyness, skill

**cram** [krăm] *verb*, to fill or force in

**cramp** [krămp] *noun*, 1) a painful
muscle spasm, *verb*, 2) to keep
within narrow limits, to confine

**crane** [krān] *noun*, a machine
designed to lift heavy loads from
one place to another

**cra-ni-um** [krā′nē-əm] *noun*, the
skull of a vertebrate animal

**crank** [krăngk] *noun*, a handle that
is attached to a machine and that
turns, causing motion

**crash** [krăsh] *noun*, 1) a loud noise
caused by a collision or
something falling, *verb*, 2) to
shatter violently, scattering
pieces everywhere

**crass** [krăs] *adjective*, grossly
insensible, rude coarse

**crate** [krāt] *noun*, a large usually wooden box or container, a case

**cra-ter** [krā'tər] *noun*, a bowl-shaped cavity, a hole

**crave** [krāv] *verb*, to want something badly

**crawl** [krôl] *verb*, to move on one's hands and knees, to move slowly

**cray-on** [krā'ŏn'] *noun*, a small pencil of colored wax used for drawing or writing

**craze** [krāz] *noun*, a fad, a popular idea, a trend

**cra-zy** [krā'zē] *adjective*, insane, wild, daft, very foolish

**creak** [krēk] *verb*, to make the sound of a door that has not been oiled, a long squeak

**cream** [krēm] *adjective*, 1) the color yellowish white, ivory 2) a thick lotion, *noun*, 3) the fatty part of milk

**crease** [krēs] *noun*, the mark or line left by a fold, a wrinkle, a furrow

**cre-ate** [krē-āt'] *verb*, to make, to bring into being, to produce for the first time

**cre-a-tion** [krē-ā'shən] *noun*, the act of causing to exist, that which is produced

**cre-a-tive** [krē-ā'tĭv] *adjective*, having new or original ideas

**cre-a-tiv-i-ty** [krē-ā'tĭv-ĭ-tē] *noun*, the ability to make or invent things, originality

**crea-ture** [krē'chər] *noun*, an animal or insect or person

**cre-den-tials** [krĭ-dĕn'shəlz] *noun*, a document verifying a person's ability or authority, references

**cred-i-ble** [krĕd'ə-bəl] *adjective*, 1) believable 2) reliable or trustworthy

**cred-it** [krĕd'ĭt] *noun*, 1) a system in which merchandise is given with the understanding that it will be paid for later 2) attention and praise received for doing something

**cred-o** [krē'dō] *noun*, creed, a belief

**cred-u-lous** [krĕj'ə-ləs] *adjective*, easily imposed upon, gullible

**creed** [krēd] *noun*, a statement of religious or ethical beliefs, principles

**creek** [krēk, krĭk] *noun*, a stream smaller than a river and larger than a brook, an inlet of water

**creep** [krēp] *verb*, to move slowly and quietly, to move furtively

**cre-o-sote** [krē'ə-sōt'] *noun*, an oily liquid obtained from coal tar and used as a wood preservative

**cre-scen-do** [krə-shĕn'dō] *noun*, a musical direction used to indicate increasing loudness

**cres-cent** [krĕs'ənt] *noun*, a curved shape like a new moon

**crest** [krĕst] *noun*, 1) the feathers that stick up on top of a bird's head 2) the top of something

**crev-ice** [krĕv'ĭs] *noun*, a narrow opening in a surface resulting from a split, a cleft, a gap

**crew** [krōō] *noun*, a group of people who work together

**crib** [krĭb] *noun*, 1) a bed made for an infant 2) a container for grain

**crick-et** [krĭk'ĭt] *noun*, 1) a ball game played with two teams of eleven players 2) a small brown insect that makes a shrill chirping noise at night

**cried** [krīd] *verb,  past tense* of **cry**

**crime** [krīm] *noun*, something that is against the law, illegal acts

**crim-i-nal** [krĭm'ə-nəl] *adjective*, 1) illegal, wrong, *noun*, 2) one who has broken the law and is guilty of a crime

**cringe** [krĭnj] *verb*, to shrink back in fear, to cower in fear

**crip-ple** [krĭp'əl] *verb*, to disable or make lame

**cri-sis** [krī'sĭs] *noun, plural*, **crises** [krī'-sēz], a stressful time when something serious is happening

**crisp** [krĭsp] *adjective*, 1) dry, brittle, easily broken 2) firm and fresh 3) very clean and pressed

**criss cross** [krĭs'krôs'] *noun* , a pattern of intersecting lines

**cri-te-ri-on** [krī-tîr'ē-ən] *noun, plural*, **criteria**, a standard for judgment, a benchmark

**crit-ic** [krĭt'ĭk] *noun*, 1) a person who is paid to review a performance or art 2) one who finds faults

**crit-i-cal** [krĭt'ĭ-kəl] *adjective*, 1) very important, able or inclined to pass judgment 2) crucial, pivotal, key

**crit-i-cism** [krĭt'ĭ-sĭz'əm] *noun*, faultfinding, review

**crit-i-cize** [krĭt'ĭ-sīz'] *verb*, to examine as a critic, to censure

**croak** [krōk] *noun*, 1) a hoarse sound like that made by frogs, *verb*, 2) to make a low hoarse sound in the throat

**croc-o-dile** [krŏk'ə-dīl'] *noun*, a large reptile, like an alligator, that lives in tropical climates

**crook-ed** [krŏŏk'ĭd] *adjective*, 1) bent, not straightened 2) dishonest, deceitful

**crop** [krŏp] *noun*, food that is planted and grown in a field

**cross** [krôs] *adjective*, 1) irritated, angry, *noun*, 2) a shape with four arms, *verb*, 3) to go over, to extend across

**crouch** [krouch] *verb*, to stoop

**crow** [krō] *noun*, 1) any of a genus of large black birds including the raven, *verb*, 2) to make a sound like a rooster

**crowd** [kroud] *noun*, 1) a large gathering of people or things, *verb*, 2) to press or cram

**crown** [kroun] *noun*, 1) a circular head covering, often made of metal with precious stones, worn by royalty, *verb*, 2) to top, to culminate, to climax

**cru-ci-al** [krŏŏ'shəl] *adjective*, important or essential as decisive in determining a doubtful crisis

**cru-ci-ble** [krŏŏ'sə-bəl] *noun*, a vessel used for melting substances

**cru-ci-fix-ion** [krŏŏ'sə-fĭk'shən] *noun*, the killing of someone by nailing them to a cross

**crude** [krŏŏd] *adjective*, 1) roughly made 2) rude, ill-mannered

**cru-el** [krŏŏ'əl] *adjective*, mean, deliberately causing pain

**cru-el-ty** [krŏŏ'əl-tē] *noun*, unkindness, oppression

**cruise** [krŏŏz] *noun*,1) a holiday on ship, *verb*, 2) to sail or drive around

**crum-ble** [krŭm′bəl] *verb*, to fall or break apart into small pieces

**cru-sade** [krōō-sād′] *noun*, 1) a campaign conducted by a band of people devoted to advancing a cause, *verb*, 2) to battle for a cause

**crush** [krŭsh] *verb*, to hurt or flatten by applying pressure

**crust** [krŭst] *noun*, a hard surface on the outside of something that often preserves what is inside, such as bread, pie, or the earth

**crutch** [krŭch] *noun*, a piece of wood or metal extending from under the arm to the ground, to support a person who cannot walk unaided

**crux** [krŭks] *noun*, the crucial point

**cry** [krī] *noun*, 1) a shout or call for help, *verb*, 2) to call out loudly 3) tears flowing from the eyes

**crypt** [krĭpt] *noun*, a vault where bodies are buried, a tomb

**cryp-tic** [krĭp′tĭk] *adjective*, having a hidden meaning, puzzling

**crys-tal** [krĭs′təl] *adjective*, 1) clear, transparent, *noun*, 2) a clear mineral 3) a high-quality clear glass

**crys-tal-lize** [krĭs′tə-līz′] *verb*, 1) to form crystals 2) to become clear

**cub** [kŭb] *noun*, a young animal of certain mammals, such as a bear, lion, or fox

**cube** [kyōōb] *noun*, a solid shape with six equal square sides

**cu-bic-le** [kyōō′bĭ-kəl] *noun*, a small space for work partitioned off in a larger room

**cu-cum-ber** [kyōō′kŭm′bər] *noun*, a long, green-skinned fruit, pickled or eaten green as a salad

**cue** [kyōō] *noun*, 1) a signal or hint 2) a rod used to hit a billiard ball

**cul-de-sac** [kŭl′dĭ-săk′] *noun*, a small dead end off the main road

**cu-li-nar-y** [kyōō′lə-nĕr′ē] *adjective*, relating to cooking

**cull** [kŭl] *verb*, to select or gather, to pick out from others

**cul-mi-nate** [kŭl′mə-nāt′] *verb*, to reach the highest point of altitude, power, climax

**cul-pa-ble** [kŭl′pə-bəl] *adjective*, deserving blame, liable

**cul-prit** [kŭl′prĭt] *noun*, a person charged with or found guilty of a crime or misdeed

**cul-ti-vate** [kŭl′tə-vāt′] *verb*, 1) to improve or develop, to refine 2) to foster and promote healthy growth, as in crops, to farm

**cul-tur-al** [kŭl′chər-əl] *adjective*, relating to culture, the arts, good taste, etc.

**cul-ture** [kŭl′chər] *noun*, 1) advancement of knowledge of a civilization 2) a level of education that appreciates art and style 3) a growth of micro-organisms and bacteria

**cum-ber-some** [kŭm′bər-səm] *adjective*, heavy, hard to manage, unwieldy

**cu-mu-la-tive** [kyōōm′yə-lā′tĭv] *adjective*, increasing by successive additions

**cun-ning** [kŭn′ĭng] *noun*, cleverness, craftiness, skill

**cup** [kŭp] *noun*, 1) a bowl-shaped drinking container with a handle 2) a unit of measure equal to 8 ounces

**cup-board** [kŭb′ərd] *noun*, a small closet or recessed shelf

**cu-ra-tor** [kyŏŏ-rā′tər] *noun*, one who has the care of a museum, a custodian, keeper

**curb** [kûrb] *noun*, 1) control, restraint 2) a ledge, a boundary, especially that along a street

**cur-dle** [kûr′dl] *verb*, to sour and coagulate from liquid to a solid, e.g., milk to cheese

**cure** [kyŏŏr] *noun*, 1) the remedy that made someone who was sick well again, *verb*, 2) to make someone who is ill, healthy, to heal

**cur-few** [kûr′fyŏŏ] *noun*, a set time enforced by law when people are to be off the streets

**cu-ri-os-i-ty** [kyŏŏr′ē-ŏs′ĭ-tē] *noun*, 1) the feeling of wanting to know about something 2) something that is strange or unusual

**cu-ri-ous** [kyŏŏr′ē-əs] *adjective*, 1) eager to know about all things 2) singular, unusual, odd

**curl** [kûrl] *noun*, 1) a ringlet or spiral shape, *verb*, 2) to make straight hair wavy and curly

**cur-mudg-eon** [kər-mŭj′ən] *noun*, a mean, bad-tempered person

**cur-rant** [kûr′ənt] *noun*, a small berry, similar to a raisin

**cur-ren-cy** [kûr′ən-sē] *noun*, money in circulation

**cur-rent** [kûr′ənt] *adjective*, 1) up to date, pertaining to the present, *noun*, 2) the powerful flow of water or electricity or air

**cur-ric-u-lum** [kə-rĭk′yə-ləm] *noun*, the classes that a school requires or offers

**cur-ry** [kûr′ē, kŭr′ē] *noun*, 1) a yellow powder containing several spices, including turmeric, used to flavor cooking, *verb*, 2) to seek favor by flattery 3) to brush or groom a horse

**curse** [kûrs] *noun*, 1) something said hoping harm will come to someone, *verb*, 2) to wish bad luck or injury on someone 3) to use profanity

**cur-sive** [kûr′sĭv] *adjective*, characteristic of handwriting in which the letters flow together

**cur-tail** [kər-tāl′] *verb*, to cut short, to reduce, to decrease

**cur-tain** [kûr′tn] *noun*, a piece of cloth hung over a window or doorway as a screen or cover

**cur-tsy** [kûrt′sē] *noun*, 1) a formal bow made with bent knees by a woman, *verb*, 2) to make a bow with one foot forward, as a gesture of respect

**cur-va-ture** [kûr′və-chŏŏr′] *noun*, a curve, a bend

**curve** [kûrv] *noun*, a bend or arch

**curv-ed** [kûrvd] *adjective*, having a line with no part straight or flat

**cush-ion** [kŏŏsh′ən] *noun*, a case or bag stuffed with some soft and elastic material

**cus-tard** [kŭs′tərd] *noun*, a pudding made of milk and eggs

**cus-to-di-an** [kŭ-stō′dē-ən] *noun*, a caretaker or porter, a janitor

**cus-to-dy** [kŭs′tə-dē] *noun*, safe-keeping under penalty or under a judge's ruling, imprisonment

**cus-tom** [kŭs′təm] *noun*, a tradition passed on from one generation to the next

**cus-tom-ar-y** [kŭs′tə-mĕr′ē] *adjective*, established by common usage, habitual

**cus-tom-er** [kŭs′tə-mər] *noun*, one who makes regular purchases from a business, a patron

**cut** [kŭt] *noun*, 1) a wound or injury that may cause the skin to bleed 2) an insult, a derogatory remark 3) something that has been made shorter, *verb*, 4) to break with a knife or blade

**cute** [kyo͞ot] *adjective*, lovable, adorable, delightful

**cu-ti-cle** [kyo͞o′tĭ-kəl] *noun*, the skin surrounding the fingernail

**cy-cle** [sī′kəl] *noun*, 1) events that happen in the same order over and over again 2) a bicycle, *verb*, 3) to move in a circuit controlled by alternating negative and positive currents

**cy-clone** [sī′klōn′] *noun*, a violent windstorm, sometimes called a typhoon or hurricane, depending on location and intensity

**cyl-in-der** [sĭl′ən-dər] *noun*, a solid spherical figure with two faces that are circles

**cy-lin-dri-cal** [sə-lĭn′drĭ-kəl] *adjective*, a circular or spherical shape with straight sides

**cym-bal** [sĭm′bəl] *noun*, a large round metal plate used as a percussion instrument

**cyn-ic** [sĭn′ĭk] *noun*, a doubter, a skeptic, an unbeliever

**cyn-i-cism** [sĭn′ĭ-sĭz′əm] *noun*, an attitude given to sneering at honesty or virtue, a belief that people are self-interested

**cy-press** [sī′prĭs] *noun*, an evergreen tree with scale-like needles

**cyst** [sĭst] *noun*, a fluid-filled pouch attached to a body part

**czar** [zär, tsär] *noun*, the supreme ruler of an empire, especially the ruler of Russia before 1917

# D

**dad** [dăd] *noun*, father

**daf-fo-dil** [dăf′ə-dĭl] *noun*, a spring flowering bulb, yellow or white, with a trumpet-like center

**dag-ger** [dăg′ər] *noun*, a weapon used specifically for stabbing, a knife

**dai-ly** [dā′lē] *adjective*, done or occurring every day

**dain-ty** [dān′tē] *adjective*, delicate, fragile, small, pretty, refined

**dair-y** [dâr′ē] *noun*, a place where milk is produced and pasteurized

**da-is** [dā′ĭs] *noun*, a raised platform for honored guests

**dai-sy** [dā′zē] *noun*, a flower with a yellow or brown center surrounded by petals

**dal-ly** [dăl′ē] *verb*, to loiter, to fiddle around, to flirt

**dam** [dăm] *noun*, 1) a wall built across a river or lake that

# damage

controls water flow, *verb*, 2) to construct a wall in a lake to retain the water and to regulate its flow

**dam-age** [dăm′ĭj] *noun*, 1) loss or detriment due to injury or harm, *verb*, 2) to hurt or cause harm or injury to something, to destroy

**damp** [dămp] *adjective*, humid, somewhat wet, moist

**dance** [dăns] *noun*, 1) a set of movements designed to accompany music, *verb*, 2) to move in rhythm with music, to skip or leap, to perform

**dan-de-li-on** [dăn′dl-ī′ən] *noun*, a bitter herb with yellow flowers, often cooked and eaten

**dan-ger** [dān′jər] *noun*, the possibility of harm

**dan-ger-ous** [dān′jər-əs] *adjective*, full of risk, perilous, hazardous, likely to harm

**dan-gle** [dăng′gəl] *verb*, to hang, to suspend loosely

**dap-pled** [dăp′əld] *adjective*, spotted with color or shade

**dare** [dâr] *verb*, to be brave, bold

**dark** [därk] *adjective*, 1) without light, not reflecting light, shadowy, *noun*, 2) a space without light

**dark-ness** [därk′nĕs] *noun*, *no plural*, a lack of light

**darl-ing** [där′lĭng] *adjective*, 1) a term of affection for someone who is loved, *noun*, 2) a sweetheart, the favorite

**darn** [därn] *verb*, to mend socks

**dart** [därt] *noun*, 1) a small weapon like a tiny arrow that can be

thrown by hand, *verb*, 2) to move quickly or suddenly

**dash** [dăsh] *noun*, 1) a punctuation mark used to indicate a pause 2) a small amount, *verb*, 3) to move quickly 4) to hit, to shatter, to break, to strike

**da-ta** [dā′tə, dăt′ə, dä′tə] *noun*, information collected on a subject for reference

**da-ta-base** [dā′tə-bās′, dăt′ə-] *noun*, information arranged for computer access

**date** [dāt] *noun*, 1) the date, month, and year 2) a small, sweet, brown fruit grown in tropical climates, *verb*, 3) to measure, to mark 4) to court

**daub** [dôb] *verb*, to dab, to smear, to spread paint or another liquid

**daugh-ter** [dô′tər] *noun*, a human female considered with reference to her parents

**daunt** [dônt] *verb*, to intimidate

**daunt-less** [dônt′lĭs] *adjective*, bold

**daw-dle** [dôd′l] *verb*, to dilly dally, to waste time

**dawn** [dôn] *noun*, the break of day when the sun rises

**day** [dā] *noun*, 1) the period of 24 hours when the earth completes one rotation on its axis 2) the opposite of night, when the sun is in the sky

**daze** [dāz] *noun*, 1) a stupor, amazement, *verb*, 2) to cause to feel stunned

**daz-zle** [dăz′əl] *verb*, to awe, to impress with splendor

**dead** [dĕd] *adjective*, 1) not alive, inactive, *noun*, 2) referring to people who are no longer alive

**dead-line** [dĕd′lĭn′] *noun*, a set time when an assignment is to be finished, a time limit

**dead-lock** [dĕd′lŏk′] *noun*, a stalemate, a state in which no progress can be made

**dead-ly** [dĕd′lē] *adjective*, dangerous, possibly fatal, causing death, mortal

**deaf** [dĕf] *adjective*, 1) not able to hear 2) not listening

**deal** [dēl] *noun*, 1) a business agreement 2) an unspecified amount 3) a bargain, *verb*, 4) to barter, or buy and sell 5) to be concerned, to cope 6) to pass out or to distribute, i.e. playing cards

**deal-er** [dē′lər] *noun*, 1) a person who buys and sells things 2) in a card game, the person who holds the cards and passes them out

**dear** [dîr] *adjective*, 1) beloved 2) costly

**dear-ly** [dîr′lē] *adverb*, very much

**death** [dĕth] *noun*, the end of life

**de-ba-cle** [dĭ-bä′kəl] *noun*, a sudden downfall

**de-bat-a-ble** [dĭ-bā′tə-bəl] *adjective*, disputable, open to question

**de-bate** [dĭ-bāt′] *noun*, 1) a public discussion of a topic in which opposing points of view are presented, *verb*, 2) to argue different points of view

**de-bil-i-tate** [dĭ-bĭl′ĭ-tāt′] *verb*, to weaken

**deb-it** [dĕb′ĭt] *noun*, an entry on an account for a sum owed

**de-bris** [də-brē′, dā′brē′] *noun*, rubbish, especially such as results from destruction

**debt** [dĕt] *noun*, money owed

**debt-or** [dĕt′ər] *noun*, one who owes something, especially money

**de-but** [dā-byōō′] *noun*, 1) a beginning 2) first public appearance

**dec-ade** [dĕk′ād′] *noun*, a period of ten years

**de-cay** [dĭ-kā′] *noun*, 1) the condition of being rotten or degenerating, *verb*, 2) to rot, to decompose 3) to decline

**de-ceased** [dĭ-sēst′] *adjective*, dead, defunct, without life

**de-ceit** [dĭ-sēt′] *noun*, fraud, trickery, deception, lie

**de-ceit-ful** [dĭ-sēt′fəl] *adjective*, dishonest, deceptive, false

**de-ceive** [dĭ-sēv′] *verb*, to lead into error, to mislead, to delude, to lie to

**De-cem-ber** [dĭ-sĕm′bər] *noun*, the twelfth month of the year, having 31 days

**de-cen-cy** [dē′sən-sē] *noun*, behavior that is proper and moral

**de-cent** [dē′sənt] *adjective*, honorable, good, fitting, ethical

**de-cep-tion** [dĭ-sĕp′shən] *noun*, the act of deceiving, fraud, false representation, dishonesty

**de-cide** [dĭ-sīd′] *verb*, to determine, to make a choice, to resolve, to choose

**de-cid-u-ous** [dĭ-sĭj′ōō-əs] *adjective*, falling out at a certain stage of development (as some leaves, antlers, insect wings, or milk teeth)

**dec-i-mal** [děs′ə-məl] *adjective,* pertaining to or founded on the number ten

**de-ci-pher** [dĭ-sī′fər] *verb,* 1) to translate from coded characters 2) to make out or read

**de-ci-sion** [dĭ-sĭzh′ən] *noun,* act or result of deciding or settling, a conclusion, a resolution

**de-ci-sive** [dĭ-sī′sĭv] *adjective,* positive, able to decide quickly

**de-ci-sive-ly** [dĭ-sī′sĭv-lē] *adverb,* in a clean manner, precisely

**deck** [děk] *noun,* 1) the floor on each level of a ship 2) a pack of playing cards 3) a flat structure without a roof attached to a house

**dec-la-ra-tion** [děk′lə-rā′shən] *noun,* an announcement or statement, a proclamation

**de-clare** [dĭ-klâr′] *verb,* to formally announce, to state firmly and solemnly

**de-cline** [dĭ-klīn′] *noun,* 1) a gradual lessening of strength or numbers, *verb,* 2) to refuse 3) to steadily become less

**de-com-pose** [dē′kəm-pōz′] *verb,* 1) to rot or decay 2) to separate a chemical into constituent parts

**de-com-po-si-tion** [dē-kŏm′pə-zĭsh′ən] *noun,* the process of decay

**dec-o-rate** [děk′ə-rāt′] *verb,* to beautify, to adorn, to enhance

**dec-o-ra-tion** [děk′ə-rā′shən] *noun,* 1) an ornament 2) an award such as a ribbon or a medal

**dec-o-rous** [děk′ər-əs] *adjective,* proper, correct, polite

**de-coy** [dē′koi′] *noun,* something used as a lure or bait

**de-crease** [dĭ-krēs′] *noun,* 1) the amount by which something has been made smaller, *verb,* 2) to diminish and lessen the amount, to reduce

**de-cree** [dĭ-krē′] *noun,* 1) a pronouncement, a declaration, *verb,* 2) to proclaim, to order

**de-crep-it** [dĭ-krĕp′ĭt] *adjective,* broken down with age, feeble, worn out, dilapidated

**de-cry** [dĭ-krī′] *verb,* to discredit, to denounce publicly

**ded-i-cate** [dĕd′ĭ-kāt′] *verb,* 1) to recognize in a solemn ceremony 2) to devote oneself to something 3) to inscribe a message in the front of a book

**ded-i-ca-tion** [dĕd′ĭ-kā′shən] *noun,* 1) devotion to something 2) an acknowledgement of another person by an author

**de-duce** [dĭ-dōōs′] *verb,* to reach a conclusion by reasoning

**de-duct** [dĭ-dŭkt′] *verb,* to subtract, to take away

**deed** [dēd] *noun,* 1) an action taken, something someone has done 2) a legal document proving that someone owns a piece of land or property

**deep** [dēp] *adjective,* 1) extending or reaching a long distance beneath the surface of the earth 2) intense, heart-felt, feelings

**deer** [dîr] *noun,* an animal with hooves that eats grass and leaves; the males have antlers

**de-face** [dĭ-fās′] *verb,* to mar, to vandalize, to destroy the appearance of

**def-a-ma-tion** [dĕf′ə-mā′shən] *noun*, harm to a person's good reputation, slander, libel

**de-fault** [dĭ-fôlt′] *noun*, 1)failure to fulfill an obligation 2) a computer setting that is used if the user does not make another choice

**de-feat** [dĭ-fēt′] *noun*, 1) a loss to be overcome, *verb*, 2) to beat, to conquer, to cause to fail

**de-fect** [dē′fĕkt′] *noun*, 1) a fault, a failing, a drawback, *verb*, 2) to desert your country or cause

**de-fec-tive** [dĭ-fĕk′tĭv] *adjective*, faulty, broken, imperfect

**de-fend** [dĭ-fĕnd′] *verb*, to fight to protect something, to guard

**de-fend-ant** [dĭ-fĕn′dənt] *noun*, a person required to make an answer in a lawsuit or a criminal case

**de-fense** [dĭ-fĕns′] *noun*, 1) protection from harm 2) justification for an action 3)protection of the goal in sports

**de-fen-sive** [dĭ-fĕn′sĭv] *adjective*, guarding, protective

**de-fer** [dĭ-fûr′] *verb*, 1) to put off, to postpone 2) to submit respectfully

**de-fer-ence** [dĕf′ər-əns] *noun*, a yielding of judgment with respect to another, courtesy

**de-fi-ance** [dĭ-fī′əns] *noun*, a state of open opposition, a challenge

**de-fi-ant** [dĭ-fī′ənt] *adjective*, opposing or resisting power or authority, disobedient

**def-i-cit** [dĕf′ĭ-sĭt] *noun*, an amount that falls short of a goal or perfect balance

**de-fine** [dĭ-fīn′] *verb*, 1) to determine the boundaries of something 2) to give the meaning of

**def-i-nite** [dĕf′ə-nĭt] *adjective*, fixed, having certain limits, precise, clearly defined

**def-i-nite-ly** [dĕf′ə-nĭt-lē] *adverb*, precisely, clearly stated, certainly

**def-i-ni-tion** [dĕf′ə-nĭsh′ən] *noun*, an explanation of the meaning of a word or term

**de-fin-i-tive** [dĭ-fĭn′ĭ-tĭv] *adjective*, final, conclusive, decisive

**de-flate** [dĭ-flāt′] *verb*, 1) to let the air out 2) to dishearten, to discourage

**de-flect** [dĭ-flĕkt′] *verb*, 1) to turn aside 2) to cause something to change direction

**de-form-i-ty** [dĭ-fôr′mĭ-tē] *noun*, a lack of proper form or symmetry, distortion

**de-fraud** [dĭ-frôd′] *verb*, to deprive someone of a right or property through deceit, to swindle

**de-fray** [dĭ-frā′] *verb*, to meet the cost of something, to pay

**de-frost** [dē-frôst′] *verb*, to melt, to thaw, to remove ice by melting

**deft** [dĕft] *adjective*, able, skillful

**de-funct** [dĭ-fŭngkt′] *adjective*, ended, dead, no longer existing

**de-fy** [dĭ-fī′] *verb*, to challenge a stronger force, to disobey

**de-gen-er-ate** [dĭ-jĕn′ər-āt′] *verb*, to become worse physically, mentally or morally, to decay

**de-grade** [dĭ-grād′] *verb*, to lower someone's reputation or character, to treat disrespectfully

**de-gree** [dǐ-grē′] *noun*, 1) a unit for measuring temperature or angles 2) a grade or rank conferred by colleges or under graduates or other scholars 3) a measured portion determined on a scale 4) a proportion

**de-i-fy** [dē′ə-fī′] *verb*, to idolize or worship as a god

**de-jec-tion** [dǐ-jĕk′shən] *noun*, sadness, depression, low spirits

**Del-a-ware** [dĕl′ə-wâr′] *noun*, a state on the east coast of the United States; the capital is Dover. The state flower of **Delaware** is the peach blossom and the motto is "Liberty and Independence."

**de-lay** [dǐ-lā′] *noun*, 1) a period of waiting, *verb*, 2) to postpone, to make something take longer

**de-lec-ta-ble** [dǐ-lĕk′tə-bəl] *adjective*, delicious

**del-e-gate** [dĕl′ĭ-gāt′] *noun*, 1) one sent and empowered to act for another, a deputy, *verb*, 2) to entrust a duty or task to another, to assign

**de-lete** [dǐ-lēt′] *verb*, to erase, to mark for omission, to remove

**de-lib-er-ate** [dǐ-lĭb′ər-ĭt] *adjective*, 1) planned or done on purpose, *verb*, [dǐ-lĭb′ər-āt] 2) to think carefully in or to make up one's mind, to consider reasons for and against

**de-lib-er-ate-ly** [dǐ-lĭb′ər-ĭt-lē] *adverb*, after mature consideration, consciously, intentionally, on purpose

**del-i-ca-tes-sen** [dĕl′ĭ-kə-tĕs′ən] *noun*, a shop where meat, cheese, and salads are sold

**del-i-ca-cy** [dĕl′ĭ-kə-sē] *noun*, 1) good taste, tact 2) choice food

**de-li-cious** [dǐ-lĭsh′əs] *adjective*, giving pleasure to the senses, especially taste

**de-light** [dǐ-līt′] *noun*, 1) a joy, *verb*, 2) to please, to cause joy or happiness

**de-light-ful** [dǐ-līt′fəl] *adjective*, pleasing, causing pleasure and satisfaction

**de-lin-quent** [dǐ-lĭng′kwənt] *adjective*, 1) failing to do what is required 2) past due, *noun*, 3) a child who persistently breaks the law

**de-lir-i-ous** [dǐ-lîr′ē-əs] *adjective*, wandering in mind, light-headed

**de-liv-er** [dǐ-lĭv′ər] *verb*, 1) to carry or take to a person to whom something is addressed 2) to assist in the birth of a baby 3) to utter, to speak 4) to rescue or set free

**de-liv-er-y** [dǐ-lĭv′ə-rē] *noun*, the act of delivering goods, a letter, etc. 2) goods that have been brought to be handed over

**del-ta** [dĕl′tə] *noun*, a fan-shaped area of land where a river splits into channels at its mouth

**de-lude** [dǐ-lōōd′] *verb*, to deceive, to fool, to mislead

**de-lu-sion** [dǐ-lōō′zhən] *noun*, 1) a mirage, a fantasy 2) a mistake, a misconception, a false belief

**delve** [dĕlv] *verb*, to examine, to probe, to look through, to search

**dem-a-gogue** [dĕm′ə-gôg′] *noun*, a person who wins support by appealing to popular feelings and prejudices especially in speeches

**de-mand** [dĭ-mănd'] *noun*,
1) a strong request, *verb*, 2) to
ask for something very strongly,
to insist or require, to claim

**de-mean** [dĭ-mēn'] *verb*, to
humiliate, to lower

**de-mean-or** [dĭ-mē'nər] *noun*, a
person's posture or conduct,
behavior, attitude

**de-mise** [dĭ-mīz'] *noun*, the death
of a person, the end of
something, a failure

**de-moc-ra-cy** [dĭ-mŏk'rə-sē] *noun*,
a form of government in which
people exercise power by
electing representatives

**Dem-o-crat** [dĕm'ə-krăt'] *noun*, a
person who advocates
democracy, one who believes in
government in which all people
have a vote

**dem-o-crat-ic** [dĕm'ə-krăt' ĭk]
*adjective*, 1) favoring equality,
considerate of humanity
2) representative

**de-mol-ish** [dĭ-mŏl'ĭsh] *verb*, to
destroy, to ruin, to take down

**dem-o-li-tion** [dĕm'ə-lĭsh'ən]
*noun*, destruction

**dem-on-strate** [dĕm'ən-strāt']
*verb*, to establish beyond doubt,
to show

**dem-on-stra-tion**
[dĕm'ən-strā'shən] *noun*, 1) a
presentation of evidence, proof
2) an exhibit, a display 3) a
peaceful march, a protest

**de-mor-al-ize** [dĭ-môr'ə-līz'] *verb*,
1) to corrupt, to destroy the
morals of someone 2) to
discourage 3) to confuse

**de-mur** [dĭ-mûr'] *noun*,
1) hesitation, objection, refusal,

*verb*, 2) to make an objection, to
delay

**de-mure** [dĭ-myŏŏr'] *adjective*,
quietly modest, reserved

**den** [dĕn] *noun*, 1) a place in which
a wild animal lives, a lair 2) a
quiet, private room

**den-i-grate** [dĕn'ĭ-grāt'] *verb*, to
ridicule, to belittle, to defame

**den-im** [dĕn'ĭm] *noun*, a heavy
cotton fabric, usually blue, used
to make clothing such as jeans

**de-nom-i-na-tion**
[dĭ-nŏm'ə-nā'shən] *noun*,
1) classification, identification,
2) a branch of a religion 3) the
value of a banknote, stamp, etc.

**de-nom-i-na-tor** [dĭ-nŏm'ə-nā'tər]
*noun*, the number base or the
quantity below the line of a
fraction

**de-nounce** [dĭ-*nouns'*] *verb*, to
attack as deserving of
punishment or censure

**dense** [dĕns] *adjective*, compact,
closely packed together

**den-si-ty** [dĕn'sĭ-tē] *noun*, 1) mass
per unit of volume 2) the number
of people in a specified area

**dent** [dĕnt] *noun*, 1) an indentation,
a nick, *verb*, 2) to make a gouge

**den-tal** [dĕn'tl] *adjective*, referring
to teeth or dentistry

**de-nun-ci-a-tion**
[dĭ-nŭn'sē-ā'shən] *noun*, a public
accusation, condemnation

**de-ny** [dĭ-nī'] *verb*, to declare
something untrue

**de-part** [dĭ-pärt'] *verb*, 1) to leave,
to go away from 2) deviate, to
withdraw 3) to die

**de-part-ment** [dĭ-pärt′mənt] *noun*, a separate division of a government or a business

**de-par-ture** [dĭ-pär′chər] *noun*, the act of leaving a place or the subject

**de-pend** [dĭ-pĕnd′]*verb*, 1) to be determined, to be a result of 2) to need, to trust, to rely on

**de-pend-a-ble** [dĭ-pĕnd′ā/bəl] *adjective*, reliable

**de-pend-ant or de-pend-ent** [dĭ-pĕn′dənt] *noun*, a person supported by another

**de-pend-ent** [dĭ-pĕn′dənt] *adjective*, relying on something else for support, contingent

**de-pict** [dĭ-pĭkt′] *verb*, to portray

**de-plete** [dĭ-plēt′] *verb*, to use up

**de-plor-able** [dĭ-plôr′ə-bəl] *adjective*, shockingly bad, vile, horrible, unfortunate

**de-plore** [dĭ-plôr′] *verb*, to feel or express disapproval

**de-ploy** [dĭ-ploi′] *verb*, to move troops to the battle line to make it stronger, to position strategically

**de-port** [dĭ-pôrt′] *verb*, to force someone to leave a country

**de-pose** [dĭ-pōz′] *verb*, 1) to remove from office or power 2) to testify under oath

**de-pos-it** [dĭ-pŏz/ĭt] *noun*, 1) money placed in a bank for safekeeping 2) money to hold something until the full price is paid 3) sediment that has settled on the bottom, *verb*, 4) to put aside for safekeeping

**de-po-si-tion** [dĕp′ə-zĭsh′ən] *noun*, testimony under oath

**de-pot** [dē′pō] *noun*, a railroad or bus station 2) a warehouse

**de-praved** [dĭ-prāvd′] *adjective*, morally corrupt

**de-pre-ci-ate** [dĭ-prē′shē-āt′] *verb*, to diminish in value

**de-pre-ci-a-tion** [dĭ-prē′shē-ā′shən] *noun*, a decrease in value

**dep-re-da-tion** [dĕp′rĭ-dā′shən] *noun*, stealing, pillage, plundering, destruction

**de-press** [dĭ-prĕs′] *verb*, 1) to make someone feel sad and despondent 2) to hold down

**de-pres-sion** [dĭ-prĕsh′ən] *noun*, 1) a feeling of sadness 2) a mental illness characterized by hopelessness and despair 3) a low place or hole or basin 4) a major slump in the economy, a long recession

**de-prive** [dĭ-prīv′] *verb*, to deny, to keep from having, to prevent from enjoying something

**depth** [dĕpth] *noun*, 1) wisdom, intellect 2) the distance from the top downward

**de-ranged** [dĭ-rānjd′] *adjective*, insane, mad, crazy

**der-by** [dûr′bē] *noun*, 1) a contest or race, a horserace 2) a round hat with a narrow brim

**der-e-lict** [dĕr′ə-lĭkt′] *adjective*, 1) abandoned 2) failing in one's duty, *noun* 3) a vagrant

**de-ride** [dĭ-rīd′] *verb*, to scoff at

**de-ri-sion** [dĭ-rĭzh′ən] *noun*, ridicule, scorn, mockery

**de-riv-a-tive** [dĭ-rĭv′ə-tĭv] *noun*, something derived from another source

**de-rive** [dǐ-rīv'] *verb*, to obtain or issue from a source

**de-rog-a-to-ry** [dǐ-rŏg'ə-tôr'ē] *adjective*, negative, mean, detracting, disparaging

**der-rick** [děr'ĭk] *noun*, 1) a tall tower that fits over an oil well, that supports drilling machinery 2) a large hoisting crane

**de-scend** [dǐ-sěnd'] *verb*, to go or move down, to fall, to drop

**de-scend-ant** [dǐ-sěn'dənt] *noun*, a person descended from a particular ancestor, such as a child or a grandchild

**de-scent** [dǐ-sěnt'] *noun*, a change from higher to lower, a downward movement

**de-scribe** [dǐ-skrīb'] *verb*, 1) to set forth in words, to tell about, to recount 2) to mark out, to draw

**de-scrip-tion** [dǐ-skrĭp'shən] *noun*, act or result of representing by words, a narration

**des-e-crate** [děs'ĭ-krāt'] *verb*, to destroy something sacred or of religious significance

**des-ert** [děz'ərt] *noun*, 1) a dry region that is sandy and without trees, [dǐ-zûrt'] *verb*, 2) to leave, to leave the armed forces without permission, to abandon

**de-ser-tion** [dǐ-zûr'shən] *noun*, 1) abandonment 2) the act of leaving service in the armed forces without permission

**de-serve** [dǐ-zûrv'] *verb*, to merit or be worthy of, to earn by service

**de sign** [dǐ-zīn'] *noun*, 1) a plan, 2) a pattern, *verb*, 3) to conceive, to invent 4) to create a plan for something, to scheme

**des-ig-nate** [děz'ĭg-nāt'] *verb*, 1) to point out, to indicate 2) to give a name 3) to appoint

**de-sign-er** [dǐ-zī'nər] *noun*, a person who creates plans for clothes, buildings, products, etc.

**de-sire** [dǐ-zīr'] *noun*, 1) a want, wish, craving, *verb*, 2) to long for, to set your heart on

**desk** [děsk] *noun*, a work table usually with drawers for paper, pencils, etc.

**des-o-late** [děs'ə-lĭt] *adjective*, deserted, forsaken, comfortless, dismal, abandoned

**des-o-la-tion** [děs'ə-lā'shən] *noun*, 1) emptiness, extinction 2) extreme sadness

**de-spair** [dǐ-spâr'] *noun*, 1) the state of being without hope, *verb*, 2) to have no hope or optimism

**des-per-ate** [děs'pər-ĭt] *adjective*, hopeless, downcast, frantic, reckless because of despair

**des-per-a-tion** [děs'pə-rā'shən] *noun*, a great need, an anxious feeling out of hopelessness

**de-spise** [dǐ-spīz'] *verb*, to look down upon with contempt, to consider unworthy of respect

**de-spite** [dǐ-spīt'] *preposition*, 1) in spite of, notwithstanding, *noun* 2) malice, contemptuous disregard

**de-spoil** [dǐ-spoil′] *verb*, to plunder

**de-spond-ent** [dǐ-spǒn′dənt] *adjective*, discouraged, without hope

**des-pot-ic** [dǐ-spǒt′ǐk] *adjective*, 1) possessing unlimited power 2) tyrannical

**des-pot-ism** [děs′pə-tǐz′əm] *noun*, tyranny, dictatorship, repression

**des-sert** [dǐ-zûrt′] *noun*, usually sweet, the last course of a meal

**des-ti-na-tion** [děs′tə-nā′shən] *noun*, the place someone is going, a goal, the end of a journey

**des-ti-ny** [děs′tə-nē] *noun*, fate, a condition predetermined by divine will, providence

**des-ti-tute** [děs′tǐ-tōot′] *adjective*, without means of existence, extremely poor, penniless

**de-stroy** [dǐ-stroi′] *verb*, to put an end to, to ruin or annihilate

**de-struc-tion** [dǐ-strŭk′shən] *noun*, the act of tearing down, causing harm or damage

**de-struc-tive** [dǐ-strŭk′tǐv] *adjective*, harmful, ruinous, causing damage

**de-tach** [dǐ-tǎch′] *verb*, to separate, to remove, to disconnect, to undo

**de-tail** [dǐ-tāl′] *noun*, a small part of a larger whole, an item

**de-tain** [dǐ-tān′] *verb*, 1) to restrain, to confine, to hold back, 2) to delay, to hinder, to impede

**de-tect** [dǐ-těkt′] *verb*, to discover the presence of, to find

**de-tec-tive** [dǐ-těk′tǐv] *noun*, 1) a special policeman who is trained to investigate crimes 2) a person whose job it is to obtain information for clients

**de-ter-gent** [dǐ-tûr′jənt] *noun*, a chemical substance like soap used to wash clothes or dishes

**de-te-ri-o-rate** [dǐ-tîr′ē-ə-rāt′] *verb*, to grow worse, to rot, to decay

**de-te-ri-o-ra-tion** [dǐ-tîr′ē-ə-rā′shən] *noun*, a process of getting worse

**de-ter-mi-na-tion** [dǐ-tûr′mə-nā′shən] *noun*, a firm purpose, resolve, willpower

**de-ter-mine** [dǐ-tûr′mǐn] *verb*, to come to a decision, to realize

**de-test** [dǐ-těst′] *verb*, to hate

**de-tour** [dē′tōor′] *noun*, a temporary way around a blockage in the road

**de-tract** [dǐ-trǎkt′] *verb*, to belittle, to take away from

**det-ri-men-tal** [dět′rə-měn′tl] *adjective*, harmful, injurious

**dev-as-tate** [děv′ə-stāt′] *verb*, 1) to lay waste, to destroy 2) to cause someone sorrow

**de-vel-op** [dǐ-věl′əp] *verb*, unfold gradually, to evolve, to mature

**de-vel-op-ment** [dǐ-věl′əp-mənt] *noun*, 1) expansion, growth 2) a new piece of information

**de-vi-ate** [dē′vē-āt′] *verb*, to turn away from an accepted course of action or standard, to stray

**de-vice** [dǐ-vīs′] *noun*, 1) an instrument used for a particular purpose 2) a scheme, a trick

**dev-il** [děv′əl] *noun*, 1) an evil spirit, thought to cause destruction and bad things 2) a wicked or mischievous person

**de-vi-ous** [dē′vē-əs] *adjective*, crafty, dishonest, gone astray

**de-vise** [dĭ-vīz′] *verb*, to contrive, to invent, to plan, to create

**de-void** [dĭ-void′] *adjective*, empty, entirely without, lacking

**de-vote** [dĭ-vōt′] *verb*, to dedicate, to give entirely, to use for a specific purpose

**de-vo-tion** [dĭ-vō′shən] *noun*, 1) dedication, affection, love 2) religious worship

**de-vour** [dĭ-vour′] *verb*, to consume greedily, to eat

**de-vout** [dĭ-vout′] *adjective*, sincere, dedicated, having religious feeling

**dew-drop** [dōō′drŏp′] *noun*, drops of water that form on anything exposed to air overnight

**dex-ter-i-ty** [dĕk-stĕr′ĭ-tē] *noun*, the ability to operate skillfully by hand, adroitness

**di-a-be-tes** [dī′ə-bē′tĭs] *noun*, a metabolic disorder in which one is very thirsty, produces excessive urine, and is unable to produce or use sufficient insulin

**di-a-bol-ic-al** [dī′ə-bŏl′ĭ-kəl] *adjective*, evil, devilish

**di-ag-no-sis** [dī′əg-nō′sĭs] *noun*, an identification of a disease based on signs or symptoms

**di-ag-o-nal** [dī-ăg′ə-nəl] *adjective*, a line extending from one corner of a polygon to another corner, that is not adjacent

**di-a-gram** [dī′ə-grăm′] *noun*, 1) a figure, or plan drawn to show how something works, *verb*, 2) to represent by a drawing

**di-al** [dī′əl] *noun*, 1) a round face on a machine, often with numbers on it, that sets the instrument to perform a specific task 2) the face of a clock, watch, etc. .3) to make a telephone call

**di-a-lect** [dī′ə-lĕkt′] *noun*, a form of speech characterized by local peculiarities

**di-a-logue** [dī′ə-lôg′] *noun*, 1) a conversation between two or more people, especially in a play or narrative 2) a discussion

**di-am-e-ter** [dī-ăm′ĭ-tər] *noun*, any straight line passing from side to side, through the center of a figure or body

**dia-mond** [dī′ə-mənd] *noun*, 1) a hard clear stone that is very precious 2) a plane shape with four equal sides with two acute angles and two obtuse angles 3) a baseball field

**di-a-phragm** [dī′ə-frăm′] *noun*, the muscle for breathing located between the lungs and the stomach

**di-ar-rhe-a** [dī′ə-rē′ə] *noun*, a purging or looseness of the bowels

**di-a-ry** [dī′ə-rē] *noun*, a journal in which a person makes daily entries of observations and personal experiences

**di-a-tribe** [dī′ə-trīb′] *noun*, a tirade, a scolding, a forceful and bitter verbal attack against someone or something

**dice**, [dīs] *noun*, *plural* 1) a small square cube with a different number of dots on each side ranging from 1-6, often used in games of chance, 2) *verb*, to cut into small cubes

# dichotomy

**di-chot-o-my** [dī-kŏt′ə-mē] *noun*, a division into two parts

**dic-tate** [dĭk′tāt′] *verb*, 1) to speak into a recording device or so that someone else can write or type what is said 2) to impose, to decree, to command

**dic-ta-tion** [dĭk/tā′/chən] *noun*, speaking words to be written down or transcribed

**dic-ta-tor** [dĭk/tā′tər] *noun*, an absolute ruler, a tyrant

**dic-tion** [dĭk′shən] *noun*, enunciation of words

**dic-tion-ar-y** [dĭk/shə-nĕr′ē] *noun*, a word list, usually with definitions, pronunciations, etc.

**did** [dĭd] *past tense* of **do**

**did-n't** [dĭd′nt] the *contraction* of the words **did** and **not**

**die** [dī] *verb*, 1) to stop living or existing 2) to lose strength, to fade away

**die-sel** [dē′zəl, -səl] *noun*, 1) an engine that burns oil instead of gasoline 2)the petroleum fuel used in a diesel engine

**di-et** [dī′ĭt] *noun*, 1) the food someone eats, *verb*, 2) to reduce the intake of food

**dif-fer** [dĭf′ər] *verb*, to be unlike, to vary, to disagree

**dif-fer-ence** [dĭf′ər-əns] *noun*, 1) contrast, unlikeness 2) disagreement, dissension 3) the answer in subtraction

**dif-fer-ent** [dĭf′ər-ənt] *adjective*, 1) not alike 2) not the same as the rest, strange 3) separate

**dif-fer-ent-ial** [dĭf′ə-rĕn′shəl] *adjective*, 1) showing or making a difference, *noun* 2) a gear that allows two wheels to rotate at different speeds

**dif-fi-cult** [dĭf′ĭ-kŭlt′] *adjective*, hard to do, not easy, hard to manage or please, tough

**dif-fi-cul-ty** [dĭf′ĭ-kŭl′tē] *noun*, a hardship, a problem

**dif-fuse** *adjective,* [dĭ-fyoō′ s′] 1) not concentrated, [dĭ-fyoōz′] *verb*, 2) to spread or circulate 3) to cause to flow on all sides

**dif-fu-sion** ən] *noun*, the process of spreading in all directions like gas

**dig** [dĭg] *verb*, 1) to unearth dirt with tools or a machine to make a hole 2) to search, to probe

**di-gest** [dī-jĕst′]*noun*, 1) a condensed literary work, article, etc. *verb*, 2) to convert food into an absorbable form 3) to think over and arrange

**di-ges-tion** [dī-jĕs′chən] *noun*, the process by which food is converted into a source of energy that can be easily assimilated by the body

**di-ges-tive tract** *noun*, the alimentary canal where food is processed and broken down into sugars for energy and wastes are eliminated

**dig-it** [dĭj′ĭt] *noun*, 1) a finger or toe 2) any number 0 through 9

**dig-ni-fy** [dĭg′nə-fī] *verb,* to give honor to

**dig-ni-tar-y** [dĭg′nĭ-tĕr′ē] *noun*, a person holding high rank or position

**dig-ni-ty** [dĭg′nĭ-tē] *noun*, 1) an office or rank 2) nobleness of manner, aspect, or style 3) the quality of being respected and respecting oneself

**di-gres-sion** [dī-grĕsh′ən, dĭ-] *noun*, an act or instance of wandering away from a subject temporarily

**dike** [dīk] *noun*, a dam or wall that holds back water

**di-lap-i-dat-ed** [dĭ-lăp′ĭ-dā′tĭd] *adjective*, falling into ruin, decaying, in disrepair

**di-late** [dī-lāt′] *verb*, to expand, to enlarge or become wider

**dil-a-to-ry** [dĭl′ə-tôr′ē] *adjective*, delaying, wasting time

**di-lem-ma** [dĭ-lĕm′ə] *noun*, a case in which a person must make a difficult choice, a quandary

**dil-i-gence** [dĭl′ə-jəns] *noun*, careful attention and application to work, a constant effort to accomplish something

**dil-i-gent** [dĭl′ə-jənt] *adjective*, careful, tireless in work

**di-lute** [dī-lōōt′] *verb*, to make thinner or weaker by mixing in something else

**dim** [dĭm] *adjective*, 1) poorly lit, 2) less bright or distinct

**dime** [dīm] *noun*, a coin worth ten cents in the United States

**di-men-sion** [dĭ-mĕn′shən] *noun*, size in a particular direction such as length or width, scope, extent

**di-min-ish** [dĭ-mĭn′ĭsh] *verb*, to make or grow less, to reduce

**dim-i-nu-tion** [dĭm′ə-nōō′shən] *noun*, a lessening, a reduction in size or duration

**dim-ple** [dĭm′pəl] *noun*, a small dent in a surface

**din-gy** [dĭn′jē] *adjective*, dirty, soiled, dull and drab, shabby

**din-ner** [dĭn′ər] *noun*, the main meal of the day served in the evening

**di-no-saur** [dī′nə-sôr′] *noun*, extinct gigantic reptiles of the Mesozoic era that were either herbivores, carnivores, or omnivores

**dip** [dĭp] *noun*, 1) a decline 2) a plunge, a soaking, an immersion 3) a mixture into which foods are dunked, *verb*, 4) to put something into a liquid and then take it out again 5) to slope

**diph-thong** [dĭf′thông′] *noun*, a combination of two vowels forming a compound sound

**di-plo-ma** [dĭ-plō′mə] *noun*, a document under seal attesting a degree conferred on a person

**di-plo-ma-cy** [dĭ-plō′mə-sē] *noun*, the business of conducting international negotiations

**dip-lo-mat** [dĭp′lə-măt′] *noun*, 1) an ambassador 2) a tactful person

**dire** [dīr] *adjective*, disastrous, serious, threatening

**di-rect** [dĭ-rĕkt′, dī-] *adjective*, 1) straight to something without stopping, *verb*, 2) to aim 3) to guide, to control, to manage

**di-rec-tion** [dĭ-rĕk′shən] *noun*, 1) the way in which someone is going or pointing 2) **di-rec-tions** instructions explaining how to do something

**di-rect-ly** [dĭ-rĕkt′lē] *adverb*, 1)at once, immediately 2) in a forthright manner

**di-rec-to-ry** [dĭ-rĕk′tə-rē] *noun*, 1) a list of people and their addresses 2) a computer file listing other files

**dirge** [dûrj] *noun*, sorrowful music, a lament for someone who has died

**dir-i-gi-ble** [dĭr'ə-jə-bəl] *noun*, an airship, a blimp

**dirt** [dûrt] *noun*, loose soil, something which causes filth

**dirt-y** [dûr'tē] *adjective*, 1) not clean, soiled 2) obscene

**dis-a-bil-i-ty** [dĭs'ə-bĭl'ĭ-tē] *noun*, a physical or mental incapacity, an inability to do something

**dis-a-ble** [dĭs-ā'bəl] *verb*, to impair the activity of something, to make incapable

**dis-ad-van-tage** [dĭs'əd-văn'tĭj] *noun*, something that makes things more difficult, a detriment

**dis-a-gree** [dĭs'ə-grē'] *verb*, to be of a different opinion, to differ

**dis-a-gree-a-ble** [dĭs'ə-grē'ə-bəl] *adjective*, unpleasant, irritating, obnoxious, bad-tempered

**dis-a-gree-ment** [dĭs'ə-grē'mənt] *noun*, an argument, a dispute

**dis-ap-pear** [dĭs'ə-pîr'] *verb*, to vanish, to go away or become hidden, to fade away

**dis-ap-point** [dĭs'ə-point'] *verb*, to frustrate the hopes of someone

**dis-ap-point-ment** [dĭs'ə-point'mənt] *noun*, failure, frustration, a feeling of being let down

**dis-ap-prove** [dĭs'ə-proōv'] *verb*, to object, to have a bad opinion of

**dis-arm** [dĭs-ärm'] *verb*, 1) to take weapons away from someone, to subdue 2) to win over

**dis-as-ter** [dĭ-zăs'tər] *noun*, something very bad that happens, a catastrophe

**dis-be-lief** [dĭs'bĭ-lēf'] *noun*, doubt, skepticism

**dis-burse** [dĭs-bûrs'] *verb*, to pay out money

**dis-burse-ment** [dĭs-bûrs'mənt] *noun*, 1) the act of paying out money 2) money paid out

**dis-card** [dĭ-skärd'] *verb*, to shed, to eliminate, to throw away

**dis-cern** [dĭ-sûrn'] *verb*, to distinguish, to perceive

**dis-charge** [dĭs-chärj'] *noun*, 1) something that is sent out from its source, *verb*, 2) to unload 3) to send away, to dismiss from duty or a job

**dis-ci-ple** [dĭ-sī'pəl] *noun*, a follower, an apostle

**dis-ci-pline** [dĭs'ə-plĭn] *noun*, 1) strict training to teach self-control 2) an advanced area of knowledge *verb*, 3) to instruct, to prepare 4) to punish

**dis-close** [dĭ-sklōz'] *verb*, to reveal, to make known, to uncover

**dis-com-fort** [dĭs-kŭm'fərt] *noun*, 1) annoyance, embarrassment 2) ache

**dis-con-nect** [dĭs'kə-nĕkt'] *verb*, to cut off, to detach, to sever

**dis-con-tent** [dĭs'kən-tĕnt'] *noun*, dissatisfaction, restlessness, unhappiness

**dis-con-tin-ue** [dĭs'kən-tĭn'yoō] *verb*, to cease, to stop

**dis-cord** [dĭs'kôrd'] *noun*, a conflict, opposition, differences

**dis-count** [dĭs'kount'] *noun*, 1) a reduction in the price of something , *verb,* 2) to disregard or disbelieve someone

**dis-cour-age** [dĭ-skûr′ĭj] *verb,* to dishearten, to deter

**dis-course** [dĭs′kôrs′] *noun,* a talk, a long written or verbal discussion

**dis-cov-er** [dĭ-skŭv′ər] *verb,* 1) to make known the existence of something 2) to find out through study or observation

**dis-cov-er-y** [dĭ-skŭv′ə-rē] *noun,* something seen or learned for the first time

**dis-cred-it** [dĭs-krĕd′ĭt] *verb,* to destroy confidence in, to cause to disbelieve

**dis-creet** [dĭ-skrēt′] *adjective,* prudent, careful, tactful, unobtrusive

**dis-crep-an-cy** [dĭ-skrĕp′ən-sē] *noun,* inconsistency between facts or figures, failure to match

**dis-cre-tion** [dĭ-skrĕsh′ən] *noun,* discernment, wise conduct and management, freedom to decide something, the act of being discreet

**dis-crim-i-nate** [dĭ-skrĭm′ə-nāt′] *verb,* to make a difference or distinction, to treat differently

**dis-crim-i-na-tion** [dĭ-skrĭm′ə-nā′shən] *noun, no plural,* 1) the ability to make fine distinctions 2) treatment based on differences, prejudice

**dis-cuss** [dĭ-skŭs′] *verb,* to talk about, to exchange ideas

**dis-cus-sion** [dĭ-skŭsh′ən] *noun,* the exchange of ideas, a debate

**dis-dain** [dĭs-dān′] *noun,* scorn or contempt

**dis-ease** [dĭ-zēz′] *noun,* 1) any mental or physical disorder 2) any quality or social condition considered harmful

**dis-en-gage** [dĭs′ĕn-gāj′] *verb,* to release, to detach, to become free

**dis-fig-ure** [dĭs-fĭg′yər] *verb,* to deform, to injure, to spoil

**dis-grace** [dĭs-grās′] *noun,* 1) something to feel ashamed of *verb,* 2) to shame, to discredit

**dis-grace-ful** [dĭs-grās′fəl] *adjective,* causing shame

**dis-grunt-led** [dĭs-grŭn′tld] *adjective,* resentful, annoyed, discontented, angry

**dis-guise** [dĭs-gīz′] *noun,* 1) things worn to change the appearance, *verb,* 2) to change the appearance of someone or something, to cover up

**dis-gust** [dĭs-gŭst′] *noun,* 1) a strong feeling of dislike, revulsion, *verb,* 2) to cause someone a strong feeling of dislike or offense

**dish** [dĭsh] *noun,* 1) a container used at a meal to serve food 2) food served

**dis-hon-est** [dĭs-ŏn′ĭst] *adjective,* deceitful, lying, corrupt

**disk** [dĭsk] *noun,* any flat round object, a circular plate

**dis-like** [dĭs-līk′] *noun,* 1) distaste, hostility *verb,* 2)to detest, to hate

**dis-mal** [dĭz′məl] *adjective,* dark or gloomy, dreary, depressing

**dis-man-tle** [dĭs-măn′tl] *verb,* to take apart, to break down to basic parts to see how something is made

**dis-may** [dĭs-mā′] *noun*, 1) an uneasy feeling of alarm, *verb*, 2) to feel alarm and distress

**dis-miss** [dĭs-mĭs′] *verb*, to send away, to cause or permit to go

**dis-obed-i-ent** [dĭs′ə-bē′dē-ənt] *adjective*, refusing to obey

**dis-o-bey** [dĭs′ə-bā′] *verb*, not to do what you are told, to resist

**dis-or-der** [dĭs-ôr′dər] *noun*, 1) sickness, ailment 2) confusion, chaos

**dis-or-gan-ized** [dĭs-ôr′gə-nīzd′] *adjective*, not properly planned

**dis-par-age** [dĭ-spăr′ĭj] *verb*, to belittle, to criticize

**dis-pa-rate** [dĭs′pər-ĭt] *adjective*, very different in kind, containing unrelated elements

**dis-par-i-ty** [dĭ-spăr′ĭ-tē] *noun*, a noticeable difference, inequality

**dis-patch** [dĭ-spăch′] *noun*, 1) a message 2) promptness, *verb*, 3) to send off to a destination

**dis-pel** [dĭ-spĕl′] *verb*, to drive or clear away

**dis-pense** [dĭ-spĕns′] *verb*, to distribute, to give out medicine

**dis-perse** [dĭ-spûrs′] *verb*, to scatter, to distribute in different directions, to disseminate

**dis-per-sion** [dĭ-spûr′zhən] *noun*, scattering, diffusion, distribution

**dis-place** [dĭs-plās′] *verb*, 1) to rearrange, to move around 2) to force people from their homes 3) to take the place of

**dis-play** [dĭ-splā′] *noun*, 1) a show, an exhibit, *verb*, 2) to show or exhibit something, to present

**dis-pose** [dĭ-spōz′] *verb*, 1) to get rid of 2) to adjust, to settle 3) to place or arrange 4) to influence in favor of

**dis-po-si-tion** [dĭs′pə-zĭsh′ən] *noun*, 1) nature, personality, makeup 2) arrangement

**dis-pro-por-tion-ate** [dĭs′prə-pôr′shə-nĭt] *adjective*, relatively too large or too small, uneven, out of proportion

**dis-prove** [dĭs-proov′] *verb*, to refute, to prove false

**dis-pute** [dĭ-spyoot′] *noun*, 1) an argument, a strong difference of opinion, *verb*, 2) to call into question, to debate

**dis-qual-i-fy** [dĭs-kwŏl′ə-fī′] *verb*, to invalidate, to judge ineligible

**dis-re-gard** [dĭs′rĭ-gärd′] *noun*, 1) indifference, disrespect, neglect, *verb*, 2) to fail to notice

**dis-re-spect-ful** [dĭs′rĭ-spĕkt′fəl] *adjective*, rude, lacking respect

**dis-rupt** [dĭs-rŭpt′] *verb*, to interrupt, to disturb

**dis-sat-is-fac-tion** [dĭs-săt′ĭs-făk′shən] *noun*, discontent, uneasiness

**dis-sat-is-fied** [dĭs-săt′ĭs-fīd′] *adjective*, displeased, fed up, disgruntled, unhappy

**dis-sect** [dĭ-sĕkt′] *verb*, 1) to divide into separate parts 2) to analyze

**dis-sec-tion** [dĭ-sĕk′shən] *noun*, analysis, the act of cutting apart in order to examine internal structure

**dis-sem-i-nate** [dĭ-sĕm′ə-nāt′] *verb*, to scatter, to spread around

**dis-sem-i-na-tion** [dĭ-sĕm′ə-nā′shən] *noun*, a scattering or spreading around, diffusion

**dis-sen-sion** [dĭ-sĕn′shən] *noun*, a disagreement causing strife

**dis-sent** [dĭ-sĕnt′] *noun*, disagreement, a quarrel

**dis-sim-i-lar** [dĭ-sĭm′ə-lər] *adjective*, not alike, different

**dis-si-pate** [dĭs′ə-pāt′] *verb*, 1) to lessen, to diminish, to scatter 2) to fritter away

**dis-solve** [dĭ-zŏlv′] *verb*, 1) to make a solid disappear into a liquid solution 2) to break up an assembly, to end an agreement

**dis-so-nance** [dĭs′ə-nəns] *noun*, discord, noise, harsh sounds

**dis-suade** [dĭ-swād′] *verb*, to discourage by persuasion, to deter

**dis-tance** [dĭs′təns] *noun*, 1) the space between two points, an interval 2) a place far away

**dis-tant** [dĭs′tənt] *adjective*, 1) far 2) cool, reserved in manner

**dis-tend** [dĭ-stĕnd′] *verb*, to expand, to bloat, to stretch

**dis-tinct** [dĭ-stĭngkt′] *adjective*, 1) distinguished by nature or station 2) individual, unique 3) well-defined, very clear

**dis-tinc-tion** [dĭ-stĭngk′shən] *noun*, 1) notable difference as in a feature 2)excellence, recognition of an accomplishment

**dis-tin-guish** [dĭ-stĭng′gwĭsh] *verb*, 1) to stand out, to be different 2) to recognize as different

**dis-tort** [dĭ-stôrt′] *verb*, to twist out of shape, to bend, to falsify

**dis-tract** [dĭ-străkt′] *verb*, to take one's attention from something

**dis-trac-tion** [dĭ-străk′shən] *noun*, 1) mental distress 2) something that distracts or amuses

**dis-traught** [dĭ-strôt′] *adjective*, very worried, disturbed, overcome with anxiety, upset

**dis-tress** [dĭ-strĕs′] *noun*, 1) a feeling of worry, sadness or difficulty, *verb*, 2) to make someone sad or worried

**dis-trib-ute** [dĭ-strĭb′yoot] *verb*, 1) to allot or divide among several 2) to spread out over an area, to give out

**dis-tri-bu-tion** [dĭs′trə-byoo′shən] *noun*, the passing out of things, circulation

**dis-trict** [dĭs′trĭkt] *noun*, 1) a division of territory 2) a defined portion of a state, county, or city

**dis-trust** [dĭs-trŭst′] *noun*, 1) suspicion, doubt, *verb*, 2) to lack confidence or trust in

**dis-turb** [dĭ-stûrb′] *verb*, to bother or interrupt, to make anxious

**ditch** [dĭch] *noun*, 1) a long narrow channel, a shallow waterway *verb*, 2) to discard

**dive** [dīv] *noun*, 1) a downward plunge, *verb*, 2) to plunge head first into water 3) to move downward, to drop sharply

**div-er** [dī′vər] *noun*, 1) a person who dives into water 2) a person who works underwater

**di-verge** [dĭ-vûrj′] *verb*, to go off in different directions from the same starting point

**di-verse** [dĭ-vûrs′] *adjective*, various, many and different

**di-ver-sion** [dĭ-vûr′zhən] *noun*, amusement, play, distraction

**di-ver-si-ty** [dĭ-vûr′sĭ-tē] *noun*, variety, a wide range

**di-vert** [dĭ-vûrt′] *verb*, to distract, to draw aside, to entertain, to change the course of

**di-vest** [dĭ-vĕst′] *verb*, to strip, to take away from, to get rid of

**di-vide** [dĭ-vīd′] *verb*, 1) to calculate how many times one number can go into another 2) to separate 3) to share or distribute

**div-i-dend** [dĭv′ĭ-dĕnd′] *noun*, 1) the share of profits earned by any policy or company 2) a number to be divided by another number 3) a benefit from an action

**di-vine** [dĭ-vīn′] *adjective*, of or relating to God, holy, sacred

**di-vis-i-ble** [dĭ-vĭz′ə-bəl] *adjective*, capable of being divided or separated

**di-vi-sion** [dĭ-vĭzh′ən] *noun*, 1) the act or result of separating anything into parts 2) a difference in opinion or feeling 3) an operation on two numbers that results in a quotient 4) a military group 5) a section of a company

**di-vorce** [dĭ-vôrs′] *noun*, 1) a legal end of a marriage, *verb*, 2) to arrange by law for a husband and wife to separate and end their marriage

**di-vulge** [dĭ-vŭlj′] *verb*, to reveal

**do** [dōō] *verb*, 1) to act, to produce 2) to travel 3) to be enough 4) to give 5) used with another verb to ask a question

**doc-ile** [dŏs′əl] *adjective*, easy to control, gentle, submissive

**dock** [dŏk] *noun*, 1) a pier where ships load and unload cargo, *verb*, 2) to tie a ship up at a port

or wharf or boat landing 3) to deduct from someone's wages

**doc-tor** [dŏk′tər] *noun*, a person trained and licensed to practice medicine

**doc-trine** [dŏk′trĭn] *noun*, a tenet, a principle of faith or religion

**doc-u-ment** [dŏk′yə-mənt] *noun*, 1) an original or official paper 2) any writing that conveys information, *verb*, 3) to write down or put on paper 4) to provide information as proof

**dodge** [dŏj] *verb*, to avoid something by moving out of the way, to evade, to escape

**doe** [dō] *noun*, a female deer

**does** [dŭz] *verb*, the part of the verb **do** used with he, she and it

**does-n't** [dŭz′ənt] the *contraction* of the words **does** and **not**

**dog** [dôg] *noun*, a domesticated mammal with four legs that eats meat, a canine

**dog-ma** [dôg′mə] *noun*, 1) opinion or beliefs widely held but not based on facts 2) doctrine

**dol-drums** [dōl′drəmz′] *noun*, 1) listlessness, an inactive period, depression 2) an ocean region near the equator with calm waters and little wind

**dol-lar** [dŏl′ər] *noun*, 1) currency used in the United States and Canada, valued at 100 cents 2) the basic unit of currency used in many countries

**dol-phin** [dŏl′fĭn] *noun*, 1) any of various small cetaceans with the snout in the shape of a beak and the neck vertebrae partially fused like a whale 2) any of various fish

**do-main** [dō-mān′] *noun*, specialty area ruled over, jurisdiction, field

**dome** [dōm] *noun*, a roof that resembles a half circle

**do-mes-tic** [də-měs′tĭk] *adjective*, found in the home or in one's home land

**dom-i-nant** [dŏm′ə-nənt] *adjective*, governing, controlling, bossy

**dom-i-nate** [dŏm′ə-nāt′] *verb*, to have control over someone

**dom-i-no** [dŏm′ə-nō′] *noun*, a game played with uniform blocks with one side divided into two halves, each half showing any number from 0 to 6

**do-nate** [dō′nāt′] *verb*, to make a contribution, to bestow, to give

**do-na-tion** [dō-nā′shən] *noun*, a gift of money or goods given to a charitable organization

**done** [dŭn] *adjective*, 1) finished or complete 2) cooked, *verb*, 3) the *past tense* of **do**

**don-key** [dŏng′kē] *noun*, an animal like a small horse with long ears

**do-nor** [dō′nər] *noun*, a person who gives money or something of value

**don't** [dōnt] the *contraction* of the words **do** and **not**

**doom** [do͞om] *noun*, 1) a grim fate, *verb*, 2) to make certain that something fails or is destroyed

**door** [dôr] *noun*, the moveable piece of wood or metal standing at an entrance, a portal

**door-way** [dôr′wā′] *noun*, the opening for an entrance to a building or a room

**dor-mant** [dôr′mənt] *adjective*, sleeping, inactive, inert

**dor-mi-to-ry** [dôr′mĭ-tôr′ē] *noun*, a building containing rooms for sleeping, a residence hall 2) a large room with many beds

**dor-sal** [dôr′səl] *adjective*, of or on the back of an animal

**dose** [dōs] *noun*, the amount of medicine that is to be taken at one time to be effective

**dot** [dŏt] *noun*, a very small round spot or mark, a point, a fleck

**dou-ble** [dŭb′əl] *adjective*, 1) twice as much, *noun*, 2) a stand in or look alike 3) a two-base hit in baseball, *verb*, 4) to make twice as much, to fold in two

**doubt** [dout] *noun*, 1) a question, a feeling of uncertainty, mistrust, *verb*, 2) to question, to wonder 3) to hesitate, to ponder

**doubt-ful** [dout′fəl] *adjective*, 1) questionable, unlikely 2) feeling uncertain

**dough** [dō] *noun*, a mixture of mostly flour and a liquid to be baked to make bread or cake

**douse** [dous] *verb*, to drench, to saturate, to put out a light

**dove** [dŭv] *noun*, 1) one of many of a small type of pigeon, *verb*, [dōv] 2) *past tense* of **dive**

**down** [doun] *adverb*, 1) toward the ground, *noun*, 2) soft feathers, *preposition*, 3) in or to a lower place

**down-stairs** [doun′stârz′]*adverb*, 1) on or to a lower floor, *noun*, 2) a lower floor of a building

**downtown** [doun′toun′] *noun*, the main business area of a city or town

103

**down-ward** [doun′wərd] *adverb*, descending from a higher to a lower level, moving toward the ground

**doze** [dōz] *verb*, to take a nap, to sleep for a brief time, to sleep lightly

**doz-en** [dŭz′ən] *noun*, twelve

**Dr**. the abbreviation of doctor

**drab** [drăb] *adjective*, dull in color, dreary, dingy, not interesting

**draft** [drăft] *noun*, 1) the first unedited copy of a manuscript 2) an order for payment of money 3) a current of air 4) forced military service

**drag** [drăg] *verb*, to pull along with effort, to haul

**drag-on** [drăg′ən] *noun*, a mythical creature that breathes fire

**drain** [drān] *noun*, 1) a pipe used to transport water into a sewer, *verb*, 2) to relieve the pressure of fluid in a wound 3) to become dry as water flows away 4) to make weak

**dra-ma** [drä′mə] *noun*, 1) a story that can be performed on stage 2) excitement

**dra-mat-ic** [drə-măt′ĭk] *adjective*, theatrical, exciting, stirring

**dra-mat-i-cal-ly** [drə-măt′ĭk-lē] *adverb*, in a sudden or alarming way, impressively

**drank** [drăngk] *past tense* of **drink**

**drape** [drāp] *noun*, 1) a heavy curtain, *verb*, 2) to cover with a piece of cloth

**dra-per-y** [drā′pə-rē] *noun*, a heavy curtain or fabric designed to cover a window

**dras-tic** [drăs′tĭk] *adjective*, forceful, severe, extreme

**draw** [drô] *noun*, 1) a tie score, *verb*, 2) to get, to take, to understand 3) to pull along 4) to make a picture with a writing instrument 5) to choose at random 6) to formulate, to prepare 7) to suck

**draw-bridge** [drô′brĭj′] *noun*, a bridge that can be raised or turned to allow boats and ships to pass

**drawl** [drôl] *noun*, a manner of speaking that stretches out the sound of a word or vowels

**drawn** [drôn] *adjective*, thin, gaunt

**dread** [drĕd] *noun*, 1) fear, horror, terror, *verb*, 2) to anticipate with anxiety, to fear greatly

**dream** [drēm] *noun*, 1) images seen while you sleep 2) desires, goals, *verb*, 3) to picture something with your imagination 4) to see images while sleeping

**drear-y** [drîr′ē] *adjective*, gloomy, depressing

**dredge** [drĕj] *verb*, 1) to remove something from deep water 2) to cover food with sugar, flour, etc.

**drench** [drĕnch] *verb*, to make completely wet, to soak

**dress** [drĕs] *noun*, 1) a piece of clothing that covers the bust, waist and thighs 2) a general term for clothing or attire, *verb*, 3) to put clothes on 4) to adorn

**dress-er** [drĕs′ər] *noun*, 1) a chest of drawers, a bureau 2) a person who helps another to dress 3) a person who dresses a certain way

**drew** [droo] *past tense* of **draw**

**drift** [drĭft] *noun*, 1) the general meaning 2) a pile of snow, leaves, etc. *verb*, 3) to float

**drill** [drĭl] *noun*, 1) a tool made of hard material used to make holes in something 2) a practice, an exercise, *verb*, 3) to make a hole in something with a special machine 4) to be trained

**drink** [drĭngk] *noun*, 1) liquid refreshment, a beverage, *verb*, 2) to consume liquid through the mouth, to swallow, to imbibe

**drip** [drĭp] *verb*, to fall in drops

**drive** [drīv] *noun*, 1) a short journey or trip made in a vehicle, *verb*, 2) to steer and control a moving vehicle 3) to force to go, to push through 4) to make, to compel, to urge

**driv-er** [drī/vər] *noun*, 1) the person steering and controlling a moving vehicle 2) a golf club for hitting long shots

**droll** [drōl] *adjective*, odd, strange and amusing

**drone** [drōn] *noun*, 1) a male bee with no stinger that mates with the queen bee, *verb*, 2) to talk dully, to buzz or murmur like a bee

**drop** [drŏp] *noun*, 1) a small amount of a liquid, *verb*, 2) to let something fall 3) to decrease

**dross** [drŏs] *noun*, waste, impurity

**drought** [drout] *noun*, a long period without rain

**drown** [droun] *verb*, to suffocate by immersion under water

**drow-sy** [drou/zē] *adjective*, sleepy, sluggish

**drudg-er-y** [drŭj/ə-rē] *noun*, dull routine work

**drug** [drŭg] *noun*, 1) a substance that changes the body's chemistry, medicine 2) a narcotic

**drug-gist** [drŭg/ĭst] *noun*, a pharmacist, one who is licensed to sell drugs

**drum** [drŭm] *noun*, 1) a percussion instrument consisting of a hollow cylinder with a taut covering 2) a cylindrical metal container, *verb*, 3) to make music or beat on a drum

**drunk** [drŭngk] *adjective*, showing the effect of too much alcohol, losing control of one's movement or speech because of alcohol

**dry** [drī] *adjective*, 1) without moisture or water, *verb*, 2) to expel or remove moisture

**dry-er** [drī/ər] *noun*, a machine that adds heat and tumbles clothes to evaporate and remove moisture

**dual** [doo/əl] *adjective*, having two purposes or parts

**duch-ess** [dŭch/ĭs] *noun*, the wife or widow of a duke

**duck** [dŭk] *noun*, 1) a bird that swims and is hunted for its eggs and meat, *verb*, 2) to crouch or lower one's head to avoid something, to dodge

**duct** [dŭkt] *noun*, a tube or channel, a ventilation shaft

**due** [doo] *adjective*, 1) owed, unpaid 2) expected, appropriate, *noun*, 3) a charge or fee for membership

**duel** [doo/əl] *noun*, 1) a fight or competition, *verb*, 2) to fight

**du-et** [doo-ĕt′] *noun*, a song or a piece of music for two people

**duke** [dook] *noun*, the title of a man who is a high-ranking nobleman

**dull** [dŭl] *adjective*, 1) not sharp, blunt 2) boring, slow, dim

**dumb** [dŭm] *adjective*, 1) unable to speak, mute, silent 2) unintelligent, stupid

**dump** [dŭmp] *noun*, 1) a public place where garbage is collected and usually buried, *verb*, 2) to leave, to drop or throw away

**dune** [doon] *noun*, a rounded hill of sand heaped up by the wind

**dun-geon** [dŭn′jən] *noun*, a close, dark prison, an underground cell

**dupe** [doop] *verb*, to fool, to trick

**du-pli-cate** [doo′plĭ-kĭt] *adjective*, 1) alike, twin, *noun*, 2) a copy, a reproduction, [doo′pl ĭ-kāt′]*verb*, 3) to reproduce, to remake, to do again

**du-ra-ble** [door′ə-bəl] *adjective*, able to endure, lasting

**du-ra-tion** [doo-rā′shən] *noun*, the length of time something continues or exists

**dur-ing** [door′ĭng] *preposition*, in the course of a period of time, throughout the course of

**dusk** [dŭsk] *noun*, evening, the time just after the sun has set, twilight

**dust** [dŭst] *noun*, 1) fine particles or powder of matter, *verb*, 2) to remove the powder by cleaning or wiping

**du-ty** [doo′tē] *noun*, 1) an obligation or a commitment 2) the responsibilities of one's

job 3) a tax on goods, especially imports and exports

**dwarf** [dwôrf] *noun*, 1) an unusually small person, *verb*, 2) to make something look small by comparison

**dwell** [dwĕl] *verb*, 1) to inhabit, to live in 2) to emphasize, to think about for a long time, to ponder

**dwell-ing** [dwĕl′ĭng] *noun*, a home to live in, a residence, an abode

**dwin-dle** [dwĭn′dl] *verb*, to reduce

**dye** [dī] *noun*, 1) a substance used to color cloth, hair, etc. *verb*, 2) fixing colors permanently in the fibers of materials, to change the color

**dy-na-mic** [dī-năm′ĭk] *adjective*, relating to the forces producing motion, forceful, energetic

**dy-na-mite** [dī′nə-mīt′] *noun*, an explosive of nitroglycerin absorbed in porous matter

**dy-nas-ty** [dī′nə-stē] *noun*, a series of rulers from the same family

**dys-func-tion-al** [dĭs-fŭngk′shən-əl] *adjective*, functioning abnormally

# E

**each** [ēch] *adjective*, every, one of two or more things, all

**ea-ger** [ē′gər] *adjective*, very willing to do something, enthusiastic

**ea-gle** [ē′gəl] *noun*, a very large keen-sighted bird of prey

**ear** [îr] *noun*, 1) the organ, one on each side of the head, used to hear 2) the sleeve in a cereal plant used to hold seeds or flowers

**ear-ly** [ûr′lē] *adjective*, 1) near the beginning of a time period, *adverb*, 2) before the set time

**earn** [ûrn] *verb*, 1) to get something through work, to achieve, to gain money 2) to achieve by one's own efforts

**ear-nest** [ûr′nĭst] *adjective*, fervent, serious, sincere

**ear-ring** [îr′rĭng, îr′ĭng] *noun*, an ornament worn on the earlobe

**Earth** [ûrth] *proper noun*, 1) the name of the planet on which we live, our world, , 2) **earth** *common noun*, soil, dirt, ground

**earth-quake** [ûrth′kwāk′] *noun*, a shaking movement of the earth caused by underground movement

**ease** [ēz] *noun*, 1) relaxation, relief, *verb*, 2) to move carefully 3) to make less painful or difficult

**ea-sel** [ē′zəl] *noun*, a tripod frame used to support an artist's canvas

**eas-i-ly** [ē′zə-lē] *adverb*, without difficulty, effortlessly

**east** [ēst] *noun*, one of the four points of a compass, pointing right of north, where the sun rises

**east-ern** [ē′stərn] *adjective*, 1) belonging to or characteristic of the east 2) Asian

**eas-y** [ē′zē] *adjective*, 1) effortless, not difficult 2) relaxed, comfortable 3) free from pain or worry 4) not strict

**eat** [ēt] *verb*, 1) to put food in the mouth, chewing it and swallowing it 2) to corrode

**eaves** [ēvz] *noun*, *plural*, the lower edges of a roof that overhang a building

**ebb** [ĕb] *noun*, 1) the receding of the tide, *verb*, 2) to fall back

**eb-on-y** [ĕb′ə-nē] *adjective*, 1) black, *noun*, 2) a hard, heavy and durable wood 3) a tropical Asian tree

**ec-cen-tric** [ĭk-sĕn′trĭk] *adjective*, 1) off-center from the regular or normal, *noun*, 2) an odd person

**ec-cle-si-as-tic** [ĭ-klē′zē-ăs′tĭk] *adjective*, pertaining to the Christian church or clergy

**ech-o** [ĕk′ō] *noun*, 1) a series of reflected sound waves that repeat as they bounce back from an object, repeating the sound *verb*, 2) to reverberate, to reflect a sound back

**e-clipse** [ĭ-klĭps′] *noun*, 1) a period of time when the light from one celestial object is blocked by another, *verb*, 2) to overshadow and cause a loss of light

**e-col-o-gy** [ĭ-kŏl′ə-jē] *noun*, the study of how plants and animals interact with the environment

**e-co-nom-ic** [ĕk′ə-nŏm′ĭk] *adjective*, related to business and the production of goods

**e-co-nom-i-cal** [ĕk′ə-nŏm′ĭ-kəl] *adjective*, affordable, inexpensive

**e-co-nom-ics** [ĕk′ə-nŏm′ĭks] *noun*, the study of the way people secure goods and services and the necessities of life

**e-con-o-my** [ĭ-kŏn′ə-mē] *noun*, 1) the careful or thrifty management of resources 2) a system for the management of resources, money, and jobs

**ec-o-sys-tem** [ĕk′ō-sĭs′təm] *noun*, living things that work together and their environment

**ec-sta-sy** [ĕk′stə-sē] *noun*, intense delight, bliss

**ec-ze-ma** [ĕk′sə-mə] *noun*, a rash, inflammatory disease of the skin

**edge** [ĕj] *noun*, 1) the segment where two surfaces meet 2) the rim or brink of something 3) the sharp blade of a cutting instrument such as a knife 4) the point farthest from the middle of a surface 5) an advantage, *verb*, 6) to take small, cautious steps 7) to put a border on something

**ed-i-ble** [ĕd′ə-bəl] *adjective*, fit to be eaten as food

**ed-i-fice** [ĕd′ə-fĭs] *noun*, a large, imposing building or structure

**ed-i-fy** [ĕd′ə-fĭ′] *verb*, to educate, to instruct, to guide spiritually

**ed-it** [ĕd′ĭt] *verb*, to revise and correct, to prepare something for publication, to cut a part of

**e-di-tion** [ĭ-dĭsh′ən] *noun*, an issue of a book, newspaper or magazine

**ed-i-tor** [ĕd′ĭ-tər] *noun*, one who reads and revises books or newspapers before they are published

**ed-u-cate** [ĕj′ə-kāt′] *verb*, to teach people, to provide knowledge

**ed-u-ca-tion** [ĕj′ə-kā′shən] *noun*, teaching and learning, acquired knowledge

**eel** [ēl] *noun*, a long fish that looks like a snake that lives in freshwater and the sea

**ee-rie** [îr′ē] *adjective*, spooky, strange, causing dread

**ef-fect** [ĭ-fĕkt′] *noun*, a result, consequence, outcome

**ef-fec-tive** [ĭ-fĕk′tĭv] *adjective*, having a positive result, helpful

**ef-fer-ves-cence** [ĕf′ər-vĕs′sĭns] *noun,* 1) the process of gas escaping in innumerable small bubbles 2) irrepressible enthusiasm

**ef-fi-ca-cious** [ĕf′ĭ-kā′shəs] *adjective*, producing a desired result, effective, efficient

**ef-fi-cien-cy** [ĭ-fĭsh′ən-sē] *noun*, productivity with little or no wasted effort

**ef-fi-cient** [ĭ-fĭsh′ənt] *adjective*, working well with no waste of money or effort, capable

**ef-fi-gy** [ĕf′ə-jē] *noun*, a likeness in the form of a dummy, an image of a hated person usually hung

**ef-fort** [ĕf′ərt] *noun*, an attempt, an action, strenuous exertion

**ef-fu-sion** [ĭ-fyo͞o′zhən] *noun*, a pouring forth of liquid, light, etc.

**e.g.** for example

**egg** [ĕg] *noun*, 1) a shell covered fetus of a baby bird, fish or insect 2) an ovum, a female reproductive cell

**e-go** [ē′gō, ĕg′ō] *noun*, a person's self-importance, self-esteem

**e-go-tist** [ē′gə-tĭst] *noun*, one who is excessively interested in herself or himself

**eight** [āt] *noun*, the number 8, one plus seven

**eight-een** [ā-tēn′] *noun*, the number 18, ten plus eight

**eight-eenth** [ā-tēnth′] *noun*, *adjective*, the number eighteen in order, 18th

108

**eighth** [ātth] *noun, adjective,* the number eight in order, one of eight equal parts

**eight-i-eth** [ā'tē-ĭth] *noun,* the number 80 in order, one of eighty equal parts

**eight-y** [ā'tē] *adjective, noun,* the number 80, eight times ten

**ei-ther** [ē'thər, ī'thər] *adjective, pronoun,* one or the other of two

**e-ject** [ĭ-jĕkt'] *verb,* to exit suddenly and forcefully, to expel

**e-lab-o-rate** [ĭ-lăb'ər-ĭt] *adjective,* 1) made with great care, carefully planned, complicated, [ĭ-lă-bə-rāt' ]*verb,* 2) to explain in detail

**e-lapse** [ĭ-lăps'] *verb,* to pass by

**e-las-tic** [ĭ-lăs'tĭk] *adjective,* 1) able to return to an original size and shape after having been stretched completely, *noun,* 2) fabric with fine strings of rubber woven in it

**e-la-tion** [ĭ-lā' shən] *noun,* excitement, joy

**el-bow** [ĕl'bō'] *noun,* the joint in the arm that allows it to bend in the middle

**eld-er** [ĕl'dər] *adjective,* 1) older, more aged, *noun,* 2) one who is older than others 3) an influential older person

**e-lect** [ĭ-lĕkt'] *verb,* to choose by vote, to decide a course of action or representative

**e-lec-tion** [ĭ-lĕk'shən] *noun,* the process of making a choice by voting

**e-lec-tor-ate** [ĭ-lĕk'tər-ĭt] *noun,* the people qualified to vote

**e-lec-tric** [ĭ-lĕk'trĭk] *adjective,* relating to or powered by electricity

**e-lec-tri-cian** [ĭ-lĕk-trĭsh'ən] *noun,* one who is licensed to install and repair electrical equipment

**e-lec-tric-i-ty** [ĭ-lĕk-trĭs'ĭ-tē] *noun,* a form of energy resulting from the activity of electrons and protons

**e-lec-tro-cute** [ĭ-lĕk'trə-kyōōt']*verb,* to kill by electric shock

**e-lec-trode** [ĭ-lĕk'trōd'] *noun,* a conductor by which an electric unit enters or leaves a region or object

**e-lec-tron** [ĭ-lĕk'trŏn'] *noun,* a particle smaller than an atom and having a negative electric charge

**e-lec-tron-ic** [ĭ-lĕk'trŏnĭk] *adjective,* operating by transistors, microchips, etc. that control an electric current

**el-e-gant** [ĕl'ĭ-gənt] *adjective,* lovely, gorgeous, refined

**el-e-ment** [ĕl'ə-mənt] *noun,* 1) a basic substance of which the universe is composed, *plural,* 2) the forces that constitute the weather

**el-e-men-ta-ry** [ĕl'ə-mĕn'tə-rē] *adjective,* of or related to the first principles or basic facts of a subject

**el-e-phant** [ĕl'ə-fənt] *noun,* a huge, herbivore mammal that lives in Africa and India, weighs 3-7 tons, stands 8-13 feet high, has thick skin, two tusks and a long nose called a trunk

**el-e-vate** [ĕl'ə-vāt'] *verb,* to raise to a higher level, to lift up

**el-e-va-tion** [ĕl′ə-vā′shən] *noun*, the altitude, the height of something from a reference point such as sea level

**el-e-va-tor** [ĕl′ə-vā′tər] *noun*, a machine with hoisting equipment for conveying persons, goods, etc. to or from different levels

**e-lev-en** [ĭ-lĕv′ən] *noun*, the number 11, one plus ten

**e-lev-enth** [ĭ-lĕv′ənth] *noun*, the number 11 in order, 11th

**elic-it** [ĭ-lĭs′ĭt] *verb*, to draw forth, to evoke a response

**el-i-gi-ble** [ĕl′ĭ-jə-bəl] *adjective*, qualified to be chosen

**e-lim-i-nate** [ĭ-lĭm′ə-nāt′] *verb*, to get rid of, to exclude from consideration, to leave out

**e-lite** [ĭ-lēt′] *adjective*, choice, select, superior, considered best

**elk** [ĕlk] *noun*, an animal similar to a moose, a large deer

**elm** [ĕlm] *noun*, a tall hardwood shade tree

**e-lope** [ĭ-lōp′] *verb*, to run away to marry secretly

**el-o-quence** [ĕl′ə-kwəns] *noun*, persuasive use of language

**else** [ĕls] *adverb*, 1) otherwise, instead of 2) more, in addition

**else-where** [ĕls′hwâr′] *adverb*, in some other place

**e-lude** [ĭ-lōōd′] *verb*, to get away from, to avoid, to escape

**e-lu-sive** [ĭ-lōō′sĭv] *adjective*, hard to grasp or catch, hard to remember

**em-a-nate** [ĕm′ə-nāt′] *verb*, to flow out, to radiate, to come out

**e-man-ci-pate** [ĭ-măn′sə-pāt′] *verb*, to set free from restrictions or slavery

**e-man-ci-pa-tion** [ĭ-măn′sə-pā′shən] *noun*, the act or condition of being freed from oppression or slavery

**em-bar-go** [ĕm-bär′gō] *noun*, a law that prevents a country from trading with another

**em-bark** [ĕm-bärk′] *verb*, 1) to board an airplane or boat 2) to begin an undertaking

**em-bar-rass** [ĕm-băr′əs] *verb*, to make ill at ease or self-conscious

**em-bar-rass-ment** [ĕm-băr′əs-mənt] *noun*, a feeling of self-consciousness, distress or shame

**em-bas-sy** [ĕm′bə-sē] *noun*, the building in which people work to represent their own country in another country

**em-bed** [ĕm-bĕd′] *verb*, to implant into something, to fix firmly

**em-bel-lish** [ĕm-bĕl′ĭsh] *verb*, to adorn, to make beautiful by adding decoration

**em-bez-zle** [ĕm-bĕz′əl] *verb*, to steal money from one's company or from savings accounts entrusted to one

**em-blem** [ĕm′bləm] *noun*, a badge or symbol of something

**em-bod-y** [ĕm-bŏd′ē] *verb*, 1) to include as a part of a whole 2) to represent

**em-brace** [ĕm-brās′] *verb*, 1) to hold closely in one's arms, to hug 2) to accept something, to include 3) to take up seriously

**em-broi-der** [ĕm-broi′dər] *verb*,
1) to sew ornamental patterns on
fabric 2) to embellish, to add
false details

**em-bry-o** [ĕm′brē-ō′] *noun*, an
early stage of development of an
animal or plant organism

**em-bry-on-ic** [ĕm′brē-ŏn′ĭk]
*adjective*, in an early stage of
development of an organism

**em-er-ald** [ĕm′ər-əld] *noun*, a
precious stone of rich, bright
green color, a variety of beryl

**e-merge** [ĭ-mûrj′] *verb*, to come out
or become visible, to appear

**e-mer-gen-cy** [ĭ-mûr′jən-sē] *noun*,
an unexpected event that calls
for immediate action, a crisis

**em-i-grant** [ĕm′ĭ-grənt] *noun*, a
person leaving one country to
live in another

**em-i-grate** [ĕm′ĭ-grāt′] *verb*, to
leave one country to go and live
in another

**em-i-nent** [ĕm′ə-nənt] *adjective*,
high, lofty, noted, famous

**e-mis-sion** [ĭ-mĭsh′ən] *noun*, a
substance given off into the air

**e-mo-tion** [ĭ-mō′shən] *noun*,
feelings, passion, excitement

**e-mo-tion-al** [ĭ-mō′shə-nəl]
*adjective*, excitable, showing
emotions more than usual,
fervent

**em-pa-thize** [ĕm′pə-thīz′] *verb*, to
relate to the feelings of others

**em-pa-thy** [ĕm′pə-thē] *noun*, the
ability to share the feelings of
another person

**em-per-or** [ĕm′pər-ər] *noun*, the
male ruler of a country or empire

**em-pha-sis** [ĕm′fə-sĭs] *noun*,
importance or stress given to
something

**em-pha-size** [ĕm′fə-sīz′] *verb*, to
call to someone's attention, to
bring out clearly, to stress

**em-pire** [ĕm′pīr′] *noun*, a group of
nations or states united under a
single sovereign power

**em-pir-i-cal** [ĕm-pîr′ĭ-kəl] *adjective*,
based on observation and
experience rather than theory

**em-ploy** [ĕm-ploi′] *verb*, to put into
use, to engage, to hire for work

**em-ploy-ee** [ĕm-ploi′ē] *noun*, one
who works for another for wages

**em-ploy-er** [ĕm-ploi′ər] *noun*, a
person or business that employs
or hires one or more persons

**em-ploy-ment** [ĕm-ploi′mənt]
*noun*, a job, an occupation

**em-pow-er** [ĕm-pou′ər] *verb*, to
authorize, to enable

**emp-ty** [ĕmp′tē] *adjective*,
1) having nothing inside, without
content or meaning, *verb*, 2) to
remove the contents completely,
to make vacant, to unload

**em-u-late** [ĕm′yə-lāt′] *verb*, to
follow or copy in the hope of
equaling

**en-a-ble** [ĕ-nā′bəl] *verb*, to make
possible, to empower

**en-act** [ĕn-ăkt′] *verb*, 1) to make
into law 2) to act, to perform

**e-nam-el** [ĭ-năm′əl] *noun*, 1) a
smooth glossy surface finish  2)
a hard glassy colored substance
fused to metal, glass or pottery
3) the outer covering of the teeth

**en-chant** [ĕn-chănt′] *verb*, 1) to put a spell on 2) to captivate, to delight

**en-chant-ment** [ĕn-chănt′mənt] *noun*, 1) a magical spell, 2) a fascination, appeal, charm

**en-clave** [ĕn′klāv′] *noun*, territory enclosed in a foreign land

**en-close** [ĕn-klōz′] *verb*, to put something inside of something else, to shut in on all sides

**en-clo-sure** [ĕn-klōz′hər] *noun*, something that surrounds on all sides

**en-com-pass** [ĕn-kŭm′pəs] *verb*, 1) to enclose in a circle, to surround 2) to include as a part of

**en-core** [ŏn′kôr′] *noun*, an additional performance given in response to calls from the audience, as by applause

**en-coun-ter** [ĕn-koun′tər] *noun*, 1) a casual meeting 2) a skirmish, *verb*, 3) to meet by chance 4) to confront in battle

**en-cour-age** [ĕn-kûr′ĭj] *verb*, to give praise or hope to someone, to urge

**en-cour-age-ment** [ĕn-kûr′ĭj-mənt, -kûr′-] *noun*, support, assurance

**en-croach-ment** [ĕn-krōch′mənt] *noun*, the act of overstepping boundaries or someone's rights

**en-cy-clo-pe-di-a** [ĕn-sī′klə-pē′dē-ə] *noun*, a comprehensive summary of knowledge on many subjects or a specialilzed subject written in a set of volumes

**end** [ĕnd] *noun*, 1) the farthest point or edge of anything 2) completion, finish 3) the aim, reason, design, *verb*, 4) to finish

**en-dan-ger** [ĕn-dān′jər] *verb*, to put in danger, to hazard

**en-deav-or** [ĕn-dĕv′ər] *noun*, 1) an attempt, a serious effort, *verb*, 2) to try, to make an earnest effort, to strive

**end-less** [ĕnd′lĭs] *adjective*, without end, infinite, ceaseless

**en-dorse** [ĕn-dôrs′] *verb*, 1) to write on the back of a check to cash it or give it to another person 2) to sanction, to declare approval of

**en-dow** [ĕn-dou′] *verb*, 1) to provide or bestow income or property 2) to give a quality to

**en-dow-ment** [ĕn-dou′mənt] *noun*, giving of money to provide a regular income

**en-dur-ance** [ĕn-dŏŏr′əns] *noun*, the ability to survive, the will to persevere

**en-dure** [ĕn-dŏŏr′] *verb*, to bear, to put up with, to tolerate, to suffer

**en-e-my** [ĕn′ə-mē] *noun*, a hostile person or group or country, a foe

**en-er-gize** [ĕn′ər-jīz′] *verb*, to make active, to invigorate, to give energy to

**en-er-gy** [ĕn′ər-jē] *noun*, 1) the capacity for performing work 2) power that makes machines work

**en-fold** [ĕn-fōld′] *verb*, to envelope, to enclose

**en-force** [ĕn-fôrs′] *verb*, to impose by force, to require compliance

**en-gage** [ĕn-gāj′] *verb*, 1) to put in gear 2) to fight 3) to hire 4) to become involved 5) to be busy or occupied 6) to promise

**en-gage-ment** [ĕn-gāj′mənt] *noun*,
1) an encounter, a military action
2) a promise by two people to
marry  3) an appointment

**en-gen-der** [ĕn-jĕn′dər] *verb*, to
cause, to give rise to

**en-gine** [ĕn′jĭn] *noun*, 1) a machine
that converts energy into motion
2) a locomotive 3) a source of
power

**en-gi-neer** [ĕn′jə-nîr′] *noun*, 1) one
who designs machines 2) one
who drives an engine, *verb*, 3) to
bring about an event

**Eng-lish** [ĭng′glĭsh] *adjective*,
1) the language of the people of
Britain, America, Canada,
Australia, and other countries
2) relating to or belonging to the
people of England

**en-grave** [ĕn-grāv′] *verb*, 1) to cut
into a surface  2) to leave an
impression

**en-gulf** [ĕn-gŭlf′] *verb*, to cover
completely, to close over

**en-hance** [ĕn-hăns′] *verb*, to make
better, to increase the value or
quality of something

**e-nig-ma** [ĭ-nĭg′mə] *noun*,
something hard to explain, a
puzzle, a mysterious person

**en-joy** [ĕn-joi′] *verb*, to take
pleasure in

**en-joy-ment** [ĕn-joi′mənt] *noun*,
delight, satisfaction, happiness,
pleasure

**en-large** [ĕn-lärj′] *verb*, to increase

**en-light-en** [ĕn-līt′n] *verb*, to
educate, to inform, to give
spiritual insight

**en-list** [ĕn-lĭst′] *verb*, to sign up, to
enroll in the armed forces

**en-mi-ty** [ĕn′mĭ-tē] *noun*, hatred

**e-nor-mous** [ĭ-nôr′məs] *adjective*,
monstrous, huge, immense

**e-nough** [ĭ-nŭf′] *adjective*, 1) as
much as is needed, ample,
*adverb*, 2) to an adequate or
sufficient degree, *noun*,
3) the required amount

**en-rage** [ĕn-rāj′] *verb*, to anger, to
inflame, to make furious

**en-rich** [ĕn-rĭch′] *verb*, to improve,
to make rich, to enhance

**en-roll** [ĕn-rōl′] *verb*, to register in
a list or as a student in a school,
to become a member

**en-roll-ment** [ĕn-rōl′mənt] *noun*,
the total number  registered

**en-sem-ble** [ŏn-sŏm′bəl] *noun*, the
whole, all the parts taken
together as a group

**en-sue** [ĕn-sōō′] *verb*, to make sure
or certain, to follow up

**en-sure** [ĕn-shōōr′] *verb*, to
guarantee, to make sure of, to
insure

**en-ter** [ĕn′tər] *verb*, to go into, to
become involved in

**en-ter-prise** [ĕn′tər-prīz′] *noun*, a
bold undertaking, a project or
business activity, a venture

**en-ter-tain** [ĕn′tər-tān′] *verb*, 1) to
hold the interest of the people
you are talking to or performing
for 2) to amuse, to delight
3) to have in mind

**en-ter-tain-ment** [ĕn′tər-tān′mənt]
*noun*, a performance that tries to
interest an audience

**en-thrall** [ĕn-thrôl′] *verb*, to
fascinate,  to mesmerize

**en-thu-si-asm** [ĕn-thōō′zē-ăz′əm]
*noun*, eager interest, excitement

**en-thu-si-as-tic** [ĕn-thōō′zē-ăs′tĭk] *adjective*, showing a passionate and devoted interest in a belief or idea

**en-tice** [ĕn-tīs′] *verb*, to lure, to attract, to tempt, to persuade

**en-tire** [ĕn-tīr′] *adjective*, whole, complete, with no parts missing

**en-ti-tle** [ĕn-tīt′l] *verb*, 1) to give as a right 2) to give a title to

**en-ti-ty** [ĕn′tĭ-tē] *noun*, a being, an individual, an existence

**en-trance** [ĕn′trəns] *noun*, 1) a means of entry or access 2) the act of coming in

**en-tree** [ŏn′trā] *noun*, the main dish of a meal

**en-tre-pre-neur** [ŏn′trə-prə-nûr′] *noun*, a person who starts a business and assumes financial risk for it

**en-trust** [ĕn-trŭst′] *verb*, to confide, to give to for safekeeping

**en-try** [ĕn′trē] *noun*, 1) entrance, a way in 2) an item in a log

**e-nun-ci-ate** [ĭ-nŭn′sē-āt′] *verb*, to pronounce, to state clearly

**en-vel-op** [ĕn-vĕl′əp] *verb*, to cover, to enclose, to surround

**en-vel-ope** [ĕn′və-lōp′] *noun*, a folded paper cover like a pocket for a letter

**en-vi-ous** [ĕn′vē-əs] *adjective*, jealous, full of envy

**en-vi-ron-ment** [ĕn-vī′rən-mənt] *noun*, the surroundings or place in which something lives

**en-vy** [ĕn′vē] *noun*, 1) a feeling of anger or bitterness because someone has more of something, or a better life, *verb*, 2) to want something someone has, to be jealous

**e-on** [ē′ŏn′, ē′ən] *noun*, a billion years, a long time

**e-phem-er-al** [ĭ-fĕm′ər-əl] *adjective*, short-lived, fleeting

**ep-ic** [ĕp′ĭk] *noun*, a long poem about a hero and his deeds

**ep-i-dem-ic** [ĕp′ĭ-dĕm′ĭk] *adjective*, 1) affecting many in the community, widespread, *noun*, 2) a contagious disease infecting many among the population

**ep-i-der-mis** [ĕp′ĭ-dûr′mĭs] *noun*, the outer layer of the skin

**ep-i-gram** [ĕp′ĭ-grăm′] *noun*, a pithy phrase, a witty saying

**ep-i-lep-sy** [ĕp′ə-lĕp′sē] *noun*, a disorder of the nervous system accompanied by convulsions and loss of consiousness

**ep-i-logue** [ĕp′ə-lôg′] *noun*, a short conclusion added to the end of a book, play, etc.

**ep-i-sode** [ĕp′ĭ-sōd′] *noun*, 1) a distinctive occurrence 2) a separate incident in a longer story or poem

**ep-i-taph** [ĕp′ĭ-tăf′] *noun*, an inscription on a monument in memory of a dead person who is buried there

**e-pit-o-me** [ĭ-pĭt′ə-mē] *noun*, a typical or perfect example of a group or type

**ep-och** [ĕp′ək] *noun*, 1) a time period characterized by a distinctive development 2) a date marking the beginning of a new period of history 3) a division of geological time

**e-qual** [ē′kwəl] *adjective*, 1) being the same as 2) alike, *noun*, 3) something valued as the same 4) a symbol = that shows both sides have the same value, *verb*, 5) to be as good as someone or something else

**e-qual-i-ty** [ĭ-kwŏl′ĭ-tē] *noun*, the state of being the same as

**e-qual-ize** [ē′kwə-līz′] *verb*, to make even, to balance

**e-qual-ly** [ē′kwə-lē] *adverb*, in an equal way, to an equal degree

**e-qua-tion** [ĭ-kwā′shən] *noun*, 1) the act or process of considering or making equal 2) a statement that the values of two mathematical expressions are equal (=)

**e-qua-tor** [ĭ-kwā′tər] *noun*, the imaginary band circling the middle of the earth, at an equal distance from the North and South Poles

**e-ques-tri-an** [ĭ-kwĕs′trē-ən] *adjective,* 1) relating to horseback riding, *noun*, 2) a rider on horseback

**e-qui-lib-ri-um** [ē′kwə-lĭb′rē-əm] *noun*, a state of balance between opposing forces

**e-qui-lat-er-al tri-angle** [ē′kwə-lăt′ər-əl trī′ăng′gəl] *noun*, a triangle with 60 degree angles and three equal sides

**e-qui-nox** [ē′kwə-nŏks′] *noun*, either of two times in the year when night and day are of equal length: March 21; October 21

**e-quip** [ĭ-kwĭp′] *verb*, to provide what is needed, to outfit

**e-quip-ment** [ĭ-kwĭp′mənt] *noun*, tools, supplies, etc., needed for a job or a special activity

**eq-ui-ty** [ĕk′wĭ-tē] *noun*, 1) the value of property or stock after subtracting liens against it 2) just, impartial, fairness

**e-quiv-a-lent** [ĭ-kwĭv′ə-lənt] *noun*, 1) equal in value or worth 2) similar in force, measure, meaning or effect, identical

**e-quiv-o-cate** [ĭ-kwĭv′ə-kāt′] *verb*, to use deliberately evasive language

**e-ra** [îr′ə, ĕr′ə] *noun*, a distinct period of time, or history

**e-rad-i-cate** [ĭ-răd′ĭ-kāt′] *verb*, to destroy completely, to get rid of

**e-rase** [ĭ-rās′] *verb*, to rub out, to remove all traces of

**e-rect** [ĭ-rĕkt′] *adjective*, 1) standing straight, upright, *verb*, 2) to build or construct

**er-mine** [ûr′mĭn] *noun*, a small weasel with white fur and a black-tipped tail in winter

**e-rode** [ĭ-rōd′] *verb*, 1) to wear away gradually 2) to destroy slowly

**e-ro-sion** [ĭ-rō′zhən] *noun*, the process of wearing down, breaking up, and carrying off land, soil, and rock, by wind and water

**err** [ûr, ĕr] *verb*, to be mistaken

**er-rand** [ĕr′ənd] *noun*, a short trip to accomplish a task

**er-rat-ic** [ĭ-răt′ĭk] *adjective*, irregular, inconsistent

**er-ro-ne-ous** [ĭ-rō′nē-əs] *adjective*, false, incorrect

115

**er-ror** [ĕr'ər] *noun*, 1) a belief in what is untrue 2) an act involving a departure from truth and accuracy, a mistake

**er-satz** [er'säts] *adjective*, 1) made or used as a substitute 2) not real or genuine

**er-u-dite** [ĕr'yə-dīt] *adjective*, learned, well-educated, scholarly

**e-rupt** [ĭ-rŭpt'] *verb*, 1) to burst out suddenly, to explode 2) to express an emotion suddenly and forcefully

**es-ca-la-tor** [ĕs'kə-lā'tər] *noun*, moving stairs attached to a circulating belt

**es-cape** [ĭ-skāp'] *noun*, 1) a means to get away from danger or unpleasantness, *verb*, 2) to free oneself

**es-chew** [ĕs-chōō'] *verb*, to avoid, to keep away from, to evade

**es-cort** [ĕs'kôrt'] *noun*, 1) a guide, an attendant, *verb*, 2) to accompany someone, to go with them as protection or an honor

**es-crow** [ĕs'krō'] *noun*, money, a bond or a deed held by a third person until a specified condition is met

**Es-ki-mo** [ĕs'kə-mō'] *noun*, a member of a people living in Russia, Alaska, Canada, and Greenland, the Inuit

**e-soph-a-gus** [ĭ-sŏf'ə-gəs] *noun*, the tube that leads from the pharynx to the stomach

**es-o-ter-ic** [ĕs'ə-tĕr'ĭk] *adjective*, understood only by a chosen few

**es-pe-cial-ly** [ĕ-spĕsh'ə-lē] *adverb*, particularly, to a great extent

**es-pi-o-nage** [ĕs'pē-ə-näzh'] *noun*, of spying, the practice of spying

**es-say** [ĕs'ā', ĕ-sā'] *noun*, 1) a literary composition expressing personal observations, *verb*, 2) to try out, to test, to attempt

**es-sence** [ĕs'əns] *noun*, 1) the real character or nature of something 2) perfume

**es-sen-tial** [ĭ-sĕn'shəl] *adjective*, 1) indispensable 2) of or pertaining to the essential nature, *noun*, 3) a necessity, the basic elements

**es-tab-lish** [ĭ-stăb'lĭsh] *verb*, 1) to make stable or firm, to settle or set up, *verb*, 2)to prove to be true

**es-tab-lish-ment** [ĭ-stăb'lĭsh-mənt] *noun*, 1) a place of business or residence 2) an organization

**es-tate** [ĭ-stāt'] *noun*, 1) a property 2) property left at someone's death

**es-teem** [ĭ-stēm'] *noun*, 1) respect, honor, *verb*, 2) to regard favorably

**es-ti-mate** [ĕs'tə-mĭt'] *noun*, 1) an educated guess, an approximation, [ĕs'tə-māt']*verb*, 2) to calculate the approximate value or amount of something 3) to give an approximate rather than an exact answer, to guess

**et cet-er-a** [ĕt sĕt'ər-ə] *abbr.* **etc.,** and so on

**etch** [ĕch] *verb*, to engrave by biting out with an acid

**e-ter-nal** [ĭ-tûr'nəl] *adjective*, endless, infinite, forever

**e-ter-ni-ty** [ĭ-tûr'nĭ-tē] *noun*, forever

**eth-i-cal** [ĕth'ĭ-kəl] *adjective*, having or relating to morals

**eth-ics** [ĕth'ĭks] *noun*, *plural*, rules of moral principles governing a group

**eth-nic** [ĕth′nĭk] *adjective*, relating to different races, ancestry, or culture

**eth-nol-o-gy** [ĕth-nŏl′ə-jē] *noun*, the study of different races and their characteristics

**et-i-quette** [ĕt′ĭ-kĕt′] *noun*, good manners, the rules for polite behavior

**et-y-mol-o-gy** [ĕt′ə-mŏl′ə-jē] *noun*, the study of the origin and derivation of words

**eu-gen-ics** [yōō-jĕn′ĭks]*noun*, the study of genetic traits by controlling breeding

**eu-lo-gy** [yōō′lə-jē] *noun*, a speech or written tribute lauding a deceased person

**eu-phe-mism** [yōō′fə-mĭz′əm] *noun*, a mild expression to replace an offensive remark

**eu-re-ka** [yŏŏ-rē′kə] *exclamation*, an expression of triumph concerning a discovery

**Eu-rope** [yŏŏr′əp] *noun*, one of the seven continents, the second smallest continent

**eu-tha-na-sia** [yōō′thə-nā′zhə] *noun*, mercy killing

**e-vac-u-ate** [ĭ-văk′yōō-āt′] *verb*, to abandon, to empty out

**e-vade** [ĭ-vād′] *verb*, to avoid, to escape by cleverness

**e-val-u-ate** [ĭ-văl′yōō-āt′] *verb*, to measure the value, to appraise

**e-vap-o-rate** [ĭ-văp′ə-rāt′] *verb*, 1) to turn from solid or liquid into vapor 2) to lose moisture, to dry up 3) to vanish

**e-vap-o-ra-tion** [ĭ-văp′ə-rā′shən] *noun*, the process in which water disappears from a surface as it becomes vapor, the loss of water into the air

**e-va-sive** [ĭ-vā′sĭv] *adjective*, 1) avoiding something, elusive 2) intentionally not answering

**eve** [ēv] *noun*, the night before

**e-ven** [ē′vən] *adjective*, 1) level, flat, smooth 2) able to be divided by two 3) equal, *adverb*, 4) more than expected 5) indeed 6) exactly

**eve-ning** [ēv′nĭng] *noun*, the time between the end of the afternoon and bedtime, dusk

**e-ven-ly** [ē′vən-lē] *adverb*, in an equal way, smoothly

**e-vent** [ĭ-vĕnt′] *noun*, something that takes place, an activity

**e-ven-tu-al-ly** [ĭ-vĕn′chōō-ə-lē] *adverb*, at long last, after the passing of some time

**ev-er** [ĕv′ər] *adverb*, 1) always, at all times 2) at any time

**ev-er-green** [ĕv′ər-grēn′] *noun*, a plant that keeps its leaves all year long, including holly, rhododendrons, pine trees, and others

**eve-ry** [ĕv′rē] *adjective*, each, all possible

**eve-ry-bod-y** [ĕv′rē-bŏd′ē] *pronoun*, every person

**eve-ry-day** [ĕv′rē-dā′] *adjective*, ordinary, commonplace, normal

**eve-ry-one** [ĕv′rē-wŭn′] *pronoun*, each person, everybody

**eve-ry-thing** [ĕv′rē-thĭng′]*pronoun*, all together, all things

**eve-ry-where** [ĕv′rē-hwâr′] *adverb*, in every place

**ev-i-dence** [ĕv′ĭ-dəns] *noun*, 1) one or more facts or items 2) testimony 3) the basis on which one believes something to be true

**ev-i-dent** [ĕv′ĭ-dənt] *adjective*, clear, apparent, obvious

**e-vil** [ē′vəl] *adjective*, very bad, corrupt, immoral, wicked

**e-voke** [ĭ-vōk′] *verb*, 1) to call forth, 2) to bring to mind

**ev-o-lu-tion** [ĕv′ə-lōō′shən] *noun*, the natural process of growth and change, development

**e-volve** [ĭ-vŏlv′] *verb*, to come into being, to develop gradually

**ex-ac-er-bate** [ĭg-zăs′ər-bāt′] *verb*, to make worse

**ex-act** [ĭg-zăkt′] *adjective*, precise, correct, completely accurate

**ex-ag-ger-ate** [ĭg-zăj′ə-rāt′] *verb*, to enlarge beyond the bounds of truth, to overstate

**ex-alt** [ĭg-zôlt′] *verb*, to praise, to elevate, to raise in rank

**ex-am-i-na-tion** [ĭg-zăm′ə-nā′shən] *noun*, scrutiny, inquiry, a test

**ex-am-ine** [ĭg-zăm′ĭn] *verb*, 1) to inspect carefully, to look at every point 2) to scrutinize 3) to question

**ex-am-ple** [ĭg-zăm′pəl] *noun*, 1) a model, a sample of what others are like 2) a person punished as a warning to others

**ex-as-per-ate** [ĭg-zăs′pə-rāt′] *verb*, to irritate, to provoke, to enrage

**ex-ceed** [ĭk-sēd′] *verb*, 1) to pass beyond the measure of something, 2) to surpass

**ex-cel** [ĭk-sĕl′] *verb*, to be better than others at something, to do well

**ex-cel-lent** [ĕk′sə-lənt] *adjective*, superior, very good

**ex-cel-si-or** [ĕk′sə-l′sē′ər] *adjective*, higher, always upward

**ex-cept** [ĭk-sĕpt′] *preposition*, 1) apart from, not including, *verb*, 2) to exclude

**ex-cep-tion** [ĭk-sĕp′shən] *noun*, 1) a circumstance not conforming to the general rule 2) an omission

**ex-cep-tion-al** [ĭk-sĕp′shə-nəl] *adjective*, superior, unusually good

**ex-cerpt** [ĕk′sûrpt′] *noun*, section that has been removed from a longer text

**ex-cess** [ĭk-sĕs′] *adjective*, 1) extra, more than expected, *noun*, 2) an amount that is more than enough 3) immoderate behavior

**ex-change** [ĭks-chānj′] *noun*, 1) the process of settling accounts or trading items between parties, *verb*, 2) to change something for something else, to replace, to trade

**ex-cise** [ĕk′sīz′] *noun*, a tax levied upon specific articles and services within a country

**ex-cite** [ĭk-sīt′] *verb*, to be energized or to have strong feeling

**ex-cite-ment** [ĭk-sīt′mənt] *noun*, 1) ado, commotion 2) a thrill

**ex-claim** [ĭk-sklām′] *verb*, to speak suddenly and with strong feeling

**ex-cla-ma-tion mark** [ĕk′sklə-mā′shən märk] *noun*,

the sign ! used to show surprise, humor, or strong feeling

**ex-clude** [ĭk-sklōōd′] *verb*, to keep out

**ex-clu-sive** [ĭk-sklōō′sĭv] *adjective*, restricted to a particular group of people

**ex-cru-ci-at-ing** [ĭk skrōō′shē-ā′tĭng] *adjective*, very painful, agonizing

**ex-cur-sion** [ĭk-skûr′zhən] *noun*, a journey chiefly for recreation, a brief tour, an outing

**ex-cuse** [ĭk′skyōōs] *noun*, 1) a reason, a defense, [ĭk-skyōōz′] *verb*, 2) to free, to allow an interruption 3) to give a reason for a fault

**ex-e-cute** [ĕk′sĭ-kyōōt′] *verb*, 1) to kill someone legally as punishment for a crime 2) to take action

**ex-e-cu-tion** [ĕk′sĭ-kyōō′shən] *noun*, 1) accomplishment, implementation 2) the act of putting to death a condemned person

**ex-ec-u-tive** [ĭg-zĕk′yə-tĭv] *noun*, 1) a business person responsible for making decisions, a manager 2) one of the three branches of the United States government

**ex-em-pla-ry** [ĭg-zĕm′plə-rē] *adjective*, commendable, serving as a desirable model

**ex-em-pli-fy** [ĭg-zĕm′plə-fī′] *verb*, to show or illustrate by example

**ex-empt** [ĭg-zĕmpt′] *verb*, to excuse from an obligation or rule, to make immune

**ex-er-cise** [ĕk′sər-sīz′] *noun*, 1) an activity used to train the body,

*verb*, 2) to train the body by using one's muscles

**ex-ert** [ĭg-zûrt′] *verb*, 1) to make an effort 2) to bring to bear

**ex-er-tion** [ĭg-zûr′shən] *noun*, hard work, a strong effort

**ex-hale** [ĕks-hāl′] *verb*, to breathe out, to blow, to emit

**ex-haust** [ĭg-zôst′] *verb*, 1) to be thorough covering all points 2) to use up 3) the waste fumes from an engine

**ex-haus-tion** [ĭg-zôs′chən] *noun*, fatique, tiredness

**ex-haus-tive** [ĭg-zô′stĭv] *adjective*, complete, thorough, attending to every detail, comprehensive

**ex-hib-it** [ĭg-zĭb′ĭt] *noun*, 1) a display of a collection, *verb*, 2) to display

**ex-hi-bi-tion** [ĕk′sə-bĭsh′ən] *noun*, a public display of art or other items

**ex-hil-a-ra-tion** [ĭg-zĭl′ə-rā′shən] *noun*, a feeling of excitement and joy

**ex-i-gen-cy** [ĕk′sə-jən-sē] *noun*, a pressing necessity, a case demanding immediate action

**ex-ile** [ĕg′zīl′] *noun*, 1) one who is not allowed to live in his or her own country as a form of punishment, *verb*, 2) to be forced out of a place and not allowed to return

**ex-ist** [ĭg-zĭst′] *verb*, 1) to be, to live, to be present, to occur

**ex-ist-ence** [ĭg-zĭs′təns] *noun*, 1) state of being actual, life 2) reality 3) all that which lives

**ex-it** [ĕg′zĭt] *noun*, 1) a way to go out, the door leading out of a building 2) the ramp leading off a major highway, *verb*, 3) to leave, to go out, to depart

**ex-o-dus** [ĕk′sə-dəs] *noun*, mass departure of people, migration

**ex-o-skel-e-ton** [ĕk′sō-skĕl′ĭ-tn] *noun*, an outer structure that provides protection to an insect, shellfish, turtle, etc.

**ex-ot-ic** [ĭg-zŏt′ĭk] *adjective*, strange, interesting, or unusual

**ex-pand** [ĭk-spănd′] *verb*, to grow or make larger, to extend

**ex-panse** [ĭk-spăns′] *noun*, a large open space, an area of land

**ex-pa-tri-ate** [ĕk-spā′trē-āt′] *noun*, someone who left his native land

**ex-pect** [ĭk-spĕkt′] *verb*, to wait for something that is supposed to happen, to anticipate

**ex-pec-ta-tion** [ĕk′spĕk-tā′shən] *noun*, anticipation, calculation

**ex-pe-di-en-cy** [ĭk-spē′dē-ən-sē] *noun*, that which is practical

**ex-pe-di-tion** [ĕk′spĭ-dĭsh′ən] *noun*, a journey or excursion for a specific purpose, a trip

**ex-pe-di-tious** [ĕk′spĭ-dĭsh′əs] *adjective*, efficient and speedy

**ex-pel** [ĭk-spĕl′] *verb*, to drive out

**ex-pend-i-ture** [ĭk-spĕn′də-chər] *noun*, a laying out, as of money or labor, the cost

**ex-pense** [ĭk-spĕns′] *noun*, 1) cost, payment 2) detriment, sacrifice

**ex-pen-sive** [ĭk-spĕn′sĭv] *adjective*, costing a lot of money

**ex-pe-ri-ence** [ĭk-spîr′ē-əns] *noun*, 1) an encounter that provokes a reaction 2) knowledge gained by observation or trial, *verb*, 3) to live, to feel by participating

**ex-per-i-ment** [ĭk-spĕr′ə-mənt] *noun*, 1) a test done to see if something is valid or true, *verb*, 2) to carry out a plan in order to test a prediction

**ex-pert** [ĕk′spûrt′] *noun*, a very knowledgeable person in his or her particular field, an authority

**ex-per-tise** [ĕk′spûr-tēz′] *noun*, specialized knowledge or skill

**ex-pi-ra-tion** [ĕk′spə-rā′shən] *noun*, a coming to an end

**ex-pire** [ĭk-spīr′] *verb*, 1) to end, to cease to exist 2) to breath out

**ex-plain** [ĭk-splān′] *verb*, to clarify or to give a reason, to account for

**ex-pla-na-tion** [ĕk′splə-nā′shən] *noun*, the act of interpreting an action or giving a description

**ex-ple-tive** [ĕk′splĭ-tĭv] *noun*, a curse word, an obscenity

**ex-plic-it** [ĭk-splĭs′ĭt] *adjective*, plain, definite, expressed clearly

**ex-plode** [ĭk-splōd′] *verb*, 1) to release energy with a loud noise as something is destroyed by bursting outward 2) to increase suddenly

**ex-ploit** [ĕk′sploit′] *noun*, 1) a deed or act, especially one of renown, *verb*, 2) to make use of for one's own profit

**ex-plo-ra-tion** [ĕk′splə-rā′shən] *noun*, a search in order to discover, an investigation

**ex-plore** [ĭk-splôr′] *verb*, 1) to look into closely, to examine or investigate 2) to go into new or unknown places to find new things and learn about them

**ex-plo-sion** [ĭk-splō′zhən] *noun* blast, a bomb bursting, a

**ex-plo-sive** [ĭk-splō′sĭv] *adjective*, flammable, combustible

**ex-port** [ĭk-spôrt′] *noun*, 1) something sold abroad as part of international trade, *verb*, 2) merchandise conveyed from one country to another

**ex-pose** [ĭk-spōz′] *verb* 1) to make something easy to see 2) to reveal, to make known 3) to leave unprotected

**ex-po-si-tion** [ĕk′spə-zĭsh′ən] *noun*, a statement of intent, a public exhibition or display

**ex-po-sure** [ĭk-spō′zhər] *noun*, not sheltered from the elements such as cold, sun, rain, wind, etc.

**ex-press** [ĭk-sprĕs′] *adjective*, 1) the fastest means available, *verb*, 2) to indicate, to show

**ex-pres-sion** [ĭk-sprĕsh′ən] *noun*, 1) the look on someone's face, a facial gesture 2) a remark, a cliché 3) a way of showing feelings or emotion through actions or words

**ex-pul-sion** [ĭk-spŭl′shən] *noun*, a driving or forcing out

**ex-punge** [ĭk-spŭnj′] *verb*, to cancel, to remove

**ex-quis-ite** [ĕk′skwĭ-zĭt] *adjective*, 1) carefully crafted or executed, 2) delicately beautiful

**ex-tend** [ĭk-stĕnd′] *verb*, 1) to stretch out, to lengthen 2) to offer

**ex-ten-sion** [ĭk-stĕn′shən] *noun*, a part added on

**ex-ten-sive** [ĭk-stĕn′sĭv] *adjective*, having wide reach, broad

**ex-tent** [ĭk-stĕnt′] *noun*, the area covered or affected by something, the amount

**ex-ten-u-ate** [ĭk-stĕn′yōō-āt′] *adjective*, out of reach, beyond your grasp or control

**ex-te-ri-or** [ĭk-stûr′ē-ər] *noun*, 1) external, outward 2) on the surface or appearance

**ex-ter-mi-nate** [ĭk-stûr′mə-nāt′] *verb*, to drive out, to destroy completely, to kill

**ex-ter-nal** [ĭk-stûr′nəl] *adjective*, 1) on or relating to the outside of the subject 2) the outer part

**ex-tinct** [ĭk-stĭngkt′] *adjective*, no longer existing or living

**ex-tin-guish** [ĭk-stĭng′gwĭsh] *verb*, to put out as a fire or a light

**ex-tort** [ĭk-stôrt′] *verb*, to get money by making threats and by intimidation or coercion

**ex-tor-tion** [ĭk-stôr′shən] *noun*, demanding money by making threats, blackmail

**ex-tra** [ĕk′strə] *adjective*, 1) a surplus, more than needed, *adverb*, 2) in addition

**ex-tract** [ĭk-străkt′] *verb*, 1) to take out 2) to distill or remove

**ex-tra-di-tion** [ĕk′strə-dĭsh′ən] *noun*, the surrender of a prisoner by another authority

**ex-tra-ne-ous** [ĭk-strā′nē-əs] *adjective*, not essential, foreign

**ex-traor-di-nar-y** [ĭk-strôr′dn-ĕr′ē, ĕk′strə-ôr′-] *adjective*, unusual, rare, exceptional, uncommon

**ex-tra-ter-res-tri-al** [ĕkstrətə′restrēəl] *adjective*, of or from outside the earth's atmosphere

**ex-trav-a-gant** [ĭk-străv′ə-gənt] *adjective*, wasteful, exceeding reasonable limits, spending too much, very expensive

**ex-treme** [ĭk-strēm′] *adjective*, 1) to the highest or a very high degree 2) the utmost limit or degree, radical 3) final, last

**ex-trem-i-ty** [ĭk-strĕm′ĭ-tē] *noun*, 1) the end or the boundary 2) an appendage such as a hand or foot

**ex-tri-cate** [ĕk′strĭ-kāt′] *verb*, to clear away, to free, to untangle

**ex-trin-sic** [ĭk-strĭn′sĭk] *adjective*, external, from outside

**ex-u-ber-ant** [ĭg-zōō′bər-ənt] *adjective*, joyful, high spirits

**ex-ude** [ĭg-zōōd′] *verb*, to discharge, to ooze, to give forth

**ex-ul-ta-tion** [ĕk′səl-tā′shən] *noun*, joy, celebration, showing delight

**eye** [ī] *noun*, 1) the organ located on the head used to see 2) the tiny hole at the end of a needle

**eye-lash** [ī′lăsh′] *noun*, one of the hairs growing on the eyelid

**eye-lid** [ī′lĭd′] *noun*, the skin which covers the eye

# F

**fa-ble** [fā′bəl] *noun*, a fictitious short story with a moral in which animals talk

**fab-ric** [făb′rĭk] *noun*, 1) any cloth that is woven or knit from fibers 2) make up, substance

**fab-ri-cate** [făb′rĭ-kāt′] *verb*, 1) to build, to construct 2) to lie

**fab-u-lous** [făb′yə-ləs] *adjective*, marvelous, wonderful, amazing

**fa-cade** [fə-säd′] *noun*, the decorated entrance of a building

**face** [fās] *noun*, 1) the front of the head, with the eyes, nose and mouth 2) the front of something 3) a flat surface of a space figure, *verb*, 4) to stand in front of or turn to confront

**fac-et** [făs′ĭt] *noun*, 1) one of the polished plane surfaces of a precious stone 2) an aspect of a subject, a side, a feature

**fa-ce-tious** [fə-sē′shəs] *adjective*, joking, sportive, kidding around, not serious, flippant, glib

**fac-ile** [făs′əl] *adjective*, easy

**fa-cil-i-tate** [fə-sĭl′ĭ-tāt′] *verb*, to make easier, to aid, to help

**fac-sim-i-le** [făk-sĭm′ə-lē] *noun*, an exact copy or likeness of anything, a reproduction

**fact** [făkt] *noun*, an indisputable piece of information, something that is true, a certainty

**fac-tion** [făk′shən] *noun*, a dissenting party, an inner circle, a clique, a group within a group

**fac-tious** [făk′shəs] *adjective*, broken into groups

**fac-tor** [făk′tər] *noun*, 1) a condition that causes a result 2) the numbers multiplied or divided to give a product

**fac-to-ry** [făk′tə-rē] *noun*, a building where products are manufactured

**fac-ul-ty** [făk′əl-tē] *noun*, 1) the professors in an institution of higher learning 2) a physical or mental ability, talent, capacity

**fad** [făd] *noun*, temporary fashion or style, the "in" thing

**fade** [fād] *verb*, to lose light or color, to become dull or dim

**Fahr-en-heit** [făr′ən-hīt′] *adjective*, of or relating to the temperature scale in which the freezing point of water is 32 degrees and the boiling point of water is 212 degrees under normal atmospheric pressure

**fail** [fāl] *verb*, to not accomplish what you set out to

**fail-ure** [fāl′yər] *noun*, lack of success, a debacle

**faint** [fānt] *adjective*, 1) hard to see, dim 2) inaudible, indistinct, soft, *verb*, 3) to feel weak or dizzy, to collapse unconscious

**fair** [fâr] *adjective*, 1) treating everyone equally, not favoring one more than another, 2) so-so, mediocre 3) pale, light-skinned complexion, *noun*, 4) a gathering for buying and selling goods

**fair-y** [fâr′ē] *noun*, an imaginary person with magical powers

**faith** [fāth] *noun*, 1) a belief in something that is not seen, relying on trust 2) religion

**faith-ful** [fāth′fəl] *adjective*, loyal, trustworthy, full of faith

**fake** [fāk] *noun*, 1) forgery, imitation, *verb*, 2) to pretend, to falsify 3) to counterfeit

**fall** [fôl] *noun*, 1) the season of autumn, *verb*, 2) to come down, to tumble 3) to lose power

**fal-lacy** [făl′ə-sē] *noun*, an error in reasoning, an erroneous idea

**fal-li-ble** [făl′ə-bəl] *adjective*, liable to err, vulnerable

**fall line** *noun*, a place where the height of the land drops

suddenly and is usually marked by many waterfalls and rapids

**false** [fôls] *adjective*, 1) not true 2) artificial, not real

**false-hood** [fôls′hŏŏd′] *noun*, a lie

**fal-ter** [fôl′tər] *verb*, to hesitate

**fame** [fām] *noun*, *no plural*, wide recognition, to become a household name, celebrity

**fa-mil-iar** [fə-mĭl′yər] *adjective*, to have some knowledge of something or someone

**fam-i-ly** [făm′ə-lē] *noun*, 1) a parent or parents and children 2) all of a person's relatives

**fam-ine** [făm′ĭn] *noun*, 1) general scarcity of food 2) extreme scarcity of something

**fam-ish-ed** [făm′ĭshd] *adjective*, extremely hungry

**fa-mous** [fā′məs] *adjective*, well known, celebrated, noted

**fan** [făn] *noun*, 1) any device designed to circulate air 2) an ardent follower or supporter, *verb*, 3) to move air, to cool with a fan 4) to spread out

**fa-nat-ic** [fə-năt′ĭk] *adjective*, 1) carrying an interest or enthusiasm to extremes, *noun*, 2) a person with a very strong interest in something

**fan-cy** [făn′sē] *adjective*, elaborate, unusually decorated, not plain

**fang** [făng] *noun*, a long sharp tooth, the incisor

**fan-tas-tic** [făn-tăs′tĭk] *adjective*, imaginary, fanciful, unreal

**fan-ta-sy** [făn′tə-sē] *noun*, a daydream, an imaginary situation, make believe

**far** [fär] *adjective*, 1) at a great distance, not near or close by, *adverb*, 2) exceedingly 3) a certain point

**fare** [fâr] *noun*, 1) money paid for a trip by bus or train for example 2) food and drink *verb* 3) to get along well

**fare-well** [fâr-wĕl'] *noun*, goodbye, adieu, parting

**farm** [färm] *noun*, buildings or land in the country where people grow food as cash crops or raise animals to sell

**farm-er** [fär'mər] *noun*, a person who owns and or cultivates crops on a portion of land

**far-ther** [fär'thər] *preposition*, to be far away, in a remote place

**fas-ci-nate** [făs'ə-nāt'] *verb*, to attract and hold interest, to captivate, to excite

**fas-ci-na-tion** [făs'ə-nā'shən] *noun*, personal attraction, infatuation

**fash-ion** [făsh'ən] *noun*, 1) clothing or articles that are in style, in vogue, *verb*, 2) to shape or form

**fast** [făst] *adjective*, 1) quick, rapid 2) fixed in place, cannot move, *verb*, 3) to go for an extended period of time without eating

**fas-tid-i-ous** [făst'ĭd'ē-əs]*adjective*, hard to please, very critical

**fat** [făt] *adjective*, 1) with a wide round shape 2) thick, *noun*, 3) an oily substance from cooked meat

**fa-tal** [fāt'l] *adjective*, in a manner that results in death, lethal

**fate** [fāt] *noun*, an invisible hand that seems to cause certain things to happen over which people have no control, destiny

**fa-ther** [fä'thər] *noun*, the male parent

**fa-ther-in-law** [fä'thər-ĭn-lô'] *noun*, the father of your wife or husband

**fath-om** [făth'əm] *verb*, to understand, to comprehend

**fa-tigue** [fə-tēg'] *noun*, 1) the condition of being very tired or exhausted, *verb*, 2) to become or make tired

**fau-cet** [fô'sĭt] *noun*, a fixture for drawing liquid from a pipe and regulating the flow

**fault** [fôlt] *noun*, 1) mistake, failure to perform a duty 2) a fracture in the earth's surface causing a displacement 3) a defect

**fa-vor** [fā'vər] *noun*, 1) an act of kindness, *verb*, 2) to prefer, to patronize, to fancy, to like

**fa-vor-ite** [fā'vər-ĭt] *adjective*, something preferred above others, liked the best

**fawn** [fôn] *noun*, a young deer less than a year old

**fear** [fîr] *noun*, 1) expecting harm, *verb*, 2) to dread or be afraid of

**fear-ful** [fîr'fəl] *adjective*, afraid, timid, frightened, scared

**fea-si-ble** [fē'zə-bəl] *adjective*, capable of being done, practical, possible, achievable

**feast** [fēst] *noun*, 1) an elaborate meal, a banquet, *verb*, 2) to eat large amounts of food and drink

**feat** [fēt] *noun*, an accomplishment, a remarkable achievement

**feath-er** [fĕth'ər] *noun*, a soft thing which covers birds, like a toothpick covered with fine hairs

**fea-ture** [fē'chər] *noun*, 1) a distinctive aspect on a person, a characteristic 2) an article in the newspaper

**Feb-ru-ar-y** [fĕb'rōō-ĕr'ē] *noun*, the second month in the year, having 28 days but 29 every four years on the leap year

**fed** [fĕd] *past tense* of **feed**

**fed-er-al** [fĕd'ər-əl] *adjective*, belonging or pertaining to a state formed by the consolidation of several states

**fed-er-a-tion** [fĕd'ə-rā'shən] *noun*, an alliance, an association

**fee** [fē] *noun*, money charged for something, the cost or expense

**fee-ble** [fē'bəl] *adjective*, weak, frail, unsteady, infirm

**feed** [fēd] *noun*, 1) food for animals, *verb*, 2) to give someone food, to nourish

**feel** [fēl] *verb*, 1) to perceive in a way other than your five senses, to sense with emotions 2) to acknowledge with the sense of touch 3) to form an opinion

**feign** [fān] *verb*, to pretend

**feist-y** [fī'stē] *adjective*, very active or spirited, exuberant

**fe-lic-i-ty** [fĭ-lĭs'ĭ-tē] *adjective*, the state of being happy

**fell** [fĕl] *adjective*, 1) cruel, deadly, *verb*, 2) *past tense* of **fall**

**fel-low** [fĕl'ō] *noun*, 1) a man 2) a companion, a comrade

**fel-on** [fĕl'ən] *noun*, a person convicted of a serious crime

**fel-o-ny** [fĕl'ə-nē] *noun*, any offense that is punishable by confinement in prison

**felt** [fĕlt] *noun*, 1) a soft synthetic fabric without a nap 2) the *past tense* of **feel**

**fe-male** [fē'māl'] *adjective*, 1) referring to a woman, feminine, *noun*, 2) attributes of a woman and characteristics

**fem-i-nine** [fĕm'ə-nĭn] *adjective*, of or pertaining to the female sex

**fence** [fĕns] *noun*, 1) a partition made of wood or wire 2) a person who receives stolen goods, *verb*, 3) to put in an enclosure 4) to duel with a sword

**fend-er** [fĕn'dər] *noun*, the strip of metal over the wheels of a car, bicycle, or other vehicle to protect against mud or water

**fer-ment** [fər-mĕnt'] *verb*, to ripen, to acidify with bacteria

**fern** [fûrn] *noun*, a bright green plant that does not have flowers, and grows in shady places

**fe-ro-cious** [fə-rō'shəs] *adjective*, savage, fierce, cruel

**fer-ret** [fĕr'ĭt] *noun*, 1) a small rodent like a weasel, *verb*, 2) to drive or hunt out of hiding

**fer-ry** [fĕr'ē] *noun*, a boat used to transport people or goods from one side to the other

**fer-tile** [fûr'tl] *adjective*, fruitful, able to produce abundantly

**fer-ti-lize** [fûr'tl-īz'] *verb*, to make ready for planting by providing proper amounts of nitrogen, potash, oxygen, etc.

**fer-vent** [fûr'vənt] *adjective*, hot, showing intense feeling

**fes-ter** [fĕs'tər] *verb*, to become worse due to infection or anger

**fes-ti-val** [fĕs′tə-vəl] *noun*, 1) a big party that takes place on a holiday or at another special time 2) a program of cultural events 3) a carnival

**fetch** [fĕch] *verb*, 1) to go after something and bring it back, to retrieve 2) to bring in

**fet-ish** [fĕt′ĭsh] *noun*, 1) a quirky habit based on a belief in magic 2) a compulsion

**feud** [fyo͞od] *noun*, 1) a long bitter quarrel, especially between two families, verb, 2) to fight like enemies, to quarrel

**fe-ver** [fē′vər] *noun*, when the body temperature rises above 98.6 degrees the body is trying to fight off bacteria and infection

**few** [fyo͞o] *adjective*, three or more, not many, hardly any

**fi-an-cé** [fē′än-sā′, fē-än′sā′] *noun*, a man engaged to be married

**fi-an-cée** [fē′än-sā′] *noun*, a woman engaged to be married

**fi-as-co** [fē-ăs′kō] *noun*, a situation that is a total failure, an upheaval

**fi-ber** [fī′bər] *noun*, 1) thread-like structures combined with others to create tissue 2) a filament

**fick-le** [fĭk′əl] *adjective*, moody, flighty, liable to change, inconsistent, not loyal

**fic-tion** [fĭk′shən] *noun*, that which is not true or based in fact, make-believe

**fic-ti-tious** [fĭk-tĭsh′əs] *adjective*, imaginary, unreal, false

**fid-dle** [fĭd′l] *noun*, 1) another word for a violin, *verb*, 2) to tinker with something

**fid-dler** [fĭd′l-ər] *noun*, a person who plays a hand-held stringed instrument

**fi-del-i-ty** [fĭ-dĕl′ĭ-tē, fī-] *noun*, faithfulness, loyalty, honesty

**field** [fēld] *noun*, 1) land put to special use for sports or farming 2) a sphere or range of activities, *verb*, 3) to receive a ball in a game and pass it to another player

**fiend** [fēnd] *noun*, a person who is wicked, cruel, or malicious

**fierce** [fîrs] *adjective*, furious, violent or aggressive

**fier-y** [fîr′ē] *adjective*, burning, heated, impassioned

**fif-teen** [fĭf-tēn′] *adjective, noun*, the number 15, ten plus five

**fif-teenth** [fĭf-tēnth′] *adjective, noun*, number 15 in order, 15th

**fifth** [fĭfth] *adjective, noun*, number five in order, written 5th

**fif-ti-eth** [fĭf′tē-ĭth] *adjective*, the ordinal of fifty, written 50th

**fif-ty** [fĭf′tē] *adjective, noun*, the number 50, 5 times 10

**fig** [fĭg] *noun*, a small fruit grown in warm climates, full of seeds

**fight** [fīt] *noun*, 1) the use of the body or weapons against someone, *verb*, 2) to engage in a physical struggle 3) to quarrel 4) to struggle in any way

**fig-ment** [fĭg′mənt] *noun*, an imaginary thing

**fig-ur-a-tive** [fĭg′yər-ə-tĭv] *adjective*, not literal, metaphorical

**fig-ure** [fĭg′yər] *noun*, 1) the shape or outline of something 2) numbers or digits in an equation or used as measurements, *verb*, 3) to calculate numbers 4) to try to simplify something that is hard to understand

**fig-ure-head** [fĭg′yər-hĕd′] *noun*, 1) a carved figure set at the front of a sailing ship 2) a leader in name only who has no power or authority

**fil-a-ment** [fĭl′ə-mənt] *noun*, a slender thread-like structure

**filch** [fĭlch] *verb*, to steal

**file** [fīl] *noun*, 1) a drawer for papers 2) a metal tool with a rough edge for making things smooth 3) a line of people 4) a stored collection of data, *verb*, 5) to organize papers or other items into a system 6) to make a surface smooth through friction with a tool 7) to walk in a straight and orderly line 8) to register

**fil-i-al** [fĭl′ē-əl] *adjective*, referring to the duty of a son or daughter

**fill** [fĭl] *verb*, 1) to occupy with as much as possible 2) to make full

**fil-let** [fĭl′ĭt] *noun*, 1) a boneless piece of meat or fish, *verb*, 2) to remove bones from

**film** [fĭlm] *noun*, 1) a solid layer that floats on liquid 2) a sensitized coating which receives photographic impressions 3) a movie shown in a theater or on television, *verb*, 4) to photograph something on film 5) to make a movie using a camera

**filth-y** [fĭl′thē] *adjective*, 1) very dirty, nasty, squalid 2) obscene

**fil-tra-tion** [fĭl-trā′shən] *noun*, purification, processing

**fin** [fĭn] *noun*, part of a fish that sticks out, may be fan-shaped, used for steering or balance

**fi-nal** [fī′nəl] *adjective*, the last

**fi-na-le** [fə-năl′ē] *noun*, the last part of a show or a musical composition, the culmination

**fi-nal-ly** [fī′nə-lē] *adverb*, at last, reaching the end, ultimately, eventually, concluding

**fi-nance** [fə-năns′] *noun*, 1) the management of money, *verb*, 2) to use money to pay for something through a loan

**find** [fīnd] *verb*, to uncover or see something after a search

**fine** [fīn] *adjective*, 1) pleasant, nice, refined, *noun*, 2) a penalty, *verb*, 3) to punish someone by making them pay money

**fin-esse** [fə-nĕs′] *noun*, 1) a delicate skill, dexterity 2) tact

**fin-ger** [fĭng′gər] *noun*, 1) one of five digits on a hand, *verb*, 2) to handle, to touch or feel

**fin-ger-nail** [fĭng′gər-nāl′] *noun*, the claw or talon on the end of a finger or foot

**fin-ick-y** [fĭn′ĭ-kē] *adjective*, very fussy, hard to please, picky

**fin-ish** [fĭn′ĭsh] *noun*, 1) a surface appearance, *verb*, 2) to end or complete 3) to use up

**fi-nite** [fī′nīt′] *adjective*, 1) limited in number 2) having boundaries

**fir** [fûr] *noun*, an evergreen tree

**fire** [fīr] *noun*, 1) animation, excitement, inspiration 2) things that are burning, *verb*, 3) to discharge or dismiss from a job

**firm** [fûrm] *adjective*, 1) solid, hard, *noun*, 2) a company managing a business

**firm-ly** [fûrm′lē] *adverb*, solidly, resolutely, unwaveringly

**first** [fûrst] *adjective*, 1) the most important 2) initial, beginning

**first aid** [fûrst′ād′] *noun*, the emergency help given someone who has been hurt

**fish** [fĭsh] *noun*, 1) any animal that lives in the sea, seafood, *verb*, 2) to try to catch a fish or get something from someone

**fis-sure** [fĭsh′ər] *noun*, a crack, a narrow groove, a cleft

**fist** [fĭst] *noun*, the hand with fingers closed tightly together

**fit** [fĭt] *adjective*, 1) healthy, active, vibrant 2) good enough, *verb*, 3) to be able to wear the right size 4) to be in harmony

**five** [fĭv] *adjective, noun*, the number 5, one plus four

**fix** [fĭks] *noun*, 1) a dilemma, a predicament, *verb*, 2) to repair 3) to set, to arrange, to put in place 4) to focus on

**fix-ture** [fĭks′chər] *noun*, that which is attached to something permanently, apparatus

**flac-cid** [flăk′sĭd, flăs′ĭd] *adjective*, flabby, hanging loosely

**flag** [flăg] *noun*, 1) cloth with a special pattern on it, used as the sign of a country, club, etc., *verb*, 2) to wave to someone as a signal to stop 3) to droop

**flag-rant** [flā′grənt] *adjective*, plainly wicked, unashamed

**flail** [flāl] *verb*, to move wildly as if beating something, to thrash

**flair** [flâr] *noun*, an aptitude or talent for doing something well

**flake** [flāk] *noun*, 1) a small sliver of something, *verb*, 2) to peel off in shavings or tiny bits

**flam-boy-ant** [flăm-boi′ənt] *adjective*, showy, flashy

**flame** [flām] *noun*, burning gas seen in a fire

**flam-ma-ble** [flăm′ə-bəl] *adjective*, capable of igniting easily and burning quickly

**flank** [flăngk] *noun*, a side, the lateral edge, on either side

**flan-nel** [flăn′əl] *noun*, a soft woolen cloth of loose texture

**flap** [flăp] *noun*, 1) the covering of an opening, hanging loose, *verb*, 2) to wave to and fro

**flare** [flâr] *noun*, 1) a torch or brilliant light, *verb*, 2) to shine, to burn brightly 3) to spread out like a fan, to expand outward

**flash** [flăsh] *noun*, 1) a split second, a gleam, an instant, *verb*, 2) to show a bright light

**flash-back** [flăsh′băk] *noun*, an interruption in the continuity of a story, play, etc. by the presentation of an earlier episode

**flash-light** [flăsh′līt′] *noun*, a hand held light operated by batteries

**flat** [flăt] *adjective*, a level, horizontal surface, smooth

**flat-ter-y** [flăt′ə-rē] *noun*, no plural, excessive compliments

**flaunt** [flônt] *verb*, to boast, to wave under one's nose

**fla-vor** [flā′vər] *noun*, 1) the seasoning of food, the taste of something, *verb*, 2) to add something to make food taste better 3) to savor

**flaw** [flô] *noun*, a defect, a weak spot, an imperfection

**flax** [flăks] *noun*, a slender plant with blue flowers whose stalks are used to make thread

**flay** [flā] *verb*, to whip, to beat with a strap or stick, to hit

**flea** [flē] *noun*, a jumping insect the size of a pinhead that sucks blood from people and animals

**fled** [flĕd] *past tense* of **flee**

**flee** [flē] *noun*, to run away

**fleece** [flēs] *noun*, 1) the wool on sheep, *verb*, 2) to shake someone down for money 3) to swindle

**fleet** [flēt] *noun*, a group of ships sailing together, or vehicles, or aircraft under one command

**fleet-ing** [flē/tĭng] *adjective*, swift in motion, passing quickly

**flex** [flĕks] *verb*, to bend

**flex-i-ble** [flĕk/sə-bəl] *adjective*, 1) able to bend easily 2) willing to change a course of action, easily adaptable

**flick-er** [flĭk/ər] *verb*, 1) to change unsteadily from bright to dim light 2) a brief sensation

**flight** [flīt] *noun*, 1) the act of flying 2) an airplane trip

**flim-sy** [flĭm/zē] *adjective*, 1) weak and easily broken 2) ineffectual, not well thought out

**flinch** [flĭnch] *verb*, to move back suddenly in fear, to make a nervous movement

**flint** [flĭnt] *noun*, stone, slate

**flip** [flĭp] *adjective*, 1) sarcastic, kidding, joking 2) a somersault in the air, *verb*, 3) to turn suddenly or swiftly in the air

**flip-pant** [flĭp/ənt] *adjective*, glib, sarcastic, disrespectful

**flirt** [flûrt] *verb*, to tease affectionately

**float** [flōt] *noun*, 1) a portable display in a parade, *verb*, 2) to be supported by liquid or gas

**flock** [flŏk] *noun*, 1) a company of birds, animals, or people 2) to gather, to congregate, to huddle

**flood** [flŭd] *noun*, 1) water that stays on land that is below sea level, *verb*, 2) when water overflows or invades a dry area

**floor** [flôr] *noun*, 1) the part of the room you walk on 2) a level of a building, *verb*, 3) to knock down

**flo-ral** [flôr/əl] *adjective*, decorated with flowers

**Flor-i-da** [flôr/ĭ-də] *noun*, on of the 50 United States, located in the Southeast, the capital is Tallahassee. The **Florida** state flower is the orange blossom, the motto is "In God we trust."

**floss** [flôs] *noun*, 1) a soft silky substance found in the husks of some plants 2) a thin silk thread used for embroidery 3) a thread covered with wax used to clean between the teeth, *verb*, 4) to run thread through the teeth to remove food and tarter

**flo-til-la** [flō-tĭl/ə] *noun*, a small fleet of ships

**floun-der** [floun/dər] *noun*, 1) any member of the flatfish family, *verb*, 2) to flail about

**flour** [flour] *noun*, the finely ground meal of wheat or other cereal plants like oats, rice, corn

**flour-ish** [flûr/ĭsh] *noun*, 1) a handwritten decoration, *verb*, 2) to prosper, to grow well

**flout** [flout] *verb*, to scoff at, to ridicule, to disobey a law

**flow** [flō] *noun*, *no plural*, 1) a current, a steady stream, *verb*, 2) the movement of gases or fluid

**flow-er** [flou′ər] *noun*, the part of a plant that bears the seeds, the blossom where fruit develops

**flu** [floo] *noun*, an illness characterized by fever, chills and coughing

**fluc-tu-ate** [flŭk′choo-āt′] *verb*, 1) to move back and forth like a wave, 2) to vary in degree or value

**fluc-tu-a-tion** [flŭk′choo-ā′shən] *noun*, 1) wavering 2) the change of the level or degree of something

**flu-ent** [floo′ənt] *adjective*, spoken smoothly and easily

**flu-id** [floo′ĭd] *adjective*, 1) not fixed or settled, able to flow, *noun*, 2) a liquid that flows

**fluo-res-cent** [floo-rĕs′ənt] *adjective*, absorption of light from another source

**flur-ry** [flûr′ē] *noun*, a brief excitement, quick movement

**flush** [flŭsh] *adjective*, 1) even, *noun*, 2) in poker, five cards of the same suit, *verb*, 3) to turn red in the face 4) to wash out

**flust-er** [flŭs′tər] *verb*, to confuse, to embarrass, to agitate

**flute** [floot] *noun*, a musical instrument like a pipe with keys to control the flow of air that can make different sounds

**flut-ter** [flŭt′ər] *verb*, to flap, to move wings hurriedly

**flux** [flŭks] *noun*, a flowing series of continuous changes

**fly** [flī] *noun*, 1) a small flying insect, *verb*, 2) to move through the air 3) to move very fast

**foam** [fōm] *noun*, froth formed on the surface of liquids by agitation, a mass of small bubbles

**fo-cal** [fō′kəl] *adjective*, central, midway, of or at a focus

**fo-cus** [fō′kəs] *noun*, 1) a central point, *verb*, 2) to concentrate, to pay attention to something

**foe** [fō] *noun*, an enemy, an adversary, an opponent

**fog** [fôg] *noun*, a cloud of fine water drops of vapor found close to the ground or sea

**foil** [foil] *noun*, 1) a paper-like sheet of metal, *verb*, 2) to throw off someone's plans

**fo-li-age** [fōlē′ĭj] *noun*, the leaves of trees and other plants

**fold** [fōld] *noun*, 1) a part of something that has been wrapped or enclosed *verb*, 2) to double or bend over, to envelope 3) to withdraw or quit

**fold-er** [fōl′dər] *noun*, a cardboard cover to protect papers and keep them together

**folk** [fōk] *noun*, people

**fol-low** [fōl′ō] *verb*, 1) to go after, to pursue 2) to come after or behind 3) to pay close attention

**fol-ly** [fōl′ē] *noun*, foolishness

**fond** [fŏnd] *adjective*, to have feelings of affection

**fon-dle** [fŏn′dl] *adverb*, to caress, to stroke lovingly

**food** [food] *noun*, a source of nourishment, what you eat

**fool** [fool] *noun*, 1) a silly person, *verb*, 2) to trick or deceive

**fool-ish** [foo′lĭsh] *adjective*, crazy, silly, senseless, ridiculous

**foot** [fŏŏt] *noun*, *plural*, **feet**, 1) the part of the leg that touches the ground 2) a measure of length equal to 12 inches 3) any base that resembles a foot

**foot-ball** [fŏŏt'bôl'] *noun*, 1) a game in which two teams of eleven players try to score points by passing a ball to each other in a period of time 2) an oval shaped inflated ball

**for** [fôr, fər when unstressed] *conjunction*, 1) because, *preposition*, 2) being as 3) to be given or used by 4) at a certain price 5) to be going toward 6) to show the meaning of as in an example

**for-age** [fôr'ĭj] *verb*, to look for food or supplies

**for-ay** [fôr'ā'] *noun*, a raid, an attempt at something unfamiliar

**for-bear** [fôr-bâr'] *verb*, to hold back, to wait, to refrain from

**for-bear-ance** [fôr-bâr'əns] *adjective*, the act of refraining from anything, self-restraint

**for-bid** [fər-bĭd'] *verb*, to prohibit, to order someone not to do something

**force** [fôrs, fōrs] *noun*, 1) power 2) a group of people trained in the same manner, *verb*, 3) to cause to happen with conviction

**fore-bod-ing** [fôr-bō'dĭng] *noun*, a warning or sign that something bad or evil will happen

**fore-cast** [fôr'kăst'] *noun*, 1) a prediction that something will happen, *verb*, 2) to anticipate, to figure out and say what will happen before it takes place

**fore-close** [fôr-klōz'] *verb*, to take away land from a person who owes money on it

**for-eign** [fôr'ĭn] *adjective*, belonging to another country

**for-eign-er** [fôr'ə-nər] *noun*, someone from another country

**fore-man** [fôr'mən] *noun*, 1) the overseer of a set of workmen 2) the spokesman of a jury

**fore-most** [fôr'mōst'] *adjective*, first in importance, time or place

**fo-ren-sic** [fə-rĕn'sĭk] *adjective*, information that is a suitable argument in court

**fore-see-a-ble** [fôr-sē'ə-bəl] *adjective*, predictable, able to be seen in the future

**fore-sight** [fôr'sīt'] *noun*, the ability to foresee future happenings or needs

**for-est** [fôr'ĭst] *noun*, a large place where trees grow together

**fore-stall** [fôr-stôl'] *verb*, to keep safe by taking action first

**fore-tell** [fôr-tĕl'] *verb*, to predict, to make a prophecy, to forecast

**for-ev-er** [fôr-ĕv'ər] *adverb*, until the end of time, always

**for-feit** [fôr'fĭt] *verb*, to lose the right, to surrender, to give up

**forge** [fôrj] *verb*, 1) to move ahead or progress with difficulty 2) to mold metal with heat and then hammering it into shapes 3) to invent or create something 4) to counterfeit with intent to defraud

**for-ger-y** [fôr'jə-rē] *noun*, the making of a false or altered document for the purpose of fraud, counterfeit

**for-get** [fər-gĕt′] *verb*, 1) to fail to recall or remember 2) to neglect

**for-give** [fər-gĭv′] *verb*, to accept an apology, to get rid of a grudge, to cease to feel angry

**for-got** [fər-gŏt′] *past tense* of **forget**

**for-got-ten** [fər-gŏt′n] *adjective*, left behind

**fork** [fôrk] *noun*, 1) a utensil with prongs on the end used to stab food 2) a place in a road where it separates in different directions

**for-lorn** [fər-lôrn′] *adjective*, sad and unhappy, lonely

**form** [fôrm] *noun*, 1) the shape of something 2) a document with questions that need to be answered, *verb*, 3) to shape or create, to develop, to mold

**for-mal** [fôr′məl] *adjective*, following the customs of an occasion, ceremonious

**for-mal-i-ty** [fôr-măl′ĭ-tē] *noun*, adherence to established rules of etiquette and convention

**for-ma-tion** [fôr-mā′shən] *noun*, 1) a creation 2) an arrangement

**form-er** [fôr′mər] *adjective*, the one mentioned first of two

**for-mi-da-ble** [fôr′mĭ-də-bəl] *adjective*, very large, alarming

**for-mu-la** [fôr′myə-lə] *noun*, 1) substances mixed together in specific amounts to create something 2) a mathematical statement

**for-mu-late** [fôr′myə-lāt′] *verb*, to give form to, to express precisely in a few words

**fort** [fôrt] *noun*, a place for protecting soldiers

**forte** [fôrt] *noun*, a strong point or special talent or ability

**for-ti-eth** [fôr′tē-ĭth] *noun*, the ordinal of forty, 40th

**for-ti-fy** [fôr′tə-fī′] *verb*, 1) to make stronger or more secure 2) to strengthen against attack 3) to empower, to invigorate

**for-ti-tude** [fôr′tĭ-tood′] *noun*, courage, strength of mind

**for-tress** [fôr′trĭs] *noun*, a building with strong walls made to be defended against attack, a fort

**for-tu-nate** [fôr′chə-nĭt] *adjective*, lucky, favorable, advantageous

**for-tune** [fôr′chən] *noun*, 1) whatever good or bad happens to people, luck 2) a large amount of money, wealth, riches

**for-ty** [fôr′tē] *noun*, the number 40, four times ten

**fo-rum** [fôr′əm] *noun*, a public meeting place and market square

**for-ward** [fôr′wərd] *adjective*, 1) near or at the front part, ahead 2) onward 3) bold, confident

**fos-sil** [fŏs′əl] *noun*, the impression in a rock of the petrified remains of an organism or animal

**fos-ter** [fô′stər] *verb*, to help, to raise, to encourage

**fought** [fôt] *past tense* of **fight**

**foul** [foul] *adjective*, 1) dirty, filthy, squalid, *noun*, 2) a ball hit outside the first or third base line

**found** [found] *verb*, 1) to establish, to lay a foundation 2) *past tense* of **find**

**foun-da-tion** [foun-dā′shən] *noun*, 1) the base of a building 2) the principles of a program or agency 3) a charitable institution

**found-er** [foun'dər] *noun*, 1) the author or prime mover, *verb*, 2) to take on water, to sink

**found-ry** [foun'drē] *noun*, a plant refining metal or glass, a factory

**foun-tain** [foun'tən] *noun*, water spraying into the air from a pipe

**four** [fôr] *adjective, noun*, the number 4, one plus three

**four-teen** [fôr-tēn'] *noun*, 4+10=14

**four-teenth** [fôr-tēnth'] *adjective, noun*, number 14 in order, 14th

**fourth** [fôrth] *adjective, noun*, the ordinal number after third, one of four equal parts, 4th

**fowl** [foul] *noun*, a bird eaten as food or kept for its eggs

**fox** [fŏks] *noun*, a wild animal the size of a dog with a pointed muzzle and bushy tail

**foy-er** [foi'ər] *noun*, the entry way in a hall, a hotel lobby

**frac-tion** [frăk'shən] *noun*, 1) a piece of something 2) a number that names part of a group, not a whole number

**frac-ture** [frăk'chər] *noun*, 1) a break, a fissure, *verb*, 2) to break

**frag-ile** [frăj'əl, -īl'] *adjective*, easily broken, delicate

**frag-ment** [frăg'mənt] *noun*, a piece broken off, a particle

**fra-grance** [frā'grəns] *noun*, having a sweet smell, perfume, aroma

**frail** [frāl] *adjective*, weak, fragile, delicate, sickly, infirm, ill

**frame** [frām] *noun*, 1) the structure that supports something 2) the outline of something encasing

something, *verb*, 3) to enclose in a frame 4) to make someone appear guilty of a crime by arranging false evidence

**fran-chise** [frăn'chīz'] *noun*, a special right or privilege granted by a government to do business

**frank** [frăngk] *adjective*, candid, honest in expressing your thoughts

**fran-tic** [frăn'tĭk] *adjective*, wild

**fra-ter-ni-ty** [frə-tûr'nĭ-tē] *noun*, a fellowship of men in a college

**fraud** [frôd] *noun*, 1) an imposter, a fake 2) criminal deception

**fraud-u-lent** [frô'jə-lənt] *adjective*, tricky, deceitful, dishonest

**fray** [frā] *noun*, 1) a conflict, a commotion, *verb*, 2) to unravel

**freak** [frēk] *noun*, odd, a strange event or person, out of the ordinary, an aberration

**freck-le** [frĕk'əl] a small, brownish spot on the skin

**free** [frē] *adjective*, 1) able to do as you please, unrestrained 2) something that doesn't cost any money 3) available, *verb*, 4) to release something from captivity, to turn loose

**free-dom** [frē'dəm] *noun*, liberty, independence, being free

**freeze** [frēz] *verb*, to become chilled by cold, to change to ice

**freez-er** [frē'zər] *noun*, an appliance that preserves food by keeping it frozen

**freight** [frāt] *noun*, transportation of products in bulk, cargo

**freight-er** [frā'tər] *noun*, a ship or aircraft laden with cargo

**fren-zy** [frĕn'zē] *noun*, craziness, wild excitement, fury

**fre-quen-cy** [frē'kwən-sē] *noun*, a common occurrence, returning often or repeatedly

**fre-quent** [frē'kwənt] *adjective*, 1) happening often, repeated, many times, *verb*, 2) to go to a place often for visits

**fresh** [frĕsh] *adjective*, new, unused, arrived recently

**fresh-man** [frĕsh'mən] *noun*, a person in his first year of high school or college

**fret** [frĕt] *verb*, to fuss, to fume, to feel anxious, to worry

**fric-tion** [frĭk'shən] *noun*, 1) the force that resists movement between two things that are in contact with each other 2) an argument caused by differences of opinion, rivalry

**Fri-day** [frī'dē, -dā']*noun*, the sixth day of the week

**friend** [frĕnd] *noun*, a person who knows and likes another

**friend-ship** [frĕnd- shĭp] *noun*, mutual respect, companionship

**fright** [frīt] *noun*, sudden fear, alarm, horror, a shock

**fright-en** [frīt'n] *verb*, to scare or alarm, to fill with fear

**frig-id** [frĭj'ĭd] *adjective*, very cold

**frill** [frĭl] *noun*, a doodad, bells and whistles, an unnecessary extra feature or luxury

**fringe** [frĭnj] *noun*, 1) an edge made of short lengths of thread, used to decorate clothes, curtains, etc. 2) an outside edge

**frisk-y** [frĭs'kē] *adjective*, playful, active, lively, bouncy

**frit-ter** [frĭt'ər] *verb*, to waste

**friv-o-lous** [frĭv'ə-ləs] *adjective*, 1) of little weight or importance 2) given to trifling, silly

**frog** [frôg] *noun*, 1) a jumping amphibian that can swim in water or live on land 2) a tool designed to sit in the bottom of the bowl or vase to hold flower stems in place for Ikebana

**frol-ic** [frŏl'ĭk] *verb*, merry making, to play happily about

**from** [frŭm] *preposition*, 1) used to show a starting point 2) used to show a point of separation 3) used to show material source or cause, given by

**front** [frŭnt] *adjective*, 1) first, ahead of the others, *noun*, 2) the face or the part of something that faces forward 3) the facade

**fron-tier** [frŭn-tîr'] *noun*, 1) the line between two countries 2) the outer limits of a settled part of a country 3) the outer limits of knowledge

**frost** [frôst] *noun*, *no plural*, the frozen water that covers the surface of everything outdoors when the temperature goes below freezing, 32 degrees

**froth** [frôth] *noun*, 1) fine bubbles, foam, effervescence, *verb*, 2) to cause to foam

**frown** [froun] *noun*, 1) a stern look, *verb*, 2) to scowl or look unhappy, to show disapproval

**froze** [frōz] *past tense* of **freeze**

**fro-zen** [frō'zən] *adjective*, the temperature cooled to the point that liquid turns to solid

**fru-gal** [frōō'gəl] *adjective*, careful management of resources, stingy

**fruit** [frōōt] *noun*, 1) an edible product of a flower, bearing seeds 2) the results, the outcome

**fruit-ful** [frōōt'fəl] *adjective*, successful, productive

**fru-i-tion** [frōō-ĭsh'ən] *noun*, fulfillment, realization

**frus-trate** [frŭs'trāt'] *verb*, to prevent from attaining a purpose

**fry** [frī] *verb*, to cook in hot oil

**fudge** [fŭj] *noun*, a soft candy usually made with chocolate

**fuel** [fyōō'əl] *noun*, something that gives off heat when it is burned

**fu-gi-tive** [fyōō'jĭ-tĭv] *noun*, one who flees from pursuit

**ful-fill** [fŏŏl-fĭl'] *verb*, 1) to satisfy a contract 2) to complete

**full** [fŏŏl] *adjective*, 1) leaving no empty space, holding as much as possible, *adverb*, 2) entirely

**full-ness** [fŏŏl'nĭs] *noun*, the state of being full or complete

**fumes** [fyōōmz] *noun*, *plural*, gases

**fu-mi-gate** [fyōō'mĭ-gāt'] *verb*, to apply smoke or vapor as a means of disinfecting or killing bugs

**fun** [fŭn] *noun*, *no plural*, light-hearted, amusement

**func-tion** [fŭngk'shən] *noun*, 1) the natural and proper action of anything 2) a service, duty, purpose 3) how something works

**fund** [fŭnd] *noun*, 1) a sum of money collected to help a special purpose, *verb*, 2) to provide money to support a cause

**fun-da-men-tal** [fŭn'də-mĕn'tl] *adjective*, 1) of first importance, essential 2) elementary

**fu-ner-al** [fyōō'nər-əl] *noun*, a ceremony honoring the life of someone who died

**fun-gus** [fŭng'gəs] *noun*, a plant that lacks chlorophyll, leaves, and a flower, i.e., mushrooms, mold, yeast

**fun-nel** [fŭn'əl] *noun*, an open cone wide at the top with a smaller end to pour liquids from one container to another

**fun-ny** [fŭn'ē] *adjective*, 1) amusing, entertaining, to make someone laugh 2) strange, unusual, odd

**fur** [fûr] *noun*, a soft hair covering on some animals, the pelt

**fu-ri-ous** [fyŏŏr'ē-əs] *adjective*, 1) very angry 2) very fast, strong or wild, intense

**fur-nace** [fûr'nĭs] *noun*, 1) an enclosed place in which heat is produced by the combustion of fuel 2) a large structure containing a very hot fire

**fur-nish** [fûr'nĭsh] *verb*, to supply, to stock, or provide, to give

**fur-ni-ture** [fûr'nĭ-chər] *noun*, *no plural*, the articles in a home that make it more comfortable, such as beds, chairs, tables, etc.

**fu-ror** [fyŏŏr'ôr'] *noun*, frenzy, a state of great excitement

**fur-ther** [fûr'thər] *adjective*, at a greater distance, beyond

**fur-tive** [fûr tĭv] *adjective*, done in a sneaky way, hoping to be unnoticed

**fu-ry** [fyŏŏr'ē] *noun*, 1) great anger 2) wild or uncontrolled force

**fur-ry** [fûr'ē] *adjective*, covered with hair, like fur

**fuse** [fyo͞oz] *noun*, 1) tinder, kindling, a wick, *verb*, 2) to combine, to blend, to mix

**fu-sion** [fyo͞o′zhən] *noun*, the process of joining two or more things together as one

**fuss** [fŭs] *noun*, 1) complaint, bother, commotion, *verb*, 2) to behave in an excited, worried way, to be overly emotional

**fu-tile** [fyo͞ot′l, fyo͞o′tĭl′] *adjective*, ineffective, fruitless, pointless

**fu-ture** [fyo͞o′chər] *adjective*, 1) coming after the present, *noun*, 2) a time that has not yet arrived

# G

**gadg-et** [găj′ĭt] *noun*, a mechanical device or tool, a thingamajig

**gag** [găg] *noun*, 1) something used to keep people from talking, *verb*, 2) to restrain someone from speaking 3) to choke

**gain** [gān] *noun*, 1) an increase, *verb*, 2) to win, to acquire

**gait** [gāt] *noun*, a manner of walking, skipping or running

**gal-ax-y** [găl′ək-sē] *noun*, a group of billions of stars held together by mutual gravitation

**gale** [gāl] *noun*, a strong wind

**gall** [gôl] *noun*, 1) bitter feeling 2) bile, the greenish fluid secreted by the liver, *verb*, 3) to annoy, to anger 4) to make sore by rubbing

**gal-lant** [găl′ənt] *adjective*, brave

**gal-le-on** [găl′ē-ən] *noun*, a large sailing ship of earlier times

**gal-ler-y** [găl′ə-rē] *noun*, 1) a long, narrow, room-like corridor or passageway 2) a room for the exhibition of works of art

**gal-ley** [găl′ē] *noun*, 1) an oblong tray to hold type which has been set 2) the lower part of a ship

**gal-lon** [găl′ən] *noun*, a unit of liquid measure equal to 4 quarts or 128 ounces

**gal-lop** [găl′əp] *verb*, to trot, to run like a horse

**gal-lows** [găl′ōz] *noun*, a public place where criminals are hung

**gal-va-nize** [găl′və-nīz′] *verb*, to stimulate with shock, to stir up

**gam-ble** [găm′bəl] *verb*, to try to win money by betting, to take a risk

**gam-bler** [găm′blər] *noun*, a risk taker, one who plays games of chance for money

**game** [gām] *noun*, a form of entertainment played with rules that tests skill and knowledge

**gam-ut** [găm′ət] *noun*, the entire range from beginning to end

**gan-der** [găn′dər] *noun*, a male goose

**gang** [găng] *noun*, an organized group of people who intimidate and harass

**gang-plank** [găng′plăngk′] *noun*, a temporary board or ramp used to board or leave a ship

**gan-grene** [găng′grēn′] *noun*, the death of a limb such as a leg due to infection

**gap** [găp] *noun*, a hole, an opening, the distance between two places

**ga-rage** [gə-räzh′] *noun*, 1) a place for housing automobiles 2) a place where automobiles or buses are repaired

**gar-bage** [gär′bĭj] *noun*, another word for solid waste, especially household waste, trash

**gar-den** [gär′dn] *noun*, 1) a plot of land where flowers or vegetables grow, *verb*, 2) to look after the plants by watering and pruning

**gar-den-er** [gärd′nər] *noun*, one who makes and tends a garden

**gar-gle** [gär′gəl] *verb*, to rinse the throat with a liquid kept in motion by air forced through it from the lungs

**gar-goyle** [gär′goil′] *noun*, figures of demons carved as a roof spout

**gar-ish** [gâr′ĭsh, gär′-] *adjective*, in bad taste, gaudy, showy

**gar-lic** [gär′lĭk] *noun*, a plant like an onion with a strong taste and smell, used to season food

**gar-ment** [gär′mənt] *noun*, a piece of clothing

**gar-ner** [gär′nər] *verb*, to gather up, to accumulate, to amass

**gar-net** [gär′nĭt] *noun*, a precious stone of a deep red color

**gar-nish** [gär′nĭsh] *noun*, 1) a decoration for food, *verb*, 2) to decorate or adorn 3) to take from someone a little at a time by order of the court to pay a debt

**gar-ri-son** [găr′ĭ-sən] *noun*, troops stationed in a fort or fortified town, a military post

**gas** [găs] *noun*, 1) a state of matter in which a substance like air is capable of infinitely expanding, has no fixed form or volume and takes the shape of its container 2) the short word for gasoline

**gas-e-ous** [găs′ē-əs, găsh′əs] *adjective*, in vapor form

**gas-ket** [găs′kĭt] *noun*, a piece of rubber sealing a joint between metal surfaces

**gas-o-line** [găs′ə-lēn′] *noun*, petroleum or diesel motor fuel

**gasp** [găsp] *noun*, 1) a short breath, *verb*, 2) to pant with a short, excited breath 3) to wheeze

**gas-tron-o-my** [gă-strŏn′ə-mē] *noun*, the science of preparing and serving good food

**gate** [gāt] *noun*, a doorway which closes an opening in a wall or fence with a hinged door

**gath-er** [găth′ər] *verb*, 1) to bring together or accumulate, to harvest 2) to infer from what someone has said

**gauche** [gōsh] *adjective*, clumsy, lacking social grace, awkward

**gaud-y** [gô′dē] *adjective*, showy in a tasteless way, ostentatious

**gauge** [gāj] *noun*, 1) an instrument used to find the exact measurement, *verb*, 2) to measure or estimate

**gaunt** [gônt] *adjective*, thin, lean

**gauze** [gôz] *noun*, 1) a cotton bandage 2) a thin fabric

**gaze** [gāz] *verb*, to stare, to look at steadily and intently, to gawk

**gaz-et-teer** [gaezə′tir] *noun*, a geographical dictionary

**gear** [gîr] *noun*, 1) a toothed wheel that passes motion and power along 2) equipment, supplies

**gel-a-tin** [jĕl′ə-tn] *noun*, a tasteless, transparent, substance, obtained from connective animal tissue such as skin, hooves, or horns

**gem** [jĕm] *noun*, a precious stone used as an ornament

**gen-der** [jĕn′dər] *noun*, a set of categories applied to nouns as masculine or feminine

**ge-ne-al-o-gy** [jē′nē-ŏl′ə-jē] *noun*, a record of family history

**gen-er-al** [jĕn′ər-əl] *adjective*, 1) of or from the whole  2) not particular or definite 3) usual or customary, common, lacking detail, *noun*, 2) the title of the commander in an army

**Gen-er-al As-sem-bly** *noun*, 1) the law-making body in the United States 2) the assembly of the representatives of the United Nations

**gen-er-al-i-ty** [jĕn′ə-răl′ĭ-tē] *noun*, a vague statement, a theory

**gen-er-al-ize** [jĕn′ər-ə-līz′] *verb*, to make a broad statement

**gen-er-al-ly** [jĕn′ər-ə-lē] *adverb*, usually, as a rule, normally

**gen-er-ate** [jĕn′ə-rāt′] *verb*, to make or create, to produce

**gen-er-a-tion** [jĕn′ə-rā′shən] *noun*, 1) the average time interval between the birth of parents and the birth of their offspring 2) all of the people born at the same time 3) the act or process of producing something

**gen-er-a-tor** [jĕn′ə-rā′tər] *noun*, a machine by which mechanical energy is changed into electrical energy

**gen-er-os-i-ty** [jĕn′ə-rŏs′ĭ-tē] *noun*, given freely, unselfishness

**gen-er-ous** [jĕn′ər-əs] *adjective*, liberal, open-handed, abundant

**gen-er-ous-ly** [jĕn′ər-əs-lē] *adverb*, plentifully, unselfishly

**ge-ni-al** [jēn′yəl] *adjective*, kind, cheerful, gracious  friendly

**gen-ius** [jēn′yəs] *noun*, extraordinary mental superiority

**gen-re** [zhän′rə] *noun*, a category, art or music characterized by a particular style, class

**gen-til-i-ty** [jĕn-tĭl′ĭ-tē] *noun*, men or women who are born to money, well-bred

**gen-tle** [jĕn′tl] *adjective*, 1) kind, courteous, amiable 2) soft and mild 3) not steep, moderate

**gen-tle-man** [jĕn′tl-mən] *noun*, a well-mannered man

**gent-ly** [jĕnt′lē] *adverb*, carefully

**gen-u-flect** [jĕn′yə-flĕkt′] *verb*, to bend one knee and bow in worship or reverence

**gen-u-ine** [jĕn′yōō-ĭn] *adjective*, the real thing, not false

**gen-u-ine-ly** [jĕn′yōō-ĭn-lē] *adverb*, truly, really

**ge-og-ra-phy** [jē-ŏg′rə-fē] *noun*, the science that describes the surface of the earth, and its division into continents

**ge-ol-o-gist** [jē-ŏl′ə-jĭst] *noun*, a person who studies the structure of the earth, its physical changes and the causes producing these to form a hypothesis

**ge-ol-o-gy** [jē-ŏl′ə-jē] *noun*, the science that studies the history and structure of the earth, its physical changes, and the causes producing these changes

**ge-om-e-try** [jē-ŏm′ĭ-trē] *noun*, the branch of mathematics that studies the relations, properties, and measurement of solids, surfaces, lines, and angles

**Geor-gia** [jôr'jə] *noun*, one of the 50 United States located in the Southeast, the capital city is Atlanta. The state flower of **Georgia** is the cherokee rose and the motto is: "Wisdom, justice, and moderation."

**ge-ra-ni-um** [jə-rā'nē-əm] *noun*, a flower with pink, red, or white blooms and velvety leaves

**germ** [jûrm] *noun*, a micro-organism that causes disease

**ger-mi-nate** [jûr'mə-nāt'] *verb*, to cause to grow or develop

**ges-ta-tion** [jĕ-stā'shən] *noun*, the period of time a new life is in the womb until it is born, pregnancy

**ges-tic-u-late** [jĕ-stĭk'yə-lāt'] *verb*, to make a motion, to gesture

**ges-ture** [jĕs'chər] *noun*, 1) any action of the hand or face 2) something done to show one's feelings, *verb*, 2) to make a movement of the arm or hand, to signal

**get** [gĕt] *verb*, 1) to take, have or buy, to acquire 2) to become

**gey-ser** [gī'zər] *noun*, a natural hot spring that throws out a spray of steam and water occasionally

**ghet-to** [gĕt- tō] *noun*, any section of a city in which many members of a minority group live, or to which they are restricted by discrimination

**ghost** [gōst] *adjective*, the appearance of a dead person, an apparition haunting the living

**gi-ant** [jī'ənt] *adjective*, 1) very large, huge, *noun*, 2) a legendary person or animal who is a very, very large size

**gift** [gĭft] *noun*, 1) a present 2) a person's inborn ability to do something well, talent

**gi-gan-tic** [jī-găn'tĭk] *adjective*, very big, large, huge, titanic

**gig-gle** [gĭg'əl] *verb*, to laugh in a silly, undignified way

**gill** [gĭl] *noun*, respiratory organs in fish that separate dissolved oxygen from water

**gi-raffe** [jə-răf'] *noun*, a tall African animal with a very long neck and very long legs and large brown spots on its coat

**gird-er** [gûr'dər] *noun*, iron or steel beams to span an opening or carry weight of a building

**girl** [gûrl] *noun*, a female child

**gist** [jĭst] *noun*, the main point

**give** [gĭv] *verb*, 1) to present, to donate, to handover 2) to impart something 3) to provide

**giv-en** [gĭv'ən] *adjective*, 1) stated, typical 2) habitually inclined

**gla-cier** [glā'shər] *noun*, a body of ice, formed in a region of perpetual snow, moving slowly down a mountain slope or valley

**glad** [glăd] *adjective*, 1) feeling pleasure or joy 2) very willing

**glad-i-o-lus** [glăd'ē-ō'ləs] *noun*, *plural*, **gladioli**, a native bulb from Africa of the iris family, that has sword-shaped leaves stems of brightly colored flowers

**glad-ly** [glăd'lē] *adverb*, happily, willingly, joyfully, thrilled

**glam-or** [glăm'ər] *noun*, beauty, attraction, alluring charm

**glance** [glăns] *noun*, 1) a quick or a brief look, *verb*, 2) to look quickly or briefly, to glimpse

# gland

**gland** [glănd] *noun*, a vital part of a living organism that secretes a substance

**glare** [glâr] *noun*, 1) a bright light reflecting shine or a gleam 2) a frown or scowl, *verb*, 3) to stare disapprovingly, to glower

**glass** [glăs] *noun, no plural*, 1) a hard clear substance that is easily shattered, used for windows, *plural*, **glasses**, 2) a drinking container 3) specially cut lenses made of plastic or glass held in a frame to adjust vision so that a person can see better, spectacles

**glaze** [glāz] *noun*, 1) a shiny, glossy surface, *verb*, 2) to cover with a thin shiny surface

**gleam** [glēm] *noun*, 1) a brief flash of light, *verb*, 2) to shine brightly, to glisten, to glitter

**glean** [glēn] *verb*, to gather leftovers, to collect

**glee** [glē] *noun*, joy, merriment

**glib** [glĭb] *adjective*, flippant, to speak freely, sarcastic

**glide** [glīd] *verb*, to move very smoothly, effortlessly

**glid-er** [glī'dər] *noun*, an aircraft that flies without an engine

**glimpse** [glĭmps] *noun*, 1) a brief look at something, *verb*, 2) to get a quick look at something

**glit-ter** [glĭt'ər] *noun*, 1) something that sparkles or twinkles, *verb*, 2) to sparkle or twinkle as a reflection of light, to shimmer

**gloat** [glōt] *verb*, to brag, to boast

**globe** [glōb] *noun*, 1) the round replica of the Earth marked with countries, continents, oceans 2) anything round like a ball

**gloom** [gloom] *noun*, 1) darkness 2) a feeling of sadness, dejection

**gloom-y** [gloo'mē] *adjective*, 1) dark, shadowy 2) despondent, dejected, disheartened

**glo-ri-fy** [glôr'ə-fī'] *verb*, to exalt, to acclaim, to worship

**glo-ri-ous** [glôr'ē-əs] *adjective*, exhibiting qualities that deserve or receive glory or praise

**glory** [glôr'ē] *noun*, praise given to someone who has accomplished something extraordinary

**glos-sa-ry** [glô'sə-rē] *noun*, a list of specialized words used in the text with definitions

**gloss-y** [glô'sē] *adjective*, smooth and shiny, gleaming bright

**glove** [glŭv] *noun*, a covering for the hand with separate sections for the fingers and the thumb

**glow** [glō] *noun*, 1) gentle radiance, light and warmth, *verb*, 2) to radiate light or heat

**glu-cose** [gloo'kōs'] *noun*, sugar created in the body by processing starch

**glue** [gloo] *noun*, 1) a substance used to make things stick together 2) to fasten with an adhesive, to attach closely

**glut-ton** [glŭt'n] *noun*, someone who is greedy for food, a pig

**glyc-er-in** [glĭs'ər-ĭn] *noun*, a softening agent for skin

**gnarled** [närld] *adjective*, twisted in a knotted form

**gnat** [năt] *noun*, a very small flying insect which bites or sucks

**gnaw** [nô] *verb*, to bite so as to wear away persistently

**go** [gō] *noun*, 1) a try, an effort, *verb*, 2) to move along 3) to depart 4) to proceed

**goad** [gōd] *verb*, to use some object to make an animal move

**goal** [gōl] *noun*, 1) a personal level of achievement 2) the cage or line at the end of the field which the opposite team tries to penetrate 3) a score when the ball goes into the end zone or cage 4) an objective

**goat** [gōt] *noun*, a small, horned farm animal that is raised for its milk and fur

**gob-ble** [gŏb′əl] *verb*, to eat fast

**gob-lin** [gŏb′lĭn] *noun*, in folklore, an ugly, grotesque, evil creature

**god** [gŏd] *noun*, a being to whom people pray and has control of the forces in the world

**God** [gŏd] *proper noun*, the supreme being, the master of the universe

**god-dess** [gŏd′ĭs] *noun*, a female form of deity

**goes** [gōz] *present tense* of **go** used in the singular, with *he*, *she* or *it*

**gog-gles** [gŏg′əlz] *noun*, large spectacles for protecting the eyes

**gold** [gōld] *adjective*, 1) bright yellow color, *noun*, 2) the precious metal

**golf** [gŏlf] *noun*, a game played by two or more people in which a small ball is hit into 18 holes arranged on a large piece of land called a course

**gone** [gôn] *past tense* of **go**,

**gong** [gông] *noun*, a large piece of metal hung up and hit to make a loud noise

**good** [gŏŏd] *adjective*, 1) right, not wrong, the opposite of bad 2) appropriate, suitable, useful 3) well-behaved 4) nice, pleasant, *noun*, *no plural*, 5) what is virtuous and kind

**good-bye** [gŏŏd-bī′] *interjection*, an expression used to acknowledge parting

**good-ness** [gŏŏd′nĭs] *noun*, generosity, kindness, strength

**goods** [gŏŏdz] *noun*, merchandise, things made by people

**good-will** [gŏŏd wĭl] *noun*, the value of kindness in business and relationships

**goose** [gōōs] *noun*, *plural*, **geese**, a water bird like a duck but larger and having a longer neck

**gore** [gôr] *noun*, blood and guts

**gorge** [gôrj] *noun*, to stuff yourself

**gor-geous** [gôr′jəs] *adjective*, strikingly beautiful

**go-ril-la** [gə-rĭl′ə] *noun*, a very large animal similar to a monkey, the largest ape

**gos-pel** [gŏs′pəl] *noun*, the word of God according to the Bible

**gos-sa-mer** [gŏs′ə-mər] *adjective*, sheer, like cobwebs

**gos-sip** [gŏs′əp] *noun*, 1) rumors about people that are unkind or untrue 2) a person who makes false remarks about others, *verb*, 3) to talk about other people

**got** [gŏt] *past tense* of **get**

**gouge** [gouj] *noun*, 1) a chisel with a trough-like blade 2) a groove or hole, *verb*, 3) to cut or tear out

# gourd

**gourd** [gôrd] *noun*, a large fruit similar to squash, its shell is often made into a container

**gour-met** [gŏŏr-mā′] *adjective*, the finest food and drink

**gov-ern** [gŭv′ərn] *verb*, to lead or control by authority

**gov-ern-ment** [gŭv′ərn-mənt] *noun*, the offices, agencies, and people who control a nation, state, or city by making laws and seeing that they are followed

**gov-er-nor** [gŭv′ər-nər] *noun*, 1) the elected leader who controls a state or country 2) an attachment to an engine for controlling its speed

**gown** [goun] *noun*, 1) a dress worn by a woman that reaches to the floor 2) a covering over the body so that a doctor can examine you without your clothes on

**grab** [grăb] *verb*, to seize, to clutch, to snatch suddenly

**grace** [grās] *noun*, 1) elegance, refinement, charm 2) kindness, 3) holiness, devotion, love 4) mercy, pardon, 5) a blessing, giving thanks, *verb*, 6) to beautify, to enhance, to adorn

**grace-ful** [grās′fəl] *adjective*, having beauty of movement

**grace-ful-ly** [grās′fə-lē′] *adverb*, gently, calmly, smoothly

**gra-cious** [grā′shəs] *adjective*, kindly, pleasing, courteous

**grade** [grād] *noun*, 1) a rating of evaluation or class, *verb*, 2) to rate in a group, according to size, quantity or aptitude

**grad-u-al** [grăj′ŏŏ-əl] *adjective*, slow progress, step by step

**grad-u-al-ly** [grăj′ŏŏ-ə-lē] *adverb*, progressively, slowly

**grad-u-ate** [grăj′ŏŏ-āt′] *noun*, 1) someone who has received a diploma to document that he has completed a required course of study 2) a cup or cylinder marked for measuring liquid, *verb*, 3) to get one's degree by finishing school

**grad-u-a-tion** [grăj′ŏŏ-ā′shən] *noun*, a ceremony to award diplomas to graduates

**graf-fi-to** [grə-fē′tō] *noun*, *plural*, **graffiti**, words written or painted in public places to deface a building or surface

**graft** [grăft] *verb*, 1) a bud or a slit of a tree inserted into another tree to grow 2) a piece of transplanted living skin or tissue 3) use of one's position to make dishonest gains

**grain** [grān] *noun*, 1) a very small piece of something, a particle 2) seed from a cereal plant such as wheat, corn or rice 3) the design or pattern of wood

**gram** [grăm] *noun*, the metric unit of weight used to measure small objects

**gram-mar** [grăm′ər] *noun*, *no plural*, rules that govern the correct use of language

**grand** [grănd] *adjective*, very large and fine, impressive in size

**grand-child** [grănd′chīld′] *noun*, *plural* **grandchildren**, the child of someone's son or daughter

**grand-daugh-ter** [grăn′dô′tər] *noun*, the daughter of a person's son or daughter

142

**gran-deur** [grăn′jər] *noun,*
1) splendor, magnificence 2)
intellectual greatness, nobility

**grand-fa-ther** [grănd′fä′thər]
*noun,* the father of one of your
parents

**grand-moth-er** [grănd′mŭth′ər]
*noun,* the mother of one of your
parents

**grange** [g rānj] *noun,* 1) a farm with
its dwelling house, barns, etc.
2) an association of farmers
founded. in 1867 for mutual
welfare and advancement

**gran-ite** [grăn′ĭt] *noun,* a hard
igneous rock, consisting of
feldspar and quartz used in
monuments or buildings

**grant** [grănt] *noun,* 1) money
donated by the government or a
charitable foundation, *verb,* 2) to
allow, to confer, to give

**gran-u-late** [grăn′yə-lāt′] *verb,* to
process a dense solid into grains

**grape** [grāp] *noun,* a small, round
edible, juicy fruit that grows in
clusters on a vine

**grape-fruit** [grāp′frōot′] *noun,* a
bitter-tasting citrus fruit

**graph** [grăf] *noun,* 1) a picture
indicating measurements to
show change 2) a drawing used
to show information

**graph-ic** [grăf′ĭk] *adjective,*
1) pertaining to the arts of
painting and drawing 2) clearly
and vividly described

**graph-ite** [grăf′īt′] *noun,* native
carbon in the form of crystals

**grap-ple** [grăp′əl] *verb,* to grab and
struggle, to seize in a firm grip

**grasp** [grăsp] *noun,* 1) a clasp, held
in the hand, *verb,* 2) to hold or
seize 3) to understand or learn,
to comprehend, to take in

**grass** [grăs] *noun,* 1) a fine ground
cover with thin leaves that
animals eat 2) as a lawn

**grass-hop-per** [grăs′hŏp′ər] *noun,*
an insect that lives in the grass
with strong back legs for
jumping and wings for flying

**grate** [grāt] *noun,* 1) a metal frame
with wires laid in the shape of a
grid, *verb,* 2) to cut or shave into
small pieces, to shred by
rubbing on a jagged surface

**grate-ful** [grāt′fəl] *adjective,*
thankful, appreciative

**grat-i-fy** [grăt′ə-fī′] *verb,* to satisfy,
to please, to delight, to indulge

**grat-i-tude** [grăt′ĭ-tōōd′] *noun, no
plural,* a feeling of thankfulness

**gra-tu-i-ty** [grə-tōō′ĭ-tē] *noun,* a tip

**grave** [grāv] *adjective,* 1) serious,
*noun,* 2) a hole in the ground
where a dead person is buried

**grav-el** [grăv′əl] *noun,* a mixture of
pebbles and rock fragments

**grav-i-ty** [grăv′ĭ-tē] *noun,* 1) the
force that draws everything to
the earth's center 2) solemnity

**gra-vy** [grā′vē] *noun,* a sauce made
with meat drippings

**gray** [grā] *adjective,* a mixture of
white and black

**graze** [grāz] *verb,* 1) to eat grass or
vegetation 2) to rub against
something and scraping off the
surface

**grease** [grēs] *noun,* 1) a soft animal
fat, any oily matter, *verb,* 2) to

lubricate or make slippery with oils, to coat with grease

**great** [grāt] *adjective*, 1) large in size, quantity, duration 2) eminent, remarkable

**great-er** [grā/tər] *adjective*, more than something in comparison to it, bigger, larger, better

**great-est** [grā/tĭst] *adjective*, the most, superior, the best

**greed** [grēd] *noun*, *no plural*, the feeling that you want more than you need, desire for wealth

**green** [grēn] *adjective*, 1) a color made by combining yellow and blue, *noun*, 2) a plot of grass

**green-house** [grēn/hous'] *noun*, a house made of glass or transparent plastic used to grow plants in a controlled environment, year round

**greet** [grēt] *verb*, to welcome

**greet-ing** [grē/tĭng] *noun*, good wishes, a friendly expression

**gre-gar-i-ous** [grĭ-gâr/ē-əs] *adjective*, very social

**grew** [grōō] *past tense* of **grow**

**grey** [grā] see **gray**, *adjective*, a mixture of black and white

**grid** [grĭd] *noun*, 1) grate, a lead plate with perforations 2) a network of horizontal and vertical lines used to locate a particular point on a map

**grid-dle** [grĭd/l] *noun*, a flat square pan used for cooking waffles

**grief** [grēf] *noun*, very deep sorrow, sadness

**griev-ance** [grē/vəns] *noun*, cause of complaint, a protest

**grieve** [grēv] *verb*, to be upset about something lost or done, to be filled with sadness

**grill** [grĭl] *noun*, 1) a cooking unit fueled by a flame with a metal rack used for broiling food 2) a system of bars forming a lattice, *verb*, 3) to broil food 4) to question intensely

**grim** [grĭm] *adjective*, dreadful, ghastly, stern, unyielding

**grin** [grĭn] *noun*, 1) a big smile, *verb*, 2) to smile broadly

**grind** [grīnd] *verb*, to crush something so hard that it becomes powder

**grip** [grĭp] *noun*, 1) a hold, a grasp, *verb*, 2) to hold or clench something tightly

**gris-ly** [grĭz/lē] *adjective*, ghastly, horrible, gruesome, shocking

**grist** [grĭst] *noun*, corn

**grit** [grĭt] *noun*, 1) courage, fortitude, bravery 2) sand, gravel

**grits** [grĭts] *noun*, *plural*, coarsely ground hominy

**griz-zly** [grĭz/lē] *noun*, a big bear

**groan** [grōn] *noun*, 1) a moan, a complaint, a cry of distress, *verb*, 2) to emit a low cry in disapproval or pain

**gro-cer** [grō/sər] *noun*, someone who sells food and sundries

**gro-cer-y** [grō/sə-rē] *noun*, food and household items

**groom** [grōōm] *noun*, 1) the husband to be 2) a stable boy, *verb*, 3) to make oneself presentable, neat and trim 4) to train for a career

**groove** [groōv] *noun*, 1) a channel or furrow cut into something, *verb*, 2) to move to a rhythm

**grope** [grōp] *verb*, to feel your way in the dark

**gross** [grōs] *adjective*, 1) bulky, coarse, unrefined, *noun*, 2) twelve dozen

**gro-tesque** [grō-těsk′] *adjective*, distorted, abnormal, strange-looking in shape, bizarre

**ground** [ground] *noun*, *no plural*, 1) the surface of the earth, *verb*, 2) past tense of **grind**

**ground-wa-ter** [ground′wô′tər] *noun*, water beneath the earth's surface that supplies wells and springs

**group** [groōp] *noun*, 1) people or things classed together because of similar qualities 2) people who share the same needs and interests

**grove** [grōv] *noun*, a group of trees

**grov-el** [grŏv′əl] *verb*, to crawl or creep, to beg, to cringe

**grow** [grō] *verb*, 1) to become larger, to increase in size or maturity 2) to change and become 3) to sprout, to germinate, to develop

**growl** [groul] *noun*, 1) a low angry or unfriendly noise coming from the throat like a dog, *verb*, 2) to make such a sound

**grown** [grōn] *adjective*, to reach maturity or full growth

**growth** [grōth] *noun*, *no plural*, 1) development 2) a tumor or other form of swelling

**grub** [grŭb] *noun*, 1) larva, a maggot, *verb*, 2) to dig, to uproot

**grudge** [grŭj] *noun*, hatred, spite

**gruel-ing** [groō′ə-lĭng] *adjective*, exhausting, very difficult

**grue-some** [groō′səm] *adjective*, ghastly, frightening, horrible

**grum-ble** [grŭm′bəl] *verb*, to complain, to grouse, to mutter

**grunt** [grŭnt] *verb*, to make a guttural sound, to snort like a pig

**guar-an-tee** [găr′ən-tē′] *noun*, 1) a pledge, *verb*, 2) to honor a promise

**guard** [gärd] *noun*, 1) a person or thing which forms security or a defense, *verb*, 2) to watch over, to prevent an escape

**guard-i-an** [gär′dē-ən] *noun*, someone who takes care of another or their property

**guer-ril-la** [gə-rĭl′ə] *noun*, a revolutionary

**guess** [gěs] *noun*, 1) a conjecture, *verb*, 2) to imagine, to think or believe 3) to give an answer without really knowing

**guest** [gěst] *noun*, 1) a person invited to stay with someone else, a visitor 2) a customer

**guid-ance** [gīd′ns] *noun*, *no plural*, help, the act or result of guiding

**guide** [gīd] *noun*, 1) someone or something that shows the way to find something, *verb*, 2) to show the way or lead 3) to counsel

**guile** [gīl] *noun*, the ability to trick others, crafty, cunning, deceit

**guilt** [gĭlt] *noun*, *no plural*, knowing you have done wrong, accepting liability and blame for a wrongdoing

**guilt-y** [gĭl′tē] *adjective*, 1) legally charged with a crime 2) full of shame, feeling remorse

**guin-ea** [gĭn′ē] *noun*, Italian money

**guise** [gīz] *noun*, general, external appearance, manner, pretense

**gui-tar** [gĭ-tär′] *noun*, a musical instrument with six strings, a fretted neck, and a pear-shaped sound box

**gulf** [gŭlf] *noun*, 1) part of a sea partially surrounded by land, larger and deeper than a bay 2) a large empty space, or chasm

**gul-li-ble** [gŭl′ə-bəl] *adjective*, easily tricked or cheated

**gul-ly** [gŭl′ē] *noun*, a small gulch

**gulp** [gŭlp] *noun*, 1) a mouthful, *verb*, 2) to swallow quickly 3) to choke or gasp nervously

**gum** [gŭm] *noun*, 1) the tissue in your mouth above the teeth to protect the roots of each tooth 2) a sticky substance used to hold things together, like glue 3) a soft substance, flavored like candy that can be chewed but it does not dissolve in the mouth

**gun** [gŭn] *noun*, a weapon consisting of a metal tube used to shoot bullets under pressure

**gust** [gŭst] *noun*, a sudden rush of wind or strong blast of air

**gut** [gŭt] *noun*, a stomach, the belly

**gut-ter** [gŭt′ər] *noun*, drainage ditch, drainpipe, the lower ground or channel along the side of the road

**gym-na-si-um** [jĭm-nā′zē-əm] *noun*, a place where athletic exercises are performed

**gym-nas-tics** [jĭm-năs′tĭks] *noun*, *plural*, exercises designed to stretch and strengthen the body

**gyp-sy** [jĭp′sē] *noun*, a person who belongs to a wandering group of people that came from India to Europe, 4,000 years ago, and now live all over the world

# H

**hab-it** [hăb′ĭt] *noun*, a tendency to do something as part of a routine

**hab-i-tat** [hăb′ĭ-tăt′] *noun*, the natural environment in which an animal or plant lives

**hab-i-ta-tion** [hăb′ĭ-tā′shən] *noun*, home, abode, dwelling

**hab-it-u-al** [hə-bĭch′ōō-əl] *adjective*, customary regular, according to habit

**hack-les** [hăk′əlz] *noun*, hairs on the back and neck of a dog

**hack-neyed** [hăk′nēd] *adjective*, common, dull, worn-out

**had** [hăd] *past tense* of **have**

**hag-gle** [hăg′əl] *verb*, to argue about price, to bargain

**hai-ku** [hī′kōō] *noun*, a form of poetry consisting of 3 lines of 5, 7, and 5 syllables each

**hail** [hāl] *noun*, 1) frozen rain drops, *verb*, 2) to shout with enthusiasm, to call out in a greeting, to welcome

**hair** [hâr] *noun*, a strand of filament that grows out of the skin of animals

**hal-cy-on** [hăl′sē-ən] *adjective*, calm, peaceful, happy

**hale** [hāl] *adjective*, 1) healthy, strong, *verb*, 2) to haul, to draw

**half** [hăf] *noun*, 1) one of two equal parts of a whole 2) partial

**half-dol-lar** [hăf′dŏl′ər] *noun*, a coin equal to fifty cents

**half-way** [hăf′wā′] *adjective*, midway between two points

**hal-i-but** [hăl′ə-bət] *noun*, the largest species of marine flatfish

**hall** [hôl] *noun*, 1) the corridor in a building 2) a large room for entertaining 3) a building at a college or university

**hal-low** [hăl′ō] *verb*, to bless or make holy or sacred

**hal-lu-ci-na-tion** [hə-lōō′sə-nā′shən] *noun*, something that is seen or heard but is not actually happening, a delusion, a vision

**halt** [hôlt] *verb*, to cause to stop

**halt-er** [hôl′tər] *noun*, 1) a rope for a horse, a rein 2) a woman's top tied behind the neck across the back 3) a hangman's noose

**halve** [hăv] *verb*, to divide in two

**ham** [hăm] *noun*, the meat from a pig's leg, preserved with salt or smoke 2) a comedian

**ham-burg-er** [hăm′bûr′gər] *noun*, ground beef served as a patty on a sandwich or alone

**ham-mer** [hăm′ər] *noun*, 1) an instrument used for driving nails, *verb*, 2) to hit or pound with a hammer or mallet, to strike

**ham-mock** [hăm′ək] *noun*, a bed of canvas cord hanging between two supports

**ham-per** [hăm′pər] *noun*, 1) a basket for dirty clothes, *verb*, 2) to obstruct, to hinder

**ham-ster** [hăm′stər] *noun*, a rodent similar to a rat, with large cheek pouches often kept as a pet

**hand** [hănd] *noun*, 1) the part of the arm used to hold something, *verb*, 2) to deliver or pass along

**hand-i-cap** [hăn′dē-kăp′] *noun*, an impediment, a physical defect

**hand-ker-chief** [hăng′kər-chĭf] *noun*, a cloth carried for wiping hands, the face or nose

**han-dle** [hăn′dl] *noun*, 1) the part of a tool or instrument held in the hand, *verb*, 2) to touch, feel, or examine with the hand 3) to control, manage or deal with

**han-dle-bar** [hăn′dl-bär′] *noun*, the part of a bicycle used to steer when you ride it

**hand-shake** [hănd′shāk′] *noun*, a greeting made by shaking hands

**hand-some** [hăn′səm] *adjective*, good-looking, attractive, manly

**hand-writ-ing** [hănd′rī′tĭng] *noun*, penmanship, writing done with a pen usually in cursive

**hand-y** [hăn′dē] *adjective*, convenient, easy to use

**hang** [hăng] *verb*, 1) to fasten so that something can swing freely, to suspend 2) to suspend from a rope until dead 3) to linger, to wait 4) to be contingent

**hang-ar** [hăng′ər] *noun*, a building for storing aircraft

**hang-er** [hăng′ər] *noun*, a device on which something hangs

**hap** [hăp] *noun*, chance, luck

**hap-haz-ard** [hăp-hăz′ərd] *adjective*, random, by chance

**hap-less** [hăp′lĭs] *adjective*, unfortunate, unlucky

# happen

**hap-pen** [hăp′ən] *verb*, 1) to occur by chance, 2) to come to pass

**hap-pi-ly** [hăp′ə-lē] *adverb*, good-natured, graciously, kindly

**hap-pi-ness** [hăp′ē-nĭs] *noun*, conscious enjoyment of good fortune, contentment

**hap-py** [hăp′ē] *adjective*, content, delighted or pleased

**ha-rangue** [hə-răng′] *noun*, a loud address to a multitude, a noisy, ranting speech

**ha-rass** [hăr′əs] *verb*, to trouble by repeated attacks, to annoy

**har-bor** [här′bər] *noun*, 1) a port where ships or boats can dock safely, *verb*, 2) to hide, to protect, or conceal

**hard** [härd] *adjective*, 1) difficult to understand 2) firm, solid, impenetrable 3) difficult, fatiguing, challenging, *adverb*, 4) intensely, diligently

**hard drive** [hard-drīv] *noun*, the memory on a computer

**hard-en** [här′dn] *verb*, 1) to make solid 2) to become unfeeling

**hard-ly** [härd′lē] *adverb*, barely, almost never, scarcely

**hard-ship** [härd′shĭp′] *adjective*, suffering, extreme privation

**hard-ware** [härd′wâr′] *noun*, 1) the pieces of equipment that make up a computer 2) the items such as nuts and bolts needed to put something together

**hare** [hâr] *noun*, an animal similar to a rabbit, that is larger, unlike a rabbit, it does not burrow and its young are born covered with fur

**harm** [härm] *noun*, 1) injury, damage, *verb*, 2) to hurt or injure

**harm-ful** [härm′fəl] *adjective*, something that could cause damage or injury

**harm-less** [härm′lĭs] *adjective*, causing no harm or damage

**har-mon-i-ca** [här-mŏn′ĭ-kə] *noun*, a hand-held rectangular musical instrument played by exhaling and inhaling through a row of metal reeds

**har-mo-ni-ous** [här-mō′nē-əs] *adjective*, symmetrical, congruous, in agreement

**har-mo-nize** [här′mə-nīz′] *verb*, to sing in harmony, to cooperate

**har-mo-ny** [här′mə-nē] *noun*, 1) in tune 2) agreement, accord

**har-ness** [här′nĭs] *noun*, the working gear of a horse

**harp** [härp] *noun*, 1) a large stringed instrument, played with fingers, *verb*, 2) to nag

**har-poon** [här-pōōn′] *noun*, 1) a barbed spear, like a missile, *verb*, 2) to stab with a harpoon

**har-row** [hăr′ō] *noun*, 1) a tractor accessory used to turn over the soil, *verb*, 2) to cultivate

**harsh** [härsh] *adjective*, 1) hard to bear, severe, cruel 2) inharmonious, jarring, dissonant

**har-vest** [här′vĭst] *noun*, 1) the season's crop, the amount gathered, *verb*, 2) to gather or pick a crop, to reap, to gain

**has** [hăz] the part of the *verb* **have** used with *he*, *she*, and *it*

**haste** [hāst] *noun*, hurry

**hast-i-ly** [hāst′ĭ-lē] *adverb*, hurriedly, quickly, fast

**hast-y** [hā′stē] *adjective*, done in a hurry, quickly, swiftly

**hat** [hăt] *noun*, a clothing accessory used to cover the head

**hatch** [hăch] *noun*, 1) a small doorway or opening in a wall or a floor, *verb*, 2) to emerge from an egg when born

**hatch-et** [hăch/ĭt] *noun*, a small ax with a short handle

**hate** [hāt] *verb*, to dislike, to detest

**hate-ful** [hāt/fəl] *adjective*, full of hate, feeling a strong dislike

**ha-tred** [hā/trĭd] *noun*, a strong feeling of dislike, hostility

**haugh-ty** [hô/tē] *adjective*, snobbish, proud, arrogant

**haul** [hôl] *verb*, to pull or draw with force, to drag

**haunt** [hônt] *noun*, 1) a deserted place, *verb*, 2) to intrude upon continually, to annoy

**have** [hăv] *verb*, 1) to hold possession of or keep 2) a word used to indicate the *past tense* in a description 3) need to, must

**ha-ven** [hā/vən] *noun*, a safe place

**hav-oc** [hăv/ək] *noun*, widespread destruction of life and property, devastation, confusion

**Ha-waii** [hə-wä/ē] *noun*, one of the 50 United States located in the Pacific ocean, the capital city is Honolulu. The state flower of Hawaii is the red hibiscus, and the motto is "The life of the land is preserved in righteousness."

**hawk** [hôk] *noun*, 1) a large bird of prey that kills birds and small animals for food, *verb*, 2) to peddle, to sell on the street

**hay** [hā] *noun*, dry grass eaten by farm animals such as cows, goats, horses

**haz-ard** [hăz/ərd] *noun*, a danger

**haz-ard-ous** [hăz/ər-dəs] *adjective*, dangerous, risky

**haze** [hāz] *noun*, *no plural*, widely dispersed dust particles in the air that cloud the view

**ha-zel** [hā/zəl] *adjective*, a color of gray, blue, and brown

**he** [hē] *pronoun*, *plural*, **they**, the male person or animal, who is the subject of the sentence

**head** [hĕd] *noun*, 1) the boney structure at the top of humans and animals that contains the brain, the face, the ears, eyes, mouth, nose 2) the seat of reason 3) the leader 4) the top of something, *verb*, 5) to move in the direction of something 6) to lead, to be the chief of

**head-ache** [hĕd/āk/] *noun*, 1) a dispute, a nuisance 2) pain in the head behind the eyes, a migraine

**head-ing** [hĕd/ĭng] *noun*, the title or caption at the top of a piece of writing

**head-line** [hĕd/līn/] *noun*, 1) a line of type displayed conspicuously at the top of a page or column of a newspaper, etc.

**head-quar-ters** [hĕd/kwôr/tərz] *noun*, the center of operations from which orders are issued

**heal** [hēl] *verb*, to cure, to treat an illness, to remedy, to repair

**health** [hĕlth] *noun*, 1) the condition of the body or mind free from sickness or disease

**health-y** [hĕl/thē] *adjective*, 1) having a sound mind and body, strong, vibrant, robust 2) wholesome, nutritious

**heap** [hēp] *noun,* 1) a pile of things, *verb,* 2) to put into a large pile, to stack

**hear** [hîr] *verb,* 1) to take in sounds 2) to listen 3) to receive news

**heard** [hûrd] *past tense* of **hear**

**hear-ing** [hîr′ĭng] *noun,* an opportunity to be heard before a judge or peers

**hearse** [hûrs] *noun,* a car used to carry a coffin to the cemetery

**heart** [härt] *noun,* 1) the hollow muscular organ that pumps blood to the arteries and receives blood from the veins 2) the center of someone's feelings and spirit

**hearth** [härth] *noun,* 1) the bottom of a furnace where metal that is melted into a liquid, collects 2) a fireplace or fireside

**heat** [hēt] *noun, no plural,* 1) the feeling of warmth or something hot caused by friction, *verb,* 2) to raise the temperature to become hot, to make warmer

**heat-er** [hē′tər] *noun,* an appliance that warms a room

**heath-en** [hē′thən] *noun,* an atheist, someone who has no god

**heave** [hēv] *verb,* to lift or pull something of great weight

**heav-en** [hĕv′ən] *noun,* 1) the home of God, where the saved go to live after death 2) a state of supreme happiness or bliss

**heav-en-ly** [hĕv′ən-lē] *adjective,* divine, very nice or pleasant

**heav-i-er** [hĕv′ē-ər] *adjective,* more weight

**heav-y** [hĕv′ē] *adjective,* 1) a lot of weight 2) burdensome

**heck-ler** [hĕk′əl- ər] *noun,* a person who shouts and bothers a public speaker by asking impertinent questions

**hec-tic** [hĕk′tĭk] *adjective,* unsettled, confused, frenzied

**hedge** [hĕj] *noun,* a dense row of shrubs or bushes to make a wall or border forming a boundary

**heed** [hēd] *verb,* to notice, to pay careful attention to

**heel** [hēl] *noun,* 1) the back part of a foot, below the ankle 2) the back, bottom part of a shoe 3) an unpleasant person, *verb,* 4) to follow obediently or closely

**heif-er** [hĕf′ər] *noun,* a young cow

**height** [hīt] *noun,* distance upwards, how tall something is

**hei-nous** [hā′nəs] *adjective,* hateful, odious, flagrant

**heir** [âr] *noun,* one who inherits, or has the right to inherit, property after the death of its owner

**heir-ess** [âr′ĭs] *noun,* a woman who has inherited a fortune

**heir-loom** [âr′lōōm′] *noun,* a family possession that is given to a new generation

**held** [hĕld] *past tense* of **hold**

**hel-i-cop-ter** [hĕl′ĭ-kŏp′tər] *noun,* a flying machine propelled by action of screws and propeller blades rotating on a vertical axis without supporting wings

**he-li-um** [hē′lē-əm] *noun,* an inert, gaseous element occurring principally in the atmosphere of the sun and stars

**hell** [hĕl] *noun*, a place where Satan lives, and where the wicked go when they die

**hel-lo** [hĕ-lō′] a greeting

**helm** [hĕlm] *noun*,1) the wheel or tiller by which a ship is steered 2) a position of control

**hel-met** [hĕl′mĭt] *noun*, a protective head covering

**help** [hĕlp] *noun*, 1) assistance, support, guidance, *verb*, 2) to do something for someone, to assist

**help-ing** [hĕl′pĭng] *adjective*, 1) willing to assist, *noun*, 2) a portion of food, a serving

**help-less** [hĕlp′lĭs] *adjective*, unable to help oneself

**help-ful** [hĕlp′fəl] *adjective*, ready to give help, useful

**hem** [hĕm] *noun*, 1) the edge of a garment that has been sewn to keep it from fraying and to hang on the body at the correct length, *verb*, 2) to sew the bottom of a garment 3) to confine, to enclose

**hem-i-sphere** [hĕm′ĭ-sfîr′] *noun*, one of the halves of the Earth

**hem-or-rhage** [hĕm′ər-ĭj] *noun*, any discharge of blood from the blood vessels, heavy bleeding

**hen** [hĕn] *noun*, a female bird

**her** [hər, ər; hûr when stressed] *pronoun*, belonging to a female

**her-ald** [hĕr′əld] *noun*, 1) a bearer of news, *verb*, 2) to announce publicly, to proclaim

**herb** [ûrb] *noun*, a plant used for medicine or adding flavor to food or aromatherapy

**her-biv-o-rous** [hûr-bĭv′ər-əs] *adjective*, plant or grain-eating

**herd** [hûrd] *noun*, 1) a group of animals eating, traveling, or living together, *verb*, 2) to control or steer a group of animals 3) to congregate

**here** [hîr] *adverb*, referring to at this place or going to this place

**he-red-i-tar-y** [hə-rĕd′ĭ-tĕr′ē] *adjective*, an inherited trait passed on through genes

**he-red-i-ty** [hə-rĕd′ĭ-tē] *noun*, inherited characteristics or traits, from parents to offspring

**her-e-sy** [hĕr′ĭ-sē] *noun*, nonconformity, dissenting view

**her-e-tic** [hĕr′ĭ-tĭk] *noun*, a nonbeliever, a skeptic

**her-it-age** [hĕr′ĭ-tĭj] *noun*, rights and or possessions handed down from ancestors, traditions

**her-mit** [hûr′mĭt] *noun*, a recluse

**her-mit-age** [hûr′mĭ-tĭj] *noun*, home of one who lives alone

**he-ro** [hîr′ō] *noun*, a person of great strength or courage

**her-o-ine** [hĕr′ō-ĭn] *noun*, a woman admired for her brave deeds

**her-o-ism** [hĕr′ō-ĭz′əm] *noun*, courage, boldness, bravery

**her-on** [hĕr′ən] *noun*, a large bird that lives in the wetlands

**her-ring** [hĕr′ĭng] *noun*, a small fish abundant in the ocean and occasionally in fresh water

**hers** [hûrz] *pronoun*, something belonging to a woman or girl

**her-self** [hûr-sĕlf′] *pronoun*, *plural*, **themselves**, the reflexive form of **she**, belonging to her

**hes-i-tate** [hĕz′ĭ-tāt′] *verb*, to act slowly, as if in doubt, to be uncertain because of fear

151

# hesitation

**hes·i·ta·tion** [hĕz′ĭ-tā′shən] *noun,* doubt, uncertainty, skepticism

**hew** [hyōō] *verb,* to cut to pieces

**hex·a·gon** [hĕk′sə-gŏn′] *noun,* a plane figure having six sides

**hi·a·tus** [hī-ā′təs] *noun,* a gap, an interval in time, a pause

**hi·ber·nate** [hī′bər-nāt′] *verb,* to sleep during the winter

**hic·cup** [hĭk′əp] *noun,* a small belch

**hid·den** [hĭd′n] *adjective,* concealed from sight

**hide** [hīd] *noun, no plural,* 1) the skin of an animal, *verb,* 2) to put out of sight or keep a secret

**hid·e·ous** [hĭd′ē-əs] *adjective,* horribly ugly, shocking

**hi·er·ar·chy** [hī′ə-rär′kē] *noun,* a pecking order, ranking

**hi·er·o·glyph·ics** [hī′ər-ə-glĭf′ĭks] *noun, plural,* characters in the picture writing of the ancient Egyptians

**high** [hī] *adjective,* 1) how tall something is from the ground 2) expensive, above average 3) a shrill pitch 4) elated, happy

**high·land** [hī′lənd] *noun,* land that is high up in the hills

**high·ness** [hī′nĭs] *noun,* a title of a member of the royal family

**high·way** [hī′wā′] *noun,* the main public road that usually connects cities and towns

**hi·jack** [hī′jăk′] *verb,* to force the driver of a vehicle to go somewhere, to commandeer

**hike** [hīk] *noun,* 1) a walk, a journey, a trek, *verb,* 2) to go on an extended walk

**hi·lar·i·ous** [hĭ-lâr′ē-əs] *adjective,* very funny, boisterously merry

**hill** [hĭl] *noun,* a rise in land making the ground higher than the earth's surface

**him** [hĭm] *pronoun,* a man or boy

**him·self** [hĭm-sĕlf′] *pronoun,* the subject mentioned later in the sentence, *plural,* **themselves**

**hind** [hīnd] *adjective,* situated in the rear, back, posterior

**hind·er** [hĭn′dər] *verb,* to make it more difficult for someone to do something, to obstruct

**hind·rance** [hĭn′drəns] *noun,* something that slows you down, an impediment

**Hin·du** [hĭn′dōō] *noun,* 1) a native of India 2) a religion in the culture of India that embraces ancient philosophy and traditions

**hinge** [hĭnj] *noun,* 1) a joint on which a door or gate turns or swings, *verb,* 2) to hang on or attach to something

**hint** [hĭnt] *noun,* 1) a suggestion, a clue 2) a slight trace

**hip** [hĭp] *noun,* the part of your body below the stomach where your legs are connected to the rest of your body

**hip·po·pot·a·mus** [hĭp′ə-pŏt′ə-məs] *noun,* a beast with thick skin that measures 4-5 feet high, 12 feet long, and weighs 4 tons that lives in Africa

**hire** [hīr] *verb,* to pay someone to do work or perform services

**his** [hĭz] *pronoun,* belonging to a man or a boy, the possessive case of **he**

**hiss** [hĭs] *noun*, 1) a sound made by forcing air through the teeth, *verb*, 2) to make a sound like a defensive cat

**his-tol-o-gy** [hĭ-stŏl′ə-jē] *noun*, the science which treats of the minute structure of animal and vegetable tissues

**his-to-ri-an** [hĭ-stôr′ē-ən] *noun*, an authority or author of past events in history

**his-tor-ic** [hĭ-stôr′ĭk] *adjective*, something embodying people or things of the past

**his-tor-ic-al** [hĭ-stôr′ĭ-kəl] *adjective*, information or articles belonging to the past

**his-to-ry** [hĭs′tə-rē] *noun*, the story and knowledge of the past

**hit** [hĭt] *noun*, 1) a blow 2) when the ball comes in contact with the bat 3) a smash, a wow, a success, *verb*, 4) to bring something down hard onto something else, to smack

**hitch** [hĭch] *verb*, to tie something to something else, to attach

**hive** [hīv] *noun*, 1) any place busy with activity 2) a variety of allergic reactions marked by itching welts or a rash

**hoard** [hôrd] *noun*, 1) a large amount of something, *verb*, 2) to collect and save, to accumulate, to set aside and hide away

**hoarse** [hôrs] *adjective*, sounding husky and rough or harsh

**hoax** [hōks] *noun*, a practical joke, a deceitful trick, a prank

**hob-by** [hŏb′ē] *noun*, a favorite activity that holds someone's interest that one likes to do

**hock-ey** [hŏk′ē] *noun*, a game played on ice or grass by two teams of several players who use curved sticks to hit a puck or a ball into a net or goal

**hoe** [hō] *noun*, 1) a tool used to lift and loosen the earth, *verb*, 2) to turn the soil over with a hoe

**hog** [hôg, hŏg] *noun*, a large pig

**hoist** [hoist] *verb*, to lift up, especially with a pulley

**hold** [hōld] *noun*, 1) the part of the ship that holds cargo, *verb*, 2) to grasp 3) to contain 4) to host an event 5) to restrain, to keep back 6) to balance something

**hole** [hōl] *noun*, an empty space in something, a gap, a cavity

**hol-i-day** [hŏl′ĭ-dā′] *noun*, 1) a period of time that involves relaxation, not work 2) a day on which a particular event is celebrated

**hol-low** [hŏl′ō] *adjective*, 1) not solid, an empty space inside 2) feeling unworthy, small, *noun*, 3) a small valley

**hol-ly** [hŏl′ē] *noun*, an evergreen, with bright red berries and prickly and glossy leaves

**hol-o-caust** [hŏl′ə-kôst′] *noun*, great or total destruction by fire, extermination, genocide

**ho-ly** [hō′lē] *adjective*, of God or the gods, divine, sacred

**hom-age** [hŏm′ĭj] *noun*, to honor, to pay tribute and respect to a person publicly

**home** [hōm] *noun*, a place where someone lives, a residence

**home-ly** [hōm′lē] *adjective*, unattractive, plain looking

**ho-me-o-path** [hō′mē -ə-păth′]
*noun*, one who combats disease
with remedies producing a
similar complaint on a healthy
person

**home run** [hōm rŭn′] *noun*, a run
scored on a hit which enables the
batter to touch all four bases

**home-stead** [hōm′stĕd′] *verb*, to
make a place one's home

**home-work** [hōm′wûrk′] *noun*,
material from school to be
completed at home

**hom-i-cide** [hŏm′ĭ-sīd′] *noun*, the
killing of one human being by
another

**hom-i-ly** [hŏm′ə-lē] *noun*, a
sermon, a moral lesson

**ho-mo-ge-neous** [hō′mə-jē′nē-əs]
*adjective*, 1) of the same kind or
nature 2) consisting of similar
parts throughout

**ho-mog-e-nize** [hə-mŏj′ə-nīz′]
*verb*, to reduce particles in
liquids such as milk or paint to
the same size

**hom-o-phone** [hŏm′ə-fōn′] *noun*, a
word that sounds the same as
another, but is spelled
differently, and has a different
meaning,e.g. *see* and *sea*

**hone** [hōn] *verb*, to sharpen

**hon-est** [ŏn′ĭst] *adjective*, truthful,
not deceitful, trustworthy

**hon-est-ly** [ŏn′ĭst-lē] *adverb*,
truthfully, openly, candidly

**hon-es-ty** [ŏn′ĭ-stē] *noun*, telling
the truth, integrity, fairness,
truthfulness, sincerity

**hon-ey** [hŭn′ē] *noun*, a syrup made
by bees with treacle gathered
from flowers

**hon-ey-comb** [hŭn′ē-kōm′] *noun*,
six-sided wax cells made by bees
to store honey or eggs

**hon-ey-moon** [hŭn′ē-mōōn′] *noun*,
a holiday taken by a couple who
have just been married

**hon-or** [ŏn′ər] *noun*, 1) fame or a
rank of high esteem, *verb*, 2) to
hold in high respect 3) to keep an
agreement

**hon-or-a-ble** [ŏn′ər-ə-bəl]
*adjective*, respectable

**hood** [hōōd] *noun*, 1) a covering for
the head attached to a jacket or a
robe 2) an engine cover

**hoof** [hōōf] *noun*, *plural*, **hooves**,
the horny, hard covering on the
foot of a horse, cow, or goat

**hook** [hōōk] *noun*, 1) a bent piece
of metal or plastic used to catch
something, *verb*, 2) to clasp, to
hang or fasten with a hook

**hoop** [hōōp] *noun*, a circular band
such as a hoola hoop or a
basketball hoop

**hop** [hŏp] *noun*, 1) a short jump,
*verb*, 2) to move on one foot
3) to jump with both feet
together to move along like a
bird or rabbit

**hope** [hōp] *noun*, 1) a feeling of
confidence, expectation *verb*, 2)
to look forward to something
believing that it will happen

**horde** [hôrd] *noun*, crowd, a mob, a
large multitude, a swarm

**ho-ri-zon** [hə-rī′zən] *noun*, where
the earth appears to intersect the
sky, the skyline

**hor-i-zon-tal** [hôr′ĭ-zŏn′tl]
*adjective*, 1) parallel to the
horizon 2) flat, level

**horn** [hôrn] *noun*, 1) one of two hard growths growing out from the heads of some animals such as deer, elk, etc. 2) the device on a car or bicycle used to warn people 3) a musical wind instrument in the brass family with a set of keys to regulate the flow of air

**hor-net** [hôr'nĭt] *noun*, a bee similar to a wasp

**hor-o-scope** [hôr'ə-skōp'] *noun*, an astrological prediction

**hor-ri-ble** [hôr'ə-bəl] *adjective*, shocking, hideous, terrible

**hor-rid** [hôr'ĭd] *adjective*, vile, disgusting, vulgar, frightful

**hor-ri-fy** [hôr'ə-fĭ'] *verb*, to frighten, to terrify, to petrify

**hor-ror** [hôr'ər] *noun*, great fear and shock caused by something terrible, a feeling of terror

**horse** [hôrs] *noun*, an animal with long legs that eats grass and can pull a cart or carry people

**horse-back** [hôrs'băk'] *noun*, to ride on the back of a horse

**horse-pow-er** [hôrs'pou'ər] *noun*, a unit of power, 33,000 foot pounds of work per minute

**horse-shoe** [hôrs'shoo'] *noun*, a strip of iron conformed to the rim of a horse's hoof

**hor-ti-cul-ture** [hôr'tĭ-kŭl'chər] *noun*, the study of growing fruits, vegetables, flowers

**hose** [hōz] *noun*, 1) a rubber tube used to transfer liquid, *verb*, 2) to water with a hose

**hos-pi-tal** [hŏs'pĭ-tl] *noun*, a place that provides medical and surgical care for the sick and injured

**hos-pi-tal-i-ty** [hŏs'pĭ-tăl'ĭ-tē] *noun*, *no plural*, a warm welcome or reception to visitors

**host** [hōst] *noun*, 1) a person who entertains guests 2) an organism harboring a parasite 3) the communion wafer, representing the bread of the last supper, *verb*, 4) to receive guests, to entertain 5) to serve as a master of ceremonies

**hos-tage** [hŏs'tĭj] *noun*, a person or thing taken prisoner for ransom

**host-ess** [hō'stĭs] *noun*, the woman of the house, the one who entertains the guests

**hos-til-i-ty** [hŏ-stĭl'ĭ-tē] *noun*, unfriendliness, antagonism, showing ill will, rancor

**hot** [hŏt] *adjective*, 1) a very high temperature 2) a very strong, burning taste, spicy

**ho-tel** [hō-tĕl'] *noun*, a large building that offers lodging and food to paying customers, etc.

**hound** [hound] *noun*, a breed of dog used for hunting or racing

**hour** [our] *noun*, 1 )sixty minutes, a measure of time, 1/24th of a day 2) a particular time of day

**house** [hous] *noun*, 1) a building or part of a building where people live or dwell 2) a residence

**house-hold** [hous'hōld'] *noun*, all the people who live in a house together as a unit

**House of Representatives** *noun*, the lower house of the legislature of the United States

**house-wife** [hous'wīf'] *noun*, the spouse who maintains the house for the family

**hov-el** [hŭv′əl] *noun*, a shack

**hov-er** [hŭv′ər] *verb*, to stay in one place floating, flying, or fluttering in the air

**hov-er-craft** [hŭv′ər-krăft′] *noun*, a sort of boat that travels over land or water by floating on air pushed out by its engines

**how** [hou] *adverb*, 1) used in questions about time, amount, or size 2) used to ask about health 3) used to show surprise or pleasure 4) used to show the way something is done

**how-ev-er** [hou-ev′ər] *adverb*, nonetheless, despite, though, yet, after all, in whatever manner

**howl** [houl] *verb*, 1) to make a long wailing cry like a wolf, 2) to moan loudly in pain

**hub** [hŭb] *noun*, 1) the center of activity 2) the center position of a wheel or propeller

**hud-dle** [hŭd′l] *verb*, to gather together, to cluster

**hue** [hyōo] *noun*, a shade of a color

**hug** [hŭg] *noun*, 1) a close embrace with arms around the body, *verb*, 2) to put arms around someone, to hold them closely, to embrace

**huge** [hyōoj] *adjective*, very large

**hulk** [hŭlk] *noun*, a bulky body, a big clumsy person or thing

**hull** [hŭl] *noun*, 1) the body of a ship 2) a shell, a husk, a case

**hum** [hŭm] *noun*, 1) to make a low, buzzing sound like a bee, *verb*, 2) to sing a melody to yourself with lips closed

**hu-man** [hyōo′mən] *noun*, pertaining to mankind, a person

**hu-mane** [hyōo-mān′] *adjective*, kind, compassionate, loving

**hu-man-i-ty** [hyōo-măn′ĭ-tē] *noun*, mankind, people, the human race

**hum-ble** [hŭm′bəl] *adjective*, 1) modest, not proud, 2) poor, plain, small 3) respectful, courteous, *verb*, 4) to bring down to defeat, to humiliate

**hu-mid-i-ty** [hyōo-mĭd′ĭ-tē] *noun*, moisture, warm, damp air

**hu-mil-i-ate** [hyōo-mĭl′ē-āt′] *verb*, to treat in a way that takes away a person's pride or self-respect

**hu-mil-i-a-tion** [hyōo-mĭl′ē-ā′shən] *noun*, embarrassment, shame

**hu-mil-i-ty** [hyōo-mĭl′ĭ-tē] *noun*, the state of being modest, meek

**hu-mor** [hyōo′mər] *noun*, *no plural*, 1) being able to make others laugh, *verb*, 2) to indulge

**hu-mor-ous** [hyōo′mər-əs] *adjective*, full of or characterized by humor, funny, comical

**hump** [hŭmp] *noun*, a round lump

**hu-mus** [hyōo′məs] *noun*, organic material consisting of decayed vegetable matter that provides nutrients for plants

**hunch** [hŭnch] *noun*, 1) a premonition or suspicion, *verb*, 2) to sit or stand with the back bent or arched

**hun-dred** [hŭn′drĭd] *noun*, the number 100, ten times ten

**hun-dreth** [hŭn′drĭdth] *noun*, 1) the ordinal number after 99th 2) the number two digits to the right of the decimal point

**hung** [hŭng] *past tense* of **hang**

**hun-ger** [hŭng′gər] *noun*,
1) wanting food, craving, *verb*,
2) to feel a strong desire for
something 3) to yearn

**hun-gry** [hŭng′grē] *adjective*, to
desire something like food

**hunt** [hŭnt] *verb*, to seek out to
capture for food or sport, 2) to
search for

**hur-dle** [hûr′dl] *noun*, 1) a barrier,
an obstacle to overcome, *verb*,
2) to jump over, to vault

**hurl** [hûrl] *verb*, to throw hard

**hur-ri-cane** [hûr′ĭ-kān′] *noun*, a
severe storm or cyclone that
develops in tropical areas

**hur-ry** [hûr′ē] *noun*, 1) confusion,
*verb*, 2) to move quickly, to
hasten, to rush, to be quick

**hurt** [hûrt] *verb*, 1) to injure, to
inflict pain or damage 2) to
offend 3) to ache, to throb

**hur-tle** [hûr′tl] *verb*, to move at
great speed, to rush headlong

**hus-band** [hŭz′bənd] *noun*, the
male spouse in a marriage

**hus-band-ry** [hŭz′bən-drē] *noun*,
home management, careful
attention to spending money

**hush** [hŭsh] *noun*, 1) quiet, calm,
silence, *verb*, 2) to muffle, to
make silent, to quiet down

**hus-tle** [hŭs′əl] *verb*, 1) to hurry,
move, or do quickly 2) to trick
someone in business

**hut** [hŭt] *noun*, a small, usually
wooden building, a shack

**hy-brid** [hī′brĭd] *noun*, two species
fertilized to create a new breed

**hy-drant** [hī′drənt] *noun*, a pipe
located at a curb with a valve for
fire engines to connect a hose to
a source of water to fight fire

**hy-drau-lic** [hī-drô′lĭk] *noun*,
operated or moved by means of
water under pressure

**hy-dro-gen** [hī′drə-jən] *noun*, a gas
that is tasteless, odorless, and
inflammable used in rockets

**hy-dro-pho-bi-a** [hī′drə-fō′bē-ə]
*noun*, 1) fear of water 2) a
symptom of rabies

**hy-dro-plane** [hī′drə-plān′] *noun*,
1) a boat which glides on the
surface of water, *verb*, 2) to lose
control when a vehicle does not
have traction and loses the
ability to stop

**hy-e-na** [hī-ē′nə] *noun*, a large,
carnivorous wild dog that lives
in Africa and Australia

**hy-giene** [hī′jēn′] *noun*, practices
that keep people clean and
healthy, cleanliness

**hymn** [hĭm] *noun*, a religious song

**hy-per-bo-le** [hī-pûr′bə-lē] *noun*,
an expression used as a figure of
speech, *i.e., I would give him the
shirt off my back.*

**hy-phen** [hī′fən] *noun*, the mark -,
used to separate syllables, as at
the end of a line e.g. *composition*, or to join the parts of
compound words e.g.
*self-confidence, self-reliant*

**hyp-no-tize** [hĭp′nə-tīz′] *verb*, to
put in a trance in which the
subject is susceptible to
suggestion, to mesmerize

**hy-po-chon-dri-ac**
[hī′pə-kŏn′drē-ăk′] *noun*, a
person always worrying about
the state of their health

**hy-poc-ri-sy** [hǐ-pŏk′rǐ-sē]
*adjective*, the act or practice of
feigning to be what one is not,
especially the false assumption
of virtue or religion

**hyp-o-crite** [hǐp′ə-krǐt′] *noun*,
someone who says one thing and
does another, a fraud

**hy-poth-e-sis** [hī-pŏth′ǐ-sǐs] *noun*,
an educated guess

**hy-po-thet-i-cal** [hī′pə-thĕt′ǐ-kəl]
*adjective*, an assumption based
on theory or conjecture

**hys-ter-i-cal** [hǐ-stĕr′ǐ-kəl]
*adjective*, excitable, nervous

# I

**I** [ī] *pronoun*, *plural*, **we**, first
person singular, the individual
speaking

**ice** [īs] *noun*, 1) frozen water, *verb*,
2) to put frosting on a cake

**ice-berg** [īs′bûrg′] *noun*, a large
mass of ice floating in the water

**ice cream** [īs′krēm′] *noun*, cream,
milk, flavoring, and eggs mixed
together in a pot of ice and salt
to make frozen cream

**i-ch-thy-ol-o-gy** [ǐk′thē-ŏl′ə-jē]
*noun*, the study of fish

**i-cing** [ī′sǐng] *noun*, frosting

**i-ci-cle** [ī′sǐ-kəl] *noun*, a piece of
ice in the form of a spike made
by water dripping and freezing

**i-con** [ī′kŏn′] *noun*, 1) a religious
image 2) a symbol that
represents something

**i-cy** [ī′sē] *adjective*, 1) very cold,
freezing, chilly 2) slippery

**I'd** [īd] the *contraction* of the
words: **I** and **would**

**Ida-ho** [ī′də-hō′] *noun*, one of the
50 United States located in the
Northwest, the capital city is
Boise. The state flower of **Idaho**
is the syringa, and the motto is
"May she endure forever."

**i-de-a** [ī-dē′ə] *noun*, 1) a concept, a
thought, an impression 2) a
belief, a judgment, a view, an
opinion 3) a goal or intention

**i-de-al** [ī-dē′əl] *adjective*,
1) perfect, ultimate, imaginary,
*noun*, 2) an image of something
in its perfect form, a model

**i-den-ti-cal** [ī-dĕn′tǐ-kəl] *adjective*,
the very same in every way

**i-den-ti-fi-ca-tion**
[ī-dĕn′tə-fǐ-kā′shən] *noun*, the
means to verify who someone is

**i-den-ti-fy** [ī-dĕn′tə-fī′] *verb*, 1) to
classify or name 2) to equate

**i-den-ti-ty** [ī-dĕn′tǐ-tē] *noun*, who
someone is, individuality

**i-de-ol-o-gy** [ī′dē-ŏl′ə-jē] *noun*,
beliefs, opinions, political ideas

**id-i-om** [ǐd′ē-əm] *noun*, a group of
words which when used together
have a special meaning, i.e.,
*raining cats and dogs*

**id-i-o-syn-cra-sy**
[ǐd′ē-ō-sǐng′krə-sē] *noun*, a
peculiar habit, a quirk

**id-i-ot** [ǐ′ē-ət] *noun*, a nitwit, jerk

**i-dle** [īd′l] *adjective*, not busy,
unoccupied, inactive, lazy

**i-dol** [īd′l] *noun*, a figure that
people worship or honor

**i.e.** an abbreviation, for example…

**if** [ĭf] *conjunction*, 1) on condition that 2) whether

**ig-loo** [ĭg′lōō] *noun*, a home made of ice and snow used by Eskimos

**ig-ne-ous** [ĭg′nē-əs] *adjective*, produced by fire, volcanic

**ig-nite** [ĭg-nīt′] *verb*, 1) to set on fire, to burn 2) to inspire

**ig-no-ble** [ĭg-nō′bəl] *adjective*, unworthy, of low character

**ig-no-rance** [ĭg′nər-əns] *noun*, *no plural*, lack of knowledge

**ig-no-rant** [ĭg′nər-ənt] *adjective*, not knowing something

**ig-nore** [ĭg-nôr′] *verb*, to take no notice of, to pretend something is not there, to disregard

**ill** [ĭl] *adjective*, feeling unhealthy or badly, uneasy, not well

**I'll** [ĭl] the *contraction* of the words **I** and **will**

**il-le-gal** [ĭ-lē′gəl] *adjective*, against the law, prohibited, criminal

**il-leg-i-ble** [ĭ-lĕj′ə-bəl] *adjective*, so poorly written that it is unreadable

**il-le-git-i-mate** [ĭl′ĭ-jĭt′ə-mĭt] *adjective*, unlawful, illegal

**il-lic-it** [ĭ-lĭs′ĭt] *adverb*, not according to law, not permitted or allowed, forbidden

**il-lim-it-a-ble** [ĭ-lĭm′ĭ-tə-bəl] *adjective*, infinite, vast, limitless

**Il-li-nois** [ĭl′ə-noi′] *noun*, one of the 50 United States located in the Midwest, the capital is Springfield. The state flower of **Illinois** is the meadow violet, and the motto is "State sovereignty, national union."

**il-lit-er-ate** [ĭ-lĭt′ər-ĭt] *adjective*, unable to read and write

**il-log-i-cal** [ĭ-lŏj′ĭ-kəl] *adjective*, not observing the rules of correct reasoning, unreasonable

**il-lu-mi-nate** [ĭ-lōō′mə-nāt′] *verb*, 1) to fill with light 2) to make understandable, to clarify

**il-lu-sion** [ĭ-lōō′zhən] *noun*, a fantasy, a fallacy, a delusion

**il-lu-sive** [ĭ-lōō′sĭv] *adjective*, deceptive, false, evasive

**il-lus-trate** [ĭl′ə-strāt′] *verb*, 1) to explain by examples or verbal images 2) to provide with pictures or designs, to show

**il-lus-tra-tion** [ĭl′ə-strā′shən] *noun*, 1) an explanation 2) a diagram that provides a design or pictures

**il-lus-tri-ous** [ĭ-lŭs′trē-əs] *adjective*, distinguished, well known, acclaimed, celebrated

**I'm** [ĭm] the *contraction* of the words, **I** and **am**

**im-age** [ĭm′ĭj] *noun*, 1) a picture in the mind, or in a mirror 2) a figure made of stone, wood, etc.

**im-age-ry** [ĭ-măj′ĕr′ē] *noun*, 1) mental images 2) descriptions and figures of speech

**im-ag-i-nar-y** [ĭ-măj′ə-nĕr′ē] *adjective*, unreal, fanciful, existing only in the mind

**im-ag-i-na-tion** [ĭ-măj′ə-nā′shən] *noun*, fantasy, dreams

**im-ag-ine** [ĭ-măj′ĭn] *verb*, 1) to develop an idea in your mind or mental picture 2) to conceive, to suppose

**im-bue** [ĭm-byōō′] *verb*, 1) to teach, to inspire 2) to saturate with moisture or color

159

**im-i-tate** [ĭm′ĭ-tāt′] *verb*, to do something the same way as someone else, to emulate

**im-i-ta-tion** [ĭm′ĭ-tā′shən] *adjective*, 1) artificial, synthetic, counterfeit, *noun*, 2) a copy of something, a fake, a replica

**im-mac-u-late** [ĭ-măk′yə-lĭt] *adjective*, without stain or blemish, spotlessly clean

**im-ma-te-ri-al** [ĭm′ə-tîr′ē-əl] *adjective*, not applicable, irrelevant, not important

**im-ma-ture** [ĭm′ə-tyŏŏr′] *adjective*, 1) not grown up 2)using poor judgment, childish

**im-meas-ur-a-ble** [ĭ-mĕzh′ər-ə-bəl] *adjective*, vast, limitless, endless, infinite

**im-me-di-ate** [ĭ-mē′dē-ĭt] *adjective*, right away

**im-me-di-ate-ly** [ĭ-mē′dē-ĭt-lē] *adverb*, at once, without interval of time or delay, now

**im-mense** [ĭ-mĕns′] *adjective*, huge, very large, enormous

**im-men-si-ty** [ĭ-mĕn′sĭ-tē] *noun*, enormity, endlessness

**im-mi-grant** [ĭm′ĭ-grənt] *noun*, a settler from another country

**im-mi-gra-tion** [ĭm′ĭ-grā′shən] *noun*, a journey or voyage to another place

**im-mi-grate** [ĭm′ĭ-grāt′] *verb*, to go to a country of which one is not a native to live as a resident

**im-mi-nent** [ĭm′ə-nənt] *adjective*, impending, near at hand, likely to occur at any moment

**im-mo-bil-i-ty** [ĭ-mō-bĭl′-ĭ-tē] *noun*, the state of being unable to move, motionless

**im-mortal** [ĭ-môr′tl] *adjective*, undying, everlasting, perpetual

**im-mor-tal-i-ty** [ĭm′ôr-tăl′ĭ-tē] *noun*, eternal life, unending fame

**im-mune** [ĭ-myōōn′] *adjective*, 1) exempt from an obligation 2) not affected by disease

**im-mu-ni-ty** [ĭ-myōō′nĭ-tē] *noun*, freedom from natural or usual liability

**im-mu-nize** [ĭm′yə-nīz′] *verb*, to protect the body from incurable diseases by injecting an inactive form of the virus or bacteria

**im-mu-ni-za-tion** [ĭm′yə-nĭ-zā′shən] *noun*, an injection that protects the body from a virus or disease

**im-pact** [ĭm′păkt′] *noun*, 1) the striking of one object by another 2) a forceful impression, a strong effect

**im-pair** [ĭm-pâr′] *verb*, to weaken, to diminish in value, make worse

**im-pale** [ĭm-pāl′] *verb*, to pierce

**im-part** [ĭm-pärt′] *verb*, to tell, to reveal, to make known, to give

**im-par-tial** [ĭm-pär′shəl] *adjective*, fair, just, not favoring one more than another, not biased

**im-pas-sa-ble** [ĭm-păs′ə-bəl] *adjective*, a place that cannot be passed or traversed

**im-passe** [ĭm′păs′] *noun*, an inescapable situation

**im-pa-tience** [ĭm-pā′shəns] *noun*, *no plural*, anticipation, anxious expectancy, feeling anxious

**im-pa-tiens** [ĭm-pā′shəns] *noun*, a flower with white or red flowers that bloom in summer

**im-pa-tient** [ĭm-pā′shənt] *adjective*, not wanting to wait

**im-peach** [ĭm-pēch′] *verb*, to charge with a crime while in office, to discredit

**im-pec-ca-ble** [ĭm-pĕk′ə-bəl] *adjective*, faultless, perfect

**im-pede** [ĭm-pēd′] *verb*, to hinder or obstruct, to slow action

**im-ped-i-ment** [ĭm-pĕd′ə-mənt] *noun*, hindrance, obstacle

**im-pel** [ĭm-pĕl′] *verb*, to push, to motivate, to drive forward

**im-pend-ing** [ĭm-pĕn′dĭng] *adjective*, nearing, approaching

**im-per-a-tive** [ĭm-pĕr′ə-tĭv] *adjective*, 1) expressive of command 2) binding, obligatory

**im-per-fect** [ĭm-pûr′fĭkt] *adjective*, flawed, defective, faulty

**im-per-fec-tion** [ĭm′pər-fĕk′shən] *noun*, 1) a flaw, a defect 2) a failing, a shortcoming, a fault

**im-pe-ri-al** [ĭm-pîr′ē-əl] *adjective*, relating to an empire and its ruler

**im-per-il** [ĭm-pĕr′əl] *verb*, to put in danger or peril

**im-pe-ri-ous** [ĭm-pîr′ē-əs] *adjective*, bossy, domineering

**im-per-me-a-ble** [ĭm-pûr′mē-ə-bəl] *adjective*, unable to pass through something, impervious

**im-per-son-al** [ĭm-pûr′sə-nəl] *adjective*, detached, withdrawn

**im-per-son-ate** [ĭm-pûr′sə-nāt′] *verb*, to pretend to be someone by assuming their appearance

**im-per-ti-nent** [ĭm-pûr′tn-ənt] *adjective*, 1) rude, insolent, pert 2) irrelevant

**im-per-vi-ous** [ĭm-pûr′vē-əs] *adjective*, 1) impenetrable, not admitting entrance or passage through 2) unaffected

**im-pet-u-ous** [ĭm-pĕch′oo-əs] *adjective*, impulsive, rash

**im-pe-tus** [ĭm′pĭ-təs] *noun*, a driving force, motive, incentive

**im-plau-si-ble** [ĭm-plô′zə-bəl] *adjective*, unlikely, unbelievable

**im-ple-ment** [ĭm′plə-mənt] *noun*, 1) a tool, a device, *verb*, 2) to complete, to accomplish, to make good on an idea

**im-pli-ca-tion** [ĭm′plĭ-kā′shən] *noun*, something that is implied, hinted or suggested

**im-plic-it** [ĭm-plĭs′ĭt] *adjective*, 1) implied, unsaid, understood 2) trusting without reserve

**im-plore** [ĭm′plôr] *verb*, to plead with or beg for with much feeling

**im-ply** [ĭm-plī′] *verb*, to suggest a meaning not spoken, to hint

**im-po-lite** [ĭm′pə-līt′] *adjective*, rude, discourteous, disrespectful

**im-port** [ĭm-pôrt′] *noun*, 1) merchandise brought into another country 2) the significance, the meaning, *verb*, 3) to bring goods into another country 4) to signify

**im-por-tance** [ĭm-pôr′tns] *noun*, *no plural*, of great significance or consequence, prominence

**im-por-tant** [ĭm-pôr′tnt] *adjective*, significant, having a great value

**im-por-tu-nate** [ĭm-pôr′chə-nĭt] *adjective*, urging, demanding

**im-pose** [ĭm-pōz′] *verb*, 1) to take unfair advantage of 2) to force on others

**im-pos-si-ble** [ĭm-pŏs′ə-bəl] *adjective*, unrealizable, unattainable, hopeless

**im-pos-tor** [ĭm-pŏs′tər] *noun*, one who practices deception, a cheat

**im-po-tent** [ĭm′pə-tənt] *adjective*, weak, ineffective, powerless

**im-prac-ti-cal** [ĭm-prăk′tĭ-kəl] *adjective*, not easily done, infeasible, not useful

**im-pre-cate** [ĭm′prĭ-kāt′] *verb*, to hope evil will happen, to curse

**im-preg-na-ble** [ĭm-prĕg′nə-bəl] *adjective*, invulnerable, unbeatable, irrefutable

**im-press** [ĭm-prĕs′] *verb*, to affect someone's feelings or mind in a positive way

**im-pres-sion** [ĭm-prĕsh′ən] *noun*, 1) a sensation, a feeling 2) an imprint on the mind, an effect

**im-pres-sive** [ĭm-prĕs′ĭv] *adjective*, touching, stirring, convincing

**im-print** [ĭm-prĭnt′] *noun*, 1) a deep impression left by pressure, *verb*, 2) to leave a mark by applying pressure

**im-pris-on** [ĭm-prĭz′ən] *verb*, to hold someone in jail

**im-prob-a-ble** [ĭm-prŏb′ə-bəl] *adjective*, unlikely to happen

**im-prop-er** [ĭm-prŏp′ər] *adjective*, something that is considered rude or inappropriate

**im-pro-pri-e-ty** [ĭm′prə-prī′ĭ-tē] *noun*, an inappropriate expression or act

**im-prove** [ĭm-prōōv′] *verb*, to make better, to uplift, to refine

**im-prove-ment** [ĭm-prōōv′mənt] *noun*, an act, a state, or result of improving or bettering

**im-pro-vise** [ĭm′prə-vīz′] *verb*, 1) to make do with whatever is at hand 2) to perform without preparation at a moment's notice

**im-pru-dent** [ĭm-prōōd′nt] *adjective*, injudicious, indiscreet

**im-pu-dent** [ĭm′pyə-dənt] *adjective*, shameless, bold

**im-pulse** [ĭm′pŭls′] *noun*, a sudden desire to do something, a whim

**im-pul-sive** [ĭm-pŭl′sĭv] *adjective*, spontaneous, unexpected

**im-pu-ni-ty** [ĭm-pyōō′nĭ-tē] *noun*, freedom from punishment

**im-pu-ri-ty** [ĭm-pyŏŏr′ĭ-tē] *noun*, something mixed with something else that is usually not as good, contamination

**im-pute** [ĭm-pyōōt′] *verb*, to credit, to attribute, to ascribe

**in** [ĭn] *adjective*, 1) being inside, *preposition*, 2) showing where 3) at or inside of something 4) during, before the end 5) wearing 6) at hand or on hand 7) near

**in-a-bil-i-ty** [ĭn′ə-bĭl′ĭ-tē] *adjective*, not able

**in-ac-ces-si-ble** [ĭn′ăk-sĕs′ə-bəl] *adjective*, 1) out of reach, unattainable 2) hard to contact

**in-ac-cu-ra-cy** [ĭn-ăk′yər-ə-sē]
*noun*, inexactness, the state of
being incorrect, an error

**in-ad-e-quate** [ĭn-ăd′ĭ-kwĭt]
*adjective*, not sufficient,
deficient, not enough

**in-ad-ver-tent-ly** [ĭn′əd-vûr′tnt-lē]
*adverb*, not purposely,
unintentionally, accidentally

**in-al-ien-a-ble** [ĭn-āl′yə-nə-bəl]
*adjective*, not to be taken away

**in-an-i-mate** [ĭn-ăn′ə-mĭt]
*adjective*, lifeless, dull

**in-ar-tic-u-late** [ĭn′är-tĭk′yə-lĭt]
*adjective*, lacking the ability to
express oneself in speech

**in-au-gu-rate** [ĭn-ô′gyə-rāt′] *verb*,
1) to commence or enter upon, to
begin 2) to install into office in a
formal manner

**in-can-des-cent** [ĭn′kən-dĕs′ənt]
*adjective*, glowing or luminous
with intense heat or brightness

**in-can-ta-tion** [ĭn′kăn-tā′shən]
*noun*, singing or chanting of
magic spells

**in-ca-pa-ble** [ĭn-kā′pə-bəl]
*adjective*, unable, powerless

**in-ca-pac-i-tate** [ĭn′kə-păs′ĭ-tāt′]
*verb*, to disable

**in-car-cer-a-tion** [ĭn-kär′sə-rā′
shən] *noun*, imprisonment

**in-car-nate** [ĭn-kär′nĭt] *adjective*,
in the flesh, in human form

**in-car-na-tion** [ĭn′kär-nā′shən]
*noun*, the act of assuming a
human body after death

**in-cen-di-ar-y** [ĭn-sĕn′dē-ĕr′ē]
*noun*, 1) causing something to
burn 2) tending to inflame
passion, a political agitator

**in-cense** [ĭn-sĕns′] *noun*, 1) scent,
aroma, fragrance, *verb*, 2) anger

**in-cen-tive** [ĭn-sĕn′tĭv] *noun*,
encouragement, stimulus

**in-ces-sant** [ĭn-sĕs′ənt] *adjective*,
continuing without interruption

**in-ces-sant-ly** [ĭn-sĕs′ənt-lē]
*adverb*, without stopping,
continual, not ceasing

**inch** [ĭnch] *noun*, a measure of
length, 1/12 of a foot

**in-ci-dent** [ĭn′sĭ-dənt] *noun*, a
happening, an event, a casual
occurrence, an episode

**in-ci-den-tal-ly** [ĭn′sĭ-dĕn′tl-ē]
*adverb*, casually, by chance

**in-cin-er-a-tor** [ĭn-sĭn′ə-rā′tər]
*noun*, a container or facility
where garbage is burned

**in-ci-sion** [ĭn-sĭzh′ən] *noun*, a cut
or slit into tissue, a gash

**in-cite** [ĭn-sīt′] *verb*, to stir up, to
stimulate to action, to provoke

**in-cite-ment** [ĭn-sīt′mĕnt] *noun*, a
stimulus, a catalyst

**in-clem-ent** [ĭn-klĕm′ənt]
*adjective*, stormy, unkind

**in-cli-na-tion** [ĭn′klə-nā′shən]
*noun*, a preference, a tendency

**in-cline** [ĭn-klīn′] *verb*, 1) to lean,
to slant 2) likely to, to tend to

**in-clude** [ĭn-klo͞od′] *verb*, 1) to
have as part of, to comprise, to
contain 2) to count or think of
someone or something as a part
of a group, to involve

**in-clu-sive** [ĭn-klo͞o′sĭv] *adjective*,
not leaving anyone out

**in-cog-ni-to** [ĭn′kŏg-nē′tō]
*adjective*, in disguise, a secret
identity

**in-co-her-ent** [ĭn′kō-hîr′ənt]
*adjective*, incomprehensible,
lacking meaningful connection

**in-come** [ĭn′kŭm′] *noun*, the money
a person earns from work or
investments, salary

**in-com-par-able**
[ĭn-kŏm′pər-ə-bəl] *adjective*,
excellent, unequaled by
comparison, unrivaled,

**in-com-pat-i-ble**
[ĭn′kəm-păt′ə-bəl] *adjective*, not
easy to get along with

**in-com-pe-tent** [ĭn-kŏm′pĭ-tənt]
*adjective*, unfit, clumsy

**in-com-plete** [ĭn′kəm-plēt′]
*adjective*, unfinished, under
construction, lacking

**in-con-ceiv-a-ble**
[ĭn′kən-sē′və-bəl] *adjective*,
unimaginable, incredible, hard to
believe, unthinkable

**in-con-gru-ous** [ĭn-kŏng′grōō-əs]
*adjective*, not fitting, absurd

**in-con-se-quen-tial**
[ĭn-kŏn′sĭ-kwĕn′shəl] *adjective*,
of little importance or
consequence

**in-con-ven-ience** [ĭn′kən-vēn′yəns]
*adjective*, bothersome,
troublesome, bad timing

**in-con-ven-ient** [ĭn′kən-vēn′yənt]
*adjective*, untimely, awkward

**in-cor-po-rate** [ĭn-kôr′pə-rāt′]
*verb*, 1) to unite into one body
2) to form into a corporation

**in-cor-rect** [ĭn′kə-rĕkt′] *adjective*,
not right in facts, wrong

**in-cor-rect-ly** [ĭn′kə-rĕkt′-lē]
*adverb*, mistakenly, erroneously

**in-crease** [ĭn-krēs′] *noun*, 1) the
amount by which something gets

larger , *verb*, 2) to become
greater in size or quantity

**in-cred-i-ble** [ĭn-krĕd′ə-bəl]
*adjective*, surpassing belief,
unlikely, unbelievable

**in-cred-u-lous** [ĭn-krĕj′ə-ləs]
*adjective*, shocking, surprising,
full of disbelief

**in-cre-ment** [ĭn′krə-mənt, ĭng′-]
*noun*, an increase, addition

**in-crim-i-nate** [ĭn-krĭm′ə-nāt′]
*verb*, to accuse or charge with a
crime or fault

**in-crim-i-nat-ing**
[ĭn-krĭm′ə-nā′tĭng] *adjective*,
showing proof of guilt

**in-cu-bate** [ĭn′kyə-bāt′] *verb*, to
apply enough heat or warmth to
make something hatch

**in-cum-bent** [ĭn-kŭm′bənt]
*adjective*, 1) required, obligatory,
*noun*, 2) an officeholder

**in-cur** [ĭn-kûr′] *verb*, to bring
something unpleasant upon
oneself

**in-cur-a-ble** [ĭn-kyōōr′ə-bəl]
*adjective*, irreparable, incapable
of being cured, terminally ill

**in-cur-sion** [ĭn-kûr′zhən] *noun*,
temporary invasion

**in-debt-ed** [ĭn-dĕt′ĭd] *adjective*,
under obligation to repay money

**in-deed** [ĭn-dēd′] *adverb*, really,
truly, in fact, certainly

**in-def-i-nite** [ĭn-dĕf′ə-nĭt]
*adjective*, uncertain, inexact

**in-def-i-nite-ly** [ĭn-dĕf′ə-nĭt-lē]
*adverb*, no set time frame

**in-del-i-ble** [ĭn-dĕl′ə-bəl] *adjective*,
something that cannot be
removed or blotted out,
permanent

**in-dem-ni-ty** [ĭn-dĕm′nĭ-tē] *noun*, protection or exemption from loss or damage, security

**in-dent** [ĭn-dĕnt′] *verb*, 1) to set lines in from the margin 2) to form notches from the edge

**in-den-ture** [ĭn-dĕn′chər] *verb*, the written work agreement of a servant to a master

**in-de-pend-ence** [ĭn′dĭ-pĕn′dəns] *noun, no plural*, the state of acting alone or separately

**in-de-pend-ent** [ĭn′dĭ-pĕn′dənt] *adjective*, free, not relying on others, without bias

**in-de-pend-ent-ly** [ĭn′dĭ-pĕn′dənt-lē] *adverb*, to work alone, self-reliant, self-directed, autonomously

**in-de-struct-i-ble** [ĭn′dĭ-strŭk′tə-bəl] *adjective*, incapable of being destroyed

**in-dex** [ĭn′dĕks′] *noun*, a table for finding reference to topics, names, etc.

**In-di-an** [ĭn′dē-ən] *noun*, a native American

**In-di-ana** [ĭn′dē-ăn′ə] *noun*, one of the 50 United States located in the Midwest, the capital is Indianapolis. The state flower of **Indiana** is the peony, and the state motto is "The crossroads of America."

**in-di-cate** [ĭn′dĭ-kāt′] *verb*, to show or describe, to point out

**in-di-ca-tion** [ĭn′dĭ-kā′shən] *noun*, something that shows a trait

**in-di-ca-tor** [ĭn′dĭ-kā′tər] *noun*, 1) something that points to a trait 2) an instrument for automatically showing the pressure of the working fluid in an engine

**in-dict** [ĭn-dīt′] *verb*, to formally charge with a crime

**in-dict-ment** [ĭn-dīt′mənt] *noun*, a formal accusation charging someone with a crime

**in-dif-fer-ent** [ĭn-dĭf′ər-ənt] *adjective*, mediocre, unresponsive, unconcerned

**in-dig-e-nous** [ĭn-dĭj′ə-nəs] *adjective*, native to an area

**in-di-gent** [ĭn′dĭ-jənt] *adjective*, poor, homeless, destitute

**in-di-gest-i-ble** [ĭn′dĭ-jĕs′tə-bəl] *adjective*, something that cannot be swallowed or eaten

**in-di-ges-tion** [ĭn′dĭ-jĕs′chən] *noun*, a stomach ache

**in-dig-nant** [ĭn-dĭg′nənt] *adjective*, angry because of something that is not right, resentful

**in-dig-na-tion** [ĭn′dĭg-nā′shən] *noun*, anger, displeasure, rage

**in-dig-ni-ty** [ĭn-dĭg′nĭ-tē] *noun*, insulting or abusive treatment

**in-di-go** [ĭn′dĭ-gō′] *noun*, a deep blue-violet dye made from plants

**in-di-rect** [ĭn′dĭ-rĕkt′] *adjective*, in a roundabout way, circuitous

**in-di-rect-ly** [ĭn′dĭ-rĕkt′lē] *adverb*, inadvertently, not intentionally

**in-dis-creet** [ĭn′dĭ-skrēt′] *adjective*, lacking prudence or discretion, unwise, not careful, imprudent

**in-dis-pen-sa-ble** [ĭn′dĭ-spĕn′sə-bəl] *adjective*, absolutely necessary, essential

**in-dis-put-a-ble** [ĭn′dĭ-spyōō′tə-bəl] *adjective*, sure, undeniable, certain

**in-di-vid-u-al** [ĭn′də-vĭj′ōō-əl],
*adjective*, 1) unique, special
*noun* 2) a person, an entity, one

**in-di-vid-u-al-ly**
[ĭn′də-vĭj′ōō-əl-lē] *adverb*,
separately, one by one, distinctly

**in-di-vis-i-ble** [ĭn′də- vĭz′ə-bəl]
*adjective*, 1) that cannot be
divided 2) cannot be divided
without leaving a remainder

**in-do-lent** [ĭn′də-lənt] *adjective*,
lazy, inactive, slothful

**in-dom-i-ta-ble** [ĭn′dŏm′ĭ-tə-bəl]
*adjective*, unconquerable,
invincible, unyielding

**in-door** [ĭn′dôr′] *adjective*, located
or used inside of a building

**in-duce** [ĭn-dōōs′] *verb*, to
persuade, to influence

**in-duce-ment** [ĭn-dōōs′mənt] *noun*,
any motive that leads one to act

**in-duc-tive** [ĭn-dŭk′tĭv] *adjective*,
going from specific to general

**in-dulge** [ĭn-dŭlj′] *verb*, to allow,
to give way to, to foster

**in-dul-gence** [ĭn-dŭl′jəns] *noun*, a
giving way to one's desires

**in-dus-tri-al** [ĭn-dŭs′trē-əl]
*adjective*, commercial, related to
economy or industry

**in-dus-tri-ous** [ĭn-dŭs′trē-əs]
*adjective*, hard-working

**in-dus-try** [ĭn′də-strē] *noun*,
1) hard work, being active
2) center of commerce,
enterprise, business activity

**in-el-i-gi-ble** [ĭn-ĕl′ĭ-jə-bəl]
*adjective*, not qualified to be
chosen for an office

**in-ept** [ĭn-ĕpt′] *adjective*, out of
place, incapable of performing a
task, incompetent, unskilled

**in-eq-ui-ty** [ĭn-ĕk′wĭ-tē] *noun*,
unfairness, not equal, bias

**in-ert** [ĭn-ûrt′] *adjective*, without
power, inactive

**in-er-tia** [ĭ-nûr′shə] *noun*, 1) a state
of matter by which it retains its
state of rest, inactivity 2) acted
upon by an external force

**in-ev-i-ta-ble** [ĭn-ĕv′ĭ-tə-bəl]
*adjective*, not to be evaded or
shunned, unavoidable

**in-fal-li-ble** [ĭn-făl′ə-bəl] *adjective*,
unfailing, reliable, certain

**in-fa-mous** [ĭn′fə-məs] *adjective*,
notoriously bad, wicked

**in-fan-cy** [ĭn′fən-sē] *adjective*, the
first part of life, early childhood

**in-fant** [ĭn′fənt] *noun*, a very young
child in the first stage of life, a
newborn, a baby

**in-fan-try** [ĭn′fən-trē] *noun*, the
ground forces of the army

**in-fat-u-a-tion** [ĭ-făch′ōō-ā′shən]
*adjective*, the state of having
very strong love or admiration
for someone, an obsession

**in-fect** [ĭn-fĕkt′] *verb*, to share a
virus or infection with others

**in-fec-tion** [ĭn-fĕk′shən] *noun*, any
disease caused by germs

**in-fec-tious** [ĭn-fĕk′shəs] *adjective*,
capable of being spread or
communicated, contagious

**in-fer** [ĭn-fûr′] *verb*, to arrive at a
conclusion, to deduce, to guess

**in-fer-ence** [ĭn′fər-əns] *noun*, the
act of drawing a conclusion from
certain premises, a guess

**in-fe-ri-or** [ĭn-fîr′ē-ər] *adjective*,
1) lower 2) of less importance
3) inequality, subordinate

166

**in-fer-nal** [ĭn-fûr′nəl] *adjective*, referring to hell, diabolical

**in-fest** [ĭn-fĕst′] *verb*, to overrun in a troublesome manner

**in-fil-tra-tion** [ĭn′fĭl-trā′shən] *noun*, 1) the act of penetrating the pores of a substance 2) passing or joining gradually

**in-fi-nite** [ĭn′fə-nĭt] *adjective*, unending, there is no end

**in-fin-i-tes-i-mal** [ĭn′fĭn-ĭ-tĕs′ə-məl] *adjective*, immeasurably small

**in-fin-i-ty** [ĭn-fĭn′ĭ-tē] *noun*, the symbol ~, to continue indefinitely

**in-firm** [ĭn-fûrm′] *adjective*, weak, sick, in poor health, ill, not well

**in-fir-ma-ry** [ĭn-fûr′mə-rē] *noun*, a small hospital, a first-aid tent

**in-fir-mi-ty** [ĭn-fûr′mĭ-tē] *noun*, weakness or ailment

**in-flam-ma-ble** [ĭn-flăm′ə-bəl] *adjective*, explosive, volatile

**in-flam-ma-tion** [ĭn′flə-mā′shən] *noun*, swelling, redness

**in-flate** [ĭn-flāt′] *verb*, to fill with air, to enlarge, to expand

**in-fla-tion** [ĭn-flā′shən] *noun*, ever higher price levels

**in-flict** [ĭn-flĭkt′] *verb*, to force, to impose, to deal as a blow

**in-flu-ence** [ĭn′floo-əns] *noun*, 1) power, authority or control 2) the gradual or unseen operation of some cause, *verb*, 3) to act upon 4) to persuade

**in-flu-en-tial** [ĭn′floo-ĕn′shəl] *adjective*, important, able to change people's thoughts on something, compelling

**in-flu-en-za** [ĭn′floo-ĕn′zə] *noun*, *no plural*, the flu, an epidemic characterized by fever, headaches and fatigue

**in-flux** [ĭn′flŭks′] *noun*, flowing into or coming in

**in-form** [ĭn-fôrm′] *verb*, 1) to tell, to notify, to advise 2) to teach

**in-for-mal** [ĭn-fôr′məl] *adjective*, casual, not dressy or formal

**in-form-ant** [ĭn-fôr′mənt] *noun*, someone who gives information

**in-for-ma-tion** [ĭn′fər-mā′shən] *noun*, facts, data, the things you need to know, knowledge

**in-frac-tion** [ĭn-frăk′shən] *noun*, a violation, a breach of trust

**in-fringe-ment** [ĭn-frĭnj′mənt] *adjective*, an act that goes further than what is right or fair

**in-fu-ri-ate** [ĭn-fyŏŏr′ē-āt′] *verb*, to make someone angry, furious

**in-fuse** [ĭn-fyooz′] *verb*, 1) to instill a principle or quality 2) to steep in water or other fluid without boiling for the purpose of extracting useful qualities

**in-fu-sion** [ĭn-fyōō′zhən] *noun*, the act of introducing, spreading or dispersion of properties

**in-ge-nu-i-ty** [ĭn′jə-noo′ĭ-tē] *noun*, skill in discovering, inventing or planning

**in-gest** [ĭn-jĕst′] *verb*, to take in food or liquids gradually

**in-grat-i-tude** [ĭn-grăt′ĭ-tood′] *adjective*, unthankfulness

**in-gre-di-ent** [ĭn-grē′dē-ənt] *noun*, 1) a component part of any mixture 2) things that are mixed together to make something

# inhabit

**in-hab-it** [ĭn-hăb′ĭt] *verb*, to live someplace, to make a place a home, to live or dwell in

**in-hab-it-ant** [ĭn-hăb′ĭ-tənt] *noun*, an animal or person who lives at a location, a resident

**in-hale** [ĭn-hāl′] *verb*, to take a deep breath, to breathe in

**in-her-ent** [ĭn-hîr′ənt] *adjective*, part of the nature of a person or thing

**in-her-it** [ĭn-hĕr′ĭt] *verb*, to receive something, usually from a relative by will or succession

**in-her-it-ance** [ĭn-hĕr′ĭ-təns] *noun*, the estate, heritage, legacy

**in-hib-it** [ĭn-hĭb′ĭt] *verb*, 1) to intimidate, to make someone hold back in fear 2) to restrain

**in-hi-bi-tion** [ĭn′hə-bĭsh′ən] *noun*, feeling painfully self-conscious

**in-iq-ui-ty** [ĭ-nĭk′wĭ-tē] *noun*, a gross injustice, wickedness

**in-i-tial** [ĭ-nĭsh′əl] *adjective*, 1) first, *noun*, 2) the first letter of a name, *verb*, 3) to sign with one's initials

**in-i-tial-ly** [ĭ-nĭsh′ə-lē] *adverb*, at the beginning, starting with

**in-i-ti-ate** [ĭ-nĭsh′ē-āt′] *verb*, to introduce, to begin or start something, to originate

**in-i-ti-a-tion** [ĭ-nĭsh′ē-ā′shən] *noun*, an induction, an inaugural

**in-i-t-ia-tive** [ĭ-nĭsh′ə-tĭv] *noun*, 1) an act that begins 2) to do something because it needs to be done, an introductory step

**in-ject** [ĭn-jĕkt′] *verb*, 1) to introduce, to insert 2) to give someone a shot 3) to force something into

**in-jec-tion** [ĭn-jĕk′shən] *noun*, an insertion of medicine through a needle into a vein, a shot

**in-jure** [ĭn′jər] *verb*, to cause harm of any kind, to wound

**in-ju-ri-ous** [ĭn-jŏŏr′ē-əs] *adjective*, hurtful, harmful

**in-ju-ry** [ĭn′jə-rē] *noun*, 1) a wound, harm to the body 2) an offense, harm done

**in-jus-tice** [ĭn-jŭs′tĭs] *noun*, violation of the rights of another, an unfair or unjust act

**ink** [ĭngk] *noun*, a colored liquid used with a pen for writing

**in-land** [ĭn′lənd] *adjective*, away from the shore or water

**in-law** [ĭn′lô′] *noun*, used after a word to mean a person related through marriage

**in-let** [ĭn′lĕt′] *noun*, a channel of water extending into the land from the river

**in-mate** [ĭn′māt′] *noun*, a prisoner or resident of a mental hospital

**inn** [ĭn] *noun*, a small hotel that serves meals, a tavern

**in-nate** [ĭ-nāt′] *adjective*, instinct, inherited, natural behavior

**in-ner** [ĭn′ər] *adjective*, 1) further in, or in the middle, 2) spiritual

**in-ning** [ĭn′ĭng] *noun*, the period in a baseball game for both teams to get three outs

**in-no-cence** [ĭn′ə-səns] *noun*, *no plural*, 1) freedom from guilt, 2) simplicity, naive

**in-no-cent** [ĭn′ə-sənt] *adjective*, 1) not guilty of a crime, blameless 2) pure, harmless

**in-no-va-tion** [ĭn'ə-vā'shən] *noun*, making changes, modernization

**in-no-va-tive** [ĭn'ə-vā'tĭv] *adjective*, the introduction of something new, change

**in-nu-en-do** [ĭn'yōō-ĕn'dō] *noun*, a suggestion, a hint, an insinuation

**in-oc-u-late** [ĭ-nŏk'yə-lāt'] *verb*, to inject an animal or person with a virus to prevent an infection

**in-op-por-tune** [ĭn-ŏp'ər-tōōn'] *adjective*, poorly timed

**in-or-di-nate** [ĭn-ôr'dn-ĭt] *adjective*, excessive, extravagant

**in-or-gan-ic** [ĭn'ôr-găn'ĭk] *adjective*, matter that does not contain carbon atoms in its main structure

**in-put** [ĭn'pŏŏt'] *noun*, anything put in, feedback, data entry

**in-quest** [ĭn'kwĕst'] *noun*, judicial inquiry or examination

**in-quire** [ĭn-kwīr'] *verb*, to ask about, to investigate

**in-quir-y** [ĭn-kwīr'ē, ĭng'-] *noun*, investigation, study, research

**in-qui-si-tion** [ĭn'kwĭ-zĭsh'ən, ĭng'] *noun*, formal questioning

**in-quis-i-tive** [ĭn-kwĭz'ĭ-tĭv] *adjective*, curious, apt to ask questions, given to research

**in-sane** [ĭn-sān'] *adjective*, crazy, psychotic, mad, deranged

**in-sa-tia-ble** [ĭn-sā'shə-bəl] *adjective*, incapable of being satisfied or appeased

**in-scrip-tion** [ĭn-skrĭp'shən] *noun*, an engraved message

**in-scru-ta-ble** [ĭn-skrōō'tə-bəl] *adjective*, unexplainable, mysterious

**in-sect** [ĭn'sĕkt'] *noun*, a bug with six legs and two pairs of wings

**in-sec-ti-cide** [ĭn-sĕk'tĭ-sīd'] *noun*, a poison used to kill bugs

**in-sen-si-ble** [ĭn-sĕn'sə-bəl] *adjective*, not aware, unconscious, unable to feel

**in-sep-a-ra-ble** [ĭn-sĕp'ər-ə-bəl] *adjective*, incapable of being separated or disjoined

**in-sert** [ĭn-sûrt'] noun, 1) an extra piece sewn or put n place, *verb*, 2) to put something into something, to inject, to set in place

**in-side** [ĭn-sīd'] adjective, 1) internal, interior, *noun*, 2) the portion that is in the middle of something, *preposition*, 3) something contained in something else, lying within

**in-sid-i-ous** [ĭn-sĭd'ē-əs] *adjective*, evil, sly, deceitful, beguiling

**in-sight** [ĭn'sīt'] *noun*, understanding, perceptiveness

**in-sig-ni-a** [ĭn-sĭg'nē-ə] *noun*, an emblem, a symbol, a badge

**in-sig-nif-i-cance** [ĭn'sĭg-nĭf'ĭ-kəns] *noun*, lack of importance, irrelevance

**in-sig-nif-i-cant** [ĭn'sĭg-nĭf'ĭ-kənt] *adjective*, unimportant, trivial

**in-sin-cere** [ĭn'sĭn-sîr'] *adjective*, untrue, false, disingenuous

**in-sin-u-ate** [ĭn-sĭn'yōō-āt'] *verb*, to introduce artfully, to suggest, to imply, to hint slyly

**in-sip-id** [ĭn-sĭp'ĭd] *adjective*, uninteresting, dull, banal

**in-sist** [ĭn-sĭst'] *verb*, 1) to say firmly, to demand, to speak with emphasis 2) to assert or demand persistently, to reiterate

**in-so-lence** [ĭn′sə-ləns] *noun*, arrogance, rudeness, impudence

**in-so-lent** [ĭn′sə-lənt] *adjective*, rude, insulting, disrespectful

**in-sol-u-ble** [ĭn-sŏl′yə-bəl] *adjective*, incapable of being dissolved

**in-som-ni-a** [ĭn-sŏm′nē-ə] *noun*, the inability to sleep

**in-spect** [ĭn-spĕkt′] *verb*, to examine carefully and critically, to scrutinize, to look over

**in-spec-tion** [ĭn-spĕk′shən] *noun*, a careful examination

**in-spec-tor** [ĭn-spĕk′tər] *noun*, someone who investigates

**in-spi-ra-tion** [ĭn′spə-rā′shən] *noun*, something that stimulates imagination and goodwill

**in-spire** [ĭn-spīr′] *verb*, to stimulate to think and to act, to influence

**in-sta-bil-i-ty** [ĭn′stə-bĭl′ĭ-tē] *noun*, lack of stability, unsteadiness

**in-stall** [ĭn-stôl′] *verb*, 1) to place in possession of an office, rank, or order 2) to put in place

**in-stal-la-tion** [ĭn′stə-lā′shən] *noun*, hooking up, placement

**in-stall-ment** [ĭn-stôl′mənt] *noun*, one of a number of parts, an affordable payment

**in-stance** [ĭn′stəns] *noun*, an example, a case in point

**in-stant** [ĭn′stənt] *adjective*, 1) happening or done at once, *noun*, 2) a moment, a very short period of time

**in-stan-ta-ne-ous** [ĭn′stən-tā′nē-əs] *adjective*, done in an instant

**in-stant-ly** [ĭn′stənt-lē] *adverb*, at once, immediately

**in-stead** [ĭn-stĕd′] *adverb*, in place of someone or something, a substitute, replacement

**in-step** [ĭn′stĕp′] *noun*, the arched middle portion of the human foot or of a shoe

**in-sti-gate** [ĭn′stĭ-gāt′] *verb*, to urge, to start, to provoke

**in-still** [ĭn-stĭl′] *verb*, 1) to teach, to educate, to inform 2) to saturate, to infuse, to permeate

**in-stinct** [ĭn′stĭngkt′] *noun*, a natural impulse that makes animals know how to take care of themselves, innate aptitude

**in-stinc-tive-ly** [ĭn-stĭngk′tĭv-lē] *adverb*, inborn, natural habits

**in-sti-tute** [ĭn′stĭ-tōōt′] *noun*, 1) an organization devoted to research and study, *verb*, 2) to form or establish an organization

**in-sti-tu-tion** [ĭn′stĭ-tōō′shən] *noun*, 1) a building used to serve a group of people 2) a commitment to a way of life and society's rules or customs

**in-struct** [ĭn-strŭkt′] *verb*, to teach, to show someone how to do something, to direct

**in-struc-tion** [ĭn-strŭk′shən] *noun*, teaching, direction, a training manual, knowledge imparted

**in-struc-tor** [ĭn-strŭk′tər] *noun*, a teacher or mentor

**in-stru-ment** [ĭn′strə-mənt] *noun*, 1) a device, a mechanism, a tool 2) a device, such as a trumpet, piano, or drum, used to make musical sounds 3) a means

**in-stru-men-tal** [ĭn′strə-mĕn′tl] *adjective*, helpful, acting to get something done

**in-suf-fer-a-ble** [ĭn-sŭf′ər-ə-bəl] *adjective*, painful, not to be endured, agonizing, intolerable

**in-suf-fi-cient** [ĭn′sə-fĭsh′ənt] *adjective*, not enough

**in-su-late** [ĭn′sə-lāt′] *verb*, to cover, to wrap, to protect

**in-su-la-tion** [ĭn′sə-lā′shən] *noun*, a material that prevents passage of heat, electricity, or sound

**in-sult** [ĭn-sŭlt′] *noun*, 1) an unkind or rude remark, *verb*, 2) to treat with abuse

**in-sur-ance** [ĭn-shŏŏr′əns] *noun*, *no plural*, money paid to an agency that keeps it as an investment to be returned to pay the cost of an accident, property damage, death, etc.

**in-sure** [ĭn-shŏŏr′] *verb*, to guarantee, to protect

**in-sur-gent** [ĭn-sûr′jənt] *noun*, a person who rises up against the law or leadership

**in-sur-rec-tion** [ĭn′sə-rĕk′shən] *noun*, an uprising, a rebellion

**in-tan-gi-ble** [ĭn-tăn′jə-bəl] *adjective*, something that cannot be touched, like an idea

**in-te-ger** [ĭn′tĭ-jər] *noun*, a whole number, an intact unit

**in-te-grate** [ĭn′tĭ-grāt′] *verb*, to make into a whole, to combine into one unit, to merge

**in-teg-ri-ty** [ĭn-tĕg′rĭ-tē] *noun*, honesty and virtue

**in-tel-lect** [ĭn′tl-ĕkt′] *noun*, the power to understand, the mind

**in-tel-lec-tu-al** [ĭn′tl-ĕk′chŏŏ-əl] *adjective*, smart, intelligent, brainy, able to reason

**in-tel-li-gence** [ĭn-tĕl′ə-jəns] *noun*, *no plural*, 1) the faculty of understanding 2) information communicated, reasoning

**in-tel-li-gent** [ĭn-tĕl′ə-jənt] *adjective*, very smart, clever

**in-tel-li-gent-ly** [ĭn-tĕl′ə-jənt-lē] *adverb*, sensibly, skillfully

**in-tel-li-gi-ble** [ĭn-tĕl′ĭ-jə-bəl] *adjective*, capable of being understood

**in-tend** [ĭn-tĕnd′] *verb*, 1) to plan to do something 2) to signify

**in-tense** [ĭn-tĕns′] *adjective*, a strong feeling, earnest

**in-ten-si-fy** [ĭn-tĕn′sə-fī′] *verb*, to make greater or more intense

**in-ten-si-ty** [ĭn-tĕn′sĭ-tē] *noun*, great concentration of energy

**in-ten-sive** [ĭn-tĕn′sĭv] *adjective*, thorough, involving special effort

**in-tent** [ĭn-tĕnt′] *noun*, 1) purpose 2) meaning

**in-ten-tion** [ĭn-tĕn′shən] *noun*, aim, a plan, a purpose, a meaning

**in-ten-tion-al-ly** [ĭn-tĕn′shə-nəl-lē] *adverb*, to do something on purpose, deliberately

**in-tent-ly** [ĭn-tĕnt′lē] *adverb*, strongly, purposefully

**in-ter** [ĭn-tûr′] *verb*, to bury

**in-ter-act** [ĭn′tər-ăkt′] *verb*, to relate mutually to, to exchange

**in-ter-cede** [ĭn′tər-sēd′] *verb*, to mediate, to act on one's behalf

**in-ter-cept** [ĭn′tər-sĕpt′] *verb*, to stop or seize something before it reaches its intended destination

**in-ter-est** [ĭn′trĭst] *noun*, 1) a concern or pleasure from learning something 2) title or share in a thing 3) a rate percent of money paid for the use of money, *verb*, 4) to involve or gain the attention of someone

**in-ter-est-ing** [ĭn′trĭ-stĭng] *adjective*, able to hold the attention or curiosity of someone

**in-ter-face** [ĭn′tər-fās′] *noun*, 1) a surface forming a common boundary between adjacent areas 2) in computer science the software or hardware connecting one drive or system to another

**in-ter-fere** [ĭn′tər-fîr′] *verb*, to be in opposition, to meddle

**in-ter-fer-ence** [ĭn′tər-fîr′əns] *noun*, obstruction, interrupting

**in-ter-im** [ĭn′tər-ĭm] *noun*, 1) in the meantime 2) temporary

**in-te-ri-or** [ĭn-tîr′ē-ər] *adjective*, 1)having to do with the inside part of something, inside *noun*, 2) the inside part of something

**in-ter-lude** [ĭn′tər-lōōd′] *noun*, a pause, a lull, a recess

**in-ter-me-di-ate** [ĭn′tər-mē′dē-ĭt] *adjective*, in the middle

**in-ter-ment** [ĭn-tûr′mənt] *noun*, the burial ceremony

**in-ter-mi-na-ble** [ĭn-tûr′mə-nə-bəl] *adjective*, endless, prolonged

**in-ter-mis-sion** [ĭn′tər-mĭsh′ən] *noun*, a break or recess

**in-ter-mit-tent** [ĭn′tər-mĭt′nt] *adjective*, coming and going at intervals, beginning again

**in-tern** [ĭn′tûrn′] *noun*, 1) a doctor's apprentice, *verb*, 2) to imprison, to confine

**in-ter-nal** [ĭn-tûr′nəl] *adjective*, 1) inside of something, inner 2) referring to any function inside the body, in word

**in-ter-na-tion-al** [ĭn′tər-năsh′ə-nəl] *adjective*, in nations all over the world, universal, global

**in-ter-ne-cine** [ĭn′tər-nĕs′ēn′] *adjective*, mutually destructive

**In-ter-net** [ĭn′tûr-nĕt] *noun*, the link to other computers, connected by a server

**in-ter-pret** [ĭn-tûr′prĭt] *verb*, to translate, to define, to explain

**in-ter-pre-ta-tion** [ĭn-tûr′prĭ-tā′shən] *noun*, an explanation of someone's art work, a translation

**in-ter-pret-er** [ĭn-tûr′prĭ-tər] *noun*, 1) one who explains or expounds 2) a translator

**in-ter-ro-gate** [ĭn-tĕr′ə-gāt′] *verb*, to ask questions of someone

**in-ter-rupt** [ĭn′tə-rŭpt′] *verb*, to stop something from continuing, to disturb, to hinder

**in-ter-sect** [ĭn′tər-sĕkt′] *verb*, when two lines meet to form angles

**in-ter-sec-tion** [ĭn′tər-sĕk′shən] *noun*, 1) a figure formed by two lines 2) a place where two or more roads meet

**in-ter-state** [ĭn′tər-stāt′] *adjective*, pertaining to commerce between the states

**in-ter-val** [ĭn′tər-vəl] *noun*, the space of time between any two points or events, a break

**in-ter-vene** [ĭn′tər-vēn′] *verb*, 1) to come or be between 2) to occur between points of time or events

**in-ter-view** [ĭn′tər-vyōō′] *noun*, a
meeting in which people
exchange information

**in-ti-ma-cy** [ĭn′tə-mə-sē] *noun*,
close familiarity or association,
very personal

**in-ti-mate** [ĭn′tə-mĭt] *adjective*,
familiar, close, dear, private

**in-tim-i-date** [ĭn-tĭm′ĭ-dāt′] *verb*,
to make someone afraid, to
threaten someone, to scare

**in-to** [ĭn′tōō] *preposition*, to go
toward the middle of something

**in-tol-er-a-ble** [ĭn-tŏl′ər-ə-bəl]
*adjective*, unbearable,
unendurable, insufferable

**in-tol-er-ance** [ĭn-tŏl′ər-əns] *noun*,
prejudice, bias, bigoted

**in-to-na-tion** [ĭn′tə-nā′shən] *noun*,
a tone of voice, speech pattern,
inflection, melody of pitch

**in-tox-i-cate** [ĭn-tŏk′sĭ-kāt′] *verb*,
1) to enliven, to excite, to elate
2) to feel drugged or drunk

**in-trac-ta-ble** [ĭn-trăk′tə-bəl]
*adjective*, unruly, refractory

**in-tran-si-tive** [ĭn-trăn′sĭ-tĭv]
*adjective*, a verb in a sentence
that does not need a direct object
to complete its meaning

**in-trep-id** [ĭn-trĕp′ĭd] *adjective*,
fearless, dauntless

**in-tri-cate** [ĭn′trĭ-kĭt] *adjective*,
complicated, involved, complex

**in-tri-cate-ly** [ĭn′trĭ-kĭt-lē] *adverb*,
in a complex or involved manner

**in-trigue** [ĭn′trēg′] *noun*, 1) a
conspiracy, a strategy, a plan,
*verb*, 2) to be drawn into, to
fascinate, to arouse curiosity

**in-trin-sic** [ĭn-trĭn′zĭk] *adjective*,
basic and essential to what
something is

**in-tro-duce** [ĭn′trə-dōōs′] *verb*,
1) to bring into notice 2) to make
known by formal announcement
3) to bring into use, to lead in

**in-tro-duc-tion** [ĭn′trə-dŭk′shən]
*noun*, 1) a piece of writing at the
beginning of a book that
explains something about the
story 2) ) the act of formally
making persons known to each
other

**in-tro-vert** [ĭn′trə-vûrt′] *noun*, a
loner, someone who feels self-
conscious, a shy person

**in-trude** [ĭn-trōōd′] *verb*, to
trespass, to enter uninvited

**in-tru-sion** [ĭn-trōō′zhən] *noun*, the
act of forcing in without right or
welcome or permission

**in-tu-i-tion** [ĭn′tōō-ĭsh′ən] *noun*,
instinctive knowledge or feeling

**in-un-date** [ĭn′ŭn-dāt′] *verb*, to
overflow, to flood, to overwhelm

**in-ure** [ĭn-yōōr′] *verb*, to accustom,
to harden by use or exposure

**in-vade** [ĭn-vād′] *verb*, to enter by
force in order to take over

**in-va-lid** [ĭn-văl′ĭd] *adjective*,
1) null and void, insupportable,
[ĭn-val′ĭ-d] *noun*, 2) a person
who is feeble, weak, frail, sickly

**in-val-i-date** [ĭn-văl′ĭ-dāt′] *verb*, to
deprive of legal force

**in-var-i-ab-ly** [ĭn-vâr′ē-ə-blē]
*adverb*, without fail, predictably

**in-va-sion** [ĭn-vā′zhən] *noun*, an
attack, a raid

**in-vent** [ĭn-vĕnt′] *verb*, to create or design a new product

**in-ven-tion** [ĭn-vĕn′shən] *noun*, a design or creation of an idea

**in-ven-tor** [ĭn-vĕn′tər] *noun*, one who finds out or devises a new product or device

**in-ven-to-ry** [ĭn′vən-tôr′ē] *noun*, an itemized list of stock on hand with their estimated worth

**in-verse** [ĭn-vûrs′] *adjective*, the opposite, reverse in direction

**in-vert** [ĭn-vûrt′] *verb*, to overturn

**in-ver-te-brate** [ĭn-vûr′tə-brĭt] *noun*, animals without a backbone or spinal column, e.g. *a worm*

**in-vest** [ĭn-vĕst′] *verb*, to empower, to qualify, to devote time

**in-ves-ti-gate** [ĭn-vĕs′tĭ-gāt′] *verb*, to examine into, to inquire

**in-ves-ti-ga-tion** [ĭn-vĕs′tĭ-gā′shən] *noun*, an inquiry into a matter, a thorough exploration or inspection, an examination

**in-vest-ment** [ĭn-vĕst′mənt] *noun*, money used to create a source of income or profit

**in-ves-tor** [ĭn-vĕs′tər] *noun*, one who makes an investment or spends money on something with a view of obtaining income or profit

**in-vet-er-ate** [ĭn-vĕt′ər-ĭt] *adjective*, deep-rooted, habitual

**in-vig-o-rate** [ĭn-vĭg′ə-rāt′] *verb*, to fill with life and energy

**in-vin-ci-ble** [ĭn-vĭn′sə-bəl] *adjective*, irresistible, unyielding

**in-vis-i-ble** [ĭn-vĭz′ə-bəl] *adjective*, something that cannot be seen

**in-vi-ta-tion** [ĭn′vĭ-tā′shən] *noun*, a request asking for someone to attend a gathering

**in-vite** [ĭn-vīt′] *verb*, to ask someone to do something or come somewhere

**in-voke** [ĭn-vōk′] *verb*, to call upon, to ask for, to cause

**in-vol-un-tar-y** [ĭn-vŏl′ən-tĕr′ē] *adjective*, without will or choice, done unwillingly

**in-volve** [ĭn-vŏlv′] *verb*, to take part in, to make a part of

**in-vul-ner-a-ble** [ĭn-vŭl′nər-ə-bəl] *adjective*, incapable of injury

**in-ward** [ĭn′wərd] *adjective*, internal, inner, center

**in-ward-ly** [ĭn′wərd-lē] *adverb*, 1) toward the middle, halfway 2) internal, privately

**i-o-dine** [ī′ə-dīn′] *noun*, a nonmetallic element isolated as a crystalline solid

**i-o-ta** [ī-ō′tə] *noun*, the very smallest quantity or degree, a particle

**Io-wa** [ī′ə-wə] *noun*, one of the 50 United States located in the Midwest, the capital city is Des Moines. The state flower of **Iowa** is the wild rose and the state motto is "Our liberties we prize and our rights we will maintain."

**i-rate** [ī-rāt′] *adjective*, angry

**ir-i-des-cent** [ĭr′ĭ-dĕs′ənt] *adjective*, the rainbow-like play of colors, shimmering

**irk-some** [ûrk′səm] *adjective*, repetitious, tedious, annoying

**i-ron** [ī′ərn] *noun*, 1) a gray metal 2) a heated device used to smooth the wrinkles from clothes 3) an element, *verb*, 4) to press with a heated iron to remove wrinkles on clothes

**i-ron-ic** [ī-rŏn′ĭk] *adjective*, what appears to be false or contradictory, but in fact is true

**i-ro-ny** [ī′rə-nē, ī′ər-] *noun*, the outcome of events contrary to what was expected

**ir-rad-i-ate** [ĭ-rā′dē-āt′] *verb*, 1) to illuminate, to enlighten 2) to expose to ultraviolet rays

**ir-ra-tion-al** [ĭ-răsh′ə-nəl] *adjective*, absurd, unreasonable,

**ir-rec-on-cil-a-ble** [ĭ-rĕk′ən-sī′lə-bəl] *adjective*, not able to be resolved by compromise, unfriendly

**ir-reg-u-lar** [ĭ-rĕg′yə-lər] *adjective*,1) not conforming to rule 2) erratic, not uniform

**ir-rel-e-vant** [ĭ-rĕl′ə-vənt] *adjective*, not applicable or pertinent, not relevant

**ir-rep-a-ra-ble** [ĭ-rĕp′ər-ə-bəl] *adjective*, permanently damaged

**ir-re-proach-a-ble** [ĭr′ĭ-prō′chə-bəl] *adjective*, blameless, above reproach

**ir-re-sist-i-ble** [ĭr′ĭ-zĭs′tə-bəl] *adjective*, tempting

**ir-re-triev-a-ble** [ĭr′ĭ-trē′və-bəl] *adjective*, lost, gone forever

**ir-rev-er-ent** [ĭ-rĕv′ər-ənt] *adjective*, lacking proper respect

**ir-rev-o-ca-ble** [ĭ-rĕv′ə-kə-bəl] *adjective*, fixed, constant

**ir-ri-gate** [ĭr′ĭ-gāt′] *verb*, to supply with water by causing a stream to flow through, as in channels

**ir-ri-tate** [ĭr′ĭ-tāt′] *verb*, 1) to annoy, to excite to anger, to bother 2) to make skin sore, red or swollen

**ir-ri-ta-tion** [ĭr′ĭ-tā′shən] *noun*, 1) something that makes a person mildly angry 2) an allergic reaction, an irritant

**is** [ĭz] the part of the *verb* to **be** that we use with *he*, *she* and *it*

**Is-lam** [ĭs-läm′] *noun*, Muslim religion founded in Arabia in the 7th century based on the teaching of Muhammed

**is-land** [ī′lənd] *noun*, a body of land completely surrounded by water

**isle** [īl] *noun*, a small island

**is-n't** [ĭz′ənt] the *contraction* of the words **is** and **not**

**i-so-late** [ī′sə-lāt′] *verb*, 1)to separate and set apart, to place alone 2) to cut off from others

**iso-la-tion** [ī′sə-lā′shən] *noun*, solitude, detachment

**i-sos-ce-les tri-an-gle** [ī-sŏs′ə-lēz′ trī′ăng′gəl] *noun*, a triangle with two equal sides

**is-sue** [ĭsh′ōō] *noun*, 1) a subject, a topic 2) the condition or action of being made available, *verb*, 3) to give, to send, or come out

**isth-mus** [ĭs′məs] *noun*, a neck of land joining two larger portions of land bordered by water

**it** [ĭt] *pronoun, plural*, **they**, 1) the subject of the sentence 2) used about the weather, time, and dates, and in other phrases

**i-tal-ic** [ĭ-tăl′ĭk] *noun*, type in which the letters slant

**itch** [ĭch] *noun*, 1) a tickling feeling in the skin that makes one want to scratch, *verb*, 2) to scratch and rub a sore because it is irritating

**i-tem** [ī′təm] *noun*, a point, a news article, a single thing in a list

**i-tem-ize** [ī′tə-mīz′] *verb*, to list or state by particulars

**itin-er-ant** [ī-tĭn′ər-ənt] *adjective*, traveling from place to place

**itin-er-ar-y** [ī-tĭn′ə-rĕr′ē] *noun*, the detailed plan for a journey

**its** [ĭts] of **it**, belonging to **it**, the possessive of the word **it**

**it's** [ĭts] the *contraction* of the words: **it** and **is**

**it-self** [ĭt-sĕlf′] *plural*, **themselves**, referring to the subject in the sentence

**I've** [īv] the *contraction* of the words **I** and **have**

**i-vo-ry** [ī′və-rē, īv′rē] *noun*, hard, white substance taken from the tusks of elephants

**i-vy** [ī′vē] *noun*, a leafy vine

# J

**jack-al** [jăk′əl] *noun*, a wild animal like a dog that eats meat

**jack-et** [jăk′ĭt] *noun*, 1) a covering worn over clothing, similar to a coat, cut below the waist 2) a covering put over something

**jade** [jād] *noun*, a stone of a green color, but sometimes whitish, capable of a fine polish

**jad-ed** [jā′dĭd] *adjective*, tired, weary from overwork

**jag-uar** [jăg′wär′] *noun*, a wild cat with a spotted coat that lives in South America

**jail** [jāl] *noun*, a prison

**jam** [jăm] *noun*, *no plural*, 1) a sweet spread, made of boiled fruit and sugar 2) when traffic is stopped because no one can move 3) a predicament, a spot, *verb*, 4) to pack tightly together, to compress, to press or push

**jan-i-tor** [jăn′ĭ-tər] *noun*, one who takes care of the repairs and cleaning of a public building

**Jan-u-ary** [jăn′yoo-ĕr′ē] *noun*, the first month of the year, having 31 days

**jar** [jär] *noun*, a container like a bottle with a wide opening

**jar-gon** [jär′gən] *noun*, language used by a particular group, special terminology

**jaun-dice** [jôn′dĭs] *noun*, a blood condition that makes the skin look yellow

**jaunt** [jônt] *noun*, a short trip

**jave-lin** [jăv′lĭn] *noun*, a spear thrown by hand for distance as in an athletic event

**jaw** [jô] *noun*, the bony part of the face in which the teeth are set

**jazz** [jăz] *noun*, a style of music using unusual tone effects on brass instruments improvised by southern blacks in the 1900's

**jeal-ous** [jĕl′əs] *adjective*, to be unhappy because you want what someone else has, envious

**jeal-ous-y** [jĕl′ə-sē] *noun*, suspicious fear or watchfulness, resentment of someone's success

**jeans** [jēnz] *noun*, *plural*, pants made of denim fabric

**jeer** [jîr] *verb*, to make fun of someone and laugh in their face, to mock, to scorn

**jel-ly** [jĕl′ē] *noun, no plural*, 1) any substance between liquid and solid 2) a sweet spread made of fruit and pectin

**jel-ly-fish** [jĕl′ē-fĭsh′] *noun*, a soft gelatinous sea creature that looks like a squishy blob

**jeop-ard-ize** [jĕp′ər-dīz′] *verb*, to expose to danger or even death

**jerk** [jûrk] *noun*, 1) a quick pull or twist movement, *verb*, 2) to pull, to push or to twist suddenly

**jer-sey** [jûr′zē] *noun*, clothing usually made of cotton with elastic that covers the top of the body like a shirt

**jest** [jĕst] *verb*, to joke, to jeer

**jet** [jĕt] *noun*, 1) an aircraft propelled through air by an engine, which releases a stream of hot air behind itself as it travels 2) a stream of gas, air, or liquid that spurts from a hole

**jet-ti-son** [jĕt′ĭ-sən] *verb*, to throw overboard, to discard

**jet-ty** [jĕt′ē] *noun*, a kind of wall built out into water for protection against the waves

**Jew** [jo͞o] *noun*, a member of the Jewish religion

**jew-el** [jo͞o′əl] *noun*, a precious stone used as an ornament, a gem of great value

**jew-el-er** [jo͞o′ə-lər] *noun*, one who makes, or deals in jewels, gems and precious stones, etc.

**jew-el-ry** [jo͞o′əl-rē] *noun, no plural*, ornaments like rings, earrings, necklaces made with precious or semiprecious stones, gems and metals

**jilt** [jĭlt] *verb*, to break up a romantic interest

**jin-gle** [jĭng′gəl] *verb*, 1) to make a tingling sound like the sound of bells, *noun*, 2) a catchy verse

**job** [jŏb] *noun*, 1) a task or responsibility 2) work done for payment 3) a position or duty

**jog** [jŏg] *verb*, 1) to run for exercise 2) to jolt, to bump, to shake 3) to stir into activity

**join** [join] *verb*, 1) to connect, to bring together, to meet 2) to become a member

**joint** [joint] *adjective*, 1) an endeavor involving two or more people, *noun*, 2) the part of the body where bones connect 3) the place where two things are joined or connected 4) a poor quality restaurant or night club

**joke** [jōk] *noun*, 1) a funny story or funny phrase spoken to amuse people, *verb*, 2) to tell funny stories or say things to make people laugh, to fool around

**jolt** [jōlt] *noun*, 1) a sudden and unexpected movement, *verb*, 2) to cause a sudden movement

**joule** [jo͞ol, joul] *noun*, the measurement of force or energy

**jour-nal** [jûr′nəl] *noun*, a book that records daily thoughts or transactions, a diary

**jour-nal-ism** [jûr′nə-lĭz′əm] *noun, no plural*, the job of writing for a publication or broadcasting news

**jour-nal-ist** [jûr′nə-lĭst] *noun*, a professional writer for a newspaper or magazine

**jour-ney** [jûr′nē] *noun*, the passage from one place to another, a trip

**jo-vi-al** [jō′vē-əl] *adjective*, joking in a friendly manner

**joy** [joi] *noun*, *no plural*, great happiness, delight, elation

**joy-ful** [joi′fəl] *adjective*, full of joy, very glad, happy

**ju-bi-lant** [jōō′bə-lənt] *adjective*, thrilled, rejoicing, great joy

**Ju-da-ism** [jōō′dē-ĭz′əm] *noun*, the religion of people descended from the Israelites in the Bible

**judge** [jŭj] *noun*, 1) one with legal authority who applies the rules of law in a court 2) the person designated to decide the winner in a contest, *verb*, 3) to make a decision, to form an opinion

**judg-ment** [jŭj′mənt] *noun*, 1) a decision or opinion 2) intelligence, understanding

**ju-di-cial** [jōō-dĭsh′əl] *adjective*, of the administration of justice by judges, laws and the courts

**ju-di-cious** [jōō-dĭsh′əs] *adjective*, sound in judgment, wise

**ju-do** [jōō′dō] *noun*, *no plural*, a form of martial arts that uses the body as a weapon, and bans throws and blows

**jug** [jŭg] *noun*, a container with a handle for holding liquids

**jug-ger-naut** [jŭg′ər-nôt′] *noun*, an overpowering or crushing force

**jug-gle** [jŭg′əl] *verb*, to throw several things into the air and keep them moving by throwing and catching them as a trick

**jug-u-lar** [jŭg′yə-lər] *noun*, one of the large veins returning the blood from the head

**juice** [jōōs] *noun*, the natural fluid that comes from fruit, vegetables or cooked meat

**Ju-ly** [jōō-lī′] *noun*, the seventh month of the year, having 31 days

**jump** [jŭmp] *noun*, 1) a spring or leap, *verb*, 2) to lift the feet off the ground into the air, to leap 3) to rise suddenly

**jump-er** [jŭm′pər] *noun*, a sleeveless dress worn over a blouse

**junc-tion** [jŭngk′shən] *noun*, a place where roads or lines of railways meet and cross

**June** [jōōn] *noun*, the sixth month of the year, having 30 days

**jun-gle** [jŭng′gəl] *noun*, land thickly overgrown with vines, bushes, trees, etc.

**jun-ior** [jōōn′yər] *adjective*, 1) a student in his third year of a four-year course 2) the son named after his father, abbreviated **Jr**. after the name

**jun-i-per** [jōōn′pər] *noun*, an evergreen bush or tree related to cypresses, with tiny bluish cones that look like berries

**junk** [jŭngk] *noun*, stuff regarded as unwanted or useless

**jun-ket** [jŭng′kĭt] *noun*, a trip, a short pleasure excursion

**ju-ris-dic-tion** [jŏŏr′ĭs-dĭk′shən] *noun*, the legal authority of a court, to apply the law

**ju-ror** [jŏŏr′ər, -ôr′] *noun*, one of a group of peers chosen to judge someone accused of a crime

**ju-ry** [jŏŏr′ē] *noun*, a group of people chosen to decide if a person is guilty or innocent of a crime in a court of law

**just** [jŭst] *adjective*, 1) fair and right 2) normal, *adverb*, 3) to the amount needed, but no more 4) a very short time ago, by a short time 5) only 6) used to compare two things

**jus-tice** [jŭs′tĭs] *noun*, *no plural*, fairness, equity, impartiality

**jus-ti-fy** [jŭs′tə-fī′] *verb*, 1) to show or prove to be right 2) to make even or true, as lines of type by proper spacing

**ju-ve-nile** [jŏŏ′və-nīl′] *adjective*, 1) young, youthful, *noun*, 2) a youth, anyone under the legal adult age of 18

# K

**ka-lei-do-scope** [kə-lī′də-skōp′] *noun*, an optical instrument exhibiting an endless variety of colored forms

**kan-ga-roo** [kăng′gə-rŏŏ′] *noun*, a marsupial, an animal that eats only plants, lives in Australia, jumps around on its large back legs

**Kan-sas** [kăn′zəz] *noun*, one of the 50 United States, located in the Midwest, the capital city is Topeka. The state flower of **Kansas** is the sunflower, and the motto is "To the stars through difficulties."

**kar-at** [kăr′ət] *noun*, the unit measure of the purity of gold

**kay-ak** [kī′ăk′] *noun*, a canoe that holds one person

**keel** [kēl] *noun*, the bottom of the boat, the underside

**keen** [kēn] *adjective*, 1) having a sharp edge 2) mentally aware, quick to understand 3) showing a strong interest, eager

**keep** [kēp] *verb*, 1) to hold something 2) to store something, to stock it 3) to make someone stay someplace 4) to prevent someone from doing something 5) to continue on

**ken-nel** [kĕn′əl] *noun*, a place to keep and care for dogs

**Ken-tucky** [kən-tŭk′ē] *noun*, one of the 50 United States, located in the South, the capital is Frankfort. The state flower of **Kentucky** is the goldenrod, and the state motto is "United We Stand, Divided We Fall."

**kept** [kĕpt] *past tense* of **keep**

**ker-chief** [kûr′chĭf] *noun*, a woman's scarf worn as a covering for the head

**ker-nel** [kûr′nəl] *noun*, a grain or seed, the edible part of a nut

**ker-o-sene** [kĕr′ə-sēn′] *noun*, thin oil used to ignite a fire

**ket-tle** [kĕt′l] *noun*, a large metal pot with a lid and a handle and a spout

**key** [kē] *noun*, 1) a metal instrument used for locking and unlocking things 2) a lever on a musical instrument that affects the sound 3) the piece of information needed to make something understood

**key-board** [kē′bôrd′] *noun*, a common input device

**khak-i** [kăk′ē] *noun*, a tan or brownish cotton cloth

**kick** [kĭk] *noun*, 1) an impulsive move with the foot, *verb*,

# kid

2) to hit something with the foot, to move the foot suddenly

**kid** [kĭd] *noun*, 1) a young goat 2) a child, *verb*, 3) to tease or joke

**kid-nap** [kĭd′năp′] *verb*, to take someone against their will

**kid-nap-per** [kĭd′nă-pər] *noun*, someone who takes a person against their will

**kid-ney** [kĭd′nē] *noun*, one of two parts inside the body which remove waste liquid from the blood and excretes uric acid

**kill** [kĭl] *verb*, to make someone die

**kill-er** [kĭl′ər] *noun*, a person who murders or takes the life from another

**kil-o-gram** [kĭl′ə-grăm′] *noun*, a unit of weight equal to 1,000 grams

**kil-o-me-ter** [kĭ-lŏm′ĭ-tər] *noun*, a distance equal to 1,000 meters, or 3,281feet

**kil-o-watt** [kĭl′ə-wŏt′] *noun*, a unit of power equal to 1,000 watts

**kin** [kĭn] *noun*, *no plural*, family members, one s relatives

**kind** [kīnd] *adjective*, 1) nice, good, helpful, willing to please, *noun*, 2) a sort or particular one

**kin-der-gar-ten** [kĭn′dər-g r ′tn] *noun*, a preschool for children before the first grade

**kin-dle** [kĭn′dl] *verb*, 1) to set fire, to ignite 2) to arouse, to inspire

**kind-ness** [kīnd′nĭs] *noun*, *no plural*, goodness, compassion

**kin-dred** [kĭn′drĭd] *adjective*, 1) similar in nature, comparable, alike 2) related by family

**ki-net-ic** [kĭ-nĕt′ĭk] *adjective*, the changes of motion produced by forces, the force of motion

**king** [kĭng] *noun*, a male ruler of a country, especially one who comes from a family of rulers

**king-dom** [kĭng′dəm] *noun*, the lands owned by a monarchy, an empire, an independent realm

**kin-ship** [kĭn′shĭp′] *noun*, a relationship or connection between family members

**kiss** [kĭs] *noun*, 1) a slight touch with the lips, *verb*, 2) to touch with the lips as a sign of affection or love

**kit** [kĭt] *noun*, a set of instruments needed for doing something or going somewhere

**kitch-en** [kĭch′ən] *noun*, the room where food is prepared and cooked and eaten

**kite** [kīt] *noun*, a light frame covered with fabric, plastic or paper, flown in the air at the end of a long string

**kit-ten** [kĭt′n] *noun*, a baby cat

**knap-sack** [năp′săk′] *noun*, a supply bag of canvas or leather with shoulder straps, worn on the back

**knave** [nāv] *noun*, an unscrupulous, dishonest person, a rascal

**knead** [nēd] *verb*, to manipulate by pressing and stretching to mix and remove air, to massage

**knee** [nē] *noun*, the joint between the thigh and the lower leg connecting the femur and tibia

**kneel** [nēl] *verb*, to stand on your knees, to bend down so that your calf is laying on the ground

**knew** [nōō] *past tense* of **know**

**knife** [nīf] *noun, plural, **knives***, a cutting instrument consisting of a sharp blade fastened to a handle

**knight** [nīt] *noun*, 1) an armed soldier in the Middle Ages 2) a chess piece in the shape of a horse's head 3) an honorary title in Britain

**knit** [nĭt] *verb*, to join wool into a cloth using long needles

**knob** [nŏb] *noun*, a handle in the shape of a round lump

**knock** [nŏk] *noun*, 1) a noise made when something is hit *verb*, 2) to hit or strike with the fist 4) to make a noise by hitting on the surface

**knoll** [nōl] *noun*, a small round hill

**knot** [nŏt] *noun*, 1) one or more threads tied together, *verb*, 2) to tie something securely with rope or cord so that it cannot come untied

**know** [nō] *verb*, 1) to understand clearly, to learn 2) to be skilled in 3) to be acquainted with someone

**knowl-edge** [nŏl′ĭj] *noun*, something learned and remembered, gained by experience

**know-ledge-a-ble** [nŏl′ĭ-jə-bəl] *adjective*, familiar with, learned

**known** [nōn] *past participle* of **know**

**knuck-le** [nŭk′əl] *noun*, one of the joints in the finger or toe

**Ko-ran** [kə-răn′, -rän′, kô-, kō-] *noun*, the holy book of Islam containing the revelations of Muhammed

# L

**la-bel** [lā′bəl] *noun*, 1) a slip of paper indicating contents, ownership, etc. *verb*, 2) to affix a tag or sticker on something naming what it is

**la-bor** [lā′bər] *noun*, 1) work 2) the pain a woman feels birthing a baby, *verb*, 3) to work hard

**lab-o-ra-to-ry** [lăb′rə-tôr′ē] *noun*, a place devoted to experiments in natural science

**la-bo-ri-ous** [lə-bôr′ē-əs] *adjective*, hardworking, tiresome, tedious

**lab-y-rinth** [lăb′ə-rĭnth′] *noun*, a series of intricate passageways, a maze, an inexplicable difficulty

**lace** [lās] *noun*, 1) a string used to tie a shoe 2) frilly threadwork used as edging or as an embroidery design, *verb*, 3) to thread through holes with a string or cord

**lac-er-a-tion** [lăs′ə-rā′shən] *noun*, a cut, a tear made with a knife

**lack** [lăk] *noun*, 1) not enough, a shortage, *verb* 2) to be without

**lack-a-dai-si-cal** [lăk′ə-dā′zĭ-kəl] *adjective*, half-hearted, lazy, indifferent, listless

**la-con-ic** [lə-kŏn′ĭk] *adjective*, brief and to the point

**lac-quer** [lăk′ər] *noun*, a liquid that hardens into a clear tough film

**lac-tic acid** [lăk′tĭk-ăs′ĭd] *noun*, a colorless, syrupy liquid, occurring in sour milk

**lad** [lăd] *noun*, a boy

**lad-der** [lăd′ər] *noun*, a device used for climbing designed with two side pieces joined together with shorter pieces called rungs that form steps

**lad-en** [lād′n] *adjective*, heavily loaded, full of cargo

**la-dle** [lād′l] *noun*, a cup-shaped spoon with a long handle, used for serving or dipping

**la-dy** [lā′dē] *noun*, 1) a polite and considerate woman 2) in Britain, a title for the wife or daughter of a Lord

**lag** [lăg] *verb*, to move at a slower pace to stay behind the others

**la-goon** [lə-goon′] *noun*, a shallow body of water near a sea, or pond-like body of water

**laid** [lād] *past tense* of **lay**

**lair** [lâr] *noun*, a den, a hole, a hideout for a wild animal

**la-i-ty** [lā′ĭ-tē] *noun*, someone not connected to the clergy, a layman practicing religion

**lake** [lāk] *noun*, a body of water with land all around

**lamb** [lăm] *noun*, a baby sheep

**lame** [lām] *adjective*, limping or disabled in a hand or joint

**la-ment** [lə-mĕnt′] *verb*, to mourn, to express grief or regret

**lam-i-nat-ed** [lăm′ə-nā′tĭd] *adjective*, arranged in layers of plastic one upon the other

**lamp** [lămp] *noun*, a device used to project artificial light

**lam-poon** [lăm-poon′] *noun*, a cartoon or satire in print

**lance** [lăns] *noun*, 1) a spear, a harpoon, a javelin, *verb*, 2) to puncture 3) to cut into with a surgical knife

**land** [lănd] *noun*, *no plural*, 1) the dry part of the earth, not covered by water 2) a country, region, area, *verb*, 3) to arrive on the ground from the air or water

**land-fill** [lănd′fĭl′] *noun*, a large outdoor site where solid waste is covered by soil

**land-lord** [lănd′lôrd′] *noun*, a person who owns a building which he lets others use or live in, in return for money

**land-mark** [lănd′märk′] *noun*, 1) an achievement, a turning point, benchmark 2) a distinctive building or geographical marker like a bend in the river

**land-scape** [lănd′skāp′] *noun*, a view of an area with its natural surroundings

**lane** [lān] *noun*, a short road

**lan-guage** [lăng′gwĭj] *noun*, 1) any means of conveying or communicating ideas 2) human speech 3) dialect, jargon, vocabulary used by a group

**lan-guish** [lăng′gwĭsh] *verb*, to lose strength, to weaken

**lan-guor** [lăng′gər] *noun*, a feeling of depression, nervous exhaustion, weakness of mind or body

**lank** [lăngk] *adjective*, 1)thin, lean 2) hanging straight or limp

**lan-tern** [lăn′tərn] *noun*, a portable lamp, with a protective case for lights, carried with a handle often used outdoors for light

**lap** [lăp] *noun*, 1) the seat created by the legs and chest when sitting 2) the distance once around a track 3) a place of rest, *verb*, 4) to drink water with a tongue, like an animal

**lapel** [lə-pĕl′] *noun*, the flat hanging appendage on a jacket

**lapse** [lăps] *noun*, 1) an interval of time in which something stops and then starts again 2) termination of policy because of non-payment of premium when due 3) a slip or error

**lar-ce-ny** [lär′sə-nē] *noun*, taking and carrying away of things, stealing, robbery

**lard** [lärd] *noun*, grease, fat

**large** [lärj] *adjective*, greater than average in size, number, etc., immense, big

**large-ly** [lärj′lē] *adverb*, mostly

**lar-ger** [lär′jər] *adjective*, bigger

**lar-gess** [lär-zhĕs′] *noun*, the generous giving of gifts

**lar-va** [lär′və] *noun*, *plural*, *larvae or larvas*, the second stage of an insect that goes through complete metamorphosis

**lar-yn-gi-tis** [lăr′ən-jī′tĭs] *noun*, infection of the larynx or upper end of the windpipe

**lar-ynx** [lăr′ĭngks] *noun*, the voice organ in the upper throat

**la-ser** [lā′zər] *noun*, a narrow beam of high-energy light that is all exactly the same color

**lash** [lăsh] *noun*, 1) a whip, a cane, *verb*, 2) to hit hard 3) to secure something in place with a rope

**las-so** [lăs′ō] *noun*, 1) a rope with a loop at the end used for catching cattle, *verb*, 2) to catch by throwing the noose of a rope around the neck or torso

**last** [lăst] *adjective*, 1) the end, final 2) an instance when something happens 3) to come after all others 4) to be a part of for a long time, to endure, *adverb*, 5) to stay in good condition, to be preserved

**last-ing** [lăs′tĭng] *adjective*, the length of time something continues, enduring

**latch** [lăch] *noun*, 1) a small bolt used to fasten a door, *verb*, 2) to fasten something shut

**late** [lāt] *adjective*, 1) after the time agreed on 2) near the end of a day, year, etc. 3) a missed opportunity 4) deceased

**late-ly** [lāt′lē] *adverb*, recently, a short time ago, not long since

**la-tent** [lāt′nt] *adjective*, hidden, present but not visible

**lat-er** [lāt′ər] *adverb*, after a certain amount of time, subsequently

**lat-er-al** [lăt′ər-əl] *adjective*, coming from the side

**lat-est** [lā′tĭst] *adjective*, most recent, newest, popular

**lath-er** [lăth′ər] *noun*, *no plural*, the bubbles created by soap

**lat-i-tude** [lăt′ĭ-tōōd′] *noun*, *no plural*, imaginary horizontal lines on a map indicating the distance of a place, measured in degrees, north or south of the earth's equator 2) freedom to act and to choose

**lat-ter** [lăt′ər] *adjective*, the second of two things, the last mentioned

**laud** [lôd] *verb*, to praise

**laugh** [lăf] *verb*, to make a sound showing something is funny, to express happiness

**laugh-ter** [lăf′tər] *noun*, *no plural*, a giggle, mirth, a chuckle

**launch** [lônch] *noun*, 1) a small boat propelled by an engine, *verb*, 2) to send off, to put a boat into water or send a space ship into orbit 3) to plunge boldly into action

**laun-dry** [lôn′drē] *noun*, dirty clothes washed together

**lau-rel** [lôr′əl] *noun*, an evergreen shrub with pink flowers

**la-va** [lä′və] *noun*, very hot melted rock that bursts out of a volcano

**lav-a-to-ry** [lăv′ə-tôr′ē] *noun*, a room with a toilet and a sink

**lav-en-der** [lăv′ən-dər] *noun*, a fragrant plant with purple flowers, classified as an herb

**lav-ish** [lăv′ĭsh] *adjective*, 1) extravagant, excessive, 2) giving in great amounts, *verb*, 3) to give generously

**law** [lô] *noun*, a written rule of conduct made and enforced by the government

**law-mak-er** [lô′mā′kər] *noun*, a person in government who is part of the legislature

**lawn** [lôn] *noun*, a piece of ground where grass is grown and is kept short in front of a building

**law-yer** [lô′yər] *noun*, a professional who practices law, an attorney, barrister

**lax-a-tive** [lăk′sə-tĭv] *noun*, a medicine or herb that induces a bowel movement

**lay** [lā] *verb*, 1) to place something in a horizontal position 2) when an adult female produces eggs 3) to remain, to rest

**lay-er** [lā′ər] *noun*, a covering that is set between two levels

**la-zy** [lā′zē] *adjective*, disinterested in work, slow-moving, indolent

**lead** [lĕd] *noun*, 1) a heavy, metallic element, having a bright luster 2) the part of a pencil used for writing, [lēd] *verb*, 3) to guide, to show someone the way

**lead-er** [lē′dər] *noun*, the chief, the person in charge, the ruler

**lead-er-ship** [lē′dər-shĭp′] *noun*, the quality of those who take charge or show the way

**leaf** [lēf] *noun*, *plural*, *leaves*,

1) a green part of a stem that grows off a branch of a plant 2) a sheet of paper

**leaf-let** [lē′flĭt] *noun*, a brochure or a small sheet of printed matter

**league** [lēg] *noun*, 1) an association or alliance with other individuals 2) sports teams organized to compete against each other 3) three nautical miles

**leak** [lēk] *noun*, 1) a crack or hole through which liquid, gas or light can ooze, *verb*, 2) to let something escape through an unintended opening such as a crack or hole

**lean** [lēn] *adjective*, 1) thin, without fat, *verb*, 2) to bend or incline toward 3) to rest on something for support to keep from falling, to recline

**leap** [lēp] *noun*, 1) a jump, *verb*, 2) to jump or spring over a hurdle or through space

**leap year** *noun*, a year, once every four years, in which February has 29 days instead of 28

**learn** [lûrn] *verb*, 1) to acquire knowledge or skill through study or experience 2) to find out, to commit to memory

**learn-ing** [lûr'nĭng] *noun*, knowledge, education

**leash** [lēsh] *noun*, a restraining device in the form of a rope or cord, chain or strap

**least** [lēst] *adjective*, the smallest amount, degree or size

**leath-er** [lĕth'ər] *noun*, skin of a dead animal prepared for use

**leave** [lēv] *noun*, 1) permission to be absent, *verb*, 2) to go away from, to depart, to exit 3) to allow something to remain untouched 4) to bequeath

**lech-er-ous** [lĕch'ər-əs] *adjective*, impure in thought and act, lustful, perverted

**lec-tern** [lĕk'tərn] *noun*, a podium for public speaking

**lec-ture** [lĕk'chər] *noun*, 1) a speech on any subject, *verb*, 2) to speak, to talk, to teach

**ledge** [lĕj] *noun*, 1) a narrow shelf, such as at the bottom of a window 2) a narrow, flat piece of rock, on which you can stand

**ledg-er** [lĕj'ər] *noun*, a book of accounts listing names and debits and credits

**left** [lĕft] *adjective*, 1) the side of a person or thing that is to the west when facing north, the opposite

of the right side, *verb*, 2) the *past tense* of **leave**

**leg** [lĕg] *noun*, 1) the body part attached to the foot or paw, used for walking 2) one of at least three pieces on a piece of furniture, used to make it stand

**leg-a-cy** [lĕg'ə-sē] *noun*, a gift of personal property left in a will

**le-gal** [lē'gəl] *adjective*, based upon or in accordance with law

**leg-end** [lĕj'ənd] *noun*, 1) a story about someone that has no factual basis 2) a description or key accompanying a map or picture 3) an admirable person

**leg-er-de-main** [lĕj'ər-də-mān'] *noun*, slight of hand, magic

**leg-i-ble** [lĕj'ə-bəl] *adjective*, capable of being read with ease

**le-gion** [lē'jən] *noun*, a large group of soldiers, a multitude of people

**leg-is-la-ture** [lĕj'ĭ-slā'chər] *noun*, persons in a state elected by the people, having power to make, repeal, or change laws

**le-git-i-mate** [lə-jĭt'ə-mĭt] *adjective*, 1) lawful, conforming to accepted standards 2) genuine

**leg-ume** [leg'yoōm] *noun*, a plant of the pea family grown as a crop

**lei-sure** [lē'zhər] *noun*, *no plural*, free time from the demand of work or duty, spare time

**lem-ming** [lĕm'ĭng] *noun*, a small rat-like animal known for its mass migration into the sea

**lem-on** [lĕm'ən] *noun*, a yellow citrus fruit with a very sour taste, grown in tropical climates

**lem-on-ade** [lĕm′ə-nād′] *noun*, a beverage of sweetened lemon juice and water

**lend** [lĕnd] *verb*, 1) to let someone use something for a while, until they return it 2) to offer help

**length** [lĕngkth] *noun*, 1) the distance from end to end 2) the amount of time

**length-en** [lĕngk′thən-] *verb*, to make longer, drawn out

**le-ni-ent** [lē′nē-ənt] *adjective*, mild, merciful, not strict

**lens** [lĕnz] *noun*, 1) a piece of curved glass or other transparent material by which light rays meet to form an image 2) a part of the eye that focuses light rays to form an image on the retina

**leop-ard** [lĕp′ərd] *noun*, one of the big cats with a spotted coat, that weighs 100-175 pounds, is seven feet long and lives in Africa

**le-sion** [lē′zhən] *noun*, a wound, a sore, diseased tissue

**less** [lĕs] *adjective*, a smaller amount, a reduction

**less-en** [lĕs′ən] *verb*, to make smaller, to become less

**les-son** [lĕs′ən] *noun*, something that must be learned or studied

**let** [lĕt] *verb*, 1) to allow, to permit, to grant 2) to rent, to lease

**le-thal** [lē′thəl] *adjective*, deadly

**le-thar-gy** [lĕth′ər-jē] *noun*, fatigue, without energy, feeling tired, drowsy, sluggish

**let's** [lĕts] the *contraction* of the words **let** and **us**

**let-ter** [lĕt′ər] *noun*, 1) a message in writing, often sent through the mail 2) one of the characters of the alphabet

**let-tuce** [lĕt′əs] *noun*, a plant having succulent leaves that are used in salads

**lev-ee** [lĕv′ē] *noun*, an embankment, dike, dam

**lev-el** [lĕv′əl] *adjective*, 1) flat, with no higher or lower places, *noun*, 2) a place or position of a particular height, *verb*, 3) to make a surface flat or even

**lev-er** [lĕv′ər] *noun*, 1) a bar used to exert pressure or sustain weight 2) a means to an end

**lev-i-ty** [lĕv′ĭ-tē] *noun*, lightness of mind, high spirits, happiness

**le-vy** [lĕv′ē] *verb*, to put a judgment on property to collect money, to impose a tax

**lewd** [lōōd] *adjective*, obscene, indecent, lecherous, lustful

**lex-i-cog-ra-pher** [lĕk′sĭ-kŏg′rə-fər] *noun*, a person who writes dictionaries

**lex-i-con** [lĕk′sĭ-kŏn′] *noun*, a dictionary, a word list

**li-a-bil-i-ty** [lī′ə-bĭl′ĭ-tē] *noun*, 1) a responsibility, 2) a monetary obligation, a debt

**li-a-ble** [lī′ə-bəl] *adjective*, 1) legally responsible 2) likely, prone, inclined, apt

**li-ai-son** [lē′ā-zŏn′] *noun*, cooperation that facilitates a close working relationship between people or organizations

**li-ar** [lī′ər] *noun*, someone who does not tell the truth

**li-bel** [lī′bəl] *noun*, a false statement made about someone

**lib-er-al** [lĭb′ər-əl] *adjective*,
1) progressive reform
2) generous, ample, abundant

**lib-er-ate** [lĭb′ə-rāt′] *verb*, to free
from constraints, to release

**lib-er-a-tion** [lĭb′ə-rā′shən] *noun*,
freeing, emancipation

**lib-er-ty** [lĭb′ər-tē] *noun*, freedom,
independence from foreign rule

**li-bi-do** [lĭ-bē′dō] *noun*, emotional
urges behind human activity

**li-brar-i-an** [lī-brâr′ē-ən] *noun*,
one who has charge or care of
the materials in a library

**li-brar-y** [lī′brĕr′ē] *noun*, 1) a place
where books are kept for reading
and research 2) a room or
building where books and
documents are preserved for
future generations

**lib-ret-to** [lĭ-brĕt′ō] *noun*, the text
of an opera or other dramatic
musical work

**li-cense** [lī′səns] *noun*, 1) authority
given to do any act 2) excess of
liberty, *verb*, 3) to authorize

**li-cen-tious** [lī-sĕn′shəs] *adjective*,
unprincipled, unrestrained

**li-chen** [lī′kən] *noun*, a fungus that
grows like algae on rocks and
tree bark

**lick** [lĭk] *noun*, 1) a stroke of the
tongue over something *verb*,
2) to touch with the tongue 3) to
defeat

**lic-o-rice** [lĭk′ər-ĭs] *noun*, a dried
root, or an extract used in candy

**lid** [lĭd] *noun*, a cover for a pot or
pan, or some other container

**lie** [lī] *noun*, 1) the intentional
statement of an untruth, *verb*,

2) to put oneself in a reclining
position 3) to say something that
is not true, to fib

**lien** [lēn] *noun*, a legal claim upon
real or personal property

**lieu** [lōō] *preposition*, in place, as
in the phrase "in lieu of"

**lieu-ten-ant** [lōō-tĕn′ənt] *noun*,
1) a substitute for another in
performance of any duty 2) a
commissioned officer in the
military below captain

**life** [līf] *noun*, 1) the ability of
living organisms to grow and
reproduce 2) the period between
birth and death

**lift** [lĭft] *noun*, 1) a free ride in a car
or other form of transportation 2)
the means by which something is
raised, *verb*, 3) to pick up, to
raise, to elevate 4) to go up, to
ascend

**lig-a-ment** [lĭg′ə-mənt] *noun*, a
tough band of fibrous tissue
connecting bones, or to support
an organ in place in the body

**light** [līt] *adjective*, 1) buoyant, not
heavy 2) carefree, *noun*, *no
plural*, 3) the opposite of
darkness, *verb*, 4) to ignite a fire
5) to illuminate, to brighten

**light-ning** [līt′nĭng] *noun*, *no
plural*, flashing of light by
electricity discharged from one
cloud to another during a storm

**like** [līk] *adjective*, 1) similar to,
equal to, *preposition*,
2) resembling, typical of, *verb*,
3) to enjoy, to find agreeable

**like-ly** [līk′lē] *adjective*,
1) expected, probable, suitable,
*adverb*, 2) probably, certainly

**like-ness** [līk′nĭs] *noun,*
1) similarity, resemblance, 2) a
picture of a person, a portrait

**like-wise** [līk′wīz′] *adverb,* in the
same way, also, similarly

**li-lac** [lī′lək] *noun,* a shrub in the
olive family that has fragrant
white or purple flowers

**lil-li-pu-tian** [lĭl′ə-pyōō′shən]
*adjective,* extremely small

**lil-y** [lĭl′ē] *noun,* a plant with
trumpet-like flowers and thick
tubular roots

**limb** [lĭm] *noun,* 1) a part of the
body such as an arm or leg or
wing 2) the large branch of a
tree

**lim-ber** [lĭm′bər] *adjective,*
flexible, elastic, easy to bend

**lim-bo** [lĭm′bō] *noun,* 1) a place
near heaven or hell where certain
souls are kept 2) a West Indian
dance 3) a state of oblivion

**lime** [līm] *noun,* a green citrus
fruit, similar to a lemon, grown
on trees in warm climates

**lim-it** [lĭm′ĭt] *noun,* 1) that which
terminates or confines 2) the full
extent, *verb,* 3) to set
boundaries, to restrict

**lim-i-ta-tion** [lĭm′ĭ-tā′shən] *noun,*
shortcomings, restriction

**lim-ou-sine** [lĭm′ə-zēn′] *noun,* a
long automobile with many seats
and a permanent top

**limp** [lĭmp] *adjective,* 1) without
stiffness, not firm, *noun,* 2) the
way you walk when one leg is
hurt, *verb,* 3) to walk carefully
without putting too much
pressure on the leg or foot

**lim-pid** [lĭm′pĭd] *adjective,* crystal
clear, transparent

**line** [līn] *noun,* 1) the distance
between 2 points 2) people or
things arranged in a row 3) a
business or vocation 4) a streak
made with a pencil and ruler 5) a
collection of points along a straight
path that goes on and on in
opposite directions 6) a boundary
marker 7) dialogue in performance,
*verb,* 8) to put a layer between the
container and the product 9) to
collect in a row, to watch or wait
for something 10) to draw a thin
mark

**lin-en** [lĭn′ən] *noun,* a thread or
cloth made of flax

**lin-er** [lī′nər] *noun,* a first class
passenger ship or airplane

**lin-ger** [lĭng′gər] *verb,* 1) to stay on
longer than expected, to dawdle
2) to persist

**lin-ge-rie** [län′zhə-rā′] *noun,* lacey,
silk or cotton underwear worn by
women, undergarments

**lin-guis-tic** [lĭng-gwĭs′tĭk]
*adjective,* pertaining to language

**lin-i-ment** [lĭn′ə-mənt] *noun,* a
liquid applied to soothe the skin

**lin-ing** [lī′nĭng] *noun,* a fold, an
overlay that forms a covering

**link** [lĭngk] *noun,* 1) a connection,
a bond, a tie, *verb,* 2) to be
joined together, to unite

**li-no-le-um** [lĭ-nō′lē-əm] *noun,* a
washable floor covering having
a base of solidified oil on a
canvas foundation

**lint** [lĭnt] *noun,* dirt, dust, fuzz

**li-on** [lī′ən] *noun,* one of the big
cats that lives in Africa

**lip** [lĭp] *noun*, one of the soft red rims round the mouth

**liq-uid** [lĭk'wĭd] *adjective*, 1) flowing like water, *noun*, 2) fluid, not solid or gas

**liq-ui-date** [lĭk'wĭ-dāt'] *verb*, to sell possessions for cash

**liq-uor** [lĭk'ər] *noun*, any liquid substance, an alcoholic beverage

**lisp** [lĭsp] *noun*, a speech impediment making it difficult to make an **S** sound

**list** [lĭst] *noun*, 1) names of different things written down one after another, *verb*, 2) to order things by writing them down in a sequence

**lis-ten** [lĭs'ən] *verb*, to pay attention to what someone is saying, to heed

**list-less** [lĭst'lĭs] *adjective*, lacking spirit or energy, languid, tired

**lit** [lĭt] *past tense* of **light**

**lit-a-ny** [lĭt'n-ē] *noun*, a prayer in the form of a religious song alternating with the congregation

**li-ter** [lē'tər] *noun*, a unit in the metric system used to measure liquid equal to 1.057 quarts

**lit-er-ac-y** [lĭt'ə-r'ə-sē] , *noun* the ability to listen, speak, read, write, view, represent, compute, and solve problems at levels of proficiency necessary to function in the family, in the community, and on the job

**li-ter-ate:***adjective,* able to read and write

**lit-er-al-ly** [lĭt'ər-ə-lē] *adverb,* word for word, as stated, verbatim

**lit-er-a-ture** [lĭt'ər-ə-chŏŏr'] *noun,* *no plural,* 1) the study of writing and books 2) printed material

**lithe** [līth] *adjective,* pliable, bendable, limber, supple

**lith-i-um** [lĭth'ē-əm] *noun,* a soft, silver-white metallic element of the alkali group

**lit-i-gant** [lĭt'ĭ-gənt] *noun,* a person who wants to sue another

**lit-i-ga-tion** [lĭt'ĭ-gā' shən] *noun,* the subject of a lawsuit, any matter before the court or a judge

**lit-mus** [lĭt'məs] *noun,* a coloring matter obtained from lichens, that is violet-blue, and turns red by an acid, and is restored to blue by an alkali

**lit-ter** [lĭt'ər] *noun,* 1) newborn baby animals, offspring 2) trash, small pieces of garbage thoughtlessly discarded, *verb,* 3) to throw trash on the ground, not in a garbage can

**lit-tle** [lĭt'l] *adjective,* 1) a small amount or size 2) a brief period of time

**live** [līv, lĭv] *adjective,* 1) performed unrehearsed, broadcasted directly 2) full of energy, *verb,* 3) to be, to exist 4) to reside in, to inhabit 5) to be active and to satisfy an ideal

**live-li-hood** [līv'lē hŏŏd] *noun,* the means of supporting oneself

**live-ly** [līv'lē] *adverb,* full of energy, very active, full of life

**liv-er** [lĭv'ər] *noun,* an organ inside the body which cleans the blood

**live-stock** [līv'stŏk'] *noun,* animals raised on a farm or ranch

**liv-id** [lĭv′ĭd] *adjective*, 1) angry 2) lead colored, black and blue

**liv-ing** [lĭv′ĭng] *adjective*, 1) alive, *noun*, 2) a manner of existence

**liz-ard** [lĭz′ərd] *noun*, a cold blooded reptile with four short legs and a scaly body

**lla-ma** [lä′mə] *noun*, a South American ruminant animal, related to the camel and raised for its fleecy wool

**load** [lōd] *noun*, 1) something carried by a person, vehicle or animal 2) a burden, *verb*, 3) to put cargo or materials on a truck or vehicle 4) to fill a gun with ammunition 5) to burden

**loaf** [lōf] *noun*, 1) the whole amount of bread before it is sliced, *verb*, 2) to take it easy, to idle away time, to waste time

**loan** [lōn] *noun*, 1) a thing, especially money, lent to another person, *verb*, 2) to let someone borrow something, to lend

**loathe** [lōth] *verb*, to detest, to feel intense dislike for, to abhor

**lob-by** [lŏb′ē] *noun*, 1) an entrance way, a foyer, *verb*, 2) to influence, to pressure, to sway

**lob-ster** [lŏb′stər] *noun*, an edible sea animal with a shell, a tail, and ten legs

**lo-cal** [lō′kəl] *adjective*, regional, in a confined area or place

**lo-cal-i-ty** [lō-kăl′ĭ-tē] *noun*, a position, a situation, a place

**lo-cate** [lō′kāt′] *verb*, to find, to search out, to come across

**lo-ca-tion** [lō-kā′shən] *noun*, where something is, a certain place

**lock** [lŏk] *noun*, 1) a device for fastening things like doors that can only be opened or closed with a key or secret code 2) a strand of hair, *verb*, 3) to close and make secure 4) to fasten with a lock

**lock-er** [lŏk′ər] *noun*, a box often with a lock, for keeping things

**lo-co-mo-tive** [lō′kə-mō′tĭv] *noun*, a railroad engine that pulls trains

**lo-cust** [lō′kəst] *noun*, an insect like a grasshopper that travels in swarms and eats plants

**lode** [lōd] *noun*, vein-like deposit of mineral ore

**lodge** [lŏj] *noun*, 1) a place to stay where you pay for the service, *verb*, 2) to pay to stay someplace, like a motel or inn 3) to become embedded in something

**loft** [lôft] *noun*, an upper room, a storage area, an attic

**loft-y** [lôf′tē] *adjective*, very high

**log** [lôg, lŏg] *noun*, 1) a piece of wood that was part of the trunk or limb of a tree 2) a book of records, a register of a trip

**log-ic** [lŏj′ĭk] *noun*, the art of correct reasoning, especially of inference, sound judgment

**log-i-cal** [lŏj′ĭ-kəl] *adjective*, in a way that is orderly and makes sense, reasonable

**lo-go** [lō′gō′] *noun*, a slogan or symbol that represents a name

**loi-ter** [loi′tər] *verb*, to hang around, to linger aimlessly, to proceed slowly, to waste time lone [lōn] *adjective*, single, one, standing apart, isolated

lone-li-ness [lōn′lē-nĕs] *noun*, feeling alone, solitude

lone-ly [lōn′lē] *adjective*, 1) a sad, depressing feeling because one is alone 2) desolate, remote

long [lông] *adjective*, 1) measuring a distance from one end to another 2) farther or taller than the others 3) an extended period or time, *adverb*, 4) a time in the distant past 5) conditionally, *verb*, 6) to want something badly, to pine, to yearn

lon-gev-i-ty [lŏn-jĕv′ĭ-tē] *noun*, to live the duration of a long life

long-ing [lông′ĭng] *verb*, desiring, wanting, yearning, craving

lon-gi-tude [lŏn′jĭ-tōod′] *noun, no plural*, imaginary lines shown on maps that go from north to south along the earth's surface, measured in degrees east and west from the prime meridian, which runs north and south through Greenwich, England

look [lŏok] *noun*, 1) a glance, a gaze 2) appearance, *verb*, 3) to stare, or glance at 4) to seem or appear 5) to expect, to await

loom [lōom] *noun*, 1) a machine used to weave cloth from yarn, *verb*, 2) to hover over 3) likely to happen in the future

loop [lōop] *noun*, a ring made by a rope or string crossing itself

loop-hole [lōop′hōl′] *noun*, a way of getting around a law or legal agreement, a means of escape

loose [lōos] *adjective*, 1) not fastened tightly or securely 2) free, not confined or shut in

loos-en [lōo′sən] *verb*, to become unfastened, to make less tight

loot [lōot] *noun*, 1) money or spoils, *verb*, 2) to steal, to rob, to pillage and plunder

lop-sid-ed [lŏp′sī′dĭd] *adjective*, hanging over to one side, uneven

lo-qua-cious [lōkwā′shəs] *adjective*, talkative, chatty, fond of talking

lord [lôrd] *noun*, 1) a person having great power or authority, a master or ruler 2) the title for a judge, bishop, or nobleman

lore [lôr] *noun*, a lesson, a teaching

lose [lōoz] *verb*, 1) to fail to win 2) to misplace something

loss [lôs] *noun*, 1) damage, injury, ruin 2) deprivation

lost [lôst] *adjective*, 1) confused, bewildered, disoriented 2) wasted 3) the *past tense* of **lose**

lot [lŏt] *noun*, 1) a piece of land or property 2) a large quantity of something 3) a kind or sort

lo-tion [lō′shən] *noun*, a liquid put on the skin to add moisture and make it soft or clean

lot-tery [lŏt′ə-rē] *noun*, a game of gambling in which a prize is given to the person with the matching digits drawn from a pool of numbers

lo-tus [lō′təs] *noun*, a water plant with white, yellow, blue or pink flowers, a water lily

loud [loud] *adjective*, 1) noisy, making or having a loud sound 2) offensively bright colors

Lou-i-si-ana [lōo-ē′zē-ăn′ə] *noun*, one of the 50 United States located in the South, the

191

capital is Baton Rouge. The state flower of **Louisiana** is the flower of the magnolia tree, and the motto is "Union, justice, confidence."

**lounge** [lounj] *noun,* 1) a couch with little or no back 2) a room in a bar where people relax and listen to music, *verb,* 3) to rest or recline comfortably

**louse** [lous] *noun, plural,* **lice,** a small insect without wings that lives on the skin of animals, birds, and people

**lous-y** [lou′zē] *adjective,* bad

**lov-a-ble** [lŭv′ə-bəl] *adjective,* able to be loved, warm, deep feeling

**love** [lŭv] *noun,* 1) a very strong warm feeling or deep concern for someone, commitment 2) darling, sweetheart, *verb,* 3) to feel passion, or a strong affection for someone or something

**love-ly** [lŭv′lē] *adjective,* beautiful, having pleasing qualities

**lov-ing** [lŭv′ĭng] *adjective,* showing affection or fondness

**low** [lō] *adjective,* 1) close to the ground, not very high 2) quiet, not very loud 3) coarse, mean 4) inferior quality

**low-er** [lou′ər] *adjective,* 1) inferior 2) less 3) under, *verb,* 4) to make something closer to the ground 5) to diminish the volume of sound 6) to demean, to debase in estimation

**loy-al** [loi′əl] *adjective,* true and faithful to a person

**loy-al-ty** [loi′əl-tē] *adjective,* allegiance, faithfulness

**lu-bri-cant** [loo′brĭ-kənt] *noun,* grease or gear oil

**lu-bri-cate** [loo′brĭ-kāt′] *verb,* to make smooth or slippery

**lu-cent** [loo′sənt] *adjective,* glowing with light, shining

**lu-cid** [loo′sĭd] *adjective,* 1) bright, 2) easily understood, clear

**luck** [lŭk] *noun,* 1) something good or bad that happens by chance or accident 2) good fortune

**luck-y** [lŭk′ē] *adjective,* fortunate

**lu-cra-tive** [loo′krə-tĭv] *adjective,* profitable, money making

**lu-cre** [loo′kər] *noun,* money

**lu-di-crous** [loo′dĭ-krəs] *adjective,* funny, ridiculous, absurd

**lug-gage** [lŭg′ĭj] *noun, no plural,* bags, suitcases, trunks and traveling accessories, baggage

**luke-warm** [look′wôrm′] *adjective,* not very warm, but not cold, room temperature, tepid

**lull** [lŭl] *noun,* 1) a quiet interval, a pause, *verb,* 2) to soothe, to calm

**lull-a-by** [lŭl′ə-bī′] *noun,* a soft song that puts someone to sleep

**lum-ba-go** [lŭm-bā′gō] *noun,* rheumatic pain in the loins and small of the back

**lum-ber** [lŭm′bər] *noun,* 1) logs or timber cut into planks or boards, *verb,* 2) to move along slowly and heavily, to plod

**lu-mi-nous** [loo′mə-nəs] *adjective,* 1) well lit, bright, radiating light 2) glowing in the dark

**lump** [lŭmp] *noun*, 1) a swelling on the body that becomes a mass 2) a hard form without a special shape or size, *verb*, 3) to put together in a pile

**lu-nar** [lōō′nər] *adjective*, having to do with the moon

**lu-na-tic** [lōō′nə-tĭk] *adjective*, 1) crazy, mad, psychotic, *noun*, 2) an insane person

**lunch** [lŭnch] *noun*, the meal you eat in the middle of the day

**lunch-eon** [lŭn′chən] *noun*, a midday meal enjoyed with others

**lung** [lŭng] *noun*, one of the two sac-like organs inside the chest with which we breathe

**lunge** [lŭnj] *verb*, to leap, to charge at someone suddenly

**lu-pine** [lōō′pən] *noun*, a plant related to peas and beans with tall spikes of flowers

**lure** [lōōr] *noun*, 1) something appealing, *verb*, 2) to entice, to bait, to attract, to tempt

**lu-rid** [lōōr′ĭd] *adjective*, horrible, sensational, shocking, gruesome

**lurk** [lûrk] *verb*, to wait in hiding, to watch someone without their knowledge, to go furtively

**lus-cious** [lŭsh′əs] *adjective*, appealing to taste or smell

**lust** [lŭst] *noun*, 1) a strong feeling of wanting something that would be selfish 2) sexual appetite

**lus-ter** [lŭs′tər] *noun*, shine, brightness, sheen or gloss

**lux-u-ri-ous** [lŭg-zhōōr′ē-əs] *adjective*, fine and expensive, very nice, sumptuous

**lux-u-ry** [lŭg′zhə-rē] *noun*, an item that adds to pleasure and comfort

**lynch** [lĭnch] *verb*, to hang someone in an act of mob violence

**lyr-ic** [lĭr′ĭk] *noun*, a poem intended to be a song

# M

**ma-ca-bre** [mə-kä′brə] *adjective*, horrible, gruesome, ghastly

**mac-a-ro-ni** [măk′ə-rō′nē] *noun*, a flour paste dried in long slender tubes, pasta

**ma-chet-e** [mə-shĕt′ē] *noun*, a long, curved knife used for cutting tall vegetation

**mach-i-na-tion** [măk′ə-nā′shən] *noun*, a scheme, a plot, or plan

**ma-chine** [mə-shēn′] *noun*, a device made to consume energy to produce another form of energy to do some kind of work

**ma-chin-er-y** [mə-shē′nə-rē] *noun*, *no plural*, equipment, devices

**mack-er-el** [măk′ər-əl] *noun*, a fish found traveling in schools in the North Atlantic

**mad** [măd] *adjective*, 1) insane, crazy, out of your right mind, reckless 2) angry, enraged

**mad-am** [măd′əm] *noun*, a respectful way of speaking to or writing to a woman

**made** [mād] *past tense* of **make**

**mad-ri-gal** [măd′rĭ-gəl] *noun*, a folk song or ballad of the 16th and 17th century

**mael-strom** [māl′strəm] *noun*, a powerful whirlpool

**maes-tro** [mīs′trō] *noun*, an eminent composer, a master

**mag-a-zine** [măg′ə-zēn′] *noun*, a pamphlet or news summary published periodically

**mag-ic** [măj′ĭk] *noun, no plural*, 1) the art or pretended art of controlling forces through the use of secret charms 2) clever tricks done to outsmart people, using sleight of hand

**mag-i-cal** [măj′ĭ-kəl] *adjective*, enchanting, marvelous

**ma-gi-cian** [mə-jĭsh′ən] *noun*, one who uses tricks to do things that seem impossible

**mag-is-trate** [măj′ĭ-strāt′] *noun*, a public civil officer charged with administering the law, a justice of the peace

**mag-nan-i-mous** [măg-năn′ə-məs] *adjective*, great of mind, generous and forgiving

**mag-nate** [măg′nāt′] *noun*, a person of prominence and influence, a tycoon

**mag-ne-si-um** [măg-nē′zē-əm] *noun*, a ductile silver-white metallic element

**mag-net** [măg′nĭt] *noun*, 1) a combination of metals that have a force that attract metals like iron 2) something that attracts

**mag-net-ic** [măg-nĕt′ĭk] *adjective*, 1) possessing the properties of the magnet 2) exerting a moral attractive force or charm

**mag-nif-i-cence** [măg-nĭf′ĭ-səns] *adjective*, grandeur, splendor

**mag-nif-i-cent** [măg-nĭf′ĭ-sənt] *adjective*, wonderful, impressive

**mag-ni-fy** [măg′nə-fī′] *verb*, to increase the size of what you are looking at, to enlarge

**mag-ni-fy-ing glass** [măg′nə-fī′ĭng glăs] *noun*, a lens that enlarges something small so that it is easier to see

**mag-ni-tude** [măg′nĭ-tōōd′] *noun*, great in size, or extent

**ma-hog-a-ny** [mə-hŏg′ə-nē] *noun*, a hard, reddish wood from tropical American trees

**maid** [mād] *noun*, a female servant

**maid-en name** [mād′n-nām] *noun*, a woman's last name before she is married

**mail** [māl] *noun*, letters and packages sent through and delivered by the postal service

**maim** [mām] *verb*, to injure so that part of the body is useless

**main** [mān] *adjective*, chief, most important, the center piece

**Maine** [mān] *noun*, one of the 50 United States located in New England, the capital is Augusta. The state flower of **Maine** is the eastern white pine cone and tassel, and the motto is "Direct or guide."

**main-spring** [mān′sprĭng′] *noun*, the principal spring in a mechanism, as in a watch

**main-stay** [mān′stā′] *noun*, 1) pillar, support 2) strength

**main-tain** [mān-tān′] *verb*, 1) to hold or keep in any particular condition, to preserve 2) to support, to insist

**main-te-nance** [mān′tə-nəns]
*noun*, *no plural*, upkeep

**maize** [māz] *adjective*, 1) pale
yellow, *noun*, 2) corn

**ma-jes-ti-cal-ly** [mə-jĕs′tĭk-lē]
*adverb*, with grandeur and
stately dignity, regal

**maj-es-ty** [măj′ĭ-stē] *noun*, the title
of a sovereign power, grandeur

**ma-jor** [mā′jər] *adjective*, 1) chief,
most important, the largest,
*noun*, 2) an officer in the
military between Lieutenant
Colonel and General

**ma-jor-i-ty** [mə-jôr′ĭ-tē] *noun*, the
greater number, more than half

**make** [māk] *verb*, 1) to create or
produce 2) to force 3) to earn or
win 4) to appoint or name

**mal-aise** [mă-lāz′] *noun*,
uneasiness, distress, fatigue

**mal-a-prop-ism**
[măl′ə-prŏp-ĭz′əm] *noun*, comic
misuse of a word, *i.e., a verbal
agreement isn't worth the paper
it is written on*

**ma-lar-i-a** [mə-lâr′ē-ə] *noun*, a
disease produced by the bite of a
mosquito causing a fever

**male** [māl] *adjective*, 1) belonging
to men and boys, *noun*, 2) a
grown boy, masculine, manly

**ma-lev-o-lent** [mə-lĕv′ə-lənt]
*adjective*, wishing evil or harm

**mal-ice** [măl′ĭs] *noun*, a desire to
inflict bad feelings on another

**ma-lign** [mə-līn′] *verb*, to say bad
things about someone

**ma-lig-nant** [mə-lĭg′nənt]
*adjective*, tending or threatening
to produce death as a tumor

**mal-le-a-ble** [măl′ē-ə-bəl] *adjective*,
1) capable of being extended or
shaped by beating with a hammer
2) easy to influence

**mal-let** [măl′ĭt] *noun*, a stick, a
club, a hammer-like tool

**mal-nu-tri-tion** [măl′nōō-trĭsh′ən]
*noun*, *no plural*, undernourishment
caused by poor diet

**mal-prac-tice** [măl′ prăk′tĭs] *verb*,
professional misconduct especially
by a physician

**mam-mal** [măm′əl] *noun*, any
warm-blooded vertebrate that
nurses its young

**mam-moth** [măm′əth] *adjective*,
very large, gigantic, huge

**man** [măn] *noun*, *plural*, **men**,
1) a full grown male person
2) speaking of mankind in
general *verb*, 3) to supply with
people

**man-age** [măn′ĭj] *verb*, 1) to
succeed in getting something
done, to reach a goal 2) to
control or have power over
something 3) to function

**man-age-a-ble** [măn′-ĭ-jə-bəl]
*adjective*, governable,
submitting to control

**man-age-ment** [măn′ĭj-mənt]
*noun*, people who manage any
enterprise, an administration

**man-ag-er** [măn′ĭ-jər] *noun*, a
person who looks after and
directs the activities of a
business, a supervisor

**man-date** [măn′dāt′] *noun*, an
order, a command

**man-da-to-ry** [măn′də-tôr′ē]
*adjective*, required, imperative

**man-drel** [măn′drəl] *noun*, an axis
inserted to support something

**mane** [mān] *noun*, the long hair on the back of the neck of an animal, such as a horse or lion

**ma-neu-ver** [mə-nōō'vər] *noun*, 1) a military movement 2) a scheme or manipulation, *verb*, 3) to move in a skillful way

**mange** [mānj] *noun*, a contagious skin disease of animals marked by itching and hair loss

**man-go** [măng'gō] *noun*, a juicy fruit with a large seed that grows on a tree in tropical climates

**ma-ni-ac** [mā'nē-ăk'] *noun*, a madman, an insane person

**man-i-cure** [măn'ĭ-kyŏŏr'] *noun*, a grooming of hands and fingernails

**man-i-fest** [măn'ə-fĕst'] *adjective*, 1) something obvious or clear, *noun*, 2) an invoice of a ship's, or truck's, or plane's cargo, *verb*, 3) to show, to display, to reveal

**man-i-fes-to** [măn'ə-fĕs'tō] *noun*, a statement of policy and plans

**man-i-fold** [măn'ə-fōld'] *adjective*, having many and various kinds or features

**ma-nip-u-late** [mə-nĭp'yə-lāt'] *verb*, 1) to treat or work with the hands 2) to control the action of something by management

**man-kind** [măn'kīnd'] *noun*, no *plural*, all human beings

**man-ner** [măn'ər] *noun*, 1) the way in which something is done or happens, prevailing customs *plural*, 2) ways of behaving in social situations

**man-or** [măn'ər] *noun*, a large house, a mansion,

**man-sion** [măn'shən] *noun*, a large, impressive house, a castle

**man-tel** [măn'tl] *noun*, 1) the shelf above a fireplace 2) the earth's interior layer between the crust and the core

**man-u-al** [măn'yōō-əl] *adjective*, 1) done by hand, *noun*, 2) an instruction guide

**man-u-fac-ture** [măn'yə-făk'chər] *verb*, to assemble parts into a product in a factory

**ma-nure** [mə-nōōr'] *noun*, livestock excrement

**man-u-script** [măn'yə-skrĭpt'] *noun*, a copy of a work intended for publication

**man-y** [mĕn'ē] *adjective*, containing a large number of something

**map** [măp] *noun*, 1) a representation of the physical features of the earth, *verb*, 2) to plan, to chart, to outline

**ma-ple** [mā'pəl] *noun*, a hardwood tree that produces sweet sap, boiled into syrup

**mar** [mär] *verb*, to damage, to hurt, to disfigure, to impair, to injure

**mar-ble** [mär'bəl] *noun*, no *plural*, 1) a hard stone that polishes well, used in buildings 2) a small glass or stone ball used in a game

**March** [märch] *noun*, the third month of the year, having 31 days

**march** [märch] *noun*, 1) the distance of a walk using regular steps 2) a piece of music to which soldiers walk, *verb*, 3) to walk with measured steps, to advance in this manner

**mare** [mâr] *noun*, a female horse

**mar-ga-rine** [mär′jər-ĭn] *noun*, *no plural*, a butter substitute made from vegetable oils

**mar-gin** [mär′jĭn] *noun*, 1) the border of empty space around the text on paper 2) a deposit of a portion of the value of stocks or bonds

**mar-gin-al** [mär′jə-nəl] *adjective*, borderline, passable

**mar-i-gold** [mär′ĭ-gōld′] *noun*, a yellow or orange flower that is a member of the daisy family

**ma-rine** [mə-rēn′] *noun*, having to do with the sea

**mar-i-on-ette** [mär′ē-ə-nĕt′] *noun*, a puppet manipulated by strings

**mar-i-time** [mär′ĭ-tīm′] *adjective*, bordering on the sea, nautical

**mark** [märk] *noun*, 1) a spot or a scratch, imprint 2) a point or the total of points indicating how one has scored on an examination or in a class 3) a distinguishing feature, *verb*, 4) to indicate a line or boundary 5) to leave a spot or write something 6) to distinguish

**mar-ket** [mär′kĭt] *noun*, 1) a store, an outlet, a shop 2) supply and demand, commodity market, *verb*, 3) to develop ways to sell a product by making it attractive

**mar-ma-lade** [mär′mə-lād′] *noun*, a preserve or jam made of the pulp and rind of fruit

**ma-roon** [mə-rōon′] *verb*, to leave someone isolated

**mar-riage** [mär′ĭj] *noun*, a wedding ceremony, the state of being married

**mar-row** [mär′ō] *noun*, soft tissue filling in cavities of bones

**mar-ry** [mär′ē] *verb*, to take someone as a husband or wife

**marsh** [märsh] *noun*, a low, wet place where the ground is damp and swampy, a bog

**mar-shal** [mär′shəl] *noun*, 1) the master of ceremonies of a parade or an event 2) an officer of justice similar to a sheriff, *verb*, 3) to manage, to direct

**mar-su-pi-al** [mär-sōo′pē-əl] *noun*, animals that nurse their offspring in a pouch

**mar-tial** [mär′shəl] *adjective*, pertaining to military affairs, war or battle, inclined to war

**mar-tyr** [mär′tər] *noun*, one who suffers persecution, torture or death for a cause or beliefs

**mar-vel** [mär′vəl] *noun*, 1) something that is remarkable or exciting, *verb*, 2) to be filled with wonder or astonishment

**mar-vel-ous** [mär′və-ləs] *adjective*, astonishing, causing wonder

**Mary-land** [mĕr′ə-lənd] *noun*, one of the 50 United States located on the East Coast, the capital is Annapolis. The state flower of **Maryland** is the black-eyed susan and the motto is "Manly deeds, womanly words."

**mas-cot** [măs′kŏt′] *noun*, an animal or person that represents a school, team, or other group

**mas-cu-line** [măs′kyə-lĭn] *adjective*, of or pertaining to the male sex, manly

**mash** [măsh] *verb*, to make into a pulpy mass or mush

**mask** [măsk] *noun*, 1) a covering that hides a face or its expressions *verb*, 2) to disguise or hide, to cover, to conceal

**ma-son** [mā′sən] *noun*, a person who builds with brick, stone, etc.

**mas-quer-ade** [măs′kə-rād′] *noun*, 1) a party at which people wear masks and sometimes costumes, *verb*, 2) to dress in costume, to wear a disguise, to conceal

**mass** [măs] *noun*, 1) a quantity or amount of something with no particular shape or number 2) the quantity of matter that a body contains as measured by the force of gravity on it 3) a large gathering of people 4) in the Catholic church the celebration of the Eucharist

**Mas-sa-chu-setts** [măs′ə-choo′sĭts] *noun*, one of the 50 United States, located on the East Coast, the capital is Boston. The state flower of **Massachusetts** is the mayflower, and the motto is "By the sword we seek peace, but peace only under liberty."

**mas-sa-cre** [măs′ə-kər] *noun*, 1) the killing of many defenseless people, *verb*, 2) to murder a large number of people

**mas-sage** [mə-säzh′] *noun*, 1) a rubdown, kneading of the body with the hands, *verb*, 2) to rub to stimulate circulation, to caress

**mas-sive** [măs′ĭv] *adjective*, heavy, weighty, consisting of a large amount, immense, huge

**mast** [măst] *noun*, a tall pole that holds up a ship's sail

**mas-ter** [măs′tər] *noun*, 1) an accomplished artist, a teacher , one in control 2) the title of address in front of a boy's name, *verb*, 3) to accomplish a difficult task

**mas-ter-piece** [măs′tər-pēs′] *noun*, a fine example of skill or excellence

**mat** [măt] *noun*, 1) a floor covering made of straw, rubber, vinyl, etc. 2) a tangled hair mass

**match** [măch] *noun*, 1) a slender piece of wood or cardboard tipped with a flammable mixture 2) a sports contest, 3) a person or thing equal to another, *verb*, 4) to sort similar objects, to pair up

**mate** [māt] *noun*, 1) an associate 2) one of a male and female pair of animals, birds, etc., *verb*, 3) to bring together a male and female animal to reproduce

**ma-te-ri-al** [mə-tîr′ē-əl] *adjective*, 1) pertaining to or composed of matter 2) of consequence, substantial, *noun* 3) data 4) cloth, the fabric something is made of 5) possessions, real things not spiritual things

**ma-te-ri-al-ize** [mə-tîr′ē-ə-līz′] *verb*, to take form, to emerge

**ma-ter-nal** [mə-tûr′nəl] *adjective*, motherly, relating to a mother

**ma-ter-ni-ty** [mə-tûr′nĭ-tē] *noun*, motherhood, the time during pregnancy, or for a mother to care for a newborn infant

**math-e-mat-ics** [măth′ə-măt′ĭks] *noun*, *plural*, the study of numbers, arithmetic

**ma-tin-ee** [măt′n-ā′] *noun*, an afternoon theater performance

**ma-tri-arch** [mā′trē-ärk′] *noun*, the woman who rules a family or social group, clan or tribe

**mat-ri-mo-ny** [măt′rə-mō′nē] *noun*, marriage, wedlock

**ma-trix** [mā′trĭks] *noun*, 1) an environment from which something develops or originates 2) a mold or die

**mat-ter** [măt′ər] *noun, no plural,* 1) the substance of which something is made 2) a situation or affair *verb,* 3) to be of importance, to signify

**mat-tress** [măt′rĭs] *noun*, a stuffed cushion to sleep on

**ma-ture** [mə-tyŏŏr′] *adjective*, fully grown or developed, adult

**ma-tu-ri-ty** [mə-tyŏŏr′ĭ-tē] *noun*, adulthood, full development

**maud-lin** [môd′lĭn] *adjective*, tearfully sentimental

**maul** [môl] *verb*, to handle roughly, to lacerate

**mau-so-le-um** [mô′sə-lē′əm] *noun*, a stately tomb, an above ground structure for burials

**mav-er-ick** [măv′ər-ĭk] *noun*, a rebel, a nonconformist

**max-im** [măk′sĭm] *noun*, a proverb, wise words

**max-i-mum** [măk′sə-məm] *adjective*, 1) greatest attainable, most, *noun*, 2) the largest amount possible

**May** [mā] *noun*, the fifth month of the year, having 31 days

**may** [mā] *verb*, 1) used to show that something is possible 2) to be allowed or permitted to 3) showing a hope that something will happen

**may-be** [mā′bē] *adverb*, perhaps, possibly

**may-hem** [mā′hĕm′] *noun*, commotion, disturbance

**may-on-naise** [mā′ə-nāz′] *noun*, a dressing for salad or sandwiches, usually made from eggs and oil

**may-or** [mā′ər, mâr] *noun*, the chief magistrate and leader of a city or town

**me** [mē] *pronoun*, the form of "I" used as an object, used by a speaker to refer to himself or herself

**mead-ow** [mĕd′ō] *noun*, a field of grass or flowers, grassland

**mea-ger** [mē′gər] *adjective*, small in amount, scant

**meal** [mēl] *noun*, food served and eaten, the occasion for eating

**mean** [mēn] *adjective*, 1) unkind, cruel, uncaring 2) the middle, *verb*, 3) to be the same as, to have as a definition 4) to intend to do something 5) to denote

**me-an-der** [mē-ăn′dər] *verb*, to wander around, to follow a path with twists and turns

**mean-ing** [mē′nĭng] *noun*, 1) the definition of a word 2) the significance of an action , signs or symbols

**means** [mēnz] *noun, plural,* resources that help us to do what we want to do, wealth

**meant** [mĕnt]*verb, past tense* of **mean**

**mean-while** [mēn′hwīl′] *adverb*, at the same time

**mea-sles** [mē′zəlz] *noun, plural*, a contagious disease marked by distinct red circular spots, accompanied by a fever

**meas-ure** [mĕzh'ər] *noun*, 1) a standard or test 2) dimension, size, capacity 3) step, action, proceeding, maneuver, *verb*, 4) to take measurements, to gauge, to scale, to calibrate

**meas-ure-ment** [mĕzh'ər-mənt] *noun*, the size, weight, distance, mass, etc. of something

**meat** [mēt] *noun*, the parts of an animal's body used as food

**me-chan-ic** [mǐ-kăn'ĭk] *noun*, 1) one who repairs cars or other machines, 2) *plural*, **mechanics**, the inner workings or things, the study of how machines work

**mech-an-ism** [mĕk'ə-nǐz'əm] *noun*, 1) the parts of a machine taken collectively 2)any system that works like a machine

**med-al** [mĕd'l] *noun*, a small, award, often embossed, given for achievement

**med-dle** [mĕd'l] *verb*, to interfere

**me-di-a** [mē'dē-ə] *plural, noun*, see **medium**

**me-di-an** [mē'dē-ən] *adjective*, 1) halfway, central, *noun*, 2) the middle, center, mid-point

**me-di-ate** [mē'dē-āt'] *verb*, to settle a dispute as an impartial third party

**med-i-cal** [mĕd'ĭ-kəl] *adjective*, healing, therapeutic

**me-dic-i-nal** [mǐ-dĭs'ə-nəl] *adjective*, having properties that cure disease or sickness

**med-i-cine** [mĕd'ĭ-sĭn] *noun*, 1) the study and treatment of illness 2) a remedy to treat disease and restore good health

**me-di-e-val** [mē'dē-ē'vəl] *adjective*, characteristic of the Middle Ages from about the fifth to the fifteenth centuries

**me-di-oc-ri-ty** [mē'dē-ŏk'rĭ-tē] *noun*, the average, commonplace, ordinary

**med-i-tate** [mĕd'ĭ-tāt'] *verb*, to think deeply

**med-i-ta-tion** [mĕd'ĭ-tā'shən] *noun*, deep, solemn reflection

**me-di-um** [mē'dē-əm] *adjective*, 1) sized between large and small, *noun*, 2) conditions, the environment 3) a means to communicate with the dead *plural*, **media**, 4) a network of communication such as television, radio, newspapers, etc. that reaches the public

**med-ley** [mĕd'lē] *noun*, a mixture

**meek** [mēk] *adjective*, humble, gentle, patient, quiet

**meet** [mēt] *verb*, to come face to face, to approach, to encounter

**meet-ing** [mē'tǐng] *noun*, 1) a gathering to discuss an issue or idea 2) point of contact

**meg-a-phone** [mĕg'ə-fōn'] *noun*, a cone or electric device that amplifies the sound of a voice

**mel-an-chol-y** [mĕl'ən-kŏl'ē] *adjective*, 1) filled with sorrow, very sad, *noun*, 2) a feeling of sadness characterized by depression

**mel-low** [mĕl'ō] *adjective*, 1) good-natured, relaxed, *verb*, 2) to soften with maturity

**mel-o-dy** [mĕl'ə-dē] *noun*, a harmonious tune, music

**mel-on** [měl'ən] *noun*, a large juicy fruit growing on vines

**melt** [mělt] *verb*, to change to a liquid state by applying heat

**mem-ber** [měm'bər] *noun*, 1) one of the limbs of the body, such as a leg, arm, hand, etc. 2) a part of a group, a component 3) one that belongs to a certain group

**mem-ber-ship** [měm'bər-shĭp'] *noun*, the state of belonging to a certain group

**mem-brane** [měm'brān'] *noun*, a thin piece or layer of animal or vegetable tissue that serves to cover separate cells, organs, etc.

**me-men-to** [mə-měn'tō] *noun*, a token as a reminder, a souvenir

**mem-oir** [měm'wär', -wôr'] *noun*, an autobiography

**mem-o-ra-ble** [měm'ər-ə-bəl] *adjective*, worthy of remembrance, remarkable

**mem-o-ran-dum** [měm'ə-răn'dəm] *noun*, a note made as a reminder, a written message, a memo

**me-mo-ri-al** [mə-môr'ē-əl] *noun*, a monument, a marker, a statue

**mem-o-rize** [měm'ə-rīz'] *verb*, to commit to memory, to learn by heart, to remember exactly

**mem-o-ry** [měm'ə-rē] *noun*, something a person remembers, the ability to remember

**men-ace** [měn'ĭs] *noun*, a danger

**me-nag-er-ie** [mə-năj'ə-rē] *noun*, a varied group or collection of animals, persons, or things that are strange, odd, or startling

**mend** [měnd] *verb*, 1) to repair or fix, to sew a tear, or patch a hole

2) to heal, to improve, to recover from illness 3) to set right a dispute

**me-ni-al** [mē'nē-əl] *adjective*, suitable for servants, low

**men-in-gi-tis** [měn'ĭn-jī'tĭs] *noun*, an infection of the three membranes that envelop the brain and spinal cord, that could be fatal

**men-tal** [měn'tl] *adjective*, of or existing in the mind

**men-tal-ly** [měn'tl-lē] *adverb*, in or using the mind, intellectually

**men-tion** [měn'shən] *noun*, 1) a reference, a notice, *verb*, 2) to remark, to refer to briefly

**men-tor** [měn'tôr'] *noun*, a trusted teacher, a wise counselor

**men-u** [měn'yōō] *noun*, 1) a list indicating the choice of meals at a restaurant 2) a list of options in a computer program

**mer-chan-dise** [mûr'chən-dīz'] *noun*, 1) commodities, wares, goods, *verb*, 2) to sell, to promote, to market

**mer-chant** [mûr'chənt] *noun*, a person who buys and sells goods

**mer-ci-ful** [mûr'sĭ-fəl] *adjective*, compassionate, kind-hearted

**mer-ci-less** [mûr'sĭ-lĭs] *adjective*, cruel, unkind, showing no compassion, inhumane

**mer-cu-ry** [mûr'kyŏŏrē] *noun, no plural*, a heavy, silver-white metallic chemical element, liquid at ordinary temperatures

**mer-cy** [mûr's *noun*, the act of sparing someone punishment shown to an offender or enemy

**mere** [mîr] *adjective*, not more than what is specified, only

**mere-ly** [mîr′lē] *adverb*, simply, hardly, barely

**merge** [mûrj] *verb*, to combine into one, to blend gradually

**me-rid-i-an** [mə-rĭd′ē-ən] *noun*, an imaginary great circle on the surface of the earth, passing through the poles and any given place on the earth's surface

**mer-it** [mĕr′ĭt] *noun*, 1) worth, good qualities, *verb*, 2) to deserve

**mer-maid** [mûr′mād′] *noun*, a mythical creature that lives in the water, having the head and torso of a woman and the tail of a fish

**mer-ry** [mĕr′ē] *adjective*, happy, full of laughter, joyful

**me-sa** [mā′sə] *noun*, a flat-topped hill with steep sides, common in dry areas

**mesh** [mĕsh] *noun*, 1) a net-like material of cords or wires that interlock with spaces between them, like a screen, *verb*, 2) to blend, to intertwine

**mes-mer-ize** [mĕz′mə-rīz′] *verb*, to hypnotize, to spellbind

**mess** [mĕs] *noun*, 1) many things mixed up, a jumble, *verb*, 2) to make something dirty or untidy 3) to make a muddle of

**mes-sage** [mĕs′ĭj] *noun*, 1) a letter or note 2) a communication transmitted from one person to another 3) a central theme

**mes-sen-ger** [mĕs′ən-jər] *noun*, one who does an errand, a carrier

**mes-sy** [mĕs′ē] *adjective*, untidy

**met** [mĕt] *past tense* of **meet**

**me-tab-o-lism** [mĭ-tăb′ə-lĭz′əm] *noun*, the chemical and physical changes in living cells that process energy in the body

**met-al** [mĕt′l] *noun*, 1) a chemical element such as silver or gold, or any combination of metals, such as brass, copper, or nickel

**met-al-lic** [mə-tăl′ĭk] *adjective*, resembling, pertaining to or consisting of metal

**meta-mor-phic** [mĕt′ə-môr′fĭk] *adjective*, changed in form

**met-a-mor-pho-sis** [mĕt′ə-môr′fə-sĭs] *noun*, a change from one form of development or shape into another

**met-a-phor** [mĕt′ə-fôr′] *noun*, a figure of speech in which one thing is spoken of in terms of another, *i.e., the road was a ribbon of moonlight…*

**met-a-phys-ics** [mĕt′ə-fĭz′ĭks] *noun*, speculative philosophy

**me-te-or** [mē′tē-ər′] *noun*, a fragment of solid matter that enters the earth's atmosphere and burns, leaving a bright streak in the sky

**me-te-or-ite** [mē′tē-ə-rīt′] *noun*, the metallic or stony remains of a body that has entered the earth's atmosphere

**me-te-or-ol-o-gist** [mē′tē-ə-rŏl′ə-jĭst] *noun*, a person who studies the weather

**me-ter** [mē′tər] *noun*, 1) a machine used for measuring 2) a measure of length equal to 100 centimeters or approximately 39 inches 3) the rhythm in a poem

**meth-od** [mĕth′əd] *noun*, a process or system used to do something

**me-thod-i-cal** [mə-thŏd′ĭ-kəl] *adjective*, systematic, orderly

**Me-tho-dist** [mə-thŏdĭst] *noun*, a member of the Protestant Christian denomination that developed from the teachings of John and Charles Wesley

**me-tic-u-lous** [mĭ-tĭk′yə-ləs] *adjective*, extremely careful

**met-ric sys-tem** *noun*, a system that measures length in centimeters, meters, and kilometers; capacity in liters, mass in grams and kilograms; temperature in degrees Celsius

**me-trop-o-lis** [mĭ-trŏp′ə-lĭs] *noun*, the chief city of a country, state or region, an urban center

**met-tle** [mĕt′l] *noun*, courage, spirit, fortitude, character

**Mich-i-gan** [mĭsh′ĭ-gən] *noun*, one of the 50 United States, located in the North, the capital is Lansing. The state flower of **Michigan** is the apple blossom and the motto is "If you seek a pleasant peninsula, look about you."

**mi-cro-cosm** [mī′krə-kŏz′əm] *noun*, a small world

**mi-cro-or-gan-ism** [mī′krō-ôr′gə-nĭz′əm] *noun*, an animal , bacterium, plant, or virus that can only be seen with a microscope

**mi-cro-phone** [mī′krə-fōn′] *noun*, a device that converts sounds into electrical energy signals that can then be amplified

**mi-cro-scope** [mī′krə-skōp′] *noun*, an optical instrument with a lens that makes it possible to see things too small to be seen with the naked eye

**mi-cro-scop-ic** [mī′krə-skŏp′ĭk] *adjective*, too small to be seen with a naked eye

**mid** [mĭd] *adjective*, halfway

**mid-dle** [mĭd′l] *adjective*, 1) halfway between two points, median, central, *noun*, 2) the center, the point equally distant from two sides

**mid-get** [mĭj′ĭt] *noun*, a small person who is fully mature

**mid-night** [mĭd′nīt′] *noun*, 12 o'clock at night

**midst** [mĭdst, mĭtst] *noun*, the middle, the central point

**might** [mīt] *noun*, *no plural*, 1) strength or force, *verb*, 2) *past tense* of **may**

**might-y** [mī′tē] *adjective*, strong, powerful, important, great

**mi-grant** [mī′grənt] *adjective*, one who travels from place to place in search of work

**mi-grate** [mī′grāt′] *verb*, 1) to move from one land to settle in another 2) to make a journey each year from one place to another at the same time of year

**mi-gra-tion** [mī-grā′shən] *noun*, movement to leave one area to live in another

**mild** [mīld] *adjective*, 1) gentle in feeling 2) not severe or extreme

**mile** [mīl] *noun*, a measure of length equal to 5,280 feet, 1,760 yards, or 1.6 kilometers

**mile-age** [mī'lĭj] *noun*, 1) an allowance for the cost per mile traveled 2) the total amount of miles traveled in a given time

**mile-stone** [mīl'stōn'] *noun*, a turning point, a great achievement or significant event

**mil-i-tant** [mĭl'ĭ-tənt] *adjective*, 1) warlike, combative, *noun*, 2) a revolutionary, a violent objector, a terrorist

**mil-i-tar-y** [mĭl'ĭ-tĕr'ē] *noun*, the armed forces of a country

**milk** [mĭlk] *noun*, 1) the liquid produced by a female mammal to feed her young, *verb*, 2) to force milk from a female mammal

**mill** [mĭl] *noun*, a building or group of buildings in which resources such as lumber, cotton, corn and steel, are processed

**mil-len-ni-um** [mə-lĕn'ē-əm] *noun*, a span of one thousand years

**mil-li-liter** [mĭl'ə-lē'tər] *noun*, a liquid measure equal to 1/1000 of a liter, or less than .04 fluid ounces

**mil-li-me-ter** [mĭl'ə-mē'tər] *noun*, a measure of length, 1/1000 of a meter, or about .04 inches

**mil-lion** [mĭl'yən] *noun*, ten times one hundred thousand, 1,000,000

**mil-lion-aire** [mĭl'yə-nâr'] *noun*, a person whose property and assets total $1,000,000

**mime** [mīm] *noun*, 1) a performer who only uses motion and facial expression, but no voice, to communicate, *verb*, 2) to use actions instead of speech to communicate

**mim-e-o-graph** [mĭm'ē-ə-grăf'] *noun*, a stenciling copying device fed by an ink drum

**mim-ic** [mĭm'ĭk] *verb*, to copy or repeat what someone does or says, to imitate playfully

**mim-ic-ry** [mĭm'ĭ-krē] *noun*, an imitation, an impersonation

**min-a-ret** [mĭn'ə-rĕt'] *noun*, a lofty slender tower attached to a mosque

**mince** [mĭns] *verb*, 1) to cut into very small pieces 2) to moderate or restrain words

**mind** [mīnd] *noun*, 1) thoughts, a person's reason or way of feeling, *verb*, 2) to watch over, to pay attention to, to obey

**mine** [mīn] *noun*, 1) a large hole or tunnel deep in the ground made to reach and remove metals or other natural resources from the earth, *pronoun*, 2) something that belongs to the person who is speaking, *verb*, 3) digging into land to remove metal ore or other valuable resources

**min-er-al** [mĭn'ər-əl] *noun*, any inorganic substance occurring naturally in the earth

**min-gle** [mĭng'gəl] *verb*, to join or mix together, to blend

**min-i-a-ture** [mĭn'ē-ə-chŏŏr'] *adjective*, 1) very small, done on a small scale, *noun*, 2) a very small painting, especially a portrait

**min-i-mum** [mĭn'ə-məm] *adjective*, 1) smallest, *noun*,

2) the least quantity possible or allowable in a given case

**min-is-ter** [mĭn′ĭ-stər] *noun*,

1) the head of a government department in some countries 2) a representative to a foreign country ranking under an ambassador 3) a Christian member of the clergy, *verb*, 4) to give help to someone, to care for, to serve, to attend

**min-is-try** [mĭn′ĭ-strē] *noun*, 1) a department of government headed by a minister 2) the work of the clergy 3) the act of serving

**Min-ne-so-ta** [mĭn′ĭ-sō′tə] *noun*, one of the 50 United States located in the North, the capital is St. Paul. The state flower of **Minnesota**, is the pink and white lady slipper and the motto is,"The star of the north."

**min-now** [mĭn′ō] *noun*, a small fish

**mi-nor** [mī′nər] *adjective*,

1) smaller, not very important *noun*, 2) a person younger than the legal age

**mi-nor-i-ty** [mə-nôr′ĭ-tē] *noun*, a number, part or amount forming less than half of a whole

**mint** [mĭnt] *noun*, 1) a large amount of money 2) any of the plants of the mint family, used to flavor food, gum, etc.3) a candy

**mi-nus** [mī′nəs] *preposition*, less

**min-ute** [mĭn′ĭt] *adjective*, 1) very small, *noun*, 2) a period of time equal to sixty seconds

**mi-nu-ti-a** [mĭ-nōō′shē-ə] *noun*, *plural*, **minutiae**, very small, petty details, trifling matters

**mir-a-cle** [mĭr′ə-kəl] *noun*, an occurrence that is unusual and goes beyond the laws of nature

**mi-rac-u-lous** [mĭ-răk′yə-ləs] *adjective*, supernatural, awesome, incredible

**mi-rage** [mĭ-räzh′] *noun*, an unreal reflection, an optical illusion

**mire** [mīr] *noun*, 1) a bog, a swamp, *verb*, 2) to immerse in swampy ground, to entangle

**mir-ror** [mĭr′ər] *noun*, 1) a looking glass in which one can see reflections 2) something that reflects

**mirth** [mûrth] *noun*, laughter, glee

**mis-be-have** [mĭs′bĭ-hāv′] *verb*, to behave badly, to be disruptive

**mis-cel-la-ne-ous** [mĭs′ə-lā′nē-əs] *adjective*, consisting of several different kinds, mixed, various

**mis-chief** [mĭs′chĭf] *noun*, an annoying action on the part of a person, havoc, harm or damage

**mis-chie-vous** [mĭs′chə-vəs] *adjective*, causing petty injury or annoyance to others

**mis-con-cep-tion** [mĭs′kən-sĕp′shən] *noun*, a misunderstanding, a mistake

**mis-con-duct** [mĭs-kŏn′dŭkt] *noun*, wrongdoing, improper behavior

**mis-con-strue** [mĭs′kən-strōō′] *verb*, to misunderstand

**mis-cre-ant** [mĭs′krē-ənt] *noun*, an evil person, a lawbreaker

**mis-de-mean-or** [mĭs′dĭ-mē′nər] *noun*, a crime less than a felony, any minor misdeed

**mi-ser** [mī′zər] *noun*, a tightwad, one who hoards money

**mis-er-a-ble** [mĭz′ər-ə-bəl]
*adjective*, unhappy, causing
misery

**mis-er-y** [mĭz′ə-rē] *noun*, great
unhappiness, or distress

**mis-for-tune** [mĭs-fôr′chən] *noun*,
bad luck, something bad that
happens, an unlucky event

**mis-giv-ing** [mĭs-gĭv′ĭng] *noun*, a
feeling of worry, doubt about a
future event, apprehension

**mis-hap** [mĭs′hăp′] *noun*, an
unfortunate accident

**mis-in-ter-pret** [mĭs′ĭn-tûr′prĭt]
*verb*, to confuse, to mistake

**mis-judge** [mĭs-jŭj′] *verb*, to
mistake, to underestimate

**mis-lead** [mĭs-lēd′] *verb*, to lead
astray, to deceive, to lie

**mis-lead-ing** [mĭs-lē′dĭng]
*adjective*, deceptive, vague,
unclear, not accurate

**mis-no-mer** [mĭs-nō′mər] *noun*,
the wrong name, an incorrect
identification

**mis-place** [mĭs-plās′] *verb*, to lose
temporarily, to mislay

**Miss** [mĭs] *noun*, the title before
the name of an unmarried
woman

**miss** [mĭs] *noun*, 1) a failure, an
error, a slip, *verb*, 2) to fail to
make the most of an opportunity
or moment 3) to notice
someone's absence, to feel sad
someone is gone 4) to avoid, to
fail to hit, to escape 5) to omit

**mis-sile** [mĭs′əl] *noun*, a weapon
capable of being hurled

**mis-sion** [mĭsh′ən] *noun*, a special
service, task or duty

**mis-sion-ar-y** [mĭsh′ə-nĕr′ē] *noun*,
one whose work is to teach
others about his religion

**Mis-sis-sip-pi** [mĭs′ĭ-sĭp′ē] *noun*,
one of the 50 United States,
located in the South, the capital
is Jackson. The state flower of
**Mississippi** is the magnolia
blossom, and the motto is "By
valor and arms."

**mis-sive** [mĭs′ĭv] *noun*, a letter

**Mis-sou-ri** [mĭ-zŏŏr′ē] *noun*, one
of the 50 Unieted States, located
in the Midwest, the capital is
Jefferson City. The state flower
of **Missouri** is the hawthorn, and
the motto is:"Let the welfare of
the people be the supreme law."

**mis-spell** [mĭs-spĕl′] *verb*, to spell
incorrectly

**mist** [mĭst] *noun*, a thin cloud of
fine droplets of water vapor or
fog near the ground

**mis-take** [mĭ-stāk′] *noun*, an error,
the wrong answer or action

**Mis-ter** [mĭs′tər] *noun*, a title for a
man, abbreviated, 'Mr.'

**mis-tle-toe** [mĭs′əl-tō′] *noun*, a
plant that lives off another, with
evergreen leaves and white
berries used at Christmas for
decoration

**mis-tress** [mĭs′trĭs] *noun*, a woman
who has control over others

**mis-trust** [mĭs-trŭst′] *noun*,
1) suspicion, uncertainty, doubt,
lack of confidence, *verb*, 2) to
doubt, to question, to challenge

**mist-y** [mĭs′tē] *adjective*, hazy,
damp, and foggy, consisting of a
mass of fine droplets of water
vapor in the atmosphere

**mis-un-der-stand**
[mĭs´-ŭn-dər-stănd´] *verb*, to misconstrue, to mistake

**mite** [mīt] *noun*, 1) a small amount 2) a small, usually parasitic arachnid, related to the tick

**mi-ter** [mī´tər] *verb*, to bevel the ends for the purpose of matching together, as a picture frame

**mitt** [mĭt] *noun*, a baseball glove with padding to protect the hand

**mit-ten** [mĭt´n] *noun*, a glove with a section for covering the thumb and a larger section to cover all four fingers

**mix** [mĭks] *verb*, to combine different things to make one

**mix-ture** [mĭks´chər] *noun*, a combination of different substances

**moan** [mōn] *verb*, to make a sound of pain or suffering, to complain

**mob** [mŏb] *noun*, a crowd, a horde

**mo-bile** [mō´bəl, *adjective* 1) moveable, portable, [mō´-bīl´] *noun*, 2) objects attached by a wire that move airily

**mo-bi-lize** [mō´bə-līz´] *verb*, to put into action, to move

**moc-ca-sin** [mŏk´ə-sĭn] *noun*, a heelless shoe of deerskin or other soft leather

**mock** [mŏk] *adjective*, 1) not real, pretended, 2) *verb*, to make fun of, to treat with ridicule

**mode** [mōd] *noun*, 1) manner 2) fashion, style

**mod-el** [mŏd´l] *noun*, 1) a person who sets a good example 2) a version of something that can be studied, a copy, 3) someone

who wears clothes for advertisement, *verb*, 3) to make a copy of something 4) to wear clothes as part of an exhibit

**mod-er-a-tion** [mŏd´ər-ā´shən] *noun*, restraint, a happy medium

**mod-ern** [mŏd´ərn] *adjective*, representative of the current trends and fashions

**mod-est** [mŏd´ĭst] *adjective*, 1) humble, decent 2) simple

**mod-es-ty** [mŏd´ĭ-stē] *noun*, *no plural*, humility, decency

**mod-i-cum** [mŏd´ĭ-kəm] *noun*, a moderate or small amount

**mod-i-fi-ca-tion** [mŏd´ə-fĭ-kā´shən] *noun*, a slight change in form, an alteration

**mod-i-fy** [mŏd´ə-fī´] *verb*, to change, to adjust, to alter

**mod-u-late** [mŏj´ə-lāt´] *verb*, to adjust the sound

**mo-gul** [mō´gəl] *noun*, a powerful person, especially in business

**moist** [moist] *adjective*, a little wet, damp, humid, soggy

**mois-ture** [mois´chər] *noun*, *no plural*, small drops of water, wetness caused by water

**mo-lar** [mō´lər] *noun*, one of several back teeth used for chewing

**mo-las-ses** [mə-lăs´ĭz] *noun*, the thick brown syrup drained from sugar in the refining process

**mold** [mōld] *noun*, 1) a cast for shapes into which a substance is poured 2) a furry substance that grows on clothing or food if left damp and away from the sun, it is a kind of small fungus, *verb*, 3)

to shape something into a form
or a mold

**mold-ing** [mōl′dĭng] *noun*, a plane
or curved narrow surface, used
for ornamentation

**mole** [mōl] *noun*, 1) a small
insectivore that makes and lives
in holes underground 2) a small
round brown mark on the skin

**mol-e-cule** [mŏl′ĭ-kyōōl′] *noun*,
1) a unit of matter consisting of
two or more atoms combined
2) a particle

**mo-lest** [mə-lĕst′] *verb*, 1) to touch
without permission 2) to annoy

**molt** [mōlt] *verb*, to shed the outer
skin, feathers or exoskeleton

**mol-ten** [mōl′tən] *adjective*, made
liquid by great heat, melted

**mo-ment** [mō′mənt] *noun*, a very
brief period of time, an instant

**mo-men-tar-y** [mō′mən-tĕr′ē]
*adjective*, fleeting, passing

**mo-men-tous** [mō-mĕn′təs]
*adjective*, very important

**mo-men-tum** [mō-mĕn′təm] *noun*,
the force or speed of movement

**mon-arch** [mŏn′ərk, -ärk′] *noun*, a
king or queen 2) an orange and
black butterfly

**mon-ar-chy** [mŏn′ər-kē] *noun*, a
government headed by one
person, a king or a queen

**mon-as-ter-y** [mŏn′ə-stĕr′ē] *noun*,
a residence in which monks live

**Mon-day** [mŭn′dē, -dā′] *noun*, the
second day of the week

**mon-e-tar-y** [mŏn′ĭ-tĕr′ē]
*adjective*, of or pertaining to
money or currency, pecuniary

**mon-ey** [mŭn′ē] *noun*, currency
and coins issued by a
government to use in exchange
for goods or services

**mon-i-tor** [mŏn′ĭ-tər] *noun*, 1) a
pupil or student given authority
2) a video screen attached to a
computer, *verb*, 3) to keep watch
over, to supervise, to check

**monk** [mŭngk] *noun*, a religious
man who lives with other men
who devote their lives to prayer
and religion, a member of a
religious order

**mon-key** [mŭng′kē] *noun*, a
primate that usually has a long
tail and lives in trees

**mon-o-gram** [mŏn′ə-grăm′] *noun*,
initials consisting of two or more
letters interwoven, usually
written, embroidered, or
engraved

**mon-o-logue** [mŏn′ə-lôg′] *noun*, a
long speech, a soliloquy

**mo-nop-o-lize** [mə-nŏp′ə-līz′]
*verb*, to have exclusive
possession of something

**mo-nop-o-ly** [mə-nŏp′ə-lē] *noun*,
exclusive control of the supply
of any commodity

**mon-o-the-ism** [mŏn′ə-thē-ĭz′əm]
*noun*, belief in one God

**mon-o-tone** [mŏn′ə-tōn′] *noun*, a
voice that never changes in pitch

**mo-not-o-nous** [mə-nŏt′n-əs]
*adjective*, 1) unvarying in pitch
2) repetitiously dull, being the
same all the time

**mon-soon** [mŏn-sōōn′] *noun*,
heavy rains and strong winds in
southern Asia

**mon-ster** [mŏn′stər] *noun*, 1) an animal or person with a strange or unusual shape 2) an imaginary and usually frightening creature

**Mon-tana** [mŏn-tăn′ə] *noun*, one of the 50 United States located in the Northwest, the capital is Helena. The state flower of **Montana** is the bitteroot, and the motto is "Gold and silver."

**month** [mŭnth] *noun*, a period of 30 days, four weeks, or 1/12 of the year

**mon-u-ment** [mŏn′yə-mənt] *noun*, a statue or building erected as a tribute to someone who has died

**mon-u-men-tal** [mŏn′yə-mĕn′tl] *adjective*, massive, enormous, exceptionally great

**mood** [mōōd] *noun*, the way a person feels, state of mind

**moon** [mōōn] *noun*, the large body in the sky that shines at night, a satellite of a planet

**moose** [mōōs] *noun*, a large North American and Eurasian deer

**moot** [mōōt] *adjective*, questionable, debatable

**mop** [mŏp] *noun*, 1) a tool with a long handle and a sponge or fabric on the bottom used for cleaning floors, *verb*, 2) to clean the floor, usually with soap and water or to remove spilled liquids

**mor-al** [môr′əl] *adjective*, ethical, honest, concerned with right conduct, virtuous, upright

**mo-rale** [mə-răl′] *noun*, spirit, confidence, resolve,

**mo-ral-i-ty** [mə-răl′ĭ-tē] *noun*, virtue, righteousness, ethics

**mor-al-ly** [môr′ə-lē] *adverb*, in accordance with ethical duty, righteously, respectfully

**mor-a-to-ri-um** [môr′ə-tôr′ē-əm] *noun*, 1) a suspension, an interval 2) a legal delay of payment

**mor-bid** [môr′bĭd] *adjective*, depressing, having to do with disease, gruesome

**more** [môr] *adjective*, 1) larger in amount or number, *adverb*, 2) again, in addition

**mo-res** [môr′āz′] *noun*, *plural*, the customs of a society, the code of acceptable conduct

**morgue** [môrg] *noun*, a place where dead bodies go to be identified before burial

**Mor-mon** [môr mŭn] *noun*, a member of the Church of Jesus Christ of Latter-day Saints founded in the U.S. in 1830 by Joseph Smith

**morn-ing** [môr′nĭng] *noun*, the time from when the sun rises until noon or the time from midnight to noon

**mo-rose** [mə-rōs′] *adjective*, sad, dejected, gloomy or sullen

**mor-phine** [môr′fēn′] *noun*, a narcotic derived from opium

**morse code** [môrs kōd] *noun*, *no plural*, a way of sending messages using flashing lights or a pattern of sounds

**mor-sel** [môr′səl] *noun*, a little piece of food, a crumb

**mor-tal** [môr′tl] *adjective*, 1) destructive to life, fatal 2) human and therefore able to die

**mor-tal-i-ty** [môr-tăl/ĭ-tē] *noun*, the condition of being mortal

**mor-tar** [môr/tər] *noun*, 1) a mixture made of cement, lime, sand, and water, used to hold bricks or stone together 2) a short cannon used to fire shells at a high angle 3) a bowl in which substances are crushed to a powder with a pestle

**mort-gage** [môr/gĭj] *noun*, a legal agreement regarding property between a borrower and a lender

**mor-ti-cian** [môr-tĭsh/ən] *noun*, an undertaker, a funeral director

**mor-ti-fy** [môr/tə-fī/] *verb*, to shame, to belittle, to humiliate

**mor-tu-ar-y** [môr/chōō-ĕr/ē] *noun*, a place where dead bodies are kept until burial or cremation

**mo-sa-ic** [mō-zā/ĭk] *noun*, a surface decoration made by inlaying small pieces of variously colored material such as tile, marble, or glass

**Mos-lem** [mŏz/ləm] *noun*, *adjective*, see Muslim

**mosque** [mŏsk] *noun*, a holy building where Muslims worship

**mos-qui-to** [mə-skē/tō] *noun*, an insect capable of puncturing the skin of humans and other animals and sucking blood

**moss** [môs, mŏs] *noun*, a bright green plant that grows flat on wet ground and stones

**most** [mōst] *adjective*, 1) greatest in amount or number, *adverb*, 2) very, *noun*, 3) the largest amount or number

**mote** [mōt] *noun*, a small speck

**moth** [môth] *noun*, an insect with four wings, like a butterfly that flies at night

**moth-er** [mŭth/ər] *noun*, the female parent

**moth-er-in-law** [mŭth/ər-ĭn-lô/] *noun*, the mother of one's spouse

**mo-tion** [mō/shən] *noun*, the action or process of moving

**mo-tion-less** [mō/shən-lĭs] *adjective*, not moving

**mo-ti-vate** [mō/tə-vāt/] *verb*, to provide the inner drive that causes one to act

**mo-ti-va-tion** [mō/tə-vā/shən] *noun*, the feeling that moves one to act

**mo-tive** [mō/tĭv] *noun*, the reason for doing something, incentive

**mo-tor** [mō/tər] *noun*, a compact engine that makes things move or work

**mo-tor-boat** [mō/tər-bōt/] *noun*, a small boat with an engine

**mo-tor-cy-cle** [mō/tər-sī/kəl] *noun*, a two-wheeled vehicle without a top, moved by a motor

**mot-tled** [mŏt/ld] *adjective*, spotted with different colors

**mot-to** [mŏt/ō] *noun*, a saying or catch-phrase that expresses a belief, a guiding principle

**mound** [mound] *noun*, 1) a heap of earth or a small hill, a knoll 2)any small pile

**mount** [mount] *noun*, 1) a mountain named after someone, *verb*, 2) to rise 3) to get on 4)to ascend 5)to prepare by putting in place

**moun-tain** [moun′tən] *noun*, a large hill or raised part of land with steep sides that rises from the earth's surface

**mourn** [môrn] *verb*, to feel sadness at a loss or death of someone

**mourn-ing** [môr′nĭng] *noun*, *no plural*, a period of grief to honor someone who died

**mouse** [mous] *noun*, *plural*, **mice**, 1) a small rodent, similar to a rat 2) a hand-held device that guides the cursor or pointer on a computer

**mouth** [mouth] *noun*, 1) the opening through which all animals consume food 2) an entry

**move** [mo͞ov] *verb*, 1) to change position or cause something to change position 2) to go to live in a new place 3) to affect, to arouse, or influence 3) to budge, to change opionion, to go on

**move-ment** [mo͞ov′mənt] *noun*, 1) an inclination, a tendency toward change 2) action, transit, change

**mov-ie** [mo͞o′vē] *noun*, a film, a motion picture

**mov-ing** [mo͞o′vĭng] *adjective*, touching, emotional

**mow** [mō] *verb*, to cut grass

**Mr.** *noun*, a title put before a man's name

**Mrs.** *noun*, a title put before a married woman's name

**Ms**. *noun*, a title put before a woman's name

**much** [mŭch] *adjective*, 1) of a large amount, great. *adverb*, 2) often, to a great degree *noun*, 3) a large amount or a lot of

**mucus** [myo͞o′kəs] *noun*, spit, of or relating to mucus, a shiny substance coating the inside of the body cavities

**mud** [mŭd] *noun*, wet soft earth

**mud-dy** [mŭd′ē] *adjective*, 1) murky, dirty 2) not clear or pure

**muf-fin** [mŭf′ĭn] *noun*, a quick bread made from batter and baked in a cup-shaped pan

**muf-fle** [mŭf′əl] *verb*, to cover or suppress a sound, to tone down

**muf-fler** [mŭf′lər] *noun*, 1) any of various devices to deaden the noise of escaping gases or vapors 2) a scarf worn around the neck

**mug** [mŭg] *noun*, 1) a cup with a handle, *verb*, 2) to assault someone, usually to rob them

**mug-gy** [mŭg′ē] *adjective*, warm and very damp, humid

**mulch** [mŭlch] *noun*, a protective layer of decomposing organic matter

**mule** [myo͞ol] *noun*, an animal whose parents were a female horse and a male donkey

**mul-ti-form** [mŭl′tə-fôrm′] *adjective*, having many shapes or forms

**mul-ti-ple** [mŭl′tə-pəl] *adjective*, 1) many 2) having many parts

**mul-ti-pli-ca-tion** [mŭl′tə-plĭ-kā′shən] *noun*, *no plural*, the process of finding the number or quantity by repeated addition of a specified number

**mul-ti-ply** [mŭl′tə-plī′] *verb*, to increase by a number of times

**mul-ti-tude** [mŭl′tĭ-to͞od′] *noun*, a crowd, a large gathering

**mum-my** [mŭm′ē] *noun*, a dead body preserved with chemicals and wrapped in cloth

**mumps** [mŭmps] *noun, plural*, an illness that causes fever and swelling in the neck and throat

**mun-dane** [mŭn-dān′] *adjective*, commonplace, worldly as opposed to spiritual

**mu-nic-i-pal** [myōō-nĭs′ə-pəl] *adjective*, having a local self-government, as in a city or town

**mu-ral** [myŏŏr′əl] *noun*, a picture painted directly on a wall

**mur-der** [mûr′dər] *noun*, 1) the act of killing someone, either after first planning to do so or during another crime, such as a robbery, *verb*, 2) to kill a person intentionally

**mur-der-er** [mûr′dər-ər] *noun*, a person who intends to kill someone and does so

**mur-mur** [mûr′mər] *verb*, to speak very softly, to whisper

**mus-cle** [mŭs′əl] *noun*, an organ whose special function is to produce movement

**muse** [myōōz] *noun*, 1) one's inner voice as a source of creativity, **Muse**, 2) one of the nine Greek goddesses, responsible for art, music, and literature, *verb*, 3) to ponder, to meditate, to think, to reflect

**mu-se-um** [myōō-zē′əm] *noun*, a building that exhibits a collection of things of interest

**mush-room** [mŭsh′rōōm′] *noun*, a plant that is not green and is a fungus, it usually has a stem with a cap on it

**mu-sic** [myōō′zĭk] *noun*, the art or science of harmonic sounds

**mu-si-cian** [myōō-zĭsh′ən] *noun*, one who plays a musical instrument and performs

**mus-ket** [mŭs′kĭt] *noun*, a gun with a long barrel, used by soldiers before rifles were invented

**musk-rat** [mŭs′krăt′] *noun*, a rodent that lives in or near water

**Mus-lim** [mŭz′ləm] *noun*, a follower of the religion that believes in Allah as the one god and the teachings of Muhammed as written in the Koran

**must** [mŭst] *verb*, 1) used with another verb to show what is necessary or what has to be done 2) showing what is sure or likely

**mus-tache** [mŭs′tăsh′] *noun*, the hair covering an upper lip

**mus-tang** [mŭs′tăng′] *noun*, a wild horse of the American plains

**mus-tard** [mŭs′tərd] *noun*, 1) a plant with yellow flowers and a seed in pods 2) powder or sauce made of ground mustard seed

**mu-ta-ble** [myōō′tə-bəl] *adjective*, 1) changing in form 2) fickle

**mute** [myōōt] *adjective*, voiceless, speechless, unable to speak

**mu-ti-late** [myōōt′l-āt′] *verb*, to cut off or remove an essential part

**mu-ti-nous** [myōōt′n-əs] *adjective*, unruly, rebellious, insurgent

**mu-ti-ny** [myōōt′n-ē] *noun*, a revolt, a rebellion, an uprising

**mu-tual** [myōō′chōō-əl] *adjective*, having a common interest

**muz-zle** [mŭz′əl] *noun*, 1) a fastening on the mouth of an animal to prevent it from biting or eating 2) the open end of a gun from which the bullet comes out when the gun is fired, *verb*, 3) to gag, to silence, to hush, to restrain speech and expression

**my** [mī] *adjective*, belonging to the person speaking

**my-op-ic** [mī-ŏp′ĭk] *adjective*, 1) nearsighted 2) self-centered, showing lack of imagination or foresight, or intellectual insight

**myr-i-ad** [mĭr′ē-əd] *noun*, a very large number

**my-self** [mī-sĕlf′] *pronoun*, the same person as the one speaking

**mys-ter-y** [mĭs′tə-rē] *noun*, something not explained or beyond human comprehension

**mys-ti-cal** [mĭs′tĭ-kəl] *adjective*, beyond understanding, spiritual

**mys-ti-fy** [mĭs′tə-fī′] *verb*, to confuse, to puzzle, to bewilder

**myth** [mĭth] *noun*, a legendary story used to explain nature or religion and often featuring heroes or supernatural beings

**my-thol-o-gy** [mĭ-thŏl′ə-jē] *noun*, the study of stories and legends

# N

**nag** [năg] *verb*, to pester, to annoy, to bother, to find faults

**nail** [nāl] *noun*, 1) a piece of pointed metal to be put into wood with a hammer 2) the horny tip on the ends of fingers and toes, *verb*, 3) to fasten with a hammer and nail

**na-ive** [nä-ēv′] *adjective*, unsophisticated, innocent

**na-ked** [nā′kĭd] *adjective*, without clothes, uncovered, nude

**name** [nām] *noun*, 1) a word given to someone or something for identification, *verb*, 2) to decide what someone or something will be called, to specify

**name-ly** [nām′lē] *adverb*, that is

**name-sake** [nām′sāk′] *noun*, one having the same name as another one, named after another

**nap** [năp] *noun*, 1) a short rest 2) a textured surface on fabric

**nap-kin** [năp′kĭn] *noun*, a piece of cloth or paper used at a meal to keep one's clothes, hands, and mouth clean while eating

**nar-cot-ic** [när-kŏt′ĭk] *noun*, a drug that relieves pain, blunts the senses and produces sleep

**nar-rate** [năr′āt′] *verb*, to make known, to tell a story, to recount

**nar-ra-tive** [năr′ə-tĭv] *noun*, a story, a history, a recital

**nar-ra-tor** [năr′āt′ ər] *noun*, a person who relates a story

**nar-row** [năr′ō] *adjective*, limited in width, breadth, or scope

**na-sal** [nā′zəl] *adjective*, associated with the nose

**nas-cent** [năs′ənt] *adjective*, coming into existence, the beginning

**na-tion** [nā′shən] *noun*, a group of people living in a particular territory under the same government, a federation

**na-tion-al** [năsh′ə-nəl] *adjective*, of or pertaining to a country or territory

**na-tion-al-i-ty** [năsh′ə-năl′ĭ-tē] *noun*, the identification of a person based on the country where he or she was born or holds citizenship

**na-tive** [nā′tĭv] *adjective*, 1) belonging to the place where a person is born, indigenous, *noun*, 2) a person born and raised in a certain place

**nat-u-ral** [năch′ər-əl] *adjective*, 1) produced by nature, not man-made 2) inborn, an innate ability

**nat-u-ral-ly** [năch′ər-ə-lē] *adverb*, as one would expect

**na-ture** [nā′chər] *noun*, *no plural*, 1) that which is not man-made, the physical world 2) traits characteristic of someone, disposition, personality

**nau-se-a** [nô′zē-ə] *noun*, 1) a stomach sickness accompanied by a desire to vomit 2) disgust

**nau-se-ate** [nô′zē-āt′] *verb*, to cause to become sick, to fill with disgust, causing a sick feeling

**nau-ti-cal** [nô′tĭ-kəl] *adjective*, having to do with the sea

**na-val** [nā′vəl] *adjective*, seafaring, nautical, relating to the navy

**na-vel** [nā′vəl] *noun*, the belly button, where the umbilical cord was attached before birth

**nav-i-gate** [năv′ĭ-gāt′] *verb*, to control in which direction a vehicle will go on a route

**nav-i-ga-tion** [năv′ĭ-gā′shən] *noun*, *no plural*, the ability to travel through water or plan and follow a specific route

**nav-i-ga-tor** [năv′ĭ-gā′tər] *noun*, one who directs and controls the course of a vehicle

**na-vy** [nā′vē] *noun*, the officers and personnel of warships

**near** [nîr] *adverb*, 1) a short distance away, *preposition*, 2) close to

**near-by** [nîr′bī′] *adverb*, close at hand, not far away

**near-ly** [nîr′lē] *adverb*, almost

**near-sight-ed** [nîr′sī′tĭd] *adjective*, able to see only things close by

**neat** [nēt] *adjective*, clean and orderly, well arranged

**Ne-bras-ka** [nə-brăs′kə] *noun*, one of the 50 United States, centrally located west of the Missouri River, the capital is Lincoln. The state flower of **Nebraska** is the goldenrod, and the motto is "Equality before the law."

**nec-es-sar-y** [nĕs′ĭ-sĕr′ē] *adjective*, needing to be done, essential

**ne-ces-si-tate** [nə-sĕs′ĭ-tāt′] *verb*, to demand, to require

**ne-ces-si-ty** [nə-sĕs′ĭ-tē] *noun*, 1) something indispensable or necessary 2) an urgent matter

**neck** [nĕk] *noun*, 1) the part of the body connecting the head and the torso 2) a narrow connecting part, as of a bottle

**neck-lace** [nĕk′lĭs] *noun*, jewelry worn around the neck

**nec-tar** [nĕk′tər] *noun*, a sweet liquid made by flowers

**need** [nēd] *noun*, 1) a lack, *verb*, 2) to lack something that is necessary or essential 3) must

**nee-dle** [nēd′l] *noun*, an instrument for sewing, made of steel, sharp at one end, with an eyehole for thread at the other end

**need-y** [nē′dē] *adjective*, poor, penniless, impoverished

**neg-a-tive** [nĕg′ə-tĭv] *adjective*, 1) expressing denial, refusal or resistance, not positive, *noun*, 2) an image on developed film

**ne-glect** [nĭ-glĕkt′] *noun*, *no plural*, 1) disregard, carelessness, lack of care or attention, *verb*, 2) to not look after something, letting it deteriorate, to ignore

**neg-li-gence** [nĕg′lĭ-jəns] *noun*, failure to give the care the occasion demands

**neg-li-gi-ble** [nĕg′lĭ-jə-bəl] *adjective*, very small, insignificant

**ne-go-ti-a-ble** [nĭ-gō′shə-bəl] *adjective*, 1) transferable or able to be assigned to another person 2) able to be compromised about, open to discussion

**ne-go-ti-ate** [nĭ-gō′shē-āt′] *verb*, to settle, to work out, to deal or bargain with others, to compromise

**Ne-gro** [nē′grō] *noun*, a member of the human species having black or brown skin color

**neigh-bor** [nā′bər] *noun*, a person who lives near another

**neigh-bor-hood** [nā′bər-hood′] *noun*, a small part of a community shared by a group of people who live near each other

**nei-ther** [nē′thər] *adjective*, *pronoun*, 1) not the one nor the other, *conjunction*, 2) not either

**ne-on** [nē′ŏn′] *noun*, an inert gaseous element often used in display lights

**neph-ew** [nĕf′yoo] *noun*, the son of a brother or a sister

**nep-o-tism** [nĕp′ə-tĭz′əm] *noun*, favoritism to a relative in a business situation

**nerve** [nûrv] *noun*, a thread in the body that carries feelings and messages to and from the brain

**nerv-ous** [nûr′vəs] *adjective*, very worried and a little scared

**nest** [nĕst] *noun*, a temporary home built by an animal or insect

**nes-tle** [nĕs′əl] *verb*, to be very close to someone else in a comfortable way

**net** [nĕt] *noun* 1) a fabric made of tying threads together in a uniform design to form a mesh 2) remaining income after deducting taxes and expenses

**net-tle** [nĕt′l] *noun*, 1) a weed with small thorns, *verb*, 2) to annoy, to bother, to irritate, to vex

**neu-rot-ic** [noo-rŏt′ĭk] *adjective*, suffering from a mental disorder characterized by anxiety and worry and phobias

**neu-ter** [noo′tər] *verb*, to make sterile, to spay or castrate

**neu-tral** [noo′trəl] *adjective*, 1) neither positive nor negative 2) not on either side during a war 3) in the middle 4) a position in which gears are not engaged

**neu-tron** [noo′trŏn′] *noun*, an uncharged particle in an atomic nucleus

**Ne-va-da** [nə-văd′ə] *noun*, one of the 50 United States, located in the West, the capital is Carson City. The state flower of **Nevada** is the sagebrush, and the motto is "All for our country."

**nev-er** [nĕv′ər] *adverb*, not at any time, absolutely not

**nev-er-the-less** [nĕv′ər-thə-lĕs′] *adverb*, notwithstanding, in spite of that, yet, however

**new** [nōō] *adjective*, 1) not having been seen or used before 2) additional

**New Hampshire** [nōō hămp′shər] *noun*, one of the 50 United States located in New England, the capital is Concord. The state flower of **New Hampshire** is the purple lilac, the motto is "Live free or die."

**New Jersey** [nōō, jûr′zē] *noun*, one of the 50 United States located in the East, the capital is Trenton. The state flower of **New Jersey** is the purple violet and the motto is "Liberty and prosperity."

**New Mexico** [nōō mĕk′sĭ-kō′] *noun*, one of the 50 United States, located in the Southwest, the capital is Santa Fe. The state flower of **New Mexico** is the yucca and the motto is "It grows as it goes."

**news** [nōōz] *noun, plural*, a report of current events, things that happened recently

**news-pa-per** [nōōz/pā′pər] *noun*, a publication that appears daily or weekly, containing recent information

**New York** [nōō yôrk] *noun*, one of the 50 United States located in the Northeast, the capital is Albany. The state flower of **New York** is the rose and the motto is "Excelsior", which expresses the idea of still higher, ever upward.

**next** [nĕkst] *adverb*, 1) in the nearest position, without anything between 2) immediately following

**nib-ble** [nĭb′əl] *verb*, to eat small bites of something

**nice** [nīs] *adjective*, 1) kind, good 2) pleasant, socially agreeable

**niche** [nĭch] *noun*, 1) a small, suitable place 2) the position of a particular population in an ecological community

**nick-el** [nĭk′əl] *noun*, 1) five cents, equal to five pennies 2) a hard, silvery metallic element of the iron group

**nick-name** [nĭk′nām′] *noun*, a name given to someone which is not his real name

**nic-o-tine** [nĭk′ə-tēn′] *noun*, a toxic alkaloid, the addictive property of tobacco

**niece** [nēs] *noun*, the daughter of one's brother or sister

**nig-gard-ly** [nĭg′ərd-lē] *adjective*, meanly stingy, meager

**night** [nīt] *noun*, the time of day after the sun goes down

**night-mare** [nīt′mâr′] *noun*, a terrifying dream or event

**nine** [nīn] *adjective, noun*, the number 9, eight plus one

**nine-teen** [nīn-tēn′] *noun*, nine plus ten, written 19

**nine-teenth** [nīn-tēnth′]*adjective*, the number 19 in order, 19th

**nine-ti-eth** [nīn′tē-ĭth] *adjective*, the number ninety in order, 90th

**nine-ty** [nīn′tē] *noun*, written 90, 9 X 10

**ninth** [nīnth] *noun, adjective*, number 9 in order, 9th

**nip-ple** [nĭp′əl] *noun*, 1) the tip of the breast where the milk ducts discharge 2) the rubber cap on a baby bottle

**nir-va-na** [nîr-vä′nə] *noun*, in Buddhist teachings, the ideal state, freedom from pain and worry, perfect bliss

**ni-tro-gen** [nī′trə-jən] *noun*, a gas necessary for life that is colorless, tasteless and odorless

**no** [nō] *adjective*, 1) not any, *adverb*, 2) a word we use to answer a question, or indicate disagreement

**no-bil-i-ty** [nō-bĭl′ĭ-tē] *adjective*, a member of the royal circle

**no-ble** [nō′bəl] *adjective*, 1) aristocratic, born to wealth 2) unselfish, of good character

**no-bod-y** [nō′bŏd′ē] *pronoun*, no one, a person of no importance

**noc-tur-nal** [nŏk-tûr′nəl] *adjective*, active or functioning at night

**nod** [nŏd] *noun*, 1) an inclination of the head, *verb*, 2) to tip the head slightly to acknowledge something

**noise** [noiz] *noun*, 1) a loud harsh sound, 2) sound of any kind

**no-mad** [nō′măd′] *noun*, a person who travels about with a tribe and has no address or home

**nom-i-nate** [nŏm′ə-nāt′] *verb*, to name for an office or place

**nom-i-na-tion** [nŏm′ə-nā′shən] *noun*, to submit a name for an award or appointment

**nom-i-nee** [nŏm′ə-nē′] *noun*, a person selected or appointed to run for a position

**non-cha-lant** [nŏn′shə-länt′] *adjective*, showing a jaunty coolness, aloof, unconcerned

**none** [nŭn] *adjective*, not any, nothing, no one, not one

**non-ex-ist-ent** [nŏn′ĭg-zĭs′tənt] *adjective*, not real

**non-fic-tion** [nŏn-fĭk′shən] *noun*, a true story

**non-sense** [nŏn′sĕns′] *noun*, folly, silliness, absurdity, meaningless

**noon** [nōōn] *noun*, midday, twelve o'clock, daytime

**nor** [nôr; nər when unstressed] *conjunction*, a word used between two choices after neither

**nor-mal** [nôr′məl] *adjective*, not unusual, common, every day

**nor-mal-ly** [nôr′mə-lē] *adverb*, generally, ordinarily, frequently

**north** [nôrth] *adjective*, 1) facing or coming from the north, *adverb*, 2) to or toward the north *noun*, 3) the direction to the left of one facing east, the compass point opposite to south, **North**, 4) regions or countries north of a point that is mentioned or understood

**North America** [nôrth-ə-mĕr′ĭ-kə] *noun,* one of the seven continents containing 7.9% of the world's population

**North Carolina** [nôrth kăr′ə-lĭ′nə] *noun,* one of the 50 United States located in the Southeast, the capital is Raleigh. The state flower of **North Carolina** is the dogwood, the state motto is "To be rather than to seem."

**North Dakota** [nôrth də-kō′tə] *noun,* a state located in the Northwest of the United States, the capital is Bismark. The state flower of **North Dakota** is the wild prairie rose, and the state motto is "Liberty and union, now and forever, one and inseparable."

**north-east** [nôrth-ēst′] *noun,* the point between north and east on a compass

**north-west** [nôrth-wĕst′] *noun,* the point between north and west on the compass

**nose** [nōz] *noun,* 1) the part of the face that contains the nostrils and the organs of smell 2) the front of a plane, rocket, etc.

**nose-gay** [nōz′gā′] *noun,* a small hand-held fragrant bouquet

**nos-tal-gia** [nŏ-stăl′jə] *noun,* homesickness, a sentimental longing for something in the past

**nos-tril** [nŏs′trəl] *noun,* either of the external openings of the nose

**not** [nŏt] *adverb,* a word that forms a contradiction in a sentence

**no-ta-ble** [nō′tə-bəl] *adjective,* remarkable, worthy of notice

**no-ta-ry** [nō′tə-rē] *noun,* an officer who witnesses and verifies commercial papers and is authorized to take affidavits

**no-ta-tion** [nō-tā′shən] *noun,* notes or marks to indicate something

**notch** [nŏch] *noun,* 1) a nick, a dent, *verb,* 2) to make a notch

**note** [nōt] *noun,* 1) an observation stuck in the mind 2) a bill, IOU, paper money 3) a single sound of music on the scale 4) a brief written message, *verb,* 5) to make an observation and commit it to memory 6) to mention

**noth-ing** [nŭth′ĭng] *adjective,* not anything, zero, insignificant

**no-tice** [nō′tĭs] *noun,* 1) a written warning indicating that something has happened or will happen, *verb,* 2) to observe, to become aware of

**no-tice-a-ble** [nō′tĭ-sə-bəl] *adjective,* capable of being observed, conspicuous

**no-ti-fi-ca-tion** [nō′tə-fĭ-kā′shən] *noun,* something made known to someone

**no-ti-fy** [nō′tə-fī′] *verb,* to inform someone of something, to give notice

**no-tion** [nō′shən] *noun,* a general or vague idea, a thought, a whim

**no-to-ri-e-ty** [nō′tə-rī′ĭ-tē] *noun,* fame, renown, celebrity status

**no-to-ri-ous** [nō-tôr′ē-əs] *adjective,* widely or commonly known, usually unfavorable

**not-with-stand-ing** [nŏt′wĭth-stăn′dĭng] *adverb,* 1) all the same, nevertheless, *preposition,* 2) in spite of

**noun** [noun] *noun*, a word that refers to a person, place, or thing

**nour-ish** [nûr'ĭsh] *verb*, 1) to feed or foster the growth of something 2) to keep healthy, to nurture, to strengthen

**nour-ish-ment** [nûr'ĭsh-mənt] *noun*, food that strengthens the body and helps it grow

**nov-el** [nŏv'əl] *adjective*, 1) new, unusual, *noun*, 2) a work of fiction or romance

**nov-el-ist** [nŏv'ə-lĭst] *noun*, a person who writes fictional stories

**nov-el-ty** [nŏv'əl-tē] *noun*, something new

**No-vem-ber** [nō-věm'bər] *noun*, the eleventh month of the year, having 30 days

**nov-ice** [nŏv'ĭs] *noun*, 1) a beginner 2) a person admitted to a religious order before taking the final vows

**now** [nou] *adverb*, at the present time, immediately

**no-where** [nō'hwâr'] *adverb*, 1) not anywhere, *noun*, 2) a place that does not exist

**nox-ious** [nŏk'shəs] *adjective*, harmful, deadly fumes

**noz-zle** [nŏz'əl] *noun*, a short outlet or pipe as of a hose, a spout

**nu-ance** [nōō'äns'] *noun*, a shade or trace of differences in meaning, or color, or tone

**nu-cle-ar** [nōō'klē-ər] *adjective*, using the very great power made by splitting an atom or joining atoms in nuclear fission

**nu-cle-us** [nōō'klē-əs] *noun*, 1) a central mass of an atom about which matter is concentrated 2) the seed of the cell is the positively charged central region of an atom

**nude** [nōōd] *adjective*, naked, bare

**nudge** [nŭj] *noun*, 1) a gentle push, *verb*, 2) to push someone lightly

**nug-get** [nŭg'ĭt] *noun*, a small lump, especially of natural gold

**nui-sance** [nōō'səns] *noun*, anything which annoys or gives trouble, a disturbance

**nul-li-fy** [nŭl'ə-fī'] *adjective*, to render invalid or void

**numb** [nŭm] *adjective*, 1) insensitive from excessive cold 2) unable to feel pain

**num-ber** [nŭm'bər] *noun*, 1) a symbol representing a quantity 2) abundance, *verb*, 3) to identify with a number 4) to amount to

**nu-mer-al** [nōō'mər-əl] *noun*, a symbol used to represent a number

**nu-mer-ous** [nōō'mər-əs] *adjective*, very many, myriad, several

**nun** [nŭn] *noun*, a woman who gives her life to serving God

**nup-tial** [nŭp'shəl] *adjective*, marriage vows, a wedding

**nurse** [nûrs] *noun*, 1) a person who takes care of the sick and dying, *verb*, 2) to look after and attend to the needs of the sick

**nurs-er-y** [nûr'sə-rē] *noun*, 1) a child's room or playroom 2) a greenhouse for young plants

**nur-ture** [nûr'chər] *verb*, to care for, to feed and protect

**nut** [nŭt] *noun*, 1) the edible kernel of a seed 2) a small piece of metal with a hole in it, used to hold a bolt in place

**nut-meg** [nŭt′mĕg′] *noun*, the aromatic seed of an East Indian tree used as a spice

**nu-tri-ent** [noō′trē-ənt] *noun*, vitamins and minerals derived from food, proteins

**nu-tri-tion** [noō-trĭsh′ən] *noun*, a healthy diet, that nourishes the body

**nu-tri-tious** [noō-trĭsh′əs] *adjective*, wholesome, healthy

**ny-lon** [nī′lŏn′] *noun*, a strong man-made elastic thread

**nymph** [nĭmf] *noun*, 1) the young of an insect that has not fully developed the structural proportions and size of an adult 2) a fairy

# O

**oaf** [ōf] *noun*, a clumsy person

**oak** [ōk] *noun*, a tree of hard wood bearing the acorn as a fruit

**oar** [ôr, ōr] *noun*, a paddle with a flat blade at the end, used to row or push a boat

**o-a-sis** [ō-ā′sĭs] *noun*, a fertile spot in a desert having a spring

**oat** [ōt] *noun*, a member of the cereal family having edible seeds such as rice, wheat or corn

**oath** [ōth] *noun*, a promise, a commitment, a solemn appeal

**o-be-di-ence** [ō-bē′dē-əns] *noun*, *no plural*, compliance with authority, submission

**o-be-di-ent** [ō-bē′dē-ənt] *adjective*, willing to do what one is told to do

**ob-e-lisk** [ŏb′ə-lĭsk] *noun*, a tall 4-sided column tapering and ending in a pyramid apex

**o-bese** [ō-bēs′] *adjective*, very fat

**o-bey** [ō-bā′] *verb*, to follow or carry out an order or law

**ob-fus-cate** [ŏb′fə-skāt′] *verb*, to confuse, to muddle, to obscure

**o-bit-u-ar-y** [ō-bĭch′oō-ĕr′ē] *noun*, an announcement of someone's death often with a short biography

**ob-ject** [ŏb′jĭkt] *noun*, 1) a thing, *verb*, 2) to oppose, to disagree

**ob-jec-tion** [əb-jĕk′shən] *noun*, a statement, a complaint

**ob-jec-tive** [əb-jĕk′tĭv] *adjective*, 1) not influenced by emotions, fair, *noun*, 2) a purpose or goal

**ob-jur-gate** [ŏb′jər-gāt′] *verb*, to scold, to rebuke severely

**ob-li-ga-tion** [ŏb′lĭ-gā′shən] *noun*, 1) the binding power of a promise 2) a debt of gratitude

**ob-lig-a-to-ry** [ə-blĭg′ə-tôr′ē] *adjective*, necessary, binding in law or conscience, mandatory

**o-blige** [ə-blīj′] *verb*, 1) to put under obligation, to accommodate 2) to do a favor for, to help, to assist

**o-blique** [ō-blēk′] *adjective*, 1) sloping or slanting 2) indirect or evasive, not explicit

**ob-lit-er-ate** [ə-blĭt′ə-rāt′] *verb*, to erase or blot out, to efface

**ob-liv-i-on** [ə-blĭv′ē-ən] *noun*, being utterly forgotten

**ob-liv-i-ous** [ə-blĭv′ē-əs] *adjective*, forgetful, lost in thought

**ob-long** [ŏb′lông′] *adjective*, a flat shape with four straight sides and four equal angles, that is longer than it is wide

**ob-nox-ious** [ŏb-nŏk′shəs]
*adjective*, annoying, offensive

**ob-scure** [ŏb-skyŏŏr′] *adjective*,
1) unclear, vague, unknown
2) not easily seen or heard
3) dark, hidden

**ob-scu-ri-ty** [ŏb-skyŏŏr′ĭ-tē] *noun*,
oblivion, no where

**ob-se-qui-ous** [ŏb-sē′kwē-əs]
*adjective*, submissive, fawning

**ob-ser-vance** [əb-zûr′vəns] *noun*,
1) noticing with attention 2)
compliance as a duty or custom

**ob-ser-va-tion** [ŏb′zər-vā′shən]
*noun*, the noting and recording
of facts and events

**ob-serv-a-to-ry** [əb-zûr′və-tôr′ē]
*noun*, a building equipped with
instruments for observing the
heavenly bodies, such as the
stars, moon, etc.

**ob-serve** [əb-zûrv′] *verb*, 1) to see
or notice 2) to comment 3) to
mark an event or day

**ob-ses-sion** [əb-sĕsh′ən, ŏb-] *noun*,
a fixed idea, continued brooding

**ob-so-lete** [ŏb′sə-lēt′] *adjective*, no
longer in use, outdated

**ob-sta-cle** [ŏb′stə-kəl] *noun*,
something that stands in the
way, an obstruction

**ob-ste-tri-cian** [ŏb′stĭ-trĭsh′ən]
*noun*, a physician specializing in
the delivery of babies

**ob-sti-nate** [ŏb′stə-nĭt] *adjective*,
not yielding to reason, stubborn

**ob-struct** [əb-strŭkt′] *verb*, to get
in the way of something or stop
it completely, to hinder

**ob-struc-tion** [əb-strŭk′shən] *noun*,
a barrier, an interference

**ob-tain** [əb-tān′] *verb*, to acquire or
win through effort or request

**ob-tain-a-ble** [əb-tān′ə-bəl]
*adjective*, capable of being
acquired or won

**ob-trude** [ŏb-trōōd′] *verb*, 1) to get
in on, to meddle, 2) to stick out

**ob-tuse** [ŏb-tōōs′] *adjective*, an
angle greater than 90 degrees

**ob-vi-ous** [ŏb′vē-əs] *adjective*,
easily seen or understood,
evident, apparent to everyone

**ob-vi-ous-ly** [ŏb′vē-əs-lē] *adverb*,
apparently, clearly, evidently

**oc-ca-sion** [ə-kā′zhən] *noun*, 1) an
event, a happening, an important
time 2) a chance, an opportunity

**oc-cas-ion-al-ly** [ə-kā′zhə-nə-lē]
*adverb*, once in a while

**oc-cult** [ə-kŭlt′] *adjective*, the
mysterious, secret, supernatural

**oc-cu-pant** [ŏk′yə-pənt] *noun*, the
inhabitant, a resident, a tenant

**oc-cu-pa-tion** [ŏk′yə-pā′shən]
*noun*, 1) a job, a way of using
time, *no plural*, 2) being in a
certain place or space

**oc-cu-py** [ŏk′yə-pī′] *verb*, 1) to
make or hold possession of
something 2) to live in a place

**oc-cur** [ə-kûr′] *verb*, 1) to happen
2) to come to mind, to appear

**oc-cur-rence** [ə-kûr′əns] *noun*,
something that happens

**o-cean** [ō′shən] *noun*, a body of
salt water covering three fifths of
the earth

**o-cea-nog-ra-phy** [ō′shə-nŏg′rə-fē]
*noun*, the study of life in the sea

o'clock [ə-klŏk′] *adverb*, according to the clock

Oc-to-ber [ŏk-tō′bər] *noun*, the tenth month of the year having 31 days

oc-to-pus [ŏk′tə-pəs] *noun*, a sea creature that has eight long limbs

oc-u-list [ŏk′yə-lĭst] *noun*, a doctor who treats the eyes

odd [ŏd] *adjective*, 1) any number that cannot be evenly divided by two 2) unusual, very different

odds [ŏdz] *noun*, *plural*, uncertain advantages, doubtful chances

odi-ous [ō′dē-əs] *adjective*, hateful, repulsive, repugnant

odi-um [ō′dē-əm] *noun*, repugnance, intense hatred

o-dom-e-ter [ō-dŏm′ĭ-tər] *noun*, a device in a vehicle used to measure distance traveled

o-dor [ō′dər] *noun*, a smell

o-dor-ous [ō′dər-əs] *adjective*, having a strong smell

of [ŭv] *preposition*, 1) belonging to 2) from among 3) made from 4) about 5) in relation to

off [ôf] *adverb*, 1) away from 2) not on or not working, *preposition*, 3) at a distance

of-fend [ə-fĕnd′] *verb*, to hurt someone's feelings, to insult

of-fense [ə-fĕns′] *noun*, a misdeed, an insult, a sense of insult or injury, an act of aggression

of-fen-sive [ə-fĕn′sĭv] *adjective*, 1) insulting, in poor taste, *noun*, 2) the position of an attack

of-fer [ô′fər] *noun*, 1) a proposal, a suggestion, *verb*, 2) to present to be accepted or refused

of-fice [ô′fĭs] *noun*, 1) a place in which business or professional work is done 2) a position that requires certain duties and tasks

of-fi-cer [ô′fĭ-sər] *noun*, a person lawfully invested with a position of trust or authority

of-fi-cial [ə-fĭsh′əl] *adjective*, 1) having the right or permission to do something, *noun*, 2) a person who is in charge of something 3) of or pertaining to the holding of an office

of-fi-ci-ate [ə-fĭsh′ē-āt′] *verb*, to act as an officer in performing a duty such as a minister

off-spring [ôf′sprĭng′] *noun*, descendants, children, progeny

of-ten [ô′fən] *adverb*, many times, frequently, repeatedly

o-ha-na [ōhŏna] *noun*, family, no one left behind

Ohio [ō-hī′ō] *noun*, one of the 50 United States located in the Midwest region, the capital is Columbus. The state flower of **Ohio** is the scarlet carnation and the motto is "With God all things are possible."

ohm [ōm] *noun*, the unit of electrical resistance

oil [oil] *noun*, 1) any liquid substance that does not dissolve in water 2) a nutrient derived from a pressed nut 3) a dark, thick mineral liquid, found deep in the ground 4) a substance used to burn in a lantern or lamp post, *verb*, 5) to lubricate with grease or oil

**oint-ment** [oint′mənt] *noun*, a
lubricant put on the skin,
containing medicine

**Okla-ho-ma** [ō′klə-hō′mə] *noun*,
one of the 50 United States
located in the Southwest, the
capital is Oklahoma City. The
state flower of **Oklahoma** is the
mistletoe, and the motto is
"Labor conquers all things."

**old** [ōld] *adjective*, 1) not young,
having lived a long time 2) the
word we use to show our age
3) not new 4) something that has
lasted over time, antique

**ol-fac-to-ry** [ŏl-făk′tə-rē] *adjective*,
referring to the nose and the
sense of smell

**ol-i-gar-chy** [ŏl′ĭ-gär′kē] *noun*, a
government run by a few leaders

**ol-ive** [ŏl′ĭv] *noun*, the fruit of an
olive tree eaten as a relish

**om-i-nous** [ŏm′ə-nəs] *adjective*,
looking or sounding as if
something bad will happen,
portending evil or harm

**o-mis-sion** [ō-mĭsh′ən] *noun*,
failure to do something,
something that is left out

**o-mit** [ō-mĭt′] *verb*, to leave
something out, to fail to include

**om-e-lette** [ŏm′ə-lĭt] *noun*, eggs
beaten together and cooked in
hot fat in a flat pan

**om-nip-o-tent** [ŏm-nĭp′ə-tənt]
*adjective*, having power over all

**om-ni-pres-ent** [ŏm′nĭ-prĕz′ənt]
*adjective*, universally present at
the same time, everywhere

**om-nis-cient** [ŏm-nĭsh′ənt]
*adjective*, all-knowing

**om-ni-vore** [ŏm′nə-vôr′] *noun*, an
animal that eats both plants and
animals

**on** [ŏn] *adverb*, 1) to be precise
2) a location 3) to show time or
date 4) about 5) to continue,
*preposition*, 6) atop

**once** [wŭns] *adverb*, 1) one time
2) a long time ago

**one** [wŭn] *adjective*, 1) the number 1
2) the same, unified 3) act as the
same, *noun*, 4) a single thing
5) any person 6) a unit

**one-self** [wŭn-sĕlf′] *pronoun*, the
same person who is the subject
of the sentence

**on-ion** [ŭn′yən] *noun*, a garden
vegetable having an edible bulb
with pungent taste and odor

**on-ly** [ōn′lē] *adjective*, 1) sole, no
one else, nothing more, 2) but,
*adverb*, 3) merely, just

**on-o-mat-o-poe-ia**
[ŏn′ə-măt′ə-pē′ə] *noun*, a term
used to describe words that
actually sound like the noises
they depict such as *boom*

**on-slaught** [ŏn′slôt′] *noun*, a
vicious assault, a massacre

**on-to** [ŏn′tōō′] *preposition*, to a
place, to a position on

**o-nus** [ō′nəs] *noun*, 1) a burden
2) a responsibility, blame

**on-ward** [ŏn′wərd] *adverb*, moving
toward a point ahead, forward

**ooze** [ōōz] *verb*, to flow out slowly

**o-pal** [ō′pəl] *noun*, a precious stone
of milky hue, with a play of
iridescent colors

**o-paque** [ō-pāk′] *adjective*, not reflecting or giving out light, not transparent; dull, dark

**o-pen** [ō′pən] *adjective*, 1) not shut or covered 2) ready for business 3) not surrounded by other things 4) unbiased, free thinking, *verb*, 5) to allow entrance 6) to start, to unfold 7) to remove the cover or door 8) to undo, to untie

**o-pe-ra** [ŏp′ər-ə] *noun*, a dramatic presentation set to music

**op-er-ate** [ŏp′ə-rāt′] *verb*, to make something work or function

**op-er-a-tion** [ŏp′ə-rā′shən] *noun*, 1) any methodical action 2) a plan put into action 3) surgery

**op-er-a-tor** [ŏp′ə-rā′tər] *noun*, one who operates equipment or works as a manager

**o-pi-ate** [ō′pē-ĭt] *noun*, a drug which causes rest or sleep, a narcotic or sedative

**o-pin-ion** [ə-pĭn′yən] *noun*, a belief stronger than an impression, a point of view, a conclusion

**o-pos-sum** [ə-pŏs′əm] *noun*, a rodent that sleeps upside down hanging from a tree during the day, and travels at night

**op-po-nent** [ə-pō′nənt] *noun*, a member of the other team, an antagonist, an adversary

**op-por-tune** [ŏp′ər-tōōn′] *adjective*, timely, well chosen

**op-por-tun-ist** [ŏp′ər-tōō′nĭst] *noun*, an individual who takes advantage of a situation and ignores ethics to achieve a goal

**op-por-tu-ni-ty** [ŏp′ər-tōō′nĭ-tē] *noun*, a fit or convenient time, occasion, a good chance

**op-pose** [ə-pōz′] *verb*, to go against, to defend, to combat, to object, to resist, to fight

**op-po-site** [ŏp′ə-zĭt] *adjective*, 1) facing, set over against 2) one that is contrary to another

**op-po-si-tion** [ŏp′ə-zĭsh′ən] *noun*, against, hostile or contrary action, a negative response

**op-press** [ə-prĕs′] *verb*, to overpower, to subdue, to treat harshly, to hold down

**op-pres-sion** [ə-prĕsh′ən] *noun*, hardship, cruelty, persecution

**op-pres-sive** [ə-prĕs′ĭv] *adjective*, 1) unreasonably burdensome 2) tyrannical, cruel, unfair

**op-tic** [ŏp′tĭk] *adjective*, pertaining to the eye, light and vision

**op-ti-cal** [ŏp′tĭ-kəl] *adjective*, visual, seeing

**op-ti-cian** [ŏp-tĭsh′ən] *noun*, a person who makes glasses, a dealer in optical goods

**op-ti-mal** [ŏp′tə-məl] *adjective*, most favorable condition

**op-ti-mist** [ŏp′tə-mĭst] *noun*, one who looks on the bright side of things, positive thinking

**op-ti-mis-tic** [ŏp′tə-mĭs-tĭk] *adjective*, having a positive outlook, upbeat, hopeful

**op-tion** [ŏp′shən] *noun*, 1) a choice 2) a stock available at a certain time at a stated price

**op-tom-e-trist** [ŏp-tŏm′ĭ-trĭst] *noun*, one who examines eyes and fits glasses to help a person see better

**op-u-lence** [ŏp′yə-ləns] *adjective*, having property, wealthy, rich, affluent, luxurious

**o-pus** [ō′pəs] *noun*, a great creative literary or musical work

**or** [ôr;] *conjunction*, used to connect words when given a choice

**o-ral** [ôr′əl] *adjective*, 1) spoken information 2) of the mouth

**or-ange** [ôr′ĭnj] *adjective*, 1) a color made when red and yellow are mixed together, *noun*, 2) a sweet, juicy fruit grown on trees in tropical climates

**or-a-tor** [ôr′ə-tər] *noun*, a public speaker of great eloquence

**or-a-to-ri-o** [ôr′ə-tôr′ē-ō′] *noun*, a dramatic poem set to music

**or-a-to-ry** [ôr′ə-tôr′ē] *noun*, a moving or powerful speech

**or-bit** [ôr′bĭt] *noun*, 1) the course an object follows in space around another, *verb*, 2) to travel through space in a cycle

**or-chard** [ôr′chərd] *noun*, a grove where fruit trees grow for food

**or-ches-tra** [ôr′kĭ-strə] *noun*, 1) a band of performers on various instruments 2) the lower floor in a theater for instruments

**or-chid** [ôr′kĭd] *noun*, an exotic tropical flower with three petals

**or-dain** [ôr-dān′] *verb*, to appoint, to install, to elect, to decree

**or-deal** [ôr-dēl′] *noun*, an extremely stressful situation

**or-der** [ôr′dər] *noun*, 1) a careful arrangement 2) a special system used to organize information 3) grouping, placement 4) a request telling someone to do something, *verb*, 5) to arrange carefully 6) to issue a command, to instruct

**or-di-nal num-ber** [ôr′dn-əl-nŭm′bər] *noun*, a number expressing degree or order in a series such as 1$^{st}$, 2$^{nd}$,

**or-di-nance** [ôr′dn-əns] *noun*, 1) a local law, an edict or decree 2) a prescribed practice or usage

**or-di-nar-i-ly** [ôr′dn-âr′ə-lē] *adverb*, usually, generally

**or-di-nar-y** [ôr′dn-ĕr′ē] *adjective*, 1) according to custom or established order 2) regular, commonplace, normal

**ore** [ôr, ōr] *noun*, a kind of rock in which metal is found

**Or-e-gon** [ôr′ĭ-gən] *noun*, one of the 50 United States in the Northwest, the capital is Salem. The state flower of **Oregon** is the Oregon grape, and the motto is "The Union."

**or-gan** [ôr′gən] *noun*, 1) a musical instrument similar to a piano, with long pipes through which air travels through to make the sound 2) a part of the body that serves a specific function

**or-gan-ic** [ôr-găn′ĭk] *adjective*, grown naturally without pesticides or fertilizers

**or-gan-ism** [ôr′gə-nĭz′əm] *noun*, any individual life form

**or-gan-i-za-tion** [ôr′gə-nĭ-zā′shən] *noun*, an association, a group of people working together for a common purpose

**or-gan-ize** [ôr′gə-nīz′] *verb*, 1) to plan, to arrange and implement in an orderly way 2) to establish or construct a plan or a scheme

**o-ri-en-tal** [ôr′ē-ĕn′tl] *adjective*, pertaining to the Orient or East Asia

**o-ri-en-ta-tion** [ôr′ē-ĕn-tā′shən] *noun*, the act of getting your bearings, an introduction

**or-i-fice** [ôr′ə-fĭs] *noun*, a mouthlike opening, a slit, any hole in a body

**or-i-gin** [ôr′ə-jĭn] *noun*, the first use or the beginning

**o-rig-i-nal** [ə-rĭj′ə-nəl] *adjective*, the first of its kind, new and different, inventive

**o-rig-i-nal-i-ty** [ə-rĭj′ə-năl′ĭ-tē] *noun*, creativeness, innovation

**o-rig-i-nate** [ə-rĭj′ə-nāt′] *verb*, 1) to bring into existence, to initiate 2) to produce as new

**or-na-ment** [ôr′nə-mənt] *noun*, a decoration, beautification

**or-na-men-tal** [ôr′nə-mĕn′tl] *adjective*, decorative, adorned, beautiful, embellished

**or-nate** [ôr-nāt′] *adjective*, excessively decorated, adorned

**or-ni-thol-o-gist** [ôr′nə-thŏl′ə-jĭst] *noun*, one who studies birds

**or-phan** [ôr′fən] *noun*, a child whose parents are dead

**or-phan-age** [ôr′fə-nĭj] *noun*, a home for children who have no family

**or-tho-dox** [ôr′thə-dŏks′] *adjective*, accepted, traditional doctrine, very conservative

**or-thog-ra-phy** [ôr-thŏg′rə-fē] *noun*, correct spelling

**os-cil-late** [ŏs′ə-lāt′] *verb*, 1) to swing backward and forward, to vibrate 2) varying above or below a mean value

**os-si-fy** [ŏs′ə-fī′] *verb*, 1) to change or harden cartilage into bone 2) to set into a repeating pattern

**os-ten-si-ble** [ŏ-stĕn′sə-bəl] *adjective*, shown, professed, apparent, pretended

**os-ten-ta-tious** [ŏs′tĕn-tā′shəs] *adjective*, pretentious, conspicuous, showiness as an attempt to attract attention

**os-tra-cize** [ŏs′trə-sīz′] *verb*, to banish, to cast out from social favor or fellowship

**os-trich** [ŏs′trĭch] *noun*, a very large bird, with long legs, that is black and white, and cannot fly

**oth-er** [ŭth′ər] *adjective*, 1) not the same, a different one, *adverb*, 2) differently, *pronoun*, 3) someone or something not mentioned specifically

**oth-er-wise** [ŭth′ər-wīz′] *adverb*, 1) if not 2) except for that 3) of a different kind

**ought** [ôt] *verb*, should

**ounce** [ouns] *noun*, 1) a weight measurement equal to 28.35 grams 2) a tiny bit

**our** [our] *adjective*, belonging to us

**our-selves** [our-sĕlvz′] *pronoun*, referring to the subjects in a sentence, we or us

**oust** [oust] *verb*, to dismiss, to kick out, to expel, to force out

**out** [out] *adverb*, 1) not in or inside, away from 2) absent, away 3) not shining or burning 4) to bring to a conclusion 5) excluded, omitted

**out-cast** [out′kăst′] *noun*, a displaced person, an exile

**out-come** [out′kŭm′] *noun*, a possible result as in an experiment, a final product

**out-doors** [out-dôrz′, -dōrz′] *adjective*, not inside a building, located outside in the open air

**out-doors-man** [out-dôrz′mən, -dōrz′-] *noun*, a person who enjoys nature and outdoor activities

**out-er** [ou′tər] *adjective*, on the outside or edge of something

**out-fit** [out′fĭt′] *noun*, 1) clothing used for a particular purpose, *verb*, 2) to provide clothes or equipment

**out-grow** [out-grō′] *verb*, to change as one develops

**out-growth** [out′grōth′] *noun*, development, product

**out-ing** [ou′tĭng] *noun*, a short trip

**out-let** [out′lĕt′, -lĭt] *noun*, 1) an opening, 2) manufacturer

**out-line** [out′līn′] *noun*, 1) a line showing the shape of something 2) the plan or format for a composition, *verb*, 3) to give the main points of

**out-live** [out-lĭv′] *verb*, to outlast, to live or last longer than

**out-rage** [out′rāj′] *noun*, 1) anger caused by injury or insult 2) anything that causes resentment or anger, a wicked or brutal act or remark *verb*, 2) to fill with anger of resentment

**out-side** [out-sīd′] *adverb*, 1) on or to the exterior surface, *noun*, 2) the outer part or surface

**out-stand-ing** [out-stăn′dĭng] *adjective*, 1) very good, excellent 2) not paid or settled

**o-val** [ō′vəl] *adjective*, a round flat shape like an egg

**ov-en** [ŭv′ən] *noun*, an electric appliance like a sealed box used to bake food

**o-ver** [ō′vər] *adjective*, 1) in control of 2) finished, *adverb*, 3) from start to finish again 4) unused, extra 5) to go beyond the top, *preposition*, 6) covering 7) across, from one side to the other 8) in every part

**o-ver-all** [ō′vər-ôl′] *adjective*, including all things, as a whole

**o-ver-alls** [ō′vər-ôlz′] *noun*, a kind of loose trousers with a bib

**o-ver-board** [ō′vər-bôrd′] *adverb*, over the side of a boat into the water

**o-ver-cast** [ō′vər-kăst′] *adjective*, cloudy, sunless, gloomy

**o-ver-coat** [ō′vər-kōt′] *noun*, a coat worn over the other clothing

**o-ver-come** [ō′vər-kŭm′] *verb*, to beat, to conquer, to lick

**o-ver-due** [ō′vər-dōō′] *adjective*, delinquent, late, past due

**o-ver-es-ti-mate** [ō′vər-ĕs′tə-māt′] *verb*, to calculate over the actual amount

**o-ver-flow** [ō′vər-flō′] *verb*, 1) to pour over the edge of a container when filled 2) to flood

**o-ver-haul** [ō′vər-hôl′] *verb*, to restore, to repair, to rebuild

**o-ver-head** [ō′vər-hĕd′] *adjective*, 1) above our heads, in the sky, *noun*, *no plural*, 2) the fixed costs to maintain something

**o-ver-lap** [ō′vər-lăp′] *verb*, 1) to rest on top of or over something and cover part of it 2) to partially coincide

**o-ver-look** [ō′vər-lŏŏk′] *verb*, 1) to fail to notice 2) to excuse

**o-ver-night** [ō′vər-nīt′] *adjective*, 1) from one day to the next, *adverb*, 2) during the night

**o-ver-seas** [ō′vər-sēz′] *adjective*, across the ocean, abroad

**o-ver-seer** [ō′vər-sē′ər] *noun*, one who watches over an area or institution, a supervisor

**o-ver-sight** [ō′vər-sīt′] *noun*, an error, a blunder, a failure

**o-vert** [ō-vûrt′] *adjective*, open to view, not concealed

**o-ver-take** [ō′vər-tāk′] *verb*, to chase and catch up to

**o-ver-ture** [ō′vər-chŏŏr′] *noun*, a proposal, an introduction

**o-ver-whelm** [ō′vər-hwĕlm′] *verb*, 1) to overpower in mind and feeling 2) to engulf, to inundate

**owe** [ō] *verb*, 1) to have to give or pay 2) to feel grateful to someone for something

**owl** [oul] *noun*, a large bird that lives in the forest, it flies at night and eats small animals

**own** [ōn] *adjective*, 1) of or belonging to oneself or itself, *verb*, 2) to have or possess

**own-er** [ō′nər] *noun*, the person who has the right to something

**own-er-ship** [ō′nər-shĭp′] *noun*, a right of possession, a lawful claim or title

**ox** [ŏks] *noun*, *plural*, **oxen**, a full-grown male of domestic cattle used for farm work

**ox-i-dize** [ŏk′sĭ-dīz′] *verb*, to combine with oxygen

**ox-y-gen** [ŏk′sĭ-jən] *noun*, a colorless, tasteless, odorless, chemically active gas, the part of air that animals, plants and people need to stay alive

**oys-ter** [oi′stər] *noun*, an edible shellfish, a bivalve mollusk

**o-zone** [ō′zōn′] *noun*, a faintly blue gas obtained by the silent discharge of electricity in air

# P

**pace** [pās] *noun*, 1) a steady step or speed that is maintained, *verb*, 2) to walk back and forth

**pach-y-derm** [păk′ĭ-dûrm′] *noun*, a thick-skinned animal

**pac-i-fist** [pə-sĭf′ĭ-st] *noun*, someone who looks for peaceful means, opposed to force

**pac-i-fy** [păs′ə-fī′] *verb*, to appease, to calm, to soothe

**pack** [păk] *noun*, 1) a bundle or a collection of things 2) a group of wild animals that hunt together, *verb*, 3) to bundle or place a group of things into a container

**pack-age** [păk′ĭj] *noun*, a box or bundle containing one or more objects

**pact** [păkt] *noun*, an agreement, a contract, a treaty, a bargain

**pad** [păd] *noun*, 1) a soft material used to protect a wound 2) a number of sheets of paper stuck together at one edge

**pad-dle** [păd′l] *noun*, 1) an ore or long stick used to row a boat, verb, 2) to spank, to whack on the bottom 3) to row a boat 4) to move the hands and feet in shallow water

**pad-dock** [păd'ək] noun, a field or enclosure where horses are kept

**pad-dy** [păd'ē] noun, a field for growing rice

**pad-lock** [păd'lŏk'] noun, a portable lock, jointed at one end

**page** [pāj] noun, 1) one side of a piece of paper in a book 2) a person who delivers messages verb, 2) to summon or call indirectly through an intercom or paging system

**pag-eant** [păj'ənt] noun, an exhibition, a show, a parade

**paid** [pād] verb, the past tense of **pay**

**pail** [pāl] noun, a bucket or container with a handle

**pain** [pān] noun, physical suffering from injury or illness, distress

**pain-ful** [pān'fəl] adjective, a feeling of hurt, aching

**paint** [pānt] noun, 1) a liquid in a variety of colors that is used to cover a surface to protect or decorate it, verb, 2) to coat or color with paint 3) to convey an image by creating it using paints

**paint-er** [pān'tər] noun, a person who paints pictures or buildings

**paint-ing** [pān'tǐng] noun, completed pictures done with paint, a representation

**pair** [pâr] noun, 1) two like things put together as a match 2) an instrument with two parts joined together, e.g. scissors, verb, 3) to separate into groups of two

**pa-ja-mas** [pə-jä'mə] noun, plural, loose fitting clothes worn to bed

**pal** [păl] noun, a friend, chum

**pal-ace** [păl'ĭs] noun, a beautiful home of a wealthy person

**pal-at-a-ble** [păl'ə-tə-bəl] adjective, 1) tasty 2) acceptable to the mind, pleasing

**pa-la-tial** [pə-lā'shəl] adjective, suitable for a palace, impressively spacious

**pale** [pāl] adjective, 1) light in color, faded, noun, 2) the area enclosed by a boundary

**pal-ette** [păl'ĭt] noun, a board on which a painter mixes paints

**pal-i-sade** [păl'ĭ-sād'] noun, a partition formed as a barrier

**pal-lid:** [păl'id] adjective, pale

**palm** [päm] noun, 1) a tree with a long trunk without branches and large leaves at the top 2) the wide part inside the hand

**pal-pa-ble** [păl'pə-bəl] adjective, 1) capable of being touched or felt, obvious 2) tangible

**pal-pi-tate** [păl'pǐ-tāt'] verb, to throb, to pound with emotion or exertion, to quiver, to shake

**pal-try** [pôl'trē] adjective, insignificant, petty, trifling

**pam-per** [păm'pər] verb, to coddle, to indulge, to baby, to spoil

**pam-phlet** [păm'flĭt] noun, a book of a few sheets of printed matter

**pan** [păn] noun, a round metal pot for cooking things over heat

**pan-a-ce-a** [păn'ə-sē'ə] noun, a solution to all problems or sickness, a cure-all

**pan-cre-as** [păng′krē-əs] *noun*, a large gland under and behind the stomach that secretes insulin to the intestine to help digest food

**pan-da** [păn′də] *noun*, a large black and white animal like a bear restricted to China

**pan-de-mo-ni-um** [păn′də-mō′nē-əm] *noun*, a wild tumult, an uproar, confusion

**pan-der** [păn′dər] *verb*, to cater to the low desires of others

**pane** [pān] *noun*, a piece of glass used in windows or doors

**pan-el** [păn′əl] *noun*, 1) a sunken compartment with raised margins in a ceiling 2) a complete jury 3) a group assembled to judge a contest or conduct a public discussion

**pan-ic** [păn′ĭk] *noun*, 1) a sudden fear which can spread quickly, *verb*, 2) to feel frightened or alarmed, filled with terror

**pan-sy** [păn′zē] *noun*, a flower that blooms through the winter

**pant** [pănt] *verb*, to breathe quickly

**pan-ther** [păn′thər] *noun*, one of the large wild cats, a cougar

**pan-to-mime** [păn′tə-mīm′] *noun*, a play in which actors use gestures without speech

**pan-try** [păn′trē] *noun*, a small room where food is stored

**pants** [pănts] *noun*, *plural*, trousers

**pa-pa** [pä′pə] *noun*, a father, a dad

**pa-per** [pā′pər] *noun*, 1) sheets of thin material used for writing, wrapping, etc. 2) a newspaper 3) paper with writing or printing on it verifying identity

**pap-ri-ka** [pă-prĕ′kə] *noun*, a Turkish red pepper

**pa-py-rus** [pə-pī′rəs] *noun*, a reed plant that grows in the Nile Valley once used as paper

**par** [pär] *noun*, average, standard, the norm, equality in value

**par-a-ble** [păr′ə-bəl] *noun*, a short, simple story teaching a lesson

**par-a-chute** [păr′ə-shōōt′] *noun*, 1) a light device made of silk or nylon, designed in an umbrella shape, used to retard the free fall from an aircraft, *verb*, 2) to eject from an aircraft by jumping out equipped with a parachute used to slow something's fall to the ground from a great height

**pa-rade** [pə-rād′] *noun*, 1) a number of people walking or marching together, a public procession, *verb*, 2) to walk or march with a group of people

**par-a-digm** [păr′ə-dīm′] *noun*, a model, an example, a pattern

**par-a-dise** [păr′ə-dīs′] *noun*, a place of complete happiness or beauty, like heaven

**par-a-dox** [păr′ə-dŏks′] *noun*, a statement that contradicts itself, but is in fact true

**par-af-fin** [păr′ə-fĭn] *noun*, a white wax used to make candles and seal preserves

**par-a-gon** [păr′ə-gŏn′] *noun*, a model of perfection

**par-a-graph** [păr′ə-grăf′] *noun*, a subdivision in writing, beginning with an indent on a new line

**par-a-keet** [păr′ə-kēt′] *noun*, a small blue or green domestic song bird

**par-al-lel** [păr′ə-lĕl′] *adjective*,
1) lying in the same direction and always the same distance apart, never intersecting 2)similar

**par-al-lel-o-gram** [păr′ə-lĕl′ə-grăm′] *noun*, a four sided plane figure with opposite sides equal and parallel

**pa-ral-y-sis** [pə-răl′ĭ-sĭs] *adjective*, loss of sensation and motion of body parts, a helpless state

**par-a-lyze** [păr′ə-līz′] *verb*, to destroy the energy of something, to stop all movement or feeling

**pa-ram-e-ter** [pə-răm′ĭ-tər] *noun*, the limit, a set standard

**par-a-mount** [păr′ə-mount′] *adjective*, most important

**par-a-noi-a** [păr′ə-noi′ə] *noun*, insanity marked by delusions of persecution or glory

**par-a-phrase** [păr′ə-frāz′] *verb*, to restate a passage in one's own words for clarity

**par-a-site** [păr′ə-sīt′] *noun*, animal or plant living off another, using it as its only source of food

**par-cel** [păr′səl] *noun*, 1) a package wrapped in paper, for mailing or carrying, *verb*, 2) to divide into portions to hand out

**parch** [pärch] *verb*, to dry in the sun, to dehydrate, to scorch

**parch-ment** [pärch′mənt] *noun*, the skin of a goat or sheep prepared for writing

**par-don** [pär′dn] *noun*, *no plural*, 1) forgiveness, *verb*, 2) to excuse, to forgive, to absolve

**par-don-a-ble** [pär′dn-ə-bəl] *adjective*, excusable, forgivable

**pare** [pâr] *verb*, 1) to peel, to cut off the outer edge, 2) to reduce

**par-ent** [pâr′ənt] *noun*, 1) the father or mother 2) the source

**pa-ren-the-sis** [pə-rĕn′thĭ-sĭs] *noun*, one of the curved lines which enclose an aside ( )

**par-ish** [păr′ĭsh] *noun*, an area served by one church

**park** [pärk] *noun*, 1) a place in town designated for recreation, rest, and beauty, *verb*, 2) to put a car or vehicle in place

**par-ka** [pär′kə] *noun*, a heavy winter coat with a hood

**par-ley** [pär′lē] *noun*, a conference between two opponents, a discussion to settle a dispute

**par-lia-ment** [pär′lə-mənt] *noun*, an assembly in Great Britain similar to the United States Congress

**par-lor** [pär′lər] *noun*, a room that is usually used for talking or entertaining, a living room

**pa-ro-chi-al** [pə-rō′kē-əl] *adjective*, of or pertaining to a parish, a local area

**par-o-dy** [păr′ə-dē] *noun*, a humorous imitation, satire

**pa-role** [pə-rōl′] *noun*, an early conditional release from prison, free on probation

**par-rot** [păr′ət] *noun*, a brightly colored bird with a short curved beak that can mimic speech

**par-si-mo-ny** [pär′sə-mō′nē] *noun*, selfishness, stinginess

**pars-ley** [pär′slē] *noun*, an herb with flat or curled leaves used to flavor soups, etc., or to garnish food

**par·snip** [pär′snĭp] *noun*, a fleshy white root, in the carrot group

**part** [pärt] *noun*, 1) some of a thing or things 2) a share in an activity 3) a character in a play or film, *verb*, 4) to separate, to leave from 5) to break apart

**par·tial·ly** [pär′shə-lē] *adverb*, partly, somewhat, slightly

**par·ti·al·i·ty** [pär′shē-ăl′ĭ-tē] *adjective*, biased, inclined to favor one side

**par·tic·i·pate** [pär-tĭs′ə-pāt′] *verb*, to have a share in common with others, to take part, to join in

**par·tic·i·pa·tion** [pär-tĭs′ə-pā′shən] *noun*, the act of getting involved with others

**par·ti·ci·ple** [pär′tĭ-sĭp′əl] *noun*, one of two forms of a verb forming the past or future tense

**par·ti·cle** [pär′tĭ-kəl] *noun*, the smallest form of matter

**par·tic·u·lar** [pər-tĭk′yə-lər] *adjective*, relating to a part, individual, precise, specific

**par·tic·u·lar·ly** [pər-tĭk′yə-lər-lē] *adverb*, specifically, in detail

**par·ti·san** [pär′tĭ-zən] *adjective*, an adherent to a party or faction

**par·ti·tion** [pär-tĭsh′ən] *noun*, 1) a division, a dividing wall, *verb*, 2) to divide, to separate

**part·ly** [pärt′lē] *adverb*, to some extent, partially, somewhat

**part·ner** [pärt′nər] *noun*, 1) an associate in business 2) a companion in dancing or sports

**par·ty** [pär′tē] *noun*, 1) a meeting of friends to enjoy themselves 2) a group of people who have the same interests or goals, *verb*, 3) to celebrate

**pass** [păs] *noun*, 1) a high mountain road **2)** a paper allowing you to go somewhere or have something 3) a forward gesture, *verb*, 4) to give something to someone else 5) to be allowed to advance to the next level

**pas·sage** [păs′ĭj] *noun*, 1) an excerpt from a chapter, a clause or quotation 2) the act or process of passing as through time or from place to place, a journey 3) a path 4) a part of a written work or a piece of music

**pass·é** [pă-sā′] *adjective*, behind the times, old fashioned

**pas·sen·ger** [păs′ən-jər] *noun*, a traveler in a vehicle such as a car, boat, bus, etc.

**pas·sion** [păsh′ən] *noun*, a strong feeling or desire, enthusiasm

**pas·sion·ate** [păsh′ə-nĭt] *adjective*, ardent in feeling or desire

**pas·sive** [păs′ĭv] *adjective*, to be unresponsive, not active

**pass·port** [păs′pôrt′] *noun*, an official permission issued to a person allowing travel out of the country and return, a document of identification

**past** [păst] *adjective*, 1) referring to time and events in history, *noun*, *no plural*, 2) time gone by, *preposition*, 3) to or on the further side of 4) beyond in time

**pas·ta** [päs′tə] *noun*, noodles made from flour, water, salt, and eggs

**paste** [pāst] *noun*, 1) a sticky substance that glues things together, *verb*, 2) to put in place, for example with an adhesive

**pas-tel** [păˈstĕlʹ] *noun*, a sketch or drawing of a soft color or hue

**pas-teur-ize** [păsʹchə-rīzʹ] *verb*, to subject fluids to a high temperature (131 degrees Celsius, 158 degrees Fahrenheit) to prevent the growth of bacteria

**pas-time** [păsʹtīmʹ] *noun*, something that you do to amuse yourself or to relax, like a hobby

**pas-tor** [păsʹtər] *noun*, a reverend, the clergyman of a church

**pas-to-ral** [păsʹtər-əl] *adjective*, rural, in the country, rustic

**pas-try** [pāʹstrē] *noun*, sweet baked foods, such as cakes or pies

**pas-ture** [păsʹchər] *noun*, grassland for grazing livestock

**pat** [păt] *noun*, 1) a light touch with an open hand, a gentle tap, *verb*, 2) to touch lightly with a hand

**patch** [păch] *noun*, 1) a small piece of cloth used to mend a tear, *verb*, 2) to put a piece of material on a surface to repair a hole or strengthen a worn area

**pat-ent** [pătʹnt] *adjective*, 1) obvious, plain, *noun*, 2) the right given to an inventor by the government, to exclusively produce a product for a number of years

**pa-ter-nal** [pə-tûrʹnəl] *adjective*, fatherly, kind, devoted

**path** [păth] *noun*, a track worn by people or animals walking on it

**pa-thet-ic** [pə-thĕtʹĭk] *adjective*, causing pity or grief, full of pathos and sympathy

**pa-thol-o-gy** [pă-thŏlʹə-jē] *noun*, the science of treating disease, their natural causes, results, etc.

**pa-thos** [pāʹthŏsʹ] *noun*, human or animal experience that cause feelings of pity, compassion

**pa-tience** [pāʹshəns] *noun*, *no plural*, the act of waiting calmly for someone or something

**pa-tient** [pāʹshənt] *adjective*, 1) able to bear quietly or wait for something calmly, *noun*, 2) a person under medical treatment

**pat-i-o** [pătʹē-ōʹ] *noun*, a paved outdoor space that is used for eating, cooking or relaxing

**pa-tri-arch** [pāʹtrē-ärkʹ] *noun*, 1) father and ruler of a family or tribe 2) a venerable old man

**pa-tri-ot** [pāʹtrē-ət] *noun*, one who loves and defends his country

**pa-tri-ot-ic** [pāʹtrē-ŏtʹĭk] *adjective*, public-spirited, flag-waving

**pa-tri-ot-ism** [pāʹtrē-ə-tĭzʹəm] *adjective*, love of one's country

**pa-trol** [pə-trōlʹ] *noun*, 1) a small group of soldiers or police officers, *verb*, 2) to follow a route regularly looking for criminal activity

**pa-tron** [pāʹtrən] *noun*, 1) someone who provides financial support to a cause 2) a customer

**pa-tron-ize** [pāʹtrə-nīzʹ] *verb*, 1) to act as a supporter 2) to treat with condescension, to look down on

**pat-tern** [pătʹərn] *noun*, 1) anything used as a guide or model for making things 2) a repeated sequence 3) to make by following a prototype or model

**pau-per** [pô′pər] *noun*, destitute, a very poor person, a beggar

**pause** [pôz] *noun*, 1) a break in action of speech, *verb*, 2) to stop briefly, to delay action or speech

**pave** [pāv] *verb*, 1) to cover the surface with asphalt bricks or cement 2) to prepare the way

**pave-ment** [pāv′mənt] *noun*, highway surface, asphalt

**paw** [pô] *noun*, the foot of a four-legged animal that has claws

**pawn** [pôn] *noun*, 1) a victim 2) a chess piece, *verb*, 3) to sell

**pay** [pā] *noun*, 1) the compensation received for work, *verb*, 2) to give someone money for goods and services

**pay-ment** [pā′mənt] *noun*, compensation, installment

**pay-roll** [pā′rōl′] *noun*, the money used to pay workers

**pea** [pē] *noun*, a seed from a pod bearing vine that can be eaten

**peace** [pēs] *noun*, 1) a period of harmony among nations when there is no war 2) a calm ordered condition,

**peach** [pēch] *noun*, *plural*, **peaches** 1) a juicy yellow-orange fruit with downy skin, from an orchard tree that has pink flowers 2) a yellowish-pink color

**pea-cock** [pē′kŏk′] *noun*, a bird with a large brightly colored tail

**peak** [pēk] *noun*, 1) the pointed top of a mountain or ridge 2) the point of greatest development

**peal** [pēl] *noun*, 1) a loud ringing of bells *verb*, 2) to resound

**pea-nut** [pē′nŭt′] *noun*, a legume that bears edible pods that taste like nuts

**pear** [pâr] *noun*, a juicy yellow, brown or green fruit from an orchard tree

**pearl** [pûrl] *noun*, a precious white substance like a bead found inside an oyster, used in jewelry

**peas-ant** [pĕz′ənt] *noun*, a person who makes a living from working the soil, especially in poorer countries

**peb-ble** [pĕb′əl] *noun*, a small stone worn by erosion

**pe-can** [pĭ-kän′] *noun*, the edible kernel nut from a hickory tree grown in the south

**peck** [pĕk] *noun*, 1) ¼ of a bushel, *verb*, 2) to cut or lift with the beak

**pec-to-ral** [pĕk′tər-əl] *adjective*, pertaining to the chest

**pe-cu-liar** [pĭ-kyōōl′yər] *adjective*, oddly different from the usual, strange, distinctive, particular

**pe-cu-ni-ar-y** [pĭ-kyōō′nē-ĕr′ē] *adjective*, pertaining to or consisting of money

**ped-a-gogue** [pĕd′ə-gŏg′] *noun*, a narrow-minded teacher

**ped-al** [pĕd′l] *noun*, 1) a lever acted on by the foot, *verb*, 2) to push with the feet when riding a bicycle in order to get the bicycle to move

**ped-dle** [pĕd′l] *verb*, to sell on the street or door to door

**ped-es-tal** [pĕd′ĭ-stəl] *noun*, a base or support for a column

**pe-des-tri-an** [pə-dĕs′trē-ən] *noun*, a person who walks

**pe-di-a-tri-cian** [pē′dē-ə-trĭsh′ən] *noun*, a doctor who is an expert in children's diseases

**ped-i-gree** [pĕd′ĭ-grē′] *noun*, a register of a line of ancestors, descent, ancestry, lineage

**peek** [pēk] *noun*, 1) a glance, *verb*, 2) to look at, to catch sight of

**peel** [pēl] *noun*, *no plural*, 1) the outside covering of a fruit or vegetable, *verb*, 2) to cut the outside covering off of a fruit or vegetable to eat the food inside

**peer** [pîr] *noun*, 1) someone your own age or someone with similar interests, an equal, *verb*, 2) to take a closer look

**peg** [pĕg] *noun*, a wooden or metal object used as a hook when put on a wall or as a fastening

**pe-jo-ra-tive** [pĭ-jôr′ə-tĭv] *adjective*, a deteriorating effect on the meaning of a word

**pel-i-can** [pĕl′ĭ-kän′] *noun*, a large water bird with webbed feet and an expandable pouch in the lower beak for holding fish

**pelt** [pĕlt] *noun*, 1) the furry skin of an animal 2) to strike over and over with repeated blows

**pen** [pĕn] *noun*, 1) an instrument for writing using ink 2) an enclosure for animals

**pe-nal-ize** [pē′nə-līz′] *verb*, to scold, to punish, to chastise

**pen-al-ty** [pĕn′əl-tē] *noun*, the suffering or fine imposed as a punishment for a violation

**pen-chant** [pĕn′chənt] *noun*, a strong mental leaning or attraction, a decided taste

**pen-cil** [pĕn′səl] *noun*, a writing instrument with a gray substance in the middle that marks paper

**pend-ant** [pĕn′dənt] *noun*, a hanging ornament or piece of jewelry, like a necklace

**pend-ent** [pĕn′dənt] *adjective*, hanging or suspended

**pend-ing** [pĕn′dĭng] *adjective*, 1) about to happen, imminent, *preposition*, 2) until 3) during

**pen-du-lum** [pĕn′jə-ləm] *noun*, a weight which swings from side to side under the combined action of gravity and momentum

**pen-e-trate** [pĕn′ĭ-trāt′] *verb*, 1) to enter into, 2) to affect deeply

**pen-guin** [pĕng′gwĭn] *noun*, a large flightless sea bird of Antarctica that has flipper-like wings

**pen-in-su-la** [pə-nĭn′syə-lə] *noun*, a piece of land extending from the mainland, surrounded by water on three sides

**pen-i-ten-tia-ry** [pĕn′ĭ-tĕn′shə-rē] *noun*, a federal prison

**pen-nant** [pĕn′ənt] *noun*, a flag or banner with an insignia

**pen-ni-less** [pĕn′ē-lĭs] *adjective*, without any money, destitute

**Penn-syl-va-nia** [pĕn′səl-vān′yə] *noun*, one of the 50 United States located in the Northeast, the capital is Harrisburg. The state flower of **Pennsylvania** is the mountain laurel and the motto is "Virtue, liberty, and independence."

**pen-ny** [pĕn′ē] *noun*, a copper coin worth one cent

**pen-sion** [pĕn′shən] *noun*, an allowance of money given to someone regularly starting at retirement

**pen-sive** [pĕn′sĭv] *adjective*, a deep thinker, thoughtful with a hint of sadness, reflective

**pen-ta-gon** [pĕn′tə-gŏn′] *noun*, a shape with five equal sides

**pent-house** [pĕnt′hous′] *noun*, an apartment on the top floor of a building

**pe-on** [pē′ŏn′] *noun*, an unskilled laborer, a menial worker

**peo-ple** [pē′pəl] *noun, plural* of **person**, 1) human beings, men, women, and children 2) a nation

**pep-per** [pĕp′ər] *noun, no plural*, 1) a powder made from seeds of some plants and used to flavor food 2) the fruit of pepper plants, which can be used in cooking or eaten raw in salads

**pep-per-mint** [pĕp′ər-mĭnt′] *noun*, 1) oil from an herb used to give a taste of mint 2) a candy that tastes like mint

**per** [pûr] *preposition*, for or in each, according to

**per-ceive** [pər-sēv′] *verb*, to comprehend, to obtain knowledge through the senses

**per-cent** [pər-sĕnt′] *noun*, a number in proportion to 100

**per-cent-age** [pər-sĕn′tĭj] *adjective*, allowance or commission on a hundred

**per-cep-ti-ble** [pər-sĕp′tə-bəl] *adjective*, capable of being perceived, discernible

**per-cep-tion** [pər-sĕp′shən] *noun*, viewpoint, observation

**perch** [pûrch] *noun*, 1) a place for a bird to sit, *verb*, 2) to sit on a narrow branch or stick

**per-co-late** [pûr′kə-lāt′] *verb*, to pass or trickle through

**per-cus-sion** [pər-kŭsh′ən] *noun*, the group of musical instruments, such as a drum, whose sound is produced by striking or hitting

**per-emp-to-ry** [pə-rĕmp′tə-rē] *adjective*, closed to further discussion or action

**per-en-ni-al** [pə-rĕn′ē-əl] *adjective*, 1) lasting through the year 2) never failing

**per-fect** [pûr′fĭkt] *adjective*, 1) beyond improvement, having nothing wrong, *verb*, 2) to improve, to make better

**per-fec-tion** [pər-fĕk′shən] *noun*, the state of being without fault the highest degree of excellence

**per-fect-ly** [pûr′fĭkt-lē] *adverb*, completely, ideally, flawlessly

**per-fi-dy** [pûr′fĭd′ē] *noun*, betrayal of trust, treachery

**per-fo-rate** [pûr′fə-rāt′] *verb*, to make a small hole, to prick

**per-form** [pər-fôrm′] *verb*, 1) to act in a play or a musical event 2) to do, to carry out a task

**per-for-mance** [pər-fôr′məns] *noun*, a show or act presented before an audience

**per-form-er** [pər-fôrm′ər] *noun*, one who entertains before an audience

**per-fume** [pûr′fyōōm′] *noun, no plural*, liquid that has a sweet smell, a fragrant oil 2) a delightful odor

**per-func-to-ry** [pər-fŭngk′tə-rē] *adjective*, done merely as a duty with little interest or care

**per-haps** [pər-hăps′] *adverb*, by chance, possibly, maybe

**per-il** [pĕr′əl] *noun*, a danger, a grave risk, a hazard

**pe-rim-e-ter** [pə-rĭm′ĭ-tər] *noun*, the measurement of the distance around a two-dimensional figure

**pe-ri-od** [pĭr′ē-əd] *noun*, 1) an interval of time having a specific length or character 2) a punctuation mark used at the end of a sentence 3) a session in school

**pe-ri-od-i-cal** [pĭr′ē-ŏd′ĭ-kəl] *noun*, a publication appearing with a fixed interval between issues

**pe-riph-er-al** [pə-rĭf′ər-əl] *adjective*, having to do with, or situated on the outside

**pe-riph-er-y** [pə-rĭf′ə-rē] *noun*, the edge, usually of a round surface

**per-i-scope** [pĕr′ĭ-skōp′] *noun*, an optical instrument that allows observation of objects from a position not in a direct line of sight, used in submarines

**per-ish** [pĕr′ĭsh] *verb*, to die

**per-ish-a-ble** [pĕr′ĭ-shə-bəl] *adjective*, likely to spoil, something that rots in air, it has to be refrigerated to make it last

**per-ju-ry** [pûr′jə-rē] *noun*, false testimony under oath

**per-ma-nent** [pûr′mə-nənt] *adjective*, meant to last without changing, lasting, durable

**per-ma-nent-ly** [pûr′mə-nənt-lē] *adverb*, lasting indefinitely

**per-me-a-ble** [pûr′mē-ə-bəl] *adjective*, 1) capable of receiving fluids or transmitting magnetic effects 2) allowing liquids to pass through

**per-me-ate** [pûr′mē-āt′] *verb*, to pass through the pores of, to spread throughout, to pervade

**per-mis-sion** [pər-mĭsh′ən] *noun*, formal consent, authorization

**per-mit** [pər-mĭt′] *noun*, 1) a written notice that allows you to do something, *verb*, 2) to allow

**per-ni-cious** [pər-nĭsh′əs] *adjective*, destructive, ruinous, causing insidious harm

**per-pen-dic-u-lar** [pûr′pən-dĭk′yə-lər] *adjective*, 1) perfectly upright 2) at right angles to a horizontal plane

**per-pe-trate** [pûr′pĭ-trāt′] *verb*, to do or to perform, to carry through, to commit

**per-pet-u-al** [pər-pĕch′ōō-əl] *adjective*, never ceasing, continuing forever, endless

**per-pet-u-ate** [pər-pĕch′ōō-āt′] *verb*, to continue, indefinitely

**per-plex** [pər-plĕks′] *verb*, to embarrass, to bewilder, to cause to doubt, to puzzle, to baffle

**per-plex-i-ty** [pər-plĕk′sĭ-tē] *noun*, the quality or state of being puzzled, bewilderment

**per-se-cute** [pûr′sĭ-kyōōt′] *verb*, to bother, to oppress, to punish

**per-se-cu-tion** [pûr′sĭ-kyōō′shən] *noun*, the act of persistently injuring, harassing or annoying

**per-se-ver-ance** [pûr′sə-vîr′əns] *noun*, the will to keep working until the job is done, persistence

**per-se-vere** [pûr′sə-vîr′] *verb*, to work to accomplish a goal despite difficulty

**per-sist** [pər-sĭst′] *verb*, to keep doing something, to persevere, to keep trying

**per-sist-ence** [pər-sĭs′təns] *noun*, the act of continuing to do something, not giving up

**per-son** [pûr′sən] *noun*, **people**, *plural*, , a human being, such as a man, woman or child, an unnamed individual

**per-son-a-ble** [pûr′sə-nə-bəl] *adjective*, good-natured, agreeable, charming, attractive

**per-son-al** [pûr′sə-nəl] *adjective*, of or concerning a particular person, concerning a person's private life, confidential

**per-son-al-i-ty** [pûr′sə-năl′ĭ-tē] *noun*, distinctive personal character, individuality

**per-son-al-ly** [pûr′sə-nə-lē] *adverb*, 1) from one's own viewpoint 2) in person

**per-son-i-fi-ca-tion** [pər-sŏn′ə-fĭ-kā′shən] *noun*, 1) to think of or represent as a person 2) an embodiment or example of someone

**per-son-nel** [pûr′sə-nĕl′] *noun*, the staff of an organization

**per-spec-tive** [pər-spĕk′tĭv] *noun*, as one sees it, a point of view

**per-spi-ra-tion** [pûr′spə-rā′shən] *noun*, sweat, a salty water fluid secreted from the sweat glands

**per-spire** [pər-spīr′] *verb*, to sweat

**per-suade** [pər-swād′] *verb*, to influence or gain over by argument or advice

**per-sua-sive** [pər-swā′sĭv] *adjective*, an influential argument

**pert** [pûrt] *adjective*, bold, flippant, forward, impertinent, saucy

**per-tain** [pər-tān′] *verb*, to relate, to be connected as a part

**per-ti-nent** [pûr′tn-ənt] *adjective*, belonging or relating to the subject at hand, relevant

**per-turb** [pər-tûrb′] *verb*, to trouble, or disturb, to agitate

**pe-ruse** [pə-rōōz′] *verb*, to read

**per-vade** [pər-vā′d] *verb*, to pass through, to permeate

**per-va-sive** [pər-vā′sĭv] *adjective*, to become spread throughout all parts, universal, permeating

**per-ver-sion** [pər-vûr′zhən] *noun*, turning from right to wrong

**per-vert** [pər-vûrt′] *verb*, to make contrary or obstinate remarks

**pes-ky** [pĕs′kē] *adjective*, annoying, being like a pest

**pes-si-mist** [pĕs′ə-mĭst] *noun*, one who looks on the dark side of things and expects the worst

**pes-si-mism** [pĕs′ə-mĭz′əm] *adjective*, belief that life is basically bad or evil

**pest** [pĕst] *noun*, an annoying and destructive insect or person

**pes-ti-cide** [pĕs′tĭ-sīd′] *noun*, any substance designed to kill living organisms, such as insects, plants, fungi and rodents

**pes-ti-lence** [pĕs′tə-ləns] *noun*, any deadly contagious epidemic of a disease or virus

**pet** [pĕt] *noun*, 1) an animal you look after and keep in your house, *verb*, 2) to stroke

**pet-al** [pĕt′l] *noun*, one of the parts of the corolla of a flower that are usually colorful

**pe-tite** [pə-tēt′] *adjective*, small, little, a woman or girl of small size

**pe-ti-tion** [pə-tĭsh′ən] *noun*, 1) a formal request accompanied by signatures as an endorsement, *verb*, 2) to request change by making a written formal request

**pet-ri-fy** [pĕt′rə-fī′] *verb*, to turn to stone, to harden, to deaden

**pet-ro-le-um** [pə-trō′lē-əm] *noun*, mineral oil, a dark brown or green inflammable liquid

**pet-ty** [pĕt′ē] *adjective*, a small matter of little importance, insignificant, trivial

**pew** [pyōō] *noun*, one of a number of fixed benches, like a seat, with backs in a church

**pew-ter** [pyōō′tər] *noun*, an alloy consisting mainly of tin and other metals

**phan-tom** [făn′təm] *noun*, an apparition, a ghost, a vision

**phar-ma-cy** [fär′mə-sē] *noun*, a place where medicines are dispensed, a drug store

**phase** [fāz] *noun*, a stage in a process of development

**pheas-ant** [fĕz′ənt] *noun*, a game bird with long tail feathers that lives in the woods

**phe-nom-e-non** [fĭ-nŏm′ə-nŏn′] *noun*, *plural*, **phenomena**, a marvel, an event, a happening

**phil-an-throp-ic** [fĭl′ən-thrŏp′ĭk] *adjective*, love for mankind, benevolent, generous

**phi-lol-o-gist** [fĭ-lŏl′ə-jĭst] *noun*, the study of languages, their structure and origin

**phi-los-o-pher** [fĭ-lŏs′ə-fər] *noun*, a wise person, a reflective thinker, a sage

**phi-los-o-phy** [fĭ-lŏs′ə-fē] *noun*, the study of moral and mental sciences, metaphysics

**pho-bi-a** [fō′bē-ə] *noun*, dislike, an irrational fear of something

**phone** [fōn] *noun*, the short term for telephone

**pho-net-ic** [fə-nĕt′ĭk] *adjective*, the sound of letters in a word that create speech

**pho-no-graph** [fō′nə-grăf′] *noun*, a record player

**phos-pho-res-cence** [fŏs′fə-rĕs′əns] *noun*, any bright and luminous radiating light

**phos-pho-rus** [fŏs′fər-əs] *noun*, a nonmetallic element used in matches

**pho-to-graph** [fō′tə-grăf′] *noun*, 1) a picture produced using film and a camera, *verb*, 2) to take a picture with a camera

**pho-to-graph-ic** [fō′tə-grăf′ĭk] *adjective*, the process of photography

**pho-to-syn-the-sis** [fō′tō-sĭn′thĭ-sĭs] *verb*, the process by which chlorophyll-containing cells in green plants use light as an energy source to synthesize carbohydrates from carbon dioxide and water

**phrase** [frāz] *noun*, 1) a part of a sentence 2) an expression, a saying, *verb*, 3) to express in words or a particular way

**phys-i-cal** [fĭz′ĭ-kəl] *adjective*, of or pertaining to nature or the human body

**phy-si-cian** [fĭ-zĭsh′ən] *noun*, a doctor of medicine

**phys-ics** [fĭz′ĭks] *noun*, the science that deals with matter and energy such as light, motion, sound, heat, electricity, or force, and the laws that govern them

**phys-i-ol-o-gy** [fĭz′ē-ŏl′ə-jē] *noun*, that part of biology which studies living organisms

**phy-sique** [fĭ-zēk′] *noun*, the development and bodily structure or appearance of a person, the frame, figure

**pi-an-ist** [pē-ăn′ĭst] *noun*, a skilled performer on the piano

**pi-a-no** [pē-ăn′ō] *noun*, a musical instrument played by hitting its keys on a keyboard with fingers, which hit felt-covered hammers which strike metal strings

**pick** [pĭk] *noun*, 1) a choice or selection 2) a tool used to break the earth, *verb*, 3) to choose 4) to hold with your fingers

**pick-et** [pĭk′ĭt] *noun*, 1) a stake, a peg, *verb*, 2) to strike, to boycott

**pick-le** [pĭk′əl] *noun*, 1) any food which has been preserved in brine or in vinegar 2) an awkward situation

**pic-nic** [pĭk′nĭk] *noun*, a pleasure trip with a meal eaten in the open air

**pic-to-graph** [pĭk′tə-grăf′] *noun*, a rudimentary diagram or symbol used to represent an idea as the primitive writing of stone tablets and cave drawings

**pic-ture** [pĭk′chər] *noun*, 1) visual representation such as a drawing, painting, photograph, etc., *verb*, 2) to imagine in your mind, to visualize

**pic-tur-esque** [pĭk′chə-rĕsk′] *adjective*, forming a pleasing picture, graphic, quaint

**pie** [pī] *noun*, a dish made with fruit, meat or vegetables, surrounded by a pastry crust on the bottom and sometimes on top

**piece** [pēs] *noun*, 1) a fragment or part separated from the whole, *verb*, 2) to put together, to repair

**pier** [pîr] *noun*, a wharf or dock extending into the water from the land used as a place to moor ships

**pierce** [pîrs] *verb*, 1) to pass or break through 2) to make a hole through

**pierc-ing** [pîrsĭng] *adjective*, very loud and shrill

**pig** [pĭg] *noun*, any swine raised for pork and bacon

**pi-geon** [pĭj′ən] *noun*, a plump bird with a small head

**pig-ment** [pĭg′mənt] *noun*, the color of something, a hue

**pile** [pīl] *noun*, 1) a heap of things laying one on another 2) the nap of a fabric 3) a post in a pier that goes into the soil beneath the water, *verb*, 4) to amass, to gather together in a heap, to accumulate, to stack

**pil-grim** [pĭl′grəm] *noun*, a person who journeys to pray at a holy place as an act of religious devotion

**pil-grim-age** [pĭl′grə-mĭj] *noun*, a journey to a holy place

**pill** [pĭl] *noun*, a small tablet or capsule of medicine that can be easily swallowed

**pil-lage** [pĭl'ĭj] *verb*, to strip of money, ransack, rob, destroy

**pil-lar** [pĭl'ər] *noun*, 1) a strong post 2) a column, a vertical support or structure

**pil-low** [pĭl'ō] *noun*, a cloth case filled with feathers or other soft material put under the head during sleep

**pil-low-case** [pĭl'ō-kās'] *noun*, the cloth bag put over a pillow to keep it clean

**pi-lot** [pī'lət] *noun*, someone who is qualified to guide or navigate a ship or a plane

**pin** [pĭn] *noun*, 1) a slender piece of metal or wood, sharp on one end round on the other, used to join and fasten things together, *verb*, 2) to fasten with a sharp instrument 3) to hold in a spot

**pin-cers** [pĭn'sərz] *noun*, an instrument or an appendage having two grasping jaws working on a pivot

**pinch** [pĭnch] *noun*, 1) a very small amount, *verb*, 2) to squeeze between the finger and thumb 3) to make something feel tight

**pine** [pīn] *noun*, 1) an evergreen tree with leaves that look like needles, *verb*, 2) to want something very badly

**pine-ap-ple** [pīn'ăp'əl] *noun*, 1) the fruit of a tropical plant, resembling the shape of a pinecone 2) a symbol of hospitality

**pin-ion** [pĭn'yən] *noun*, a cogwheel with a small number of teeth, designed to interlock its gear with a larger wheel

**pink** [pĭngk] *adjective*, 1) a pastel color of red and white *noun*, 2) the color made by mixing red and white

**pin-na-cle** [pĭn'ə-kəl] *noun*, 1) a small turret above the rest of the building 2) a lofty peak

**pint** [pīnt] *noun*, a liquid measurement equal to 2 cups or 16 fluid ounces

**pi-o-neer** [pī'ə-nîr'] *noun*, one of the first to explore an area or field of study, an innovator

**pi-ous** [pī'əs] *adjective*, devout

**pipe** [pīp] *noun*, 1) a tube, a cylinder used to convey liquid or gas 2) a device with a bowl at the end of a short straw used to smoke tobacco 3) a musical instrument through which air is blown, *verb*, 4) to make a high pitched sound

**pi-quant** [pē'kənt] *adjective*, 1) pleasantly tart-tasting, spicy 2) provocative

**pique** [pēk] *noun*, slight anger or resentment, wounded pride

**pi-rate** [pī'rĭt] *noun*, a person who robs ships at sea

**pis-til** [pĭs'təl] *noun*, the part of a flower that produces seeds

**pis-tol** [pĭs'təl] *noun*, a small gun like a revolver, a firearm

**pis-ton** [pĭs'tən] *noun*, a metal disk which moves up and down in a cylinder exerting pressure

**pit** [pĭt] *noun*, 1) a deep hole in the ground 2) the seed of a fruit

**pitch** [pĭch] *noun*, 1) a gummy substance used for sealing roads and caulking 2) a ball thrown or tossed 3) the tone of a voice or a sound, *verb*, 4) to put in place or set up 5) to toss or throw a ball 6) when a boat leans to an angle while traveling in the water

**pitch-er** [pĭch'ər] *noun*, 1) a container with a lip and a handle to pour liquid 2) the person who throws the ball to the batter in a baseball game

**pitch-fork** [pĭch'fôrk'] *noun*, a fork with a long handle used to lift and toss hay

**pit-fall** [pĭt'fôl'] *noun*, a trap, a snare or hazard not easily avoided, a manhole

**pith-y** [pĭth'ē] *adjective*, concise, short and to the point

**pit-i-ful** [pĭt'ĭ-fəl] *adjective*, something that causes sympathy

**pit-tance** [pĭt'ns] *noun*, a small amount, next to nothing

**pit-y** [pĭt'ē] *noun*, 1) the sadness felt when someone else is hurt or in trouble, *verb*, 2) to feel sorry for someone, to feel sympathy

**piv-ot** [pĭv'ət] *noun*, a fixed pin on which something turns

**piz-za** [pēt'sə] *noun*, a baked flat crust covered with cheese, tomato sauce, etc.

**pla-cate** [plā'kāt'] *verb*, to pacify, to satisfy, to please someone

**place** [plās] *noun*, 1) a designated area or a particular space, *verb*, 2) to put in a particular spot 3) to identify by recalling

**plac-id** [plăs'ĭd] *adjective*, calm, peaceful, tranquil, untroubled

**pla-gia-rism** [plā'jə-rĭz'əm] *noun*, the act of copying someone's work and claiming it as your own

**plague** [plāg] *noun*, 1) anything troublesome 2) an infectious disease, *verb*, 3) to annoy

**plaid** [plăd] *adjective*, a pattern on cloth with stripes of different colors that cross each other

**plain** [plān] *adjective*, 1) open to view, clear, easy to understand, 2) simple, *noun*, 3) a stretch of gently rolling land with few trees

**plain-ly** [plān'lē] *adverb*, clearly

**plain-tiff** [plān'tĭf] *noun*, one who commences a legal action or suit

**plan** [plăn] *noun*, 1) a drawing made to scale of a new building or a project 2) a scheme indicating how to accomplish something, *verb*, 3) to design, to scheme or devise

**plane** [plān] *noun*, 1) a hand tool used to smooth the surface of wood 2) the short term for airplane 3) any flat or level surface

**plan-et** [plăn'ĭt] *noun*, a large mass like the earth that revolves around the sun

**plank** [plăngk] *noun*, a long, flat, thin piece of wood

**plank-ton** [plăngk'tən] *noun*, plant and animal organisms, generally microscopic, that float and or drift in great numbers in fresh or salt water

**plant** [plănt] *noun*, 1) a living thing that is not a mineral or animal 2) a factory, a work place, *verb*, 3) to put into the ground to grow

**plan-ta-tion** [plăn-tā'shən] *noun*, a large estate or farm cultivated by workers living on it

**plaque** [plăk] *noun*, 1) a marker, a tablet with an inscription 2) tarter calcified on the teeth

**plas-ma** [plăz'mə] *noun*, the fourth state of matter, composed of broken up atoms

**plas-tic** [plăs'tĭk] *adjective*, 1) referring to any pliable petroleum based product, *noun*, 2) any of a group of substances made chemically and molded by heat to form, fibers, bottles, etc.

**plate** [plāt] *noun*, a shallow dish from which food is eaten

**pla-teau** [plă-tō'] *noun*, 1) an elevated plane 2) inactive period

**plat-form** [plăt'fôrm'] *noun*, 1) a part of a station where you get on and off trains 2) a raised stage or dais so the audience can see the speaker or performers 3) beliefs, principles

**plat-i-tude** [plăt'ĭ-tōōd'] *noun*, a commonplace statement

**pla-ton-ic** [plə-tŏn'ĭk] *adjective*, a friendly relationship

**pla-toon** [plə-tōōn'] *noun*, a military unit of troops

**plat-ter** [plăt'ər] *noun*, 1) a large serving of food 2) a large shallow plate for serving food

**plau-dits** [plô'dĭts] *noun, plural*, enthusiastic approval, applause

**plau-si-ble** [plô'zə-bəl] *adjective*, apparently right, seeming to be reasonable, credible

**play** [plā] *noun*, 1) the performance of a story on the stage, *verb*, 2) to amuse or entertain 3) to

take part in a game 4) to perform on a musical instrument

**plea** [plē] *noun*, 1) an appeal, an urgent request 2) a defense

**plead** [plēd] *verb*, 1) to ask for something that is felt to be very important, to appeal earnestly 2) to respond to a charge by a court of law

**pleas-ant** [plĕz'ənt] *adjective*, 1) agreeable, amiable, friendly 2) fair, mild, comfortable

**pleas-ant-ly** [plĕz'ənt-lē] *adverb*, agreeably, politely, kindly

**please** [plēz] *noun*, 1) a word added to a request to make it sound polite, *verb*, 2) to make someone happy 3) to wish

**pleased** [plēzd] *adjective*, glad

**plea-sur-ably** [plĕzh'ər-ə-bəl] *adverb*, capable of affording satisfaction, pleasant

**pleas-ure** [plĕzh'ər] *noun*, enjoyment or satisfaction

**pledge** [plĕj] *noun*, 1) a promise, a guarantee, *verb*, 2) to take an oath, to bind by a promise

**plen-ty** [plĕn'tē] *adjective*, enough, all that is needed

**pleth-o-ra** [plĕth'ər-ə] *noun*, a large or excessive amount of something, an abundance

**pli-ant** [plī'ənt] *adjective*, bendable

**pli-ers** [plī'ərz] *noun*, a small pincers with long jaws, used for bending metal rods or wire, or holding small objects

**plod** [plŏd] *verb*, to walk heavily, to trudge, to work steadily

**plot** [plŏt] *noun*, 1) a piece of land 2) a secret plan, usually to commit a crime 3) the story of a book, film, etc. *verb*, 4) to plan a secret activity, to conspire

**plow** [plou] *noun*, 1) a farm tool used to overturn earth for planting *verb*, 2) to turn over the soil to prepare the earth for planting 3) to move forcefully

**pluck** [plŭk] *verb*, to pull off or pull out 2) to grasp or grab

**plug** [plŭg] *noun*, 1) a stopper used to keep water from draining out of a basin 2) a device put in a wall socket to conduct electricity, *verb*, 3) to put an electric cord into a socket 4) to put a stopper into a drain hole, to fill a hole 5) to persevere

**plum** [plŭm] *noun*, a sweet juicy red fruit with a pit as a seed

**plumb-er** [plŭm'ər] *noun*, a tradesman who fits, and repairs gas and water pipes

**plumb-ing** [plŭm'ĭng] *noun*, *no plural*, all the water pipes, containers, etc. put in a building so that there can be running water and drainage

**plume** [ploom] *noun*, a large or conspicuous feather

**plum-met** [plŭm'ĭt] *verb*, to fall straight down quickly

**plump** [plŭmp] *adjective*, a little fat, rounded in form

**plunge** [plŭnj] *noun*, 1) a sudden dive or fall, *verb*, 2) to fall quickly from a great height 3) to throw oneself into

**plung-er** [plŭn'jər] *noun*, 1) a rubber suction cup on a handle, used to clear drains 2) a piston-

like part that acts with a thrusting movement in a pump

**plu-ral** [ploor'əl] *adjective*, of or involving more than one

**plus** [plŭs] *preposition*, in addition to, increased by

**ply-wood** [plī'wŏod'] *noun*, sheets of wood arranged in thin layers where the grain is in opposite directions to give it strength

**p.m.** *adjective*, post meridian, the afternoon, the period between noon and midnight

**pneu-mo-nia** [nŏo-mōn'yə] *noun*, infection of the lungs caused by bacteria or viruses

**poach** [pōch] *verb*, 1) to hunt or fish illegally 2) to cook a raw egg in boiling water

**pock-et** [pŏk'ĭt] *noun*, an envelope made by sewing a piece of cloth into clothing to hold things

**pod** [pŏd] *noun*, a long, slender part of a vine plant in which the seeds grow, like a pea or bean

**po-di-um** [pō'dē-əm] *noun*, a pedestal, a raised platform

**po-em** [pō'əm] *noun*, a composition, usually in verse, with regular rhythm and sounds that express images in powerful or beautiful language

**po-et** [pō'ĭt] *noun*, one who writes verse in a specific form

**po-et-ic** [pō-ĕt'ĭk] *adjective*, pertaining to poetry, imaginative

**po-et-ry** [pō'ĭ-trē] *noun*, *no plural*, words written in verse

**poign-ant** [poin'yənt] *adjective*, touching, piercing, sharp, keen, affecting the emotions

**point** [point] *noun*, 1) the tip of something, usually sharp 2) the purpose of a verbal illustration 3) the number of goals for a team 4) at a particular time 5) the location of an ordered pair of numbers, *verb*, 6) to indicate

**point-less** [pointlĕs] *adjective*, meaningless, senseless

**poise** [poiz] *noun*, 1) composure, self-assurance, confidence, *verb*, 2) to balance, to keep steady

**poi-son** [poi′zən] *noun*, 1) any substance dangerous to life and health, *verb*, 2) to kill with toxic chemicals 3) to ruin

**poi-son-ous** [poi′zə-nəs] *adjective*, deadly, toxic, noxious

**poke** [pōk] *verb*, to push something pointed into something, to prod

**po-lar** [pō′lər] *adjective*, 1) of or near the North or South Poles 2) at opposite ends

**pole** [pōl] *noun*, 1) a round piece of wood, metal or plastic,etc. a rod 2) one end of the earth or at the end of the axis of a sphere

**po-lice** [pə-lēs′] *noun, no plural*, 1) a department of government that maintains order and enforces the law 2) members of that department

**pol-i-cy** [pŏl′ĭ-sē] *noun*, 1) a course of action adopted by an individual or group 2) an insurance contract

**pol-ish** [pŏl′ĭsh] *noun*, 1) a substance such as oil or cleanser used to make a surface shine when rubbed with a cloth, *verb*, 3) rubbing something to make it shine or glossy

**po-lite** [pə-līt′] *adjective*, showing good manners, courteous

**po-lit-i-cal** [pə-lĭt′ĭ-kəl] *adjective*, of or pertaining to the conduct of government or politics

**pol-i-ti-cian** [pŏl′ĭ-tĭsh′ən] *noun*, a person who runs for public office

**pol-i-tics** [pŏl′ĭ-tĭks] *noun*, the conduct of government

**pol-i-ty** [pŏl′ĭ-tē] *noun*, form of government of a nation or a state

**poll** [pōl] *noun*, 1) a survey, *verb*, 2) to interview, to canvass

**pol-len** [pŏl′ən] *noun*, a fine yellow dust on the anthers of seed bearing flowers, which serves as the male agent in reproduction

**pol-li-nate** [pŏl′ə-nāt′] *verb*, to fertilize a flower so that it will reproduce itself by conveying pollen to the stigma

**pol-lute** [pə-lōot′] *verb*, to contaminate, to make dirty or unusable, to make foul

**pol-lu-tion** [pə-lōo′shən] *noun*, substances in the air, in water and on land that contaminate the earth

**pol-y-gon** [pŏl′ē-gŏn′] *noun*, a many sided plane or figure

**pomp-ous** [pŏm′pəs] *adjective*, arrogant, showing off

**pon-cho** [pŏn′chō] *noun*, a sleeveless cover for the upper body, a waterproof cloak

**pond** [pŏnd] *noun*, a small body of water, smaller than a lake

**pon-der** [pŏn′dər] *verb*, to think about something, to contemplate, to consider carefully

**po-ny** [pō′nē] *noun*, a small horse

**pool** [pōol] *noun*, 1) any amount of still liquid, a basin 2) a collection of things 3) billiards 4) to gather or combine resources for mutual benefit

**poor** [po͝or] *adjective*, 1) not having much money 2) needing kindness or help 3) not good

**pop** [pŏp] *noun*, *no plural*, 1) a sudden noise made when air is released 2) part of the popular culture of the 1960s, *verb*, 3) to make a sudden, sharp, explosive sound

**pope** [pōp] *noun*, the leader of the Roman Catholic Church

**pop-py** [pŏp′ē] *noun*, a red flower that has seeds that have a narcotic effect

**pop-u-lar** [pŏp′yə-lər] *adjective*, pleasing to people in general

**pop-u-lar-i-ty** [pŏp′yə-lăr′ĭ-tē] *noun*, *no plural*, a measurement of how happy people are with something

**pop-u-late** [pŏp′yə-lāt′] *verb*, to occupy, to reside in

**pop-u-la-tion** [pŏp′yə-lā′shən] *noun*, the count of people or organisms who live in an area

**pop-u-lous** [pŏp′yə-ləs] *adjective*, crowded with people

**por-ce-lain** [pôr′sə-lĭn] *noun*, a delicate form of china, made with a special clay

**porch** [pôrch] *noun*, a covered platform in front of a doorway

**por-cu-pine** [pôr′kyə-pīn′] *noun*, a small animal that has long spikes all over its body for protection

**pore** [pôr] *noun*, a small hole in the skin for perspiration

**pork** [pôrk] *noun*, *no plural*, the meat from a pig used as food

**po-rous** [pôr′əs] *adjective*, a rough surface, full of holes or texture

**por-ridge** [pôr′ĭj] *noun*, food made by boiling grain in water or milk until it is very soft, i.e., oatmeal

**port** [pôrt] *noun*, 1) a harbor or community where ships and boats dock 2) the left handed side of a ship when facing forward 3) a sweet red wine 4) an opening in a ship for cargo

**port-a-ble** [pôr′tə-bəl] *adjective*, easily carried by hand

**por-tal** [pôr′tl] *noun*, an entrance, a large doorway, a gate

**por-tend** [pôr-tĕnd′] *verb*, to foretell, to predict, to forecast

**por-tent** [pôr′tĕnt′] *noun*, a sign, an omen, forewarning of a threat

**por-tent-ous** [pôr-tĕn′təs] *adjective*, ominous, serious

**por-ter** [pôr′tər] *noun*, a person hired to carry luggage in a hotel or a train station or airport

**port-fo-li-o** [pôrt-fō′lē-ō′] *noun*, a portable case holding papers, prints, drawings, etc.

**por-ti-co** [pôr′tĭ-kō′] *noun*, a colonnade at the entrance of a building

**por-tion** [pôr′shən] *noun*, a part of a whole, a segment, a share

**port-ly** [pôrt′lē] *adjective*, overweight, heavy set, fat

**por-trait** [pôr′trĭt] *noun*, a painting or photograph of someone

**por-tray** [pôr-trā′] *verb*, to describe, to represent

**pose** [pōz] *noun*, 1) a stance or posture, *verb*, 2) to model, to stand 3) to ask a question

**po-si-tion** [pə-zĭsh′ən] *noun*, 1) a posture, an attitude 2) a job

**pos-i-tive** [pŏz′ĭ-tĭv] *adjective*, 1) the affirmative, the opposite of negative 2) confident attitude

**pos-sess** [pə-zĕs′] *verb*, to have as property, to own, to control

**pos-ses-sion** [pə-zĕsh′ən] *noun*, that which one owns, property

**pos-si-bil-i-ty** [pŏs′ə-bĭl′ĭ-tē] *noun*, likelihood, probability, chance

**pos-si-ble** [pŏs′ə-bəl] *adjective*, what may happen or exist

**post** [pōst] *noun*, 1) a piece of wood or metal placed in the ground as a support 2) a place where a person is stationed, a job or responsibility 3) sending mail through the post office, *verb*, 4) to make known by putting notices or flyers in public places 5) to station at a place

**post-age** [pō′stĭj] *noun*, *no plural*, the amount of money paid for something sent through the mail

**post-card** [pōst′kärd′] *noun*, a small note card with a written message sent through the mail

**post-er** [pō′stər] *noun*, a large advertisement usually hung on a wall in a public place

**pos-ter-i-ty** [pŏ-stĕr′ĭ-tē] *noun*, the future generation, descendents

**post-hu-mous** [pŏs′chə-məs] *adjective*, occurring after death

**post-pone** [pōst-pōn′] *verb*, to put off, to defer to a later time

**post-script** [pōst′skrĭpt′] *noun*, 1) a note added to a signed letter 2) an addition to a book

**pos-tu-late** [pŏs′chə-lāt′] *noun*, 1) a self-evident truth, *verb*, 2) to presume, theorize, speculate

**pos-ture** [pŏs′chər] *noun*, a stance, an unnatural attitude, position

**pot** [pŏt] *noun*, a container, usually round made for cooking

**pot-ash** [pŏt′ăsh′] *noun*, wood ashes, potassium hydrochloride

**po-tas-si-um** [pə-tăs′ē-əm] *noun*, 1) a soft, white metallic element of the alkali group, 2) Vitamin K

**po-ta-to** [pə-tā′tō] *noun*, an underground starchy vegetable

**po-tent** [pōt′nt] *adjective*, powerful, effective, mighty

**po-ten-tial** [pə-tĕn′shəl] *noun*, the capability someone has to accomplish something

**po-tion** [pō′shən] *noun*, a dose of a liquid with magical powers

**pot-pour-ri** [pō′pŏŏ-rē′] *noun*, any miscellaneous grouping

**pot-ter-y** [pŏt′ə-rē] *noun*, *no plural*, ceramic dishes and pots made of baked clay

**pouch** [pouch] *noun*, 1) a bag, purse 2) a sack on a marsupial for their young

**poul-tice** [pōl′tĭs] *noun*, a compress used to heal a bruise or sprain

**poul-try** [pōl′trē] *noun*, any domestic fowl used as food

**pounce** [pouns] *verb*, to jump on something, to seize eagerly

**pound** [pound] *noun*, 1) a form of money in Britain and some other countries 2) a measure of weight equal to 2 cups, 16 oz. 3) a place to keep stray animals *verb*, 4) to crush something by striking it over and over

**pour** [pôr] *verb*, to flow or cause to flow, as in making a stream

**pout** [pout] *verb*, to make a long face, to sulk, to mope

**pov-er-ty** [pŏv'ər-tē] *noun*, the state of being poor, destitute, or without money or resources

**pow-der** [pou'dər] *noun*, *no plural*, fine grains of matter, like dust

**pow-er** [pou'ər] *noun*, the ability to do something, strength or force

**pow-er-ful** [pou'ər-fəl] *adjective*, strong, forceful, mighty

**prac-ti-cal** [prăk'tĭ-kəl] *adjective*, 1) derived from actual use and experience, virtual 2) given to action rather than to speculation

**prac-ti-cal-ly** [prăk'tĭk-lē] *adverb*, almost, nearly

**prac-tice** [prăk'tĭs] *noun*, 1) an exercise 2) an habitual action 3) the work of a profession, *verb*, 4) to perform over and over to learn a skill 5) to do something as a principle of living 6) to work at a profession

**prag-mat-ic** [prăg-măt'ĭk] *adjective*, practical, matter of fact, using common sense

**prai-r-ie** [prâr'ē] *noun*, a meadow of grassland with no trees

**praise** [prāz] *noun*, 1) applause, approval, admiration, *verb*, 2) to say nice things about someone, to applaud, to compliment

**prance** [prăns] *verb*, to frolic, to dance about in a lively manner

**prank** [prăngk] *noun*, a playful trick, a joke, a caper

**prate** [prāt] *verb*, to speak foolishly, to boast idly

**pray** [prā] *verb*, to talk to God or a god, often asking for something or expressing gratitude

**pray-er** [prâr] *noun*, words spoken aloud or silently to God

**preach** [prēch] *verb*, to talk to people about how they should live a better life

**preach-er** [prē'chər] *noun*, a person who talks about living life according to the words of the Bible, a minister

**pre-am-ble** [prē'ăm'bəl, prē-ăm'-] *noun*, an introduction or preface

**pre-car-i-ous** [prĭ-kâr'ē-əs] *adjective*, depending on the will of another, uncertain

**pre-cau-tion** [prĭ-kô'shən] *noun*, something that is done beforehand to guard against harm, danger, mistakes, or accidents

**pre-cede** [prĭ-sēd'] *adjective*, to go before, to introduce or preface

**prec-e-dent** [prĕs'ĭ-dənt] *noun*, 1) an authoritative example 2) preceding in time or rank serving as an example

**pre-cept** [prē'sĕpt'] *noun*, a principle of conduct

**pre-cinct** [prē'sĭngkt'] *noun*, a district with certain boundaries

**pre-cious** [prĕsh'əs] *adjective*, 1) of great value, much loved by someone 2) costly, expensive

**prec-i-pice** [prĕs'ə-pĭs] *noun*, a very high and steep cliff

**pre-cip-i-tate** [prĭ-sĭp'ĭ-tāt'] *adjective*, 1) headlong, rash, *noun,* 2) a solid formed in a solvent in which it will not dissolve and settles as particles, *verb,* 3) to condense from vapor and fall to the earth's surface like snow or rain

**pre-cip-i-ta-tion** [prĭ-sĭp′ĭ-tā′shən] *noun,* water that falls as rain or snow from the atmosphere

**pre-cip-i-tious** [prĭ-sĭp′ĭ- tious] *adjective,* 1) very steep 2) hasty, done without careful thought

**pre-cise** [prĭ-sīs′] *adjective,* exact, accurate, clearly expressed

**pre-ci-sion** [prĭ-sĭzh′ən] *adjective,* accuracy, exactness

**pre-clude** [prĭ-klōōd′] *verb,* to prevent from happening, to hinder, to make impossible

**pre-co-cious** [prĭ-kō′shəs] *adjective,* showing skills at an earlier age than usual

**pre-cur-sor** [prĭ-kûr′sər] *noun,* forerunner, predecessor

**pred-a-tor** [prĕd′ə-tər, -tôr′] *noun,* an animal that eats other animals

**pred-e-ces-sor** [prĕd′ĭ-sĕs′ər] *noun,* one that comes before another in business or sequence

**pre-dic-a-ment** [prĭ-dĭk′ə-mənt] *noun,* a stressful position, dilemma, or situation

**pre-dict** [prĭ-dĭkt′] *verb,* to make a reasonable statement about what might happen, to foretell

**pre-dic-tion** [prĭ-dĭk′shən] *noun,* foretelling the future, prophecy

**pre-di-lec-tion** [prĕd′l-ĕk′shən] *noun,* an inclination toward something, preference

**pre-dom-i-nance** [prĭ-dŏm′ə-nəns] *noun,* power over someone

**pre-em-i-nent** [prē-ĕm′ə-nənt] *noun,* distinction above others, outstanding, superior

**pref-ace** [prĕf′ĭs] *noun,* an explanation to the reader at the beginning of a book

**pre-fer** [prĭ-fûr′] *verb,* to like one thing better than another

**pref-er-a-ble** [prĕf′ər-ə-bəl] *adjective,* a better choice

**pref-er-ence** [prĕf′ər-əns] *noun,* one thing that is liked more than another, inclination

**pre-fix** [prē′fĭks′] *noun,* letters added at the front of a word to alter the meaning

**preg-nant** [prĕg′nənt] *adjective,* having a child or offspring developing in the body

**pre-his-tor-ic** [prē′hĭ-stôr′ĭk] *adjective,* a time prior to recorded history

**prej-u-dice** [prĕj′ə-dĭs] *noun,* a strong feeling against something

**prel-ude** [prĕl′yōōd′] *noun,* the introduction, forerunner

**pre-ma-ture** [prē′mə-tyo͝or′] *adjective,* too early, undeveloped

**pre-mier** [prĭ-mîr′] *adjective,* a head of government in many nations, such as Russia

**pre-miere** [prĭ-mîr′] *noun,* the first public showing or display

**pre-mi-um** [prē′mē-əm] *noun,* 1) a bonus given as an inducement to purchase products 2) the amount usually paid in installments by a policy holder for coverage under a contract

**pre-mo-ni-tion** [prē'mə-nĭsh'ən]
*noun*, a dream or image in which
one sees what is to come

**prep-a-ra-tion** [prĕp'ə-rā'shən]
*noun*, the act of doing something
beforehand to get ready for
something

**pre-pare** [prĭ-pâr'] *verb*, to make
or get ready for something

**pre-pon-der-ance**
[prĭ-pŏn'dər-əns] *adjective*,
superiority of weight, influence,
overwhelming power

**prep-o-si-tion** [prĕp'ə-zĭsh'ən]
*noun*, a word used before a noun
or pronoun to indicate where or
to express connections and
relationships

**pre-pos-ter-ous** [prĭ-pŏs'tər-əs]
*adjective*, absurd, ridiculous

**pre-req-ui-site** [prē-rĕk'wĭ-zĭt]
*noun*, an essential condition,
required beforehand

**pre-rog-a-tive** [prĭ-rŏg'ə-tĭv] *noun*,
an exclusive or peculiar right or
privilege of a certain rank

**pres-age** [prĕs'ĭj] *verb*, to foretell

**pre-scribe** [prĭ-skrīb'] *verb*, to give
directions to guide someone

**pre-scrip-tion** [prĭ-skrĭp'shən]
*noun*, a written direction for
preparation of a medicine

**pres-ence** [prĕz'əns] *noun*, the act
or state of being present

**pres-ent** [prĕz'ənt] *adjective*,
1) not past or future, now  2) in
attendance, being in a certain
place *noun*, 3) the present time,
right now 4) a gift, *verb*, 5) to
show, to perform 6) to introduce
one person to another 7) to give
as a gift

**pres-en-ta-tion** [prĕz'ən-tā'shən]
*noun*, exhibition, demonstration,
display or lecture

**pre-ser-va-tion** [prē-zûr-vā'shən]
*noun*, protection from harm,
danger, or rot

**pre-serve** [prĭ-zûrv'] *noun*, 1) an
area for the protection of wildlife
and natural resources, *verb*, 2) to
keep something in its original
form, to protect

**pre-serves** [prĭ-zûrvz'] *noun*
*plural*, fruits preserved in syrup

**pre-side** [prĭ-zīd'] *verb*, to control,
to lead, to manage, to oversee

**pres-i-dent** [prĕz'ĭ-dənt] *noun*,
1) the elected leader of the
United States government 2) the
head of a university, college or
corporation

**press** [prĕs] *noun*, 1) the newspaper
business or media generated
news stories, *verb*, 2) to push on
steadily with pressure 3) trying
to get someone to do something
4) pushing something to cause
an effect 5) to iron out the
wrinkles in clothing

**pres-sure** [prĕsh'ər] *noun*, the
action of a force against an
opposing force

**pres-tige** [prĕ-stēzh'] *noun*,
influence derived from past
success or reputation

**pre-sume** [prĭ-zo͞om'] *verb*, to
assume, to conclude, to suppose

**pre-sump-tion** [prĭ-zŭmp'shən]
*noun*, an assumption

**pre-sup-pose** [prē'sə-pōz'] *verb*, to
assume, to consider beforehand

**pre-tend** [prĭ-tĕnd'] *verb*, to fake,
to make believe, to imitate

**pre-tense** [prē'těns'] *noun*, the act of pretending to be or have something you are not

**pre-ten-sion** [prĭ-těn'shən] *adjective*, when one assumes an air of superiority

**pre-text** [prē'tĕkst'] *noun*, a false reason to justify an action

**pret-ty** [prĭt'ē] *adjective*, 1) attractive, pleasing to the eye, *adverb*, 2) close to, quite, fairly

**pre-vail** [prĭ-vāl'] *verb*, to command, to control, to win

**prev-a-lent** [prĕv'ə-lənt] *adjective*, widespread, generally accepted

**pre-vent** [prĭ-věnt'] *verb*, to keep something from happening

**pre-ven-tion** [prĭ-věn'shən] *noun*, that which hinders or obstructs

**pre-view** [prē'vyoo'] *noun*, 1) a look at something before it is reproduced, *verb*, 2) to see in advance

**pre-vi-ous** [prē'vē-əs] *adjective*, existing or occurring earlier, prior, preceding

**pre-vi-ous-ly** [prē'vē-əs-lē] *adverb*, formerly, at one time, before

**prey** [prā] *noun*, any animal that serves as food for another animal

**price** [prīs] *noun*, the cost of something, what you have to pay

**prick** [prĭk] *verb*, to make a small hole with something sharp

**pride** [prīd] *noun*, *no plural*, the feeling of doing your personal best, self-respect

**priest** [prēst] *noun*, a clergyman of the Catholic Church

**prim** [prĭm] *adjective*, very precise and formal, exceedingly proper

**pri-ma-ry** [prī'měr'ē] *adjective*, 1) pertaining to elementary education or schools 2) first

**prime** [prīm] *adjective*, 1) best, choice, excellent, *verb*, 2) to prepare for operation, to make ready

**prime min-is-ter** [prīm-mĭn'ĭ-stər] *noun*, the head of government in the parliamentary system

**prim-i-tive** [prĭm'ĭ-tĭv] *adjective*, characterized by the manner of an early time, crude

**prince** [prĭns] *noun*, 1) the son of a king or queen 2) the ruler of a small country or state

**prin-cess** [prĭn'sĭs] *noun*, 1) the daughter of a king or queen 2) the wife of a prince

**prin-ci-pal** [prĭn'sə-pəl] *noun*, 1) occupying the first place or rank, most important 2) the person in charge of a school

**prin-ci-ple** [prĭn'sə-pəl] *noun*, 1) a source or origin 2) a fundamental truth or doctrine

**print** [prĭnt] *noun*, 1) the size and style of lettering in a book or poster, *verb*, 2) to press words and pictures on paper or cloth by machine 3) to write

**print-er** [prĭn'tər] *noun*, a device connected to a computer to make paper copies of a document

**pri-or** [prī'ər] *adjective*, earlier, before, preceding in time

**pri-or-i-ty** [prī-ôr'ĭ-tē] *noun*, most important

**prism** [prĭz'əm] *noun*, 1) a three dimensional object with all sides equal 2) a transparent solid that refracts light

**pris-on** [prĭz'ən] *noun*, a place where criminals are kept while they are punished

**pris-on-er** [prĭz'ə-nər] *noun*, a person who is guilty of a crime and must serve a sentence of time away from society, living among other criminals

**pris-tine** [prĭs'tēn'] *adjective*,
1) part of earlier times, primitive
2) unspoiled, spotless

**pri-va-cy** [prī'və-sē] *noun*, isolation, seclusion, solitude

**pri-vate** [prī'vĭt] *adjective*,
1) confidential, personal, secret, *noun*, 2) an enlisted soldier

**pri-va-tion** [prī-vā'shən] *noun*, hardship, want, lack of comfort

**priv-i-lege** [prĭv'ə-lĭj] *noun*, a peculiar benefit, favor, or advantage of a group

**prize** [prīz] *noun*, 1) a reward for winning a contest, *verb*, 2) to cherish, to hold dear

**prob-a-bil-i-ty** [prŏb'ə-bĭl'ĭ-tē] *adjective*, the chance an event will occur, likelihood

**prob-a-ble** [prŏb'ə-bəl] *adjective*, likely to occur, plausible

**prob-a-bly** [prŏb'ə-blē] *adverb*, very likely to prove true

**pro-bate** [prō'bāt'] *noun*, proof before an officer of the county that a will is valid

**pro-ba-tion** [prō-bā'shən] *noun*, a trial period, an experiment

**probe** [prōb] *verb*, to explore with a pointed object or tool

**prob-lem** [prŏb'ləm] *noun*, 1) a dilemma, something that needs to be solved or worked out

2) a question on a test

**pro-ce-dure** [prə-sē'jər] *noun*, a manner of proceeding in any action, a process, conduct

**pro-ceed** [prō-sēd'] *verb*, to go onward or forward, to advance

**proc-ess** [prŏs'ĕs'] *noun*, 1) a method of operation 2) to change by a special treatment

**pro-ces-sion** [prə-sĕsh'ən] *noun*, people following one another as part of a ceremony

**pro-claim** [prō-klām'] *verb*, to announce officially, to declare

**proc-la-ma-tion** [prŏk'lə-mā'shən] *noun*, an announcement

**pro-cliv-i-ty** [prō-klĭv'ĭ-tē] *noun*, an inclination, a natural tendency

**pro-cras-ti-nate** [prō-krăs'tə-nāt'] *verb*, to postpone, to put off doing something, to delay

**pro-cras-ti-na-tion** [prō-krăs'tə-nā' shən] *noun*, hesitation, delaying, tarrying

**prod** [prŏd] *verb*, 1) to poke, to stir up, to jab 2) to urge, to nag

**prod-i-gal** [prŏd'ĭ-gəl] *adjective*, one who is reckless with money

**pro-di-gious** [prə-dĭj'əs] *adjective*, marvelous, enormous, huge

**prod-i-gy** [prŏd'ə-jē] *noun*, a highly gifted child, a marvel

**pro-duce** [prə-dōōs'] *noun*,
1) fruits of the harvest, *verb*, 2) to create, to bring forth, to provide 3) to present, to display, to exhibit 4) to cause, to make

**pro-duc-er** [prə-dōō'sər] *noun*, someone in charge of making a movie or film

**prod-uct** [prŏd′əkt] *noun*,
1) something that has an economic
value such as refined natural
resources or a man-made material
2) the outcome of an endeavor
3) the result of multiplying two
numbers together

**pro-duc-tion** [prə-dŭk′shən] *noun*,
1) creation, construction 2) that
which is the result of effort

**pro-fane** [prō-fān′] *adjective*, not
sacred, irreverent, secular

**pro-fan-i-ty** [prō-făn′ĭ-tē] *noun*,
cursing, swearing, expletive

**pro-fess** [prə-fĕs′] *verb*, to lay
claim to, to affirm, to declare

**pro-fes-sion** [prə-fĕsh′ən] *noun*, an
employment which needs
specialized study and training

**pro-fes-sion-al** [prə-fĕsh′ə-nəl]
*adjective*, 1) engaged in an
activity as a paid job 2) highly
competent

**pro-fes-sor** [prə-fĕs′ər] *noun*, a
teacher of the highest rank in a
university or college

**prof-fer** [prŏf′ər] *verb*, to offer, to
give, to present, to submit

**pro-fi-cient** [prə-fĭsh′ənt]
*adjective*, advanced in any
occupation or study, skillful

**pro-file** [prō′fīl′] *noun*, a drawing
or other representation of a view

**prof-it** [prŏf′ĭt] *noun*, 1) a
monetary gain, *verb*, 2) to be of
advantage, to gain, to benefit

**prof-li-gate** [prŏf′lĭ-gĭt] *adjective*,
1) wasteful 2) licentious

**pro-found** [prə-found′] *adjective*,
1) intense, intellectual 2) very
deep, endless, bottomless

**pro-fuse** [prə-fyoos′] *adjective*,
existing in large amounts

**pro-fu-sion** [prə-fyoo′zhən] *noun*,
plenty, abundance

**prog-e-ny** [prŏj′ə-nē] *noun*,
children, offspring

**prog-no-sis** [prŏg-nō′sĭs] *noun*,
foretelling the course and
termination of a disease

**prog-nos-ti-cate** [prŏg-nŏs′tĭ-kāt′]
*verb*, to predict, to plan for the
future, to foretell

**pro-gram** [prō′grăm′] *noun*, 1) a
plan of action 2) a written
outline of the order of events in a
public exercise presented as a
leaflet 3) a set of instructions
that tells a computer to do a
specific job 4) a planned
activity, verb 5) to use create a
set of instructions for a computer

**pro-gress** [prŏg′rĕs′] *noun*, *no
plural*, 1) a moving toward a
goal, development, *verb*, 2) to go
forward, 3) to advance to a
higher stage, to improve

**pro-gres-sion** [prə-grĕsh′ən] *noun*,
the act of moving forward

**pro-gres-sive** [prə-grĕs′ĭv]
*adjective*, favoring reform,
forward thinking

**pro-hib-it** [prō-hĭb′ĭt] *verb*, to
prevent, to forbid, to hinder

**pro-hi-bi-tion** [prō′ə-bĭsh′ən]
*noun*, a law forbidding the sale
of alcoholic liquors

**proj-ect** [prŏj′ĕkt′] *noun*, 1) an
activity that requires planning
and materials, *verb*, [prō-jĕkt′]
2) to cause an image to be shown
on a screen 3) to stick out, to
protrude 4) to estimate

**pro-jec-tile** [prə-jĕk′təl] *noun*, an object propelled through the air

**pro-jec-tion** [prə-jĕk′shən] *noun*, 1) a bulge, something sticking out 2) a forecast, a prediction

**pro-le-tar-i-at** [prō′lĭ-târ′ē-ĭt] *noun*, a member of the working class

**pro-lif-ic** [prə-lĭf′ĭk] *adjective*, abundantly fruitful, plentiful

**pro-logue** [prō′lôg′] *noun*, an introduction to a play or a story

**pro-long** [prə-lông′] *verb*, to lengthen, to extend

**prom-e-nade** [prŏm′ə-nād′] *noun*, 1) a walk in a public place, *verb*, 2) to walk arm in arm

**prom-i-nent** [prŏm′ə-nənt] *adjective*, important, noticeable

**prom-ise** [prŏm′ĭs] *noun*, 1) a declaration, binding one to do or not to do a specific act, *verb*, 2) to engage to do, to pledge

**prom-is-so-ry** [prŏm′ĭ-sôr′ē] *adjective*, containing or implying a promise, an informal contract such as an I.O.U. note

**pro-mote** [prə-mōt′] *verb*, to further, to encourage, to advance

**pro-mo-tion** [prə-mō′shən] *noun*, advancement in rank, improvement, support

**prompt** [prŏmpt] *adjective*, 1) without delay, without too much time passing, *verb*, 2) to cause to act, to urge

**prompt-ly** [prŏmpt′lē] *adverb*, instantly, quickly, without delay

**prone** [prōn] *adjective*, 1) inclined to, apt 2) lying face down

**prong** [prông] *noun*, a sharp projecting part, a spike

**pro-noun** [prō′noun′] *noun*, a word like **he**, **she**, **it**, **they**, used instead of using a noun again

**pro-nounce** [prə-nouns′] *verb*, 1) to assert, to declare, to proclaim 2) to speak emphasizing proper sounds and accents, to enunciate

**pro-nun-ci-a-tion** [prə-nŭn′sē-ā′shən] *noun*, the act of saying words with the proper sound and accent

**proof** [prōōf] *noun*, *no plural*, facts which prove something

**prop** [prŏp] *noun*, 1) an accessory, *verb*, 2) to support, to reinforce 3) to encourage

**prop-a-gan-da** [prŏp′ə-găn′də] *noun*, an effort to spread an idea

**prop-a-gate** [prŏp′ə-gāt′] *verb*, to multiply, to spread around

**pro-pel** [prə-pĕl′] *verb*, to impel, to cause to move or continue in motion, to push forward

**pro-pel-ler** [prə-pĕl′ər] *noun*, blades turned by a motor to move a boat or airplane through water or air

**pro-pen-si-ty** [prə-pĕn′sĭ-tē] *noun*, a natural inclination, a tendency

**prop-er** [prŏp′ər] *adjective*, fitting, appropriate, respectable

**prop-er noun** [prŏp′ər noun] *noun*, a particular person, place or thing, the first letter is capitalized

**prop-er-ly** [prŏp′ər-lē] *adverb*, correctly, rightly, absolutely

**prop-er-ty** [prŏp′ər-tē] *noun*, land, buildings, cars, boats, and other things people own

**prop-er-ty tax** [prŏp′ər-tē-tăks] *noun*, a certain amount of money

paid as a tax on the land,
buildings, cars, and boats a
person owns

**proph-e-cy** [prŏf′ĭ-sī′] *noun*, a
prediction made after receiving a
sign or a vision

**proph-e-sy** [prŏf′ĭ-sī′] *verb*, to
predict, to foretell, to foresee

**proph-et** [prŏf′ĭt] *noun*, 1) a person
who predicts what is going to
happen in the future 2) a person
who claims to be selected by
God to lead

**pro-phy-lac-tic** [prō′fə-lăk′tĭk]
*noun*, a medicine or device that
prevents disease, a preventive

**pro-por-tion** [prə-pôr′shən] *noun*,
the relation of one portion to
another in size, the ratio

**pro-pos-al** [prə-pō′zəl] *noun*, a
formal suggestion, an offer

**pro-pose** [prə-pōz′] *verb*, to offer
for consideration, to put forward

**prop-o-si-tion** [prŏp′ə-zĭsh′ən]
*noun*, a plan, a scheme

**pro-pri-e-tor** [prə-prī′ĭ-tər] *noun*,
an owner, one who has legal
right to a business

**pro-pri-e-ty** [prə-prī′ĭ-tē] *noun*,
established standards of proper
behavior, appropriateness

**pro-pul-sion** [prə-pŭl′shən] *noun*,
driving forward, thrust

**prose** [prōz] *noun*, ordinary
language, not poetry or verse

**pros-e-cute** [prŏs′ĭ-kyōot′] *verb*, to
enforce the law by legal process,
to seek justice for a crime

**pros-pect** [prŏs′pĕkt′] *noun*, 1) an
expectation, a possibility, odds
2) a view, an outlook, *verb*, 3) to
explore, to search

**pros-pec-tus** [prə-spĕk′təs] *noun*, a
summary of a plan, an outline

**pros-per** [prŏs′pər] *verb*, to do
well, to become rich, to succeed

**pros-per-i-ty** [prŏ-spĕr′ĭ-tē] *noun*,
material well-being, success

**pros-per-ous** [prŏs′pər-əs]
*adjective*, doing well, successful

**pros-the-sis** [prŏs-thē′sĭs] *noun*, an
artificial device to replace a
missing part of the body

**pros-trate** [prŏs′trāt′] *adjective*,
1) lying down *verb*, 2) to stretch
out full on the ground

**pro-tect** [prə-tĕkt′] *verb*, to guard
or defend, to keep from harm

**pro-tec-tion** [prə-tĕk′shən] *noun*,
preservation from loss, injury, or
annoyance, safe keeping

**pro-té-gé** [prō′tə-zhā′] *noun*, one
under the care and protection of
another, often learning a craft
under the guidance of a more
experienced person

**pro-tein** [prō′tēn′] *noun*, a nutrient
found in amino acids essential to
the growth and repair of animal
tissue found in eggs, meat, etc.

**pro-test** [prə-tĕst′] *noun*, 1) a
complaint or formal
disagreement, *verb*, 2) to
disagree strongly, to object

**Prot-es-tant** [prŏt′ĭ-stənt] *noun*,
*adjective*, a person belonging to
any of the Christian churches
resulting from the Reformation
under the leadership of Calvin,
Wesley, Luther, etc.

**pro-to-col** [prō′tə-kôl′] *noun*,
decorum, formalities, proper
manners, a set of rules

**pro-ton** [prō'tŏn'] *noun*, a particle
of matter, a part of an atom

**pro-to-type** [prō'tə-tīp'] *noun*,
original work used as a model by
others, an example

**pro-trac-tor** [prō-trăk'tər-] *noun*, a
device for measuring angles on a
plane or on paper

**pro-trude** [prō-trōōd'] *verb*, to
stick out, to cause to jut out

**proud** [proud] *adjective*,
a feeling of satisfaction over
something one owns, is, or does

**proud-ly** [proud'lē] *adverb*, feeling
a sense of accomplishment after
doing your personal best

**prove** [prōōv] *verb*, 1) to show that
something is true with evidence
and tests 2) to turn out

**prov-e-nance** [prŏv'ə-nəns] *noun*,
place or source of origin

**pro-verb** [prŏv'ûrb'] *noun*, a short
saying that speaks the truth

**pro-vide** [prə-vīd'] *verb*, 1) to look
out for in advance 2) to furnish

**prov-i-dence** [prŏv'ĭ-dəns] *noun*,
divine direction, foresight

**prov-ince** [prŏv'ĭns] *noun*, part of a
country, with its own
government

**pro-vin-cial** [prə-vĭn'shəl]
*adjective*, limited to a small
area, parochial

**pro-vi-sion** [prə-vĭzh'ən] *noun*,
requirement, a formal stipulation

**pro-voke** [prə-vōk'] *verb*, 1) to
make someone angry, to annoy,
2) to incite to action

**prowl** [proul] *verb*, to sneak, to
rove about stealthily

**prox-im-i-ty** [prŏk-sĭm'ĭ-tē] *noun*,
nearness, neighborhood, vicinity

**prox-y** [prŏk'sē] *noun*, 1) a person
authorized to act for another 2) a
document giving such consent

**pru-dent** [prōōd'nt] *adjective*,
cautious, sagacious, advisory

**prune** [prōōn] *noun*, 1) a dried
plum, *verb*, 2) to cut off
branches of a plant

**pry** [prī] *verb*, 1) to lift off or open
by pushing with leverage 2) to
snoop, to spy, to search

**psalm** [säm] *noun*, a sacred song or
poem used to praise God

**pseu-do-nym** [sōōd'n-ĭm'] *noun*, a
fictitious name, a pen name

**psy-che** [sī'kē] *noun*, 1) the soul or
spirit 2) the mind's force

**psy-chic** [sī'k'ĭk] *adjective*, 1)
apprently sensitive to
supernatural forces 2) a person
who predicts the future

**psy-chi-a-trist** [sĭ-kī'ə-trĭst] *noun*,
a doctor who analyzes and treats
mental problems

**psy-cho** [sī'kē'ō] *noun*, the mind or
mental processes

**psy-chol-o-gy** [sī-kŏl'ə-jē] *noun*,
the study of mental states, the
mind and its processes

**psy-cho-sis** [sī-kō'sĭs] *noun*, a
major mental disorder in which
the personality is very seriously
disorganized and one's sense of
reality is usually altered

**pto-maine** [tō'mān'] *noun*, an
alkaloid from decomposing
animals that is usually poisonous

**pub-lic** [pŭb'lĭk] *adjective*, 1) open
to everyone, *noun*, 2) the people
constituting a community

**pub-li-ca-tion** [pŭb'lĭ-kā'shən]
*noun*, published material

**pub-lic-i-ty** [pŭ-blĭs'ĭ-tē] *noun*, public notice and attention

**pub-lish** [pŭb'lĭsh] *verb*, to print and sell a manuscript

**pub-lish-er** [pŭb'lĭ-shər] *noun*, one who creates and offers for sale books, magazines, or newspapers

**pud-ding** [pŏŏd'ĭng] *noun*, a custard made of milk, sugar and eggs boiled together

**pud-dle** [pŭd'l] *noun*, a small pool of water on the ground

**puff** [pŭf] *noun*, 1) a quick burst of air, smoke, etc. *verb*, 2) to make short quick breaths of air

**pu-is-sant** [pwĭs'ənt] *adjective*, powerful, strong, potent

**pul-chri-tude** [pŭl'krĭ-tōōd'] *noun*, beauty, loveliness, charm

**pull** [pŏŏl] *noun*, 1) a force, a power, strength, *verb*, 2) to move something toward oneself through grasping and drawing with force 3) to put on

**pul-ley** [pŏŏl'ē] *noun*, a wheel used to transmit power by means of a band, rope, or chain

**pul-mo-nar-y** [pŏŏl'mə-nĕr'ē] *adjective*, affecting the lungs

**pulp** [pŭlp] *noun*, 1) a soft, moist, sticky mass of fibers made up of wood, straw, etc. and used to make paper and paperboard 2) the soft moist part of fruit that is left after the seeds and peels are removed

**pul-pit** [pŏŏl'pĭt] *noun*, an elevated desk or platform in a church for a preacher or orator

**pul-sate** [pŭl'sāt'] *verb*, to throb

**pulse** [pŭls] *noun*, a heart beat

**pul-ver-ize** [pŭl'və-rīz'] *verb*, to reduce to a fine powder or dust

**pum-mel** [pŭm'əl] *verb*, to beat

**pump** [pŭmp] *noun*, 1) a machine for making liquid or gas move by putting air into something or to extract water or other liquid from the ground using a special lever, *verb*, 2) to draw up using up and down action

**pump-kin** [pŭmp'kĭn] *noun*, a large orange gourd-like fruit, used in cooking

**punch** [pŭnch] *noun*, 1) a hit aimed squarely with a fist 2) a fruit drink, *verb*, 3) to hit someone very hard with a fist

**punc-tu-al** [pŭngk'chōō-əl] *adjective*, on time

**punc-tu-al-i-ty** [pŭngk'chōō-ăl'ĭ-tē] *adverb*, being prompt, making a point of being on time

**punc-tu-ate** [pŭngk'chōō-āt'] *verb*, to add proper signs and marks of grammar to writing

**punc-tu-a-tion** [pŭngk'chōō-ā'shən] *noun*, no plural, signs like ,, : , ? and ! used in writing so that the reader emphasizes certain ideas expressed on paper

**punc-ture** [pŭngk'chər] *noun*, 1) perforation with something pointed, *verb*, 2) to penetrate, to pierce, to make a hole

**pun-dit** [pŭn'dĭt] *noun*, a critic, a commentator, an expert

**pun-gent** [pŭn'jənt] *adjective*, powerful or strong odor or flavor

**pun-ish** [pŭn'ĭsh] *verb*, to discipline, to reprove, to correct

**pun-ish-ment** [pŭn′ĭsh-mənt] *noun*, 1) a penalty 2) rough or injurious treatment inflicted for an offense

**pu-ny** [pyōō′nē] *adjective*, insignificant, tiny, weak

**pu-pa** [pyōō′pə] *noun*, the inactive stage of development of an insect before reaching the adult, often in a cocoon or a cell

**pu-pil** [pyōō′pəl] *noun*, 1) a boy or girl being taught by a teacher 2) a black dot, the expanding and contracting opening in the iris of the eye, in the middle of the eye that receives light

**pup-pet** [pŭp′ĭt] *noun*, a small doll that looks like a person or an animal that is moved by wires or with hands on a small stage

**pup-py** [pəpē] *noun*, a young dog

**pur-chase** [pûr′chĭs] *noun*, 1) something that has been paid for, an acquisition, *verb*, 2) to acquire for a price, to buy

**pure** [pyōōr] *adjective*, without anything mixed into it, clean, unpolluted, spotless

**pur-ga-to-ry** [pûr′gə-tôr′ē] *noun*, 1) a place where a sinner makes amends 2) limbo

**purge** [pûrj] *verb*, 1) to clean by removing impurities 2) to remove all criminal charges from public record

**pu-ri-fy** [pyōōr′ə-fī′] *verb*, to make clean, to free from imperfection

**pu-ri-ty** [pyōōr′ĭ-tē] *noun*, cleanliness, pureness, innocence

**pur-loin** [pər-loin′] *verb*, to steal

**pur-ple** [pûr′pəl] *adjective*, 1) the color of violets, *noun*, 2) a color made by mixing red and blue pigments

**pur-pose** [pûr′pəs] *noun*, the reason for which something exists or has been done

**purse** [pûrs] *noun*, 1) a small hand bag to hold money and personal items 2) prize money from a race

**pur-sue** [pər-sōō′] *verb*, to follow with a view to overtake, to persecute, to capture

**pur-suit** [pər-sōōt′] *noun*, an aim, an objective, a search

**pur-vey-or** [pər-vā′ər] *noun*, someone who provides food

**push** [pŏŏsh] *noun*, 1) a shove, a rigorous effort, *verb*, 2) to press or lean against, so as to move

**put** [pŏŏt] *verb*, 1) to move, to place 2) to impose, to assign

**pu-trid** [pyōō′trĭd] *adjective*, foul, rotten, decayed, disgusting

**put-ty** [pŭt′ē] *noun*, an adhesive, glue, compound to seal something

**puz-zle** [pŭz′əl] *noun*, 1) a picture cut into many pieces to be put back together 2) a game designed to make it difficult for you to finish, *verb*, 3) to exercise one's mind  4) to perplex

**pyg-my** [pĭg′mē] *noun*, a dwarf, a very small person in Africa

**pyr-a-mid** [pĭr′ə-mĭd] *noun*, 1) a solid shape with a square base and pointed top, whose faces are triangles with a common corner 2) huge monuments in the desert of Egypt, built as burial vaults for ancient Egyptian kings

**py-ro-ma-ni-ac** [pī′rō-mā′nē-ăk′] *noun*, a person who likes to set fires and watch them burn

# Q

**quack** [kwăk] *noun*, 1) an imposter, a fake, *verb*, 2) to make noises like a duck

**quad-ri-lat-er-al** [kwŏd′rə-lăt′ər-əl] *noun*, a four-sided polygon

**quad-ru-ped** [kwŏd′rə-pĕd′] *noun*, a four-footed animal

**quad-ru-ple** [kwŏ-drōō′pəl] *verb*, to multiply by four

**quaff** [kwŏf] *verb*, to drink with enthusiasm

**quag-mire** [kwăg′mīr′] *noun*, a bog, a marsh, muddy soil

**quail** [kwāl] *noun*, 1) a game bird that lives in the woods, *verb*, 2) to cower in fear

**quaint** [kwānt] *adjective*, pleasing in an unusual way, peculiar, odd

**quake** [kwāk] *verb*, to shake, to shudder, to tremble, to quiver

**qual-i-fi-ca-tion** [kwŏl′ə-fĭ-kā′shən] *noun*, special training or knowledge

**qual-i-fy** [kwŏl′ə-fī′] *verb*, 1) to meet the set criteria 2) to make less harsh or strict

**qual-i-ty** [kwŏl′ĭ-tē] *noun*, 1) a characteristic that distinguishes one person or thing from another 2) a degree of excellence

**qualm** [kwäm] *noun*, misgiving, remorse, uneasiness

**quan-ti-ty** [kwŏn′tĭ-tē] *noun*, an amount of something

**quar-an-tine** [kwôr′ən-tēn′] *noun*, 1) separation of people with a contagious disease, *verb*, 2) to be separated from society while suffering from an infectious disease in order to prevent the disease from spreading

**quar-rel** [kwôr′əl] *noun*, 1) an angry dispute, *verb*, 2) to argue or disagree, to fight with words

**quar-ry** [kwôr′ē] *noun*, 1) a deep pit where stone is cut out of the gound to use for buildings 2) prey, an animal that is being hunted

**quart** [kwôrt] *noun*, a liquid measurement equal to 32 ounces, 1.13 liters, ¼ of a gallon, 2 pints

**quar-ter** [kwôr′tər] *noun*, 1) a coin worth 25 cents 2) one of four equal parts, one fourth

**quar-ters** [kwôr′tərz] *noun*, *plural*, a place where people live, especially if they live where they work

**quar-tet** [kwôr-tĕt′] *noun*, a group of musicians or singers, also, a piece of music for four instruments or voices

**quartz** [kwôrts] *noun*, a mineral compound of silica

**queen** [kwēn] *noun*, 1) the wife of the king 2) any woman who rules a country born to that title, a female monarch 4) any woman who is very important

**queer** [kwîr] *adjective*, odd, different in a strange way

**quell** [kwĕl] *verb*, to put down, to quiet, to suppress, to pacify

**quench** [kwĕnch] *verb*, 1) to satisfy one's thirst or appetite 2) to extinguish, to put out

**que-ry** [kwîr′ē] *noun*, 1) a question, *verb*, 2) to doubt or question, to interrogate

**quest** [kwĕst] *noun*, a search, a journey, an exploration

**ques-tion** [kwĕs′chən] *noun*, 1) an inquiry, *verb*, 2) to ask, to inquire 3) to doubt, to quiz

**ques-tion mark** [kwĕs′chən-märk] *noun*, the sign ? used at the end of a sentence which asks a question

**ques-tion-naire** [kwĕs′chə-nâr′] *noun*, a survey submitted to obtain information, a printed set of questions

**queue** [kyōō] *noun*, a line of people waiting for something

**quib-ble** [kwĭb′əl] *verb*, to equivocate, to play with words

**quick** [kwĭk] *adjective*, very fast,

**quick-en** [kwĭk′ən] *verb*, to hurry, to rush, to hasten, to accelerate

**quick-ly** [kwĭk′lē] *adverb*, in a hurry, fast, promptly

**qui-et** [kwī′ĭt] *adjective*, 1) making little or no sound, not moving , still, *noun*, 2) silence

**qui-et-ly** [kwī′ĭt- lē] *adverb*, calmly, peacefully, silently

**quill** [kwĭl] *noun*, 1) a large feather from a bird's tail or wing 2) a sharp spine of a porcupine

**quilt** [kwĭlt] *noun*, a blanket made by sewing small pieces of fabric together in a design

**quince** [kwĭns] *noun*, a bitter fruit resembling a large yellow apple

**quin-tes-sence** [kwĭn-tĕs′əns] *noun*, the purest and highest essence of something

**quip** [kwĭp] *noun*, a taunting remark, a witty remark

**quit** [kwĭt] *verb*, to give up, to surrender, to depart, to leave

**quite** [kwīt] *adverb*, completely, entirely, actually, really

**quiv-er** [kwĭv′ər] *noun*, 1) a case for holding arrows 2) a trembling, *verb*, 2) to shake a little, to tremble nervously

**quix-ot-ic** [kwĭk-sŏt′ĭk] *adjective*, romantically idealistic

**quiz** [kwĭz] *noun*, 1) a small test, *verb*, 2) to ask a few questions

**quo-rum** [kwôr′əm] *noun*, the number of members of any body legally necessary to transact business

**quo-ta** [kwō′tə] *noun*, the amount, quantity, proportion

**quo-ta-tion** [kwō-tā′shən] *noun*, 1) words spoken or written lifted from their context 2) the naming or publishing of the current prices of stocks, bonds, etc., the price named

**quote** [kwōt] *verb*, to say or write something that has been said before by another person

**quo-tient** [kwō′shənt] *noun*, the product from the division of one number by another

# R

**rab-bi** [răb′ī] *noun*, the leader or teacher of the Jewish religion

**rab-bit** [răb′ĭt] *noun*, a small furry animal with long ears and long back legs that burrows holes and lives underground

**rab-ies** [rā′bēz] *noun*, disease caused by organisms called a virus that attacks the nervous system

**rac-coon** [răk-kōōn′] *noun*, a large black and white nocturnal rodent that lives in trees

**race** [rās] *noun*, 1) a competitive event, a contest 2) a part of humanity, an ethnic background, *verb*, 3) to run in a dash or compete in a contest

**ra-cial** [rā′shəl] *adjective*, pertaining to ethnic differences

**rac-ism** [rā′sĭz′əm] *noun*, narrow-mindedness, intolerance, bigotry

**rack** [răk] *noun*, 1) a frame on which things are hung or kept, *verb*, 2) to cause pain

**rack-et** [răk′ĭt] *noun*, 1) a light bat with a netted hoop 2) a loud or confused noise

**ra-dar** [rā′där] *noun*, *no plural*, the ability to find the position of something using radio waves

**ra-di-ant** [rā′dē-ənt] *adjective*, shining, luminous, bright

**ra-di-ate** [rā′dē-āt′] *verb*, to give off energy or rays of light

**ra-di-a-tor** [rā′dē-ā′tər] *noun*, a device used to cool a liquid

**rad-i-cal** [răd′ĭ-kəl] *adjective*, unconventional, odd

**ra-di-o** [rā′dē-ō] *noun*, 1) the use of electromagnetic waves to carry messages without the use of wires, *verb*, 2) to send or transmit messages in this manner

**ra-di-o-act-ive waste** [rā′dē-ōăk′tĭvwāst] *noun,* waste left over from creating nuclear power or atomic energy which gives off radiant energy in rays

or particles by the disintegration of the atomic nuclei such as found in radium and uranium

**ra-di-um** [rā′dē-əm] *noun*, a metallic element found in minute quantities, capable of spontaneously emitting rays

**ra-di-us** [rā′dē-əs] *noun*, the distance from the center of a circle to its perimeter

**raft** [răft] *noun*, large pieces of wood joined to make a flat floating surface

**raft-er** [răf′tər] *noun*, a crossbeam

**rag** [răg] *noun*, 1) an old torn garment 2) a piece of cloth used to clean, polish or dust

**rage** [rāj] *noun*, fierce anger that continues with great force

**raid** [rād] *noun*, 1) a surprise attack, *verb*, 2) to invade, to attack, to assault

**rail** [rāl] *noun*, 1) a bar extending horizontally between two posts as in a fence or railroad ties, *verb*, 2) to scold, to rant and rave

**rail-ing** [rā′lĭng] *noun*, a fence or partition to keep people or animals from straying into places they should not go

**rail-road** [rāl′rōd′] *noun*, a road or track built with parallel steel rails and used by trains

**rain** [rān] *noun*, 1) part of a weather pattern when water droplets fall from the sky *verb*, 2) to fall as water in drops from the sky 3) to fall like rain

**rain-bow** [rān′bō′] *noun*, an arc-shaped spectrum of colors seen in the sky, caused by sunlight refracted by raindrops

**rain-coat** [rān′kōt′] *noun*, a coat that protects a person from getting wet

**rain-fall** [rān′fôl′] *noun*, the amount of water falling within a given time or area

**raise** [rāz] *noun*, 1) an increase in salary, *verb*, 2) to lift up, to elevate 3) to grow or cultivate

**rai-sin** [rā′zĭn] *noun*, a dried grape

**rake** [rāk] *noun*, 1) a long-handled tool with teeth used to gather leaves on the ground, *verb*, 2) to use a tool to gather fallen leaves or to smooth soil

**ral-ly** [răl′ē] *noun*, 1) a mass meeting, an assembly, a gathering, *verb*, 2) to restore, to recover, to renew 3) to counter attack

**ram** [răm] *noun*, a male sheep

**ram-ble** [răm′bəl] *verb*, 1) to wander in a leisurely manner 2) to chatter, to babble

**ram-i-fi-ca-tion** [răm′ə-fĭ-kā′shən] *noun*, 1) branching out, a diversion 2) a complicated outcome of a statement or plan

**ramp** [rămp] *noun*, a slanted walk or roadway that connects a lower to a higher place

**ram-page** [răm′pāj′] *noun*, a rage, violent behavior, a tantrum

**ramp-ant** [răm′pənt] *adjective*, unruly, furious, unrestrained

**ram-part** [răm′pärt′, -pərt] *noun*, a defensive mound of earth

**ran** [răn] *past tense* of **run**

**ranch** [rănch] *noun*, a rural estate where livestock are raised

**ran-cid** [răn′sĭd] *adjective*, rotten, an unpleasant smell or taste

**ran-cor** [răng′kər] *noun*, bitterness, hatred, malice, ill will

**ran-dom** [răn′dəm] *adjective*, without order or logic

**range** [rānj] *noun*, 1) a line of mountains or hills 2) an extensive variety of different things 3) the distance something can travel on its own

**rang-er** [rān′jər] *noun*, an enforcement agent assigned to patrol a certain region

**rank** [răngk] *adjective*, 1) bad smell, *noun*, 2) a class thought of as higher or lower than other groups, *verb*, 3) to classify in a group 4) to arrange in a row

**ran-kle** [răng′kəl] *verb*, to make someone annoyed and mad

**ran-sack** [răn′săk′] *verb*, to search a house thoroughly

**ran-som** [răn′səm] *noun*, the release of a person in return for payment

**rant** [rănt] *verb*, to talk wildly, to speak bombastically

**rap** [răp] *verb*, 1) to knock, to tap, to thump 2) to talk, to chat

**rap-id** [răp′ĭd] *adjective*, very fast, quick, swift, often, speedy

**rap-id-ly** [răp′ĭd-lē] *adverb*, quickly, hurriedly, swiftly

**rap-ids** [răp′ĭdz] *noun*, *plural*, a place in the river where the river descends creating swift currents producing white water

**rap-ture** [răp′chər] *noun*, joy, delight, bliss, exhilaration

**rare** [râr] *adjective*, unusual, uncommon, hard to come by

**rare-ly** [râr'lē] *adverb*, once in a great while, very seldom

**ras-cal** [răs'kəl] *noun*, a deceitful person, a mischievous child

**rash** [răsh] *adjective*, 1) acting quickly without thinking about the results, reckless, *noun*, 2) a patch of red spots on the skin, indicating an allergy

**rasp-ber-ry** [răz'bĕr'ē] *noun*, a red or purple berry that grows on a bush

**rat** [răt] *noun*, 1) a small rodent, larger than a mouse, that lives on grain 2) an informer

**rate** [rāt] *noun*, 1) a relative amount 2) the speed of something, *verb*, 3) to evaluate, to rank, to grade, to consider

**rath-er** [răth'ər, rä'thər] *adjective*, preferable, instead, somewhat

**rat-i-fy** [răt'ə-fī'] *verb*, to approve formally, to endorse, to confirm

**ra-tio** [rā'shē-ō'] *noun*, the relation between quantity, degree or rate between one thing and another

**rati-oci-na-tion**
[răsh'ē-ŏs'ə-nā'shən] *noun*, reasoning logically, the process of exact thinking

**ra-tion** [răsh'ən, rā'shən] *noun*, 1) a fixed amount of something that is given or allowed, *verb*, 2) to limit the amount of resources to each person or group

**ra-tion-al** [răsh'ə-nəl] *adjective*, reasonable, intelligent, sensible

**ra-tion-al-i-za-tion**
[răsh'ə-nə-lĭ-zā'shən] *noun*, bringing into conformity with reason, logical thinking

**ra-tion-al-ize** [răsh'ə-nə-līz'] *verb*, to explain away, to make excuses, to justify

**rat-tle** [răt'l] *noun*, 1) a toy with beads inside that makes a noise when shaken, *verb*, 2) to shake, to clatter, to move noisily

**rau-cous** [rô'kəs] *adjective*, rough in sound, harsh, strident

**rav-age** [(răv'ĭj] *verb*, to plunder, to destroy or wreck, to ruin

**rave** [rāv] *verb*, to speak enthusiastically about something

**rav-en-ous** [răv'ə-nəs] *adjective*, extremely hungry

**ra-vine** [rə-vēn'] *noun*, a long, deep ditch or valley in the earth with steep sides, a gorge

**raw** [rô] *adjective*, 1) uncooked, bloody 2) something in its natural, unadulterated state 3) cold and damp

**ray** [rā] *noun*, 1) a thin beacon of light 2) part of a line that has an endpoint and goes on and on in one direction 3) a trace, hint

**ray-on** [rā'ŏn] *noun*, a fine cloth that looks like glossy silk

**raze** [rāz] *verb*, to level to the ground, to destroy completely

**ra-zor** [rā'zər] *noun*, a keen edged cutting instrument especially used for shaving

**reach** [rēch] *noun*, *no plural*, 1) the distance that can be attained 2) grasp, *verb*, 3) to stretch out to touch or take something 4) to get to a place, to arrive at

**re-act** [rē-ăkt'] *verb*, to act because of something that has happened

**re-ac-tion** [rē-ăk'shən] *noun*, a direct response

**re-ac-tion-ar-y** [rē-ăk'shə-něr'ē] *adjective*, someone who is against progress

**read** [rēd] *verb*, to look at words and understand them

**read-i-ly** [rĕd'ə-lē] *adverb*, easily, willingly, without hesitating

**read-i-ness** [rĕd'ē-nĭs] *adjective*, willingness, eagerness, ease

**re-ad-just** [rē'ə-jŭst'] *verb*, to adapt, to fine tune

**read-y** [rĕd'ē] *adjective*, 1) willing, able, prepared 2) at hand

**re-al** [rē'əl, rēl] *adjective*, factual, actually existing, true

**re-al-ism** [rē'ə-lĭz'əm] *noun*, a philosophy that regards external objects as the most fundamentally real things, and perceptions or ideas as secondary

**re-al-ist** [rē'ə-lĭst] *noun*, 1) someone with a practical outlook 2) an attempt to make art and literature resemble life

**re-al-i-ty** [rē-ăl'ĭ-tē] *noun*, fact, truth, real things, actuality

**re-al-i-za-tion** [rē'ə-lĭ-zā'shən] *noun*, a perception, an awareness

**re-al-ize** [rē'ə-līz'] *verb*, 1) to understand, to make real, to become aware of 2) to achieve

**re-al-ly** [rē'ə-lē] *adverb*, truly, very, genuinely, indeed

**realm** [rĕlm] *noun*, region, sphere, domain or province, kingdom

**ream** [rēm] *noun*, in the paper business, 500 sheets of paper

**reap** [rēp] *verb*, to gather the harvest by cutting

**rear** [rîr] *adjective*, 1) at the back, behind, *noun*, 2) the back part, *verb*, 3) to raise children or livestock until they grow up

**rea-son** [rē'zən] *noun*, 1) the answer or explanation given as part of a belief 2) a cause for acting, thinking, or feeling a special way, *verb*, 3)) to think things through to present an opinion, to conclude, to infer

**rea-son-a-ble** [rē'zə-nə-bəl] *adjective*, governed by reason, not excessive, logical

**rea-son-a-bly** [rē'zə-nə-blē] *adverb*, adequately, fairly, sufficiently, logically

**rea-son-ing** [rē'zə-nĭng] *noun*, the thought process, logic

**re-as-sure** [rē'ə-shŏŏr'] *verb*, to help feel safe and comfortable

**re-as-sur-ance** [rē'ə-shŏŏr'əns] *noun*, restoring confidence

**re-bate** [rē'bāt'] *noun*, a deduction offered on a purchase in the form of a refund

**re-bel** [rĕb'əl] *noun*, 1) someone who fights against the leadership of a government, *verb*, 2) to defy any authority, to revolt

**re-bel-lion** [rĭ-bĕl'yən] *noun*, a revolt, resistance, mutiny

**re-bel-lious** [rĭ-bĕl'yəs] *adjective*, someone who resists the law, defying authority

**re-bound** [rē'bound'] *verb*, 1) to bounce back, to move like a boomerang 2) to recover

**re-buff** [rĭ-bŭf′] *noun*, 1) a sharp rejection, a snub, *verb*, 2) to drive back or repel 3) to refuse bluntly, to reject, to snub

**re-build** [rē-bĭld′] *verb*, to repair, to put in working order

**re-but-tal** [rĭ-bŭt′l] *noun*, an argument introduced by the other side in a debate

**re-cal-ci-trant** [rĭ-kăl′sĭ-trənt] *adjective*, obstinately stubborn

**re-call** [rĭ-kôl′] *verb*, 1) to summon or call back, 2) to remember

**re-cant** [rĭ-kănt′] *verb*, to withdraw a previous statement

**re-ca-pit-u-late** [rē′kə-pĭch′ə-lāt′] *verb*, to repeat the principal points in a program

**re-cede** [rĭ-sēd′] *verb*, to move back, to retreat, to withdraw

**re-ceipt** [rĭ-sēt′] *noun*, a written acknowledgment that something was received

**re-ceive** [rĭ-sēv′] *verb*, to take in, to come into possession of, accept

**re-cent** [rē′sənt] *adjective*, something that happened a little while ago, prior to the present

**re-cent-ly** [rē′sənt-lē] *adverb*, a short while ago

**re-cep-ta-cle** [rĭ-sĕp′tə-kəl] *noun*, 1) a container 2) a contact device in an electrical outlet

**re-cep-tion** [rĭ-sĕp′shən] *noun*, 1) a greeting, a welcome 2) a social gathering 3) receiving television or radio wave frequencies

**re-cess** [rē′sĕs′] *noun*, 1) a short intermission 2) a space formed by indentation, a niche

**re-ces-sion** [rĭ-sĕsh′ən] *noun*, an economic slow down

characterized by high unemployment

**re-cid-i-vism** [rĭ-sĭd′ə-vĭz′əm] *noun*, habitual return to crime

**rec-i-pe** [rĕs′ə-pē′] *noun*, a list of ingredients and directions for preparing something

**re-cip-i-ent** [rĭ-sĭp′ē-ənt] *noun*, the person who accepts something

**re-cip-ro-cal** [rĭ-sĭp′rə-kəl] *adjective*, mutual, exchangeable, interacting, given in return

**re-cip-ro-cate** [rĭ-sĭp′rə-kāt′] *verb*, to return the favor for something done or given, to respond in kind

**re-cit-al** [rĭ-sīt′l] *noun*, a program of music or dance before an audience

**re-cite** [rĭ-sīt′] *verb*, to repeat from memory, to narrate in detail

**reck-less** [rĕk′lĭs] *adjective*, careless and dangerous

**reck-on** [rĕk′ən] *verb*, to come to terms with, to settle matters

**re-claim** [rĭ-klām′] *verb*, to bring back, to restore, to recover

**re-cline** [rĭ-klīn′] *verb*, to lean back

**rec-luse** [rĕk′lōōs′] *noun*, a hermit

**rec-og-ni-tion** [rĕk′əg-nĭsh′ən] *noun*, 1) acknowledgment of something done or given 2) acknowledgment of acquaintance

**rec-og-nize** [rĕk′əg-nīz′] *verb*, 1) to acknowledge formally 2) to identify as previously seen or known 3) to greet, to accept

**re-coil** [rĭ-koil′] *verb*, to retreat, or drawback, to shrink back

**rec-ol-lect** [rĕk′ə-lĕkt′] *verb*, to call to mind, to remember

**rec-ol-lec-tion** [rĕk′ə-lĕk′shən] *noun*, something remembered

**re-com-mend** [rĕk′ə-mĕnd′] *verb*, to present favorably, to urge or suggest, to advise

**re-com-men-da-tion** [rĕk′ə-mĕn-dā′shən] *noun*, a suggestion for what is most suitable

**rec-om-pense** [rĕk′əm-pĕns′] *noun*, 1) compensation, payment, *verb*, 2) to pay for service received

**rec-on-cil-able** [rĕk′ən-sī′lə-bəl, rĕk′ən-sī′-] *adjective*, capable of being restored to friendship

**re-con-cile** [rĕk′ən-sīl′] *verb*, 1) to restore to friendship 2) to settle a quarrel 3) to be resigned to accept things as they are

**rec-on-dite** [rĕk′ən-dīt′] *adjective*, hard to understand, profound, hidden from view, abstruse

**re-con-nais-sance** [rĭ-kŏn′ə-səns] *noun*, a survey of the enemy by soldiers, reconnoitering

**re-con-struct** [rē′kən-strŭkt′] *verb*, to put something together or make it again, to rebuild

**re-cord** [rĭ-kôrd′,rĕk′ərd] *noun*, 1) a written account of what happened 2) a plastic disk on which sounds are recorded, *verb*, 3) to write down something that has happened 4) to register on a disk in a permanent form

**re-cord-er** [rĭ-kôr′dər] *noun*, 1) an office worker, a secretary 2) a wooden or plastic flute played like a whistle

**re-count** [rĭ-kount′] *verb*, 1) to tell a story, to narrate 2) to count again

**re-course** [rē′kôrs′] *noun*, resorting to help when in trouble

**re-cov-er** [rĭ-kŭv′ər] *verb*, 1) to get back to a normal state, to get well, to recuperate 2) to get back what was lost or stolen

**re-cov-er-y** [rĭ-kŭv′ə-rē] *noun*, a return to good health

**rec-re-a-tion** [rĕk′rē-ā′shən] *noun*, sports or play as a form of enjoyable relaxation

**re-crim-i-na-tion** [rĭ-krĭm′ə-nā′shən] *noun*, an accusation in response to another, a countercharge

**re-cruit** [rĭ-krōōt′] *noun*, 1) a new member who agrees to join a group, *verb*, 2) to enlist, to attract new members

**rec-tan-gle** [rĕk′tăng′gəl] *noun*, a flat shape with four straight sides and four right angles, the opposite sides of which are parallel

**rec-ti-fy** [rĕk′tə-fī′] *verb*, to correct, to make better

**rec-ti-tude** [rĕk′tĭ-tōōd′] *noun*, uprightness, moral virtue

**re-cu-per-ate** [rĭ-kōō′pə-rāt′] *verb*, to recover, to restore to health

**re-cur** [rĭ-kûr′] *verb*, to return again and again as an event

**re-cur-rent** [rĭ-kûr′ənt] *adjective*, returning repeatedly or coming again to mind

**re-cy-cle** [rē-sī′kəl] *verb*, to process materials so they can be made into new products

**red** [rĕd] *adjective*, 1) crimson, cherry, ruby, *noun*, 2) one of the three primary colors: blue, yellow and red

**re-deem** [rĭ-dēm′] *verb*, 1) to recover, 2) to buy back 3) to exchange 4) to fulfill

**red-o-lent** [rĕd′l-ənt] *adjective*, 1) fragrant, a pleasant odor 2) strongly reminiscent

**re-dress** [rĭ-drĕs′] *verb*, to set right, to make amends for, to remedy

**re-duce** [rĭ-dōōs′] *verb*, to diminish, to make smaller or use less

**re-duc-tion** [rĭ-dŭk′shən] *noun*, 1) the act of making less 2) the amount by which something is diminished

**re-dun-dant** [rĭ-dŭn′dənt] *adjective*, superfluous, excessively wordy, repetitious

**reed** [rēd] *noun*, 1) a small, thin, flat piece of wood, metal, or plastic used in the mouthpiece of some musical instruments, such as the clarinet 2) a tall sturdy grass that grows in the water

**reef** [rēf] *noun*, a ridge of sand, rocks, or coral, off shore but close to the water's surface

**reek** [rēk] *verb*, to give off an odor

**reel** [rēl] *noun*, 1) a spool that turns, winding or unwinding a fishing line 2) a Scottish dance *verb*, 3) to feel happy, elated with excitement

**re-enact** [rē′ĕn-ăkt′] *verb*, to perform as if for the first time

**re-fer** [rĭ-fûr′] *verb*, 1)to recommend someone go to see someone for help 2) to use a resource for help

**ref-er-ee** [rĕf′ə-rē′] *noun*, a sports official with final authority for conducting a game

**ref-er-ence** [rĕf′ər-əns] *noun*, 1) a specific direction of the attention 2) a written statement of the qualifications of another 3) a resource such as a, dictionary, encyclopedia, thesaurus

**re-fine** [rĭ- fīnd] *verb*, to reduce to a fine, unmixed, or pure state by removing all unwanted matter

**re-fined**[rĭ-fīn′d] *adjective*, 1) in a pure state 2) having good manners and good taste

**re-fin-er-y** [rĭ-fī′nə-rē] *noun*, a factory where resources like oil or sugar are made ready for use

**re-flect** [rĭ-flĕkt′] *verb*, 1) to throw or cast back the sun's rays 2) to think, to ponder, to meditate

**re-flec-tion** [rĭ-flĕk′shən] *noun*, 1) an image bounced back from a shiny surface 2) an object seen in a mirror 3) serious thought, thinking back on something

**re-flec-tor** [rĭ-flĕk′tər] *noun*, a polished surface that reflects light, heat or sound

**re-flex** [rē′flĕks′] *adjective*, mechanical, unthinking, habitual

**re-form** [rĭ-fôrm′] *noun*, 1) a change, an improvement, *verb*, 2) to correct, to revise, to renew

**re-form-a-to-ry** [rĭ-fôr′mə-tôr′ē] *noun*, a jail or prison

**re-frac-tion** [rĭ-frăk′shən] *noun*, the bending of a ray of light

**re-frain** [rĭ-frān′] *noun*, 1) a chorus, a verse, *verb*, 2) to abstain, to keep oneself from doing something

**re-fresh** [rĭ-frĕsh′] *verb*, to revive with rest or food, to renew

# refreshment

**re-fresh-ment** [rĭ-frĕsh′mənt]
*noun*, food and drink

**re-frig-er-a-tor** [rĭ-frĭj′ə-rā′tər]
*noun*, an appliance that preserves
food in cool temperatures

**ref-uge** [rĕf′yo͞oj] *noun*, a safe
place, a place to hide

**ref-u-gee** [rĕf′yo͞o-jē′] *noun*, an
exile, someone forced to leave
his country

**re-fund** [rĭ-fŭnd′] *noun*,
1) reimbursement, repayment,
*verb*, 2) to give back, to
reimburse, to repay

**re-fur-bish** [rē-fûr′bĭsh] *verb*, to
repair and make useful

**re-fus-al** [rĭ-fyo͞o′zəl] *noun*, a
denial, a refusal

**ref-use** [rĭ-fyo͞oz′] *noun*, 1) a
general term for solid waste
materials, also called garbage or
trash, *verb*, 2) to deny, not to
allow or agree, to decline to do

**re-fute** [rĭ-fyo͞ot′] *verb*, to prove
false, to disprove, to rebut

**re-gain**[rĭ- gān*] verb,* to get back

**re-gal** [rē′gəl] *adjective*, royal,
majestic, stately, splendid

**re-gale** [rĭ-gāl′] *verb*, to entertain

**re-gard** [rĭ-gärd′] *noun, plural*,
1) respect, concern, *verb*, 2) to
think of or see 3) to relate to

**re-gard-ing** [rĭ-gär′dĭng]
*preposition*, about, concerning

**re-gard-less** [rĭ-gärd′lĭs] *adverb*,
without concern for problems or
objections, despite, although

**re-gat-ta** [rĭ-gä′tə] *noun*, a boat or
yacht race

**re-gen-er-ate** [rĭ-jĕn′ə-rāt′] *verb*, to
renew, to reconstitute

**re-gen-er-a-tion** [rĭ-jĕn′ə-rā′shən]
*noun*, a spiritual rebirth

**re-gime** [rā-zhēm′] *noun*, character
of government or of a prevailing
social system

**reg-i-men** [rĕj′ə-mən] *noun*, a
systematic plan usually to
improve health

**reg-i-ment** [rĕj′ə-mənt] *noun*, 1) an
infantry unit 2) to systematize

**re-gion** [rē′jən] *noun*, an indefinite
area, a territory, a district

**reg-is-ter** [rĕj′ĭ-stər] *noun*, 1) an
entry in a book or record, *verb*,
2) to enter one's name on the
list, catalogue, record

**reg-is-trar** [rĕj′ĭ-strär′] *noun*, a
keeper of records

**reg-is-tra-tion** [rĕj′ĭ-strā′shən]
*noun*, enrollment

**re-gret** [rĭ-grĕt′] *noun*, 1) an
apology, a feeling of remorse,
*verb*, 2) to feel sadness for doing
something wrong

**re-gret-ta-ble** [rĭ-grĕt′ə-bəl]
*adjective*, unfortunate, sad

**reg-u-lar** [rĕg′yə-lər] *adjective*,
habitual, customary, routine

**reg-u-lar-i-ty** [rĕg′yə-lăr′ĭ-tē]
*noun, no plural*, uniformity,
constancy, on a regular basis

**reg-u-late** [rĕg′yə-lāt′] *verb*, to
control or direct by a rule

**reg-u-la-tion** [rĕg′yə-lā′shən]
*noun*, a rule of conduct, a law

**re-gur-gi-tate** [rē-gûr′jĭ-tāt′] *verb*,
to spit out food that has been
swallowed, to vomit

**re-ha-bil-i-tate** [rē′hə-bĭl′ĭ-tāt′]
*verb*, to restore to proper
condition, i.e., good health

**re-hears-al** [rĭ-hûr′səl] *noun*, a practice performance

**re-hearse** [rĭ-hûrs′] *verb*, to practice in preparation for a performance, to try out

**reign** [rān] *noun*, 1) the period of time when a king or queen rules, *verb*, 2) to rule or govern

**re-im-burse** [rē′ĭm-bûrs′] *verb*, to make restoration, to repay

**rein** [rān] *noun*, 1) a strap of a bridle for governing a horse or other animal, *verb*, 2) to pull back or control, to check

**rein-deer** [rān′dîr′] *noun*, a large deer of arctic regions used to pull a cart or sled

**re-in-force** [rē′ĭn-fôrs′] *verb*, to strengthen, to stiffen, to fortify

**re-it-er-ate** [rē-ĭt′ə-rāt′] *verb*, to repeat, to say or do again

**re-ject** [rĭ-jĕkt′] *verb*, to refuse to accept or use

**re-joice** [rĭ-jois′] *verb*, to celebrate, to be joyful, to delight

**re-ju-ve-nate** [rĭ-jōō′və-nāt′] *verb*, to make more lively or youthful

**re-lapse** [rĭ-lăps′] *noun*, 1) a set back 2) to return to a former state, to regress, to revert

**re-late** [rĭ-lāt′] *verb*, to tell, to connect in thought and meaning

**re-la-tion** [rĭ-lā′shən] *noun*, 1) a member of the same family 2) an association or friendship

**re-la-tion-ship** [rĭ-lā′shən-shĭp′] *noun*, 1) the association between things, the affect one thing has on another 2) kinship

**rel-a-tive** [rĕl′ə-tĭv] *adjective*, 1) in relation to or compared to, *noun*, 2) a person connected by blood or marriage, kin

**re-lax** [rĭ-lăks′] *verb*, 1) to rest, to be at ease 2) to make less rigid

**re-lax-a-tion** [rē′lăk-sā′shən] *noun*, *no plural*, a time of rest or ease, leisure, recreation

**re-lay** [rē′lā] *verb*, 1) to send, to give out, to beam 2) to convey

**re-lease** [rĭ-lēs′] *noun*, 1) freedom from confinement, *verb*, 2) to let go, to set free, to liberate, to untie 3) to relieve

**rel-e-gate** [rĕl′ĭ-gāt′] *verb*, to banish, to consign to an inferior position, place or condition

**re-lent** [rĭ-lĕnt′] *verb*, to become less strict, to become more forgiving

**rel-e-van-cy** [rĕl′ə-vəns-ē] *noun*, reference to the case at hand

**re-li-a-ble** [rĭ-lī′ə-bəl] *adjective*, dependable, trustworthy

**re-li-ance** [rĭ-lī′əns] *adjective*, confidence, something dependent on something else

**rel-ic** [rĕl′ĭk] *noun*, that which remains or is left, anything valued as a memento

**re-lief** [rĭ-lēf′] *noun*, *no plural*, 1) assistance, aid, help 2) comfort, ease, cheer 3) the contour of the front of a building

**re-lieve** [rĭ-lēv′] *verb*, to free from worry, to alleviate, to ease

**re-lig-ion** [rĭ-lĭj′ən] *noun*, possessing beliefs concerning the nature and purpose of the universe and the supernatural

**re-li-gious** [rĭ-lĭj′əs] *adjective*, 1) possessing pious beliefs in a God or gods 2) dedicated, devout

**re-lin-quish** [rĭ-lĭng′kwĭsh] *verb*, to abandon, to leave alone

**rel-ish** [rĕl′ĭsh] *noun*, 1) a condiment made of vegetables and herbs 2) great enjoyment, *verb*, 3) to savor, to appreciate, to like, to enjoy, to delight in

**re-luc-tance** [rĭ-lŭk′təns] *noun*, unwillingness or aversion marked by hesitation

**re-luc-tant** [rĭ-lŭk′tənt] *adjective*, unwilling to participate

**re-ly** [rĭ-lī′] *verb*, to depend confidently, to trust

**re-main** [rĭ-mān′] *verb*, to stay

**re-main-der** [rĭ-mān′dər] *noun*, 1) the fraction left over after a number has been divided 2) what is left over, remnant, residue

**re-mains** [rĭ-mānz′] *noun*, *plural*, parts which are left behind exposed to air, a corpse

**re-make** [rē-māk′] *noun*, something that has been redone or given a different form

**re-mark** [rĭ-märk′] *noun*, 1) something spoken, *verb*, 2) to take notice of, to observe

**re-mark-a-ble** [rĭ-mär′kə-bəl] *adjective*, uncommon, extraordinary, unusual

**re-mark-a-bly** [rĭ-mär′kə-blē] *adverb*, notably, especially

**re-me-di-al** [rĭ-mē′dē-əl] *adjective*, intended to improve poor skills

**rem-e-dy** [rĕm′ĭ-dē] *noun*, 1) a cure 2) a solution to the problem

**re-mem-ber** [rĭ-mĕm′bər] *verb*, to keep in your mind, to not forget

**re-mem-brance** [rĭ-mĕm′brəns] *noun*, a recollection, a memory

**re-mind** [rĭ-mīnd′] *verb*, to help someone remember

**rem-i-nisce** [rĕm′ə-nĭs′] *verb*, to think back or talk about past experiences, to recollect

**rem-i-nis-cence** [rĕm′ə-nĭs′əns] *noun*, the act of recalling the past, recollection, memory

**rem-i-nis-cent** [rĕm′ə-nĭs′ənt] *adjective*, suggestive, remindful

**re-miss** [rĭ-mĭs′] *adjective*, negligent, careless, neglectful

**re-mit** [rĭ-mĭt′] *verb*, to send money usually as a payment

**re-mit-tance** [rĭ-mĭt′ns] *noun*, the sending of money, bills, etc, money transmitted

**rem-nant** [rĕm′nənt] *noun*, something left over

**re-mon-strate** [rĭ-mŏn′strāt′] *verb*, to plead in protest, to argue repeatedly in opposition

**re-morse** [rĭ-môrs′] *noun*, deep regret for wrongdoing

**re-mote** [rĭ-mōt′] *adjective*, far away, a great distance from everyone, slight, aloof

**re-mov-al** [rĭ-moo′vəl] *noun*, to take something away

**re-move** [rĭ-moov′] *verb*, to take and move somewhere else

**re-mu-ner-a-tion** [rĭ-myoo′nə-rā′shən] *noun*, compensation, reward

**ren-ais-sance** [rĕn′ĭ-säns′] *noun*, a rebirth, revival, renewal

**rend** [rĕnd] *verb*, 1) to split, to tear apart with violence 2) to disturb

**rend-er** [rĕn′dər] *verb*, to cause to become, to provide, to perform

**ren-dez-vous** [rän′dā-vōō′] *noun*, a meeting place, an appointment

**ren-di-tion** [rĕn-dĭsh′ən] *noun*, the artistic interpretation of a song or dance and how it is performed

**ren-e-gade** [rĕn′ĭ-gād′] *noun*, a person who deserts a cause to join another, an outlaw

**re-new** [rĭ-nōō′] *verb*, 1) to bring up to date 2) to start again

**re-new-al** [rĭ-nōō′əl] *noun*, a new start, recurrence, a revival

**re-nounce** [rĭ-nouns′] *verb*, to abandon, to discontinue, to disown, to repudiate

**ren-o-vate** [rĕn′ə-vāt′] *verb*, to make repairs, to redecorate

**re-nown** [rĭ-noun′] *adjective*, fame, widespread recognition

**rent** [rĕnt] *noun*, 1) money paid to use property, *verb*, 2) to pay someone to use something that they own, to lease

**re-pair** [rĭ-pâr′] *noun*, 1) the result of renewing or reconditioning something, *verb*, 2) to fix or mend, to make new again

**re-par-a-tion** [rĕp′ə-rā′shən] *noun*, compensation demanded by a victorious nation from a defeated nation, amends

**rep-ar-tee** [rĕp′ər-tē′,] *noun*, a clever reply

**re-pay** [rĭ-pā′] *verb*, to give someone money owed to them

**re-peal** [rĭ-pēl′] *noun*, 1) retraction, withdrawal, *verb*, 2) to cancel

**re-peat** [rĭ-pēt′] *verb*, to cause to happen again, to duplicate

**re-peat-ed-ly** [rĭ-pē′tĭd-lē] *adverb*, said or done again and again

**re-pel** [rĭ-pĕl′] *verb*, to drive back, to oppose, to ward off

**re-pel-lent** [rĭ-pĕl′ənt] *adjective*, offensive, disgusting, repugnant

**re-pent** [rĭ-pĕnt′] *verb*, to express regret, to feel contrite

**re-pent-ance** [rĭ-pĕn′təns] *noun*, sorrow for what one has done or omitted to do, regret

**re-per-cus-sion** [rē′pər-kŭsh′ən, rĕp′ər-] *noun*, the effect of something said or done

**rep-er-toire** [rĕp′ər-twär′] *noun*, a list of musical scores which a company or a person has thoroughly rehearsed and is prepared to perform

**rep-e-ti-tion** [rĕp′ĭ-tĭsh′ən] *noun*, doing or saying something over and over

**re-place** [rĭ-plās′] *verb*, 1) to take the place of 2) to make good

**re-place-ment** [rĭ-plās′mənt] *noun*, a person or thing that takes the place of another, a substitute

**re-plen-ish** [rĭ-plĕn′ĭsh] *verb*, to fill again, to supply anew

**re-plete** [rĭ-plēt′] *adjective*, filled to capacity, abundantly supplied

**rep-li-ca** [rĕp′lĭ-kə] *noun*, a copy

**re-ply** [rĭ-plī′] *noun*, 1) an answer, a response, *verb*, 2) to give an answer, to reply

**re-port** [rĭ-pôrt′] *noun*, 1) an oral or written account containing information in an organized form, *verb*, 2) to give an account of something

**re-port-er** [rĭ-pôr′tər] *noun*, 1) a person who reports legal proceedings or legislative debates 2) a person who gathers information and writes reports for a newspaper, magazine, etc.

**re-pose** [rǐ-pōz'] *noun*, 1) a state of calm *verb*, 2) to be in a state of rest or relaxation

**re-pos-i-to-ry** [rǐ-pŏz'ǐ-tôr'ē] *noun*, a storehouse, a vault where things are kept

**rep-re-hen-si-ble** [rĕp'rǐ-hĕn'sə-bəl] *adjective*, wicked, deceitful

**rep-re-sent** [rĕp'rǐ-zĕnt'] *verb*, 1) to portray, to stand for something 2) to act or speak for someone or something

**rep-re-sen-ta-tion** [rĕp'rǐ-zĕn-tā'shən] *noun*, something that expresses a point of view or represents something else, a portrayal

**rep-re-sen-ta-tive** [rĕp'rǐ-zĕn'tə-tǐv] *adjective*, 1) typically characteristic, *noun*, 2) one acting in the place of another

**re-press** [rǐ-prĕs'] *verb*, to check, to overpower, to keep down

**re-prieve** [rǐ-prēv'] *noun*, 1) a delay, *verb*, 2) to postpone, to delay the punishment of

**rep-ri-mand** [rĕp'rə-mănd'] *verb*, to censure, to scold

**re-pris-al** [rǐ-prī'zəl] *noun*, retaliation, an act short of war by which a nation seeks to redress a wrong committed against it by another nation

**re-proach** [rǐ-prōch'] *noun*, 1) blame, censure, *verb*, 2) to blame someone, to criticize

**re-pro-duce** [rē'prə-dōōs'] *verb*, 1) to produce offspring or create babies 2) to make a copy of something, to duplicate

**re-prove** [rǐ-prōōv'] *verb*, to reprimand someone for doing something wrong, to correct someone, to rebuke, to chide

**rep-tile** [rĕp'tǐl] *noun*, a cold-blooded, egg laying vertebrate, such as a lizard or snake

**re-pub-lic** [rǐ-pŭb'lǐk] *noun*, government in which people elect their representatives

**re-pub-li-can** [rǐ-pŭb'lǐ-kən] *noun*, a person who advocates a republican government, one who believes in government elected by representatives

**Re-pub-li-can Par-ty** *noun*, A U.S. political party that developed in the 1850s from those who opposed slavery and that elected Abraham Lincoln as the first Republican president

**re-pu-di-ate** [rǐ-pyōō'dē-āt'] *verb*, to disown, to renounce, to reject

**re-pug-nant** [rǐ-pŭg'nənt] *adjective*, disgusting, vulgar, offensive, objectionable

**re-pulse** [rǐ-pŭls'] *verb*, 1)to offend 2) to drive back, to repel

**re-pul-sion** [rǐ-pŭl'shən] *noun*, a feeling of aversion or disgust

**rep-u-ta-tion** [rĕp'yə-tā'shən] *noun*, what people generally think about a person or thing

**re-quest** [rǐ-kwĕst'] *noun*, 1) something that is asked for, *verb*, 2) to ask for something

**re-quire** [rǐ-kwīr'] *verb*, to have need of, to insist or compel

**re-quire-ment** [rǐ-kwīr'mənt] *noun*, a condition that must be met to satisfy a need, something needed, a necessity

**req-ui-site** [rĕk′wĭ-zĭt] *noun*, a demand, something required

**req-ui-si-tion** [rĕk′wĭ-zĭsh′ən] *noun*, an official written request for something

**re-quite** [rĭ-kwīt′] *verb*, to repay, to seek revenge, to get even

**re-scind** [rĭ-sĭnd′] *verb*, to cut off or remove, to cancel or abolish

**res-cue** [rĕs′kyōō] *noun*, 1) help or aid offered to save someone, *verb*, 2) to aid or save from danger or confinement

**re-search** [rĭ-sûrch′] *noun*, *no plural*, 1) a careful study conducted to learn and discover something new, *verb*, 2) to investigate or study something, to make a careful inquiry

**re-sem-blance** [rĭ-zĕm′bləns] *noun*, similarity, likeness

**re-sem-ble** [rĭ-zĕm′bəl] *verb*, to have similar qualities and likeness, to be like

**re-sent** [rĭ-zĕnt′] *verb*, to feel angry with someone because they were unfair, to feel indignant

**re-sent-ment** [rĭ-zĕnt′mənt] *noun*, exasperation, ill will, anger

**res-er-va-tion** [rĕz′ər-vā′shən] *noun*, 1) a commitment to hold a space for someone 2) hesitation, qualm 3) land the government gave Indians to live on

**re-serve** [rĭ-zûrv′] *noun*, 1) restraint, *verb*, 2) to hold something for someone

**res-er-voir** [rĕz′ər-vwär′] *noun*, 1) a place where a large supply of anything is built up over time 2) a body of water stored for use

**re-side** [rĭ-zīd′] *verb*, to live, to inhabit, to remain, to dwell in

**res-i-dence** [rĕz′ĭ-dəns] *noun*, living or dwelling in a place for some time, a home

**res-i-dent** [rĕz′ĭ-dənt] *noun*, someone who resides in a place

**res-i-den-tial** [rĕz′ĭ-dĕn′shəl] *adjective*, where people live

**re-sid-u-al** [rĭ-zĭj′ōō-əl] *adjective*, effects remaining after the principal action

**res-i-due** [rĕz′ĭ-dōō′] *noun*, the remainder of something

**re-sign** [rĭ-zīn′] *verb*, 1) to relinquish, to withdraw from an office or position 2) to calmly accept an unpleasant outcome

**res-ig-na-tion** [rĕz′ĭg-nā′shən] *noun*, *no plural*, 1) reluctant acceptance of something 2) a formal statement to leave a job

**re-signed** [rĭ-zīnd′] *adjective*, unresisting, patiently submissive

**re-sil-ient** [rĭ-zĭl′yənt] *adjective*, the ability to return to the same size and condition after excessive stress and strain

**res-in** [rĕz′ĭn] *noun*, in plastics manufacturing, the different compounds used to create the different forms of plastic

**re-sist** [rĭ-zĭst′] *verb*, to oppose, to refuse to comply, to withstand

**re-sist-ance** [rĭ-zĭs′təns] *noun*, the act of resisting or opposing, any opposing force

**res-o-lute** [rĕz′ə-lōōt′] *adjective*, determined, purposeful, earnest

**res-o-lu-tion** [rĕz′ə-lōō′shən] *noun*, a firm decision, a course of action decided on

**re-solve** [rĭ-zŏlv′] *noun*,
1) determination, conviction,
*verb*, 2) to decide to take action

**res-o-nant** [rĕz′ə-nənt] *adjective*,
echoing, , vibrant, deep in sound

**re-sort** [rĭ-zôrt′] *noun*, 1) a
luxurious place visited for rest
and relaxation, *verb*, 2) to turn to
for help or support

**re-source** [rē′sôrs′] *noun*, 1) a
source of help or supply 2) a
supply or form of wealth

**re-source-ful** [rē′sôrs′ fəl]

*adjective,* able to deal promptly
and effectively with difficulties

**re-spect** [rĭ-spĕkt′] *noun*, 1) an
aspect 2) consideration for
someone, *verb*, 3) to have a good
opinion of someone, look up to

**re-spect-a-ble** [rĭ-spĕk′tə-bəl]
*adjective*, honorable, well
thought of, worthy of respect

**re-spect-ful** [rĭ-spĕkt′fəl] *adjective*,
polite, well-mannered, civil

**re-spect-ful-ly** [rĭ-spĕkt′fə-lē]
*adverb*, in a civil manner,
courteously, politely

**re-spec-tive** [rĭ-spĕk′tĭv] *adjective*,
in relation to one another

**re-spec-tive-ly** [rĭ-spĕk′tĭv-lē]
*adverb*, for each separately in
precisely the order given

**res-pi-ra-tion** [rĕs′pə-rā′shən]
*noun*, the emission of vapor,
exhaling, breathing

**res-pite** [rĕs′pĭt] *verb*,
postponement or delay

**re-splend-ent** [rĭ-splĕn′dənt]
*adjective*, brilliant, lustrous

**re-spond** [rĭ-spŏnd′] *verb*, to
answer, to act in return

**re-spond-ent** [rĭ-spŏn′dənt] *noun*,
one who answers actions in a
civil case, the defendant

**re-sponse** [rĭ-spŏns′] *noun*, an
answer, a reaction, something
said or done in reply

**re-spon-si-bil-i-ty**
[rĭ-spŏn′sə-bĭl′ĭ-tē] *noun*, a
person or thing that one is
obligated to

**re-spon-si-ble** [rĭ-spŏn′sə-bəl]
*adjective*, 1) the willingness to
respond appropriately
2) trustworthy, reliable

**rest** [rĕst] *noun*, 1) a quiet time for
relaxation 2) those remaining or
left behind, *verb*, 3) to relax and
feel at ease 4) to lean or put
something on something else

**res-tau-rant** [rĕs′tər-ənt] *noun*, a
public eating establishment

**res-ti-tu-tion** [rĕs′tĭ-tōō′shən]
*noun*, an agreement as terms of a
settlement to pay for loss or
damage

**rest-less** [rĕst′lĭs] *adjective*, not
relaxed, eager to do something
else, uneasy, fitful, anxious

**re-store** [rĭ-stôr′] *verb*, 1) to revive
2) to bring back to a former
condition, to reinstate 3) to give
back, to return

**re-strain** [rĭ-strān′] *verb*, 1) to hold
back with force 2) to limit

**re-straint** [rĭ-strānt′] *noun*, a
means of holding back from
action, a check, a control

**re-strict** [rĭ-strĭkt′] *verb*, to
confine, to keep within limits

**re-stric-tive** [rĭ-strĭk′tĭv] *adjective*,
confining, limiting, inhibiting

**re-sult** [rĭ-zŭlt′] *noun*, 1) the product or consequence of an action, the outcome, *verb*, 2) to have been the cause of something, to end up

**re-su-me** [′rez-ə-mā] *noun*, 1) a summary of personal or work history [rĭ-zōōm′] *verb*, 2) to start again after stopping for a period of time

**res-ur-rec-tion** [rĕz′ə-rĕk′shən] *noun*, 1) the act of rising from the dead 2) renewal, revival

**re-sus-ci-tate** [rĭ-sŭs′ĭ-tāt′] *verb*, to revive, especially from apparent death, to restore to consciousness

**re-tail** [rē′tāl′] *verb*, to sell goods directly to the consumer

**re-tain** [rĭ-tān′] *verb*, 1) to keep in place or hold 2) to have

**re-tal-i-a-tion** [rĭ-tăl′ē-ā′shən] *noun*, to repay like for like, especially evil for evil

**re-tard** [rĭ-tärd′] *verb*, to delay the progress of, to hinder

**re-ten-tion** [rĭ-tĕn′shən] *noun*, 1) holding something 2) having a good memory, retaining

**ret-i-cence** [rĕt′ĭ-səns] *noun*, not revealing your thoughts or feelings openly

**ret-i-na** [rĕt′n-ə] *noun*, the light-sensitive colored circle of the eye

**re-tire** [rĭ-tīr′] *verb*, 1) to withdraw to a place of privacy 2) to go to bed 3) to remove from active service, to stop working

**re-tire-ment** [rĭ-tīr′mənt] *noun*, the period at the end of a career when a person stops working to relax and enjoy their savings

**re-tort** [rĭ-tôrt′] *verb*, a response

**re-tract** [rĭ-trăkt′] *verb*, 1) to draw back as claws or fangs 2) to disavow, to recant, to disclaim

**re-treat** [rĭ-trēt′] *noun*, 1) a place to rest and relax, a place of safety *verb*, 2) to turn around and go back, to withdraw

**re-trench** [rĭ-trĕnch′] *verb*, to cut down, to economize, to reduce

**ret-ri-bu-tion** [rĕt′rə-byōō′shən] *noun*, vengeance, compensation, punishment for offenses

**re-trieve** [rĭ-trēv′] *verb*, 1) to get and bring back 2) to recover

**ret-ro-ac-tive** [rĕt′rō-ăk′tĭv] *adjective*, that which takes effect from a time in the past

**ret-ro-grade** [rĕt′rə-grād′] *verb*, going or inclined to go backward

**ret-ro-spect** [rĕt′rə-spĕkt′] *noun*, looking back on things past

**re-turn** [rĭ-tûrn′] *noun*, 1) to go to a place and come back from it 2) the income from an investment 3) a response, in kind, *verb*, 4) to give or put something back 5) to go back to the same place 6) to reply

**re-use** [rē-yōōz′] *verb*, to use again, to recycle

**re-veal** [rĭ-vēl′] *verb*, 1) to make known, to tell, to disclose, to admit 2) to bring into view

**rev-e-la-tion** [rĕv′ə-lā′shən] *noun*, a sign from heaven, a disclosure

**rev-el-ry** [rĕv′əl-rē] *noun*, boisterous merrymaking

**re-venge** [rĭ-vĕnj′] *noun*, 1) a form of getting even, retribution, *verb*, 2) to administer punishment

**rev-e-nue** [rĕv′ə-nōō] *noun*, 1) the return from an investment 2) an item of income 3) the taxes collected by a government

**re-ver-ber-ate** [rĭ-vûr′bə-rāt′] *verb*, to echo, to resound

**re-vere** [rĭ-vîr′] *verb*, to regard with respect, to admire, to look upon with awe, to honor

**rev-er-ence** [rĕv′ər-əns] *adjective*, honor or respect given to someone because of position

**rev-er-end** [rĕv′ər-ənd] *noun*, the title of the leader of a church

**rev-er-ie** [rĕv′ə-rē] *noun*, a daydream, a musing

**re-verse** [rĭ-vûrs′] *adjective*, 1) opposite, backward, *noun*, 2) a lever that makes a machine go backward, *verb*, 3) to turn around 4) to evoke or annul

**re-vert** [rĭ-vûrt′] *verb*, to return to a former habit, practice or belief

**re-view** [rĭ-vyōō′] *noun*, 1) an examination or inspection 2) a critical essay 3) a periodical, *verb*, 4) to go over or examine critically 5) to look back upon

**re-vile** [rĭ-vīl′] *verb*, to denounce using abusive language

**re-vise** [rĭ-vīz′] *verb*, to review and make changes in order to bring up to date, to correct, to improve

**re-vi-sion** [rĭ-vĭzh′ən] *noun*, the changed version of writing, or work, or doctrine

**re-vive** [rĭ-vīv′] *verb*, to bring back to life or to regain strength

**re-volt** [rĭ-vōlt′] *noun*, 1) a planned attack on a government or its leaders, *verb*, 2) to fight as a mass of rebels against leaders

3) to offend someone by making them feel ill or disgusted

**rev-o-lu-tion** [rĕv′ə-lōō′shən] *noun*, 1) the motion of a body about a center or axis 2) the overthrow of a government or system by those who are governed, usually by force, a rebellion 3) a radical change

**rev-o-lu-tion-ar-y** [rĕv′ə-lōō′shə-nĕr′ē] *noun*, an activist who promotes change

**re-volve** [rĭ-vŏlv′] *verb*, 1) to orbit the way the Earth moves slowly around the sun 2) to rotate 3) to recur in cycles

**re-volv-er** [rĭ-vŏl′vər] *noun*, a firearm with a cylinder of several chambers to be discharged repeatedly

**re-vul-sion** [rĭ-vŭl′shən] *noun*, a sickening feeling, a negative reaction

**re-ward** [rĭ-wôrd′] *noun*, 1) something given to praise good work, kindness or bravery, *verb*, 2) to give a prize in appreciation of good work

**rhap-so-dize** [răp′sə-dīz′] *verb*, to speak or write enthusiastically

**rhap-so-dy** [răp′sə-dē] *noun*, delight, happiness, enthusiasm

**rhet-o-ric** [rĕt′ər-ĭk] *noun*, the art of using language effectively

**rheu-ma-tism** [rōō′mə-tĭz′əm] *noun*, a painful disease of the muscles and joints, accompanied by swelling and stiffness

**rhi-noc-er-os** [rī-nŏs′ər-əs] *noun*, a large wild animal with tough skin and two large horns on its nose, which lives in Africa

**Rhode Island** [rōd-ī′lənd] *noun*, one of 50 United States located on the East Coast, the capital is Providence. The state flower of **Rhode Island** is the violet and the motto is "Hope."

**rhom-bus** [rŏm′bəs] *noun*, a form with four equal sides in the shape of a diamond

**rhu-barb** [roō′bärb′] *noun*, acid leafstalks of a coarse herb, used for sauce or pie

**rhyme** [rīm] *noun*, 1) correspondence of sounds in words, *verb*, 2) to end the line of a verse with the same sound

**rhythm** [rĭth′əm] *noun*, 1) repetition of a beat played throughout a musical piece 2) the recurrence of stress or a sound at regular intervals

**rib** [rĭb] *noun*, one of many narrow bones surrounding the chest

**rib-ald** [rĭb′əld] *adjective*, wanton, indecent, offensive, vulgar

**rib-bon** [rĭb′ən] *noun*, a narrow fabric usually of silk, used to trim a dress or a present

**rice** [rīs] *noun*, a grain in the cereal family from a grass-like plant grown in warm climates

**rich** [rĭch] *adjective*, 1) wealthy, having many resources 2) plentiful, abundant

**rich-es** [rĭch′ĭz] *noun, plural*, treasures, things worth a lot of money, valuable possessions

**rid** [rĭd] *verb*, to dispose of

**rid-dance** [rĭd′ns] *noun*, a cleaning up or out, relief or deliverance

**rid-dle** [rĭd′l] *noun*, 1) a clever question with an unexpected answer, a puzzling thing, *verb*, 2) to pierce with many holes

**ride** [rīd] *verb*, to travel on an animal or in a vehicle to go somewhere

**rid-er** [rī′dər] *noun*, 1) modification of a law, by adding a clause to legislation 2) a passenger on a journey

**ridge** [rĭj] *noun*, a long narrow raised part of the hill, a crest

**rid-i-cule** [rĭd′ĭ-kyoōl′] *noun*, 1) taunts, jeers, *verb*, 2) to sneer at, to mock, to make fun of

**ri-dic-u-lous** [rĭ-dĭk′yə-ləs] *adjective*, unworthy of serious consideration, absurd

**rife** [rīf] *adjective*, prevalent, common or frequent in occurrence, widespread

**ri-fle** [rī′fəl] *noun*, 1) a firearm with a long barrel, *verb*, 2) to search hurriedly through

**rift** [rĭft] *noun*, an opening, a break

**rig** [rĭg] *noun*, 1) heavy equipment, 2) a vehicle used to haul large shipments, *verb*, 3) to equip

**rig-ging** [rĭg′ĭng] *noun*, the ropes used to raise and hold the sails of a ship

**right** [rīt] *adjective*, 1) of or located to the opposite of left 2) what is fair and good 3) correct, *adverb*, 4) correctly 5) straight to, without stopping, *noun*, 6) a freedom allowed by law

**right triangle** [rīt-trī′ăng′gəl] *noun*, a triangle that has one right angle in it, the opposite side is the hypotenuse

**right-eous** [rī′chəs] *adjective*, just, virtuous, acting in a moral way

**rig-id** [rĭj/ĭd] *adjective*, hard, fixed, immovable, not flexible

**rig-or** [rĭg/ər] *noun*, severity

**rig-or-ous** [rĭg/ər-əs] *adjective*, strict, severe discipline

**rim** [rĭm] *noun*, the often-curved edge of something, a border

**rind** [rīnd] *noun*, the tough outer skin of fruit or cheese that protects it from air

**ring** [rĭng] *noun*, 1) small circular band worn on the finger 2) a circular object with a vacant center 3) an area where fights are held 4) a small group 5) the sound created by a bell, *verb*, 6) to make a sound like a bell

**rink** [rĭngk] *noun*, a playing field, a ring, a smooth floor

**rinse** [rĭns] *verb*, to wash lightly, to cleanse with water after washing

**ri-ot** [rī/ət] *noun*, 1) unrestrained fighting, vandalism, *verb*, 2) to fight in an angry crowd

**ri-ot-ous** [rī/ət-əs] *adjective*, unrestrained, tumultuous

**rip** [rĭp] *verb*, to tear away

**ripe** [rīp] *adjective*, completely mature, ready to be eaten, aged

**rip-en** [rī/pən] *verb*, to grow to maturity or when ready to eat

**rip-ple** [rĭp/əl] *noun*, 1) a little wave, *verb*, 2) to cause little waves of sound or movement

**rise** [rīz] *noun*, 1) an increase, *verb*, 2) to stand up 3) to move upward 4) to move in a positive direction 5) to get up out of bed

**risk** [rĭsk] *noun*, 1) a sense or chance of danger involved with doing something, *verb*, 2) to take a chance of injury or loss

**rite** [rīt] *noun*, a formal ceremony, a ritual, a custom

**rit-u-al** [rĭch/ōō-əl] *noun*, a set action or series of actions

**ri-val** [rī/vəl] *noun*, a competitor

**ri-val-ry** [rī/vəl-rē] *noun*, a contention, a contest, jealousy

**riv-er** [rĭv/ər] *noun*, a large natural stream of fresh water that flows into the ocean

**riv-et** [rĭv/ĭt] *noun*, 1) a metal pin for passing through holes in two or more pieces to hold them together, *verb*, 2) to hold attention firmly, to engross

**roach** [rōch] *noun*, a cockroach or small insect that eats food

**road** [rōd] *noun*, a route used for vehicles to travel, an avenue or thoroughfare, a street

**roam** [rōm] *verb*, to wander about, to travel aimlessly

**roar** [rôr, rōr] *noun*, 1) a deep angry sound, a loud growl or snarl, *verb*, 2) to growl in a loud voice 3) to laugh loudly

**roast** [rōst] *noun*, 1) a piece of meat that has been cooked over fire or will be, *verb*, 2) to cook without water over a fire or in an oven, to expose to great heat

**rob** [rŏb] *verb*, to deprive, to steal from someone, to defraud

**rob-ber** [rŏb/ər] *noun*, a thief, someone who steals

**robe** [rōb] *noun*, a piece of clothing that covers most of the body worn for lounging or relaxing

**rob-in** [rŏb′ĭn] *noun*, a brown song bird with a red breast found in North America

**ro-bot** [rō′bət] *noun*, a programmed machine designed to do the work of a person

**ro-bust** [rō-bŭst′] *adjective*, vigorous, strong, healthy

**rock** [rŏk] *noun*, 1) a hard, natural material of mineral origin, a stone 2) the mineral matter that makes up a large portion of the earth's crust *verb*, 3) to move back and forth or from side to side

**rock-et** [rŏk′ĭt] *noun*, 1) a missile, a spacecraft, *verb*, 2) to shoot into space 3) to move swiftly

**rod** [rŏd] *noun*, a thin pole

**rode** [rōd] *past tense* of **ride**

**ro-dent** [rōd′nt] *noun*, a small furry four-legged animal, like a squirrel, mouse or rat

**ro-de-o** [rō′dē-ō′] *noun*, a contest for people like cowhands to show their skill

**rogue** [rōg] *noun*, a scoundrel

**role** [rōl] *noun*, a part played by an actor, a characterization

**roll** [rōl] *noun*, 1) a long, drawn out noise 2) a small rounded portion of bread, *verb*, 3) to move along by turning over and over 4) to make something flat by pressing it with a roller

**ro-man nu-mer-als** [rō-mäɴ′nōō′mər-əlz] *noun*, *plural*, the number symbols used by Romans 2,500 years ago

**ro-mance** [rō-măns′] *noun*, 1) the state of being in love 2) a story about love between people, *verb*, 3) to court romantically

**ro-man-tic** [rō-măn′tĭk] *adjective*, 1) not based in fact, fanciful 2) thoughts of love and adventure

**roof** [rōōf] *noun*, 1) the external cover of a building 2) the top of the mouth

**rook-ie** [rŏŏk′ē] *noun*, a beginner

**room** [rōōm] *noun*, 1) one of the parts of a house separated by walls and doors 2) space

**roost** [rōōst] *noun*, 1) a perch, *verb*, 2) to sleep or rest on a perch

**roost-er** [rōō′stər] *noun*, a domestic male fowl, a cock

**root** [rōōt] *noun*, 1) the part of the plant that grows in the ground, it's purpose is to hold it in the earth, to absorb moisture and to store nourishment, *verb*, 2) to dig up with the nose or snout 3) to cheer for a team

**rope** [rōp] *noun*, a heavy cord

**rose** [rōz] *noun*, 1) a shrub with a beautiful sweet smelling flower, *verb*, 2) the *past tense* of **rise**

**ros-ter** [rŏs′tər] *noun*, a list

**ros-trum** [rŏs′trəm] *noun*, a stage for public speaking, a pulpit

**rot** [rŏt] *verb*, to decompose, to decay gradually, to spoil

**ro-ta-ry** [rō′tə-rē] *noun*, rotating parts turning on an axis

**ro-tate** [rō′tāt] *verb*, to turn around a center or axis, to revolve

**ro-ta-tion** [rō-tā′shən] *noun*, 1) a revolution, turning in a full circle 2) the growing of different crops in the same place usually in regular order

**rote** [rōt] *noun*, learning through repetition and memorization

**rot-ten** [rŏt′n] *adjective*, no good

**ro-tun-da** [rō-tŭn′də] *noun*, a round building or rooms

**rough** [rŭf] *adjective*, 1) not smooth, uneven, difficult 2) not calm or gentle 3) unfinished, crude, coarse to the touch

**rough-ly** [rŭf-lē] *adverb*, approximately

**round** [round] *adjective*, 1) in the shape of a circle or a ball, circular, *noun*, 2) a circle, an orb, a globe 3) a course, a cycle, a series, *verb*, 4) to turn a bend or corner 5) to express a number to the nearest whole number

**round-a-bout** [round′ə-bout′] *adjective*, 1) not direct or straightforward, *noun*, 2) a traffic circle

**rouse** [rouz] *verb*, to stimulate, to spur, to wake up, to excite

**rout** [rout] *noun* 1) a disorganized retreat from an attack, *verb*, 2) to drive out, to defeat decisively

**route** [rōōt, rout] *noun*, a road for traveling ffrom one place to another

**rou-tine** [rōō-tēn′] *adjective*, 1) habitual, 2) unoriginal, *noun*, 3) a regular course or procedure

**row** [rō] *noun*, 1) an arrangement set in a line 2) a quarrel or fight, *verb*, 3) to propel with oars

**roy-al** [roi′əl] *adjective*, 1) of a king or queen  2) fit for a king or queen

**roy-al-ty** [roi′əl-tē] *noun*, 1) a member of the monarchy 2) a

payment to the owner for the use of copyright material

**rub** [rŭb] *verb*, 1) to create friction by moving something back and forth 2) to massage

**rub-ber** [rŭb′ər] *noun*, *no plural*, a mix of chemicals to form a pliable substance

**rub-bish** [rŭb′ĭsh] *noun*, *no plural*, refuse, garbage, trash

**rub-ble** [rŭb′əl] *noun*, pieces or fragments of large objects

**ru-by** [rōō′bē] *noun*, a precious stone of deep red

**rud-der** [rŭd′ər] *noun*, a steering mechanism at the back of a boat

**rud-dy** [rŭd′ē] *adjective*, reddish, healthy-looking

**rude** [rōōd] *adjective*, not polite, unkind, discourteous behavior

**ru-di-men-ta-ry** [rōō′də-mĕn′tə-rē] *adjective*, the first undeveloped state, unrefined, imperfect

**ruf-fi-an** [rŭf′ē-ən] *noun*, a person who is rough and dirty

**ruf-fle** [rŭf′əl] *noun*, 1) trimming, frill, *verb*, 2) to make uneasy

**rug** [rŭg] *noun*, a floor covering made of woven fibers or wool

**rug-ged** [rŭg′ĭd] *adjective*, 1) rough and wild 2) full of rocks with a jagged surface

**ruin** [rōō′ĭn] *noun*, 1) destruction, damage, *verb*, 2) to destroy

**ru-in-ous** [rōō′ə-nəs] *adjective*, destructive, harmful

**rule** [rōōl] *noun*, 1) a law, a guide for conduct or procedure, *verb*, 2) to have power and control over someone 3) to decree

**rul-er** [roo′lər] *noun*, 1) someone who governs a body of people 2) an instrument used to measure and draw straight lines

**rum-ble** [rŭm′bəl] *noun*, 1) a loud sound, like earth moving, *verb*, 2) to make a continuous loud, low noise, like thunder

**ru-mi-nate** [roo′mə-nāt′] *verb*, 1) to chew the cud 2) to ponder, to think about, to meditate

**rum-mage** [rŭm′ĭj] *noun*, 1) odds and ends, miscellany, *verb*, 2) to look for, to rifle through

**ru-mor** [roo′mər] *noun*, gossip, common talk, hearsay

**run** [rŭn] *noun*, 1) the distance traveled, a journey 2) a score in a baseball game 3) movement that is quicker than walking, *verb*, 4) to move quickly or swiftly 5) to work or make work 6) to go over 7) to escape, to retreat 8) to ooze or pour out

**rung** [rŭng] *noun*, 1) a rod on a ladder that is a step, *verb*, 2) *past participle* of **ring**

**run-ner** [rŭn′ər] *noun*, 1) a long ski on the bottom of a sled used on snow and ice 2) a person who runs errands 3) a carpet or decorative cover placed on a walk way

**rup-ture** [rŭp′chər] *noun*, 1) a fracture, a breach, *verb*, 2) to break, to fracture, to split

**ru-ral** [roor′əl] *adjective*, having to do with, in, or like farmland, country people, or life in the country, rustic

**ruse** [roos] *noun*, a trick, gimmick

**rush** [rŭsh] *noun*, *no plural*, 1) rapid movement, haste 2) reeds that grow near the water, *verb*, 3) to move quickly or fast as in a hurry 4) to charge, to attack

**rust** [rŭst] *noun*, *no plural*, 1) a corrosive red-brown substance that forms on iron when it has been exposed to water and oxygen, *verb*, 2) to become covered with the corrosive element 3) to deteriorate

**rus-tic** [rŭs′tĭk] *adjective*, referring to country people, rural

**rus-tle** [rŭs′əl] *verb*, to make a soft rubbing sound, to crackle

**rut** [rŭt] *noun*, a deep narrow groove in the ground

**ruth-less** [rooth′lĭs] *adjective*, cruel, harsh, merciless

**rye** [rī] *noun*, a grass with seeds that are made into flour

# S

**Sab-bath** [săb′əth] *noun*, a holy day, a day of rest

**sack** [săk] *noun*, a large bag made of woven material strong enough to carry things

**sa-cred** [sā′krĭd] *adjective*, holy, worshipped, religious

**sac-ri-fice** [săk′rə-fīs′] *noun*, 1) an offering, the surrender of anything, *verb*, 2) to give up something, to forfeit

**sac-ro-sanct** [săk′rō-săngkt′] *adjective*, most sacred, holy

**sad** [săd] *adjective*, unhappy, sorrowful, affected by grief

**sad-dle** [săd/l] *noun*, 1) a seat made of leather that fits over the back of a horse, *verb*, 2) to burden

**sa-dis-tic** [sə-dĭs/tĭk] *adjective*, pleasure in being cruel

**sa-fa-ri** [sə-fär/ē] *noun*, a journey into the jungles and plains of Africa, to look at wild animals

**safe** [sāf] *adjective*, 1) not in danger, protected, secure, *noun*, 2) a vault, a chest, a repository

**safe-ty** [sāf/tē] *noun*, a way of preventing damage to workers or a machine, protection

**sag** [săg] *verb*, 1) to hang down, to droop 2) to decline in value

**sa-ga** [sä/gə] *noun*, any legend, a long drawn out story

**sa-ga-cious** [sə-gā/shəs] *adjective*, shrewd, wise, knowledgeable

**sage** [sāj] *noun*, a wise man

**said** [sĕd] *past tense* of **say**

**sail** [sāl] *noun*, 1) a large cloth used to catch the wind and move a boat, *verb*, 2) to travel on water 3) to navigate a ship equipped with sails 4) to glide

**sail-or** [sā/lər] *noun*, a seaman, someone who works on a ship

**saint** [sānt] *noun*, a person who has lived a religious life and has been recognized by a group of religious leaders for good work

**sake** [sāk] *noun*, used with **for**, to show purpose or reason

**sal-ad** [săl/əd] *noun*, a preparation of vegetables, fruit, fish, or meat, dressed with vinegar, oil, etc.

**sal-a-ry** [săl/ə-rē] *noun*, fixed wages for a year, quarter, or month, for services

**sale** [sāl] *noun*, 1) the exchange of goods for money 2) when merchandise is sold at a reduced price 3) an auction

**sales-man** [sālz/mən] *noun*, one whose occupation is to sell goods or merchandise

**sales tax** [sālz-tăks] *noun*, a tax people pay for purchases

**sa-li-ent** [sā/lē-ənt] *adjective*, standing out, conspicuous, striking, noticeable, obvious

**sa-line** [sā/lēn/] *adjective*, salty

**sa-li-va** [sə-lī/və] *noun*, a fluid secreted in the mouth to help digest food, spit

**salm-on** [săm/ən] *noun*, a species of fresh-water fish

**sa-loon** [sə-lōōn/] *noun*, a bar or tavern, a large public room

**salt** [sôlt] *noun*, a white crystal compound of chlorine and sodium found in sea water, used to flavor food and preserve meat

**sa-lu-bri-ous** [sə-lōō/brē-əs] *adjective*, promoting health

**sal-u-ta-tion** [săl/yə-tā/shən] *noun*, a greeting, something uttered

**sal-u-tar-y** [săl/yə-tĕr/ē] *adjective*, beneficial, wholesome

**sa-lute** [sə-lōōt/] *noun*, 1) a sign of respect for a superior officer *verb*, 2) to hold up the right hand to the forehead

**sal-vage** [săl/vĭj] *noun*, 1) property saved from destruction, *verb*, 2) to save, to recycle, to recover, to rescue

**sal-va-tion** [săl-vā/shən] *noun*, saved from harm or loss, deliverance from evil salve [săv] *noun*, a medicinal ointment, a lotion, a balm

same [sām] *adjective*, 1) having the same identifying characteristics, identical 2) not different

sam-ple [săm′pəl] *noun*, 1) a part of anything shown as quality, a specimen, *verb*, 2) to try or test

san-a-to-ri-um [săn′ə-tôr′ē-əm] *noun*, a place where chronically ill patients receive the care they need until they recover

sanc-ti-fy [săngk′tə-fī′] *verb*, to bless, to make holy, to anoint

sanc-tion [săngk′shən] *noun*, 1) coercive measures directed against a nation that has violated international law, *verb*, 2) to approve, to support, to confirm

sanc-tu-ar-y [săngk′chōō-ĕr′ē] *noun*, church, a place of refuge

sand [sănd] *noun*, fine grains made of rocks usually found near the sea or in deserts

san-dal [săn′dl] *noun*, a kind of shoe consisting of a sole strapped to the foot

sand-bar [sănd′ bär] *noun*, a ridge of sand formed in a river or along a shore by the action of currents or tides

sand-wich [sănd′wĭch, săn′-] *noun*, slices of bread with something between them such as meat, cheese or jelly

sane [sān] *adjective*, reasonable, sensible, sound in mind

sang [săng] *past tense* of sing

san-i-tar-y [săn′ĭ-tĕr′ē] *adjective*, very clean, antiseptic

san-i-ta-tion [săn′ĭ-tā′shən] *noun*, the job of keeping things clean

san-i-ty [săn′ĭ-tē] *noun*, a healthy outlook, a state of being sane

sank [săngk] *verb*, *past tense* of sink

sap [săp] *noun*, 1) the fluid in a plant that gives nourishment, *verb*, 2) to take strength from something, to weaken gradually

sapi-ent [sā′pē-ənt] *adjective*, wise, shrewd, showing great wisdom

sap-ling [săp′lĭng] *noun*, a young tree, a sprout of a tree

sap-phire [săf′īr′] *noun*, a precious gemstone of a blue color

sar-casm [sär′kăz′əm] *noun*, scornful remarks, ridicule

sar-cas-tic [sär-kăs′tĭk] *adjective*, taunting, satirical, scornful

sar-coph-a-gus [sär-kŏf′ə-gəs] *noun*, a coffin, a casket

sar-dine [sär-dēn′] *noun*, a small herring preserved in olive oil

sash [săsh] *noun*, a wide ribbon worn around the waist or over the shoulder

sat-el-lite [săt′l-īt′] *noun*, 1) a small, heavenly body orbiting around a planet 2) an artificial object launched to orbit the earth or other celestial bodies

sa-ti-ate [sā′shē-āt′] *verb*, to satisfy fully, to supply to excess

sat-ire [săt′īr′] *noun*, a form of writing that makes fun of habits, ideas or customs

sat-is-fac-tion [săt′ĭs-făk′shən] *noun*, the feeling of having what you need and want

sat-is-fac-to-ry [săt′ĭs-făk′tə-rē] *adjective*, sufficient, fulfilling all requirements

**sat-is-fy** [săt′ĭs-fī′] *verb*, 1) to be enough or good enough, to meet a need 2) to make sure

**sat-u-rate** [săch′ə-rāt′] *verb*, to become thoroughly soaked

**Sat-ur-day** [săt′ər-dē′] *noun*, the seventh day of the week

**sauce** [sôs] *noun*, a liquid of a variety of ingredients eaten with food to improve its taste

**sauc-er** [sô′sər] *noun*, a small plate put under a cup to catch the drips

**saun-ter** [sôn′tər] *verb*, to stroll, to walk slowly, to meander

**sau-sage** [sô′sĭj] *noun*, minced and seasoned meat, commonly enclosed in an edible casing

**sav-age** [săv′ĭj] *adjective*, wild, untamed, uncivilized

**sa-van-nah** [sə-văn′ə] *noun*, a grassy plain that has very few trees in a tropical climate

**sa-vant** [să-vänt′] *noun*, a scholar, a learned person, a sage

**save** [sāv] *verb*, 1) to rescue from harm or danger 2) to set aside for future use, to store 4) to copy on a disk or the hard drive of a computer

**sav-ings** [sā′vĭngz] *noun*, *plural, no singular*, money set aside to use in the future, reserve funds

**sav-ior** [sāv′yər] *noun*, someone who saves others from danger

**savoir faire** [săv′wär-fâr′] *noun*, ease and dexterity in social and practical affairs from the French, meaning "to know how to act"

**sa-vor** [sā′vər] *noun*, 1) a taste or aroma, *verb*, 2) to taste or enjoy a distinctive flavor, smell or quality, to appreciate

**saw** [sô] *noun*, 1) a tool with a jagged blade and handle used to cut wood, *verb*, 2) *past tense* of **see** 3) to cut with a serrated blade or saw

**say** [sā] *verb*, to speak something

**say-ing** [sā′ĭng] *noun*, a wise statement that is full of truth like a proverb or aphorism

**scab** [skăb] *noun*, 1) a hard covering of coagulated blood on a wound 2) a worker who stays on the job while others go on strike

**scaf-fold** [skăf′əld] *noun*, 1) a temporary platform built to hold laborers while working on a building 2) the gallows

**scald** [skôld] *verb*, 1) to injure or burn with hot liquid 2) to heat to just below the boiling point

**scale** [skāl] *noun*, 1) a balance to measure weight 2) a range, degree, or progression 3) a protective crust or plate, *verb*, 4) to adjust to a standard of measure 5) to climb or ascend

**sca-lene tri-an-gle** [skā′lēn′ trī′ăng′gəl] *noun*, a triangle with unequal sides

**scalp** [skălp] *noun*, 1) the skin and hair of the head, *verb*, 2) to remove the hair from someone

**scam-per** [skăm′pər] *verb*, to scurry, to run quickly

**scan** [skăn] *verb*, to look over, to review, to examine closely

**scan-dal** [skăn′dl] *noun*, an incident which offends conscience or moral feelings

**scape-goat** [skāp′gōt′] *noun*, someone who bears the blame for others

**scar** [skär] *noun*, 1) a mark left where a wound has been, *verb*, 2) to make a deep cut or to cause deep unforgettable pain

**scar-ab** [skăr′əb] *noun*, a large beetle with a dark shell

**scarce** [skârs] *adjective*, hard to find or come by, not plentiful

**scarce-ly** [skârs′lē] *adverb*, with difficulty, barely, hardly

**scare** [skâr] *noun*, 1) a sudden fright, *verb*, 2) to make someone afraid, to frighten, to terrify

**scarf** [skärf] *noun, plural, scarves,* a triangular or rectangular piece of cloth worn around the head, neck, or shoulders

**scat-ter** [skăt′ər] *verb*, to throw things everywhere, to disperse

**scav-en-ger** [skăv′ən-jər] *noun*, collector of garbage, an animal that devours refuse

**scene** [sēn] *noun*, 1) a setting, a view 2) a specific place 3) a shocking incident, a fight

**scen-er-y** [sē′nə-rē] *noun, no plural*, the setting of a place or landscape, the panorama

**sce-nic** [sē′nĭk] *adjective*, full of natural splendors, breathtaking

**scent** [sĕnt] *noun*, a smell that characterizes things

**sched-ule** [skĕj′ōol] *noun*, 1) a written formal list or inventory, *verb*, 2) to arrange tasks to fit into a specific time frame

**scheme** [skēm] *noun*, 1) a plan, purpose, arrangement, *verb*, 2) to make secret plans, to plot

**schol-ar** [skŏl′ər] *noun*, a person who studies a particular subject at great length, a student

**schol-ar-ship** [skŏl′ər-shĭp′] *noun*, money granted to a worthy student to pay for their education

**scho-las-tic** [skə-lăs′tĭk] *noun*, pertaining to a school or education

**school** [skōol] *noun*, 1) a place of instruction 2) a style, manner, method 3) a company of fish

**schoon-er** [skōo′nər] *noun*, a sailing ship with fore and aft rigging

**sci-ence** [sī′əns] *noun*, classified knowledge of the physical world

**sci-en-tif-ic** [sī′ən-tĭf′ĭk] *adjective*, in conformity to the principles of the physical world

**sci-en-tist** [sī′ən-tĭst] *noun*, a person who studies information about natural phenomena

**scis-sors** [sĭz′ərz] *noun*, a tool with two blades and handles, pivoted together that is used for cutting

**scoff** [skŏf] *verb*, to ridicule or make fun of, to deride, to jeer

**scold** [skōld] *verb*, to angrily tell someone they did something wrong, to reprimand

**scoop** [skōop] *noun*, 1) a large spoonful, *verb*, 2) to take some from the whole thing with a spoon or the hands

**scoot** [skōot] *verb*, to move quickly

**scope** [skōp] *noun*, 1) a range of one's mind 2) opportunity to function, capacity

**scorch** [skôrch] *verb*, to burn lightly leaving a brown stain

**score** [skôr] *noun*, 1) the points you get on a test or in a game 2) the reason, the purpose 3) a copy of a musical composition showing all parts for instruments and voices 4) a period of twenty years, *verb*, 5) to make points in a game 6) to achieve success

**scorn** [skôrn] *noun*, 1) disrespect, disdain, hate, *verb*, 2) to act like someone is worthless

**scor-pi-on** [skôr′pē-ən] *noun*, an arachnid that kills with its poisonous tail

**scoun-drel** [skoun′drəl] *noun*, a villain, a rascal, a mean person

**scour** [skour] *verb*, 1) to search an area thoroughly 2) to clean and polish by rubbing

**scout** [skout] *noun*, a person sent out ahead to obtain information

**scowl** [skoul] *noun*, 1) an angry, disgusted expression on the face, *verb*, 2) to make an angry expression showing disapproval

**scram-ble** [skrăm′bəl] *verb*, to move quickly on hands and knees, to hurry along

**scrap** [skrăp] *noun*, waste with some value, particularly material left over from construction or manufacturing suitable for reprocessing

**scrap-book** [skrăp′bŏŏk′] *noun*, a blank book filled with mementos, cards and souvenirs

**scrape** [skrāp] *noun* 1) a predicament, *verb*, 2) to take something off by rubbing it with a sharp edge 3) to make a grating sound

**scratch** [skrăch] *noun*, 1) a mark or wound made with something

pointed, *verb*, 2) to make marks with something pointed 3) to remove a layer by rubbing

**scream** [skrēm] *noun*, 1) a loud, shrill cry made in pain or fear, *verb*, 2) to make a sharp cry

**screech** [skrēch] *noun*, 1) a loud high-pitched noise, *verb*, 2) to make a harsh shrill noise

**screen** [skrēn] *noun*, 1) a portable covered framework in the nature of a partition 2) a grating of fine wire 3) protection, *verb*, 4) to eliminate applicants

**screw** [skrōō] *noun*, 1) a cylinder, grooved in an advancing spiral on its surface, *verb*, 2) to turn around and around

**scrib-ble** [skrĭb′əl] *verb*, to write or draw in an unintelligible manner

**scrim-mage** [skrĭm′ĭj] *noun*, a football or soccer practice

**script** [skrĭpt] *noun*, 1) a form of handwriting that connects the letters in a word 2) written words to be spoken from a text

**scrip-ture** [skrĭp′chər] *noun*, any sacred writing or book

**scroll** [skrōl] *noun*, 1) a rod with a roll of paper attached, *verb*, 2) to move a cursor smoothly, vertically or sideways, to review data on a computer screen

**scrub** [skrŭb] *verb*, to rub with a hard brush to clean off a spot

**scru-pu-lous** [skrōō′pyə-ləs] *adjective*, careful, cautious, exact, punctilious, precise

**scru-ti-nize** [skrōōt′n-īz′] *verb*, to examine closely and critically

**scru-ti-ny** [skrōōt′n-ē] *noun*, close examination, minute inspection

**sculpt** [skŭlpt] *verb*, to make or shape a statue

**sculp-tor** [skŭlp′tər] *noun*, one who carves or cuts wood or stone into statues

**sculp-ture** [skŭlp′chər] *noun*, works of art made from stone, clay or metal, a statue

**scythe** [sīth] *noun*, a long, curved-blade instrument for cutting grass by hand

**sea** [sē] *noun*, part of an ocean that is partially surrounded by land

**sea-gull** [sē′gŭl′] *noun*, a bird that lives near the ocean and scavenges for food

**seal** [sēl] *noun*, 1) an emblem affixed to a document to prove authenticity 2) a mammal with sleek skin, and limbs in the form of flippers, that lives in the water and on land, *verb*, 3) to close tightly so that something cannot be opened

**seam** [sēm] *noun*, 1) the stitches joining two pieces of cloth together 2) a fissure

**search** [sûrch] *noun*, 1) a careful investigation, a hunt, *verb*, 2) to look for someone or something

**sea-son** [sē′zən] *noun*, 1) a special time of year devoted to a certain activity 2) one of the four divisions of the year: fall, winter, spring, summer, *verb*, 3) to flavor or add zest to food

**seat** [sēt] *noun*, 1) a place to sit or a cushion to sit on 2) a location

**se-cede** [sĭ-sēd′] *verb*, to withdraw from association or fellowship

**se-ces-sion** [sĭ-sĕsh′ən] *noun*, withdrawal

**se-clu-sion** [sĭ-kloo′zhən] *noun*, 1) hiding, isolation 2) privacy

**sec-ond** [sĕk′ənd] *adjective*, 1) coming directly after the first, *noun*, 2) a very short period of time, a moment, *verb*, 3) to endorse, to support a motion

**se-cre-cy** [sē′krĭ-sē] *noun*, keeping things quiet without the knowledge of others

**se-cret** [sē′krĭt] *adjective*, 1) kept from the knowledge of most people, *noun*, 2) something known only to oneself or a few

**sec-re-tar-y** [sĕk′rĭ-tĕr′ē] *noun*, 1) a person who writes letters, files documents 2) a government officer who is a member of the President's Cabinet

**se-crete** [sĭ-krēt′] *verb*, to produce a liquid discharge

**se-cre-tion** [sĭ-krē′shən] *noun*, a fluid emitted from a gland

**sec-tion** [sĕk′shən] *noun*, a piece of the whole, a portion, a part

**sec-tor** [sĕk′tər, -tôr′] *noun*, region, area, zone, a distinct part

**sec-u-lar** [sĕk′yə-lər] *adjective*, worldly, not pertaining to church matters, temporal, earthly

**se-cure** [sĭ-kyoor′] *adjective*, 1) safe 2) strong and fixed firmly, *verb*, 3) to assure

**se-cu-ri-ty** [sĭ-kyoor′ĭ-tē] *noun*, 1) safety, assurance, freedom from danger 2) stocks and bonds

**se-date** [sĭ-dāt′] *adjective*, dignified, composed, calm

**sed-a-tive** [sĕd′ə-tĭv] *noun*, a tranquilizer, a narcotic

**sed-en-tar-y** [sĕd′n-tĕr′ē] *adjective*, accustomed to sitting most of the day

**sed-i-ment** [sĕd′ə-mənt] *noun*, the solid matter that settles to the bottom in a liquid

**se-di-tion** [sĭ-dĭsh′ən] *noun*, resistance to authority, insubordination

**sed-ul-ous-ly** [sĕj′ə-ləs-lē] *adjective*, diligently, loyally

**see** [sē] *verb*, 1) to perceive or acknowledge with the eye 2) to understand, to comprehend 3) to go and look 4) to meet 5) to think about something and to act if necessary

**seed** [sēd] *noun*, a small grain from which a plant grows

**seek** [sēk] *verb*, to look for

**seem** [sēm] *verb*, to appear to be true or probable

**seen** [sēn] past perfect of **see**

**seep** [sēp] *verb*, a liquid flowing slowly or leaking through

**seg-ment** [sĕg′mənt] *noun*, any part which separates from the whole

**seg-re-ga-tion** [sĕg′rĭ-gā′shən] *noun*, the act of setting groups apart, separation, racial discrimination

**seis-mic** [sīz′mĭk] *adjective*, pertaining to an earthquake

**seize** [sēz] *verb*, 1) to grasp suddenly, to take possession of by force

**sel-dom** [sĕl′dəm] *adjective*, rarely, not often, infrequently

**se-lect** [sĭ-lĕkt′] *adjective*, 1) first rate, *verb*, 2) to choose, to pick

**se-lec-tion** [sĭ-lĕk′shən] *noun*, a collection of things chosen

**self** [sĕlf] *noun*, your person, what you are, individuality

**self-ish** [sĕl′fĭsh] *adjective*, to think only of oneself and not others

**self-ish-ness** [sĕl′fĭsh- nĭs] *noun*, pettiness, being small-minded

**sell** [sĕl] *verb*, 1) to offer in exchange for money 2) to deal in

**sem-blance** [sĕm′bləns] *noun*, likeness, resemblance, similarity

**se-mes-ter** [sə-mĕs′tər] *noun*, either of two terms into which the period of instruction is divided in an academic year

**sem-i-cir-cle** [sĕm′ĭ-sûr′kəl] *noun*, the shape of half a circle

**sem-i-co-lon** [sĕm′ĭ-kō′lən] *noun*, a mark of punctuation (;) used to separate two independent clauses when there is no conjunction, as *When you make a mistake, admit it; learn from it and don't repeat it. Bear Bryant*

**sen-ate** [sĕn′ĭt] *noun*, one of the groups that constitutes the legislative government

**sen-a-tor** [sĕn′ə-tər] *noun*, an elected representative who serves in the Senate

**send** [sĕnd] *verb*, to cause something or someone to go somewhere, to dispatch

**se-nil-i-ty** [sĭ-nĭl′ĭ-tē] *noun*, feeble mindedness of old age

**sen-ior** [sēn′yər] *adjective*, 1) older, *noun*, 2) a student in the final year of a four year course

**sen-sa-tion** [sĕn-sā′shən] *noun*, 1) a feeling 2) excited interest

**sense** [sĕns] *noun*, 1) reason or understanding 2) a reasonable meaning 3) a feeling, *verb*, 4) to recognize, to detect

**sense-less** [sĕns′lĭs] *adjective*, stupid, unconscious

**sen-si-bil-i-ty** [sĕn′sə-bĭl′ĭ-tē] *noun*, awareness, understanding

**sen-si-ble** [sĕn′sə-bəl] *adjective*, reasonable, possessing good sense, smart, perceptive

**sen-si-tive** [sĕn′sĭ-tĭv] *adjective*, quick to notice or feel, easily affected by slight change

**sen-su-ous** [sĕn′shoo-əs] *adjective*, exuding sexuality, appealing

**sen-tence** [sĕn′təns] *noun*, 1) a combination of words which express a thought, beginning with a capital letter, ending with a period 2) the judgment of a court, *verb*, 3) to pass judgment on, to inflict punishment

**sen-ti-ment** [sĕn′tə-mənt] *noun*, feelings, thoughts, emotions

**sen-ti-men-tal** [sĕn′tə-mĕn′tl] *adjective*, expressing feelings of love, pity, etc. to excess

**sen-ti-nel** [sĕn′tə-nəl] *noun*, a soldier set to guard an army from surprise, a sentry

**sen-try** [sĕn′trē] *noun*, a lookout, guard, watchman, a soldier

**sep-a-rate** [sĕp′ə-rāt′] *adjective*, 1) not together, not joined, *verb*, 2) to divide, to disconnect, to keep apart

**sep-a-ra-tion** [sĕp′ə-rā′shən] *noun*, time apart from each other

**Sep-tem-ber** [sĕp-tĕm′bər] *noun*, the ninth month of the year, having 30 days

**sep-tic** [sĕp′tĭk] *adjective*, decaying, putrid or toxic, rotten

**sep-ul-cher** [sĕp′əl-kər] *noun*, a tomb, a burial place

**se-quel** [sē′kwəl] *noun*, the continuation of a story

**se-quence** [sē′kwəns] *noun*, a succession, a following or coming after in a series

**se-ques-ter** [sĭ-kwĕs′tər] *verb*, to go into isolation, to remove, to seclude, to set apart

**sere-nade** [sĕr′ə-nād′] *verb*, to court, to play music under a window to charm a sweetheart

**ser-en-dip-i-tous** [sĕr′ən-dĭp′ĭ-t əs] *adjective*, fortunate discoveries made by accident

**se-rene** [sə-rēn′] *adjective*, calm, tranquil, placid, clear, peaceful

**se-ren-i-ty** [sə-rĕn′ĭ-tē] *noun*, tranquility, peace

**ser-geant** [sär′jənt] *noun*, a noncommissioned officer ranking next above a corporal

**se-ries** [sîr′ēz] *noun*, a number of things connected in a sequence

**se-ri-ous** [sîr′ē-əs] *adjective*, 1) grave in manner or disposition, earnest, solemn, sincere 2) weighty

**se-ri-ous-ly** [sîr′ē-əs-lē] *adverb*, thoughtfully, sincerely

**ser-mon** [sûr′mən] *noun*, a talk given by a religious leader

**ser-pent** [sûr′pənt] *noun*, a snake

**ser-pen-tine** [sûr′pən-tēn′] *adjective*, winding, twisting

**ser-rat-ed** [sĕr′ā′tĭd] *adjective*, having a saw-toothed or jagged edge

**se-rum** [sîr′əm] *noun*, the watery protein of an animal fluid

**serv-ant** [sûr′vənt] *noun*, one who works for another especially in a home to perform chores

**serve** [sûrv] *verb*, 1) to do work for other people, to give assistance or help 2) to offer food to someone 3) to answer a purpose

**serv-ice** [sûr′vĭs] *noun*, 1) a job that one performs for others 2) a church ceremony

**ser-vile** [sûr′vəl] *adjective*, subservient, groveling, cringing

**ses-sion** [sĕsh′ən] *noun*, the sitting of an organized body for the transaction of business, a term

**set** [sĕt] *noun*, 1) a group of things thought of together, *verb*, 2) to put in a place 3) to make something happen, to begin 4) to sink in the sky below the horizon

**set-ting** [sĕt′ĭng]] *noun*, 1) the position of something, as a dial, that has been set 2) time and place, environment, etc. of an event, story, play, etc. 3) actual physical surroundings, real or artificial

**set-tle** [sĕt′l] *verb*, 1) to go and live in a place 2) to make comfortable 3) to come to a mutual agreement, to decide

**set-tle-ment** [sĕt′l-mənt] *noun*, 1) an agreement 2) a new place for people to live, a colony

**sev-en** [sĕv′ən] *adjective, noun*, the number 7, one plus six

**sev-en-teen** [sĕv′ən-tēn′] *adjective*, *noun*, the number 17, 7 + 10

**sev-en-teenth** [sĕv′ən-tēnth′] *adjective, noun*, number 17 in order, written 17th

**sev-enth** [sĕv′ənth] *adjective*, *noun*, number 7 in order, 7th

**sev-en-ti-eth** [sĕv′ən-tē-ĭth] *adjective, noun*, number 70 in order, written 70th

**sev-en-ty** [sĕv′ən-tē] *noun*, *adjective*, the number 70, 7 X 10

**sev-er** [sĕv′ər] *verb*, to cut off, to separate, to disconnect

**sev-er-al** [sĕv′ər-əl] *adjective*, 1) separate or distinct, *pronoun*, 2) being more than two but fewer than many

**se-vere** [sə-vîr′] *adjective*, 1) strict in judgment or discipline, harsh 2) hard to deal with

**se-ver-i-ty** [sə-vĕr′ĭ-tē] *noun*, harshness, intensity

**sew** [sō] *verb*, to bind two pieces of cloth together with a needle and thread, to repair with a thread

**sew-age** [sōō′ĭj] *noun*, liquid waste from homes and businesses transported away by sewers

**sew-er** [sōō′ər] *noun*, 1) a gutter, a disposal system 2) one who works with needle and thread

**sex** [sĕks] *noun*, to be male or female

**shab-by** [shăb′ē] *adjective*, old, cheap, dirty, falling apart

**shack-le** [shăk′əl] *noun*, 1) chains, handcuffs, *verb*, 2) to confine, to restrain with chains

**shade** [shād] *noun*, *no plural*, 1) shelter from the sun or light, *verb*, 2) to cut off from a bright light 3) to dim or darken

**shad-ow** [shăd′ō] *noun*, 1) the image cast on a surface when something blocks the light 2) a faint indication

**shaft** [shăft] *noun*, 1) a long thin pole 2) a long hole leading to a mine 3) a ray or beam

**shake** [shāk] *verb*, 1) to move quickly up and down or from side to side 2) to tremble

**shall** [shăl] *verb*, 1) a word used instead of will with *I* and *we*, to indicate something is going to happen 2) used with *I* and *we* in questions when asking or offering to do something

**shal-low** [shăl′ō] *adjective*, 1) not deep 2) superficial, with little seriousness or deep thought

**sham** [shăm] *noun*, a farce

**sham-bles** [shăm′bəlz] *noun*, *plural,* a scene of disorder

**shame** [shām] *noun*, 1) dishonor, guilt, humiliation, *verb*, 2) to humiliate or embarrass

**sham-poo** [shăm-poo′] *noun*, 1) a liquid soap used to wash hair, *verb*, 2) to wash hair with soap

**shape** [shāp] *noun*, 1) the outline or form of something, 2) a form or condition in which something exists, *verb*, 3) to mold or give form to something

**share** [shâr] *noun*, 1) a portion of something after it has been divided, *verb*, 2) to use, experience, or enjoy with others 3) to participate in  4) to disclose to others

**shark** [shärk] *noun*, a large predatory fish with a huge jaw

**sharp** [shärp] *adjective*, 1) having a thin cutting edge 2) the ability to see things far away that are small 3) severe or intense, having a strong odor or flavor 4) alert 5) quick and forceful

**sharp-en** [shär′pən] *verb*, 1) to make a pointed edge 2) to make acute or more sensitive to feeling

**sharp-ly** [sharp-lē] *adverb*, clearly, suddenly, distinctly

**shat-ter** [shăt′ər] *verb*, to break into many pieces or fragments

**shave** [shāv] *verb*, to cut very close

**shawl** [shôl] *noun*, a long piece of cloth worn over the shoulders and head

**she** [shē] *pronoun*, the female person or subject in the sentence

**sheaf** [shēf] *noun*, 1) a quantity of grain bound together 2) any bundle of things such as papers

**shear** [shîr] *verb*, to cut wool from a sheep, to cut hair, to clip

**shears** [shîrz] *noun*, *plural*, large-sized scissors

**sheath** [shēth] *noun*, a case that holds a sword or dagger

**sheathe** [shēth] *verb*, to put into a case or covering

**shed** [shĕd] *noun*, 1) a hut for tools, *verb*, 2) to let something fall or come off naturally 3) to pour forth, to stream out

**sheep** [shēp] *noun*, *no plural*, an animal that is kept for meat and wool from its thick, fleecy coat

**sheep-ish-ly** [shē′pĭsh-lē] *adverb*, with a feeling of embarrassment

**sheer** [shîr] *adjective*, 1) totally, entirely 2) transparent

**sheet** [shēt] *noun*, 1) a large flat piece of something such as paper or cloth 2) a rope used to secure a ship's sail

**shelf** [shĕlf] *noun*, *plural*, **shelves,** a board attached to a wall to put things on it

**shell** [shĕl] *noun*, the hard protective covering of fruit, eggs or some fish and reptiles

**shel-lac** [shə-lăk′] *noun*, a wood finishing such as varnish, lacquer or polyurethane

**shell-fish** [shĕl′fĭsh′] *noun*, any fish with a hard armor such as crabs, lobsters, or oysters

**shel-ter** [shĕl′tər] *noun*, 1) a safe place, a place to hide, *verb*, 2) to hide someone, to guard or keep safe from harm, to protect

**shep-herd** [shĕp′ərd] *noun*, a person who herds and tends sheep, goats, or livestock

**sher-bet** [shûr′bĭt] *noun*, flavored dessert ice

**sher-iff** [shĕr′ĭf] *noun*, a law enforcement officer of a county

**shib-bo-leth** [shĭb′ə-lĭth] *noun*, a slogan, a catchword

**shield** [shēld] *noun*, 1) a piece of defensive armor carried on the arm, protection, *verb*, 2) to defend or protect 3) to conceal

**shift** [shĭft] *noun*, 1) a set of people who work together at one time 2) the length of time that one group works, *verb*, 3) to move, to transfer, to displace

**shil-ling** [shĭl′ĭng] *noun*, English currency equal to a dollar

**shim-mer** [shĭm′ər] *verb*, to glimmer intermittently, to glisten

**shin** [shĭn] *noun*, the part of the leg between the knee and the ankle

**shine** [shīn] *verb*, to give off light

**shin-gle** [shĭng′gəl] *noun*, a tile made of wood or tar used to protect a roof or wall

**ship** [shĭp] *noun*, a boat which travels in deep water like the sea

**ship-ment** [shĭp′mənt] *noun*, the act of sending goods by air, water, or, on the road

**shirt** [shûrt] *noun*, a garment which covers the upper part of the body consisting of a collar, sleeves, and buttons, similar to a blouse

**shiv-er** [shĭv′ər] *verb*, to shake from feeling cold or afraid

**shoal** [shōl] *noun*, 1) a sandbar or piece of rising ground in shallow water 2) a school of fish

**shock** [shŏk] *noun*, 1) the feeling caused by a horrible unpleasant surprise 2) a pain caused by electricity going through the body, *verb*, 3) to startle, to disturb or surprise

**shod-dy** [shŏd′ē] *adjective*, not genuine, inferior quality

**shoe** [shoo] *noun*, an outer covering for the foot consisting of a sole and a covering made of leather, vinyl, or cloth

**shoot** [shoot] *noun*, 1) new growth, a sprout, *verb*, 2) to discharge a weapon 3) to move quickly, to dart 4) to photograph or film

**shop** [shŏp] *noun*, 1) a place to go and buy different things that you need, *verb*, 2) to visit stores to make purchases

**shore** [shôr] *noun*, 1) land bordering water such as a lake or the sea, *verb*, 2) to prop up

**short** [shôrt] *adjective*, 1) the opposite of tall, small 2) not long, brief, concise

**short-age** [shôr′tĭj] *noun*, not enough, a deficiency

**short-en** [shôr′tn] *verb*, to cut down

**short-en-ing** [shôr′tn-ĭng] *noun*, lard or oil used in cooking

**shorts** [shôrts] *noun*, *plural*, pants worn above the knee

**shot** [shŏt] *noun*, 1) injection with a hypodermic needle 2) a try, an attempt 3) lead for a shotgun

**should** [shŏŏd] *verb*, obligated to do something, ought to

**shoul-der** [shōl′dər] *noun*, 1) part of the body between the neck and the chest, connected to the arms, *verb*, 2) to carry a burden

**shouldn't** [shŏŏd′nt] the *contraction* of the words **should** and **not**

**shout** [shout] *noun*, 1) a sudden cry in a loud voice, *verb*, 2) to speak or yell in a loud voice

**shove** [shŭv] *noun*, 1) a push, *verb*, 2) to push roughly or rudely

**shov-el** [shŭv′əl] *noun*, 1) a broad scoop with a long handle for lifting dirt, *verb*, 2) to lift things from the ground or another surface with a shovel

**show** [shō] *noun*, 1) a display in which things are gathered for people to see 2) a performance for an audience, *verb*, 3) to let someone see something

**show-er** [shou′ər] *noun*, 1) precipitation from clouds in the form of rain 2) a bath in which water is sprayed from a nozzle, 3) a party to honor someone, *verb*, 4) to pour down or fall on 5) to bestow

**shred** [shrĕd] *noun*, 1) a small amount, *verb*, 2) to tear or cut into small pieces

**shrew** [shrōō] *noun*, 1) a scolding woman, a nag 2) a mouse-like rodent with a long snout

**shrewd** [shrōōd] *adjective*, clever in business, sharp-witted

**shriek** [shrēk] noun, 1) a high-pitched scream, *verb*, 2) to utter a shrill cry, to scream

**shrill** [shrĭl] *adjective*, having a high-pitched sound, piercing

**shrimp** [shrĭmp] *noun*, a shellfish that is considered a delicacy

**shrine** [shrīn] *noun*, 1) a place for worship and keeping sacred relics 2) a saint's tomb

**shrink** [shrĭngk] *verb*, 1) to withdraw, to pull away from 2) to lessen, to make smaller

**shriv-el** [shrĭv′əl] *verb*, to contract in size, to shrink and wrinkle

**shrub** [shrŭb] *noun*, a bush

**shrug** [shrŭg] *verb*, 1) to raise the shoulders to show uncertainty about something 2) to disregard

**shud-der** [shŭd′ər] *noun*, a quick, light shaking motion, a shiver

**shuf-fle** [shŭf′əl] *verb*, 1) to walk dragging your feet 2) to rearrange the order, to mix together like a deck of cards

**shun** [shŭn] *verb*, to deliberately avoid, to stay away from

**shut** [shŭt] *verb*, to close, to adjust something so that it is not open

**shut-ter** [shŭt′ər] *noun*, 1) a wooden cover for a window 2) a mechanical device for opening and closing the aperture of a camera lens to expose the film

**shy** [shī] *adjective*, bashful, wary

**sib-ling** [sĭb′lĭng] *noun*, a brother or sister

**sick** [sĭk] *adjective*, not feeling well

**sick-ness** [sĭk′nĭs] *noun*, illness, nausea, ailment, disease

**side** [sīd] *noun*, 1) the right or left portion of the body 2) the surface of something flat that has a top and bottom 3) the boundaries of a surface or image 4) a perspective, a way of looking at something, an aspect

**siege** [sēj] *noun*, a continued attempt of an army to gain possession around a fortified place to compel its surrender

**sieve** [sĭv] *noun*, a bowl with holes in the bottom to let water drain out, or used to separate fine matter from the coarser materials

**sigh** [sī] *noun*, 1) a deep breath indicating that you are tired, sad, etc, *verb*, 2) to let out a deep breath, to exhale

**sight** [sīt] *noun*, 1) the ability or power to see 2) something worth seeing 3) a scene, an incident

**sign** [sīn] *noun*, 1) a gesture which sends a message to the person who sees it 2) an indication 3) a plaque with a message, *verb*, 4) to write your name 5) to hire or transfer by written agreement

**sig-nal** [sĭg′nəl] *noun*, 1) a movement or thing which tells you what to do, *verb*, 2) to warn someone, or send another message through motions

**sig-na-ture** [sĭg′nə-chər] *noun*, 1) a name written in ink, in cursive, as an endorsement to an agreement 2) the printed sheet so marked as to leave an imprint

**sig-net** [sĭg′nĭt] *noun*, an emblem

**sig-nif-i-cance** [sĭg-nĭf′ĭ-kəns] *noun*, *no plural*, the meaning

**sig-nif-i-cant** [sĭg-nĭf′ĭ-kənt] *adjective*, expressive or suggestive, important

**sig-ni-fy** [sĭg′nə-fī′] *verb*, to indicate, to signal, to denote

**si-lence** [sī′ləns] *noun*, *no plural*, 1) complete quiet 2) secrecy

**si-lent** [sī′lənt] *adjective*, making no sound, quiet, speechless

**si-lent-ly** [sī′lənt-lē] *adverb*, quietly, without a sound

**sil-hou-ette** [sĭl′ōō-ĕt′] *noun*, an outline of something against a light background

**sil-i-con** [sĭl′ĭ-kən, -kŏn′] *noun*, a nonmetallic element, very abundant in nature

**silk** [sĭlk] *noun*, a fine fabric made by the threads from a silkworm

**sill** [sĭl] *noun*, the rim on a window

**sil-ly** [sĭl′ē] *adjective*, not serious, or reasonable, playful, foolish

**silt** [sĭlt] *noun*, sediment of fine particles that hangs in stagnant water or forms on the bottom left there by running water

**sil-ver** [sĭl′vər] *adjective*, 1) the color of this metal, *noun*, *no plural*, 2) a soft shiny gray metal used for jewelry, coins, and ornaments

**sim-i-an** [sĭm′ē-ən] *adjective*, like a monkey or an ape

**sim-i-lar** [sĭm′ə-lər] *adjective*, somewhat like, nearly, corresponding, resembling

**sim-i-lar-i-ty** [sĭm′ə-lăr′ĭ-tē] *noun*, likeness, resemblance

**sim-i-le** [sǐm′ə-lē] *noun*, a phrase comparing unlike subjects using like or as, i.e., *he is as slow as a turtle; she sings like a bird*

**sim-ple** [sǐm′pəl] *adjective*, 1) easy to understand 2) plain, common, not complicated, not showy

**sim-plic-i-ty** [sǐm-plǐs′ǐ-tē] *adjective*, freedom from duplicity, absence of excess

**sim-pli-fy** [sǐm′plə-fī′] *verb*, to make easier to understand

**sim-ply** [sǐm′plē] *adverb*, only, or merely, absolutely

**sim-u-late** [sǐm′yə-lāt′] *verb*, to feign, to pretend, to fake

**si-mul-ta-ne-ous** [sī′məl-tā′nē-əs] *adjective*, occurring at the same time, concurrent

**si-mul-ta-ne-ous-ly** [sī′məl-tā′nē-əs-lē] *adverb*, happening at the same time

**sin** [sǐn] *noun*, 1) an act that harms someone, *verb*, 2) to err, to violate a moral principle

**since** [sǐns] *adverb*, 1) between a moment in the past and now, *conjunction*, 2) because, *preposition*, 3) after, from a certain time until the present

**sin-cere** [sǐn-sîr′] *adjective*, being in reality what it appears to be, genuine 3) free of hypocrisy

**sin-cere-ly** [sǐn-sîr′lē] *adverb*, honestly, truly

**sin-cer-i-ty** [sǐn-sĕr′ǐ-tē] *adverb*, honesty, truthfulness

**sin-ew** [sǐn′yōō] *noun*, 1) a tendon, a muscle 2) strength, power

**sing** [sǐng] *verb*, to make music with the voice

**singe** [sǐnj] *verb*, to scorch or burn the surface or ends

**sin-gle** [sǐng′gəl] *adjective*, 1) consisting of only one person or thing, alone, *noun*, 2) in baseball, a hit in which the batter reaches first base

**sin-gu-lar** [sǐng′gyə-lər] *adjective*, 1) when speaking of one, *noun*, 2) unique, particular, individual

**sin-is-ter** [sǐn′ǐ-stər] *adjective*, dishonest, indicative of lurking evil, wicked, menacing

**sink** [sǐngk] *noun*, 1) a basin that holds water, *verb*, 2) to go down 3) to become submerged in water 4) to permeate the mind

**sin-ner** [sǐn′ər] *noun*, one who does wrong to others

**sip** [sǐp] *noun*, 1) a small amount of liquid swallowed, *verb*, 2) to drink a very small amount

**si-phon** [sī′fən] *noun*, a bent tube, having one end longer than the other, used for drawing liquids from a higher to a lower level

**sir** [sûr] *noun*, 1) the title of a knight 2) a respectful term to use when talking to a man

**si-ren** [sī′rən] *noun*, a device that makes a loud warning sound

**sis-ter** [sǐs′tər] *noun*, 1) a girl who shares the same parents with a sibling 2) the title for a nun

**sit** [sǐt] *verb*, to rest in a chair or on the floor, with the back straight

**site** [sīt] *noun*, a particular piece of land or a building whose location has a specific use

**sit-u-ate** [sǐch′ōō-āt′] *verb*, to put in place, to position, to locate

**sit-u-a-tion** [sĭch′o͞o-ā′shən] *noun*, 1) circumstances, the state of affairs, a case 2) a position

**six** [sĭks] *adjective, noun*, the number 6, five plus one

**six-teen** [sĭk-stēn′] *adjective, noun*, the number 16, six plus ten

**six-teenth** [sĭk-stēnth′] *adjective, noun*, the number 16 in order, written 16$^{th}$

**sixth** [sĭksth] *adjective, noun*, the number 6 in order, written 6$^{th}$

**six-ti-eth** [sĭk′stē-ĭth] *adjective, noun*, number 60 in order, 60$^{th}$

**six-ty** [sĭks′tē] *adjective*, the number 60, six times ten

**size** [sīz] *noun*, ) the amount of space that something takes up

**skate** [skāt] *noun*, 1) a runner or set of wheels with a frame to fit the shoe, *verb*, 2) to glide over the ground with shoes fit with a runner or wheels

**skel-e-ton** [skĕl′ĭ-tn] *noun*, the bones of a person or animal that show its size and structure

**skep-tic** [skĕp′tĭk] *noun*, a doubter, a cynic, a questioner

**skep-ti-cal** [skĕp′tĭ-kəl] *adjective*, distrustful, not convinced

**sketch** [skĕch] *noun*, 1) a drawing that lacks detail, an image, *verb*, 2) to draw in a rough manner

**ski** [skē] *noun, plural*, **skis**, one of a pair of long, flat, wood or metal runners used for gliding on snow or water *verb*, 2) to slide over snow on blades using poles for balance

**skid** [skĭd] *noun*, 1) a pallet to elevate something off the ground, *verb*, 2) to slip on a wet surface 3) to lose traction

**skill** [skĭl] *noun*, having the ability and knowledge to do something

**skil-let** [skĭl′ĭt] *noun*, a small metal pan with a handle, a frying pan

**skill-ful** [skĭl′fəl] *adjective*, very good at doing something

**skill-ful-ly** [skĭl′fə-lē] *adverb*, intelligently, sensibly

**skim** [skĭm] *verb*, 1) to read over quickly 2) to take off the floating layer 3) to glide in a sail boat

**skimp** [skĭmp] *verb*, to hold back, to offer small portions

**skin** [skĭn] *noun*, 1) the covering of the body, or fruit, often covered with hairs, *verb*, 2) to remove the outer layer of something

**skip** [skĭp] *verb*, 1) to move by alternately hopping or stepping, to move with light steps 2) to omit, to pass over, to miss

**skirt** [skûrt] *noun*, 1) woman's clothing that hangs from the waist, *verb*, 2) to avoid

**skit** [skĭt] *noun*, a short play or theatrical performance

**skit-tish** [skĭt′ĭsh] *adjective*, lively, frisky, nervous

**skulk** [skŭlk] *verb*, 1) to move slyly and secretly in a sneaking manner 2) to lie in hiding

**skull** [skŭl] *noun*, the bony structure of the head enclosing the brain

**skunk** [skŭngk] *noun*, a rodent with black fur distinguished by a white strip that goes down its back and tail and sprays a horrible smell when scared

**sky** [skī] *noun*, the space above the Earth which can be seen when you look up

**sky-scrap-er** [skī′skrā′pər] *noun*, a very tall building

**slack** [slăk] *adjective*, 1) lazy, slow, barely moving 2) a mixture of small pieces of coal, dust, and dirt left from screening coal

**slacks** [slăks] *noun*, *plural*, pants or trousers for casual wear

**slain** [slān] *past tense* of **slay**

**slam** [slăm] *verb*, 1) to fling or put down violently, with a loud noise 2) to shut, to close

**slan-der** [slăn′dər] *noun*, 1) a malicious, false statement made about a person, *verb*, 2) to lie about someone, to malign

**slang** [slăng] *noun*, *no plural*, language used in conversation, that is crude, disrespectful, or inappropriate, an expletive

**slant** [slănt] *verb*, to lean or slope

**slap** [slăp] *noun*, 1) the blow or hit caused by something flat, *verb*, 2) to hit with something flat, such as an open hand

**slate** [slāt] *adjective*, 1) a gray color, *noun*, 2) a fine-grained metamorphic rock used as a roof tile or writing tablet with chalk

**slaugh-ter** [slô′tər] *noun*, *no plural*, 1) a killing of a large number of people or animals, *verb*, 2) to kill animals or people as a group

**slave** [slāv] *noun*, a person owned as property, subject to the will of his owner

**slav-er-y** [slā′və-rē] *noun*, *no plural*, the concept of owning people as property

**slay** [slā] *verb*, to kill or murder

**slea-zy** [slē′zē] *adjective*, low class

**sled** [slĕd] *noun*, a wooden device with runners on the bottom used to carry people or things on snow or ice as a vehicle

**sleek** [slēk] *adjective*, smooth, neat, glossy, well-groomed

**sleep** [slēp] *noun*, *no plural*, 1) a time of rest, when not awake and alert, *verb*, 2) to rest semi-unconscious with eyes closed

**sleet** [slēt] *noun*, 1) a combination of ice and rain falling from the sky, *verb*, 2) to shower frozen rain

**sleeve** [slēv] *noun*, the part of clothing that covers the arm

**sleigh** [slā] *noun*, a horse drawn vehicle with runners used for carrying people over snow

**sleight** [slīt] *noun*, skill, cunning

**slen-der** [slĕn′dər] *adjective*, 1) slim, thin, narrow 2) meager

**slice** [slīs] *noun*, 1) a piece cut from the whole, a share, *verb*, 2) to cut a flat piece off from a whole

**slick** [slĭk] *adjective*, 1) a surface that is slippery when wet 2) clever, deceitful

**slide** [slīd] *noun*, 1) a piece of playground equipment you can sit on and slip on the surface, an image for projection on a screen, *verb*, 3) to move smoothly along a surface, to slip

**slight** [slīt] *adjective*, of a small degree, of little importance

**slim** [slĭm] *adjective*, slender, thin, lean, narrow, meager

**slime** [slīm] *noun*, mire, mud

**sling** [slĭng] *noun*, 1) a piece of cloth holding something in place, *verb*, 2) to throw

**slip** [slĭp] *noun*, 1) a piece of paper 2) a garment worn under a dress 3) a mistake 4) a stall to keep something 5) a cutting from a plant, *verb*, 6) to lose your balance and fall off your feet 7) to enter or exit unobserved 8) to escape, to pass from

**slip-per** [slĭp'ər] *noun*, a light shoe which may be slipped on easily

**slip-per-y** [slĭp'ə-rē] *adjective*, 1) smooth and slick or slimy, hard to grip 2) devious, not trustworthy, shifty

**slit** [slĭt] *noun*, 1) a long narrow opening, *verb*, 2) to make a small cut as an opening

**slith-er** [slĭth'ər] *verb*, to move, walk or slide like a snake

**slo-gan** [slō'gən] *noun*, a catch phrase, a motto

**slope** [slōp] *noun*, 1) a surface which is higher on one side than the other, *verb*, 2) to lean on an incline, to slant up or downward

**slot** [slŏt] *noun*, a long, narrow opening for receiving something

**sloth** [slôth] *noun*, a lazy person

**slov-en-ly** [slŭv'ən-lē] *adjective*, untidy, careless in work habits

**slow** [slō] *adjective*, 1) to move without much speed, not fast 2) behind others, sluggish

**slow-ly** [slō'lē] *adverb*, to crawl or move sluggishly, not quickly

**slug** [slŭg] *noun*, 1) a soft, slimy creature without bones or legs that eats plants 2) a false coin, *verb*, 3) to hit with a fist

**sluice** [slōōs] *noun*, an artificial channel for water with a gate

**slum** [slŭm] *noun*, a poor neighborhood, a ghetto

**slum-ber** [slŭm'bər] *noun*, 1) a deep sleep, a long nap, *verb*, 2) to sleep, to doze

**slump** [slŭmp] *noun*, 1) a drop, a decline, a decrease, *verb*, 2) to sink, to slouch, to stoop

**slur** [slûr] *noun*, 1) a disrespectful remark, *verb*, 2) to insult, to offend 3) to garble, to speak unintelligibly

**slush** [slŭsh] *noun*, partially melting snow or ice

**sly** [slī] *adjective*, clever and deceiving, calculating

**smack** [smăk] *noun*, 1) a kiss, a pat, a peck, *verb*, 2) to hit with a hand as a slap 3) to put the lips together after a tasty meal

**small** [smôl] *adjective*, 1) little, not big 2) mean-spirited, petty

**small-er** [smôl'ər] *adjective*, not as big, shorter, less, fewer

**small-est** [smôl'ĕst] *adjective*, tiny, very little

**smart** [smärt] *adjective*, 1) intelligent, bright 2) well dressed, attractive, fashionable, *verb*, 3) to feel a painful, stinging sensation

**smash** [smăsh] *verb*, to break violently into many pieces

**smat-ter-ing** [smăt'ər-ĭng] *noun*, slight knowledge, a few facts

**smell** [smĕl] *noun*, 1) the identifying scent that distinguishes something, *verb*, 2) to use one of the five senses to recognize a scent

**smelt** [smĕlt] *verb*, to melt in a furnace, to purify an ore

**smile** [smīl] *noun*, 1) an expression formed by the upward curve of the mouth, to show pleasure, amusement, etc., 2) to look pleased, happy, or amused

**smirk** [smûrk] *noun*, a twisted smile, a smug expression

**smog** [smŏg] *noun*, a mixture of pollutants, principally ground-level ozone, produced by chemical reactions in the air

**smoke** [smōk] *noun*, 1) visible fumes, *verb*, 2) to puff or inhale the vapor from a lit cigarette, 3) to make fumes come from fire

**smol-der** [smōl′dər] *verb*, 1) to burn without flame 2) anger, liable to break out at any moment

**smooth** [smōōth] *adjective*, 1) even, level, without bumps 2) calm, composed, unruffled

**smoth-er** [smŭth′ər] *verb*, to hide or suppress, to suffocate

**smudge** [smŭj] *noun*, 1) a dirty mark, a smear, *verb*, 2) to make dirty with streaks, to blur

**smug-gle** [smŭg′əl] *verb*, to bring things across borders secretly or illegally to avoid tariffs or border police

**snack** [snăk] *noun*, 1) food eaten between meals, *verb*, 2) to eat when you are hungry

**snail** [snāl] *noun*, a slug in a spirally coiled shell

**snake** [snāk] *noun*, 1) a cold-blooded reptile without legs that slithers on the ground, *verb*,

2) to move like a snake by slithering and sliding

**snap** [snăp] *noun*, 1) the sharp sound of something breaking 2) a clothing fastener like a button that locks together, *verb*, 3) to make a crackling sound 4) to try to nip or bite someone

**snare** [snâr] *noun*, 1) a trap that entangles its victim, *verb*, 2) to trap with a noose, to entangle

**snarl** [snärl] *verb*, 1) to make an angry noise with bared teeth 2) to talk in a vicious tone

**snatch** [snăch] *verb*, to take something directly from someone in a rough manner

**sneak** [snēk] *noun*, 1) a cheater, a rascal, *verb*, 2) to creep, to slink

**sneer** [snîr] *verb*, to laugh at someone to make fun of them

**sneeze** [snēz] *noun*, to blow air through the nose and mouth without warning

**sniff** [snĭf] *verb*, to breathe in, to inhale, to get a whiff, to smell

**snif-fle** [snĭf′əl] *verb*, to gasp as if to hold back tears

**snob** [snŏb] *noun*, someone who thinks he is better than others

**snore** [snôr] *verb*, to make a loud guttural noise in the nose or throat when sleeping

**snout** [snout] *noun*, the part of an animal's head projecting forward containing the nose and jaws

**snow** [snō] *noun*, *no plural*, 1) precipitation that forms in the cloud as ice and falls to the ground as white crystals, *verb*, 2) a flurry of crystals or snowflakes falling to the earth from the sky

**snug** [snŭg] *adjective*, close fitting, comfortable, cozy, compact

**so** [sō] *adverb*, 1) in such a way, to such a point 2) also 3) very, very much 4) therefore 5) in order that 6) the same thing 7) used to show agreement 8) factual

**soak** [sōk] *verb*, to leave something immersed in liquid for awhile

**soap** [sōp] *noun*, a substance used for cleaning, manufactured as bars, flakes, or liquid, mixed with water

**soar** [sôr] *verb*, to fly or ascend quickly and easily upward

**sob** [sŏb] *verb*, to cry aloud in large gasps, to weep convulsively

**so-ber** [sō′bər] *adjective*, serious, somber, not gay or laughing

**so-bri-e-ty** [sə-brī′ĭ-tē] *noun*, self-restraint, recovery from abusing alcohol, not drunk

**so-bri-quet** [sō′brĭ-kā′] *noun*, a nickname, a pet name

**soc-cer** [sŏk′ər] *noun*, *no plural*, a game of football as played in South America and Europe

**so-cial** [sō′shəl] *adjective*, pertaining to men as living in society, friendly, gregarious

**so-cial-ism** [sō′shə-lĭz′əm] *adjective*, a communist philosophy of equal sharing

**so-ci-e-ty** [sə-sī′ĭ-tē] *noun*, a group of persons associated together

**so-ci-ol-o-gy** [sō′sē-ŏl′ə-jē] *noun*, the science of the development of human society

**sock** [sŏk] *noun*, 1) a short stocking made of soft material to cover the foot, *verb*, 2) to punch

**sock-et** [sŏk′ĭt] *noun*, any device that holds a complementary part

**sod** [sŏd] *noun*, earth, dirt, soil

**so-da** [sō′də] *noun*, a carbonated beverage flavored with syrup

**so-di-um** [sō′dē-əm] *noun*, a silver-white, metallic element of the alkali group, also known as salt

**so-fa** [sō′fə] *noun*, a long couch, usually upholstered and having a back and arms

**soft** [sôft] *adjective*, 1) tender 2) not hard 3) low volume, not loud 4) smooth or silky

**soft-en** [sô′fən] *verb*, 1) to ease, to relax, 2) to melt

**soft-ly** [sôft′lē] *adverb*, 1) quietly 2) mildly, gently

**soft-ware** [sôft′wâr′] *noun*, instructions that allow a computer to do specific tasks

**soil** [soil] *noun*, 1) the earth where plants and organisms grow, the top layer of the earth, *verb*, 2) to make something dirty

**so-journ** [sō′jûrn′] *noun*, 1) a brief stay, *verb*, 2) to stay temporarily

**sol-ace** [sŏl′ĭs] *noun*, comfort in trouble, or sorrow, or distress

**so-lar** [sō′lər] *adjective*, referring to or relating to the sun

**sold** [sōld] *verb*, *past tense* of **sell**

**sol-der** [sŏd′ər] *noun*, a metal or a metallic alloy used to join by fusing metallic surfaces together

**sol-dier** [sōl′jər] *noun*, a man or woman enlisted in the army

**sole** [sōl] *adjective*, 1) single, one *noun*, 2) the part of the shoe on which the bottom of the foot rests 3) an edible flat fish

**sole-ly** [sōl′lē] *adverb*, the only one

**sol-emn** [sŏl′əm] *adjective*, serious, grave, formal and dignified

**so-le-noid** [sō′lə-noid′] *noun*, a cylindrical round coil

**so-lic-it** [sə-lĭs′ĭt] *verb*, to ask someone to buy something or commit themselves

**so-lic-i-tor** [sə-lĭs′ĭ-tər] *noun*, the law officer of a city or government

**sol-id** [sŏl′ĭd] *adjective*, 1) not hollow, hard, firm, *noun*, 2) any substance that cannot flow, takes up space and has a definite shape and volume

**sol-id-ify** [sə-lĭd′ə-fī′] *verb*, to change from liquid to solid

**so-lil-o-quy** [sə-lĭl′ə-kwē] *noun*, the act of talking to one's self, a monologue in a drama

**sol-i-taire** [sŏl′ĭ-târ′] *noun*, 1) a gem set by itself 2) a card game involving one person

**sol-i-tar-y** [sŏl′ĭ-tĕr′ē] *adjective*, living or being by one's self, single, alone, secluded

**sol-i-tude** [sŏl′ĭ-tōōd′] *noun*, state of being alone, a lonely place

**so-lo** [sō′lō] *noun*, 1) something accomplished by one person 2) an unaccompanied performance

**sol-stice** [sŏl′stĭs] *noun*, either of two times a year when the sun is farthest from the equator, June 21 and December 22

**sol-u-ble** [sŏl′yə-bəl] *adjective*, something that dissolves

**so-lu-tion** [sə-lōō′shən] *noun*, 1) a liquid containing another substance dissolved in it 2) the answer found

**solve** [sŏlv] *verb*, to find the answer by studying the problem

**sol-vent** [sŏl′vənt] *adjective*, 1) debt free, able to pay one's debts, *noun*, 2) a usually liquid substance in which another substance can dissolve

**som-ber** [sŏm′bər] *adjective*, gloomy, serious, melancholy

**some** [sŭm] *adjective*, 1) an amount of, not all, *pronoun*, 2) referring to people or things without saying exactly who or what

**some-bod-y** [sŭm′bŏd′ē] *pronoun*, any person, an unknown or unnamed individual

**some-how** [sŭm′hou′] *adverb*, in some unknown way

**some-one** [sŭm′wŭn′] *pronoun*, a person or an individual

**some-place** [sŭm′plās′] *noun*, a location, somewhere

**som-er-sault** [sŭm′ər-sôlt′] *noun*, the act of turning upside down with your head between your legs as though rolling in a ball

**some-thing** [sŭm′thĭng] *pronoun*, an unknown amount or identity

**some-time** [sŭm′tīm′] *adverb*, a time in the past or future

**some-times** [sŭm′tīmz′] *adverb*, occasionally, not always

**some-what** [sŭm′hwŏt′] *adverb*, slightly, to some degree

**some-where** [sŭm′hwâr′] *adverb*, in or to, in an unspecified space

**som-nam-bu-list** [sŏm-năm′byə-lĭst] *noun*, a sleepwalker

301

**son** [sŭn] *noun*, a male child, or offspring

**song** [sông] *noun*, 1) a piece of music with words 2) poetry

**son-net** [sŏn′ĭt] *noun*, a poem, fourteen lines in iambic pentameter

**soon** [so͞on] *adverb*, something that will happen in a short time from now, promptly, quickly

**soon-er** [so͞o′nər] *adjective*, before long, earlier than

**soot** [so͝ot] *noun*, *no plural*, a black powder separated from fuel during combustion, smoke residue, cinders, ash

**soothe** [so͞oth] *verb*, 1) to ease or comfort 2) to quiet, to pacify

**so-phis-ti-ca-tion** [sə-fĭs′tĭ-kā′shən] *noun*, intelligence, social grace, elegance, style, good taste

**soph-o-more** [sŏf′ə-môr] *noun*, a student in his second year of a four-year course

**so-pran-o** [sə-prăn′ō] *noun*, a singer who can reach the high notes in music

**sor-cer-ess** [sôr′sər-ĭs] *noun*, a magician, a witch

**sor-did** [sôr′dĭd] *adjective*, filthy, base, vile, squalid, selfish

**sore** [sôr, sōr] *adjective*, 1) hurting, painful, *noun*, 2) a painful, injured place on the body

**so-ror-i-ty** [sə-rôr′ĭ-tē] *noun*, a society or club of girls or women

**sor-row** [sŏr′ō] *noun*, sadness

**sor-ry** [sŏr′ē] *adjective*, feeling pity or sorrow, regret

**sort** [sôrt] *noun*, 1) a special kind, *verb*, 2) to separate into different categories, to classify

**sought** [sôt] *past tense* of **seek**

**soul** [sōl] *noun*, the part of you that is not body, and that some people think does not die with your body, the spirit of a person

**sound** [sound] *adjective*, 1) healthy, strong 2) deep or undisturbed, *noun*, 3) something heard from transmitted vibrations, *verb*, 4) to make a noise

**soup** [so͞op] *noun*, a liquid food made by boiling meat, fish, or vegetables and seasonings

**sour** [sour] *adjective*, 1) having a sharp, biting, acid taste, tart, tangy, 2) soured, curdled

**source** [sôrs] *noun*, 1) the thing or place from which something comes 2) someone who provides information 3) a reference book

**south** [south] *adjective*, just opposite the north

**South America** [south-ə-měr′ĭ-kə] *noun*, one of the seven continents, containing 5.9% of the world's population

**South Carolina** [south-kăr′ə-lī′nə] *noun*, one of the 50 United States, located in the Southeast, the capital is Columbia. The state flower of **South Carolina** is the yellow jasmine, and the motto is "Prepared in mind and resources." or "While I breathe I hope."

**South Dakota** [south-də-kō′tə] *noun*, one of the 50 United States, located in the Northwest, the capital is Pierre. The state flower of **South Dakota** is the pasque flower and the motto is "Under God the people rule."

**sou-ve-nir** [soo′və-nîr′] *noun*, that which serves as a reminder, a keepsake, a memento

**sov-er-eign** [sŏv′ər-ĭn] *adjective*, highest in power, chief

**sow** *noun*, 1) [sou] *noun*, an adult female pig, [sō]*verb*, 2) to scatter seeds over the ground where they will grow to produce a crop

**soy-bean** [soi′bēn′] *noun*, a bean plant grown for its edible, nutritious seeds

**space** [spās] *noun*, 1) the limitless three-dimensional area all around 2) an empty place or unoccupied time

**space-ship** [spās′shĭp′] *noun*, a rocket orbiting the earth

**spa-cious** [spā′shəs] *adjective*, vast in extent, roomy, sizeable

**spade** [spād] *noun*, 1) a small hand-held shovel 2) one of the four suits in a deck of cards

**spa-ghet-ti** [spə-gĕt′ē] *noun*, a variety of macaroni made in cords of small diameter

**span** [spăn] *noun*, a stretch, the measure, the distance

**spare** [spâr] *adjective*, 1) kept in addition to what is already available, *verb*, 2) to give something extra, to share 3) to omit, to leave out

**spark** [spärk] *noun*, 1) a tiny burning particle, *verb*, 2) to stimulate, to set in motion

**spar-kle** [spär′kəl] *verb*, to shine with bright points of light

**spark plug** [spärk′plŭg′] *noun*, a device with two electrodes between which an electric jump spark is made

**spar-row** [spăr′ō] *noun*, a small brownish-gray bird

**sparse** [spärs] *adjective*, not thick, thinly scattered or distributed

**spasm** [spăz′əm] *noun*, a seizure, a fit, a convulsive movement

**spa-tial** [spā′shəl] *adjective*, relating to space

**spat-u-la** [spăch′ə-lə] *noun*, an instrument with a broad blade used for spreading or mixing

**spawn** [spôn] *verb*, to lay eggs

**spay** [spā] *verb*, to remove the reproductive organs, to castrate

**speak** [spēk] *verb*, to say words aloud, to talk, to express ideas

**speak-er** [spē′kər] *noun*, 1) the one talking 2) an orator, a lecturer

**spear** [spîr] *noun*, a long thin weapon with a pointed end

**spe-cial** [spĕsh′əl] *adjective*, 1) individual, peculiar, particular, different from the others 2) extra nice, distinct 3) having a particular function or purpose

**spe-cial-ist** [spĕsh′ə-lĭst] *noun*, one who studies a subject at great length, an expert, an authority

**spe-cial-ize** [spĕsh′ə-līz′] *verb*, to focus on a particular profession

**spe-cies** [spē′shēz] *noun*, *plural*, 1) a distinct sort, kind, or variety 2) a group of living things that can breed together

**spe-cif-ic** [spĭ-sĭf′ĭk] *noun*, special, explicit, precise, peculiar

**spec-i-fy** [spĕs′ə-fī′] *verb*, to
designate, to name explicitly, to
indicate, to point out in detail

**spec-i-men** [spĕs′ə-mən] *noun*, a
part of anything to show the
quality of the whole

**spe-cious** [spē′shəs] *adjective*,
something false that appears to
be true, deceptively attractive

**speck** [spĕk] *noun*, a small piece or
particle of something

**spec-ta-cle** [spĕk′tə-kəl] *noun*, 1) a
public scene that attracts a lot of
attention  2) a display, a show

**spec-ta-cles** [spĕk′tə-kəlz] *noun*,
*plural*, glasses for the eyes to
improve vision set in a frame
that rests on the nose and ears

**spec-tac-u-lar** [spĕk-tăk′yə-lər]
*adjective*, impressive, amazing,
breath-taking, dramatic

**spec-ta-tor** [spĕk′tā′tər] *noun*, one
who looks on and watches, an
observer, a bystander

**spec-ter** [spĕk′tər] *noun*, any object
of dread, a ghost, an apparition

**spec-tro-scope** [spĕk′trə-skōp′]
*noun*, an optical instrument

**spec-trum** [spĕk′trəm] *noun*, a
broad range or sequence,
especially of light separated into
its constituent colors

**spec-u-late** [spĕk′yə-lāt′] *verb*,
1) to gamble, to buy and sell on
the market 2) to consider, to
contemplate, to hypothesize

**spec-u-la-tion** [spĕk′yə-lā′shən]
*noun*, theory, hypothesis,
conjecture, contemplation

**speech** [spēch] *noun*, 1) a long talk
usually prepared in advance
2) language, words, dialect

**speed** [spēd] *noun*, 1) the rate at
which something moves, *verb*,
2) to quicken, to hasten

**speed-om-e-ter** [spĭ-dŏm′ĭ-tər]
*noun*, an instrument for
indicating speed or velocity

**spell** [spĕl] *noun*, 1) a charm that
captivates some and holds their
attention 2) a short period of
time, *verb*, 3) to indicate the
correct arrangement of letters in
a word 4) to be a sign of

**spell-ing** [spĕl′ĭng] *noun*, the
correct use of the proper letters
composing a word

**spend** [spĕnd] *verb*, 1) to give
money for something 2) to use or
consume energy or time

**spent** [spĕnt] *past tense* of **spend**

**sphere** [sfîr] *noun*, 1) a ball or
globe 2) a social position

**spher-i-cal** [sfîr′ĭ-kəl] *adjective*,
globular, round like a ball

**spice** [spīs] *noun*, a seed or root of
a plant used to add flavor to food

**spi-der** [spī′dər] *noun*, a bug that
uses threads from its body to
make a web to capture insects

**spill** [spĭl] *noun*, 1) a fall, *verb*,
2) to accidentally allow a liquid
to flow out of a container

**spin** [spĭn] *verb*, 1) to whirl quickly
2) to twist into a thread from
wool or other natural fibers

**spin-ach** [spĭn′ĭch] *noun*, an edible
green leafy vegetable

**spine** [spīn] *noun*, the long row of
bones in your back

**spi-ral** [spī′rəl] *noun*, helical, like
the thread of a screw

**spire** [spīr] *noun*, the pointed top of a
tower or steeple

**spir-it** [spĭr′ĭt] *noun*, 1) a mysterious part of you which is not the body, the soul 2) an eager state of mind, enthusiasm 3) a supernatural being such as a ghost or a fairy 4) an alcoholic drink such as liquor

**spir-it-u-al** [spĭr′ĭ-choo-əl] *adjective*, airy, motivated by the soul, holy, religious

**spit** [spĭt] *noun*, 1) saliva, *verb*, 2) to spray water or saliva out of the mouth

**spite** [spīt] *noun*, *no plural*, hatred, feelings of malice, wanting to hurt or annoy another person

**splash** [splăsh] *noun*, 1) the sound made when a solid falls into liquid, *verb*, 2) to make a wave of water in a pool

**splen-did** [splĕn′dĭd] *adjective*, excellent, magnificent, very fine

**splice** [splīs] *verb*, to insert a shoot, to join, to graft, to unite

**splint** [splĭnt] *noun*, a board used to keep a thing from bending, a way of protecting a broken limb

**splin-ter** [splĭn′tər] *noun*, a thin piece of wood split off from a larger piece, a sliver

**split** [splĭt] *noun*, 1) a tear or a break, *verb*, 2) to break lengthwise 3) to share

**spoil** [spoil] *verb*, 1) to damage or injure, to ruin 2) to become rotten or decayed 3) to overindulge or corrupt by coddling someone

**spoke** [spōk] *noun*, 1) one of the bars joining the rim of a wheel to the center to support weight, *verb*, 2) *past tense* of **speak**

**sponge** [spŭnj] *noun*, 1) a substance that absorbs water, used to clean and wipe 2) a primitive marine animal having a soft elastic skeleton with many pores, *verb*, 3) to live off the generosity of others

**spon-sor** [spŏn′sər] *noun*, 1) a patron, supporter, mentor, backer, *verb*, 2) to offer financial support for a program

**spon-ta-ne-i-ty** [spŏn′tə-nē′ĭ-tē] *noun*, acting at the spur of the moment, impromptu

**spon-ta-ne-ous** [spŏn-tā′nē-əs] *adjective*, 1) acting on impulse, a result of natural law 2) energy

**spool** [spool] *noun*, a round object used to wind thread or wire

**spoon** [spoon] *noun*, a utensil consisting of a shallow bowl with a long handle attached to it, used for eating or stirring

**spoon-ful** [spoon′fool′] *noun*, the quantity that sits in a spoon

**spo-rad-ic** [spə-răd′ĭk] *adjective*, occurring irregularly

**spore** [spōr] *noun*, a cell that reproduces itself such as fungus, fern, or bacterium

**sport** [spōrt] *noun*, 1) games and exercises done for pleasure 2) a rascal 3) a teammate

**spot** [spŏt] *noun*, 1) a small mark, drop, or blemish 2) a location, *verb*, 3) to see something

**spouse** [spous] *noun*, a partner in marriage, husband or wife

**spout** [spout] *noun*, 1) the lip of a container from which liquid is poured, *verb*, 2) to spurt, to discharge, to gush forth

**sprain** [sprān] *verb*, to strain a body part by twisting it, causing it to swell

**sprawl** [sprôl] *verb*, to stretch, to spread out, to extend

**spray** [sprā] *noun*, 1) liquid dispersed in very fine drops 2) a small branch of flowers or foliage, *verb*, 3) to blow or scatter liquid in very fine drops

**spread** [sprĕd] *verb*, 1) to cover a surface with a thin layer 2) to unfold or stretch out 3) to circulate, to disseminate 4) to extend over a large area

**spring** [sprĭng] *noun*, 1) a river or pond coming up from the ground 2) a piece of wire twisted into a spiral 3) the season following winter, when plants begin to grow, *verb*, 4) to jump 5) to come from 6) to grow

**sprin-kle** [sprĭng′kəl] *verb*, 1) to spatter, to disperse in drops 2) to drizzle 3) to dust lightly

**sprint** [sprĭnt] *noun*, 1) a short fast run, *verb*, 2) to dash at top speed

**sprock-et** [sprŏk′ĭt] *noun*, a projection shaped so as to engage with a chain

**sprout** [sprout] *verb*, to grow out of a seed, to start to grow

**spruce** [sprōōs] *noun*, one of the softwood evergreen trees

**sprung** [sprŭng] *past tense* of **spring**

**spry** [sprī] *adjective*, vigorous, quick, energetic, agile

**spun** [spŭn] *past tense* of **spin**

**spur** [spûr] *noun*, 1) a short side track connecting with the main railroad 2) a sharp blade on the back of a boot used to urge horses to run faster 3) an impetus, a cause to action, *verb*, 4) to urge, to goad, to stimulate

**spu-ri-ous** [spyŏŏr′ē-əs] *adjective*, counterfeit, false, not genuine

**spurn** [spûrn] *verb*, to reject, to scorn, to despise, to shun

**spy** [spī] *noun*, *plural*, **spies** 1) an agent hired to secretly obtain information *verb*, 2) to see or catch sight of 3) to keep secret watch

**squad** [skwŏd] *noun*, a small group of soldiers who work, train, and fight together 2) a sports team

**squad-ron** [skwŏd′rən] *noun*, armed military aircraft

**squal-id** [skwŏl′ĭd] *adjective*, dirty through neglect, foul, filthy

**squan-der** [skwŏn′dər] *verb*, to spend money or resources without being accountable

**square** [skwâr] *noun*, 1) a surface with four equal sides and right angle corners 2) an open area in the center of town surrounded by stores and businesses

**square number** [skwâr- nŭm′bər] *noun*, the product of two equal factors, e.g., 12 x 12 = 144

**squash** [skwŏsh] *noun*, 1) a vegetable that grows on a vine 2) a game similar to racquetball, *verb*, 3) to repress 4) to flatten by pressing or from pressure

**squat** [skwŏt] *adjective*, 1) wide, stocky, *verb*, 2) to stoop

**squeak** [skwēk] *noun*, 1) a very sharp, high-pitched sound, *verb*, 2) to make a short high-pitched sound

**squeal** [skwēl] *noun*, 1) a shrill cry, *verb*, 2) to make such a sound 3) to turn informer

**squeeze** [skwēz] *verb*, to press hard upon 2) to put pressure on to extract liquid 3) to force one's way 4) to crowd

**squid** [skwĭd] *noun*, a sea creature similar to an octopus

**squint** [skwĭnt] *verb*, to scrunch one's eyes to strain to see

**squirm** [skwûrm] *verb*, to wiggle

**squir-rel** [skwûr′əl, skwŭr′-] *noun*, a small rodent with a bushy tail that lives in trees

**sta-bil-i-ty** [stə-bĭl′ĭ-tē] *adjective*, firmness, constancy, strength

**sta-ble** [stā′bəl] *adjective*, 1) firm, steady, *noun*, 2) a building in which horses are kept

**stac-ca-to** [stə-kä′tō] *adjective*, music played in a quick, abrupt manner

**stack** [stăk] *noun*, 1) a large pile arranged in some sort of order 2) a chimney, *verb*, 3) to pile up

**sta-di-um** [stā′dē-əm] *noun*, an open arena where concerts, sports, or events are held

**staff** [stăf] *noun*, a long stick carried in the hand for support

**stag** [stăg] *noun*, a male deer

**stage** [stāj] *noun*, 1) a raised floor or platform in a theatre or auditorium 2) a period of time or a step in development

**stage-coach** [stāj′kōch′] *noun*, a carriage on wheels pulled by horses on a fixed route

**stag-ger** [stăg′ər] *verb*, to stand or walk unsteadily, to reel

**stag-nant** [stăg′nənt] *adjective*, not moving or flowing, motionless

**stag-nate** [stăg′nāt′] *verb*, to be or become stagnant, motionless, to become impure or foul

**staid** [stād] *adjective*, sober, sedate

**stain** [stān] *noun*, 1) a mark that changes the appearance of something, a blot, *verb*, 2) to make a strong mark that cannot be removed 3) to disgrace

**stair** [stâr] *noun*, a step connecting different levels, *plural*, **stairs,** a series or flight of steps

**stake** [stāk] *noun*, 1) a pointed post in the ground 2) a gamble, a risk

**stale** [stāl] *adjective*, 1) old, dry, not fresh, tasteless 2) dull, bored

**stale-mate** [stāl′māt′] *noun*, a deadlock, a situation in which no side may take action

**stalk** [stôk] *noun*, 1) the long part of a plant that supports leaves or flowers, *verb*, 2) to follow someone with the intention of harming them 3) to pursue prey

**stall** [stôl] *noun*, 1) a small open room, as in a barn or a market place, *verb*, 2) to stop due to a mechanical failure

**stal-lion** [stăl′yən] *noun*, a male horse used for breeding

**stal-wart** [stôl′wərt] *adjective*, 1) sturdy, strong 2) brave 3) firm, steadfast

**stam-i-na** [stăm′ə-nə] *noun*, the power to endure, strength

**stamp** [stămp] *noun*, 1) a small piece of paper purchased to put on an envelope or package to send it through the mail 2) the imprint left from a device used to leave a mark, *verb*, 3) to mark with a special sign or design 4) to set the foot down heavily

**stam-pede** [stăm-pēd/] *verb*, to rush wildly in a group

**stance** [stăns] *noun*, 1) posture 2) political or social position

**stand** [stănd] *verb*, 1) to be your feet 2) to take a position 3) to mean or signify, to represent

**stand-ard** [stăn/dərd] *adjective*, 1) regular, official, basic, *noun*, 2) a fixed quality by which things are compared

**stands** [stăndz] *noun, plural*, the bleachers where spectators watch sports events

**stan-za** [stăn/zə] *noun*, a verse in a poem, a song, or a refrain

**sta-ple** [stā/pəl] *noun*, 1) principle commodity, an essential element 2) a wire used to attach things together such as cloth or paper, *verb*, 3) to bond two things together with staples applied by a stapler

**star** [stär] *noun*, 1) a point of light that can be seen in the sky at night 2) a five-pointed shape, *verb*, 3) to stand out in a positive way, to be outstanding

**star-board** [stär/bərd] *adjective*, the right-hand side of a ship as one faces the bow

**starch** [stärch] *noun*, a carbohydrate, that turns into sugar in the body

**stare** [stâr] *verb*, to look at someone or something with a steady gaze, to glare

**stark** [stärk] *adjective*, extremely

simple or severe, bleak

**start** [stärt] *noun*, 1) an act of beginning, *verb*, 2) to begin

**star-tle** [stär/tl] *verb*, to surprise, to greet unexpectedly, to shock

**star-va-tion** [stär-vā/shən] *noun*, to suffer from hunger and lack of food or nourishment

**starve** [stärv] *verb*, to be hungry, unfed, deprived of food

**state** [stāt] *noun*, 1) the condition of something 2) a mood 3) a group of people living under an independent government, that is part of a country or federal union which governs itself as a republic or commonwealth, *verb*, 5) to say, to declare

**state-ment** [stāt/mənt] *noun*, 1) a spoken or written commitment 2) a summary of an account showing the balance

**states-man** [stāts/mən] *noun*, a leader of government

**stat-ic** [stăt/ĭk] *noun*, applicable to electricity not in motion

**sta-tion** [stā/shən] *noun*, a stopping place for the convenience of passengers, a depot

**sta-tion-ar-y** [stā/shə-něr/ē] *adjective*, fixed in a place, not changing, not moving

**sta-tion-er-y** [stā/shə-něr/ē] *noun*, writing paper, pens, and ink

**sta-tis-tic** [stə-tĭs/tĭk] *noun*, a fact stated as a number or in tables

**stat-ue** [stăch/ōō] *noun*, replica of a figure, real or imaginary made of plaster, bronze, marble, etc.

**stat-ure** [stăch/ər] *noun*, 1) a person's status or place in the community 2) the height of a person or animal

**sta-tus** [stā′təs] *noun*, position, high standing, prestige

**stat-ute** [stăch′ōōt] *noun*, a law enacted by a legislature

**stat-u-to-ry** [stăch′ə-tôr′ē] *adjective*, authorized, made as a law, regulated by statute

**stay** [stā] *verb*, to continue to be

**stead-fast** [stĕd′făst′] *adjective*, firmly fixed or established, unwavering, constant

**stead-i-ly** [stĕd′ə-lē] *adverb*, constantly, continually, regularly

**stead-y** [stĕd′ē] *adjective*, 1) regular 2) firm, immovable

**steak** [stāk] *noun*, a thick flat piece of meat or fish

**steal** [stēl] *verb*, 1) to take or carry away without permission 2) to move or pass very quietly without making noise

**stealth** [stĕlth] *noun*, secrecy, sneakiness, surreptitious

**steam** [stēm] *noun*, 1) the vapor created by boiling water, *verb*, 2) to cook using the intense heat of steam 3) to expose to steam

**steel** [stēl] *noun*, a hard metal made of specially treated iron, used in machines, knives, hardware, etc.

**steep** [stēp] *adjective*, 1) having a sharp incline or slope, *verb*, 2) to soak in liquid, to saturate

**stee-ple** [stē′pəl] *noun*, a free-standing column or tower

**steer** [stîr] *noun*, 1) a form of long horned cattle, *verb*, 2) to drive, to fly, to conduct, or navigate

**stel-lar** [stĕl′ər] *adjective*, 1) star-like, referring to heavenly bodies, celestial 2) outstanding

**stem** [stĕm] *noun*, 1) the stalk of a plant that supports the flower and leaves, *verb*, 2) to develop from 3) to stop the flow of

**sten-cil** [stĕn′səl] *noun*, a thin sheet with perforations in the form of a design through which ink or paint may be forced

**step** [stĕp] *noun*, 1) a stair 2) the movement with a foot 3) one of a series of events in a program, *verb*, 4) to walk or go on foot

**ster-e-o** [stĕr′ē-ō′] *noun*, an electronic device that makes sounds or plays music

**ster-e-o-type** [stĕr′ē-ə-tīp′] *noun*, 1) a typical example or pattern 2) a conventional, oversimplified conception

**ste-rile** [stĕr′əl, -īl′] *adjective*, clean, antiseptic, germ free

**ster-i-lize** [stĕr′ə-līz′] *verb*, 1) to render incapable of germination, 2) to disinfect, to clean

**ster-ling** [stûr′lĭng] *adjective*, 1) genuine, superior, excellent, of the highest quality *noun*, 2) made of pure silver

**stern** [stûrn] *adjective*, 1) unsympathetic, firm, strict 2) the back of the boat

**steth-o-scope** [stĕth′ə-skōp′] *noun*, an instrument used to convey to the ear, sounds produced by the body, especially in the chest

**stew** [stōō] *noun*, 1) a thick soup, *verb*, 2) to cook in liquid

**stew-ard** [stōō′ərd] *noun*, 1) one who watches over something

2) one in charge of provisions and dinner arrangements

**stew-ard-ess** [stoo͞o′ər-dĭs] *noun*, a woman who serves passengers on an airplane, a flight attendant

**stick** [stĭk] *noun*, 1) a short branch or twig, *verb*, 2) to make something adhere to a surface 3) to push in or out 4) to stay with something, to persevere

**stiff** [stĭf] *adjective*, 1) something that cannot be moved or bent easily 2) difficult or hard to accomplish 3) sore

**stiff-en** [stĭf′ən] *verb*, to harden, to brace, to become rigid

**stig-ma** [stĭg′mə] *noun*, 1) the apex of a flower pistil where pollen is placed 2) a disgraceful blot

**stig-ma-tize** [stĭg′mə-tīz′] *verb*, to brand, to mark as wicked

**still** [stĭl] *adjective*, 1) without movement, *adverb*, 2) up to this or that time 3) even so

**still-ness** [stĭl′nĭs] *noun*, the state of being still or without sound

**stim-u-late** [stĭm′yə-lāt′] *verb*, to rouse to action, to excite

**stim-u-lus** [stĭm′yə-ləs] *noun*, an incentive, an impetus

**sting** [stĭng] *noun*, 1) the pain or wound of an insect or bug bite 2) a sharp or smarting pain 3) the attack of an insect on its prey or an enemy

**stin-gy** [stĭn′jē] *adjective*, not generous, miserly

**stink** [stĭngk] *noun*, 1) an unpleasant or awful odor, *verb*, 2) to give off a bad smell

**sti-pend** [stī′pĕnd′] *noun*, payment given for services

**stip-u-late** [stĭp′yə-lāt′] *verb*, to bargain, to specify as a condition of an agreement

**stir** [stûr] *verb*, to mix or blend

**stir-ring** [stûr′ĭng] *adjective*, moving, touching, exciting

**stitch** [stĭch] *noun*, 1) a needle and thread, piercing cloth and then coming out again to form a link of thread in a fabric 2) a loop added to a knitting needle, *verb*, 3) to sew, to mend

**stock** [stŏk] *noun*, goods kept on hand, merchandise

**stock-ade** [stŏ-kād′] *noun*, a barricade, a fence, an obstacle

**stock-hold-er** [stŏk′hōl′dər] *noun*, an owner of stocks or shares in a corporation

**stock-ing** [stŏk′ĭng] *noun*, a sheer leg covering made of nylon

**sto-ic** [stō′ĭk] *noun*, one who is indifferent to pleasure or pain, stern, impassive, cold

**stoke** [stōk] *verb*, to provide with fuel, to feed abundantly

**stole** [stōl] *past tense* of **steal**

**stom-ach** [stŭm′ək] *noun*, a large muscular bag in the body that receives food, digests some of it, and passes it on, to the intestines

**stone** [stōn] *noun*, 1) a small piece of rock, *verb*, 2) to pelt or kill

**stool** [stool] *noun*, 1) a seat with three or four legs and no back 2) a bowel movement

**stoop** [stoop] *verb*, 1) to bend or squat the body over forwards 2) to lower oneself, to condescend

**stop** [stŏp] *verb*, 1) to end, to make something come to an end 2) to prevent something from happening, moving, etc. 3) to complete the action

**stor-age** [stôr′ĭj] *noun*, the act of keeping things for future use

**store** [stōr] *noun*, 1) supply of things saved for use later 2) a shop, a place to buy things, *verb*, 3) to put away for later use

**stork** [stôrk] *noun*, a large bird with long legs and a large beak

**storm** [stôrm] *noun*, a period of high winds, possibly thunder and lightning, rain, or snow

**sto-ry** [stōr′ē] *noun*, 1) telling of events with words spoken or written in a book 2) an account of something either true or fictitious, a report, a description 3) the floor of a building

**stout** [stout] *adjective*, 1) short, heavy-set 2) resolute, firm

**stove** [stōv] *noun*, an appliance which is heated and used for cooking or heating

**stow** [stō] *verb*, to store, to put away for future use

**straight** [strāt] *adjective*, 1) not curved, *adverb*, 2) without going anywhere else or doing anything else 3) moving on a path that is unchanged 4) without delay, *noun*, 5) a poker hand of 5 cards in consecutive order

**straight-en** [strāt′n] *verb*, to fix or arrange in order

**strain** [strān] *noun*, 1) the change of a body produced by an external force 2) a new species or breed 3) a suggestion, a hint, a

trace, *verb*, 4) to cause stress, to stretch to reach

**strait** [strāt] *noun*, a narrow channel between two bodies of water, an inlet

**strand** [strănd] *noun*, 1) seashore, waterfront 2) a piece of something long and thin like a rope or a piece of hair

**strange** [strānj] *adjective*, unusual, odd, unfamiliar, exotic

**strange-ly** [strānj′lē] *adverb*, unusually, seldom, rarely

**stran-ger** [strān′jər] *noun*, a person you do not know, an outsider

**stran-gle** [străng′gəl] *verb*, 1) to kill by suffocating 2) to suppress

**strap** [străp] *noun*, 1) a narrow piece of leather, plastic, cloth, etc, used for fastening something, *verb*, 2) to fasten something on with a tie

**strat-e-gy** [străt′ə-jē] *noun*, a plan

**strat-o-sphere** [străt′ə-sfîr′] *noun*, the upper atmosphere extending 12-30 miles above the earth's surface, the ozone

**stra-tum** [strā′təm] *noun*, *plural* **strata**, a layer of the earth's surface, sedimentary rock

**straw** [strô] *noun*, 1) a dry stem 2) something that people use to suck a drink out of a glass

**straw-ber-ry** [strô′bĕr′ē] *noun*, the edible red berry of a small plant, that grows on the ground

**stray** [strā] *adjective*, 1) anything that does not seem to be part of a group, *verb*, 2) to wander away from home or the rest of the group 3) to digress

**streak** [strēk] *noun*, 1) a long mark like a band or a stripe, *verb*, 2) to draw stripes on something in a wild pattern

**stream** [strēm] *noun*, 1) a small river, a small body of running water 2) a steady or continuous flow, *verb*, 3) to flow, to pour

**street** [strēt] *noun*, a public paved road as in a town or city

**strength** [strĕngkth] *noun*, power, capacity for exertion or endurance, force in numbers

**strength-en** [strĕngk′thən] *verb*, to reinforce, to make stronger

**stren-u-ous** [strĕn′yo͞o-əs] *adjective*, characterized by vigorous exertion, difficult

**stress** [strĕs] *noun*, 1) anxiety, tension, *verb*, 2) to apply force to cause strain 3) to emphasize

**stretch** [strĕch] *noun*, 1) an expanse, a range or reach, *verb*, 2) to exaggerate 3) to extend across a given space 4) to extend one s body or limbs to feel limber

**stretch-er** [strĕch′ər] *noun*, a framework consisting of two poles with a cloth fastened between them used to carry an injured person

**strict** [strĭkt] *adjective*, close adherence to the rules

**stride** [strīd] *noun*, 1) a large step or movement, *verb*, 2) to step

**stri-dent** [strīd′nt] *adjective*, loud and harsh in sound, grating

**strike** [strīk] *noun*, 1) an unsuccessful attempt by a batter to hit a ball 2) a protest of wages that stops work in order to bargain for better working conditions, *verb*, 3) to hit or attack 4) to refuse to work discover, to uncover 6) to eliminate 7) to find, to reach

**string** [strĭng] *noun*, 1) a thin twine made by twisting several threads together 2) a fine piece of wire used in some musical instruments, *verb*, 3) to thread a bead onto a string

**strin-gent** [strĭn′jənt] *adjective*, strict, inflexible, exacting

**stripe** [strīp] *noun*, a long thin line

**strive** [strīv] *verb*, to exert oneself, to try, to make a strenuous effort

**stroke** [strōk] *noun*, 1) a mild heart attack, *verb*, 2) to caress, to rub

**stroll** [strōl] *verb*, to walk leisurely

**strong** [st rŏng] *adjective*, 1) able to take stress or strain 2) intense in degree 3) physically powerful

**struck** [strŭk] *verb*, *past tense* of **strike**

**struc-ture** [strŭk′chər] *noun*, 1) the framework of something, 2) a complete building

**strug-gle** [strŭg′əl] *noun*, 1) the fight, the effort, *verb*, 2) to continue to endure set backs

**strut** [strŭt] *verb*, to swagger, to walk with bravado

**stub-born** [stŭb′ərn] *adjective*, unwilling to give in or compromise, obstinate

**stuck** [stŭk] *verb*, *past tense* of **stick**

**stu-dent** [sto͞od′nt] *noun*, a person enrolled at a school or college

**stud-y** [stŭd′ē] *noun*, 1) a room to read and write 2) a subject or area of learning, *verb*, 3) to apply the mind to the effort to learn by reading and thinking

**stuff** [stŭf] *noun*, 1) substance, material, *verb*, 2) to fill by crowding, to push or crowd in

**stum-ble** [stŭm′bəl] *verb*, to walk unsteadily so that you appear to be about to fall, to trip while running 2) to come upon unexpectedly 3) to stammer

**stump** [stŭmp] *noun*, 1) what is left of a tree after it has been cut down, *verb*, 2) to perplex

**stun** [stŭn] *verb*, to astonish, to amaze, to confound, to shock

**stunt** [stŭnt] *noun*, 1) a performance, a skit, an act, *verb*, 2) to suppress, to retard the growth of something

**stu-pen-dous** [stoō-pĕn′dəs] *adjective*, astonishing, wonderful, amazing

**stu-por** [stoō′pər] *noun*, a state of apathy, a daze, lack of awareness

**stur-dy** [stûr′dē] *adjective*, very strongly built, durable

**stut-ter** [stə′tər] *verb*, to speak with difficulty, to stammer

**sty** [stī] *noun*, 1) a painful red swelling on the end of an eyelid 2) a pig pen

**style** [stīl] *noun*, 1) the fashion or design 2) elegance or flair

**sty-mie** [stī′mē] *verb*, to present an obstacle, to stump, to hinder

**suave** [swäv] *adjective*, smoothly, agreeable, courteous, polite

**sub-due** [səb-doō′] *verb*, to calm down, to bring under control

**sub-ject** [sŭb′jĭkt] *adjective*, 1) owing obedience to 2) likely to be affected by, *noun*, 3) an area of study 4) a person under the authority or control of another 5) in a sentence the word about which the predicate makes a statement, *verb*, 6) to expose to

**sub-jec-tive** [səb-jĕk′tĭv] *adjective*, based on personal feelings or opinions

**sub-lime** [sə-blīm′] *adjective*, great, noble, majestic, superior

**sub-lim-i-nal** [sŭb-lĭm′ə-nəl] *adjective*, affecting the subconscious, below the threshold of consciousness

**sub-ma-rine** [sŭb′mə-rēn′] *noun*, a naval warship armed with torpedoes and missiles that operates under water

**sub-merge** [səb-mûrj′] *verb*, to put or sink under water

**sub-mis-sive** [səb-mĭs′ĭv] *adjective*, to take orders without questioning authority

**sub-mit** [səb-mĭt′] *verb*, 1) to put something forward for someone else's reaction 2) to give in to someone or something

**sub-or-di-nate** [sə-bôr′dn-ĭt] *adjective*, 1) being in a lower rank or class, subject to another's authority *noun*, 2) one lower in rank, inferior

**sub-poe-na** [sə-pē′nə] *noun*, a writ commanding a person listed in it to appear in court

**sub-scribe** [səb-scrīb′] *verb*, 1) to sign up for something 2) to give permission or consent

**sub-scrip-tion** [səb-skrĭp′shən] *noun*, money paid as a form of membership for service

**sub-se-quent** [sŭb′sĭ-kwĕnt′] *adjective*, following, after

**sub-ser-vi-ent** [səb-sûr′vē-ənt] *adjective*, useful in an inferior capacity, subordinate

**sub-side** [səb-sīd′] *verb*, to settle down to become calm

**sub-si-dize** [sŭb′sĭ-dīz′] *verb*, 1) to add to 2) to provide financial aid

**sub-si-dy** [sŭb′sĭ-dē] *noun*, direct financial aid by the government

**sub-stance** [sŭb′stəns] *noun*, the material something is made of

**sub-stan-tial** [səb-stăn′shəl] *adjective*, 1) strong 2) having considerable property

**sub-stan-ti-ate** [səb-stăn′shē-āt′] *verb*, to verify, to support

**sub-stan-tive** [sŭb′stən-tĭv] *adjective*, essential, pertaining to

**sub-sti-tute** [sŭb′stĭ-to͞ot′] *noun*, 1) a person or thing put in place of another, a replacement *verb*, 2) to act in place of another

**sub-ter-fuge** [sŭb′tər-fyo͞oj′] *noun*, a device or plan by which one can hide an objective

**sub-ter-ra-ne-an** [sŭb′tə-rā′nē-ən] *adjective*, 1) under the earth's surface 2) hidden, secret

**sub-tle** [sŭt′l] *adjective*, difficult to to detect, not obvious, slight

**sub-tle-ty** [sŭt′l-tē] *noun*, cunning, delicately understated

**sub-tract** [səb-trăkt′] *verb*, to take away one number from another

**sub-trac-tion** [səb-trăk′shən] *noun*, an equation in which one number is taken from another

**sub-urb** [sŭb′ûrb′] *noun*, a residential community on the outskirts of a city or town

**sub-ur-ban** [sə-bûr′bən] *adjective*, pertaining to a smaller district next to a city or town

**sub-ver-sive** [səb-vûr′sĭv] *adjective*, tending to overthrow or ruin, corruption

**sub-way** [sŭb′wā′] *noun*, an underground electric train or urban transit system

**suc-ceed** [sək-sēd′] *adjective*, to follow in order, to be successful

**suc-cess** [sək-sĕs′] *noun*, accomplishment, achievement

**suc-cess-ful** [sək-sĕs′fəl] *adjective*, prosperous, enjoying abundance

**suc-ces-sion** [sək-sĕsh′ən] *noun*, sequence, order, descent

**suc-ces-sive** [sək-sĕs′ĭv] *adjective*, following one after another in a line or series, consecutive

**suc-ces-sor** [sək-sĕs′ər] *noun*, someone appointed to a title or position to replace another

**suc-cinct** [sək-sĭngkt′] *adjective*, concise, terse, brief, to the point

**suc-cor** [sŭk′ər] *noun*, aid, help, assistance, relief

**suc-cul-ent** [sŭk′yə-lənt] *adjective*, 1) juicy 2) delicious, tasty

**suc-cumb** [sə-kŭm′] *verb*, 1) to yield, to give way 2) to die

**such** [sŭch] *pronoun*, 1) of this or that kind 2) used in some phrases to mean like

**suck** [sŭk] *verb*, to draw into the mouth by action of the lips and tongue when inhaling

**suc-tion** [sŭk′shən] *noun*, the pulling force of a partial vacuum

**sud-den** [sŭd′n] *adjective*, when
something happens unexpectedly

**sud-den-ly** [sŭd′n-lē] *adverb*,
happening at once without
warning, unexpectedly

**sue** [soo] *verb*, to ask a court to
solve a problem legally

**suede** [swād] *noun*, a leather made
when the flesh, or underside of
the leather is buffed or
sandpapered to produce a nap

**suf-fer** [sŭf′ər] *verb*, 1) to feel pain
or hurt 2) to tolerate, to allow

**suf-fer-ing** [sŭf′ər-ĭng] *noun*,
enduring pain and sadness

**suf-fice** [sə-fĭs′] *verb*, 1) to be
enough for 2) to satisfy a need

**suf-fi-cient** [sə-fĭsh′ənt] *adjective*,
adequate for the purpose

**suf-fix** [sŭf′ĭks] *noun*, letters added
to the end of a word, to change
the meaning

**suf-fo-cate** [sŭf′ə-kāt′] *verb*, 1) to
smother, to choke 2) to kill by
depriving of oxygen

**suf-frage** [sŭf′rĭj] *noun*, the right to
vote, a vote

**sug-ar** [shoog′ər] *noun*, a sweet
substance made from sugar cane
or sugar beets and used in food
products

**sug-gest** [səg-jĕst′] *verb*, 1) to
bring up or call to mind, to
propose for consideration 2) to
imply, to indicate

**sug-ges-tion** [səg-jĕs′chən] *noun*,
1) a proposal, an idea, advice, a
recommendation 2) a slight
trace, a hint, an implication

**su-i-cide** [soo′ĭ-sīd′] *noun*, the act
of taking one's own life

**suit** [soot] *noun*, 1) a set of clothes
made from the same fabric, *verb*,
2) to adapt, to perform

**suit-a-ble** [soo′tə-bəl] *adjective*,
fitting, proper, appropriate

**suit-case** [soot′kās′] *noun*, a
rectangular piece of luggage

**suite** [swēt] *noun*, a number of
rooms connected together

**suit-or** [soo′tər] *noun*, a beau, a
man who courts a woman

**sul-fur** [sŭl′fər] *noun*, a
nonmetallic yellow element used
in gunpowder, matches and
medicine

**sulk** [sŭlk] *verb*, to pout and feel
angry or sorry for yourself

**sul-len** [sŭl′ən] *adjective*, silent
from anger or hurt, moody,
indulging in self-pity

**sul-ly** [sŭl′ē] *verb*, 1) to disgrace, to
tarnish someone's character 2) to
soil, to stain

**sul-try** [sŭl′trē] *adjective*,
sweltering, hot and humid

**sum** [sŭm] *noun*, the total of
different amounts added together

**sum-ma-ry** [sŭm′ə-rē] *noun*, a
shorter version of an article

**sum-ma-tion** [sə-mā′shən] *noun*,
the act of finding the total

**sum-mer** [sŭm′ər] *noun*, the third
season of the year, between
spring and autumn

**sum-mit** [sŭm′ĭt] *noun*, 1) the top
leaders, the highest point 2) the
top of a mountain

**sum-mon** [sŭm′ən] *verb*, 1) to call,
to send for by command 2) to
gather, to call forth

**sum-mons** [sŭm′ənz] *noun*, a formal letter requesting a response in court

**sump-tu-ous** [sŭmp′choo-əs] *adjective*, luxurious, splendid

**sun** [sŭn] *noun*, the central star of the solar system around which the planets revolve which gives off light, heat and energy

**sun-dae** [sŭn′dē] *noun*, a dish of ice cream covered with toppings such as chocolate syrup, nuts and whipped cream

**Sun-day** [sŭn′dē] *noun*, the first day of the week, observed as the Sabbath by most Christians

**sun-der** [sŭn′dər] *verb*, to separate, to cut apart

**sun-dry** [sŭn′drē] *adjective*, various, more than one or two

**sun-flow-er** [sŭn′flou′ər] *noun*, a plant with large yellow-rayed flower heads that produces edible seeds that yield an oil

**sun-rise** [sŭn′rīz′] *noun*, the early morning, the crack of dawn

**sun-set** [sŭn′sĕt′] *noun*, close of the day, twilight

**sun-shine** [sŭn′shīn′] *noun*, no plural, bright light, day light

**su-per** [soo′pər] *adjective*,
1) outstanding, exceptionally fine,
2) great, extreme or excessive

**su-perb** [soo-pûrb′] *adjective*, exceptional, extraordinary

**su-per-cil-i-ous** [soo′pər-sĭl′ē-əs] *adjective*, lofty with pride, haughty, contemptuous

**su-per-fi-cial** [soo′pər-fĭsh′əl] *adjective*, 1) relating to the surface or appearance only

2) actions thoughtlessly done, insincere, shallow

**su-per-flu-ous** [soo-pûr′floo-əs] *adjective*, excessive, more than needed, unnecessary

**su-per-in-tend-ent** [soo′pər-ĭn-tĕn′dənt] *noun*, one having oversight and direction of some place or agency

**su-pe-ri-or** [soo-pîr′ē-ər] *adjective*, 1) beyond power or influence of another 2) greater in number or amount 3) above average

**su-per-mar-ket** [soo′pər-mär′kĭt] *noun*, a large store with shelves that have a variety of household products, a large grocery store

**su-per-nat-u-ral** [soo′pər-năch′ər-əl] *adjective*, beyond what is explainable by natural law, metaphysical

**su-per-sede** [soo′pər-sēd′] *adjective*, to come to take the place of something that is not as modern, efficient,or appropriate

**su-per-son-ic** [soo′pər-sŏn′ĭk] *adjective*, faster than sound

**su-per-sti-tion** [soo′pər-stĭsh′ən] *noun*, reverence for that which is unknown or mysterious

**su-per-sti-tious** [soo′pər-stĭsh′əs] *adjective*, awe of that which is unknown or mysterious based on an irrational belief

**su-per-vise** [soo′pər-vīz′] *verb*, to direct, to watch over

**su-per-vi-sion** [soo′pər-vĭzh′ən] *noun*, no plural, overseeing someone's work

**su-per-vi-sor** [soo′pər-vī′zər] *noun*, a person who oversees a department of workers

**sup-per** [sŭp′ər] *noun*, dinner, a meal eaten in the evening

**sup-ple** [sŭp′əl] *adjective*, 1) flexible, pliant, bending easily without breaking 2) limber

**sup-ple-ment** [sŭp′lə-mənt] *noun*, a part added, an appendix

**sup-ply** [sə-plī′] *noun*, 1) a resource, *verb*, 2) to provide something needed

**sup-port** [sə-pôrt′, -pōrt′] *noun*, 1) aid, assistance 2) an abutment, a brace, a stay, *verb*, 3) to advocate, to back, to uphold 4) to provide food and clothing and other necessities

**sup-pose** [sə-pōz′] *verb*, to hold that something is true, to assume that something is true

**sup-posi-tion** [sŭp′ə-zĭsh′ən] *noun*, presumption, theory, principle

**sup-press** [sə-prĕs′] *verb*, to subdue, to quell, to inhibit, to keep from being known

**su-preme** [soo-prēm′] *adjective*, highest in authority, highest in degree, above all

**Su-preme Court** [soo-prēm′kôrt] *noun*, the most important court in the United States, consisting of 9 members appointed by the President

**sure** [shoor] *adjective*, certain beyond question, having no doubt

**sure-ly** [shoor′lē] *adverb*, certainly

**surf** [sûrf] *noun*, *no plural*, 1) the waves of the sea as they hit the shores, *verb*, 2) to ride a surfboard 3) to search the Internet on a computer

**sur-face** [sûr′fəs] *noun*, 1) a plane, the outside or topside face 2) the

top of the water, *verb*, 3) to rise to the top of a body of water

**sur-feit** [sûr′fĭt] *noun*, 1) excess *verb*, 2) to over-indulge, to give to use in excess

**surge** [sûrj] *noun*, 1) a rush, a flow, *verb*, 2) to swell, to pour out

**sur-geon** [sûr′jən] *noun*, one whose profession it is to cure diseases or injuries by performing an operation

**sur-ger-y** [sûr′jə-rē] *noun*, an operation when a doctor cuts into a person's body with instruments to help cure them

**sur-ly** [sûr′lē] *adjective*, rude, cross

**sur-mise** [sər-mīz′] *noun*, 1) a guess, speculation, likelihood, *verb*, 2) to assume, to guess, to suppose, to conjecture

**sur-mount** [sər-mount′] *verb*, to be overcome, to prevail over

**sur-name** [sûr′nām′] *noun*, a person's last name

**sur-pass** [sər-păs′] *verb*, to exceed, to do better, to go beyond

**sur-plus** [sûr′pləs, -plŭs′] *noun*, the amount that is more than needed

**sur-prise** [sər-prīz′] *noun*, 1) something sudden and unexpected, *verb*, 2) to cause to feel astonished

**sur-real** [sûr′rēl] *adjective*, seeming like a dream; something that is real but feels imaginary or impossible, bizarre

**sur-ren-der** [sə-rĕn′dər] *verb*, to give up, to yield

**sur-rep-ti-tious** [sûr′əp-tĭsh′əs] *adjective*, kept secret (especially if it would not be approved of), hidden, unauthorized

**sur-ro-gate** [sûr′ə-gĭt] *adjective*, substitute, replacement

**sur-round** [sə-round′] *verb*, to encircle, to enclose on all sides

**sur-round-ings** [sə-roundĭngs] *noun, plural,* the conditions or things around a person or place

**sur-veil-lance** [sər-vā′ləns] *noun*, a close watch over something

**sur-vey** [sər-vā′] *noun*, 1) a study, a poll, a review, *verb*, 2) to examine, to inspect, to watch

**sur-vey-or** [sər-vā′ər] *noun*, 1) one who collects data 2) one whose business it is to measure land

**sur-viv-al** [sər-vī′vəl] *noun, no plural,* what one needs to stay alive or exist

**sur-vive** [sər-vīv′] *verb*, to continue to exist, to live longer

**sur-vi-vor** [sər-vīv′ər] *noun*, the one to make it when the others died or failed

**sus-cep-ti-ble** [sə-sĕp′tə-bəl] *adjective*, capable of being affected emotionally

**sus-pect** [sə-spĕkt′] *noun*, 1) a person who is believed to have done something wrong, *verb*, 2) to suppose that something is true

**sus-pend** [sə-spĕnd′] *verb*, 1) to hang 2) to stop temporarily

**sus-pend-ers** [sə-spĕn′dərz] *noun*, two adjustable bands or straps arranged to pass over the shoulders to hold the trousers up

**sus-pense** [sə-spĕns′] *noun, no plural,* a pause or delay which leaves people anxious

**sus-pen-sion** [sə-spĕn′shən] *noun*, a delay, postponement

**sus-pi-cion** [sə-spĭsh′ən] *noun*, 1) distrust, doubt, 2) trace

**sus-pi-cious** [sə-spĭsh′əs] *adjective*, having a feeling that something is wrong, distrustful

**sus-tain** [sə-stān′] *verb*, to bear, to hold up, to keep going

**sus-te-nance** [sŭs′tə-nəns] *noun*, that which supports life, a food or nourishment

**su-ture** [sōō′chər] *noun*, stitches sewn to hold the cut edges of a wound or incision

**swag-ger** [swăg′ər] *verb*, to walk in a boastful and proud manner

**swal-low** [swŏl′ō] *noun*, 1) a small bird with a tail split into two parts, *verb*, 2) to consume food through the mouth into the stomach, to take in

**swamp** [swŏmp, swômp] *noun*, 1) wet, boggy ground which is always soft, wet land, *verb*, 2) to overwhelm with too much of something, to inundate

**swan** [swŏn] *noun*, a large white bird with a long neck that lives in the water and on land

**swap** [swŏp] *verb*, to exchange

**swarm** [swôrm] *noun*, 1) a large group of insects or bugs, *verb*, 2) to travel in a large group, to teem, to crowd

**swarth-y** [swôr′thē] *adjective*, having a dark complexion

**swat** [swŏt] *verb*, to hit, to whack

**sway** [swā] *verb*, to swing gently

**swear** [swâr] *verb*, 1) to curse 2) to promise, to make a solemn declaration

**sweat** [swĕt] *noun*, 1) moisture which comes out of the skin due to exertion, *verb*, 2) to give off water through the skin

**sweat-er** [swĕt'ər] *noun*, a wool or woven garment worn over the top of the body

**sweep** [swēp] *noun*, 1) a continuous search, *verb*, 2) to clean or clear with a brush or broom

**sweet** [swēt] *adjective*, 1) tasting like sugar or honey 2) a pleasant or kind personality 3) having a pleasant smell

**swell** [swĕl] *verb*, to become larger

**swel-ter** [swĕl'tər] *verb*, to be tired by the heat, to perspire, to sweat

**swept** [swĕpt] *past tense* of **sweep**

**swerve** [swûrv] *verb*, to move suddenly to one side when you are moving along

**swift** [swĭft] *adjective*, very fast or quick to act, nimble, prompt

**swim** [swĭm] *noun*, 1) the act of staying afloat or traveling in water, *verb*, 2) to move through the water by using movements of the body

**swin-dle** [swĭn'dl] *verb*, to cheat, to deceive or defraud

**swing** [swĭng] *noun*, 1) a seat hanging on ropes or chains, *verb*, 2) to move freely from a fixed point, to pivot, to turn

**swirl** [swûrl] *noun*, 1) a spiral, *verb*, 2) to turn in a circular motion

**switch** [swĭch] *noun*, 1) a device that can be used to turn something on or off, *verb*, 2) to exchange 3) to turn something

on or off 4) to change as in direction, to shift, to transfer

**swiv-el** [swĭv'əl] *verb*, to turn or pivot on a bolt or pin

**swol-len** [swō'lən] *adjective*, inflamed, puffed up, enlarged

**swoon** [swoon] *noun*, 1) a fainting spell, *verb*, 2) to faint

**swoop** [swoop] *verb*, to fly down very quickly like a bird

**sword** [sôrd] *noun*, a weapon similar to a knife with a very long blade

**swore** [swôr] *past tense* of **swear**

**syl-la-ble** [sĭl'ə-bəl] *noun*, a combination of letters indicating a sound in a word

**syl-lo-gism** [sĭl'ə-jĭz'əm] *noun*, logical formula using a major premise, a minor premise leading to a conclusion

**sym-bol** [sĭm'bəl] *noun*, anything that stands for or represents something else

**sym-met-ri-cal** [sĭ-mĕt'rĭ-kəl] *adjective*, alike on both sides, proportional

**sym-me-try** [sĭm'ĭ-trē] *noun*, the balance of things on opposite sides, excellence of proportion

**sym-pa-thet-ic** [sĭm'pə-thĕt'ĭk] *adjective*, kind, warm, compassionate, tender

**sym-pa-thize** [sĭm'pə-thīz'] *verb*, to feel sorry for another, to share in a feeling

**sym-pa-thy** [sĭm'pə-thē] *noun*, the understanding of another person's feelings, pity

**sym-pho-ny** [sĭm'fə-nē] *noun*, a musical composition performed by an orchestra

**symp-tom** [sĭm′təm] *noun*, a sign indicating the presence of an illness or something

**syn-a-gogue** [sĭn′ə-gŏg′] *noun*, a house of worship, a temple

**syn-chro-nic-i-ty** [sĭng′krə-nĭs′ĭ-tē] *noun*, the simultaneous occurrence of unrelated events

**syn-chro-nize** [sĭng′krə-nīz′] *verb*, to agree in time, to move together simultaneously

**syn-di-cate** [sĭn′dĭ-kĭt] *verb*, a network of businesses that sell news to the media

**syn-er-gy:** [sĭn′/ər-jē] *noun,* the interaction or cooperation of two or more organizations, substances, or other agents to produce a combined effect greater than the sum of their separate effects

**syn-o-nym** [sĭn′ə-nĭm′] *noun*, a word that means the same as another

**syn-op-sis** [sĭ-nŏp′sĭs] *noun*, a general view of a whole, an abstract or summary

**syn-the-sis** [sĭn′thĭ-sĭs] *noun*, combining parts into a whole

**syn-thet-ic** [sĭn-thĕt′ĭk] *adjective*, produced by artificial processes, not real or genuine

**sy-ringe** [sə-rĭnj′] *noun*, an instrument with a needle used to inject a fluid into the blood stream through a vein

**syr-up** [sĭr′əp] *noun*, a sugar liquid

**sys-tem** [sĭs′təm] *noun*, a network of things working together as a functioning unit

**sys-tem-at-ic** [sĭs′tə-măt′ĭk] *adjective*, methodical, proceeding according to method

# T

**ta-ble** [tā′bəl] *noun*, 1) a piece of furniture with a flat top and legs used for placing things on or using as a work space 2) a list, often using lines or boxes to arrange facts

**tab-leau** [tăb′lō′] *noun*, a scene of persons in costume remaining silent and motionless

**ta-ble-cloth** [tā′bəl-klôth′] *noun*, a decorative cloth spread over the top of a table

**tab-let** [tăb′lĭt] *noun*, a hard flat piece or block of something

**ta-boo** [tə-bōō′] *adjective*, 1) forbidden, banned by religion or custom, *noun*, 2) a restriction, a ban or prohibition

**tac-it** [tăs′ĭt] *adjective*, implied or indicated, but not expressed

**tac-i-tur-n** [tăs′ĭ-tûr′n] *adjective*, habitually silent, not given to conversation, saying little

**tack** [tăk] *noun*, a small nail with a broad, flat head on it

**tack-le** [tăk′əl] *noun*, 1) ropes and pulleys arranged for hoisting or pulling 2) equipment used for fishing 3) downing a player 4) a football player, *verb*, 5) to undertake, to get down to business to solve a problem 6) to bring to the ground

**tact** [tăkt] *noun*, *no plural*, to do or say the right thing at the right time, diplomacy

**tac-tic** [tăk′tĭk] *noun*, a maneuver

**tac-tile** [tăk′təl, -tīl′] *adjective*, referring to the sense of touch

**tag** [tăg] *noun*, 1) a small identifying card or label 2) a game children play in which one player chases the others, *verb*, 3) to follow along

**tail** [tāl] *adjective*, 1) coming from behind, *noun*, 2) the part of an animal which sticks out at the end of its back

**tai-lor** [tā'lər] *noun*, one who cuts out and makes clothes

**taint** [tānt] *noun*, 1) a trace of something bad, *verb*, 2) to contaminate, to corrupt

**take** [tāk] *verb*, 1) to get hold of something 2) to carry something or go with someone to another place 3) to swallow something 4) to travel 5) to accept

**tak-en** [tā'kən] *adjective*, 1)held, seized 2) accepted

**tale** [tāl] *noun*, a story

**tal-ent** [tăl'ənt] *noun*, a natural ability, aptitude

**tal-is-man** [tăl'ĭs-mən] *noun*, an amulet or lucky charm

**talk** [tôk] *verb*, to speak or be able to speak, to consult or confer

**talk-a-tive** [tô'kə-tĭv] *adjective*, inclined to talk a lot, loquacious

**tall** [tôl] *adjective*, above average height, high

**tal-ly** [tăl'ē] *noun*, 1) a mark made to keep score or to count, *verb*, 2) to keep track of an account

**tal-on** [tăl'ən] *noun*, a claw, especially of a bird of prey

**tame** [tām] *adjective*, 1) trained to live with man, not wild, *verb*, 2) to make a wild animal obedient and friendly to people

**tan** [tăn] *adjective*, 1) light brown, tawny 2) to convert into leather

**tan-gent** [tăn'jənt] *noun*, a straight line that touches a curve without intersecting it

**tan-ge-rine** [tăn'jə-rēn'] *noun*, a variety of a small-sized orange

**tan-gi-ble** [tăn'jə-bəl] *adjective*, capable of being touched, real

**tank** [tăngk] *noun*, 1) a large container to hold liquid or gas fuel 2) an armed vehicle used in combat 3) the metal box in the back of the car to hold gasoline

**tan-ta-lize** [tăn'tə-līz'] *verb*, to tease, to tempt, to promise by offering a reward

**tan-ta-mount** [tăn'tə-mount'] *adjective*, equal in value

**tan-trum** [tăn'trəm] *noun*, an exaggerated display of anger, a fit of irritability, bad temper

**tap** [tăp] *noun*, 1) the faucet attached to a pipe to release liquid or gas, *verb*, 2) to hit or touch lightly 3) to drain by making a hole 4) to draw from

**tape** [tāp] *noun*, 1) a narrow piece of cloth or other material, *verb*, 2) to bind or secure with an adhesive material 3) to record

**tap-er** [tā'pər] *verb*, to decrease in amount or size by becoming narrower or smaller

**tap-es-try** [tăp'ĭ-strē] *noun*, a heavy, decorative, woven fabric used especially for wall hangings

**tap-i-o-ca** [tăp'ē-ō'kə] *noun*, cassava, a coarse granular preparation used in puddings

**tar** [tär] *noun*, a thick black liquid made from heating coal or wood

**ta-ran-tu-la** [tə-răn′chə-lə] *noun*, a hairy, large, poisonous spider

**tar-get** [tär′gĭt] *noun*, 1) somebody or something aimed at 2) an objective, a goal, *verb*, 3) to make the focus or object of something

**tar-iff** [tăr′ĭf] *noun*, a tax on goods exported or imported

**tar-nish** [tär′nĭsh] *verb*, 1) to dull the luster of metal 2) to taint

**tart** [tärt] *adjective*, 1) sour to the taste, *noun*, 2) a piece of pastry with fruit cooked on top of it

**task** [tăsk] *noun*, a chore or small job that must be done

**tas-sel** [tăs′əl] *noun*, a pendant ornament ending in a tuft of loose threads

**taste** [tāst] *noun*, 1) a preference, liking 2) the sense that distinguishes the flavor of things placed in the mouth 3) a flavor itself, *verb*, 4) to sample a food by taking it in the mouth

**tat-too** [tă-tōō′] *noun*, a design on the skin made using a needle filled with dye

**taught** [tôt] *past tense* of **teach**

**taunt** [tônt] *verb*, to tease or make fun of someone, to ridicule

**taut** [tôt] *adjective*, stretched tight

**tau-tol-o-gy** [tô-tŏl′ə-jē] *noun*, needless repetition of an idea in different words

**taw-dry** [tô′drē] *adjective*, cheap and showy or flashy, gaudy

**tax** [tăks] *noun*, 1) a sum of money to be paid to the government imposed by the elected leaders, *verb*, 2) to put a fee on service or goods that are given to the government

**tax-i** [tăk′sē] *noun*, a car for hire to take people from one place to another

**tax-i-der-mist** [tăk′sĭ-dûr′mĭst] *noun*, one who prepares dead animals to look life-like

**tea** [tē] *noun*, 1) prepared dried leaves of a plant 2) a small meal or snack in the afternoon 3) a cup of a beverage made with leaves steeped in hot water

**teach** [tēch] *verb*, to show someone how to do something

**teach-er** [tē′chər] *noun*, a person whose occupation is to instruct

**team** [tēm] *noun*, 1) persons working or playing together as a group 2) two or more animals harnessed together to pull a vehicle

**tear** [tûr] *noun*, 1) a drop of water that comes out of the eye 2) a hole or cut in material, *verb*, 3) to make a hole in material by pulling on it

**tease** [tēz] *verb*, to make fun of someone, to annoy

**tea-spoon** [tē′spōōn′] *noun*, a small spoon used to measure

**tech-ni-cal** [tĕk′nĭ-kəl] *adjective*, having knowledge of a mechanical or scientific subject

**tech-ni-cian** [tĕk-nĭsh′ən] *noun*, a person who works with machines or instruments

**tech-nique** [tĕk-nēk′] *noun*, a procedure used to perform a task

**tech-nol-o-gy** [tĕk-nŏl′ə-jē] *noun*, the use of science to produce useful things for practical purposes that improve life

**te-di-ous** [tē′dē-əs] *adjective*, tiresome, dull, boring

**tel-e-phone** [tĕl′ə-fōn′] *noun*, 1) an instrument for reproducing sounds at a distance, *verb*, 2) to call to someone on an instrument that communicates voices through airwaves or wires

**tel-e-scope** [tĕl′ĭ-skōp′] *noun*, an optical instrument for viewing distant objects

**tel-e-vi-sion** [tĕl′ə-vĭzh′ən] *noun*, a set used to transmit visual images onto a screen

**tell** [tĕl] *verb*, 1) to speak to someone, to inform, to narrate 2) to deduce, to differentiate

**tell-er** [tĕl′ər] *noun*, a bank employee who handles customer transactions

**tem-per** [tĕm′pər] *noun*, 1) a person's state of mind, mood, *verb*, 2) to tone down, to moderate, to bring under control

**tem-per-a-ment** [tĕm′prə-mənt] *noun*, the physical and mental character of an individual

**tem-per-ance** [tĕm′pər-əns] *noun*, habitual moderation of the appetites and passions

**tem-per-a-ture** [tĕm′pər-ə-chŏor′] *noun*, the degree of heat or cold

**tem-ple** [tĕm′pəl] *noun*, 1) a holy building 2) the part of the head above and in front of the ear

**tem-po** [tĕm′pō] *noun*, the rate of speed of a musical passage

**tem-po-ral** [tĕm′pər-əl] *adjective*, not lasting forever, limited by time, the present

**tem-po-rar-y** [tĕm′pə-rĕr′ē] *adjective*, intended to last a short period of time, not permanent

**tempt** [tĕmpt] *verb*, to entice someone to do something unwise or wrong, to provoke

**temp-ta-tion** [tĕmp-tā′shən] *noun*, an instant urge or desire

**ten** [tĕn] *noun*, the number 10, one plus nine

**te-na-cious** [tə-nā′shəs] *adjective*, holding fast, stubborn

**te-nac-i-ty** [tə-năs′ĭ-tē] *noun*, firmness, persistency

**ten-ant** [tĕn′ənt] *noun*, someone who lives in a house or apartment, an occupant

**tend** [tĕnd] *verb*, 1) to be likely to, to do something habitually 2) to take care of something

**ten-den-cy** [tĕn′dən-sē] *noun*, inclination, propensity, leaning

**tend-er** [tĕn′dər] *adjective*, 1) kind and gentle 2) sensitive to touch or movement 3) cooked so that the food is easy to eat, *noun*, 4) a car attached to a train for carrying food and water

**ten-der-ness** [tĕn′dər-nĭs] *noun*, affection, gentleness

**ten-e-ment** [tĕn′ə-mənt] *noun*, a building divided into flats

**ten-et** [tĕn′ĭt] *noun*, doctrine, dogma, belief, conviction

**Ten-nes-see** [tĕn′ĭ-sē′] *noun*, one of the 50 United States located in the South, the capital city is Nashville. The state flower of **Tennessee** is the iris, and the motto is "Agriculture and commerce."

**ten-nis** [tĕn′ĭs] *noun*, a game played on a court by two or four people in which a ball is hit over a net with rackets

**ten-or** [tĕn′ər] *noun*, 1) a tendency, a trend 2) the highest range of the male singing voice

**tense** [tĕns] *adjective*, 1) full of excitement 2) tightly stretched, taut, *noun*, 3) the form of a verb that shows when the action happens – past, present, or future

**ten-sion** [tĕn′shən] *noun*, 1) act of stretching, 2) mental or nervous state or condition of strain

**tent** [tĕnt] *noun*, a shelter of canvas or nylon, supported by poles

**ten-ta-cle** [tĕn′tə-kəl] *noun*, a long, arm-like structure growing out of an animal's body, used for movement or catching food

**ten-ta-tive** [tĕn′tə-tĭv] *adjective*, experimental, based on trials

**tenth** [tĕnth] *adjective*, the number after nine in series, written 10th

**ten-u-ous** [tĕn′yōō-əs] *adjective*, weak and unconvincing

**ten-ure** [tĕn′yər] *noun*, the period of time during which an office is held, occupation

**te-pee** [tē′pē] *noun*, a cone shaped tent in which some Indians live

**tep-id** [tĕp′ĭd] *adjective*, 1) not hot or cold, lukewarm 2) showing little enthusiasm

**term** [tûrm] *noun*, 1) a fixed amount of time 2) an expression or form of language 3) a condition or stipulation

**ter-min-al** [tûr′mə-nəl] *adjective*, 1) end, final, concluding, *noun*, 2) a depot where buses or trains

make connections 3) a conducting circuit arranged for connection in an electrical circuit

**ter-mi-nate** [tûr′mə-nāt′] *verb*, to end, to finish, to cancel

**ter-mi-na-tion** [tûr′mə-nā′shən] *noun*, the ending

**ter-mi-nol-o-gy** [tûr′mə-nŏl′ə-jē] *noun*, vocabulary used in a specialized subject

**ter-race** [tĕr′ĭs] *noun*, 1) a level area cut out from the side of a hill 2) a flat area outside a house

**ter-rain** [tə-rān′] *noun*, the features of an area of land

**ter-rar-i-um** [tə-râr′ē-əm] *noun*, a transparent container in which land animals or plants are kept

**ter-res-tri-al** [tə-rĕs′trē-əl] *adjective*, of the earth

**ter-ri-ble** [tĕr′ə-bəl] *adjective*, appalling, dreadful

**ter-rif-ic** [tə-rĭf′ĭk] *adjective*, awesome, wonderful

**ter-ri-fy** [tĕr′ə-fī′] *verb*, to fill or overwhelm with fear or horror

**ter-ri-to-ry** [tĕr′ĭ-tôr′ē] *noun*, a portion of land belonging to someone else, a region

**ter-ror** [tĕr′ər] *adjective*, fear

**terse** [tûrs] *adjective*, concise, abrupt, a short answer

**ter-ror-ist** [tĕr′ər] *noun*, one who uses violence to intimidate

**tes-sel-la-tion** [tĕs′ə-lā′shən] *adjective*, a mosaic pattern

**test** [tĕst] *noun*, 1) a trial 2) an examination to assess the level of knowledge of a subject, *verb*,

3) to try something out to see how it works 4) to examine

**tes-ta-ment** [tĕs′tə-mənt] *noun*, 1) a will 2) scripture from the Bible

**tes-ti-fy** [tĕs′tə-fī′] *verb*, to establish some fact, under oath to serve as evidence

**tes-ti-mo-ny** [tĕs′tə-mō′nē] *noun*, the statement of a witness under oath, evidence or proof

**tet-a-nus** [tĕt′n-əs] *noun*, a painful, often fatal, infectious disease, marked by painful spasms of the muscles, frequently of the jaw

**teth-er** [tĕth′ər] *noun*, 1) a cord, a link, a supply line, *verb*, 2) to tie up with a rope, to hitch, to fasten

**Tex-as** [tĕk′səs] *noun*, one of the 50 United States located in the Southwest, the capital city is Austin. The state flower of **Texas**, is the bluebonnet, and the motto is "Friendship."

**text** [tĕkst] *noun*, the words used in a book, a written work

**text-book** [tĕkst′bŏŏk′] *noun*, an instruction book, a manual

**tex-tile** [tĕks′tīl′] *noun*, fabrics such as cotton, wool, linen, silk, rayon, and polyester

**tex-ture** [tĕks′chər] *noun*, the feel or appearance of something – soft, smooth, rough, etc.

**than** [thăn] used as a *conjunction*, to introduce the second part of a comparison

**thank** [thăngk] *verb*, to express gratitude and appreciation

**thank-ful** [thăngk′fəl] *adjective*, to be grateful, to show appreciation or praise

**thanks** [thăngks] *noun*, an acknowledgment of a kindness, favor, or the like

**Thanks-giv-ing** [thăngks-gĭv′ĭng] *noun*, a national holiday celebrated the fourth Thursday in November

**that** [thăt] *pronoun, plural*, **those**, 1) the one singled out 2) used instead of which 3) used to join two parts of a sentence 4) so 5) used to show the result

**that's** [thăts] the *contraction* of the words **that** and **is**

**thatch** [thăch] *noun*, bundles of straw woven together

**thaw** [thô] *verb*, to pass from a frozen to a liquid state

**the** [thē before a vowel, thə before a consonant] *article*, a word that usually goes before a noun

**the-a-ter** [thē′ə-tər] *noun*, a building where dramatic performances are presented

**the-at-ri-cal** [thē-ăt′rĭ-kəl] *adjective*, dramatic, eloquent

**thee** [thē] *pronoun*, the objective case of thou

**theft** [thĕft] *noun*, the act or instance of stealing

**their** [thâr] *pronoun*, belonging to them, a form of the possessive case of **they** used attributively, e.g., *their school*

**theirs** [thârz] *pronoun*, showing personal ownership

**them** [thĕm] *pronoun*, the objective case of **they**, *plural*, **them-selves**, the same people, animals, or things mentioned in the sentence as the subject

**theme** [thēm] *noun*, the subject on which one writes or speaks

**then** [thĕn] *adverb*, 1) at another time, not now 2) afterwards, next 3) if that is true

**the-ol-o-gy** [thē-ŏl′ə-jē] *noun*, the science of God or of religion

**the-o-rem** [thē′ər-əm] *noun*, a principle, a theoretical proposition, a thesis

**the-o-ret-i-cal** [thē′ə-rĕt′ĭ-kəl] *adjective*, depending on conjecture, speculative

**the-o-ry** [thē′ə-rē] *noun*, an abstract plan, an hypothesis

**ther-a-peu-tic** [thĕr′ə-pyōō′tĭk] *adjective*, curative, healing, good for personal growth and health

**ther-a-py** [thĕr′ə-pē] *noun*, exercises and treatment designed to rehabilitate a person

**there** [thâr] *adverb*, 1) referring to that place 2) referring to at that moment

**there's** [thârz] the *contraction* of the words **there** and **is**

**there-fore** [thâr′fôr′] *adverb*, for that reason, as a result

**ther-mal** [thûr′məl] *adjective*, pertaining to heat

**ther-mo-dy-nam-ics** [thûr′mō-dī-năm′ĭks] *noun*, the relationship between heat and other forms of energy

**ther-mom-e-ter** [thər-mŏm′ĭ-tər] *noun*, a device for measuring how hot or cold something is

**ther-mos** [thûr′məs] *noun*, a vacuum bottle for keeping liquids hot or cold for hours

**ther-mos-tat** [thûr′mə-stăt′] *noun*, a mechanical device used to control temperature

**the-sau-rus** [thĭ-sôr′əs] *noun*, a dictionary of synonyms and antonyms

**these** [thēz] *pronoun, adjective,* the *plural* of **this**

**the-sis** [thē′sĭs] *noun*, an essay presented by a candidate for a degree or diploma

**they** [thā] *pronoun*, the *plural* of **he**, **she** or **it**

**they'll** [thāl] the *contraction* of the words **they** and **will**

**they're** [thâr] the *contraction* of the words **they** and **are**

**thick** [thĭk] *adjective*, 1)occupying much space in depth or from side to side, measuring between sides 2) a dense fluid

**thief** [thēf] *noun, plural,* **thieves,** one who steals

**thigh** [thī] *noun*, the thick part of the leg above the knee and below the hip

**thim-ble** [thĭm′bəl] *noun*, a metal cap put over the finger to keep it from being pricked by a needle

**thin** [thĭn] *adjective*, 1) not thick, slender 2) lacking volume or density 3) sparse, insufficient, inadequate, flimsy

**thing** [thĭng] *noun*, 1) an object, a creature, a form of life 2) conditions 3) an act or event

**think** [thĭngk] *verb*, 1) to form or have on the mind 2) to use the power of reason 3) to believe, to suppose

**third** [thûrd] *adjective, noun*, the number three in order after second, written 3$^{rd}$

**thirst** [thûrst] *noun, no plural*, the need to drink something

**thirst-y** [thûr′stē] *adjective*, needing something to drink

**thir-teen** [thûr-tēn′] *adjective, noun*, the number 13, 3+10

**thir-teenth** [thûr-tēnth′] *adjective, noun*, number 13 in order, 13$^{th}$

**thir-ti-eth** [thûr′tē-ĭth] *adjective, noun*, number 30 in order, 30$^{th}$

**thir-ty** [thûr′tē] *adjective, noun*, the number 30, ten times three

**this** [thĭs] *adjective*, 1) being the one present, near or just mentioned 2) being the one nearer or last mentioned, *adverb* 3) the thing the speaker is talking about, *pronoun*, 4) the one nearer than that one in time or space 5) what is in the present or being talked about

**this-tle** [thĭs′əl] *noun*, a plant with prickly leaves and stems and a purple flower

**thorn** [thôrn] *noun*, a sharp projection on a stem

**thor-ough** [thûr′ō] *adjective*, complete, perfect, absolute

**thor-ough-ly** [thûr′ō-lē] *adverb*, completely done

**those** [thōz] *pronoun*, the ones over there, the ones further away than this one

**thou** [thou] you

**though** [thō] *adverb*, 1) however, *conjunction*, 2) although

**thought** [thôt] *noun*, 1) an idea, the process of thinking 2) intention

3) attention, *verb*, 4) the *past tense* of **think**

**thought-ful** [thôt′fəl] *adjective*, showing consideration for others, kind, discreet

**thou-sand** [thou′zənd] *noun, adjective*, the number 1,000, ten times 100

**thread** [thrĕd] *noun*, 1) a fine string made of cotton, linen, or silk, *verb*, 2) to wind through openings 3) to pass a thread through the eye of a needle

**threat** [thrĕt] *noun*, a warning, that one may do harm

**threat-en** [thrĕt′n] *verb*, to torment, to scare, to pose a danger

**three** [thrē] *adjective, noun*, the number 3, one plus two, 3

**thresh-old** [thrĕsh′ōld′] *noun*, a piece of timber which lies under a door, an entrance

**thrift** [thrĭft] *noun*, the practice of being careful with money

**thrift-y** [thrĭf′tē] *adjective*, careful about money, economical

**thrill** [thrĭl] *noun*, 1) an excited feeling, *verb*, 2) to fill with excitement

**thrive** [thrīv] *verb*, 1) to grow abundantly 2) to prosper, to flourish, to succeed

**throat** [thrōt] *noun*, the passage inside of the neck attached to the mouth, lungs, and stomach

**throb** [thrŏb] *verb*, to beat strongly, to pulsate steadily

**throne** [thrōn] *noun*, a special chair for a king or queen

**throng** [thrông, thrŏng] *noun*, a crowd of people, a multitude

**throt-tle** [thrŏt′l] *noun,* 1) a lever or pedal that helps an engine start and run, *verb,* 2) to strangle, to suppress 3) to regulate the speed of an engine

**through** [throo] *adjective,* 1) finished, *adverb,* 2) from one side or end of something to the other, *preposition,* 3) in one side and out the other 4) by the agency of, by way of, via 5) among or between 6) past or beyond, in the midst of

**through-out** [throo-out′] *preposition,* all over, from end to end, from inside and out

**throw** [throo] *noun,* 1) the distance something is tossed, cast or projected, *verb,* 2) to toss, fling, or hurl something through the air

**thrust** [thrŭst] *verb,* to push suddenly and hard

**thud** [thŭd] *noun,* a dull sound made when something heavy falls and lands

**thumb** [thŭm] *noun,* the short, thick finger on the hand which is separate from the others

**thun-der** [thŭn′dər] *noun, no plural,* the loud sound heard in the sky during a storm

**Thurs-day** [thûrz′dē] *noun,* the fifth day of the week

**thus** [thŭs] *adverb,* in this way

**thy** [thī] *pronoun,* your

**thyme** [tīm] *noun,* a pungent aromatic plant used in seasoning

**tick** [tĭk] *noun,* 1) the sound made by a clock 2) a check mark 3) a small parasite that sucks blood from animals and people, *verb,* 4) to make a soft, steady, rhythmic sound 5) to check off

things on a list that fit a certain criteria

**tick-et** [tĭk′ĭt] *noun,* 1) the ballot of a political party 2) an admission 3) a fine 4) a price tag

**tick-le** [tĭk′əl] *noun,* 1) a tingling sensation, *verb,* 2) to touch a person lightly to make them laugh 3) to delight, to amuse

**tid-al** [tīd′l] *adjective,* action of the sea caused by the tides

**tide** [tīd] *noun,* regular rise and fall of the ocean caused by the pull of the sun and the moon

**ti-dy** [tī′dē] *adjective,* 1) neat and orderly 2) substantial, more than enough, *verb,* 3) to make neat and well organized

**tie** [tī] *noun,* 1) a narrow piece of cloth used as a man's dress accessory worn around the neck with a shirt, a necktie 2) a bond 3) a standoff, *verb,* 4) to fasten something with string or rope 5) to come out equal in a contest

**tier** [tîr] *noun,* one of several levels

**ti-ger** [tī′gər] *noun,* a fierce animal, one of the big cats, which has yellow fur with black stripes

**tight** [tīt] *adjective,* 1) so close in structure that air cannot pass through 2) drawn close together

**tight-en** [tīt′n] *verb,* to draw closer together, to squeeze

**tight-ly** [tīt′lē] *adverb,* pulled closely together, tautly

**tile** [tīl] *noun,* a flat piece of baked clay that has been painted with glaze or linoleum used as a floor covering

**till** [tĭl] *adverb,* 1) before, up to, *noun,* 2) a cash box, a place to store money, *verb,* 3) to plow

**till-er** [tĭl′ər] *noun*, a handle used to steer a boat

**tilt** [tĭlt] *verb*, to make something lean so that it is not straight

**tim-ber** [tĭm′bər] *noun*, a piece of wood, lumber, hardwood

**tim-bre** [tăm′bər] *noun*, quality of a musical tone produced by a musical instrument

**time** [tīm] *noun*, 1) minutes, hours, days, weeks, months, years, etc. 2) a limited duration 3) a period or event 4) a certain hour or part of the day 5) a moment, *verb*, 6) to measure how long it takes to do something 7) a number multiplied by another

**time-ly** [tīm′lē] *adjective*, prompt, well-timed, favorable

**tim-id** [tĭm′ĭd] *adjective*, shy, afraid, uncertain, hesitant

**tim-id-i-ty** [tĭm′ĭ-dĭ-tē] *noun*, lack of self-confidence or courage

**tim-or-ous** [tĭm′ər-əs] *adjective*, fearful and hesitant

**tin** [tĭn] *noun*, *no plural*, a soft white metal mixed with alloys

**tinc-ture** [tĭngk′chər] *noun*, a slight quality added to anything, a trace or tinge, pigment

**tin-gle** [tĭng′gəl] *verb*, 1) to get excited 2) to have a prickling sensation

**tin-ker** [tĭng′kər] *verb*, to fool around, to dabble, to putter

**tin-sel** [tĭn′səl] *noun*, showy or flashy decorations

**tint** [tĭnt] *noun*, 1) the color, shade, hue, *verb*, 2) to color, to shade

**ti-ny** [tī′nē] *adjective*, very small

**tip** [tĭp] *noun*, 1) a point, a peak 2) a hint, advice, a pointer 3) compensation for a service, gratuity, *verb*, 4) to tilt, to lean to one side, to slant 5) to give someone money for a small service 6) to cause something to fall over and become unbalanced

**tip-toe** [tĭp′tō′] *noun*, 1) the tip of the toe, *verb*, 2) to walk on toes so that the step is not heard

**ti-rade** [tī′rād′] *noun*, extended scolding, denunciation

**tire** [tīr] *noun*, 1) a rubber, air-filled part of a car or bicycle wheel that cushions the ride, *verb*, 2) to make someone feel that he needs to rest 3) to become bored, fatigued

**tir-ed** [tīrd] *adjective*, feeling sleepy, needing rest

**tis-sue** [tĭsh′oo] *noun*, very thin paper that feels soft

**ti-tan-ic** [tī-tăn′ĭk] *adjective*, gigantic, of great size or power

**tithe** [tīth] *noun*, a payment of one tenth of an income given to the church

**ti-tle** [tīt′l] *noun*, 1) the name of a story, a book, a film, etc. 2) a word used in front of a person's name 3) a sport's championship

**to** [too; tə when unstressed] *adverb*, 1) in a direction toward *preposition*, 2) in the direction of 3) as far as 4) on or against 5) until 6) used to show why 7) used with the infinitive of a verb 8) for the purpose of, in order to 9) belonging to

**toad** [tōd] *noun*, an animal that looks like a frog but does not live in water

**toast** [tōst] *noun*, 1) sliced bread broiled to make it crisp, *verb*, 2) to praise someone when raising your drink in a glass 3) to brown by the heat of a fire

**to-bac-co** [tə-băk′ō] *noun*, the dried leaves of a plant used for smoking and chewing

**to-bog-gan** [tə-bŏg′ən] *noun*, a very long, flat-bottomed sled used to glide on snow

**to-day** [tə-dā′] *adverb*, 1) on or for this very day, *noun*, 2) modern times, present day, contemporary

**toe** [tō] *noun*, 1) one of the five digits at the end of the foot 2) the part of a shoe or sock that covers this end of the foot

**tof-fee** [tô′fē] *noun*, a hard, chewy candy made of caramel candy, brown sugar and butter

**to-ga** [tō′gə] *noun*, Roman outer robe of free born men

**to-geth-er** [tə-gĕth′ər] *adverb*, 1) at the same time 2) in conjunction, with each other, in cooperation

**toil** [toil] *verb*, to work very hard

**toi-let** [toi′lĭt] *noun*, an instrument to flush human waste into a sewage system, a bathroom

**to-ken** [tō′kən] *noun*, 1) a sign or symbol or gesture to indicate something 2) a souvenir 3) a coin used as a currency for travel

**told** [tōld] *past tense* of **tell**

**tol-er-ance** [tŏl′ər-əns] *noun*, compassion, open-mindedness

**tol-er-ant** [tŏl′ər-ənt] *noun*, broad minded, liberal, accepting

**toll** [tōl] *noun*, 1) the charge for a privilege or a service 2) the number lost or taken, *verb*, 3) to ring a bell slowly

**to-ma-to** [tə-mā′tō] *noun*, a red berry with seeds and a pulpy fruit eaten as a vegetable

**tomb** [tōōm] *noun*, a sacred place where a dead person is buried

**tomb-stone** [tōōm′stōn′] *noun*, the carved stone with an inscription identifying the person on a grave

**tome** [tōm] *noun*, a large volume

**to-mor-row** [tə-môr′ō] *adverb* 1) the day after today, *noun*, 2) sometime in the future

**ton** [tŭn] *noun*, the weight of measure of a very heavy quantity, e.g., 2,000 pounds

**tone** [tōn] *noun*, 1) the sound of a voice or a musical instrument 2) manner, expression

**tongs** [tôngz] *noun*, *plural*, (pair of) a tool with two legs used to pick up or to hold something

**tongue** [tŭng] *noun*, 1) the organ of speech covered by taste buds 2) the flap of leather or cloth under the lacing of a shoe 3) the language spoken 4) dialect

**ton-ic** [tŏn′ĭk] *noun*, a refreshing drink that invigorates

**to-night** [tə-nīt′] *adverb*, 1) the night following today, *noun*, 2) on or during the night of today

**too** [tōō] *adverb*, 1) also 2) more than is needed or wanted

**took** [tōōk] *past tense* of **take**

**tool** [tōōl] *noun*, an instrument used to do work or make repairs

**tooth** [tōōth] *noun*, *plural* **teeth**, 1) a white bony material that grows in the mouth, set in sockets around the jaw, used for chewing 2) the projections on a blade

**tooth-ache** [tooth′āk′] *noun*, a pain in the mouth due to an infection from a tooth

**top** [tŏp] *adjective*, 1) best, first, chief, *noun*, 2) the highest part of something 3) the lid or cover of something 4) a toy that spins quickly on a point

**to-paz** [tō′păz′] *noun*, a precious stone, usually yellow or tan

**top-ic** [tŏp′ĭk] *noun*, the subject of a conversation, speech, or essay

**to-pog-ra-phy** [tə-pŏg′rə-fē] *noun*, detailed representation of the features of a region

**top-ple** [tŏp′əl] *verb*, to make or become unsteady and fall over

**torch** [tôrch] *noun*, an instrument that gives off a very hot flame

**tor-ment** [tôr′mĕnt′] *noun*, 1) abuse, agony, chaos, *verb*, 2) to torture, to annoy, to abuse, to afflict with mental suffering

**tor-na-do** [tôr-nā′dō] *noun*, a storm with a strong wind which spins very fast, a violent windstorm

**tor-pe-do** [tôr-pē′dō] *noun*, a self-propelled underwater missile containing explosives fired through the water from a ship to destroy another ship

**tor-pid** [tôr′pĭd] *adjective*, dormant, dull, lethargic

**tor-rent** [tôr′ənt] *noun*, a fast flow of water or energy

**tor-ren-tial** [tô-rĕn′shəl] *adjective*, a rushing, violent stream of water

**tor-rid** [tôr′ĭd] *adjective*, 1) passionate 2) tropical, sweltering, oppressively hot

**tor-so** [tôr′sō] *noun*, the trunk of a statue with head and limbs missing, the upper part of the human body

**tort** [tôrt] *noun*, a civil wrong, independent of a contract

**tor-toise** [tôr′tĭs] *noun*, a very large turtle that lives on the land

**tor-tu-ous** [tôr′chōō-əs] *adjective*, winding, full of curves

**tor-ture** [tôr′chər] noun1) 1) the act of causing great pain or suffering 2) distress of mind or body, *verb*, 3) to inflict pain on someone mercilessly, in order to dominate and control

**toss** [tôs, tŏs] *verb*, 1) to throw 2) to move about up and down

**to-tal** [tōt′l] *adjective*, 1) making up the whole, *noun*, 2) the sum of numbers in addition, entire

**to-tal-ly** [tōt′l-ē] *adverb*, wholly, entirely, completely

**touch** [tŭch] *noun*, 1) one of the five senses that communicates texture, temperature, and density to the brain through feeling, *verb*, 2) to make physical contact with something or someone

**tough** [tŭf] *adjective*, 1) yielding to force without breaking, strong 2) brave 3) difficult to chew

**tour** [tŏŏr] *noun*, 1) a journey that ends where it starts, *verb*, 2) to make a trip through a place

**tour-ist** [tŏŏr′ĭst] *noun*, a person traveling for pleasure

**tour-na-ment** [tŏŏr′nə-mənt] *noun*, a set number of contests that

includes many teams or players
and produces one winner

**tow** [tō] *verb*, to pull or haul with a
rope or a chain

**to-ward** [tôrd] *preposition*, 1) in
the direction of, in relation to 2)
facing from the opposite
direction

**tow-el** [tou/əl] noun, a piece of
cloth or paper used for wiping
or drying

**tow-er** [tou/ər] *noun*, 1) a tall
building or structure that stands
above the rest 2) a turret or spire
attached to a building or fortress,
*verb*, 3) to stand or reach above
everything

**town** [toun] *noun*, buildings
creating a hamlet, larger than a
village and smaller than a city

**tox-ic** [tŏk/sĭk] *adjective*,
poisonous, harmful

**toy** [toi] *noun*, an ornament or
article that children play with

**trace** [trās] *noun*, 1) a small
amount of something, *verb*,
2) to draw an image using paper
to duplicate it 3) to try to follow
the path of someone by using
evidence that indicates what they
are doing or have done

**track** [trăk] *noun*, 1) a mark left
by something that has passed 2)
a path or roadway, *verb*, 3) to
follow or trace, to trail

**trac-ta-ble** [trăk/tə-bəl] *adjective*,
1) obedient, willing, compliant
2) easily shaped, malleable

**trac-tion** [trăk/shən] *noun*,
adhesive friction of being
drawn or pulled, the grip of the
wheels on the ground

**trac-tor** [trăk/tər] *noun*, a machine
used to plow and to till soil

**trade** [trād] *noun, no plural*, 1) the
exchange of goods 2) a form of
business or enterprise 3) a
specific type of work that
requires training, *verb*, 4) to
buy and sell goods, to barter

**tra-di-tion** [trə-dĭsh/ən] *noun*, a
custom or belief passed within
families or other groups from
one generation to another

**tra-di-tion-al** [trə-dĭsh/ə-nəl]
*adjective*, following a custom
that has been handed down
through generations

**traf-fic** [trăf/ĭk] *noun*,
1) commerce, trade, the
interchange of goods 2) the
movement of cars and people on
streets or of planes and ships

**trag-e-dy** [trăj/ĭ-dē] *noun*, 1) drama
that deals with sad or terrible
themes, as opposed to comedy 2)
a fatal or unfortunate event

**trag-ic** [trăj/ĭk] *adjective*, very sad,
dreadful, unfortunate

**trail** [trāl] *noun*, 1) the marks or
evidence left behind in a place
by someone or something that
was there earlier, *verb*, 2) to
follow someone, to track

**train** [trān] *noun*, 1) railroad cars
for people or freight pulled by an
engine, *verb*, 2) to teach
someone or yourself to do
something difficult that is
considered a skill

**train-ing** [trā/nĭng] *noun*,
preparation, instruction

**trait** [trāt] *noun*, a distinguishing
characteristic or feature

**trai-tor** [trā′tər] *noun*, one who betrays a cause or any trust

**tra-jec-to-ry** [trə-jĕk′tə-rē] *noun*, a path taken by a projectile, or a flying object in its flight

**tramp** [trămp] *noun*, a person with no home or job who travels from place to place begging, a vagrant

**tram-ple** [trăm′pəl] *verb*, to crush into the ground, to walk heavily on something

**trance** [trăns] *noun*, a dream-like state of deep relaxation

**tran-quil** [trăng′kwəl] *adjective*, calm, peaceful, quiet, serene

**tran-quil-li-ty** [trăng-kwĭl′ĭ-tē] *noun*, calmness, composure

**tran-quil-iz-er** [trăng′kwə-līz′ər] *noun*, a sleeping pill, sedative

**trans-ac-tion** [trăn-săk′shən] *noun*, the doing of any business

**tran-scend** [trăn-sĕnd′] *verb*, to rise above and beyond the ordinary limits, to surpass, to exist independent of

**tran-scen-den-tal** [trăn′sĕn-dĕn′tl] *adjective*, beyond understanding, supernatural, spiritual

**trans-con-ti-nen-tal** [trăns′kŏn-tə-nĕn′tl] *adjective*, spanning a continent

**tran-scribe** [trăn-skrīb′] *verb*, to write out a spoken message

**tran-script** [trăn′skrĭpt′] *noun*, a written copy of a broadcast or a student's academic record

**trans-fer** [trăns-fûr′] *noun*, 1) the act of moving something from one place to another, *verb*, 2) to convey from one place to another

**trans-fer-a-ble** [trăns-fûr′ə-bəl] *noun*, capable of being moved from one place to another

**trans-form** [trăns-fôrm′] *verb*, 1) to change the form or appearance of something 2) to glorify

**trans-form-er** [trăns-fôr′mər] *noun*, a device that transfers electrical energy from one circuit to another

**trans-fu-sion** [trăns-fyōō′zhən] *noun*, the introduction into a person's bloodstream of blood from another

**trans-gres-sion** [trăns-grĕsh′ən] *noun*, violation of law, a going beyond some limit

**tran-sient** [trăn′shənt] *adjective*, of short duration, not permanent

**tran-sis-tor** [trăn-zĭs′tər] *noun*, an electrical device like a radio that sends and amplifies voices

**tran-sit** [trăn′sĭt] *noun*, 1) a passage 2) the state of being carried 3) a surveyor's instrument for measuring angles

**tran-si-tion** [trăn-zĭsh′ən] *noun*, going from one state of action or position to another

**tran-si-tive** [trăn′sĭ-tĭv] *adjective*, when the action of a verb is done to something or somebody

**tran-si-to-ry** [trăn′sĭ-tôr′ē] *adjective*, temporary, brief, lasting only a short time

**trans-late** [trăns-lāt′] *verb*, to pass along the message from one language to another

**trans-la-tion** [trăns-lā′shən] *noun*, the conversion of a message into another language

**trans-lu-cent** [trăns-lōō′sənt] *adjective*, a material that lets

light in diffusively, but cannot
be seen through

**trans-mis-sion** [trăns-mĭsh′ən]
*noun*, 1) the apparatus by which
the power is transmitted from
high-speed motor power to the
wheels 2) the sending of
pictures or sounds through the
air, as by radio or television

**trans-mit** [trăns-mĭt′] *verb*, 1) to
send information over wires or
air waves 2) to convey or send
from one person or place to
another 3) to pass along

**trans-mit-ter** [trăns-mĭt′ər] *noun*,
the part of a telegraph or
telephone instrument used to
send a message

**trans-mute** [trăns-myo͞ot′] *verb*, to
change, to convert from one
substance to another

**trans-par-ent** [trăns-pâr′ənt]
*adjective*, easily or capable of
being seen through, clear

**tran-spire** [trăn-spīr′] *verb*, 1) to
exhale 2) to happen, to occur

**trans-plant** [trăns-plănt′] *verb*,
1) to take out of the ground to
plant somewhere else 2) a
medical operation that
exchanges a body organ

**trans-port** [trăns-pôrt′] *noun*,
1) a means of carrying people or
goods, *verb*, 2) to carry

**trans-por-ta-tion**
[trăns′pər-tā′shən] *noun*, the act
of carrying things from one
place to another

**trans-pose** [trăns-pōz′] *verb*, 1) to
switch 2) to put into a different
key in music

**trap** [trăp] *noun*, 1) a device used
to capture someone or something
2) a strategy used to capture or
entrap someone, *verb*, 3) to
capture something or someone
so that they cannot escape

**tra-peze** [tră-pēz′] *noun*, a short
horizontal bar suspended by two
parallel ropes, one at each end

**trap-e-zoid** [trăp′ĭ-zoid′] *noun*, a
closed figure of four sides, two
sides are parallel but unequal in
length

**trash** [trăsh] *noun*, something
considered worthless that is
thrown away, garbage

**trau-mat-ic** [trou′măt′ĭk] *adjective*,
upsetting, stressful, disturbing

**tra-vail** [trə-vāl′] *noun*, 1) painful
labor, hard work 2) anguish

**trav-el** [trăv′əl] *noun*, 1) taking a
trip, seeing the world, *verb*, 2) to
go from one place to another 3)
to be transmitted

**trav-erse** [trə-vûrs′] *verb*, to cross
in traveling, to pass over

**trawl-er** [trô′lər] *noun*, a fishing
boat which drags a cone-shaped
net across the floor of the ocean

**tray** [trā] *noun*, a flat shallow
receptacle with raised edges on
which things can be carried

**treach-er-ous** [trĕch′ər-əs]
*adjective*, dangerous

**trea-cle** [trē′kəl] *noun*, syrup
obtained in refining sugar

**tread** [trĕd] *noun*, 1) the part
touching the ground, *verb*, 2) to
stand on, to walk on, to step

**trea-son** [trē′zən] *noun*, *no plural*,
the crime of helping the enemy
of a group or country one is
loyal to

**treas-ure** [trĕzh′ər] *noun*, 1) an accumulation of wealth such as money or jewels, *verb*, 2) to regard as precious, to cherish

**treas-ur-er** [trĕzh′ər-ər] *noun*, one who is in charge of the disbursement of money

**treas-ur-y** [trĕzh′ə-rē] *noun*, a place to store and control money such as a bank

**treat** [trēt] *noun*, 1) something that gives pleasure or enjoyment, *verb*, 2) to behave toward 3) to deal with, to serve 4) to give medicine as a doctor

**trea-tise** [trē′tĭs] *noun*, an article treating a subject systematically and thoroughly

**treat-ment** [trēt′mənt] *noun*, 1) handling, processing 2) therapeutic care

**trea-ty** [trē′tē] *noun*, a formal agreement between two or more nations

**tree** [trē] *noun*, a large plant with a trunk, branches, and leaves

**trek** [trĕk] *verb*, to travel with hardship, a difficult journey

**trem-ble** [trĕm′bəl] *verb*, to shake, to feel nervous, to quiver

**tre-men-dous** [trĭ-mĕn′dəs] *adjective*, 1) marvelously great 2) very large 3) extraordinary

**trem-or** [trĕm′ər] *noun*, trembling, involuntary shaking of the body

**trem-u-lous** [trĕm′yə-ləs] *adjective*, quivering, wavering

**trench** [trĕnch] *noun*, a long narrow ditch, dug into the earth

**trench-ant** [trĕn′chənt] *adjective*, cutting, sarcastic, critical, keen

**trench-er-man** [trĕn′chər-mən] *noun*, a person with a hearty appetite

**trend** [trĕnd] *noun*, the popular course, direction, tendency

**trep-i-da-tion** [trĕp′ĭ-dā′shən] *noun*, fear, apprehension

**tres-pass** [trĕs′pəs] *noun*, 1) an intrusion, *verb*, 2) to encroach on another's right 3) to unlawfully enter land of another

**tri-al** [trī′əl] *noun*, 1) when people in a court of law decide whether a person is guilty of a crime 2) a test to see if something is good or bad 3) suffering or adversity

**tri-an-gle** [trī′ăng′gəl] *noun*, a plane figure with three sides and three angles

**tri-an-gu-lar** [trī-ăng′gyə-lər] *adjective*, having three points like a triangle

**tribe** [trīb] *noun*, a group of people descended from a common ancestor who practice the same traditions, customs, and rituals, lead by a chief, a clan

**trib-u-la-tion** [trĭb′yə-lā′shən] *noun*, distress, suffering

**tri-bu-nal** [trī-byoo′nəl] *noun*, a court or forum for justice

**trib-u-tar-y** [trĭb′yə-tĕr′ē] *adjective*, 1) under another's control, *noun*, 2) a stream or river that flows into a larger river

**trib-ute** [trĭb′yoot] *noun*, a gesture to show respect for someone, an accolade, a statement of praise

**trick** [trĭk] *noun*, 1) a clever prank, a sly or ingenious feat, *verb*, 2) to deceive by cunning

**trick-le** [trĭk/əl] *verb*, to flow in a small, gentle stream

**tri-cy-cle** [trī/sĭk/əl] *noun*, a light three-wheeled vehicle

**tried** [trīd] *verb, past tense* of **try**

**tri-fle** [trī/fəl] *noun*, 1) a small amount, *verb*, 2) to play or toy

**tri-fling** [trī/flĭng] *adjective*, of little value or importance

**trig-ger** [trĭg/ər] *noun*, 1) the firing mechanism on a gun, *verb*, 2) to set something off

**trig-o-nom-e-try** [trĭg/ə-nŏm/ĭ-trē] *noun*, measuring the sides and angles of triangles

**tril-lion** [trĭl/yən] *noun*, a million million: 1,000,000,000,000

**tril-o-gy** [trĭl/ə-jē] *noun*, a novel or play in three separate works that are closely related

**trim** [trĭm] *noun*, 1) ornaments or decorations, *verb*, 2) to decorate 3) to cut back to make tidy

**tri-o** [trē/ō] *noun*, a set of three

**trip** [trĭp] *noun*, 1) a journey, a jaunt, an excursion, a pilgrimage, *verb*, 2) to skip, to stumble 3) to release a lever suddenly

**tri-ple** [trĭp/əl] *adjective*, three-way, multiplied three times

**tri-pod** [trī/pŏd/] *noun*, a stand or support with three legs

**trite** [trīt] *adjective*, 1) trivial, insignificant 2) hackneyed

**tri-umph** [trī/əmf] *noun*, 1) exultation over success, *verb*, 2) to gain victory

**tri-um-phant** [trī-ŭm/fənt] *adjective*, feeling thrilled and happy about winning

**triv-i-a** [trĭv/ē-ə] *noun*, small, unimportant matters, trifles

**triv-i-al** [trĭv/ē-əl] *adjective*, of little worth or importance

**trol-ley** [trŏl/ē] *noun*, a public bus that travels on a train track

**troop** [troŏp] *noun*, 1) a collection of people 2) a body of cavalry

**tro-phy** [trō/fē] *noun*, something as a prize or award, given to show success in an activity

**trop-ic** [trŏp/ĭk] *noun*, a place between the two imaginary lines that run parallel above and below the equator, where it is hot and humid all year long

**trop-i-cal** [trŏp/ĭ-kəl] *adjective*, temperatures of a jungle or warm climate near the equator

**trot** [trŏt] *verb*, to keep at a steady pace, to canter, to gallop

**trou-ble** [trŭb/əl] *noun*, 1) a problem, a difficulty 2) a dangerous or difficult situation 3) extra work or effort, *verb*, 4) to impose on 5) to distress

**troupe** [troŏp] *noun*, a troop or company of musicians or performers

**trou-sers** [trou/zərz] *noun, plural*, loose fitting pants

**trout** [trout] *noun*, a small fresh-water fish in the salmon family

**trow-el** [trou/əl] *noun*, 1) a hand-held spade 2) a tool with a flat blade used to apply mortar or cement

**tru-ant** [troŏ/ənt] *noun*, 1) absent from school without good reason or permission 2) neglectful

**truce** [tro͞os] *noun*, a peace agreement, cease-fire

**truck** [trŭk] *noun*, a large, heavy vehicle with at least four wheels used to transport heavy materials or large quantities

**true** [tro͞o] *adjective*, 1) honest, real, based on fact 2) loyal

**tru-ism** [tro͞o′ĭz′əm] *noun*, a self-evident obvious truth

**tru-ly** [(tro͞o′lē) *adverb*, in fact or in truth, sincerely, really

**trump** [trŭmp] *verb*, 1) to fabricate or invent 2) to beat someone's hand in bridge

**trum-pet** [trŭm′pĭt] *noun*, a horn, one of the brass instruments with several keys and a flaring bell

**trunk** [trŭngk] *noun*, 1) a chest, a storage box 2) the main stem of a tree 3) a compartment in a car 4) the snout of an elephant

**trust** [trŭst] *noun*, 1) belief in someone's goodness and integrity, *verb*, 2) to believe that someone will do as they say

**trust-ee** [trŭ-stē′] *noun*, one entrusted to administer the property of another

**truth** [tro͞oth] *noun*, the facts, what actually happened, reality

**try** [trī] *verb*, 1) to attempt, to make an effort 2) to sample

**try-ing** [trī′ĭng] *adjective*, difficult, straining one's patience

**tryst** [trĭst] *noun*, an appointed meeting, a rendezvous

**tsu-nami** [tso͞o-nä′mē] *noun*, a giant, fast-moving ocean wave produced by an earthquake

**tub** [tŭb] *noun*, a container used to take a bath or wash clothes

**tu-ba** [to͞o′bə] *noun*, the lowest-pitched of the brass instruments

**tube** [to͞ob] *noun*, 1) a pipe made of metal, plastic 2) a glass usually used to conduct liquids or gases

**tu-ber-cu-lo-sis** [to͞o-bûr′kyə-lō′sĭs] *noun*, a disease due to the presence of small granular tumors in an organ marked by coughing

**tuck** [tŭk] *noun*, 1) a pleat, fold or gather, *verb*, 2) to wrap snugly

**Tues-day** [to͞oz′dē] *noun*, the third day of the week

**tuft** [tŭft] *noun*, a cluster, a clump

**tug** [tŭg] *verb*, to jerk, to yank, to pull with force or effort

**tu-i-tion** [to͞o-ĭsh′ən] *noun*, the price paid for instruction

**tu-lip** [to͞o′lĭp] *noun*, a flower grown from a bulb in a variety of colors, in the shape of a cup

**tulle** [to͞ol] *noun*, a thin, fine net of acetate, silk or rayon, often used for veils or a tutu

**tum-ble** [tŭm′bəl] *verb*, 1) to turn over and over 2) to fall down

**tu-mult** [to͞o′mŭlt′] *noun*, commotion, a riot, noise

**tu-mul-tu-ous** [to͞o-mŭl′cho͞o-əs] *adjective*, wild, chaotic

**tu-na** [to͞o′nə] *noun*, a large fish that lives in the ocean

**tun-dra** [tŭn′drə] *noun*, the vast treeless plains in Siberia and arctic North America

**tune** [to͞on] *noun*, 1) musical notes arranged as a medley, *verb*, 2) to put the right amount of tension on a stringed instrument so that it gives a certain sound 3) to be in sync, to put in harmony

**tung-sten** [tŭng′stən] *noun*, a hard, brittle, whitish-gray metal with an extremely high melting point at 6100 degrees Fahrenheit

**tun-nel** [tŭn′əl] *noun*, 1) a long passageway dug underground, *verb,* 2) to dig, to burrow

**tur-ban** [tûr′bən] *noun*, a man's headdress having no brim

**tur-bid** [tûr′bĭd] *adjective*, muddy, having the sediment disturbed

**tur-bine** [tûr′bĭn] *noun*, a machine that uses the gas from liquid to turn a shaft

**tur-bu-lence** [tûr′byə-ləns] *noun*, 1) wind currents that move very quickly 2) confusion, excited activity

**tur-bu-lent** [tûr′byə-lənt] *adjective*, 1) agitated, violent, stormy 2) full of disorder

**tu-reen** [tŏŏ-rēn′] *noun*, a deep table dish for holding soup

**tur-key** [tûr′kē] *noun*, a bird of the pheasant family, originally found wild in North America

**tur-moil** [tûr′moil′] *adjective*, a state of great confusion, agitation or disturbance

**turn** [tûrn] *noun*, 1) a chance or opportunity to participate 2) a bend, a twist or a bend in the road 3) a reversal, *verb,* 4) to cause to rotate or revolve 5) to change or to transform

**tur-nip** [tûr′nĭp] *noun*, a thick, edible, roundish root in the mustard family, eaten when boiled

**tur-pen-tine** [tûr′pən-tīn′] *noun*, a thin flammable oil made from certain pine trees used as a solvent to thin paint

**tur-quoise** [tûr′kwoiz′] *noun*, a bluish green or greenish gray mineral used as a gem

**tur-tle** [tûr′tl] *noun*, a reptile with a soft body protected by a hard shell covering, into which it can draw its head, legs and tail

**tusk** [tŭsk] *noun*, a long pointed tooth, as of an elephant or walrus

**tu-tor** [tōō′tər] *noun*, a private teacher

**tweed** [twēd] *noun*, a soft, flexible fabric made of wool

**tweez-ers** [twē′zərz] *noun*, *plural*, a pincer-like tool for picking up small things

**twelfth** [twĕlfth] *adjective*, the ordinal of twelve, written 12th

**twelve** [twĕlv] *noun, adjective*, the number 12, the number after eleven

**twen-ti-eth** [twĕn′tē-ĭth] *adjective*, the number 20 in order, 20th, the ordinal of 20

**twen-ty** [twĕn′tē] *adjective, noun*, the number 20, ten times two

**twice** [twīs] *adverb*, two times, in double amount or degree

**twig** [twĭg] *noun*, a small outshoot of a branch or stem

**twi-light** [twī′līt′] *noun*, the light as the sun sets from the west

**twin** [twĭn] *adjective*, 1) two of the same, matched 2) an identical couple 3) either of two offspring brought forth at birth

**twine** [twīn] *noun*, 1) a strong cord of threads twisted together, *verb,* 2) to wrap around

**twinge** [twĭnj] *verb*, to feel a sharp physical or mental pain

**twin-kle** [twĭng′kəl] *verb*, to sparkle, to shimmer, to flicker

**twins** [twĭnz] *noun, plural*, two children born at the same time from the same mother

**twirl** [twûrl] *verb*, to whirl or spin in a circle, to rotate rapidly

**twitch** [twĭch] *verb*, to jerk or make spastic movements

**two** [tōō] *adjective, noun*, the number that follow one, written 2, one plus one

**type** [tīp] *noun*, 1) the letters in different fonts used to print words 2) category, sort, *verb*, 3) to use a keyboard to write words printed on a computer

**type-writ-er** [tīp′rī′tər] *noun*, an instrument for writing by means of type

**ty-phoid** [tī′foid′] *noun*, a fever which eats up the walls of the intestines causing internal bleeding

**ty-phoon** [tī-fōōn′] *noun*, a cyclone in the region of the Philippines or the China Sea

**typ-i-cal** [tĭp′ĭ-kəl] *adjective*, representing something by a model, characteristic

**ty-rant** [tī′rənt] *noun*, an absolute ruler who is usually cruel

# U

**u-biq-ui-tous** [yōō-bĭk′wĭ-təs] *adjective*, being everywhere at the same time, omnipresent

**UFO** [yōō′ĕf-ō′] *noun*, **U**nidentified **F**lying **O**bject, a thing in the sky that seems too strange to be real

**ug-ly** [ŭg′lē] *adjective*, revolting to look at, unattractive

**ul-cer** [ŭl′sər] *noun*, a sore on the skin filled with pus and infection that is painful, a lesion

**ul-te-ri-or** [ŭl-tîr′ē-ər] *adjective*, intentionally concealed

**ul-ti-mate** [ŭl′tə-mĭt] *adjective*, 1) final, supreme 2) farthest

**ul-ti-mate-ly** [ŭl′tə-mĭt-lē] *adverb*, finally, at the end, totally

**ul-ti-ma-tum** [ŭl′tə-mā′təm] *noun*, a final proposition or condition offered to end a dispute

**um-brage** [ŭm′brĭj] *noun*, resentment, anger, a sense of injury or insult, offense

**um-brel-la** [ŭm-brĕl′ə] *noun*, a covering held in the hand as protection from the rain

**um-pire** [ŭm′pīr′] *noun*, the judge or referee in a baseball game

**un-a-ble** [ŭn-ā′bəl] *adjective*, not capable of doing something

**un-alienable** [ŭn-āl′yə-nə-bəl] *adjective*, cannot be taken away

**u-nan-i-mous** [yōō-năn′ə-məs] *adjective*, being of one mind, showing complete agreement

**u-nan-i-mous-ly** [yōō-năn′ə-məs-lē] *adverb*, with all voters voting the same way

**un-as-sum-ing** [ŭn′ə-sōō′mĭng] *adjective*, modest, simple, plain

**un-a-void-a-ble** [ŭn′ə-voi′də-bəl] *adjective*, inevitable

**un-bear-a-ble** [ŭn-bâr′ə-bəl]
*adjective*, not capable of being
endured, intolerable

**un-bri-dled** [ŭn-brīd′ld] *adjective*,
not restrained, uninhibited

**un-can-ny** [ŭn-kăn′ē] *adjective*,
strange, mysterious, seeming to
have a supernatural basis

**un-cer-tain-ty** [ŭn-sûr′tn-tē] *noun*,
doubtfulness, not reliable

**un-cle** [ŭng′kəl] *noun*, the brother
of one of your parents, or the
husband of the sister of one of
your parents

**un-com-fort-a-ble**
[ŭn-kŭm′fər-tə-bəl] *adjective*,
uneasy, causing discomfort

**un-com-mon** [ŭn-kŏm′ən]
*adjective*, not usual, unique, odd

**un-con-cern** [ŭn′kən-sûrn′]
*adjective*, indifference, lack of
interest, freedom from anxiety

**un-con-scion-a-ble**
[ŭn-kŏn′shə-nə-bəl] *adjective*,
unscrupulous, something done
that shows no conscience,
excessive, unreasonable

**un-con-scious** [ŭn-kŏn′shəs]
*adjective*, not knowing what is
happening, lacking awareness

**un-cov-er** [ŭn-kŭv′ər] *verb*, 1) to
take something from on top of
something 2) to find out

**un-der** [ŭn′dər] *adjective*, 1) less
than 2) working for or obeying,
*preposition*, 3) below, beneath
the surface

**un-der-es-ti-mate**
[ŭn′dər-ĕs′tə-māt′] *verb*, to
undervalue, to minimize

**un-der-go** [ŭn′dər-gō′] *verb*, 1) to
experience 2) to suffer or endure

**un-der-grad-u-ate**
[ŭn′dər-grăj′ōō-ĭt] *noun*, a
student at a college who has not
received a bachelor's degree

**un-der-ground** [ŭn′dər-ground′]
*adjective*, 1) in the recesses of
the earth 2) in secrecy

**un-der-growth** [ŭn′dər-grōth′]
*noun*, *no plural*, thickly growing
plants underneath trees

**un-der-line** [ŭn′dər-līn′] *verb*, to
put a line under a word or words

**un-der-neath** [ŭn′dər-nēth′]
*adverb*, down from below

**un-der-rate** [ŭn′dər-rāt′] *verb*, to
evaluate too low, to undervalue

**un-der-stand** [ŭn′dər-stănd′] *verb*,
1) to grasp the nature of 2) to
know what something means

**un-der-take** [ŭn′dər-tāk′] *verb*, to
take upon oneself as a task

**un-der-tak-er** [ŭn′dər-tā′kər]
*noun*, one whose business is to
take charge of funerals

**un-der-tak-ing** [ŭn′dər-tā′kĭng]
*noun*, a duty, an obligation, a
job, a task

**un-der-wear** [ŭn′dər-wâr′] *noun*,
the garments worn next to the
skin under outside clothing

**un-der-write** [ŭn′dər-rīt′] *verb*, to
insure, to guarantee

**un-do** [ŭn-dōō′] *verb*, 1) to untie or
unfasten 2) to reverse or annul

**un-doubt-ed-ly** [ŭn-dou′tĭd-lē]
*adverb*, certainly, indeed

**un-du-late** [ŭn′jə-lāt′] *verb*, to
move with a wave-like motion

**un-earth** [ŭn-ûrth′] *verb*, to dig up

**un-eas-y** [ŭn-ē′zē] *adjective*, a little
afraid, worried, uncomfortable

**un-em-ployed** [ŭn′ĕm-ploid′] *adjective*, having no paid work

**un-equal** [ŭn-ē′kwəl] *adjective*, unmatched, not even

**un-e-quiv-o-cal** [ŭn′ĭ-kwĭv′ə-kəl] *adjective*, plain, obvious

**un-err-ing-ly** [ŭn-ûr′ĭng-lē] *adverb*, correctly, precisely

**un-e-ven** [ŭn-ē′vən] *adjective*, not level or flat, not uniform

**un-ex-pect-ed** [ŭn′ĭk-spĕk′tĭd] *adjective*, sudden, coming without warning, unforeseen

**un-fair** [ŭn-fâr′] *adjective*, unjust, unethical, biased, dishonest

**un-faltering** [ŭn-fôl′tər-ĭng] *adjective*, steadfast

**un-fas-ten** [ŭn-făs′ən] *verb*, to undo, to detach, to separate

**un-fit** [ŭn-fĭt′] *adjective*, made unsuitable, not prepared or adapted, not competent

**un-fold** [ŭn-fōld′] *verb*, 1) to open out 2) to explain, to evolve

**un-for-tu-nate** [ŭn-fôr′chə-nĭt] *adjective*, unlucky, regrettable

**un-for-tu-nate-ly** [ŭn-fôr′chə-nĭt-lē] *adverb*, having bad luck, unsuccessful

**un-friend-ly** [ŭn-frĕnd′lē] *adjective*, not nice, unkind

**un-grate-ful** [ŭn-grāt′fəl] *adjective*, thankless

**un-hap-py** [ŭn-hăp′ē] *adjective*, dissatisfied, not content, sad

**un-health-y** [ŭn-hĕl′thē] *adjective*, 1) ill, sickly 2) food or habits that make a person feel tired

**u-ni-corn** [yōō′nə- kôrn] *noun*, a mythical horse-like animal with a horn growing from the center of its forehead

**u-ni-form** [yōō′nə-fôrm′] *adjective*, 1) unvaried, regular, constant, *noun*, 2) clothes worn for a special job or school

**u-ni-form-i-ty** [yōō′nə-fôrm′ĭ-tē] *noun*, sameness, consistency, identical with others

**u-ni-fy** [yōō′nə-fī′] *verb*, to combine, to integrate, to connect

**u-ni-lat-er-al** [yōō′nə-lăt′ər-əl] *adjective*, one sided

**un-im-ag-i-na-tive** [ŭn-ĭ-măj′ə-nə-tĭv] *adjective*, uninspired, common, everyday

**un-impeach-a-ble** [ŭn′ĭm-pē′chə-bəl] *adjective*, blameless and exemplary

**un-im-por-tant** [ŭn′ĭm-pôr′tnt] *adjective*, 1) trivial, trite 2) extraneous, irrelevant

**un-in-hib-it-ed** [ŭn′ĭn-hĭb′ĭ-tĭd] *adjective*, not restrained by convention, free and easy

**un-in-tel-li-gi-ble** [ŭn′ĭn-tĕl′ĭ-jə-bəl] *adjective*, not capable of being understood

**un-ion** [yōōn′yən] *noun*, 1) a coming together 2) a group of people who join to support a cause 3) a combination, **Union** 4) the army fighting for northern states during the Civil War

**u-nique** [yōō-nēk′] *adjective*, single in kind or excellence

**u-ni-son** [yōō′nĭ-sən] *noun*, unity of pitch, complete accord

**u-nit** [yōō′nĭt] *noun*, 1) a complete set 2) a specific amount, a form of measurement 3) a single entity

**u-nite** [yōō-nīt′] *verb*, to join, to connect, to put together as one

# United States

**United States**
[yōō-nī′tĭd-stāts-ŭv-ə-měr′ĭ-kə]
*noun*, the country made up of the
land between the Pacific Ocean
and the Atlantic Ocean, between
Canada and Mexico, including
Alaska and Hawaii, the capital,
is the District of Columbia

**u-ni-ver-sal** [yōō′nə-vûr′səl]
*adjective*, mutual understanding,
totally accepted everywhere

**u-ni-verse** [yōō′nə-vûrs′] *noun*, all
existing things including the
earth and all of space

**u-ni-ver-si-ty** [yōō′nə-vûr′sĭ-tē]
*noun*, an institution of higher
learning empowered to confer
degrees in the arts and sciences

**un-just** [ŭn-jŭst′] *adjective*, unfair,
biased, unworthy

**un-kempt** [ŭn-kěmpt′] *adjective*, a
messy, uncared for appearance

**un-kind** [ŭn-kīnd′] *adjective*,
indifferent, unfeeling, rude

**un-known** [ŭn-nōn′] *adjective*,
1) unfamiliar 2) unexplored

**un-less** [ŭn-lěs′] *adjective*, under
different conditions, or else

**un-like** [ŭn-līk′] *adjective*,
dissimilar, different

**un-load** [ŭn-lōd′] *verb*, 1) to take
something off a vehicle such as
cargo 2) to dispose of

**un-luck-y** [ŭn-lŭk′ē] *adjective*,
unsuccessful, unfortunate

**un-mis-tak-a-ble** [ŭn′mĭ-stā′kə-
bəl] *adjective*, clear, obvious

**un-mis-take-a-bly**
[ŭn′mĭ-stā′kə-blē] *adverb*,
undoubtedly, obviously

**un-nec-es-sar-y** [ŭn-něs′ĭ-sěr′ē]
*adjective*, uncalled for, needless

**un-ob-tru-sive** [ŭn′əb-trōō′sĭv]
*adjective*, not noticeable

**un-pleas-ant** [ŭn-plěz′ənt]
*adjective*, disagreeable

**un-prec-e-dent-ed**
[ŭn-prěs′ĭ-děn′tĭd] *adjective*,
novel, unparalleled

**un-pre-pare-ed** [ŭn′prĭ-pârd′]
*adjective*, unaware, not ready

**un-rav-el** [ŭn-răv′əl] *verb*, to
untangle, to unwind, to unfold

**un-rea-son-a-ble** [ŭn-rē′zə-nə-bəl]
*adjective*, absurd, illogical, not
guided by sound judgment

**un-re-li-a-ble** [ŭn′rĭ-lī′ə-bəl]
*adjective*, not dependable

**un-ru-ly** [ŭn-rōō′lē] *adjective*,
disobedient, lawless

**un-safe** [ŭn-sāf′] *adjective*,
hazardous, dangerous, risky

**un-sat-is-fac-to-ry**
[ŭn-săt′ĭs-făk′tə-rē] *adjective*,
not good enough, inadequate

**un-scru-pu-lous**
[ŭn-skrōō′pyə-ləs] *adjective*,
unprincipled, devious, deceptive

**un-seem-ly** [ŭn-sēm′lē] *adjective*,
unbecoming, inappropriate

**un-so-phis-ti-cat-ed**
[ŭn′sə-fĭs′tĭ-kā′tĭd] *adjective*,
innocent, showing inexperience

**un-stead-y** [ŭn-stěd′ē] *adjective*,
1) not safe 2) unsure, wavering

**un-suit-a-ble** [ŭn-sōō′tə-bəl]
*adjective*, inappropriate,
unsatisfactory, something that
does not fit in, irregular

**un-sure** [ŭn-shŏŏr] *adjective*, uncertain, doubtful

**un-ten-a-ble** [ŭn-těn′ə-bəl] *adjective*, not able to be maintained or supported against criticism

**un-ti-dy** [ŭn-tī′dē] *adjective*, messy, cluttered, not orderly

**un-tie** [ŭn-tī′] *verb*, to unfasten a string or rope, to loosen

**un-til** [ŭn-tĭl′] *conjunction*, 1) up to the time that, or when, *preposition*, 2) up to the time of, as far as, before

**un-to-ward** [ŭn-tôrd′] *adjective*, unfortunate, annoying

**un-true** [ŭn-trōō′] *adjective*, false, incorrect, deceptive, disloyal

**un-u-su-al** [ŭn-yōō′zhōō-əl] *adjective*, strange, odd

**un-veil** [ŭn-vāl′] *verb*, to remove the covering from something

**un-well** [ŭn-wĕl′] *adjective*, ill, sick, upset, ailing

**un-wield-y** [ŭn-wēl′dē] *adjective*, not easily carried, bulky

**un-will-ing** [ŭn-wĭl′ĭng] *adjective*, reluctant, resistant, averse

**un-wind** [ŭn-wīnd′] *verb*, 1) to undo something, to loosen 2) to relax, to get rid of tension

**un-wise** [ŭn-wīz′] *adjective*, not reasonable or sensible

**un-wit-ting** [ŭn-wĭt′ĭng] *adjective*, unintentional, not knowing

**un-wrap** [ŭn-răp′] *verb*, to remove the protective covering on a package or product

**up** [ŭp] *adverb*, 1) to put in a higher place, *preposition*, 2) to position something so that it is standing 3) toward

**up-braid** [ŭp-brād′] *verb*, to scold, to reproach, to criticize

**up-heav-al** [ŭp-hē′vəl] *noun*, an eruption, a change, a quake

**up-hold** [ŭp-hōld′] *verb*, to maintain, to support, to sustain

**up-hol-ster-y** [ŭp-hōl′stə-rē] *noun*, furniture with stuffing, springs, covers or trim

**up-lift** [ŭp-lĭft′] *noun*, 1) upgrade, restoration, *verb*, 2) to raise up 3) to improve socially or morally

**up-on** [ə-pŏn′] *adverb*, 1) on, *preposition*, 2) on top of something

**up-per** [ŭp′ər] *adjective*, 1) in a higher position, further up 2) the part of the shoe above the sole

**up-right** [ŭp′rīt′] *adjective*, 1) straight up and down 2) righteous, honest, honorable

**up-set** [ŭp-sĕt′] *verb*, 1) to knock over 2) to make unhappy or worried 3) to spoil something that was planned, to disrupt

**up-stairs** [ŭp′stârz′] *adverb*, 1) up the steps, *noun*, *plural*, 2) the next level, the upper level

**up-ward** [ŭp′wərd] *adjective*, to a higher place or position

**u-ra-ni-um** [yŏŏ-rā′nē-əm] *noun*, a rare radioactive, metallic element found in certain minerals used in nuclear weapons

**ur-ban** [ûr′bən] *noun*, characteristic of a city

**ur-bane** [ûr-bān′] *adjective*, suave, refined, elegant, sophisticated, charming, courteous, polite

**ur-chin** [ûr′chǐn] *noun*, a needy or mischievous child

**urge** [ûrj] *noun*, 1) a strong wish, *verb*, 2) to try to make someone do something, to push along

**ur-gen-cy** [ûr′jən-sē] *adverb*, calling for quick action

**ur-gent** [ûr′jənt] *adjective*, pressing, calling for immediate attention or action, insistent

**us** [ŭs] *pronoun*, the person who is speaking, and the others mentioned in the sentence, the objective case of **we**

**us-age** [yōō′sǐj] *noun*, a long continued practice, a custom

**use** [yōōz] *noun*, 1) a purpose, *verb*, 2) to find a purpose for something, to utilize

**used to** [yōōst-tōō] *adjective*, 1) knowing what something or someone is like, familiar 2) something done in the past but is not done now

**use-ful** [yōōs′fəl] *adjective*, helpful, serviceable

**use-less** [yōōs′lǐs] *adjective*, hopeless, valueless, vain

**u-su-al** [yōō′zhōō-əl] *adjective*, something that happens regularly, not uncommon

**u-su-al-ly** [yōō′zhōō-əl-lē] *adverb*, almost always, frequently

**u-surp** [yōō-sûrp′] *verb*, to seize, to take possession of by force or without right or authority

**u-sur-pa-tion** [yōō′sər-pā′shən] *noun*, the act of seizing power and rank of another

**u-su-ry** [yōō′zhə-rē] *noun*, interest in excess of a legal rate

**Utah** [yōō′tô′] *noun*, one of the 50 United States, the capital is Salt Lake City. The state flower of **Utah** is the sego lily; and the motto is "Industry."

**u-ten-sil** [yōō-tĕn′səl] *noun*, a tool, a dining instrument

**u-til-i-ty** [yōō-tĭl′ĭ-tē] *noun*, a company that provides products such as gas, water, or electricity

**u-ti-lize** [yōōt′l-īz′] *verb*, to make use of something

**ut-most** [ŭt′mōst′] *adjective*, the furthest or most extreme

**u-to-pi-a** [yōō-tō′pē-ə] *noun*, heaven on earth, an ideal place

**ut-ter** [ŭt′ər] *verb*, to speak

**ut-ter-ance** [ŭt′ər-əns] *noun*, vocal expression, articulation, speech

**ut-ter-ly** [ŭt′ər-lē] *adverb*, completely, entirely, without doubt, totally, absolutely

# V

**va-can-cy** [vā′kən-sē] *noun*, 1) emptiness 2) an unfilled place, job or position 3) an opening

**va-cant** [vā′kənt] *adjective*, empty

**va-cate** [vā′kāt′] *verb*, 1) to leave, to empty, to abandon 2) to annul

**va-ca-tion** [vā-kā′shən] *noun*, time away from work for rest, amusement, and relaxation

**vac-ci-nate** [văk′sə-nāt′] *verb*, to inoculate with a vaccine as a form of protection

**vac-ci-na-tion** [văk′sə-nā′shən] *noun*, a remedy which is the injection of the virus itself

**vac-cine** [văk-sēn] *noun*, a weakened germ of a virus used to protect a person from the often fatal or debilitating effects of a virus

**vac-il-late** [văs′ə-lāt′] *verb*, to change one's mind often, to waffle, to waver

**vac-u-um** [văk′yōō-əm] *noun*, 1) the absolute absence of matter 2) an appliance used to rid carpets of dust and litter 3) a kind of bottle that keeps liquids hot or cold, such as a thermos

**vag-a-bond** [văg′ə-bŏnd′] *noun*, a tramp, an outcast, a vagrant

**va-grant** [vā′grənt] *adjective*, 1) wandering, begging, *noun*, 2) one who wanders around outside from place to place

**vague** [vāg] *adjective*, not clearly understood, indistinct

**vain** [vān] *adjective*, 1) conceited, too proud of the way one looks 2) fruitless, unsuccessful

**vale** [vāl] *noun*, valley, lowland

**val-en-tine** [văl′ən-tīn′] *noun*, a love poem, a card expressing love and affection

**val-et** [văl′ĭt] *noun*, a manservant who takes care of the clothes and personal needs of his employer

**val-iant** [văl′yənt] *adjective*, full of courage, brave

**val-iant-ly** [văl′yənt-lē] *adverb*, unafraid of danger, boldly, courageously, bravely

**val-id** [văl′ĭd] *adjective*, 1) significant, sound 2) legally effective or binding

**val-i-date** [văl′ĭ-dāt′] *verb*, to confirm, to ratify, to substantiate

**va-lid-i-ty** [və-lĭ′dĭ-tē] *noun*, confirmation that proves something is what it says it is

**val-ley** [văl′ē] *noun*, a region of low land situated between hills or mountains, a dale

**val-or** [văl′ər] *noun*, bravery, courage, boldness

**val-u-a-ble** [văl′yōō-ə-bəl] *adjective*, precious, of considerable worth, costly

**val-ue** [văl′yōō] *noun*, 1) what something is worth, what someone will pay, *verb*, 2) to think that something is important and meaningful 3) to say how much something is worth on the market, to rate

**valve** [vălv] *noun*, any device by which the flow of liquid, air, or gas may be regulated

**van** [văn] *noun*, a small, covered truck carrying goods or passengers or animals

**van-dal-ism** [văn′dl-ĭz′əm] *noun*, willful destruction of property

**vane** [vān] *noun*, a piece of metal or cloth set up high to swing with the wind to tell which way the wind is blowing

**va-nil-la** [və-nĭl′ə] *noun*, a flavoring made from the beans of the vanilla plant

**van-ish** [văn′ĭsh] *verb*, to disappear, to dissolve, to end

**van-i-ty** [văn′ĭ-tē] *noun*, 1) too proud of oneself 2) a small table for putting on makeup

**van-quish** [văng′kwĭsh] *verb*, to conquer, to overcome, to overpower in battle

**van-tage** [văn′tĭj] *noun*, the position giving an advantage

**va-por** [vā′pər] *noun*, 1) condensation 2) a substance in the gaseous state such as fog

**var-i-a-ble** [vâr′ē-ə-bəl] *noun*, changeable, liable to vary

**var-i-ance** [vâr′ē-əns] *noun*, degree of difference, disagreement

**var-i-a-tion** [vâr′ē-ā′shən] *noun*, a change in form, position, or condition

**va-ri-e-ty** [və-rī′ĭ-tē] *noun*, many different things, assortment

**var-i-ous** [vâr′ē-əs] *adjective*, , several different kinds, diverse

**var-nish** [vär′nĭsh] *noun*, 1) a liquid that hardens into a clear, tough film, *verb*, 2) to paint with a clear protective sealant

**var-si-ty** [vär′sĭ-tē] *adjective*, a principal team in sports representing a school or college

**var-y** [vâr′ē] *verb*, to change

**vase** [vās] *noun*, a decorated pot for cut flowers or for decoration

**vas-sal** [văs′əl] *noun*, in feudalism, one who held land of a superior lord

**vast** [văst] *adjective*, limitless, expansive, very great in size, quantity or degree, widespread

**vat** [văt] *noun*, a large container for liquids, a barrel

**vaude-ville** [vôd′vĭl′] *noun*, a theatrical performance with music, songs, and dance

**vault** [vôlt] *noun*, 1) a room constructed to protect its contents, *verb*, 2) to jump or leap over with hands holding a pole

**veer** [vîr] *verb*, to change in direction or position

**veg-e-ta-ble** [vĕj′tə-bəl] *noun*, an edible plant grown for food

**veg-e-tate** [vĕj′ĭ-tāt′] *verb*, to live in a monotonous, inactive way

**veg-e-ta-tion** [vĕj′ĭ-tā′shən] *noun*, plant growth, foliage, flowers

**veg-e-tar-i-an** [vĕj′ĭ-t′ər ′ē-ən] *noun*, one who does not eat meat, one who believes in a vegetable diet as best for people

**ve-he-ment** [vē′ə-mənt] *adjective*, fervent, impassioned, fiery

**ve-hi-cle** [vē′ĭ-kəl] *noun*, something used to carry or transport people or things

**veil** [vāl] *noun*, a piece of transparent material worn to hide or protect the face, a cover

**vein** [vān] *noun*, 1) one of the vessels which conveys blood back to the heart 2) a crack in a rock filled with mineral matter

**vel-lum** [vĕl′əm] *noun*, a form of paper made out of animal skin that will hold ink

**ve-loc-i-ty** [və-lŏs′ĭ-tē] *noun*, speed, rapidity of motion

**vel-vet** [vĕl′vĭt] *noun*, *no plural*, a type of cloth with a soft surface

**ven-det-ta** [vĕn-dĕt′ə] *noun*, revenge for a dispute

**ven-dor** [vĕn′dər] *noun*, someone who sells something, a merchant

**ve-neer** [və-nîr′] *noun*, 1) a thin layer of finished wood, glued on a cheap surface 2) a superficial show of quality

**ven-er-a-ble** [vĕn′ər-ə-bəl] *adjective*, deserving high respect

**ven-er-a-tion** [věn′ə-rā′shən] *noun*, deep, respectful love, adoration

**venge-ance** [věn′jəns] *noun*, retribution, revenge, reprisal

**ve-ni-al** [vē′nē-əl] *adjective*, capable of being forgiven

**ven-i-son** [věn′ĭ-sən] *noun*, deer meat used for food

**venn di-a-gram** [věn-dī′ə-grăm′] *noun*, a tool to indicate the relationship of elements

**ven-om** [věn′əm] *noun*, poison stored in some animals

**ven-om-ous** [věn′ə-məs] *adjective*, poisonous, deadly, toxic

**vent** [věnt] *noun*, a small opening or outlet to let out air

**ven-ti-late** [věn′tl-āt′] *verb*, to cause fresh air to circulate through, to admit air into

**ven-tril-o-quist** [věn-trĭl′ə-kwĭst] *noun*, one who can make a voice seem to come from another person or thing

**ven-ture** [věn′chər] *noun*, 1) doing something that involves the risk of a loss *verb*, 2) to dare to go, to do or to say

**ven-tur-ous** [věn′chər-əs] *adjective*, daring, bold

**ven-ue** [věn′yōō] *noun*, an agreed place where something will take place, the scene of an event

**ve-rac-i-ty** [və-răs′ĭ-tē] *noun*, habitual observance of truth, truthfulness, accuracy

**ve-ran-da** [və-răn′də] *noun*, a long porch with a roof along the outside of a building

**verb** [vûrb] *noun*, the word expressing action in a sentence

**ver-ba-tim** [vər-bā′tĭm] *adverb*, word for word, literal

**ver-bi-age** [vûr′bē-ĭj] *noun*, a pompous array of words

**ver-dant** [vûr′dnt] *adjective*, green with vegetation

**ver-dict** [vûr′dĭkt] *noun*, the decision of a jury given to the court, a judgment or decision

**verge** [vûrj] *noun*, 1) the point beyond which something begins, the brink, *verb*, 2) to tend to incline

**ver-i-fy** [věr′ə-fī′] *verb*, to prove to be true, to confirm, to ascertain

**ver-i-si-mil-i-tude** [věr′ə-sĭ-mĭl′ĭ-tōōd′] *noun*, appearance of truth, likelihood

**ver-i-ty** [věr′ĭ-tē] *noun*, truth, reality, a statement that is true

**ver-mi-cel-li** [vûr′mĭ-chěl′ē] *noun*, a pasta dried in a slender tube form, like spaghetti

**ver-mic-u-lite** [vər-mĭk′yə-līt′] *noun*, slivers of mica that expand when heated, used for insulation, and water absorption

**Ver-mont** [vər-mŏnt′] *noun*, one of the 50 United States located in New England, the capital is Montpelier. The state flower of **Vermont** is the red clover, the motto is "Freedom and unity."

**ver-nal** [vûr′nəl] *adjective*, of or occurring in spring

**ver-sa-tile** [vûr′sə-təl′] *adjective*, having the capability of doing many different things

**verse** [vûrs] *noun*, 1) lines of writing which have a rhythm often a rhyme 2) a few lines of this from a longer piece called a poem 3) a small part of the Bible, the Jewish Koran, or Talmud

**ver-sion** [vûr′zhən] *noun*, a description from a particular point of view, a standpoint

**ver-sus** [vûr′səs] *preposition*, against, in contrast with

**ver-te-brate** [vûr′tə-brĭt] *noun*, an animal with a backbone

**ver-tex** [vûr′tĕks′] *noun*, 1) the point where two planes intersect to form an angle 2) the highest point

**ver-ti-cal** [vûr′tĭ-kəl] *adjective*, straight up and down, perpendicular to the horizon

**verve** [vûrv] *noun*, enthusiasm, liveliness, energy, vitality

**ver-y** [vĕr′ē] *adjective*, 1) the same 2) the right or appropriate one, *adverb*, 3) to emphasize the word to make it stronger

**ves-sel** [vĕs′əl] *noun*, 1) a hollow utensil for holding anything 2) a boat 3) a channel for delivering blood, a vein or capillary

**vest** [vĕst] *noun*, a sleeveless top worn over a shirt with pockets

**ves-ti-bule** [vĕs′tə-byo͞ol′] *noun*, foyer, lobby, entry way

**ves-tige** [vĕs′tĭj] *noun*, a trace or visible sign of something gone

**vet-er-an** [vĕt′ər-ən] *noun*, experienced, old in service, especially in military life

**vet-er-i-nar-i-an** [vĕt′ər-ə-nâr′ē-ən] *noun*, a doctor who specializes in animal health and surgery

**ve-to** [vē′tō] *noun*, 1) a denial, a rejection, *verb*, 2) to deny, to reject, to turn down

**vex** [vĕks] *verb*, to annoy, to distress, to irritate

**vex-a-tion** [vĕk-sā′shən] *noun*, irritation, a cause of trouble or disquiet, annoyance

**vi-a** [vī′ə, vē′ə] *preposition*, traveling through, by way of

**vi-a-ble** [vī′ə-bəl] *adjective*, capable of maintaining life

**vi-a-duct** [vī′ə-dŭkt′] *noun*, a bridge for carrying a road, resting on masonry arches, often in water to allow boats through

**vi-and** [vī′ənd] *noun*, food, provision

**vi-brate** [vī′brāt′] *verb*, 1) to shake, to quiver or tremble 2) to echo, to reverberate, to move to and fro

**vi-bra-tion** [vī-brā′shən] *noun*, shaking, quivering, pulsation

**vi-car-i-ous-ly** [vī-kâr′ē-əs-lē] *adverb*, acting as a substitute, done in place of another

**vice** [vīs] *noun*, corruption, weakness, faults, foible

**vice president** [vīs′prĕz′ĭ-dənt] *noun*, the person chosen to replace the president

**vi-cin-i-ty** [vĭ-sĭn′ĭ-tē] *noun*, the region near or close by

**vi-cious** [vĭsh′əs] *adjective*, corrupt, wicked, mean

**vi-cis-si-tude** [vĭ-sĭs′ĭ-to͞od′] *noun*, change or succession from one thing to another

**vic-tim** [vĭk′tĭm] *noun*, 1) someone who suffers from an illness or action 2) a person who is deceived or cheated

**vic-to-ri-ous** [vĭk-tôr′ē-əs] *adjective*, conquering, triumphant in war, winning

**vic-to-ry** [vĭk′tə-rē] *noun*, winning a contest or a battle, a triumph

**vict-uals** [vĭt′lz] *noun*, *plural*, food for human beings, provisions

**vid-e-o** [vĭd′ē-ō′] *noun*, film for showing on a television set

**vie** [vī] *verb*, to contend, to strive in competition, to struggle

**view** [vyo͞o] *noun*, 1) ideas, beliefs, opinion 2) something you see

**vig-i-lance** [vĭj′ə-ləns] *noun*, watchfulness, caution

**vi-gnette** [vĭn-yĕt′] *noun*, a scene depicting a moment in time

**vig-or** [vĭg′ər] *noun*, physical or mental strength, stamina, energy

**vig-or-ous** [vĭg′ər-əs] *adjective*, exhibiting strength, powerful, energetic, intense, robust

**vig-or-ous-ly** [vĭg′ər-əs-lē] *adverb*, very fast, with a great deal of energy, healthy, spirited

**vile** [vīl] *adjective*, disgusting

**vil-i-fy** [vĭl′ə-fī′] *verb*, to slander, to malign, to slur, to revile

**vil-lage** [vĭl′ĭj] *noun*, a group of houses that form a community, usually smaller than a town

**vil-lain** [vĭl′ən] *noun*, one capable or guilty of great crimes, a rascal

**vin-di-cate** [vĭn′dĭ-kāt′] *verb*, to support or maintain as true, to free from suspicion

**vin-dic-tive** [vĭn-dĭk′tĭv] *adjective*, revengeful, retaliatory, mean

**vine** [vīn] *noun*, a name given to some plants with climbing stems

**vin-e-gar** [vĭn′ĭ-gər] *noun*, a sour liquid made by fermentation of wine or cider

**vi-o-late** [vī′ə-lāt′] *verb*, 1) to break the rules, to disregard as a promise 2) to break in on

**vi-o-lence** [vī′ə-ləns] *noun*, commotion, disorder, outrage, brutality, intense force

**vi-o-lent** [vī′ə-lənt] *adjective*, brutal, vicious, forceful, rough

**vi-o-lent-ly** [vī′ə-lənt-lē] *adverb*, harshly, with destructive force

**vi-o-let** [vī′ə-lĭt]) *adjective*, 1) the color that is a combination of blue and red, *noun*, 2) a purple flower that grows wild as a ground cover

**vi-o-lin** [vī′ə-lĭn′] *noun*, one of the small stringed instruments played with a bow

**vi-o-lin-ist** [vī′ə-lĭn′ĭst] *noun*, a person who plays a violin

**vi-per** [vī′pər] *noun*, a poisonous snake, a serpent

**vir-gin** [vûr′jĭn] *adjective*, pure, chaste, unused

**Vir-gin-i-a** [vər-jĭn′yə] *noun*, one of the 50 United States located in the Southeast, the capital is Richmond. The state flower of **Virginia** is the flowering dogwood and the motto is "Ever thus to tyrants."

**vir-ile** [vîr′əl] *adjective*, manly, showing masculine strength

**vir-tue** [vûr′cho͞o] *noun*, uprightness, moral excellence

**vir-tu-ous** [vûr′cho͞o-əs] *adjective*, righteous, honest, moral

**vi-rus** [vī′rəs] *noun*, an group of infectious submicroscopic agents that cause various diseases in plants or animals

**vis-age** [vĭz′ĭj] *noun*, the face, countenance, or look of a person

**vis-cer-al** [vĭs′ər-əl] *adjective*, felt in one's inner organs

**vis-cous** [vĭs′kəs] *adjective*, thick and sticky in consistency

**vise** [vīs] *noun*, a clamp, clasp, grip

**vis-i-ble** [vĭz′ə-bəl] *adjective*, as seen by the eye, in view

**vi-sion** [vĭzh′ən] *noun*, 1) something imagined, as in a dream, 2) a look into the future, unusual foresight 3) eyesight

**vi-sion-ar-y** [vĭzh′ə-nĕr′ē] *noun*, existing only in the imagination

**vis-it** [vĭz′ĭt] *noun*, 1) a social call, an appointment, *verb*, 2) to go to see someone 3) to chat casually

**vis-i-tor** [vĭz′ĭ-tər] *noun*, one who comes and goes to see another

**vi-sor** [vī′zər] *noun*, a sunshade or shield to block out glare

**vi-su-al** [vĭzh′ōō-ə-l] *adjective,* of or used in seeing, pleasing to the sight

**vi-su-al-ize** [vĭzh′ōō-ə-līz′] *verb*, 1) to imagine 2) to see something in the mind

**vi-tal** [vīt′l] *adjective*, necessary to life, important, indispensable

**vi-tal-i-ty** [vī-tăl′ĭ-tē] *noun*, spirit, energy, the capacity to develop

**vi-ta-min** [vī′tə-mĭn] *noun*, nutrients that give the body nourishment to help balance the metabolism

**vi-ti-ate** [vĭsh′ē-āt′] *verb*, to spoil the effect of something, to make less effective or imperfect

**vit-ri-ol-ic** [vĭt′rē-ŏl′ĭk] *adjective*, mean, causing bad feelings

**vi-tu-per-a-tive** [vī-tōō′pər-ə-tĭv] *adjective*, abusive, scolding

**vi-va-cious** [vĭ-vā′shəs] *adjective*, lively, sprightly, energetic

**viv-id** [vĭv′ĭd] *adjective*, easy to see, life-like, bright, colorful

**vo-cab-u-lar-y** [vō-kăb′yə-lĕr′ē] *noun*, the words of a language

**vo-cal** [vō′kəl] *adjective*, 1) voiced, outspoken 2) expressed by singing 3) relating to the sound made by the voice

**vo-ca-tion** [vō-kā′shən] *noun*, a job, employment or occupation, a profession

**vogue** [vōg] *adjective*, fashionable, in style, popular

**voice** [vois] *noun*, 1) the sounds coming through a person's mouth made by the respiratory system 2) to express an idea in writing or speaking

**void** [void] *noun*, an empty space

**vol-ca-no** [vŏl-kā′nō] *noun*, an opening in the earth's crust where melted rock, lava, gases, and ash are thrust onto the land

**vo-li-tion** [və-lĭsh′ən] *noun*, the act of making a conscious choice

**vol-ley** [vŏl′ē] *noun*, 1) a barrage, a bombardment, *verb*, 2) to return a ball before it hits the ground

**vol-ley-ball** [vŏl′ē-bôl′] *noun*, *no plural*, a game in which a large ball is knocked back and forth across a net, by hand

**volt** [vōlt] *noun*, 1) a measure of electricity, the unit of electromotive force 2) a turning movement of a horse, sideways around a center

**vol-ume** [vŏl'yōōm] *noun,* 1) a single book, *no plural,* 2) the space something occupies 3) the amount of sound something makes, loudness of a sound

**vo-lu-mi-nous** [və-lōō'mə-nəs] *adjective,* bulky, large

**vol-un-tar-y** [vŏl'ən-těr'ē] *adjective,* proceeding from the will, to give or perform freely

**vol-un-teer** [vŏl'ən-tîr'] *noun,* 1) one who offers his services of his own free will, *verb,* 2) to give freely of your time

**vo-lup-tu-ous** [və-lŭp'chōō-əs] *adjective,* shapely, full in form

**vom-it** [vŏm'ĭt] *noun,* 1) something from the stomach that comes out of the mouth, *verb,* 2) to throw up, to regurgitate food

**vo-ra-cious** [vô-rā'shəs] *adjective,* 1) someone who has a large appetite 2) exceedingly eager

**vor-tex** [vôr'těks'] *noun,* whirlpool, a whirling mass of water

**vote** [vōt] *noun,* 1) a choice made during an election, *verb,* 2) to decide by general consent

**vot-er** [vōt'ər] *noun,* a person registered to participate in an election

**vouch** [vouch] *verb,* to certify, to assure, to provide proof

**vouch-er** [vou'chər] *noun,* a document exchangeable for certain goods or services

**vow** [vou] *noun,* 1) an oath, a solemn pledge, *verb,* 2) to promise something important

**vow-el** [vou'əl] *noun,* the letters – **a,e,i,o,u,** and sometimes **y**

**voy-age** [voi'ĭj] *noun,* a long journey by sea, water, air, or space from one place to another

**vul-gar** [vŭl'gər] *adjective,* rude or rough in behavior, taste, etc, lacking good taste or refinement

**vul-ner-a-ble** [vŭl'nər-ə-bəl] *adjective,* capable of being easily harmed or injured

**vul-ture** [vŭl'chər] *noun,* a large bird that eats as a scavenger of dead animals

# W

**wade** [wād] *verb,* to walk through a substance such as water or snow

**waf-fle** [wŏf'əl] *noun,* 1) a cake baked in an iron skillet, *verb,* 2) to change one's mind often

**waft** [wäft] *verb,* to move or be moved lightly over water or air, to drift

**wag** [wăg] *verb,* to move or cause to move briskly from side to side or up and down

**wage** [wāj] *noun,* 1) money paid for work or services, salary, *verb,* 2) to carry on (a war or campaign)

**wa-ger** [wā'jər] *noun,* the amount of money or property risked in an uncertain event, a bet

**wag-on** [wăg'ən] *noun,* a vehicle with four wheels that is pulled

**waif** [wāf] *noun,* a homeless child or animal, an orphan

**wail** [wāl] *verb,* to make a long cry showing sadness or pain, to sob

**waist** [wāst] *noun*, the part of the body between the ribs and the hips where the stomach is

**wait** [wāt] *noun*, 1) a time of anticipation, *verb*, 2) to expect, to anticipate, to be ready

**wait-er** [wā′tər] *noun*, a person hired to serve meals

**waive** [wāv] *verb*, to give up temporarily, to yield

**waiv-er** [wā′vər] *noun*, the act of giving up a right or claim

**wake** [wāk] *noun*, 1) the ripple of waves created by the motion of a boat, *verb*, 2) to stop sleeping, to be aroused from sleep

**walk** [wôk] *noun*, 1) a journey on foot, *verb*, 2) to take one step at a time, to proceed along

**wall** [wôl] *noun*, 1) a partition made of bricks or stone that separates space 2) one of the sides of a room or building, *verb*, 3) to divide, to partition

**wal-let** [wŏl′ĭt] *noun*, a small flat case for money, cards, etc., usually carried in a pocket

**wal-low** [wŏl′ō] *verb*, to tumble in the mud 2) move slowly

**wall-pa-per** [wôl′pā′pər] *noun*, *no plural*, decorative paper used to cover walls of a room

**wal-nut** [wôl′nŭt′] *noun*, 1) a hard, dark-colored wood, valuable for furniture 2) the nut or seed from the walnut tree in a hard shell

**wal-rus** [wôl′rəs] *noun*, a sea animal like the sea lion and the seal, with outside ears and tusks

**waltz** [wôlts] *verb*, a dance with four beats per measure

**wand** [wŏnd] *noun*, a baton, a rod, a fairy's magic stick

**wan-der** [wŏn′dər] *verb*, 1) to travel from place to place with no plan or purpose in mind 2) to slip easily off the subject

**wane** [wān] *verb*, to grow gradually smaller or decrease in strength, to decline, to dwindle

**wan-gle** [wăng′gəl] *verb*, to bring about by manipulation or trickery, to scheme

**want** [wŏnt] *noun*, 1) a need, lack, not having something necessary, *verb*, 2) to desire or feel a need for something, to require

**wan-ton** [wŏn′tən] *adjective*, unruly, wild, excessive

**war** [wôr] *noun*, a deadly conflict

**war-ble** [wôr′bəl] *verb*, to sing melodiously, to trill as a bird

**ward** [wôrd] *noun*, 1) a child in the care of someone other than his family 2) a district, a division, *verb*, 3) to fend off, to avert

**war-den** [wôrd′n] *noun*, the chief administrator of a prison

**ward-robe** [wôr′drōb′] *noun*, a closet of clothes

**ware** [wâr] *noun*, a product, merchandise, stock

**ware-house** [wâr′hous′] *noun*, a storehouse for wares or goods

**war-i-ly** [wâr′ĭ-lē] *adverb*, in a watchful and suspicious way

**warm** [wôrm] *adjective*, 1) a temperature between hot and cold, moderately hot, *verb*, 2) to add heat to make something no longer cold

**warmth** [wôrmth] *noun*,
1) friendship, 2) bodily heat

**warn** [wôrn] *verb*, 1) to inform someone that something bad will happen or of impending danger 2) to admonish, to exhort

**warn-ing** [wôr′nĭng] *noun*, the act of telling someone to proceed with caution, notification

**warp** [wôrp] *verb*, 1) to twist out of shape, to distort 2) to pervert

**war-rant** [wôr′ənt] *noun*, 1) a written request by a judge to make an arrest, *verb*, 2) to be sure of something, to justify

**war-ran-ty** [wôr′ən-tē] *noun*, a guarantee that a contract will be carried out by a manufacturer

**war-ri-or** [wôr′ē-ər] *noun*, a man engaged in war, a soldier

**wart** [wôrt] *noun*, a small growth or lump that looks like a blemish on skin often caused by a virus

**war-y** [wâr′ē] *adjective*, very cautious, on guard, watchful

**was** [wŭz] *verb*, *past tense* of **be**, used in the 3rd singular, **he**, **she** or **it**

**wash** [wŏsh] *noun*, 1) a batch of clothes that are to be or have been washed, *verb*, 2) to clean with soap and water

**wash-er** [wŏsh′ər] *noun*, 1) a machine for washing clothes or dishes 2) a round piece of metal put under a bolt to reinforce it

**Wash-ing-ton** [wŏsh′ĭng-tən] *noun*, one of the 50 United States located in the Northwest, the capital is Olympia. The state flower of **Washington** is the coast rhododendron and the motto is "By and by."

**wasn't** [wŭz′ənt] the *contraction* of the words **was** and **not**

**wasp** [wŏsp] *noun*, a flying insect like a bee, the female inflicts the sting

**waste** [wāst] *adjective*, 1) useless, *noun*, 2) anything discarded that is not considered useful, *verb*, 3) to throw away, to spend or use carelessly, to squander

**waste-ful** [wāst′fəl] *adjective*, squandering or spending in a needless manner

**waste-wa-ter** [wāst′wô′tər] *noun*, water that has been used either to manufacture a product or in the home, which requires treatment and purification before it can be used again

**watch** [wŏch] *noun*, 1) a small clock worn on the wrist or hung from a chain, *verb*, 2) to observe, to look at attentively 3) to guard, to be on the lookout

**wa-ter** [wô′tər] *noun*, 1) a molecule made of one oxygen atom and two hydrogen atoms, that covers 75% of the earth's surface, *verb*, 2) to moisten or soak with water 3) to dilute

**wa-ter-fall** [wô′tər-fôl′] *noun*, a cascade of water coming down from a precipice or cliff

**wa-ter-way** [wô′tər-wā′] *noun*, a body of water that ships can use

**wa-ter-wheel** [wô′tər-hwēl] *noun*, a wheel turned by water running against or falling on paddles or steps, used as a source of power

**watt** [wŏt] *noun*, a measure of electrical power equivalent to one joule per second

**wave** [wāv] *noun*, 1) a breaker, a surge, surf, *verb*, 2) to greet

**wa-ver** [wā′vər] *verb*, 1) to be unsteady and show signs of falling or giving way 2) to be indecisive

**wax** [wăks] *noun*, a substance made from fats and oils that melts when heated

**way** [wā] *noun*, 1) the manner, custom, style 2) means, process 3) a passage, a road

**way-ward** [wā′wərd] *adjective*, unruly, disobedient, willful

**we** [wē] *plural*, *pronoun*, referring to one or more people, including oneself and others

**weak** [wēk] *adjective*, not strong, fragile, feeble, lacking strength

**weak-ness** [wēk′nĭs] *noun*, inclination, tendency

**wealth** [wĕlth] *noun*, riches, abundance of property

**wealth-y** [wĕl′thē] *adjective*, rich

**wean** [wēn] *verb*, 1) to accustom a baby not to nurse 2) to give up a cherished activity or habit

**weap-on** [wĕp′ən] *noun*, an instrument used for attack or defense in combat

**wear** [wâr] *noun*, 1) the diminished value caused by use, *verb*, 2) to put on, to carry on the body or over the body 3) to exhibit a certain expression on the face 4) to diminish through friction 5) to cause someone to be weary or exhausted 6) to impair by use

**wear-y** [wîr′ē] *adjective*, 1) tired, fatigued, physically or mentally exhausted 2) bored or resigned

**weath-er** [wĕth′ər] *noun*, 1) the condition of the atmosphere with regard to temperature, moisture, wind, etc., *verb*, 2) to endure the elements and the conditions outside in the atmosphere

**weath-er-ing** [wĕth′ər-ĭng] *noun*, the effects of the elements such as wind and water on rock surfaces, and homes or buildings

**weave** [wēv] *verb*, 1) to interlace threads into cloth 2) to wind or curve in and out

**web** [wĕb] *noun*, an entanglement, a mesh, an intricate network

**web-li-og-ra-phy** [wĕb′lē-ŏg′rə-fē] a bibliography of Internet sites used for research

**we'd** [wĕd] the *contraction* of the words **we** and **would**

**wed** [wĕd] *verb*, to join in marriage

**wed-ding** [wĕd′ĭng] *noun*, the ceremony when two people are married

**wedge** [wĕj] *noun*, 1) a flat edge used to split objects or to lift them up 2) a chunk or a block of something, *verb*, 3) to force something to split apart 4) to press in closely, to cramp

**Wednes-day** [wĕnz′dē, -dā′] *noun*, the fourth day of the week

**weed** [wēd] *noun*, 1) an unwanted or unwelcome plant, *verb*, 2) to remove as being undesirable

**week** [wēk] *noun*, the seven days between Sunday and Saturday

**weep** [wēp] *verb*, 1) to cry, to shed tears 2) to grieve, to mourn 3) to exude liquid

**weigh** [wāt] *verb*, to measure the heaviness of someone or something by use of a scale

**weight** [wāt] *noun*, 1) the force with which a body is attracted to the earth or other celestial bodies 2) how heavy a thing is

**weight-less** [wāt′lĭs] *adjective*, having little or no weight

**weird** [wîrd] *adjective*, strange

**wel-come** [wĕl′kəm] *verb*, to receive gladly or hospitably

**weld** [wĕld] *verb*, 1) to join or connect by fusing two metals with heat 2) to unite

**wel-fare** [wĕl′fâr′] *noun*, assistance from the government, a state of well-being, health, happiness

**well** [wĕl] *adjective*, 1) healthy, strong, fit, *adverb*, 2) in a thoroughly manner, *noun*, 3) a narrow, deep hole made in the ground to reach water, oil, or natural gas, *verb*, 4) to rise to the surface and flow out

**welt** [wĕlt] *noun*, a large blister caused by heat or a beating

**went** [wĕnt] past participle of **go**

**were** [wûr] *past tense* of the *verb* **to be** used with **we**, **you** and **they**

**west** [wĕst] *noun*, the direction in which the sunsets

**west-ern** [wĕs′tərn] *adjective*, of or typical of Europe and the Americas

**West Vir-gin-i-a** [wĕst- vər-jĭn′yə] *noun*, one of the 50 United States, located in the Southeast, the capital is Charleston. The state flower of **West Virginia** is the great rhododendron, and the motto is "Mountaineers are always free."

**wet** [wĕt] *adjective*, 1) covered with water, moistened, *verb*, 2) to soak with water

**wet-lands** [wĕt′lăndz′] *noun*, *plural*, a habitat of swamps and marshes for wildlife

**whale** [hwāl] *noun*, the largest animal in the sea, it is not a fish, it feeds its young with milk

**wharf** [hwôrf] *noun*, a dock along a shore where boats moor and wait to load or unload

**what** [hwŏt, hwŭt, wôt] *adjective*, 1) used to ask about the identity of a person, object, or matter 2) how remarkable, *adverb*, 3) how, in what way? *pronoun*, 4) which thing, an event, etc. 5) used to ask a question

**what-ev-er** [hwŏt-ĕv′ər] *pronoun*, anything that, so what

**what's** [hwŏts] the *contraction* of the words **what** and **is**

**wheat** [hwēt] *noun*, one of the cereal plants used to make flour

**whee-dle** [hwēd′l] *verb*, to coax

**wheel** [hwēl] *noun*, 1) a circular frame or disk attached to an axis that rolls, *verb*, 2) to move on rollers or wheels, to turn

**wheel-bar-row** [hwēl′băr′ō] *noun*, a hand cart with three wheels

**when** [hwĕn] *adverb*, at what time

**when-ev-er** [hwĕn-ĕv′ər] *adjective*, any time, no matter when

**where** [hwâr] *adverb*, 1) to or toward a certain place 2) at or in what place

**wher-ev-er** [hwâr-ĕv′ər] *adjective*, at or any place at all

**whet** [hwĕt] *verb*, 1) to sharpen by friction 2) to stimulate, to stir

**wheth-er** [hwĕth′ər] *conjunction*, used to express two choices

**which** [hwĭch] *noun*, the one, that

**while** [hwĭl] *noun*, a period of time

**whim-per** [hwĭm′pər] *verb*, to pout, to whine, to cry

**whim-si-cal** [hwĭm′zĭ-kəl] *adjective*, capricious, given to fanciful notions, playful

**whine** [hwīn] *verb*, 1) to make a high and sad sound 2) to complain in an annoying manner

**whip** [hwĭp] *noun*, 1) an instrument made with a handle attached to a long lash made of leather or rope used to hit animals, *verb*, 2) to strike with a lash, to flog 3) to beat to a froth 4) to defeat

**whirl** [hwûrl] *verb*, to move or make something move around and around very fast

**whisk** [hwĭsk] *noun*, 1) a cooking utensil used to mix ingredients, *verb*, 2) to move quickly

**whisk-er** [hwĭs′kər] *noun*, 1) hair growing on the sides of a man's face 2) one of the long stiff hairs that grow near the mouth of dogs, cats, rats, etc.

**whis-per** [hwĭs′pər] *noun*, 1) a murmur, *verb*, 2) to speak very softly, to murmur quietly

**whis-tle** [hwĭs′əl] *noun*, 1) an instrument that makes a shrill, musical sound, *verb*, 2) to make a clear, high-pitched sound by forcing breath through the teeth or by pursing the lips, or using a device

**white** [hwīt] *adjective*, the color of snow, the absence of pigment

**whit-tle** [hwĭt′l] *verb*, 1) to shape by carving or sculpting 2) to reduce gradually, to diminish

**who** [hōō] *pronoun*, 1) the person or people 2) that 3) what persons?

**who-ev-er** [hōō-ĕv′ər] *pronoun*, any one that

**whole** [hōl] *adjective*, 1) total, complete, *noun*, 2) the total amount of a thing or entity

**whole-some** [hōl′səm] *adjective*, sound, healthy, beneficial

**whom** [hōōm] *pronoun*, objective case for **who**

**whose** [hōōz] *pronoun*, of whom, possessive case of who

**why** [hwī] *adverb*, 1) for what reason or purpose, *noun*, 2) the cause or interaction

**wick** [wĭk] *noun*, the string in a candle or oil lamp that burns the flame, the fuse

**wick-ed** [wĭk′ĭd] *adjective*, evil, very bad, sinful, vicious

**wide** [wīd] *adjective*, 1) broad, expansive 2) to be fully open or accessible, of great scope

**wid-ow** [wĭd′ō] *noun*, a woman whose husband is dead

**wid-ow-er** [wĭd′ō-ər] *noun*, a man whose wife is dead

**width** [wĭdth] *noun*, the distance across, the breadth

**wield** [wēld] *verb*, to control, to sway, to manage, to use

**wife** [wīf] *noun*, *plural*, **wives**, a married woman

**wig** [wĭg] *noun*, a covering for the head, hair from other people or animals, a toupee, a hairpiece

**wig-gle** [wĭg/əl] *verb*, to move around, to squirm

**wild** [wīld] *adjective*, untamed or domesticated, a natural state

**wil-der-ness** [wĭl/dər-nĭs] *noun*, a tract of land undeveloped and uninhabited by people

**wild-life** [wīld/līf/] *noun*, any species of animals living in their natural habitat

**will** [wĭl] *noun*, 1) power in the mind or character, what we want to do 2) a declaration by a person concerning their estate, *verb*, 3) used with other verbs to show something is going to happen 4) used in questions when asking to do something

**will-ful** [wĭl/fəl] *adjective*, 1) determined, intentional, deliberate 2) obstinate, stubborn

**will-ing** [wĭl/ĭng] *adjective*, ready, given or done gladly

**wil-low** [wĭl/ō] *noun*, a tree with long drooping branches

**wilt** [wĭlt] *verb*, 1) to wither, to lose freshness 2) to lose strength

**wil-y** [wī/lē] *adjective*, sly, clever

**win** [wĭn] *verb*, 1) to achieve victory over others 2) to receive an award for a performance

**wind** [wĭnd] *noun*, 1) currents of air moving quickly with force, [wīnd] *verb*, 2) to wrap around

over and over 3) to turn round and round, to move in curves and bends, not a straight line

**win-dow** [wĭn/dō] *noun*, 1) a pane of glass 2) an opening with a transparent cover that allows light in

**win-dow-sill** [wĭn/dō-sĭl/] *noun*, a shelf or ledge below a window

**wine** [wīn] *noun*, an alcoholic drink made from fermented grapes

**wing** [wĭng] *noun*, 1) one of the two limbs of a bird or insect with which it flies 2) a side projection of an airplane 3) an extension of a building

**wink** [wĭngk] *noun*, 1) one eye closed and one eye open as a gesture of approval, *verb*, 2) to close and open one eye quickly

**win-now** [wĭn/ō] *verb*, to sift, to separate good parts from bad

**win-some** [wĭn/səm] *adjective*, agreeable, gracious, engaging

**win-ter** [wĭn/tər] *noun*, the first season of the year, between autumn and spring, when the earth is farthest from the sun

**wipe** [wīp] *verb*, to make dry or clean with a cloth

**wire** [wīr] *noun*, 1) a metal thread or strand, *verb*, 2) to connect

**Wis-con-sin** [wĭs-kŏn/sĭn] *noun*, one of the 50 United States located in the North,, the capital city is Madison. The state flower of **Wisconsin** is the violet, and the motto is "Forward."

**wis-dom** [wĭz/dəm] *noun*, learning and the capacity to use it

**wise** [wīz] *adjective*, showing good judgment, intelligent

**wish** [wĭsh] *noun*, 1) a desire that is beyond your reach, *verb*, 2) to desire, to long for, to want

**wist-ful** [wĭst′fəl] *adjective*, hopeful, yearning, longing

**wit** [wĭt] *noun*, cleverness, quickness of mind, ingenuity

**witch** [wĭch] *noun*, a woman who is believed to have magic powers

**with** [wĭth] *preposition*, 1) in the company of 2) using it 3) having 4) because of 5) next to

**with-draw** [wĭth-drô′] *verb*, to retreat, to go back on or to take back an offer, to remove

**with-drawn** [wĭth-drôn′] *adjective*, 1) taken back, removed 2) shy, introverted, retiring

**with-er** [wĭth′ər] *verb*, to shrivel, to fade, to lose freshness

**with-hold** [wĭth-hōld′] *verb*, to restrain, to hold back

**with-in** [wĭth-ĭn′] *adverb*, 1)inside, *preposition*, 2) in, not beyond

**with-out** [wĭth-out′] *adverb*, 1) outside, *preposition*, 2) lacking, wanting, not having

**wit-ness** [wĭt′nĭs] *noun*, 1) a spectator, an onlooker, a person who sees something, *verb*, 2) to see, to observe, to hear

**wiz-ard** [wĭz′ərd] *noun*, someone who performs sorcery and magic

**woe** [wō] *noun*, self-pity, sadness

**wolf** [wŏolf] *noun*, *plural*, **wolves**, a wild dog similar to a coyote

**wom-an** [wŏom′ən] *noun*, *plural*, **women**, a female, a lady

**won-der** [wŭn′dər] *noun*, 1) a feeling of surprise and admiration, amazement, *verb*, 2) to express a wish to know

**won-der-ful** [wŭn′dər-fəl] *adjective*, extra special, very good, remarkable, marvelous

**won-drous** [wŭn′drəs] *adjective*, amazing, astonishing, marvelous

**wont** [wônt] *adjective,* 1) apt or likely, *noun*, 2) custom, habitual procedure

**won't** [wōnt] the *contraction* of the words **will** and **not**

**wood** [wŏod] *noun*, 1) the material which comes from trees 2) a small forest

**wood-land** [wŏod′lənd] *noun*, the forest, land covered with trees

**wood-peck-er** [wŏod′pĕk′ər] *noun*, a black and white bird with a red head that pecks at wood with its bill to find bugs to eat

**wood-winds** [wŏod′wĭndz′] *noun*, musical instruments, usually made of wood or metal, that you blow into or use a reed to play such as a clarinet

**wool** [wŏol] *noun*, the, soft, thick fur on a sheep often used for yarn or fabric

**word** [wûrd] *noun*, 1) speech, sound or symbol used to communicate 2) a message 3) a promise 4) news, information

**work** [wûrk] *noun*, 1) a job, a form of labor, a duty 2) a deed, an accomplishment, *verb*, 3) to do a job, to labor, to perform a duty

**world** [wûrld] *noun*, the Earth and its people and all living things

**world-ly** [wûrld′lē] *adjective*, known all over, cosmopolitan

**worm** [wûrm] *noun*, a thin creature without bones or legs that lives in the earth

**wor-ry** [wûr′ē] *verb*, to fret, to show concern, to feel anxious

**worse** [wûrs] *adjective*, to go from bad to a more damaged condition, inferior, less good or well

**wor-ship** [wûr′shĭp] *noun*, 1) ardent devotion, *verb*, 2) to pray to or show reverence or respect for someone

**worth** [wûrth] *noun*, the value or importance of something

**worth-less** [wûrth′lĭs] *adjective*, without worth, valueless

**wor-thy** [wûr′thē] *adjective*, admirable, deserving, noble

**would** [wŏŏd] future perfect tense of the *verb* **be**

**wouldn't** [wŏŏd′nt] the *contraction* of the words **would** and **not**

**wound** [wŏŏnd] *noun*, 1) an injury, *verb*, 2) to injure, to hurt 3) to disturb or upset someone

**wrap** [răp] *noun*, 1) a removable covering, *verb*, 2) to cover with a substance usually to protect something, to enclose

**wrath** [răth] *noun*, anger, fury

**wreak** [rēk] *verb*, to produce rage, to perpetuate, to inflict

**wreath** [rēth] *noun*, a ring of flowers and leaves

**wreck** [rĕk] *noun*, 1) the remains of something partially destroyed like a car, building, or ship, *verb*, 2) to destroy or damage something, to tear down

**wren** [rĕn] *noun*, a brown-grey bird that lives in the south

**wrench** [rĕnch] *noun*, 1) a tool used to grip a bolt or a nut 2) a forcible twist, *verb*, 3) to pull or turn suddenly with a violent twist, to damage or injure

**wrest** [rĕst] *verb*, 1) to pull away 2) to take away by force, to seize, to wrench away

**wres-tle** [rĕs′əl] *verb*, to struggle hand to hand, to grapple

**wretch** [rĕch] *noun*, a vile, disgusting person

**wrig-gle** [rĭg′əl] *verb*, to squirm or twist like a worm, to writhe

**wring** [rĭng] *verb*, to twist, to squeeze by twisting tightly

**wrin-kle** [rĭng′kəl] *noun*, 1) a crease or fold, *verb*, 2) to pucker into folds and creases

**wrist** [rĭst] *noun*, the joint between the hand and the forearm

**write** [rīt] *verb*, to use an instrument such as a pencil to draw symbols to communicate

**writer** [rī′tər] *noun*, author, journalist, newsperson

**writhe** [rīth] *verb*, to twist or move as if in pain, to thrash

**wrong** [rông *adjective*, 1) in error, mistaken, incorrect 2) contrary to morality or laws

**wrote** [rīt′n] *past tense* of **write**

**Wy-o-ming** [wī-ō′mĭng] *noun*, one of the 50 United States, located in the Northwest, the capital is Cheyenne. The state flower of **Wyoming** is the indian paintbrush and the motto is "Equal rights."

# X

**xeno-phile** [zĕn'ə-fīl'] *noun*, one attracted to foreign people, manners, and styles

**xeno-pho-bi-a** [zĕn'ə-fō'bē-ə] *noun*, fear and hatred of foreigners or strangers

**xy-lem** [zī'ləm] *noun*, the system of a woody tissue that transports water in a plant

**xy-log-ra-phy** [zī-lŏg'rə-fē] *noun*, the art of engraving on wood

**x-ray** [ĕks'rā'] *noun*, 1) a photograph of a part of the inside of your body, *verb*, 2) to take a picture of the inside of the body

**xy-lo-phone** [zailəfoun] *noun*, a percussion instrument played by striking horizontal wooden bars with small wooden hammers

# Y

**yacht** [yät] *noun*, a boat used either for private pleasure or as a vessel of state to convey people from one place to another

**yam** [yăm] *noun*, a sweet potato, the root of a potato plant

**yard** [yärd] *noun*, 1) a length of measure equal to 36 inches 2) the lawn or property around someone's house

**yarn** [yärn] *noun*, 1) knitting thread, spun wool 2) a story, a fictional account

**yawn** [yôn] *verb*, to open the mouth wide and breathe deeply as if tired or bored

**year** [yîr] *noun*, 365 days, or each cycle that the earth rotates around the sun divided, into 12 months, 52 weeks, and 4 seasons

**yearn** [yûrn] *verb*, to desire something, to long for

**yeast** [yēst] *noun*, a fungus which produces fermentation, used as a leavening agent in dough

**yell** [yĕl] *verb*, to shout, to scream

**yel-low** [yĕl'ō] *noun*, one of the primary colors, the color of corn

**yen** [yĕn] *noun*, 1) the currency of Japan 2) a longing, an urge

**yes** [yĕs] *interjection*, a word of agreement, an affirmative reply

**yes-ter-day** [yĕs'tər-dā'] *adverb*, 1) on the day before today, *noun*, 2) the day before today

**yet** [yĕt] *conjunction*, until now

**yield** [yēld] *verb*, 1) to give way to, to submit, to surrender 2) to produce, to supply, to give forth

**yo-ga** [yō'ga] *noun*, an exercise by which one seeks union with the universal soul through deep mediation, prescribed postures, controlled breathing, etc.

**yo-gurt** [yō'gərt] *noun*, a dairy product that is thicker than milk and has a slightly sour taste

**yolk** [yōk] *noun*, the yellow and principal part inside an egg

**you** [yōō] *pronoun*, the person or persons spoken to

**you'd** [yōōd] the *contraction* of the words **you** and **would**

**you'll** [yōōl] the *contraction* of the words **you** and **will**

**young** [yŭng] *adjective*, the early stage of life, not old

**your** [yŏŏr] *pronoun*, belonging to
you

**you're** [yŏŏr] the *contraction* of
the words, **you** and **are**

**yours** [yŏŏrz, yôrz, yōrz] *pronoun*,
belonging to you

**your-self** [yŏŏr-sĕlf′] *pronoun*, a
form of you for emphasis when
the object of a verb and the
subject are the same

**youth** [yŏŏth] *noun*, a young
person, an adolescent

# Z

**za-ny** [zā′nē] *adjective*, crazy,
whimsically comical

**zeal** [zēl] *noun*, ardor in pursuit of
anything, fervor, eagerness

**zeal-ous** [zĕl′əs] *adjective*,
enthusiastic, eager, devoted

**ze-bra** [zē′brə] *noun*, an African
wild animal like a horse which
has brown and white stripes all
over its body

**Zen Buddhism** [zĕn- bŏŏ′dĭz′əm]
*noun*, a faith in which Buddha is
the embodiment of the superior
man and followers seek
enlightenment through
meditation and intuition instead
of the traditional scriptures

**ze-nith** [zē′nĭth] *noun*, the point
directly overhead in the sky, the
summit, the highest point

**zeph-yr** [zĕf′ər] *noun*, a gentle
breeze, the west wind

**ze-ro** [zîr′ō] *noun, plural,* **zeros** *or*
**zeroes**, 1) the numberical symbol 0
2) nothing 3) the temperature on
a scale indicated by this symbol

**zest** [zĕst] *noun*, feeling of
enjoyment, excitement

**zinc** [zĭngk] *noun*, a bluish white
metallic element often mixed
with other metals

**zip-per** [zĭp′ər] *noun*, a slide
fastener for clothing, briefcases,
and other objects, with two sets
of interlocking teeth

**zone** [zōn] *noun*, a division of an
area that differs or is
distinguished in some respect
from adjoining areas

**zoo** [zōō] *noun*, a place where
different animals are kept for
people to look at

**zo-ol-o-gy** [zō-ŏl′ə-jē] *noun*, the
science of animals

**zy-gote** [zī′gōt′] *noun*, the single
cell resulting from the union of
an egg and a sperm

# *Weights and Measures*

## **ENGLISH**

### Length

| | | |
|---|---|---|
| 12 inches | = | 1 foot |
| 3 feet | = | 1 yard |
| 5280 feet | = | 1 mile |
| 1760 yards | = | 1 mile |

### Area

| | | |
|---|---|---|
| 144 square inches | = | 1 square foot |
| 9 square feet | = | 1 square yard |
| 4840 square yards | = | 1 acre |
| 640 acres | = | 1 square mile |

### Volume

| | | |
|---|---|---|
| 1728 cubic inches | = | 1 cubic foot |
| 27 cubic feet | = | 1 cubic yard |

### Capacity (Dry)

| | | |
|---|---|---|
| 2 pints | = | 1 quart |
| 8 quarts | = | 1 peck |
| 4 pecks | = | 1 bushel |

### Capacity (Liquid)

| | | |
|---|---|---|
| 16 fluid ounces | = | 1 pint |
| 2 pints | = | 1 quart |
| 4 quarts | = | 1 gallon (8 pints) |

### Mass

| | | |
|---|---|---|
| 16 ounces | = | 1 pound (7000 grains) |
| 20 cwt | = | 1 ton |
| 2000 lbs | = | 1 ton |

### Troy Weights

| | | |
|---|---|---|
| 12 ounces | = | 1 pound (5760 grains) |

### Measures

| | | |
|---|---|---|
| 16 fluid ounces | = | 1 pint |

inches

metric

# METRIC

## Length
| | | |
|---|---|---|
| 1 millimeter | = | 1000 micrometers |
| 1 centimeter | = | 10 millimeters |
| 1 meter | = | 1000 millimeters |
| 1 meter | = | 100 centimeters |
| 1 kilometer | = | 1000 meters |

## Area
| | | |
|---|---|---|
| 1 square centimeter | = | 100 square millimeters |
| 1 square meter | = | 10,000 square centimeters |
| 1 square meter | = | 1,000,000 square millimeters |
| 1 square kilometer | = | 1,000,000 square meters |

## Volume
| | | |
|---|---|---|
| 1 milliliter | = | 1 cubic centimeter |
| 1 liter | = | 1000 milliliters |
| 1 liter | = | 0.001 cubic meter |

## Mass
| | | |
|---|---|---|
| 1 gram | = | 1000 milligrams |
| 1 kilogram | = | 1000 grams |
| 1 metric ton | = | 1000 kilograms |

## Volume
1 cubic inch ($in^3$) = 16.39 cubic centimeters ($cm^3$)
1,728 cubic inches = 1 cubic foot = 0.02832 cubic meters ($m^3$)
27 cubic feet ($ft^3$) = 1 cubic yard ($y^3$) = 0.7646 cubic meters

## Temperature Conversions
$^{\circ}C$ Celsius = 5/9 ($^{\circ}F$ −32)          $^{\circ}F$ Fahrenheit = (9/5 $^{\circ}C$) +32

## Square Measure
100 sq. meters = 1 sq. decameter = 119.6 sq. yards
100 sq. decameters = 1 sq. hectometer = 2.471 acres
100 sq. hectometers = 1 sq. kilometer = 0.386 sq. miles or
                                                                247.1 acres

363

# Words for Large Numbers

| Term | Calculation | # of Zeros |
|------|-------------|-----------|
| Ten | 10 Ones | 1 |
| One Hundred | 100 Ones | 2 |
| One Thousand | 1,000 Ones | 3 |
| One Million | 1,000 Thousands | 6 |
| One Billion | 1,000 Millions | 9 |
| One Trillion | 1,000 Billions | 12 |
| One Quadrillion | 1,000 Trillions | 15 |
| One Quintillion | 1,000 Quadrillions | 18 |
| One Sextillion | 1,000 Quintillions | 21 |
| One Septillion | 1,000 Sextillions | 24 |
| One Octillion | 1,000 Septillions | 27 |
| One Nonillion | 1,000 Octillions | 30 |
| One Decillion | 1,000 Nonillions | 33 |
| One Googol | 10,000,000,000,000,000,000,000,000, 000,000,000,000,000,000,000,000,00 0,000,000,000 Decillions | 100 |

# Five Big Words

**PNEUMONOULTRAMICROSCOPICSILICOVOLCANOCONIOSIS**
This word is forty-five letters and its definition is a lung disease
caused by breathing in certain particles.

**ANTITRANSUBSTANTIATIONALIST**
One who doubts the validity of transubstantiation.

**FLOCCINAUCINIHILIPILIFICATION**
The estimation of a thing as worthless.

**ANTIDISESTABLISHMENTARIANISM**
Opposition of those who oppose the link between Church and State.

**SUPERCALIFRAGILISTICEXPIALIDOCIOUS**
The word to say when you don't know what to say.

# Common Standard International Unit Symbols

$$km = kilometer$$
$$m = meter$$
$$dm = decimeter$$
$$cm = centimeter$$
$$mm = millimeter$$

$$m^3 = L = cubic\ decimeter = Liter$$
$$m^3 = cubic\ meter$$
$$mg = T = megagram$$
$$kg = kilogram$$
$$g = gram$$
$$mg = milligram$$

$$ks = kilosecond$$
$$s = second$$
$$ms = millisecond$$
$$us = microsecond$$

# Standard International Factor Prefixes

| | | | |
|---|---|---|---|
| $10^{24}$ | yotta | Y | septillion |
| $10^{21}$ | zeta | Z | sextillion |
| $10^{18}$ | exa | E | quintillion |
| $10^{15}$ | peta | P | quadrillion |
| $10^{12}$ | tera | T | trillion |
| $10^{9}$ | giga | G | billion |
| $10^{6}$ | mega | M | million |
| $10^{3}$ | kilo | k | thousand |
| $10^{2}$ | hecto | h | hundred |
| $10^{1}$ | deka | da | ten |
| $10^{-1}$ | deci | d | tenth |
| $10^{-2}$ | centi | c | hundredth |
| $10^{-3}$ | milli | m | thousandth |
| $10^{-6}$ | micro | u | millionth |
| $10^{-9}$ | nano | n | billionth |
| $10^{-12}$ | pico | p | trillionth |
| $10^{-15}$ | femto | f | quadrillionth |
| $10^{-18}$ | atto | a | quintillionth |
| $10^{-21}$ | zepto | z | sextillionth |
| $10^{-24}$ | yocto | y | septillionth |

# Periodic Table of the Elements

# Multiplication Table

| x | 1 | 2 | 3 | 4 | 5 | 6 | 7 | 8 | 9 | 10 | 11 | 12 |
|---|---|---|---|---|---|---|---|---|---|----|----|----|
| 1 | 1 | 2 | 3 | 4 | 5 | 6 | 7 | 8 | 9 | 10 | 11 | 12 |
| 2 | 2 | 4 | 6 | 8 | 10 | 12 | 14 | 16 | 18 | 20 | 22 | 24 |
| 3 | 3 | 6 | 9 | 12 | 15 | 18 | 21 | 24 | 27 | 30 | 33 | 36 |
| 4 | 4 | 8 | 12 | 16 | 20 | 24 | 28 | 32 | 36 | 40 | 44 | 48 |
| 5 | 5 | 10 | 15 | 20 | 25 | 30 | 35 | 40 | 45 | 50 | 55 | 60 |
| 6 | 6 | 12 | 18 | 24 | 30 | 36 | 42 | 48 | 54 | 60 | 66 | 72 |
| 7 | 7 | 14 | 21 | 28 | 35 | 42 | 49 | 56 | 63 | 70 | 77 | 84 |
| 8 | 8 | 16 | 24 | 32 | 40 | 48 | 56 | 64 | 72 | 80 | 88 | 96 |
| 9 | 9 | 18 | 27 | 36 | 45 | 54 | 63 | 72 | 81 | 90 | 99 | 108 |
| 10 | 10 | 20 | 30 | 40 | 50 | 60 | 70 | 80 | 90 | 100 | 110 | 120 |
| 11 | 11 | 22 | 33 | 44 | 55 | 66 | 77 | 88 | 99 | 110 | 121 | 132 |
| 12 | 12 | 24 | 36 | 48 | 60 | 72 | 84 | 96 | 108 | 120 | 132 | 144 |

## Prefix Table

| one | uni | unicorn, unilateral, universal |
| | mon, mono | monarchy, monotone, monochromatic |
| two | bi | bicycle, binoculars, bifocals, biceps |
| three | tri | triangle, trilogy, triplet, triceratops |
| four | quad | quadruped, quadrant, quadruplet |
| | tetra | tetrahedron, tetrad, tetragon, tetrapod |
| five | penta | pentagon, pentathlon, pentagram, |
| | quint | quintuplet, quintet, quintile |
| six | hexa | hexagon, hexagram, hexahedron |
| | sext | sextuplet, sextet, sextuple |
| seven | hepta | heptathlon, heptad, heptahedron, |
| | sept | septuplet, septuple, septennial |
| eight | oct | octave, octopus, octagon, octogenarian |
| nine | nona *before a vowel* | nonagon, nonet |
| ten | deca *before a vowel* | decade, decibel, decimal, decimeter |
| hundred | cent | century, centennial, centigrade |
| thousand | kilo | kilogram, kilometer, kilobyte, kilobit, |
| million | mega | megabyte, megahertz, megaton |
| billion | giga | gigabyte, gigawatt, gigaflop, gigaton |

367

# Roman Numerals

| | |
|---|---|
| I | 1 |
| II | 2 |
| III | 3 |
| IV | 4 |
| V | 5 |
| VI | 6 |
| VII | 7 |
| VIII | 8 |
| IX | 9 |
| X | 10 |
| XX | 20 |
| XXX | 30 |
| XL | 40 |
| L | 50 |
| LX | 60 |
| LXX | 70 |
| LXXX | 80 |
| XC | 90 |
| C | 100 |
| CC | 200 |
| CD | 400 |
| D | 500 |
| DC | 600 |
| DCC | 700 |
| DCCC | 800 |
| CM | 900 |
| M | 1,000 |
| $\overline{V}$ | 5,000 |
| $\overline{X}$ | 10,000 |
| $\overline{L}$ | 50,000 |
| $\overline{C}$ | 100,000 |
| $\overline{D}$ | 500,000 |
| $\overline{M}$ | 1,000,000 |

# *The United States Flag*

*I pledge allegiance to the flag of the United States of America and to the republic for which it stands, one nation under God, indivisible, with liberty and justice for all.*

Betsy Ross sewed the first American flag in May, 1776. No one wrote down the story of why the United States decided to use stars and stripes when the design was chosen for our new nation. The only record indicates that the United States flag was first authorized by the Second Continental Congress on June 14, 1777. It said: "Resolved That the Flag of the United States be 13 stripes alternate red and white, that the Union be 13 stars white in a blue field representing a new constellation." This date is now observed as "Flag Day" throughout America.

The flag has changed 26 times since 1777 – each time a new state joined the Union. The flag was first modified in 1795 to have 15 stars and 15 stripes to include Vermont and Kentucky. In 1818, when Tennessee, Ohio, Louisiana, Indiana and Mississippi became states, the flag was designed to have 20 stars and 13 stripes. At that time, Congress decreed that the flag should have 13 stripes, and that new admissions to the Union should be recognized with a new star. Since then, the only change has been the adding of new stars. The 50-star flag was raised for the first time at 12:01 a.m. on July 4, 1960, at Fort McHenry National Monument, when Hawaii joined the Union.

# Civics Lesson

Civics is the study of government and laws. Laws are made to maintain order, mutual respect and peace by defining people's rights and responsibilities toward society. They are agreed upon by people and enforced by governments. Most of the laws we use are based on English law, which was based on a judge's ruling in a dispute. This decision set a precedent and so any similar violation was considered with the most recent ruling used as a guide or common practice. These decisions created what is known as common law. Since these laws do not cover all situations, the elected officials created their own laws, known as statute law. There are three branches of government: legislative, executive and judicial.

The **Legislative** branch: Congress, which is made up of the Senate and the House of Representatives. Congress has the power to make laws, declare war, charge taxes, borrow money, and regulate business between states. To become law, a bill must be approved by both houses, the Senate and the House of Representatives and signed by the President. The **Senate** consists of 100 members, two members from each state, who serve six year terms. The Senate approves or rejects appointees made by the President to his Cabinet and to the Supreme Court and treaties made by the President.

The **House of Representatives** consists of 435 members. Members are elected from their home state based on population. Each member is elected to serve a two year term. The House of Representatives has the responsibility of initiating all bills for raising taxes and determines how money collected in taxes is spent.

The **Executive** branch consists of the President, the Vice President and the members of the President's Cabinet. The President and Vice President are elected together to a four year term by the Electoral College after a popular vote. Duties of the President: chief executive, head of state, and commander in chief of the armed forces.

The Vice President acts in the President's capacity if the President is unable to perform the duties of the office; presides over the Senate and only votes to break a tie. The Cabinet members are advisors to the President, appointed by the President. All members must be approved by the Senate. The Cabinet consists of the secretaries of the departments of State, Agriculture, Commerce, Defense, Education, Energy, Health and Human Services, Homeland Security, Housing and Urban Development, the Interior, Labor, Transportation, the Treasury, Veterans Affairs, and the Justice Department headed by the Attorney General.

The **Judicial** Branch is made up of the Supreme Court which consists of the Chief Justice and eight Associate Justices, who interpret the law of the land to implement the United States Constitution. Each justice is appointed for life terms after the President's nomination to the court is approved by the Senate. The Supreme Court is responsible for hearing appeals of cases from the federal and state court systems and all matters between individual states. It presides over all cases affecting ambassadors to the United States and public ministers including the president. Courts handle two kinds of disputes: civil and criminal. A civil dispute is between two private citizens; a criminal case is a dispute between an individual and the whole community. Our justice system is comprised of courts within 94 Federal Judicial Districts in the 50 states, Washington D.C. and Puerto Rico. Some of the other courts within the Federal Judicial Branch include the U.S. Tax Court, the U.S. Court of International Trade, 13 circuit Courts of Appeals: one Federal Circuit Court, 11 for the districts throughout the states, and one in the District of Columbia.

# THE DECLARATION OF INDEPENDENCE
## of the Thirteen Colonies In CONGRESS, July 4, 1776

### The unanimous Declaration of the thirteen united States of America,

When in the Course of human events, it becomes necessary for one people to dissolve the political bands which have connected them with another, and to assume among the powers of the earth, the separate and equal station to which the Laws of Nature and of Nature's God entitle them, a decent respect to the opinions of mankind requires that they should declare the causes which impel them to the separation.

We hold these truths to be self-evident, that all men are created equal, that they are endowed by their Creator with certain unalienable Rights, that among these are Life, Liberty and the pursuit of Happiness. – That to secure these rights, Governments are instituted among Men, deriving their just powers from the consent of the governed, – That whenever any Form of Government becomes destructive of these ends, it is the Right of the People to alter or to abolish it, and to institute new Government, laying its foundation on such principles and organizing its powers in such form, as to them shall seem most likely to effect their Safety and Happiness. Prudence, indeed, will dictate that Governments long established should not be changed for light and transient causes; and accordingly all experience hath shown, that mankind are more disposed to suffer, while evils are sufferable, than to right themselves by abolishing the forms to which they are accustomed. But when a long train of abuses and usurpations, pursuing invariably the same Object evinces a design to reduce them under absolute Despotism, it is their right, it is their duty, to throw off such Government, and to provide new Guards for their future security. --Such has been the patient sufferance of these Colonies; and such is now the necessity which constrains them to alter their former Systems of Government. The history of the present King of Great Britain [George III] is a history of repeated injuries and usurpations, all having in direct object the establishment of an absolute Tyranny over these States. To prove this, let Facts be submitted to a candid world.

He has refused his Assent to Laws, the most wholesome and necessary for the public good.

He has forbidden his Governors to pass Laws of immediate and pressing importance, unless suspended in their operation till his Assent should be obtained; and when so suspended, he has utterly neglected to attend to them.

He has refused to pass other Laws for the accommodation of large districts of people, unless those people would relinquish the right of Representation in the Legislature, a right inestimable to them and formidable to tyrants only.

He has called together legislative bodies at places unusual, uncomfortable, and distant from the depository of their public Records, for the sole purpose of fatiguing them into compliance with his measures.

He has dissolved Representative Houses repeatedly, for opposing with manly firmness his invasions on the rights of the people.

He has refused for a long time, after such dissolutions, to cause others to be elected; whereby the Legislative powers, incapable of Annihilation, have returned to the People at large for their exercise; the State remaining in the mean time exposed to all the dangers of invasion from without, and convulsions within.

He has endeavored to prevent the population of these States; for that purpose obstructing the Laws for Naturalization of Foreigners; refusing to pass others to encourage their migrations hither, and raising the conditions of new Appropriations of Lands.

He has obstructed the Administration of Justice, by refusing his Assent to Laws for establishing Judiciary powers.

He has made Judges dependent on his Will alone, for the tenure of their offices, and the amount and payment of their salaries.

He has erected a multitude of New Offices, and sent hither swarms of Officers to harass our people, and eat out their substance.

He has kept among us, in times of peace, Standing Armies without the consent of our legislatures.

He has affected to render the Military independent of and superior to the Civil power.

He has combined with others to subject us to a jurisdiction foreign to our constitution and unacknowledged by our laws; giving his Assent to their Acts of pretended Legislation:

For Quartering large bodies of armed troops among us:

For protecting them, by a mock Trial, from punishment for any Murders which they should commit on the Inhabitants of these States:

For cutting off our Trade with all parts of the world:

For imposing Taxes on us without our Consent:

For depriving us, in many cases, of the benefits of Trial by Jury:

For transporting us beyond Seas to be tried for pretended offences:

For abolishing the free System of English Laws in a neighbouring Province, establishing therein an Arbitrary government, and enlarging its Boundaries so as to render it at once an example and fit instrument for introducing the same absolute rule into these Colonies:

For taking away our Charters, abolishing our most valuable Laws, and altering fundamentally the Forms of our Governments:

For suspending our own Legislatures, and declaring themselves invested with power to legislate for us in all cases whatsoever.

He has abdicated Government here, by declaring us out of his Protection and waging War against us.

He has plundered our seas, ravaged our Coasts, burnt our towns, and destroyed the lives of our people.

He is at this time transporting large Armies of foreign Mercenaries to complete the works of death, desolation and tyranny, already begun with circumstances of Cruelty and perfidy scarcely paralleled in the most barbarous ages, and totally unworthy the Head of a civilized nation.

He has constrained our fellow Citizens taken Captive on the high Seas to bear Arms against their Country, to become the executioners of their friends and Brethren, or to fall themselves by their Hands.

He has excited domestic insurrections amongst us, and has endeavored to bring on the inhabitants of our frontiers, the merciless Indian Savages, whose known rule of warfare, is an undistinguished destruction of all ages, sexes and conditions.

In every stage of these Oppressions We have Petitioned for Redress in the most humble terms: Our repeated Petitions have been answered only by repeated injury. A Prince whose character is thus marked by every act which may define a Tyrant, is unfit to be the ruler of a free people.

Nor have We been wanting in attentions to our British brethren. We have warned them from time to time of attempts by their legislature to extend an unwarrantable jurisdiction over us. We have reminded them of the circumstances of our emigration and settlement here. We have appealed to their native justice and magnanimity, and we have conjured them by the ties of our common kindred to disavow these usurpations, which, would inevitably interrupt our connections and correspondence. They too have been deaf to the voice of justice and of consanguinity. We must, therefore, acquiesce in the necessity, which denounces our Separation, and hold them, as we hold the rest of mankind, Enemies in War, in Peace Friends.

We, therefore, the Representatives of the united States of America, in General Congress, Assembled, appealing to the Supreme Judge of the world for the rectitude of our intentions, do, in the Name, and by the Authority of the good People of these Colonies, solemnly publish and declare, That these United Colonies are, and of Right ought to be Free and Independent States; that they are Absolved from all Allegiance to the British Crown, and that all political connection between them and the State of Great Britain, is and ought to be totally dissolved; and that as Free and Independent States, they have full Power to levy War, conclude Peace, contract Alliances, establish Commerce, and to do all other Acts and Things which Independent States may of right do. And for the support of this Declaration, with a firm reliance on the protection of divine Providence, we mutually pledge to each other our Lives, our Fortunes and our sacred Honor.

**The signers of the Declaration represented the new states as follows:**

## Connecticut:

Roger Sherman, Samuel Huntington, William Williams, Oliver Wolcott

## Delaware:

Caesar Rodney, George Read, Thomas McKean

## Georgia:

Button Gwinnett, Lyman Hall, George Walton

## Maryland:

Samuel Chase, William Paca, Thomas Stone, Charles Carroll of Carrollton

## Massachusetts:

John Hancock, Samuel Adams, John Adams, Robert Treat Paine, Elbridge Gerry

## New Hampshire:

Josiah Bartlett, William Whipple, Matthew Thornton

## New Jersey:

Richard Stockton, John Witherspoon, Francis Hopkinson, John Hart, Abraham Clark

## New York:

William Floyd, Philip Livingston, Francis Lewis, Lewis Morris

## North Carolina:

William Hooper, Joseph Hewes, John Penn

## Pennsylvania:

Robert Morris, Benjamin Rush, Benjamin Franklin, John Morton, George Clymer, James Smith, George Taylor, James Wilson, George Ross

## Rhode Island:

Stephen Hopkins, William Ellery

## South Carolina:

Edward Rutledge, Thomas Heyward, Jr., Thomas Lynch, Arthur Middleton, Jr.

## Virginia:

George Wythe, Richard Henry Lee, Thomas Jefferson, Benjamin Harrison, Thomas Nelson, Jr., Francis Lightfoot Lee, Carter Braxton

\* \* \* \*

# The United States Constitution

*Preamble*

# We the People . . .

of the United States, in Order to form a more perfect Union, establish Justice, insure domestic Tranquility, provide for the common defense, promote the general Welfare, and secure the Blessings of Liberty to ourselves and our Posterity, do ordain and establish this Constitution for the United States of America.

## Article. I. *Adopted 1787*

### Section. 1.
All legislative Powers herein granted shall be vested in a Congress of the United States, which shall consist of a Senate and House of Representatives.

### Section. 2.
The House of Representatives shall be composed of Members chosen every second Year by the People of the several States, and the Electors in each State shall have the Qualifications requisite for Electors of the most numerous Branch of the State Legislature.

No Person shall be a Representative who shall not have attained to the Age of twenty five Years, and been seven Years a Citizen of the United States, and who shall not, when elected, be an Inhabitant of that State in which he shall be chosen.

Representatives and direct Taxes shall be apportioned among the several States which may be included within this Union, according to their respective Numbers, which shall be determined by adding to the whole Number of free Persons, including those bound to Service for a Term of Years, and excluding Indians not taxed, three fifths of all other Persons.

The actual Enumeration shall be made within three Years after the first Meeting of the Congress of the United States, and within every subsequent Term of ten Years, in such Manner as they shall by Law direct. The Number of Representatives shall not exceed one for every thirty Thousand, but each State shall have at Least one Representative; and until such enumeration shall be made, the State of New Hampshire shall be entitled to choose three, Massachusetts eight, Rhode Island and

Providence Plantations one, Connecticut five, New York six, New Jersey four, Pennsylvania eight, Delaware one, Maryland six, Virginia ten, North Carolina five, South Carolina five and Georgia three.

When vacancies happen in the Representation from any State, the Executive Authority thereof shall issue Writs of Election to fill such Vacancies.

The House of Representatives shall chuse their Speaker and other Officers; and shall have the sole Power of Impeachment.

### Section. 3.
The Senate of the United States shall be composed of two Senators from each State, chosen by the Legislature thereof, for six Years; and each Senator shall have one Vote.

Immediately after they shall be assembled in Consequence of the first Election, they shall be divided as equally as may be into three Classes. The Seats of the Senators of the first Class shall be vacated at the Expiration of the second Year, of the second Class at the Expiration of the fourth Year, and of the third Class at the Expiration of the sixth Year, so that one third may be chosen every second Year; and if Vacancies happen by Resignation, or otherwise, during the Recess of the Legislature of any State, the Executive thereof may make temporary Appointments until the next Meeting of the Legislature, which shall then fill such Vacancies.

No person shall be a Senator who shall not have attained to the Age of thirty Years, and been nine Years a Citizen of the United States, and who shall not, when elected, be an Inhabitant of that State for which he shall be chosen.

The Vice President of the United States shall be President of the Senate, but shall have no Vote, unless they be equally divided.

The Senate shall chuse their other Officers, and also a President pro tempore, in the absence of the Vice President, or when he shall exercise the Office of President of the United States.

The Senate shall have the sole Power to try all Impeachments. When sitting for that Purpose, they shall be on Oath or Affirmation. When the President of the United States is tried, the Chief Justice shall preside: And no Person shall be convicted without the Concurrence of two thirds of the Members present.

Judgment in Cases of Impeachment shall not extend further than to removal from Office, and disqualification to hold and enjoy any Office of honor, Trust or Profit under the United States: but the Party convicted shall nevertheless be liable and subject to Indictment, Trial, Judgment and Punishment, according to Law.

## Section. 4.

The Times, Places and Manner of holding Elections for Senators and Representatives, shall be prescribed in each State by the Legislature thereof; but the Congress may at any time by Law make or alter such Regulations, except as to the Places of chusing Senators.

The Congress shall assemble at least once in every Year, and such Meeting shall be on the first Monday in December, unless they shall by Law appoint a different Day.

## Section. 5.

Each House shall be the Judge of the Elections, Returns and Qualifications of its own Members, and a Majority of each shall constitute a Quorum to do Business; but a smaller number may adjourn from day to day, and may be authorized to compel the Attendance of absent Members, in such Manner, and under such Penalties as each House may provide.

Each House may determine the Rules of its Proceedings, punish its Members for disorderly Behaviour, and, with the Concurrence of two-thirds, expel a Member.

Each House shall keep a Journal of its Proceedings, and from time to time publish the same, excepting such Parts as may in their Judgment require Secrecy; and the Yeas and Nays of the Members of either House on any question shall, at the Desire of one fifth of those Present, be entered on the Journal.

Neither House, during the Session of Congress, shall, without the Consent of the other, adjourn for more than three days, nor to any other Place than that in which the two Houses shall be sitting.

## Section. 6.

The Senators and Representatives shall receive a Compensation for their Services, to be ascertained by Law, and paid out of the Treasury of the United States. They shall in all Cases, except Treason, Felony and Breach of the Peace, be privileged from Arrest during their Attendance at the Session of their respective Houses, and in going to and returning from the same; and for any Speech or Debate in either House, they shall not be questioned in any other Place.

No Senator or Representative shall, during the Time for which he was elected, be appointed to any civil Office under the Authority of the United States which shall have been created, or the Emoluments whereof shall have been increased during such time; and no Person holding any Office under the United States, shall be a Member of either House during his Continuance in Office.

## Section. 7.
All bills for raising Revenue shall originate in the House of Representatives; but the Senate may propose or concur with Amendments as on other Bills.

Every Bill which shall have passed the House of Representatives and the Senate, shall, before it become a Law, be presented to the President of the United States; If he approve he shall sign it, but if not he shall return it, with his Objections to that House in which it shall have originated, who shall enter the Objections at large on their Journal, and proceed to reconsider it. If after such Reconsideration two thirds of that House shall agree to pass the Bill, it shall be sent, together with the Objections, to the other House, by which it shall likewise be reconsidered, and if approved by two thirds of that House, it shall become a Law. But in all such Cases the Votes of both Houses shall be determined by Yeas and Nays, and the Names of the Persons voting for and against the Bill shall be entered on the Journal of each House respectively. If any Bill shall not be returned by the President within ten Days (Sundays excepted) after it shall have been presented to him, the Same shall be a Law, in like Manner as if he had signed it, unless the Congress by their Adjournment prevent its Return, in which Case it shall not be a Law.

Every Order, Resolution, or Vote to which the Concurrence of the Senate and House of Representatives may be necessary (except on a question of Adjournment) shall be presented to the President of the United States; and before the Same shall take Effect, shall be approved by him, or being disapproved by him, shall be repassed by two thirds of the Senate and House of Representatives, according to the Rules and Limitations prescribed in the Case of a Bill.

## Section. 8.
The Congress shall have Power To lay and collect Taxes, Duties, Imposts and Excises, to pay the Debts and provide for the common Defence and general Welfare of the United States; but all Duties, Imposts and Excises shall be uniform throughout the United States;

To borrow Money on the credit of the United States;

To regulate Commerce with foreign Nations, and among the several States, and with the Indian Tribes;

To establish an uniform Rule of Naturalization, and uniform Laws on the subject of Bankruptcies throughout the United States;

To coin Money, regulate the Value thereof, and of foreign Coin, and fix the Standard of Weights and Measures;

To provide for the Punishment of counterfeiting the Securities and current Coin of the United States;

To establish Post Offices and post Roads;

To promote the Progress of Science and useful Arts, by securing for limited Times to Authors and Inventors the exclusive Right to their respective Writings and Discoveries;

To constitute Tribunals inferior to the supreme Court;

To define and punish Piracies and Felonies committed on the high Seas, and Offences against the Law of Nations;

To declare War, grant Letters of Marque and Reprisal, and make Rules concerning Captures on Land and Water;

To raise and support Armies, but no Appropriation of Money to that Use shall be for a longer Term than two Years;

To provide and maintain a Navy;

To make Rules for the Government and Regulation of the land and naval Forces;

To provide for calling forth the Militia to execute the Laws of the Union, suppress Insurrections and repel Invasions;

To provide for organizing, arming, and disciplining the Militia, and for governing such Part of them as may be employed in the Service of the United States, reserving to the States respectively, the Appointment of the Officers, and the Authority of training the Militia according to the discipline prescribed by Congress;

To exercise exclusive Legislation in all Cases whatsoever, over such District (not exceeding ten Miles square) as may, by Cession of particular States, and the acceptance of Congress, become the Seat of the Government of the United States, and to exercise like Authority over all Places purchased by the Consent of the Legislature of the State in which the Same shall be, for the Erection of Forts, Magazines, Arsenals, dock-Yards, and other needful Buildings; And

To make all Laws which shall be necessary and proper for carrying into Execution the foregoing Powers, and all other Powers vested by this Constitution in the Government of the United States, or in any Department or Officer thereof.

## Section. 9.

The Migration or Importation of such Persons as any of the States now existing shall think proper to admit, shall not be prohibited by the Congress prior to the Year one thousand eight hundred and eight, but a Tax or duty may be imposed on such Importation, not exceeding ten dollars for each Person.

The privilege of the Writ of Habeas Corpus shall not be suspended, unless when in Cases of Rebellion or Invasion the public Safety may require it.

No Bill of Attainder or ex post facto Law shall be passed.

No capitation, or other direct, Tax shall be laid, unless in Proportion to the Census or Enumeration herein before directed to be taken.

No Tax or Duty shall be laid on Articles exported from any State.

No Preference shall be given by any Regulation of Commerce or Revenue to the Ports of one State over those of another: nor shall Vessels bound to, or from, one State, be obliged to enter, clear, or pay Duties in another.

No Money shall be drawn from the Treasury, but in Consequence of Appropriations made by Law; and a regular Statement and Account of the Receipts and Expenditures of all public Money shall be published from time to time.

No Title of Nobility shall be granted by the United States: And no Person holding any Office of Profit or Trust under them, shall, without the Consent of the Congress, accept of any present, Emolument, Office, or Title, of any kind whatever, from any King, Prince or foreign State.

## Section. 10.

No State shall enter into any Treaty, Alliance, or Confederation; grant Letters of Marque and Reprisal; coin Money; emit Bills of Credit; make any Thing but gold and silver Coin a Tender in Payment of Debts; pass any Bill of Attainder, ex post facto Law, or Law impairing the Obligation of Contracts, or grant any Title of Nobility.

No State shall, without the Consent of the Congress, lay any Imposts or Duties on Imports or Exports, except what may be absolutely necessary for executing it's inspection Laws: and the net Produce of all Duties and Imposts, laid by any State on

Imports or Exports, shall be for the Use of the Treasury of the United States; and all such Laws shall be subject to the Revision and Controul of the Congress.

No State shall, without the Consent of Congress, lay any duty of Tonnage, keep Troops, or Ships of War in time of Peace, enter into any Agreement or Compact with another State, or with a foreign Power, or engage in War, unless actually invaded, or in such imminent Danger as will not admit of delay.

## Article II. *Adopted 1787*

### Section. 1.

The executive Power shall be vested in a President of the United States of America. He shall hold his Office during the Term of four Years, and, together with the Vice-President chosen for the same Term, be elected, as follows:

Each State shall appoint, in such Manner as the Legislature thereof may direct, a Number of Electors, equal to the whole Number of Senators and Representatives to which the State may be entitled in the Congress: but no Senator or Representative, or Person holding an Office of Trust or Profit under the United States, shall be appointed an Elector.

The Electors shall meet in their respective States, and vote by Ballot for two persons, of whom one at least shall not be an Inhabitant of the same State with themselves. And they shall make a List of all the Persons voted for, and of the Number of Votes for each; which List they shall sign and certify, and transmit sealed to the Seat of the Government of the United States, directed to the President of the Senate. The President of the Senate shall, in the Presence of the Senate and House of Representatives, open all the Certificates, and the Votes shall then be counted. The Person having the greatest Number of Votes shall be the President, if such Number be a Majority of the whole Number of Electors appointed; and if there be more than one who have such Majority, and have an equal Number of Votes, then the House of Representatives shall immediately chuse by Ballot one of them for President; and if no Person have a Majority, then from the five highest on the List the said House shall in like Manner chuse the President. But in chusing the President, the Votes shall be taken by States, the Representation from each State having one Vote; a quorum for this Purpose shall consist of a Member or Members from two-thirds of the States, and a Majority of all the States shall be necessary to a Choice. In every Case, after the Choice of the President, the Person having the greatest Number of Votes of the Electors shall be the Vice President. But if there should remain two or more who have equal Votes, the Senate shall chuse from them by Ballot the Vice President.

The Congress may determine the Time of chusing the Electors, and the Day on which they shall give their Votes; which Day shall be the same throughout the United States.

No person except a natural born Citizen, or a Citizen of the United States, at the time of the Adoption of this Constitution, shall be eligible to the Office of President; neither shall any Person be eligible to that Office who shall not have attained to the Age of thirty-five Years, and been fourteen Years a Resident within the United States.

In Case of the Removal of the President from Office, or of his Death, Resignation, or Inability to discharge the Powers and Duties of the said Office, the same shall devolve on the Vice President, and the Congress may by Law provide for the Case of Removal, Death, Resignation or Inability, both of the President and Vice President, declaring what Officer shall then act as President, and such Officer shall act accordingly, until the Disability be removed, or a President shall be elected.

The President shall, at stated Times, receive for his Services, a Compensation, which shall neither be increased nor diminished during the Period for which he shall have been elected, and he shall not receive within that Period any other Emolument from the United States, or any of them.

Before he enter on the Execution of his Office, he shall take the following Oath or Affirmation:-- "I do solemnly swear (or affirm) that I will faithfully execute the Office of President of the United States, and will to the best of my Ability, preserve, protect and defend the Constitution of the United States."

## Section. 2.
The President shall be Commander in Chief of the Army and Navy of the United States, and of the Militia of the several States, when called into the actual Service of the United States; he may require the Opinion, in writing, of the principal Officer in each of the executive Departments, upon any Subject relating to the Duties of their respective Offices, and he shall have Power to Grant Reprieves and Pardons for Offenses against the United States, except in Cases of Impeachment.

He shall have Power, by and with the Advice and Consent of the Senate, to make Treaties, provided two thirds of the Senators present concur; and he shall nominate, and by and with the Advice and Consent of the Senate, shall appoint Ambassadors, other public Ministers and Consuls, Judges of the supreme Court, and all other Officers of the United States, whose Appointments are not herein otherwise provided for, and which shall be established by Law: but the Congress may by Law vest the Appointment of such inferior Officers, as they think proper, in the President alone, in the Courts of Law, or in the Heads of Departments.

The President shall have Power to fill up all Vacancies that may happen during the Recess of the Senate, by granting Commissions which shall expire at the End of their next Session.

## Section. 3.
He shall from time to time give to the Congress Information of the State of the Union, and recommend to their Consideration such Measures as he shall judge necessary and expedient; he may, on extraordinary Occasions, convene both Houses, or either of them, and in Case of Disagreement between them, with Respect to the Time of Adjournment, he may adjourn them to such Time as he shall think proper; he shall receive Ambassadors and other public Ministers; he shall take Care that the Laws be faithfully executed, and shall Commission all the Officers of the United States.

## Section. 4.
The President, Vice President and all civil Officers of the United States, shall be removed from Office on Impeachment for, and Conviction of, Treason, Bribery, or other high Crimes and Misdemeanors.

# Article III. *Adopted 1787*

## Section. 1.
The judicial Power of the United States, shall be vested in one supreme Court, and in such inferior Courts as the Congress may from time to time ordain and establish. The Judges, both of the supreme and inferior Courts, shall hold their Offices during good Behavior, and shall, at stated Times, receive for their Services a Compensation which shall not be diminished during their Continuance in Office.

## Section. 2.
The judicial Power shall extend to all Cases, in Law and Equity, arising under this Constitution, the Laws of the United States, and Treaties made, or which shall be made, under their Authority;-- to all Cases affecting Ambassadors, other public Ministers and Consuls; to all Cases of admiralty and maritime Jurisdiction;-- to Controversies to which the United States shall be a Party;-- to Controversies between two or more States; between a State and Citizens of another State;-- between Citizens of different States; between Citizens of the same State claiming Lands under Grants of different States, and between a State, or the Citizens thereof, and foreign States, Citizens or Subjects.

In all Cases affecting Ambassadors, other public Ministers and Consuls, and those in which a State shall be Party, the Supreme Court shall have original Jurisdiction. In all the other Cases before mentioned, the supreme Court shall have appellate Jurisdiction, both as to Law and Fact, with such Exceptions, and under such

Regulations as the Congress shall make.

The Trial of all Crimes, except in Cases of Impeachment, shall be by Jury; and such Trial shall be held in the State where the said Crimes shall have been committed; but when not committed within any State, the Trial shall be at such Place or Places as the Congress may by Law have directed.

### Section. 3.
Treason against the United States, shall consist only in levying War against them, or in adhering to their Enemies, giving them Aid and Comfort. No Person shall be convicted of Treason unless on the Testimony of two Witnesses to the same overt Act, or on Confession in open Court.

The Congress shall have Power to declare the Punishment of Treason, but no Attainder of Treason shall work Corruption of Blood, or Forfeiture except during the Life of the Person attainted.

## Article. IV.  *Adopted 1787*

### Section. 1.
Full Faith and Credit shall be given in each State to the public Acts, Records, and judicial Proceedings of every other State. And the Congress may by general Laws prescribe the Manner in which such Acts, Records and Proceedings shall be proved, and the Effect thereof.

### Section. 2.
The Citizens of each State shall be entitled to all Privileges and Immunities of Citizens in the several States.

A Person charged in any State with Treason, Felony, or other Crime, who shall flee from Justice, and be found in another State, shall on demand of the executive Authority of the State from which he fled, be delivered up, to be removed to the State having Jurisdiction of the Crime.

No Person held to Service or Labour in one State, under the Laws thereof, escaping into another, shall, in Consequence of any Law or Regulation therein, be discharged from such Service or Labour, but shall be delivered up on Claim of the Party to whom such Service or Labour may be due.

### Section. 3.
New States may be admitted by the Congress into this Union; but no new State shall be formed or erected within the Jurisdiction of any other State; nor any State be

formed by the Junction of two or more States, or parts of States, without the Consent of the Legislatures of the States concerned as well as of the Congress.

The Congress shall have Power to dispose of and make all needful Rules and Regulations respecting the Territory or other Property belonging to the United States; and nothing in this Constitution shall be so construed as to Prejudice any Claims of the United States, or of any particular State.

### Section. 4.
The United States shall guarantee to every State in this Union a Republican Form of Government, and shall protect each of them against Invasion; and on Application of the Legislature, or of the Executive (when the Legislature cannot be convened) against domestic Violence.

# Article. V. *Adopted 1787*

The Congress, whenever two thirds of both Houses shall deem it necessary, shall propose Amendments to this Constitution, or, on the Application of the Legislatures of two thirds of the several States, shall call a Convention for proposing Amendments, which, in either Case, shall be valid to all Intents and Purposes, as part of this Constitution, when ratified by the Legislatures of three fourths of the several States, or by Conventions in three fourths thereof, as the one or the other Mode of Ratification may be proposed by the Congress; Provided that no Amendment which may be made prior to the Year One thousand eight hundred and eight shall in any Manner affect the first and fourth Clauses in the Ninth Section of the first Article; and that no State, without its Consent, shall be deprived of its equal Suffrage in the Senate.

# Article. VI. *Adopted 1787*

All Debts contracted and Engagements entered into, before the Adoption of this Constitution, shall be as valid against the United States under this Constitution, as under the Confederation.

This Constitution, and the Laws of the United States which shall be made in Pursuance thereof; and all Treaties made, or which shall be made, under the Authority of the United States, shall be the supreme Law of the Land; and the Judges in every State shall be bound thereby, any Thing in the Constitution or Laws of any State to the Contrary notwithstanding.

The Senators and Representatives before mentioned, and the Members of the several State Legislatures, and all executive and judicial Officers, both of the United States and of the several States, shall be bound by Oath or Affirmation, to support this Constitution; but no religious Test shall ever be required as a Qualification to any Office or public Trust under the United States.

## Article. VII. *Adopted 1787*

The Ratification of the Conventions of nine States, shall be sufficient for the Establishment of this Constitution between the States so ratifying the Same.

Done in Convention by the Unanimous Consent of the States present the Seventeenth Day of September in the Year of our Lord one thousand seven hundred and Eighty seven and of the Independence of the United States of America the Twelfth. In Witness whereof We have hereunto subscribed our Names.

George Washington - President and deputy from Virginia
New Hampshire - John Langdon, Nicholas Gilman
Massachusetts - Nathaniel Gorham, Rufus King
Connecticut – Wm. Saml. Johnson, Roger Sherman
New York - Alexander Hamilton

New Jersey – Wil: Livingston, David Brearley. Wm. Paterson. Jona: Dayton
Pennsylvania - Benjamin Franklin, Thomas Mifflin, Robt. Morris, Geo. Clymer, Thos. FitzSimons, Jared Ingersoll, James Wilson, Gouverneur Morris
Delaware - Geo. Read, Gunning Bedford Junior, John Dickinson, Richard Bassett, Jaco: Broom
Maryland - James McHenry, Dan of St Thos. Jenifer, Danl Carroll
Virginia - John Blair, James Madison, Junior
North Carolina – Wm. Blount, Richd. Dobbs Spaight, Hugh Williamson
South Carolina - J. Rutledge, Charles Cotesworth Pinckney, Charles Pinckney, Pierce Butler
Georgia - William Few, Abr Baldwin
Attest: William Jackson, Secretary

ARTICLES IN ADDITON TO, AND AMENDMENT OF THE CONSTITUTION OF THE UNITED STATES OF AMERICA, PROPOSED BY CONGRESS, AND RATIFIED BY THE LEGISLATURES OF THE SEVERAL STATES, PURSUANT TO THE FIFTH ARTICLE OF THE ORIGINAL CONSTITUTION.

## Article. I.
(Adopted 1791; freedom of religion, speech, press, assembly, and petition.)

Congress shall make no law respecting an establishment of religion, or prohibiting the free exercise thereof; or abridging the freedom of speech, or of the press; or the right of the people peaceably to assemble, and to petition the Government for a redress of grievances.

## Article. II.
(Adopted 1791; the right to keep and bear arms.)

A well regulated Militia, being necessary to the security of a free State, the right of the people to keep and bear Arms, shall not be infringed.

## Article. III.
(Adopted 1791; prevention of compulsory billeting during peacetime.)

No Soldier shall, in time of peace be quartered in any house, without the consent of the Owner, nor in time of war, but in a manner to be prescribed by law.

## Article. IV.
(Adopted 1791; security of person and possessions against search and seizure.)

The right of the people to be secure in their persons, houses, papers, and effects, against unreasonable searches and seizures, shall not be violated, and no Warrants shall issue, but upon probable cause, supported by Oath or affirmation, and particularly describing the place to be searched, and the persons or things to be seized.

## Article. V.
(Adopted 1791; prevention of double-jeopardy; right against self-incrimination.)

No person shall be held to answer for a capital, or otherwise infamous crime, unless on a presentment or indictment of a Grand Jury, except in cases arising in the land or naval forces, or in the Militia, when in actual service in time of War or public danger;

nor shall any person be subject for the same offense to be twice put in jeopardy of life or limb; nor shall be compelled in any criminal case to be a witness against himself, nor be deprived of life, liberty, or property, without due process of law; nor shall private property be taken for public use, without just compensation.

## Article. VI.
(Adopted 1791; Fair, speedy, and public trial by jury; right to counsel.)

In all criminal prosecutions, the accused shall enjoy the right to a speedy and public trial, by an impartial jury of the State and district wherein the crime shall have been committed, which district shall have been previously ascertained by law, and to be informed of the nature and cause of the accusation; to be confronted with the witnesses against him; to have compulsory process for obtaining witnesses in his favor, and to have the Assistance of Counsel for his defense.

## Article. VII.
(Adopted 1791; right to trial by jury in common law suits.)

In Suits at common law, where the value in controversy shall exceed twenty dollars, the right of trial by jury shall be preserved, and no fact tried by a jury, shall be otherwise re-examined in any Court of the United States, than according to the rules of the common law.

## Article. VIII.
(Adopted 1791; prevention of cruel or unusual punishments; and excessive fines)

Excessive bail shall not be required, nor excessive fines imposed, nor cruel and unusual punishments inflicted.

## Article. IX.
(Adopted 1791; protection of rights not enumerated in the Constitution.)

The enumeration in the Constitution, of certain rights, shall not be construed to deny or disparage others retained by the people.

## Article. X.
(Adopted 1791; reservation of the rights of individual states.)

The powers not delegated to the United States by the Constitution, nor prohibited by it to the States, are reserved to the States respectively, or to the people.

# Article. XI.
(Adopted 1795; delineation of judicial powers of the US in certain cases.)

The Judicial power of the United States shall not be construed to extend to any suit in law or equity, commenced or prosecuted against one of the United States by Citizens of another State, or by Citizens or Subjects of any Foreign State.

# Article. XII.
(Adopted 1804; procedures for electing President and Vice President.)

The Electors shall meet in their respective states, and vote by ballot for President and Vice-President, one of whom, at least, shall not be an inhabitant of the same state with themselves; they shall name in their ballots the person voted for as President, and in distinct ballots the person voted for as Vice-President, and they shall make distinct lists of all persons voted for as President, and of all persons voted for as Vice-President and of the number of votes for each, which lists they shall sign and certify, and transmit sealed to the seat of the government of the United States, directed to the President of the Senate;
The President of the Senate shall, in the presence of the Senate and House of Representatives, open all the certificates and the votes shall then be counted;
The person having the greatest Number of votes for President, shall be the President, if such number be a majority of the whole number of Electors appointed; and if no person have such majority, then from the persons having the highest numbers not exceeding three on the list of those voted for as President, the House of Representatives shall choose immediately, by ballot, the President. But in choosing the President, the votes shall be taken by states, the representation from each state having one vote; a quorum for this purpose shall consist of a member or members from two-thirds of the states, and a majority of all the states shall be necessary to a choice. And if the House of Representatives shall not choose a President whenever the right of choice shall devolve upon them, before the fourth day of March next following, then the Vice-President shall act as President, as in the case of the death or other constitutional disability of the President.
The person having the greatest number of votes as Vice-President, shall be the Vice-President, if such number be a majority of the whole number of Electors appointed, and if no person have a majority, then from the two highest numbers on the list, the Senate shall choose the Vice-President; a quorum for the purpose shall consist of two-thirds of the whole number of Senators, and a majority of the whole number shall be necessary to a choice. But no person constitutionally ineligible to the office of President shall be eligible to that of Vice-President of the United States.

## Article. XIII.
(Adopted 1865, abolished slavery.)

**Section 1.** Neither slavery nor involuntary servitude, except as a punishment for crime whereof the party shall have been duly convicted, shall exist within the United States, or any place subject to their jurisdiction.

**Section 2.** Congress shall have power to enforce this article by appropriate legislation.

## Article. XIV.
*(Adopted 1868; guarantee of the rights of citizenship.)*

**Section 1.** All persons born or naturalized in the United States, and subject to the jurisdiction thereof, are citizens of the United States and of the State wherein they reside. No State shall make or enforce any law which shall abridge the privileges or immunities of citizens of the United States; nor shall any State deprive any person of life, liberty, or property, without due process of law; nor deny to any person within its jurisdiction the equal protection of the laws.

**Section 2.** Representatives shall be apportioned among the several States according to their respective numbers, counting the whole number of persons in each State, excluding Indians not taxed. But when the right to vote at any election for the choice of electors for President and Vice-President of the United States, Representatives in Congress, the Executive and Judicial officers of a State, or the members of the Legislature thereof, is denied to any of the male inhabitants of such State, being twenty-one years of age, and citizens of the United States, or in any way abridged, except for participation in rebellion, or other crime, the basis of representation therein shall be reduced in the proportion which the number of such male citizens shall bear to the whole number of male citizens twenty-one years of age in such State.

**Section 3.** No person shall be a Senator or Representative in Congress, or elector of President and Vice-President, or hold any office, civil or military, under the United States, or under any State, who, having previously taken an oath, as a member of Congress, or as an officer of the United States, or as a member of any State legislature, or as an executive or judicial officer of any State, to support the Constitution of the United States, shall have engaged in insurrection or rebellion against the same, or given aid or comfort to the enemies thereof. But Congress may by a vote of two-thirds of each House, remove such disability.

**Section 4.** The validity of the public debt of the United States, authorized by law, including debts incurred for payment of pensions and bounties for services in suppressing insurrection or rebellion, shall not be questioned. But neither the United States nor any State shall assume or pay any debt or obligation incurred in aid of insurrection or rebellion against the United States, or any claim for the loss or emancipation of any slave; but all such debts, obligations and claims shall be held illegal and void.

**Section 5**. The Congress shall have power to enforce, by appropriate legislation, the provisions of this article.

## Article. XV.

(Adopted 1870; right to vote regardless of race, color, or previous servitude.)

**Section 1**. The right of citizens of the United States to vote shall not be denied or abridged by the United States or by any State on account of race, color, or previous condition of servitude.

**Section 2**. The Congress shall have power to enforce this article by appropriate legislation.

## Article. XVI.

(Adopted 1913; right of Congress to levy income taxes.)

The Congress shall have power to lay and collect taxes on incomes, from whatever source derived, without apportionment among the several States, and without regard to any census or enumeration.

## Article. XVII.

(Adopted 1913; procedure for electing Senators.)

The Senate of the United States shall be composed of two Senators from each State, elected by the people thereof, for six years; and each Senator shall have one vote. The electors in each State shall have the qualifications requisite for electors of the most numerous branch of the State legislatures.

When vacancies happen in the representation of any State in the Senate, the executive authority of such State shall issue writs of election to fill such vacancies: *Provided*, That the legislature of any State may empower the executive thereof to make temporary appointments until the people fill the vacancies by election as the legislature may direct.

This amendment shall not be so construed as to affect the election or term of any Senator chosen before it becomes valid as part of the Constitution.

## Article. XVIII.

(Adopted 1919; introduced prohibition.)

**Section 1**. After one year from the ratification of this article the manufacture, sale, or transportation of intoxicating liquors within, the importation thereof into, or the exportation thereof from the United States and all territory subject to the jurisdiction thereof for beverage purposes is hereby prohibited.

**Section 2**. The Congress and the several States shall have concurrent power to enforce this article by appropriate legislation.

**Section 3**. This article shall be inoperative unless it shall have been ratified as an amendment to the Constitution by the legislatures of the several States, as provided in the Constitution, within seven years from the date of the submission hereof to the States by the Congress.

## Article. XIX.
(Adopted 1920; right of women to vote.)

The right of citizens of the United States to vote shall not be denied or abridged by the United States or by any State on account of sex.

Congress shall have power to enforce this article by appropriate legislation.

## Article. XX.
(Adopted 1933; presidential term and succession; terms of other offices.)

**Section 1**. The terms of the President and Vice President shall end at noon on the 20th day of January, and the terms of Senators and Representatives at noon on the 3d day of January, of the years in which such terms would have ended if this article had not been ratified; and the terms of their successors shall then begin.

**Section 2.** The Congress shall assemble at least once in every year, and such meeting shall begin at noon on the 3d day of January, unless they shall by law appoint a different day.

**Section 3.** If, at the time fixed for the beginning of the term of the President, the President elect shall have died, the Vice President elect shall become President. If a President shall not have been chosen before the time fixed for the beginning of his term, or if the President elect shall have failed to qualify, then the Vice President elect shall act as President until a President shall have qualified; and the Congress may by law provide for the case wherein neither a President elect nor a Vice President elect shall have qualified, declaring who shall then act as President, or the manner in which one who is to act shall be selected, and such person shall act accordingly until a President or Vice President shall have qualified.

**Section 4.** The Congress may by law provide for the case of the death of any of the persons from whom the House of Representatives may choose a President whenever the right of choice shall have devolved upon them, and for the case of the death of any of the persons from whom the Senate may choose a Vice President whenever the right of choice shall have devolved upon them.

**Section 5**. Sections 1 and 2 shall take effect on the 15th day of October following the ratification of this article.

**Section 6**. This article shall be inoperative unless it shall have been ratified as an amendment to the Constitution by the legislatures of three-fourths of the several States within seven years from the date of its submission.

## Article. XXI.
(Adopted 1933; repeal of prohibition, the 18th Amendment.)

**Section 1.** The eighteenth article of amendment to the Constitution of the United States is hereby repealed.

**Section 2.** The transportation or importation into any State, Territory, or possession of the United States for delivery or use therein of intoxicating liquors, in violation of the laws thereof, is hereby prohibited.

**Section 3.** The article shall be inoperative unless it shall have been ratified as an amendment to the Constitution by conventions in the several States, as provided in the Constitution, within seven years from the date of the submission hereof to the States by the Congress

## Article. XXII.
(*Adopted 1951*; limiting Presidents to two terms.)

**Section 1.** No person shall be elected to the office of the President more than twice, and no person who has held the office of President, or acted as President, for more than two years of a term to which some other person was elected President shall be elected to the office of the President more than once. But this Article shall not apply to any person holding the office of President, when this Article was proposed by the Congress, and shall not prevent any person who may be holding the office of President, or acting as President, during the term within which this Article becomes operative from holding the office of President or acting as President during the remainder of such term.

**Section 2.** This article shall be inoperative unless it shall have been ratified as an amendment to the Constitution by the legislatures of three-fourths of the several States within seven years from the date of its submission to the States by the Congress.

## Article. XXIII.
(Adopted 1961; grants Washington DC residents a vote in the Presidential elections.)

**Section 1.** The District constituting the seat of Government of the United States shall appoint in such manner as the Congress may direct: A number of electors of President and Vice President equal to the whole number of Senators and Representatives in Congress to which the District would be entitled if it were a State, but in no event more than the least populous State; they shall be in addition to those appointed by the States, but they shall be considered, for the purposes of the election of President and Vice President, to be electors appointed by a State; and they shall meet in the District and perform such duties as provided by the twelfth article of amendment.

**Section 2**. The Congress shall have power to enforce this article by appropriate legislation.

## Article. XXIV.
(Adopted 1964; bars poll (voting) tax in federal elections.)

**Section 1.** The right of citizens of the United States to vote in any primary or other election for President or Vice President, for electors for President or Vice President, or for Senator or Representative in Congress, shall not be denied or abridged by the United States or any State by reason of failure to pay any poll tax or other tax.

**Section 2**. The Congress shall have power to enforce this article by appropriate legislation.

## Article. XXV.
(Adopted 1967; order of Presidential succession.)

**Section 1**. In case of the removal of the President from office or of his death or resignation, the Vice President shall become President.

**Section 2**. Whenever there is a vacancy in the office of the Vice President, the President shall nominate a Vice President who shall take office upon confirmation by a majority vote of both Houses of Congress.

**Section 3**. Whenever the President transmits to the President pro tempore of the Senate and the Speaker of the House of Representatives his written declaration that he is unable to discharge the powers and duties of his office, and until he transmits to them a written declaration to the contrary, such powers and duties shall be discharged by the Vice President as Acting President.

**Section 4**. Whenever the Vice President and a majority of either the principal officers of the executive departments or of such other body as Congress may by law provide, transmit to the President pro tempore of the Senate and the Speaker of the House of Representatives their written declaration that the President is unable to discharge the powers and duties of his office, the Vice President shall immediately assume the powers and duties of the office as Acting President.

Thereafter, when the President transmits to the President pro tempore of the Senate and the Speaker of the House of Representatives his written declaration that no inability exists, he shall resume the powers and duties of his office unless the Vice President and a majority of either the principal officers of the executive department or of such other body as Congress may by law provide, transmit within four days to the President pro tempore of the Senate and the Speaker of the House of

Representatives their written declaration that the President is unable to discharge the powers and duties of his office. Thereupon Congress shall decide the issue, assembling within forty eight hours for that purpose if not in session. If the Congress, within twenty one days after receipt of the latter written declaration, or, if Congress is not in session, within twenty one days after Congress is required to assemble, determines by two thirds vote of both Houses that the President is unable to discharge the powers and duties of his office, the Vice President shall continue to discharge the same as Acting President; otherwise, the President shall resume the powers and duties of his office.

## Article. XXVI.
(Adopted 1971; right to vote at age eighteen.)

**Section 1.** The right of citizens of the United States, who are eighteen years of age or older, to vote shall not be denied or abridged by the United States or by any State on account of age.
**Section 2.** The Congress shall have power to enforce this article by appropriate legislation.

## Article. XXVII.
(Adopted 1992; postpones Representatives' pay raises until after new elections.)

No law, varying the compensation for the services of the Senators and Representatives, shall take effect, until an election of Representatives shall have intervened.

\* \* \* \* \* \* \*

To find additional information about the Declaration of Independence, visit these sites on the Internet:

- National Archives and Records Administration http://www.pro.gov.uk/webarchive/
- Library of Congress: http://www.loc.gov/about/sitemap/

# George Washington

*1st President.* George Washington was born in Westmoreland County, Virginia, on February 22, 1732. His father was a prosperous farmer and his grandparents emigrated from England to Virginia in the 1650s. Washington did not have formal schooling and started his first job as a surveyor when he was 16. He inherited Mount Vernon at the age of 21 when his Uncle Lawrence died. At this time, Governor Dinwiddie of Virginia sent Washington on a mission to keep the French out of the Ohio Valley. In 1755, when he was 23 he became commander in chief of the Virginia forces, and led them to victory in the French and Indian War. Washington married Martha Custis, a young widow. They did not have any children. In 1774 he served as a delegate to the first Continental Congress. He was unanimously elected commander in chief of the American forces. He helped write the peace treaty ending the American Revolution that was signed in 1783. George Washington was named president of the Federal Convention in 1787, and in 1789 was elected President of the United States. As the first president, he had to decide how to carry out the duties of the executive branch of the government. Washington felt this position should be devoid of politics and should represent all of the American people. The first Cabinet was made up of Thomas Jefferson, Secretary of State; Edmund Randolph, Attorney General; Alexander Hamilton, Secretary of the Treasury, and Henry Knox, Secretary of War. Washington stayed in office two terms and declined to serve a third term. He died at his home in Mount Vernon on December 14, 1799. **Washington was President from 1789-97 and the Vice President was John Adams.**

# John Adams

*2nd President.* John Adams was born October 19, 1735 in Quincy, Massachusetts. He attended school at a local academy. When he was 16 he enrolled in Harvard College and graduated in 1755. Adams began practicing law three years later. He married Abigail Smith in 1764. Together they had four children. In 1765 Adams wrote letters in the Boston Gazette protesting the Stamp Act imposed by the British Government that would tax public documents, newspapers, licenses, insurance policies and playing cards. Adams was elected to the Congress in 1774 and served in that capacity until 1777. He established his reputation as a champion of individual rights. He was one of the first to favor independence from Great Britain and in 1775 he recommended George Washington to be the commander in chief of the new Continental Army. He was appointed minister to the Netherlands in 1780. He successfully arranged loan and trade agreements between France, the Netherlands and America. Adams traveled to Paris in 1782 to negotiate a peace treaty with Great Britain, ending the Revolutionary War. He served as minister to Great Britain in 1785 until 1788 when he was elected vice president. Adams served as vice president two terms until he was elected President in 1797. John and Abigail Adams were the first to occupy the White House. It was undecorated and littered with building debris. Adams served only one term. He lost the election to Thomas Jefferson. He returned to Quincy, Massachusetts where he spent most of his time reading and writing essays. He died there on July 4, 1826. **Adams was President from 1797-1801 and the Vice President was Thomas Jefferson.**

## THOMAS JEFFERSON

*3rd President.* Thomas Jefferson was born in Albermarle County, Virginia on April 13, 1743. He was born into a wealthy family and tutored at home. When he turned 17 he went to the College of William and Mary in Williamsburg; he learned to speak French, Italian and Spanish. Jefferson studied law for five years; he was admitted to the bar when he was 24 and practiced law until the American Revolution closed the courts. In 1772 he married Martha Wayles Shelton; they had three daughters. In 1776 when he was 33, he was chosen to write the Declaration of Independence. The same year he became a member of the United States House of Delegates. He introduced the Bill for Establishing Religious Freedom in 1779 and it which passed seven years later. Jefferson served two terms as Governor of Virginia. In 1782 his wife died; he never remarried. He was elected to the Continental Congress in 1783 where he presented the concept of the dollar and the decimal system of money. In 1785, George Washington appointed Jefferson, Ben Franklin's successor as minister to France; he lived there for five years. Jefferson left France at the start of the French Revolution in 1789. Jefferson ran against Adams for the presidency and lost by three electoral votes. He became the Vice President. In 1800 he ran against Adams again and won the office of president; he served two terms. As president, he bought the Louisiana Territory for $15 million doubling the size of the United States. In 1819 he chartered the University of Virginia. He died at this home, Monticello, on July 4, 1826. **Jefferson was President from 1801-09 and the Vice Presidents were Aaron Burr and George Clinton.**

## JAMES MADISON

*4th President.* James Madison was born on March 16, 1751 in Port Conway, Virginia. He grew up on a family-owned tobacco farm called Montpellier, where his mother and grandmother taught him to read and write. When he turned 11 he went off to a boarding school in King and Queen County, Virginia. He loved to read. He attended Princeton University and graduated. In 1776 when Madison was 25, he was elected to the Virginia Revolutionary Convention. He served in the Virginia legislature for one year and was defeated when he ran for reelection. He was appointed a member of the Governor's Council, which managed the Revolutionary War efforts. In 1784 he was elected to the Virginia legislature. He married Dolley Payne Todd; they did not have any children. Madison attended the Annapolis Convention as a delegate and then the Constitutional Convention in Philadelphia, in 1787. His understanding of government made him a leader in creating the Constitution; he advocated a republican form of government in which the people are sovereign but rule through elected representatives. In 1789 he was elected to the United States House of Representatives, at the end of his term in 1801, he was appointed Secretary of State by Thomas Jefferson. In 1809 he was elected President. At this time, Britain and France were at war. After Britain attacked American ships, Madison reluctantly led our nation into war against Britain. During the War of 1812 the White House was burned by the British. Madison left Washington in 1817 after serving two terms as president. He lived on his farm developing new methods of agriculture until he died on June 28, 1836. **Madison was President from 1809-17 and the Vice Presidents were George Clinton and Elbridge Gerry.**

## JAMES MONROE

*5th President.* James Monroe was born on April 28, 1758 in Westmoreland County, Virginia. He left home to attend William and Mary College when he was 16. He joined the Third Virginia Regiment two years later to fight in the American Revolution. In 1782 he was elected to the Virginia House of Delegates. In 1783 he became a member of the Congress of the Confederation and served until 1786. He married Elizabeth Kortright. In 1790 he was elected United States senator and served four years, until he was appointed minister to France by George Washington. He retired from that position and two years later he was elected Governor of Virginia. In 1803 Monroe went on a diplomatic mission to France to help negotiate the Louisiana Purchase. President Jefferson appointed Monroe minister to Great Britain and a year later minister to Spain. In 1810 he was elected to the Virginia legislature. He served one year and left when he was elected Governor again in 1811. The same year he was appointed Secretary of State and also served under James Madison as the Secretary of War between 1814–1815. In 1817 Monroe was elected President. During his administration he bought Florida from Spain and established the Canadian border. He authored the Monroe doctrine that warned nations in Europe not to take over or set up colonies in North and South America. His presidency was known as the Era of Good Feeling; a period of national optimism, expansion and growth. He left office in 1825 and moved to Loudon County, Virginia with his wife. After she died he lived with his daughter in New York City, where he died July 4, 1831. **Monroe was President from 1817-25 and the Vice President was Daniel D. Tompkins.**

## JOHN Q. ADAMS

*6th President.* John Quincy Adams was born July 11, 1767 in Quincy, Massachusetts. He attended a village school until the headmaster went off to war. His parents were determined to see him elected President. He was tutored by his mother and he attended schools in Paris and the University of Leiden in the Netherlands. John Quincy Adams began a diary that he wrote in for over 60 years. He returned from the Netherlands in 1785 to attend Harvard College. He graduated in 1787 and started to practice law. At the age of 28 he was appointed minister to the Netherlands by · George Washington. He married Louisa Johnson and they had three sons. He served as the minister of Prussia in 1797 until 1801. He often traveled with his father, President John Adams. Adams was elected to the United States Senate in 1803 where he served until 1808. In 1809 President Madison appointed Adams the first American minister to Russia. In 1812 war broke out between the United States and Great Britain. Adams served on the delegation that brought about the Peace Treaty of Ghent in 1814. He later became the minister of Great Britain until 1817 when President Monroe appointed Adams Secretary of State. He negotiated the Transcontinental Treaty of 1819 with Spain, which gave the United States access to the Pacific Ocean. Adams ran for President in 1825 and won; he served one term. Adams was frustrated by the politics of the presidency, because he believed he was the people's representative. He ran for Congress in 1831 where he was an active legislator. He died two days after he collapsed on the floor of the House of Representatives, on February 23, 1848. **Adams was President from 1825-29 and the Vice President was John C. Calhoun.**

# ANDREW JACKSON

*7th President.* Andrew Jackson was born March 15, 1767 in a log cabin in the Waxhaw settlement of South Carolina, a few days after his father's death. He lived with his mother and two older brothers. He attended school enough to learn how to read. Jackson left home to fight in the Revolutionary War when he was 14; he was taken prisoner by a British officer. Shortly after he was released, his mother died. Jackson studied law in Salisbury, North Carolina and passed the bar exam. He traveled west with a group of pioneers and ended up in Tennessee where he married Rachel Donelson Robards in 1794. He was elected to the House of Representatives in 1796 and served one year in the United States Senate as the first representative from Tennessee. He had to return home when his farm failed. In 1802 he was elected major general of the Tennessee militia. In 1814 he defeated the Creek Indians during the war of 1812; he was promoted to major general of the United States Army. In 1815 he successfully fought off the British attack on New Orleans protecting the Louisiana territory. Jackson was elected Governor of the new territory of Florida in 1821. He served two years and returned to his home in Tennessee where he was elected to the Senate. Jackson ran for President in 1824 but lost to Martin Van Buren in a close race that was decided by the House of Representatives. In 1829 he was elected President and served two terms. He returned to his home in Nashville, Tennessee where he lived until he died on June 8, 1845. **Jackson was President from 1829-37 and the Vice Presidents were John C. Calhoun and Martin Van Buren**

# MARTIN VAN BUREN

*8th President.* Martin Van Buren was born March 4, 1782, in Kinderhook, New York. He was the first President to be born under the American flag. His father owned a tavern that also served as a polling place so he heard politics discussed at an early age. He was a student at the Kinderhook Academy until he took a job in a local law office when he was 13. At the age of 18 he had a job in a law office in New York City. When he was 21 he returned home to practice law; he was a very successful lawyer. He married Hannah Hoes his childhood sweetheart in 1807; together they had four sons. Van Buren was elected to the Senate in 1812. He interrupted his second term in the Senate to run for governor. Van Buren served as governor of New York for ten weeks and then moved to Washington to perform the duties of Secretary of State in 1829. He was elected to the office of Vice President under Andrew Jackson in 1832. Van Buren was elected president in 1836, the first to be elected as a member of the Democratic Party. He became president in 1837—the same year that the United States entered a major depression. During his administration he instituted the Department of the Treasury to protect government funds due to the economic depression caused by investment in land speculation that was not backed by gold or silver. He was not reelected in 1840 because he did not believe the government should help people who had lost their jobs. Van Buren tried again for the presidency in 1848 as a Free Soil candidate and lost to Zachary Taylor. Martin Van Buren died in Kinderhook, New York, in 1862. **Van Buren was President from 1837-41 and the Vice President was Richard M. Johnson.**

## WILLIAM H. HARRISON

*9th President.* William Henry Harrison was born on February 9, 1773 on his father's plantation in Charles City County, Virginia. His father was one of the signers of the Declaration of Independence and a friend of George Washington. Harrison was taught at home until he went to Hampden-Sidney College in Virginia. He joined the Army one year later— his father died the same year. In 1795 he married Anna Symmes; they had ten children. Harrison was appointed Secretary of the Northwest Territory by President John Adams and served as the delegate to Congress from that region. He was appointed Governor of the Indiana territory where he served for 12 years. He took millions of acres of land from Native Americans by battle or by treaty. And he recaptured Detroit from the British in the War of 1812. Harrison defeated the Shawnee Indians and destroyed their settlement. Harrison defeated the British and Indians at the Battle of the Thames during the War of 1812. He moved his family to North Bend, Ohio. In 1816 he was elected to Congress and in 1819 he was elected to the state senate. At the end of that term in 1825 he was elected to the United States Senate. President John Quincy Adams appointed Harrison minister to Columbia in 1828. He offended Columbian President Simon Bolivar and he was forced to leave the country in 1829. Harrison returned to his farm in North Bend. He was nominated by the Whig Party to run for President against Martin Van Buren, and lost. Harrison ran for President again four years later and won. He died of pneumonia only 30 days after taking office on April 4, 1841. **Harrison was President from March 4, 1841 to April 4, 1841. His Vice President was John Tyler.**

## JOHN TYLER

*10th President.* John Tyler was born on March 29, 1790 in Charles City County, Virginia on Greenway Plantation. His mother died when he was seven; his father was a judge who was later elected Governor of Virginia. In 1802 Tyler entered the high school of the College of William and Mary in Williamsburg. He graduated from the college when he was only 17. He went on to study law and in 1811 he began to practice law in Richmond. That same year he was elected to the Virginia House of Delegates and served for five years. He married Letitia Christian in 1813; they had eight children. In 1816 Tyler was elected to the United States House of Representatives where he served for five years. He went on to serve in the Virginia House of Delegates from 1823 until 1825. He was elected Governor of Virginia in 1825 and served for two years until he was elected to the United States Senate. He served in the Senate for nine years. Tyler was elected Vice President when William Henry Harrison won the presidential election in 1841. A month later he took the oath of office as President. His wife died while he was President and he married Julia Gardiner; he was the first president to wed, while serving in office. Together they had seven children. President Tyler was instrumental in the annexation of Texas in 1845 and he established the United States Weather Bureau. As president he established trade between China and the United States. He left office in 1845 and moved to his plantation, Sherwood Forest in Virginia, where he lived with his family until he died on January 18, 1862. **Tyler was President from 1841-45 and since he was completing Harrison's term, there was no Vice President**

# JAMES K. POLK

*11th President.* James Knox Polk was born on November 2, 1795 in Mecklenburg, Virginia. His family moved to Duck River, Tennessee when he was a child. Polk was too weak to work on the farm so his parents focused on developing his mind. He was taught by tutors and sent to private schools. In 1815 he enrolled in the University of North Carolina. He then went on to study law and he was admitted to the bar. Polk became a popular lawyer and he was elected to the state legislature. On January 1, 1824 he married Sarah Childress; they did not have any children. Polk was elected to the United States legislature in 1825. He served seven terms, until he was elected Governor of Tennessee. Polk served one term as Governor. Then he was nominated by the Democrats to run for President. He won and pledged to serve only one term. During Polk's administration, gold was discovered in 1848 in California and thousands of people migrated west. The Department of the Interior was established. Wisconsin, Iowa and Texas became states. Polk negotiated the Minnesota and Oregon boundaries with Britain, making them federal territories. He fought and won the Mexican War (1846-48) and annexed much of the southwest and California. Polk was known for working long hours, beginning his duties at daybreak and working at his desk until midnight. He was away from the White House only 37 days during his four-year term. He promised voters he would serve only one term as president. He died three months after he left office at his home in Nashville, Tennessee on June 15, 1849. **Polk was President from 1845-49 and the Vice President was George M. Dallas.**

# ZACHARY TAYLOR

*12th President.* Zachary Taylor was born November 24, 1784 in Barbour, Virginia. His father was a Lieutenant Colonel in the Revolutionary War. His only formal education was at a small schoolhouse. His parents supplemented his education by teaching him at home. He worked on his family's plantation until he left home in 1808 to join the 7th Infantry Regiment. He married Margaret Mackall South in 1810; they had six children, two daughters died in childhood. Taylor fought in the War of 1812 rising in rank to major by 1816 in the 3rd Infantry Regiment. In 1832 Taylor fought in the Black Hawk War to drive the Sac Indians out of Illinois. In 1837 he received an honorary commission as brigadier general after he defeated the Seminole Indians in Florida during the Second Seminole War. He was not able to defeat the Indians in 1840; he was relieved of his command and assigned to fight the Indians in the Southwest. He fought on the Texas-Louisiana border; his army defeated the Mexicans at Palo Alto. His final victory was in the battle of Buena Vista where his troops were outnumbered 4-1. He was promoted to major general. The Whig Party nominated Zachary Taylor for President in 1848 and he won. Taylor was a soldier most of his life; he never held political office until he was elected president. He was inaugurated President, March 1849. As president he tried to use the army to prevent states from withdrawing from the United States. He was President for only one year. On July 4th, he participated in the ceremonies laying the cornerstone of the Washington monument. He had a stomach ailment after eating that day and he died July 9, 1850. **Taylor was President from 1849-50 and the Vice President was Millard Fillmore.**

## MILLARD FILLMORE

*13<sup>th</sup> President.* Millard Fillmore was born January 7, 1800 in Locke, New York. He spent most of his early life on a farm and attended a local school. He was eager to improve his education and jumped at the chance to study law with County Judge Walter Wood as an apprentice when he was 19. In 1823 Fillmore passed the bar exam and began his law practice in East Aurora, New York. He married Abigail Powers and they had two children. The family moved to Buffalo where Fillmore was a very successful lawyer. In 1828 he was elected to the state legislature. In 1832 he was elected to the United States House of Representatives where he served for ten years. In 1842, he ran for Governor of New York and lost. Fillmore was elected Vice President in 1848 and was sworn in as President July 10, 1850 when Zachary Taylor died unexpectedly. During his administration the first practical fire engine was developed in Ohio. There was a lot of tension between the North and the South over slavery.

Many slaves were fleeing to the north. He addressed the slavery issue through the Compromise of 1850 and signed the Fugitive Slave Law. Fillmore tried to prevent the Civil War by urging the northern and southern states to agree on a settlement. He was not nominated for a second term because neither expansionists nor slaveholders were pleased with his policies. He returned to Buffalo, New York; that same year his wife died. Fillmore ran again for President in 1856 but was unsuccessful. He remarried and lived in Buffalo participating in many civic activities in his community until his death on March 8, 1874. **Fillmore was President from 1850-53 and since he was completing Taylor's term, there was no Vice President.**

## FRANKLIN PIERCE

*14<sup>th</sup> President.* Franklin Pierce was born in a log cabin on November 23,1804 in Hillsborough County, New Hampshire. He attended a local school. His father was a general in the Revolutionary War and served two terms as Governor. In 1820 Pierce enrolled in Bowdoin College in Brunswick, Maine, where he met a life long friend, Nathaniel Hawthorne. He went on to study law and was admitted to the bar in 1827. Pierce was elected to the state legislature where he served four years. He married Jane Means Appleton, they had three children, two died in childhood, only Benjamin survived. Pierce was elected to two terms in Congress and then to the United States Senate in 1832. He only served four years; he resigned his post because his wife did not like life in Washington D.C. They returned to Concord, New Hampshire where he practiced law. In 1847 Pierce enlisted as a private in the Concord Light Infantry in the Mexican War; he rose to brigadier general of volunteers commanding 2,500 men in Mexico. He could no longer fight after he suffered a leg wound from a fall from his horse. Pierce returned to practice law in Concord. He was nominated by the Democrats to run for President and won the election easily. On January 6, the Pierces were in a train wreck that killed their son Benjamin who was 11 years old. Mrs. Pierce who was brokenhearted lived in seclusion in the White House the entire term. During his presidency, Pierce bought parts of Arizona and New Mexico from Mexico. The Pierces toured Europe after he left office and returned to live in Concord, New Hampshire where he died on October 8, 1869. **Pierce was President from 1853-57 and the Vice President was William R. King, he died before their term even started.**

## JAMES BUCHANAN

15<sup>th</sup> *President.* James Buchanan was born on April 23, 1791 in a log cabin in Cove Gap, Pennsylvania. He was the oldest of nine children. They went to school in Mercersburg, where his father owned a general store. He attended Dickinson College in Carlisle, Pennsylvania, and law school in Lancaster. He was a successful lawyer who interrupted his career to join a volunteer cavalry company to fight in the War of 1812. Buchanan returned home from the war and won a seat in the legislature, serving two terms. He returned to his law practice in Lancaster. He ran for Congress and served ten years. Andrew Jackson asked him to serve as minister to Russia; he negotiated the first trade agreement between Russia and the United States. Buchanan was elected to the Senate in 1835 where he served ten years. President Polk appointed Buchanan Secretary of State. He helped to arrange the Treaty of Guadalupe Hidalgo with Mexico in 1848, by which the United States purchased the region extending west from Texas to the Pacific Ocean. He wrote the Oregon Treaty of 1846 that settled the Northwestern boundary between Canada and the United States. Buchanan ran for President in 1852 and lost. He served as minister to Great Britain. Buchanan ran for President as a Democrat and won. He never married, so his niece Harriet Lane performed the duties of First Lady. Buchanan ran for a second term and was defeated by Lincoln. Before he left office, seven states seceded from the Union. He returned to his home in Lancaster, Pennsylvania, where he lived until he died June 1, 1868. **Buchanan was President from 1857-61 and the Vice President was John C. Breckenridge.**

## ABRAHAM LINCOLN

16<sup>th</sup> *President.* Abraham Lincoln was born on February 12, 1809, in a log cabin in Hardin County, Kentucky. His parents were uneducated pioneers. His father, Thomas Lincoln, believed that there were better opportunities elsewhere, so the family migrated 100 miles to Indiana. Lincoln helped his father, who was a farmer. His mother died when he was nine and his father remarried. He attended school and loved to read. He was a master of the English language by reading every book he could hold. He practiced law in Springfield, Illinois and he was very popular in the court circuit. He married Mary Todd in 1842 and they had four boys. Edward died when he was four. Lincoln was elected to the United States House of Representatives. He ran for the Senate and lost. He was elected President in 1860 and guided the nation through the Civil War. It was his aim to preserve the union of the states. The Emancipation Proclamation was one of the most important features of his presidency. It did not free the slaves, but it gave all Americans the same rights under the Constitution. The Gettysburg Address was another important document. More than 60,000 soldiers died in a three-day battle in Gettysburg, Pennsylvania; he tried to bring the nation together in their grief. Their son William died in the White House when he was 11. Lincoln was elected to a second term in 1864 and the Civil War ended. The peace treaty was signed on April 11, 1865. Three days later, Lincoln was shot in the head by John Wilkes Booth of Virginia. He died from that gunshot wound April 15, 1865, in the White House. **Lincoln was President from 1861-65 and the Vice Presidents were Hannibal Hamlin and Andrew Johnson.**

## ANDREW JOHNSON

*17th President.* Andrew Johnson was born in Raleigh, North Carolina on December 29, 1808. His father died when he was three, so his mother and brother worked to support themselves. He did not go to school and at 17 he was sent to apprentice with a tailor, where he learned to read. In 1826 when he was 18, his family moved to Greenville, Tennessee. He married Eliza McCardle a year later; she taught him how to write. He opened his own tailor shop, where young men in the town frequently stopped by to debate politics and public affairs. He was elected mayor of Greenville in 1830 and served three years. Johnson was elected to the Tennessee legislature for two terms: from 1835-37 and 1839-43. He served in the House of Representatives for ten years until he was elected Governor in 1853. After serving one term he was voted into office as a U.S. senator until he was elected the Military Governor of Tennessee during the Civil War. In 1864 he was nominated as the Vice President from the Republican Party and was inaugurated Vice President on March 4, 1865; he took office on April 15, as President after Lincoln was assassinated. In 1868 he was impeached by the House of Representatives, accused of breaking the law by dismissing the Secretary of War, Edwin Stanton. He was acquitted in the impeachment trial in 1869. His main accomplishment as president was the purchase of Alaska from Russia. He finished his term as President and returned to Tennessee in March, 1869. He was elected to the Senate in 1874 and died of a stroke a year later, July 31, 1875. **Johnson was President, from 1865-69 and since he was completing Lincoln's term, there was no Vice President.**

## ULYSSES S. GRANT

*18th President.* Ulysses Simpson Grant was born on April 27, 1822 in Point Pleasant, Ohio. He was born to a pioneer family and he was agile with horses. He attended schools in Georgetown, Ohio. In 1839 he received an appointment to West Point Academy, he graduated as a first lieutenant, but he did not like the Army and wanted to join the cavalry but there were no openings. He fought in the Mexican-American War in 1846 until 1848 when the war ended. He married Julia Dent and they had two children. In 1854 he resigned from the Army. He tried farming and real estate and failed. He became a partner in a family leather business in Galena, Illinois. He returned to join the military when the Civil War broke out in 1861 as colonel of the 21$^{st}$, Illinois Volunteer Regiment. He captured Vicksburg, Mississippi in 1863 giving the Union control of the Mississippi River. Lincoln promoted him to lieutenant general and commander of the Union armies. Grant accepted Lee's surrender April 9, 1865 in Appomattox, Virginia. The Congress appointed Grant full General– the first man to reach this rank since George Washington. He served briefly as secretary of war. Grant was a popular leader after the Civil War. He was elected President in 1869 and served two terms. During his administration the 15$^{th}$ Amendment was ratified giving Negroes the right to vote. The telephone was invented by Alexander Graham Bell. Grant went home to Mount McGregor, New York when he left the White House to write his memoirs. He died on July 23, 1885, one week after he completed his memoirs. **Grant was President, from 1869-77 and the Vice Presidents were Schuyler Colfax and Henry Wilson.**

# RUTHERFORD B. HAYES

*19th President.* Rutherford Birchard Hayes was born in October 4, 1822 in Delaware, Ohio. His father died when he was born. He was educated at home and attended private schools. In 1838 he enrolled in Kenyon College in Gambier, Ohio. Hayes graduated in 1842 and went on to Harvard Law School. He graduated in 1845 and was admitted to the Ohio bar. He married Lucy Webb and they had eight children. In 1857 he was elected City Solicitor of Cincinnati. When the Civil War started he joined the Union Army. He was elected to Congress in 1864 but refused to leave the battlefield. Hayes advanced to the rank of brevetted major general. He was reelected to Congress in 1866 and served only one year because he was elected Governor of Ohio in 1867. He remained in office until 1871 when his term ended. He returned to Spiegel Grove where he practiced law and worked to develop public libraries. He ran again for Governor of Ohio in 1876 and won. He was nominated as the Republican candidate for President against Samuel J. Tilden. Hayes won in a close election that was disputed for four months and ultimately decided by an electoral commission. During his administration Hayes removed all federal troops from the South ending Reconstruction—the period after the Civil War during which the southern states were reorganized and made part of the Union once again. He tried to promote civil service reform. Hayes did not want to serve a second term and retired to his farm in Spiegel Grove, Ohio where he devoted his time to his philanthropic activities until he died January 17, 1893. **Hayes was President from 1877-81 and the Vice President was William A. Wheeler.**

# JAMES A. GARFIELD

*20th President.* James Abram Garfield was born in Orange, Ohio on November 19, 1831. He was the last president to be born in a log cabin. His father died when he was two; he had three brothers and sisters. Since they had to work to help support their family, they could only attend school three months out of the year. He loved to read. At the age of 16 Garfield left home and joined the Navy in Cleveland. He had to return home when he became sick with malaria. He attended Williams College in Massachusetts. He graduated and became a teacher at Hiram College where he was once a student. A year later he became President of the College. He married Lucretia Rudolph in 1858; they had five children He was elected to the Ohio Senate in 1859 where he served for two years. Garfield volunteered for the Union Army in 1861. He fought bravely in the Civil War battles at Shiloh and Chickamauga. He resigned in 1863 with the rank of major general, when President Lincoln asked him to serve in Congress. In December 1863, at the age of 32, he entered the House of Representatives. He served as a legislator for 17 years and he became minority leader. He was nominated by the Republican Party and was elected President in 1881. Garfield was the first President to use a telephone. During his administration the great railroad expansion reached Texas. James Garfield was assassinated on July 2nd, while waiting for a train, only a few months after he took office. He died two months later in Elbron, New Jersey on September 19, 1881. **Garfield was President from March 4, 1881-September 17, 1881 and the Vice President was Chester A. Arthur.**

# CHESTER A. ARTHUR

21$^{st}$ President. Chester Alan Arthur was born in Fairfield, Vermont on October 5, 1830. His father was a teacher and minister. Arthur entered Union College in Schenectady, New York when he was 15. He taught school to pay for his education and graduated with honors in 1848. He then went on to study law, while continuing to teach to support himself, until 1853 when he went to New York City to start his career as a lawyer. He took on two very controversial and groundbreaking cases. His law firm gained freedom for eight runaway slaves. He also represented Lizzie Jennings in a segregation case. She was told she was not allowed to ride on a New York City streetcar because she was black; she was awarded $500 in damages. The court decision stated that Negroes had the same right to ride on New York streetcars as anyone else. Chester Arthur married Ellen Lewis Herndon in 1859. During the Civil War, Arthur was appointed quartermaster general of New York State, supplying food, guns and tents to the soldiers. After that he became collector of customs for the port of New York. He held that job for seven years until he was elected Vice President. When James Garfield was assassinated only six months after he was sworn in as President, Chester Arthur became President on September 19, 1881. During his administration he passed the Pendleton Act, which helped to eliminate the corruption of political favors and he established the Civil Service Agency. After serving as president, he returned to New York and practice law. A year later Chester Arthur became ill and died at his home on November 18, 1886. **Arthur was President from 1881-85 and since he was completing the term of James Garfield, there was no Vice President.**

# GROVER CLEVELAND

22$^{nd}$ and 24$^{th}$ President. ( Stephen) Grover Cleveland was born in Caldwell, New Jersey on March 18, 1837. His family moved to Fayetteville, New York where he was educated in a one-room schoolhouse. In 1850 they moved to Clinton, New York where he attended the Liberal Institute. When he was 18 he visited an uncle in Buffalo, New York who asked for his help on his farm, in return for getting him a job in a law office. Four years later, Cleveland was admitted to the bar. In 1863 he became assistant district attorney of Erie County, New York for two years. His record of honesty and fairness led to his election as sheriff of Erie County; a job he held for two years. In 1882 Cleveland was elected mayor of Buffalo. He was in office one year, when the Democrats nominated him for governor of New York and he won. Two years later he was nominated for President, and won. Grover Cleveland married Frances Folsom, June 2, 1886 in a White House ceremony. He lost the 1888 presidential election to Benjamin Harrison. He returned to New York where he practiced law. He was nominated for President again by the Democrats and won. Cleveland was inaugurated as the 24$^{th}$ President in 1893. He served one term, he was not nominated by his party for a second term because he did not support the expansion of the United States into Hawaii and Cuba. His party turned to William Jennings Bryan who lost to William McKinley. Cleveland returned to Princeton, New Jersey where he lived until he died on June 24, 1908. **Cleveland was President from 1885-89 and the Vice President was Thomas A. Hendricks. He served as President again from 1893-97 and the Vice President was Adlai E. Stevenson.**

# BENJAMIN HARRISON

*23rd President.* Benjamin Harrison was born August 20, 1833 in North Bend, Ohio, the grandson of President William Henry Harrison. He attended school in a log cabin and at the age of 14 he entered the Farmer's College near Cincinnati. Three years later he transferred to Miami University at Oxford, Ohio. Harrison went on to study law and he was admitted to the bar. In 1893 Harrison married Caroline Scott; they had two children. He started a law practice in Indianapolis, Indiana. Harrison joined the Union Army in 1862 during the Civil War and earned the position of general. When the war ended he returned to his law practice. In 1876 he ran unsuccessfully for Governor of Indiana. In 1881 Harrison was elected to the Senate, he served the six-year term. He was elected President in 1889. His wife died two weeks before the election. During his administration Montana, Idaho, Washington, North and South Dakota and Wyoming were admitted into the Union. The Sherman Anti-Trust Act was passed in 1890, which was designed to regulate monopolies and prices. American women were first allowed to vote in Wyoming in 1890. The first gasoline-powered automobile was built in 1893 by the Duryea brothers. Basketball was invented by James Naismith in 1891 in Springfield, Massachusetts. He fortified the Navy and established trade policies over seas. Harrison was defeated in the 1892 presidential election. After leaving office he returned to his home in Indianapolis. He married again in 1896 to Mary Scott Lord Dimmick; they had one child. He worked at his law practice in Indianapolis until he died March 13, 1901. **Harrison was President from 1889-93 and the Vice President was Levi P. Morton.**

# WILLIAM McKINLEY

*25th President.* William McKinley was born in Niles, Ohio on January 29, 1843. He attended school in Poland, Ohio and then went to Allegheny College in Meadville, Pennsylvania. At the age of 17 he left college before he graduated and started teaching in a rural school. The Civil War broke out in 1861. He enlisted as a private in the 23rd Ohio Volunteer Regiment. He was promoted to captain and served under Rutherford B. Hayes. When the Civil War ended in 1865 he returned to Ohio to study law. He opened a law office in 1867 and two years later he was elected county solicitor. He married Ida Saxton in 1871. They had two daughters who died at an early age. His wife suffered from epilepsy and needed special attention. In 1876 McKinley was elected to the House of Representatives where he served for 17 years. In 1892 he was elected Governor of Ohio. He served one term and was nominated by the Republican Party to run for President. He won and he was a popular president. He guided the country through the Spanish-American War that lasted 100 days. As a result of the war, Cuba gained its independence from Spain. He became known for the open door policy with China, which initiated the equality of trade with China and respect for its territorial integrity. McKinley was reelected to a second term but he was assassinated only six months after he was sworn in. He died on September 14, 1901, eight days after being shot at point blank range, when he was attending a reception in Buffalo, New York. He is buried in Canton, Ohio. **McKinley was President from 1897-1901 and the Vice Presidents were Garret A. Hobart and Theodore Roosevelt.**

## THEODORE ROOSEVELT

26th *President.* Theodore Roosevelt was born on October 27, 1858 in New York City. He graduated from Harvard College. In 1880 he married Alice Hathaway Lee. He enrolled in Columbia University to study law. He was elected to the New York State Assembly and abandoned his studies. In his third term in 1884, Roosevelt's mother died, a few hours later his wife who had given birth to a baby girl also died. He served to the end of his term, and moved to the Dakota Territory to his ranch on the Little Missouri River. He married Edith Carow; they had five children. He accepted an appointment to the United States Civil Service Commission, serving for six years until he was appointed President of the New York City board of police commissioners. He resigned from the Police Board to become assistant Secretary of the Navy. A year later during the Spanish-American War, he organized and then commanded the first United States Volunteer Cavalry Regiment. In 1899 he was elected Governor of New York. Roosevelt was inaugurated Vice President of the United States, March 4, and sworn in as President upon the death of President William McKinley on September 14, 1901. Roosevelt received the Nobel Peace Prize and he served two terms. He traveled to Africa after he left the White House, staying there a year and returned to New York City to organize the Bull Moose Party to run for President in 1912. He lost to Woodrow Wilson. He wrote his autobiography and then traveled to South America in 1913. Roosevelt died in his sleep at his home in Sycamore Hill, New York, on January 6, 1919. **Roosevelt was President from 1901-09 and the Vice President was Charles W. Fairbanks.**

## WILLIAM HOWARD TAFT

27th *President.* William Howard Taft was born in Cincinnati, Ohio on September 15, 1857. His father was a judge and his son William was an excellent student. He entered Yale College in 1874 and graduated four years later. He returned to Cincinnati and became a successful lawyer. In 1881 he was appointed assistant prosecutor in a county court. He went on to become an official in the Bureau of the Internal Revenue Service. He did not like that job and resigned. He married Helen Herron in 1886; they had three children. In 1887 he was named a judge on the Ohio Superior Court. In 1890, President Benjamin Harrison offered Taft the post of Solicitor General of the United States, the second largest job of the Department of Justice. In 1892 he resigned to become a federal circuit judge. President William McKinley picked Taft to become head of a special commission to oversee the government of the Philippine Islands. In 1904 President Roosevelt appointed Taft Secretary of War. Taft was nominated for President by the Republican Party and won. He helped establish the 16th Amendment to the Constitution, which allows Congress to collect income tax. He served one term. In the next election he was opposed by Roosevelt and Woodrow Wilson. He retired to Yale University where he was a professor of constitutional law until he was appointed Chief Justice of the United States by President Harding in 1921. His administrative work as a Supreme Court justice is considered his greatest contribution to public service. He retired in 1930 due to poor health and died the same year on March 8 in Washington D.C. **Taft was President from 1909-13 and the Vice President was James S. Sherman.**

## WOODROW WILSON

28th *President.* (Thomas) Woodrow Wilson was born in Staunton, Virginia, on December 28, 1856. He attended private school in Georgia and South Carolina. He enrolled in Davidson College in North Carolina and then Princeton University in New Jersey. He studied law at the University of Virginia and went on to Johns Hopkins University in Baltimore, where he graduated with a PhD in philosophy in 1886. He married Ellen Axson in 1885 and they had three daughters. He taught at Bryn Mawr College in Pennsylvania and at Wesleyan University in Connecticut. He later taught constitutional law at Princeton University and became the president of the University. In 1911 he was elected governor of New Jersey. He was elected President in 1913 during World War I. During his presidency 1,000,000 automobiles were produced. As President, Wilson reduced tariffs and created an income tax. The United States became involved in World War I when the Germans ambushed the *Lusitania*. Wilson was awarded the Nobel Peace Prize in 1919. He tried to introduce the concept of the League of Nations when he went to Paris to present the 14 Points of Peace and to help write the Versailles Treaty. The armistice was signed on November 11, 1918. Wilson had support for the League of Nations abroad, but when he proposed the idea at home, it was defeated in the Senate. Women were given the right to vote when the 19th Amendment was added to the Constitution in 1920. He left office in 1921. He died of a stroke while on a speaking tour in Washington, D.C. to promote the League of Nations, on February 3, 1924. **Wilson was President from 1913-21 and the Vice President was Thomas R. Marshall.**

## WARREN G. HARDING

29th *President.* Warren Gamaliel Harding was born in Corsica, Ohio on November 2, 1865. He helped his father on the farm and attended school. He was the oldest of eight children; his father was a doctor. When he was 14, Harding enrolled in Ohio Central College in Iberia. He graduated and took a job as a schoolteacher but quit after one year. He moved to Marion, Ohio and studied law, but he didn't like it. He borrowed money from his father, and with two friends bought the newspaper, the Marion *Star*. His partners left the business and he ran it by himself. He married a widow, Florence Kling De Wolfe in 1891 who helped him make the newspaper successful. In 1899 he was nominated by the Republicans to the State Senate and won; he served four years. In 1903 he was elected Lieutenant Governor of Ohio and served for three years. He returned to Marion to work on the *Star*. In 1910 he ran for governor and lost. In 1914 he was elected to the United States Senate. He served a full term and he was sworn in as President in 1921. During his administration the first nonstop transcontinental airplane flight was made and the first commercial radio broadcast took place. During his presidency Harding established a budget system for the federal government but his administration was marred by the Tea Pot Dome scandal: federal oil reserves were illegally rented to private businesses. In June 1923, Harding and his wife took a trip across the country. He fell ill from food poisoning when he arrived in San Francisco after leaving Alaska. He developed pneumonia, and died suddenly on August 2, 1923. **Harding was President from 1921-23 and the Vice President was Calvin Coolidge.**

## CALVIN COOLIDGE

*30th President.* Calvin Coolidge was born on July 4, 1872 in Plymouth Notch, Vermont. He went to school in a one-room schoolhouse. He was raised on a farm and enrolled in Black River Academy in Ludlow, Vermont when he was 13. He was admitted to Amherst College in Massachusetts and after graduation in 1895 he decided to become a lawyer. He took a job in a law office in Northampton, Massachusetts. While working, he studied for the bar exam and was admitted to the bar in 1897. He opened his own law office in the same town. In 1898 he was elected city councilman. He married Grace Goodhue in 1905; they had two sons. In 1907 Coolidge was elected to the Massachusetts legislature. Three years later he was voted mayor of Northampton. In 1912 he became a Massachusetts State senator. He was elected Lieutenant Governor of Massachusetts in 1916. Coolidge was elected governor in 1919. He served one year. He was elected Vice President of the United States in 1920. In 1923 he became President of the United States when President Warren Harding died on August 3. The next year he won the presidential election and served the full term. The 18th Amendment, Prohibition, was enforced during his presidency. During his term Coolidge worked to lower the national debt, limit government spending and lower taxes. Charles Lindbergh was the first man to fly alone nonstop across the Atlantic Ocean. Coolidge did not want to run for a second term. He retired to Northampton where he wrote his biography and lived a quiet life until he died of a heart attack on January 5, 1933. **Coolidge was President from 1923-29 and the Vice President was Charles G. Dawes.**

## HERBERT C. HOOVER

*31st President.* Herbert Clark Hoover was born on August 10, 1874, in West Branch, Iowa. His father died of typhoid fever when he was six and his mother died of pneumonia when he was nine. He moved to Newberg, Oregon to live with his uncle, Dr. Henry Minthorn, where he attended a Quaker academy. When he was 16 he enrolled in Leland Stanford, a new university in Palo Alto, California. He graduated in 1895 and worked in the goldfields of Nevada. In 1927 a British company hired Hoover to manage its gold mines in Australia where he lived for two years. He returned home and married Lou Henry in 1899. During the next 15 years he worked on engineering projects in Europe, India, South Africa, and Egypt. He was rich enough to retire before he was 40 years old. Hoover was in London as Chairman of the American Relief Committee when World War I broke out. He also served on the Commission for Relief in Belgium. President Warren G. Harding appointed Hoover Secretary of Commerce at the end of World War I. Coolidge decided not to run again for President in 1928, so Hoover's opponent in the presidential election was New York Governor, Alfred E. Smith. Hoover won in a landslide victory. As president he worked to improve the standards of radio broadcasting, aviation and housing. During his administration the stock market crashed in 1929 leading to the Great Depression. He established a few programs to combat the crises, but he opposed aid through federal bureaucracy, so he did not provide enough relief and he was defeated in the 1932 election. He died on October 20, 1964 in New York City at the age of 90. **Hoover was President from 1929-33 and the Vice President was Charles Curtis.**

# FRANKLIN D. ROOSEVELT

32nd President. Franklin Delano Roosevelt was born on January 30, 1882 in Hyde Park, New York. He was tutored by a governess and he took frequent trips to Europe. He graduated in 1904 from Harvard University and attended Columbia University Law School in New York. He married Eleanor Roosevelt, a distant cousin, in 1905; together they had six children. He passed the bar and joined a law firm on Wall Street. He ran for the New York Senate and won when he was 28 years old. President Woodrow Wilson appointed Roosevelt assistant Secretary of the Navy three years later in 1913. Roosevelt traveled to Canada where he contracted polio, leaving him paralyzed from the waist down for the rest of his life. In 1929 he ran for Governor of New York and won. He served one term; he was nominated by the Democratic Party to run for President. Roosevelt won in a landslide victory. He helped the nation through its economic depression by creating the Public Works Administration. In 1937 he was elected to a second term. By then the economy had reached the prosperity levels of the 1920s. Roosevelt was elected to a third term in 1941. On December 7 of that year, the United States Naval fleet was attacked by the Japanese Air Force. The United States declared war on Japan. On December 8, Roosevelt declared war with Italy and on December 11, war with Germany. The United States was embroiled in World War II when Roosevelt was elected to his fourth term as President. He died in office before the end of his first year on April 12, 1945. **Roosevelt was President from 1933-45 and the Vice Presidents were John N. Garner, Henry A. Wallace and Harry S Truman.**

# HARRY S TRUMAN

33rd President. Harry S Truman was born in Lamar, Missouri on May 8, 1884. His father lost all of their money in the family business so Truman had to forgo college. He worked on the family farm for 10 years to help his family pay off their debts. During World War I, he joined the Missouri National Guard, commanding a field artillery battery. He married Bess Wallace in 1919; they had one daughter. Truman opened a men's clothing store in the post-war depression. He lost his life's savings and was left $20,000 in debt. He spent 15 years paying it off. He ran for County Judge and won. Truman had little knowledge about law so he attended the Kansas City School of Law in 1928. He served as a judge of the Jackson County Court until 1935 when he was elected to the United States Senate. He was elected to two terms as Senator of Missouri, but left the office to join Franklin D. Roosevelt's campaign for President. He was inaugurated Vice President of the United States, January 20, 1945 and became President four months later upon the death of Franklin D. Roosevelt, on April 12. Truman adopted Roosevelt's programs, renaming them the "Fair Deal." He worked hard for equal rights for all citizens of the United States. He was the only president to use the atomic bomb, when the United States attacked Hiroshima and Nagasaki, Japan on September 2, 1945, causing Japan to surrender and end World War II. Truman was elected to a second term but decided not to run for office in 1953. He returned to his home in Independence, Missouri where he devoted his time to the Truman Library. He died on December 26, 1972. **Truman was President from 1945-53 and the Vice President was Alben W. Barkley.**

## DWIGHT D. EISENHOWER

*34th President.* Dwight David Eisenhower was born on October 14, 1890 in Denison, Texas. His family moved to Abilene, Kansas where his father bought a house on a 10-acre farm. He worked on the farm with his four brothers. Everyone called him "Ike". In high school he worked nights at the creamery where he studied his lessons. He was accepted into West Point and graduated in 1915, commissioned as a second lieutenant. A year later he married Mamie Geneva Doud. General Douglas MacArthur asked Eisenhower to assist him in planning the defense of the Philippines. In 1942 Eisenhower became the commanding General of the American Forces in the European theater and the Commander in Chief of the Allied forces in North Africa, commanding the British and American troops. A year later he was promoted to full (4-Star) general. On June 6, 1944, also known as D-Day, he was promoted to General of the Army. May 7, 1945 the German Army surrendered. For the next three years Eisenhower was Chief of Staff of the United States Army until he was named the President of Columbia University. In 1951, he was named Commander of NATO Forces in Europe. Eisenhower was nominated by the Republicans to run for President and won; he served two terms. While President, he suffered a severe heart attack in 1955 and another stroke. During his administration he was engaged in foreign policy, ending the Korean War, and negotiating with China, Cuba and Russia. He enforced the Supreme Court's decision to integrate schools. Eisenhower died on March 28, 1969 at Walter Reed Hospital in Washington D. C. **Eisenhower was President from 1953-61 and the Vice President was Richard M. Nixon.**

## JOHN F. KENNEDY

*35th President.* John Fitzgerald Kennedy was born on May 29, 1917 in Brookline, Massachusetts; the second of nine children. He attended private schools and enrolled in Princeton University. The summer of his freshman year he traveled to London where he fell ill with jaundice. It took two years for him to fully recover. He resumed his studies at Harvard and graduated with honors in 1940. When the Japanese attacked Pearl Harbor, Kennedy signed up with the Navy and became a Naval Commander. He had to leave the Navy in 1944 after contracting malaria. He was elected to Congress in 1946 in a Boston district; and re-elected twice. In 1953 he was elected Senator of Massachusetts defeating Henry Cabot Lodge. That same year he married Jacqueline Bouvier; they had three children, Patrick Bouvier died a few days after he was born. Kennedy was sworn in as President in 1960. His administration was marked by the invasion of the Bay of Pigs in Cuba, in which anti-Castro Cubans invaded Cuba but failed to complete their mission, causing a stand off. Kennedy succeeded in forcing the Soviet Union to remove missiles from Cuba and in keeping troops in Berlin to prevent the spread of Communism. Kennedy supported the Civil Rights movement led by Martin Luther King. He advocated improved medical care for the elderly and space exploration. Kennedy initiated the Peace Corps, an organization of volunteers who carry education and skills to underdeveloped countries. Kennedy was assassinated while traveling in a motorcade through Dallas, Texas on November 22, 1963. **Kennedy was President from 1961-63 and the Vice President was Lyndon B. Johnson.**

## LYNDON B. JOHNSON

*36<sup>th</sup> President.* Lyndon Baines Johnson was born in Stonewall, Texas on August 27, 1908. He attended public schools and after realizing how hard it was to find a good job without a college education, he enrolled in Southwest Texas State Teachers College. He graduated in 1930. He taught for one year in the Texas schools and left to enter politics. He worked for a Congressman and was then appointed Texas state director of the National Youth Administration. He married Claudia Alta Taylor better known as Lady Bird; they had two daughters. Johnson was elected to the United States House of Representatives in 1937. He joined the Navy when the Japanese attacked Pearl Harbor on December 7, 1941, and fought in the Pacific Theater. He returned from the war in July 1942 when President Roosevelt ordered all members of Congress, in military service to return to their duties. In 1948 he was elected to the Senate and became the Democratic majority leader in 1954. He was elected Vice President when John F. Kennedy won the presidential election in 1959. Johnson took the oath of office 99 minutes after Kennedy was assassinated in Dallas, Texas in 1963. He passed Kennedy's bills on civil rights, poverty and conservation. Johnson ran for President in 1964 and won. During his administration he was known for creating the "Great Society" that promoted equal rights for all and provided health insurance for the elderly. Johnson decided not to run for re-election in 1968 because of the national turmoil of the Vietnam War, which escalated during his administration. He returned to his ranch in Texas where he died on January 22, 1973. **Johnson was President from 1963-69 and the Vice President was Hubert H. Humphrey.**

## RICHARD M. NIXON

*37<sup>th</sup> President.* Richard Milhous Nixon was born on January 9, 1913 in Yorba Linda, California. His family moved to Whittier, California, where he and his five brothers attended public school and worked at his father's store. He enrolled in Whittier College when he was 17. In 1934, Nixon received a scholarship to Duke University Law School in North Carolina. After graduation, he tried to get a job with a law firm in New York, but he was turned down every time and returned to Whittier, California, where he met and married Patricia Ryan. They had two daughters. Nixon joined the Navy in 1942 rising to lieutenant commander by the end of the war. He was elected to Congress in 1947 and served there until he was elected to the United States Senate in 1951. In 1959 he was elected Vice President under Eisenhower. He served eight years as an active leader when Eisenhower was sick. Nixon ran for President in 1960 and lost against Kennedy. Two years later, he ran for Governor of California and lost. He moved to New York to practice law. He was nominated for President by the Republican Party in 1968, and won. Nixon began bringing troops home from Vietnam; in his second term the war ended with the victory of North Vietnam. During his administration the Apollo 11 space flight landed a man on the moon. Nixon rebuilt ties with China, after 21 years of silence. The *Washington Post* began investigating the illegal activities of Nixon and his aides during the 1972 election campaign. In 1974 he faced impeachment and resigned as president. He retired to his home in San Clemente, California where he died on April 22, 1994. **Nixon was President from 1969-74 and the Vice Presidents were Spiro T. Agnew and Gerald R. Ford.**

## GERALD R. FORD

38th *President.* Gerald Rudolph Ford was born on July 14, 1913 in Omaha, Nebraska. Named Leslie Lynch King, Jr. at birth, he was the first and only child. He moved to Grand Rapids, Michigan with his mother when his parents divorced. In 1916 his mother married Gerald Rudolf Ford. The boy's name was not legally changed until 1935. He was a popular student and athlete– he played football in high school and college at the University of Michigan. Ford went on to law school and he was admitted to the bar. He joined the Navy in 1942 to fight in World War II; he was promoted to the rank of lieutenant commander and remained on active duty until 1946. After the war he ran for a seat in Congress and won. He spent 25 years in the United States House of Representatives. Ford married Elizabeth Bloomer Warren in 1948; they had four children. In 1973, after the resignation of Vice President Spiro T. Agnew, President Nixon asked Ford to be the Vice President. A year later, Ford replaced Nixon as President, when Nixon resigned his presidency because of the Watergate scandal. Ford is the only President and Vice President who was not elected to the office. As President, Ford gave Nixon a pardon, "for all offenses against the United States." The act made him unpopular with many people. He successfully controlled inflation during his administration, but there was high unemployment during his term in office. He was successful with his foreign policies– he championed détente, and peace among nations. Ford tried to bring the nation together but failed to be reelected in 1976. He died at his home in Rancho Mirage, California, December 26, 2006. **Ford was President from 1974-77 and the Vice President was Nelson A. Rockefeller.**

## JAMES E. CARTER, JR.

39th *President.* James Earl Carter, Jr. was born on October 1, 1924 in Plains, Georgia. Carter grew up on a peanut farm. He left home to attend the United States Naval Academy at Annapolis, Maryland where he studied nuclear physics, and graduated in 1946. He served in the Navy for seven years and returned home to run the family business. He married Rosalynn Smith, they had four children. Carter served on the school board and educational advisory boards. He was a strong advocate for Civil Rights. In 1962 he was elected to the United States Senate; he served one term. He ran for Governor of Georgia and won. Carter was nominated by the Democratic Party to run for President in 1976, and won. As President he established diplomatic ties with China and helped to write the Camp David Accords; a peace treaty between Egypt and Israel. He helped negotiate the Salt II treaty with the Soviet Union. During his administration Carter was criticized for the poor economy. In 1979, a group of Iranian students took the staff of the United States Embassy, hostage. Efforts to negotiate the release of the 52 hostages in Iran consumed the later half of his term. He was not successful and this was perceived as weakness and made him unpopular. He was defeated in the 1980 election. After his term as President, Carter started the Carter Center to introduce democracy throughout the world. He won the Nobel Peace prize. Carter and his wife Rosalynn live in Plains, Georgia. They have actively promoted humanitarian programs and peace throughout the world since he left the office of President. **Carter was President from 1977-81 and the Vice President was Walter F. Mondale.**

## RONALD W. REAGAN

*40th President.* Ronald Wilson Reagan was born on February 6, 1911 in Tampico, Illinois. He attended public schools and enrolled in Eureka College in Illinois, where he studied economics and sociology. After graduating in 1932 he worked as a radio announcer in Iowa. In 1937 he started his career as an actor, appearing in more than 50 movies during his 27 year career. In 1940 he married Jane Wyman, they had a daughter and adopted a son; their marriage ended in divorce in 1948. Reagan joined the United States Air Force in 1942; he served three years. In 1952 he married actress Nancy Davis; they have a daughter and son. Reagan ran for Governor of California as a Republican in 1967 and won. He was elected President in a landslide victory over Jimmy Carter in 1980. Moments after he was sworn into office the hostages were released in Iran. During his administration he set out to strengthen military defense. He tried to stop inflation and improve business growth by instituting supply-side economics, which called for cutting taxes and government programs, but resulted in high budget deficits. He also promoted Social Security and tax reforms. In 1981 Reagan was wounded in an assassination attempt. During his second term the Berlin Wall came down, uniting East and West Germany who had been divided since World War II. His administration was criticized for the sale of weapons to Iran in exchange for hostages and the use of money to aid rebels in Nicaragua. Ten years before his death, Reagan suffered from Alzheimer's disease. He died in Bel Air, California on June 6, 2004. **Reagan was President from 1981-89 and the Vice President was George H. W. Bush.**

## GEORGE H. W. BUSH

*41st President.* George Herbert Walker Bush was born on June 12, 1924 in Milton, Massachusetts. He attended private schools in Connecticut and Phillips Academy in Andover, Massachusetts. In 1942 he served in the Navy as a pilot during World War II and received the Distinguished Flying Cross after being shot down over the Pacific in 1944. He married Barbara Pierce in 1945. They had six children; one died of leukemia when she was four. In 1948 he graduated from Yale University. He started a development company, which dealt in Texas oil and gas properties. Bush tried running for the Senate and lost. He was elected to Congress in 1966. He tried again to run for Senator of Texas, and lost. He served as the ambassador to the United Nations and head of the Central Intelligence Agency. In 1974, he was appointed by President Ford as the U.S. liaison officer to the People's Republic of China. He served eight years as Vice President when Reagan was elected President in 1980. Bush was elected President in 1988. In 1989, he ordered an invasion of Panama to remove the country's leader, General Manuel Noriega. In 1990, Iraq invaded Kuwait and President Bush led the worldwide forces against Iraq in the Persian Gulf War. During his administration Bush supported democratization in the Soviet Union, which dissolved in 1991, and in Eastern Europe. He raised taxes to combat budget deficits. His popularity diminished in late 1991 due to the economic recession. He lost the election to Bill Clinton. George Bush and his wife Barbara live in Texas. **Bush was President from 1989-93 and the Vice President was J. Danforth Quayle.**

## WILLIAM J. CLINTON

*42<sup>nd</sup> President.* William Jefferson Clinton was born William Jefferson Blythe IV on August 19, 1946, in Hope, Arkansas. His father died in a traffic accident a few months later. His mother wed Roger Clinton; he took the family name in high school. He attended public schools in Arkansas. He moved to Washington D.C. to attend Georgetown University. In 1968, he won a Rhodes Scholarship to Oxford University in London. He received a law degree from Yale University in 1973. Clinton returned to Arkansas and ran for Congress and lost. He married Hillary Rodham; they have one daughter. He taught at the University of Arkansas. In 1976, Clinton was elected Arkansas Attorney General. He ran for Governor of Arkansas in 1978 and won. He lost his bid for a second term, but he regained the office four years later, and served until he won the presidential nomination against incumbent George Bush in 1992. As President, Clinton successfully reduced the national debt. He promoted international trade and persuaded Congress to pass the North American Free Trade Agreement (NAFTA) between the United States, Canada and Mexico. Clinton was a global proponent for an expanded NATO. He was reelected in 1996. He supported use of NATO forces to remove Serbian troops from Kosovo in 1999. He improved relations with Russia and China. During his second term, in 1998 Clinton was the second president impeached by the House of Representatives. He was accused of giving false court testimony. He was tried in the Senate and found not guilty of the charges. Clinton and his wife Hillary live in New York, where she is a Senator. **Clinton was President from 1993-2001 and the Vice President was Albert Gore, Jr.**

## GEORGE W. BUSH

*43<sup>rd</sup> President.* George Walker Bush was born on July 6, 1946 in New Haven, Connecticut the son of the 41<sup>st</sup> President, George H.W. Bush. He grew up in Houston, Texas where he attended private schools. He received a bachelor's degree from Yale University in 1968, and then served as an F-102 fighter pilot in the Texas Air National Guard. He enrolled in Harvard Business School in 1975 and received a Master of Business Administration. He married Laura Welch; they have twin daughters. He bought the Texas Rangers baseball franchise in 1989 by forming a partnership with a group of investors. He served as general manager and partner of the team, until he was elected Governor of Texas in 1994. Bush was the first Governor of Texas to be elected to consecutive four-year terms when he was re-elected in 1998. Since he was sworn in as president in 2001, President Bush has signed into law initiatives to improve public schools by raising standards, requiring accountability, and strengthening local control. He has signed tax relief that lowered the income tax rate. He has increased pay and benefits for America's military. After the attacks on the World Trade Center, Bush created the Office of Homeland Security to protect Americans against terrorism by making citizens better informed of suspected attacks and more vigilant. American troops have liberated Afghanistan from the Taliban regime. An American-led coalition of a few allied countries invaded Iraq in March 2003 to overthrow Saddam Hussein. The United States is helping Iraq establish a democratic form of government under new leadership. **Bush became President in 2001 and the Vice President is Richard B. Cheney.**

# The Fifty United States

Britain's American colonies broke with the mother country in 1776 and were recognized as the new nation of the United States of America following the Treaty of Paris in 1783. During the 19th and 20th centuries, 37 new states were added to the original 13 as the nation expanded across the North American continent and acquired a number of overseas possessions. The two most traumatic experiences in the nation's history were the Civil War (1861-65) and the great Depression of the 1930s. Buoyed by victories in World Wars I and II and the end of the Cold War in 1991, the US remains the world's most powerful nation-state. The economy is marked by steady growth, low unemployment and inflation, and rapid advances in technology.

*From the CIA Factbook, 2003*

**Size:** 3,716,829 square miles          **Population:** 290,342,554

**Motto** "In God We Trust", adopted July 30, 1956. The original motto adopted September 9, 1776, was:
"E Pluribus Unum" (Out of many, one).

**The Great Seal** The Great Seal of the United States shows an American bald eagle with a ribbon in its mouth bearing the Latin words 'e pluribus unum". In its talons are the arrows of war and an olive branch of peace. On the back of the Great Seal is an unfinished pyramid with an eye (the eye of Providence) above it. The seal was approved by Congress on June 20, 1782.

**Bird** Eagle, adopted June 20, 1782

**Song** "The Star Spangled Banner," written by Francis Scott Key in 1814, was adopted by Congress as the National anthem in 1931.

**Flower** Rose, chosen by President Ronald Reagan when he was in office.

# Washington, DC  *The Nation's Capital*

Washington, DC is the capital of the United States. It became the capital of the United States in 1800, when the federal government moved from Philadelphia. The city was named after George Washington. It was built to be the legislative, administrative, and judicial center of the United States.

There are 715 libraries—only 118 fewer than New York City. The Residence Bill of July 16, 1790, established the federal district which was first called the Territory of Columbia and the federal city, the City of Washington. The name changed to the District of Columbia in 1793. The first act passed by the District's first legislative assembly on August 3, 1871, created the corporate seal of the District of Columbia.

The present system of government (since 1975) provides for an elected mayor and city council, but reserves for Congress veto power over the budget and legislation and direct control over most of the federal buildings and monuments. The Twenty-Third Amendment (1961) to the Constitution gave inhabitants the right to vote in presidential elections.

**Size**  61 square miles
**Population**  572,059
**Great Seal**  Justice, who is a woman, is shown on the seal hanging a wreath on a statue of George Washington.
**Motto**  Justia Omnibus, Justice for all
**Flower**  American beauty rose
**Bird**  Woodthrush
**Tree**  Scarlet Oak

## Alabama (AL)

*The Yellowhammer State*

*Alabama* comes from an Indian word for "tribal town."

| | |
|---|---|
| **Capital** | Montgomery |
| **Size** | 52,419 square miles |
| **Population** | 4,486,508 |
| **Statehood** | December 14, 1819; 22nd State |
| **Motto** | "We Dare Defend Our Rights" |
| **Tree** | Southern Pine |
| **Bird** | Yellowhammer |
| **Flower** | Camellia |
| **Song** | "Alabama," by Julia S. Tutwiler Music by Edna Goeckel Gussen |

---

## Alaska (AK)

*The Last Frontier*

*Alaska* comes from alakshak, the Eskimo word meaning "peninsula" or "land that is an island."

| | |
|---|---|
| **Capital** | Juneau |
| **Size** | 663,267 square miles |
| **Population** | 643,786 |
| **Statehood** | January 3, 1959, 49th State |
| **Motto** | "North to the Future" |
| **Tree** | Sitka Spruce |
| **Bird** | Willow Ptarmigan |
| **Flower** | Forget-Me-Not |
| **Song** | "Alaska's Flag" by Marie Drake Music by Elinor Dusenbury |

NOTE: The abbreviations following the state name are U.S. Postal abbreviations.

## Arizona (AZ)  *The Grand Canyon State*

*Arizona* comes from a Pima Indian word "Arizonac", meaning "little spring place."

| | |
|---|---|
| **Capital** | Phoenix |
| **Size** | 114,006 square miles |
| **Population** | 5,456,453 |
| **Statehood** | February 14, 1912<br>48th State |
| **Motto** | "Ditant Deus (God Enriches)" |
| **Tree** | Palo Verde |
| **Bird** | Cactus Wren |
| **Flower** | Saguaro Cactus Blossom |
| **Song** | "Arizona" by Margaret Rowe Clifford<br>Music by Maurice Blumenthal |

## Arkansas (AR)  *The Land of Opportunity*

*Arkansas* is a variation of Quapaw, the name of an Indian tribe, which means "south wind."

| | |
|---|---|
| **Capital** | Little Rock |
| **Size** | 53,182 square miles |
| **Population** | 2,710,079 |
| **Statehood** | June 15, 1836<br>25th State |
| **Motto** | "Regnat Populus"<br>(The People Rule) |
| **Tree** | Southern Pine |
| **Bird** | Mockingbird |
| **Flower** | Apple Blossom |
| **Songs** | "Arkansas," Music and Words by Wayland Holyfield<br>"Oh, Arkansas," Music and Words by Terry Rose & Gary Klaff |

# California (CA)                    *The Golden State*

*California* was named by Spanish explorers after an imaginary island in the story, *Las Sergas de Esplandian*, by Garcia Ordonez de Montalvo, circa 1500.

| | |
|---|---|
| **Capital** | Sacramento |
| **Size** | 163,696 square miles |
| **Population** | 35,116,033 |
| **Statehood** | September 9, 1850, 31st State |
| **Motto** | "Eureka" (I have found it) |
| **Tree** | California Redwood |
| **Bird** | California Quail |
| **Flower** | California Poppy |
| **Song** | "I Love You, California" |

# Colorado (CO)                    *The Centennial State*

*Colorado* comes from an Algonquin Indian word meaning "long river place."

| | |
|---|---|
| **Capital** | Denver |
| **Size** | 104,100 square miles |
| **Population** | 4,506,542 |
| **Statehood** | August 1, 1876 38th State |
| **Motto** | "Nil Sine Numine" (Nothing without providence)" |
| **Tree** | Colorado Blue Spruce |
| **Bird** | Lark Bunting |
| **Flower** | Columbine |
| **Song** | "Where the Columbines Grow" by A.J. Flynn |

# Connecticut (CT)

*The Constitution State*

*Connecticut* comes from an Algonquin Indian word Quinnehtukqut, meaning "beside the long tidal river."

| | |
|---|---|
| **Capital** | Hartford |
| **Size** | 5,544 square miles |
| **Population** | 3,460,503 |
| **Statehood** | January 9, 1788<br>5th State |
| **Motto** | "Quitranstulit Sustined"<br>(He who, transplanted, sustains) |
| **Tree** | White Oak |
| **Bird** | American Robin |
| **Flower** | Mountain Laurel |
| **Song** | "Yankee Doodle" |

# Delaware (DE)

*The First State*

*Delaware* is named after Sir Thomas West, Baron La Warr, the English governor of Virginia in colonial times.

| | |
|---|---|
| **Capital** | Dover |
| **Size** | 2,489 square miles |
| **Population** | 807,385 |
| **Statehood** | December 7, 1787,<br>1st State |
| **Motto** | "Liberty and Independence" |
| **Tree** | American Holly |
| **Bird** | Blue Hen Chicken |
| **Flower** | Peach Blossom |
| **Song** | "Our Delaware" |

# Florida (FL)

*Florida*, means "feast of flowers or flowery" in Spanish. The territory was named by the explorer Ponce de Leon, who discovered it on Easter.

| | |
|---|---|
| **Capital** | Tallahassee |
| **Size** | 65,755 square miles |
| **Population** | 16,713,149 |
| **Statehood** | March 3, 1845, 27th State |
| **Motto** | "In God We Trust" |
| **Tree** | Sabal Palmetto |
| **Bird** | Mockingbird |
| **Flower** | Orange Blossom |
| **Song** | "Swanee River" ("Old Folks at Home") by Stephen Foster |

# Georgia (GA)

*Georgia* was named after King George II of England, who granted the settlers the right to create a colony there in 1732.

| | |
|---|---|
| **Capital** | Atlanta |
| **Size** | 59,425 square miles |
| **Population** | 8,560,310 |
| **Statehood** | January 2, 1788 4th State |
| **Motto** | "Wisdom, Justice, and Moderation" |
| **Tree** | Live Oak |
| **Bird** | Brown Thrasher |
| **Flower** | Cherokee Rose |
| **Song** | "Georgia" by Robert Loveman; music by Lollie Belle Wylie |

# Hawaii (HI)

*The Aloha State*

*Hawaii* comes from Hawaiki, or Owhyhee, the native Polynesians' word for "homeland."

| | |
|---|---|
| **Capital** | Honolulu |
| **Size** | 10,931 square miles |
| **Population** | 1,244,898 |
| **Statehood** | August 21, 1959, 50th State |
| **Motto** | "The Life of the Land is Preserved by Righteousness" |
| **Tree** | Kukui |
| **Bird** | Hawaiian Goose |
| **Flower** | Yellow Hibiscus |
| **Song** | "Our Own Hawaii" by King Kalakaua Music by Henry Berger |

# Idaho (ID)

*The Gem State*

*Idaho* is an invented name whose meaning is unknown. It may have come from a Kiowa Apache name for the Comanche Indians.

| | |
|---|---|
| **Capital** | Boise |
| **Size** | 83,574 square miles |
| **Population** | 1,341,131 |
| **Statehood** | July 3, 1890, 43rd State |
| **Motto** | "It Endures Forever" (Esto Perpetua) |
| **Tree** | Western White Pine |
| **Bird** | Mountain Bluebird |
| **Flower** | Syringa |
| **Song** | "Here We Have Idaho" |

# Illinois (IL)

*The Prairie State*

*Illinois* comes from Illini, an Algonquin Indian word meaning "tribe of superior men" or "warriors."

| | |
|---|---|
| **Capital** | Springfield |
| **Size** | 57,918 square miles |
| **Population** | 12,600,620 |
| **Statehood** | December 3, 1818, 21st State |
| **Motto** | "State Sovereignty, National Union" |
| **Tree** | White Oak |
| **Bird** | Cardinal |
| **Flower** | Meadow Violet |
| **Song** | "Illinois" |

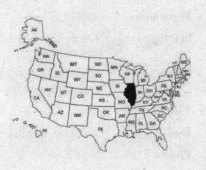

# Indiana (IN)

*the Hoosier State*

*Indiana* means "land of the Indians."

| | |
|---|---|
| **Capital** | Indianapolis |
| **Size** | 36,420 square miles |
| **Population** | 6,159,068 |
| **Statehood** | December 11, 1816, 19th State |
| **Motto** | "The Crossroads of America" |
| **Tree** | Tulip Tree |
| **Bird** | Cardinal |
| **Flower** | Peony |
| **Song** | "On the Banks of the Wabash Far Away" by Paul Dresser |

# Iowa (IA) *The Hawkeye State*

*Iowa* comes from an Indian word meaning "this is the place" or "the Beautiful land."

| | |
|---|---|
| **Capital** | Des Moines |
| **Size** | 56,276 square miles |
| **Population** | 2,936,760 |
| **Statehood** | December 28, 1846, 29th State |
| **Motto** | "Our Liberties We Prize and Our Rights We Will Maintain" |
| **Tree** | Oak |
| **Bird** | American Goldfinch |
| **Flower** | Wild Rose |
| **Song** | "The Song of Iowa" by Major S.H.M. Byers To the tune of "O Tannenbaum" |

# Kansas (KS) *The Sunflower State*

*Kansas* comes from the name of a Sioux Indian word meaning, "people of the south wind."

| | |
|---|---|
| **Capital** | Topeka |
| **Size** | 82,282 square miles |
| **Population** | 2,715,884 |
| **Statehood** | January 29, 1861 , 34th State |
| **Motto** | "To the Stars Through Difficulty" |
| **Tree** | Cottonwood |
| **Bird** | Western Meadowlark |
| **Flower** | Sunflower |
| **Song** | "Home on the Range" by Dr. Brewster M. Higley; music by Daniel Kelly |

# Kentucky (KY)

*The Bluegrass State*

From an Iroquoian word "Ken-tah-ten",
meaning "land of tomorrow."

| | |
|---|---|
| Capital | Frankfort |
| Size | 40,411 square miles |
| Population | 4,092,891 |
| Statehood | June 1, 1792,<br>15th State |
| Motto | "United We Stand, Divided We Fall" |
| Tree | Tulip Poplar |
| Bird | Cardinal |
| Flower | Goldenrod |
| Song | "My Old Kentucky Home" by Stephen Foster |

# Louisiana (LA)

*The Pelican State*

*Louisiana* is named in honor of
Louis XIV of France.

| | |
|---|---|
| Capital | Baton Rouge |
| Size | 51,840 square miles |
| Population | 4,482,646 |
| Statehood | April 30, 1812,<br>18th State |
| Motto | "Union, Justice, and Confidence" |
| Tree | Bald Cypress |
| Bird | Brown Pelican |
| Flower | Magnolia |
| Song | "Song of Louisiana" by Vashti R. Stopher |

# Maine (ME)

*The Pine Tree State*

*Maine* was first used to distinguish the mainland from the offshore islands. It has been considered a complement to Henrietta Maria, queen of Charles I of England. She was said to have owned the province of Mayne in France.

| | |
|---|---|
| **Capital** | Augusta |
| **Size** | 35,385 square miles |
| **Population** | 1,294,464 |
| **Statehood** | March 15, 1820, 23rd State |
| **Motto** | "Dirigo (I Lead)" |
| **Tree** | White Pine |
| **Bird** | Black Capped Chickadee |
| **Flower** | White Pine Cone and Tassel |
| **Song** | "State of Maine Song" by Roger Vinton Snow |

# Maryland (MD)

*The Old Line State*

*Maryland* was named in honor of Queen Henrietta Maria, who granted the right to establish an English colony there.

| | |
|---|---|
| **Capital** | Annapolis |
| **Size** | 12,407 square miles |
| **Population** | 5,458,137 |
| **Statehood** | April 28, 1788, 7th State |
| **Motto** | "Strong Deeds, Gentle Words" |
| **Tree** | White Oak |
| **Bird** | Baltimore Oriole |
| **Flower** | Black-Eyed Susan |
| **Song** | "Maryland, My Maryland" by James R. Randall |

# Massachusetts (MA)

*The Bay State*

*Massachusetts* is named after the Massachusett tribe of Native Americans, meaning "at or about the great hill."

| | |
|---|---|
| **Capital** | Boston |
| **Size** | 10,555 square miles |
| **Population** | 6,427,801 |
| **Statehood** | February 6, 1788, 6th State |
| **Motto** | "By The Sword We Seek Peace, But Peace Only Under Liberty" |
| **Tree** | American Elm |
| **Bird** | Black Capped Chickadee |
| **Flower** | Mayflower |
| **Song** | "All Hail to Massachusetts" |

# Michigan (MI)

*The Wolverine State*

*Michigan* comes from the Chippewa Indian words "mica gama" meaning "great or large lake," referring to Lake Michigan.

| | |
|---|---|
| **Capital** | Lansing |
| **Size** | 96,705 square miles |
| **Population** | 10,050,446 |
| **Statehood** | January 26, 1837, 26th State |
| **Motto** | "If You Seek a Pleasant Peninsula, Look About You" |
| **Tree** | White Pine |
| **Bird** | Robin |
| **Flower** | Apple Blossom |
| **Song** | "Michigan, My Michigan" |

# Minnesota (MN)

*The Land of 10, 000 Lakes*

*Minnesota* comes from a Dakota Sioux Indian word meaning "sky-tinted water."

| | |
|---|---|
| **Capital** | Saint Paul |
| **Size** | 86,943 square miles |
| **Population** | 5,019,720 |
| **Statehood** | May 11, 1858, 32nd State |
| **Motto** | "Star of the North" |
| **Tree** | Red (Norway) Pine |
| **Bird** | Common Loon |
| **Flower** | Lady Slipper |
| **Song** | "Hail Minnesota" |

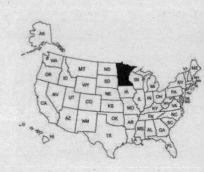

---

# Mississippi (MS)

*The Magnolia State*

*Mississippi* comes from an Indian word meaning "Father of Waters."

| | |
|---|---|
| **Capital** | Jackson |
| **Size** | 48,430 square miles |
| **Population** | 2,871,782 |
| **Statehood** | December 10, 1817, 20th State |
| **Motto** | "By Valor and Arms" |
| **Tree** | Magnolia |
| **Bird** | Mockingbird |
| **Flower** | Magnolia Blossom |
| **Song** | "Go Mississippi" |

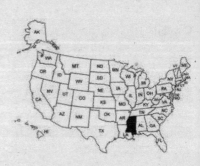

# Missouri (MO)

*Missouri* is named after the Algonquin Indian tribe; it means "town of the large canoes."

| | |
|---|---|
| **Capital** | Jefferson City |
| **Size** | 69,709 square miles |
| **Population** | 5,672,579 |
| **Statehood** | August 10, 1821, 24th State |
| **Motto** | "Let the Welfare of the People be the Supreme Law" |
| **Tree** | Flowering Dogwood |
| **Bird** | Bluebird |
| **Flower** | White Hawthorn Blossom |
| **Song** | "Missouri Waltz" by J.R. Shannon |

---

# Montana (MT)

*Montana* was chosen from a Latin dictionary by J.M. Ashley. It is a Latinized Spanish word meaning "mountainous."

| | |
|---|---|
| **Capital** | Helena |
| **Size** | 147,046 square miles |
| **Population** | 909,453 |
| **Statehood** | November 8, 1889, 41st State |
| **Motto** | "Gold and Silver" |
| **Tree** | Ponderosa Pine |
| **Bird** | Western Meadowlark |
| **Flower** | Bitterroot |
| **Song** | "Montana" by Charles C. Cohen Music by Joseph E. Howard |

# Nebraska (NE)

*The Cornhusker State*

*Nebraska* comes from an Oto Indian word meaning "flat river" or "broad water," their name for the Platte River.

| | |
|---|---|
| **Capital** | Lincoln |
| **Size** | 77,358 square miles |
| **Population** | 1,729,180 |
| **Statehood** | March 1, 1867, 37th State |
| **Motto** | "Equality Before the Law" |
| **Tree** | Cottonwood |
| **Bird** | Western Meadowlark |
| **Flower** | Goldenrod |
| **Song** | "Beautiful Nebraska" |

# Nevada (NV)

*The Silver State*

*Nevada* was given the name by Spanish explorers. It is the Spanish word meaning "snowcapped," referring to the Sierra Nevada Mountains.

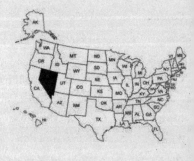

| | |
|---|---|
| **Capital** | Carson City |
| **Size** | 110,567 square miles |
| **Population** | 2,173,491 |
| **Statehood** | October 31, 1864, 36th State |
| **Motto** | "All for our Country" |
| **Tree** | Single-Leaf Pinon |
| **Bird** | Mountain Bluebird |
| **Flower** | Sagebrush |
| **Song** | "Home Means Nevada" |

## New Hampshire (NH)

*The Granite State*

*New Hampshire* comes from the English county of Hampshire.

| | |
|---|---|
| Capital | Concord |
| Size | 9,283 square miles |
| Population | 1,275,056 |
| Statehood | June 21, 1788, 9th State |
| Motto | "Live Free or Die" |
| Tree | White Birch |
| Bird | Purple finch |
| Flower | Purple Lilac |
| Song | "Old New Hampshire" by John F. Holmes; music by Maurice   Hoffman |

## New Jersey (NJ)

*The Garden State*

*New Jersey* was named for the English Channel Isle of Jersey.

| | |
|---|---|
| Capital | Trenton |
| Size | 8,721 square miles |
| Population | 8,590,300 |
| Statehood | December 18, 1787, 3rd State |
| Motto | "Liberty and Prosperity" |
| Tree | Red Oak |
| Bird | American Goldfinch |
| Flower | Violet |
| Song | *None Listed* |

# New Mexico (NM)

*Land of Enchantment*

New Mexico was given its name by 16th-century Spaniards in Mexico.

| | |
|---|---|
| **Capital** | Santa Fe |
| **Size** | 121,598 square miles |
| **Population** | 1,855,059 |
| **Statehood** | January 6, 1912,<br>47th State |
| **Motto** | "It Grows as it Goes" |
| **Tree** | Nut Pine |
| **Bird** | Roadrunner |
| **Flower** | Yucca |
| **Song** | "O Fair New Mexico" by Elizabeth Garrett |

# New York (NY)

*The Empire State*

*New York* was named in honor of the Duke of York and Albany after the English took it from Dutch settlers.

| | |
|---|---|
| **Capital** | Albany |
| **Size** | 54,556 square miles |
| **Population** | 19,157,532 |
| **Statehood** | July 26, 1788,<br>11th State |
| **Motto** | "Excelsior" |
| **Tree** | Sugar Maple |
| **Bird** | Bluebird |
| **Flower** | Rose |
| **Song** | "I Love New York" |

# North Carolina (NC)

*The Tar Heel State*

*North Carolina*, the northern part of the English colony of Carolana, was named in honor of Charles I of England.

| | |
|---|---|
| **Capital** | Raleigh |
| **Size** | 53,819 square miles |
| **Population** | 8,320,146 |
| **Statehood** | November 21, 1789, 12th State |
| **Motto** | "To Be Rather Than to Seem" |
| **Tree** | Southern Pine |
| **Bird** | Cardinal |
| **Flower** | Flowering Dogwood |
| **Song** | "The Old North State" by William Gaston |

# North Dakota (ND)

*The Peace Garden State*

North Dakota is named after the Sioux tribe, meaning "allies."

| | |
|---|---|
| **Capital** | Bismark |
| **Size** | 70,704 square miles |
| **Population** | 634,110 |
| **Statehood** | November 2, 1889, 39th State |
| **Motto** | "Liberty and Union, Now and Forever, One and Inseparable" |
| **Tree** | American Elm |
| **Bird** | Western Meadowlark |
| **Flower** | Wild Prairie Rose |
| **Song** | "North Dakota Hymn" by James W. Foley Music by C.S. Putnam |

# Ohio (OH)

*The Buckeye State*

*Ohio* comes from an Iroquoian word meaning "great river."

| | |
|---|---|
| **Capital** | Columbus |
| **Size** | 44,828 square miles |
| **Population** | 11,421,267 |
| **Statehood** | March 1, 1803, 17th State |
| **Motto** | "With God All Things Are Possible" |
| **Tree** | Ohio Buckeye |
| **Bird** | Cardinal |
| **Flower** | Red Scarlet Carnation |
| **Song** | "Beautiful Ohio" |

# Oklahoma (OK)

*The Sooners State*

*Oklahoma* comes from two Choctaw Indian words meaning "red people."

| | |
|---|---|
| **Capital** | Oklahoma City |
| **Size** | 69,903 square miles |
| **Population** | 3,493,714 |
| **Statehood** | November 16, 1907, 46th State |
| **Motto** | "Labor Conquers all Things" |
| **Tree** | Redbud |
| **Bird** | Scissor-Tailed Fly Catcher |
| **Flower** | Mistletoe |
| **Song** | "Oklahoma" by R. Rogers and O. Hammerstein |

# Oregon (OR)

*Oregon*'s name origin is unknown, however, it is generally accepted that the name, first used by Jonathan Carver in 1778, was taken from the writings of Major Robert Rogers, an English army officer.

| | |
|---|---|
| **Capital** | Salem |
| **Size** | 98,381 square miles |
| **Population** | 3,521,515 |
| **Statehood** | February 14, 1859, 33rd State |
| **Motto** | "She Flies With Her Own Wings" |
| **Tree** | Douglas Fir |
| **Bird** | Western Meadowlark |
| **Flower** | Oregon Grape |
| **Song** | "Oregon, My Oregon," by J.A. Buchman Music By Henry B. Murtagh |

# Pennsylvania (PA)

*Pennsylvania* means "Penn's Woodland," the name given to the colony founded by Admiral Sir William Penn, father of William Penn.

| | |
|---|---|
| **Capital** | Harrisburg |
| **Size** | 46,058 square miles |
| **Population** | 12,335,091 |
| **Statehood** | December, 12, 1787, 2nd State |
| **Motto** | "Virtue, Liberty and Independence" |
| **Tree** | Hemlock |
| **Bird** | Ruffed Grouse |
| **Flower** | Mountain Laurel |
| **Song** | "Pennsylvania" |

# Rhode Island (RI) *The Ocean State*

*Rhode Island's* name comes from the Greek Island of Rhodes.

| | |
|---|---|
| **Capital** | Providence |
| **Size** | 1,545 square miles |
| **Population** | 1,069,725 |
| **Statehood** | May 29, 1790, 13th State |
| **Motto** | "Hope" |
| **Tree** | Red Maple |
| **Bird** | Rhode Island Red |
| **Flower** | Wood Violet |
| **Song** | "Rhode Island" by T. Clark Brown |

# South Carolina (SC) *The Palmetto State*

*South Carolina*, the southern part of the English colony of Carolana, was named in honor of Charles I of England.

| | |
|---|---|
| **Capital** | Columbia |
| **Size** | 32,020 square miles |
| **Population** | 4,107,183 |
| **Statehood** | May 23, 1788, 8th State |
| **Motto** | "While I Breathe, I Hope" |
| **Tree** | Palmetto |
| **Bird** | Carolina Wren |
| **Flower** | Yellow Jasmine |
| **Song** | "Carolina" by Henry Timrod Music by Anna Custis Burgess |

# South Dakota (SD)

*The Mount Rushmore State*

*South Dakota* comes from a Sioux Indian word meaning "ally" or "friend."

| | |
|---|---|
| **Capital** | Pierre |
| **Size** | 77,121 square miles |
| **Population** | 761,063 |
| **Statehood** | November 2, 1889; 40th State |
| **Motto** | "Under God the People Rule" |
| **Tree** | Black Hills Spruce |
| **Bird** | Ring-necked Pheasant |
| **Flower** | Pasque flower |
| **Song** | "Hail, South Dakota" |

# Tennessee (TN)

*The Volunteer State*

*Tennessee* comes from "Tanasi," the name of Cherokee Indian villages on the Little Tennessee River.

| | |
|---|---|
| **Capital** | Nashville |
| **Size** | 42,146 square miles |
| **Population** | 5,797,280 |
| **Statehood** | June 1, 1796, 16th State |
| **Motto** | "Agriculture and Commerce" |
| **Tree** | Tulip Tree |
| **Bird** | Mockingbird |
| **Flower** | Iris |
| **Songs** | "Tennessee Waltz" (1965); "My Homeland, Tennessee" (1925); "When It's Iris Time in Tennessee" (1935); "My Tennessee" (1955); "Rocky Top" (1982); "Tennessee" (1992) |

# Texas (TX)

*The Lone Star State*

*Texas* comes from a word meaning "friends" or "allies," used by the Spanish to describe some of the American Indians living there.

| | |
|---|---|
| **Capital** | Austin |
| **Size** | 268,581 square miles |
| **Population** | 21,779,893 |
| **Statehood** | December 29, 1845; 28th State |
| **Motto** | "Friendship" |
| **Tree** | Pecan |
| **Bird** | Mockingbird |
| **Flower** | Bluebonnet |
| **Song** | "Texas, Our Texas," by William Marsh and Gladys Y. Wright |

---

# Utah (UT)

*The Beehive State*

*Utah* comes from the Ute tribe, meaning "people of the mountains."

| | |
|---|---|
| **Capital** | Salt Lake City |
| **Size** | 84,904 square miles |
| **Population** | 2,316,256 |
| **Statehood** | January 4, 1896, 45th State |
| **Motto** | "Industry" |
| **Tree** | Blue Spruce |
| **Bird** | California Gull |
| **Flower** | Sego Lily |
| **Song** | "Utah, We Love Thee" by Evan Stephens |

# Vermont (VT)

*The Green Mountain State*

*Vermont* comes from the French "vert mont," meaning "green mountain."

| | |
|---|---|
| **Capital** | Montpelier |
| **Size** | 9,615 square miles |
| **Population** | 616,592 |
| **Statehood** | March 4, 1791; 14th State |
| **Motto** | "Freedom and Unity" |
| **Tree** | Sugar Maple Tree |
| **Bird** | Hermit Thrush |
| **Flower** | Red Clover |
| **Song** | "These Green Mountains" by Diane Martin |

# Virginia (VA)

*Old Dominion State*

*Virginia* is named in honor of Elizabeth, "Virgin Queen" of England.

| | |
|---|---|
| **Capital** | Richmond |
| **Size** | 42,774 square miles |
| **Population** | 7,293,542 |
| **Statehood** | June 25, 1788, 10th State |
| **Motto** | "Thus Always to Tyrants" |
| **Tree** | Dogwood |
| **Bird** | Cardinal |
| **Flower** | Flowering Dogwood |
| **Song** | "Carry Me Back to Old Virginia" by James A. Bland |

# Washington (WA)

*Evergreen State*

*Washington* is named in honor of George Washington, the first president of the United States.

| | |
|---|---|
| **Capital** | Olympia |
| **Size** | 71,300 square miles |
| **Population** | 6,068,996 |
| **Statehood** | November 11, 1889; 42nd State |
| **Motto** | "By and By" |
| **Tree** | Western Hemlock |
| **Bird** | Willow Goldfinch |
| **Flower** | Rhododendron |
| **Song** | "Washington My Home" by Mrs. Helen Davis |

---

# West Virginia (WV)

*Mountain State*

*West Virginia* was named by the people of western Virginia, who formed their own government during the Civil War.

| | |
|---|---|
| **Capital** | Charleston |
| **Size** | 24,231 square miles |
| **Population** | 1,801,873 |
| **Statehood** | June 20, 1863, 35th State |
| **Motto** | "Mountaineers Are Always Free" |
| **Tree** | Sugar Maple |
| **Bird** | Cardinal |
| **Flower** | Rhododendron |
| **Song** | "West Virginia Hills" |

# Wisconsin (WI)

*The Badger State*

*Wisconsin* comes from a Chippewa name that is believed to mean "grassy place."

| | |
|---|---|
| **Capital** | Madison |
| **Size** | 65,499 square miles |
| **Population** | 5,441,196 |
| **Statehood** | May 29, 1848; 30th State |
| **Motto** | "Forward" |
| **Tree** | Sugar Maple |
| **Bird** | Robin |
| **Flower** | Violet |
| **Song** | "On Wisconsin" by Dr. Phillip A. Forsbeck Music by William T. Purdy |

# Wyoming (WY)

*The Equality State*

*Wyoming* is named after the Delaware Indian word, meaning "mountains and valleys alternating"; the same as the Wyoming Valley in Pennsylvania.

| | |
|---|---|
| **Capital** | Cheyenne |
| **Size** | 97,818 square miles |
| **Population** | 498,703 |
| **Statehood** | July 10, 1890, 44th State |
| **Motto** | "Equal Rights" |
| **Tree** | Cottonwood |
| **Bird** | Western Meadowlark |
| **Flower** | Indian Paintbrush |
| **Song** | "Wyoming State Song" by Charles E. Winter Music by George E. Knapp |

# MAPS OF THE WORLD

## The World

**Total area:** 510.072 million sq km (316.96 million sq mi).

**Land area:** 148.94 million sq km (92.55 million sq mi).

**Water area:** 361.132 million sq km (224.41 million sq mi).
**Note:** 70.8% of the world is water, 29.2% is land.

## The Four Oceans:
**Pacific Ocean**: 64,186,300 square miles; 12,925 feet deep
**Atlantic Ocean**: 33,420,000 square miles; 11,730 feet deep
**Indian Ocean**: 28,350,500 square miles; 12,598 feet deep
**Arctic Ocean**: 5,105,700 square miles; 3,407 feet deep

- **Terrain:** Highest elevation is Mt. Everest at 8,850 m (29,035 ft) and lowest land depression is the Dead Sea at −411 m (−1,349 ft) below sea level.

- **Land use:** Arable land: 10%. Permanent crops: 1%. Meadows and pastures: 26%. Forests and woodlands: 32%. Other: 31% (1993 est.). Irrigated land: 2,481,250 sq km (1,541,849 sq mi).

\* **Note**: *The maps of the world and the seven continents are from The World Factbook 2004.*

# ASIA

Asia measures 16,990,000 square miles and holds 61% of the world's population. Asia is comprised of many countries including Russia, China, Mongolia, Iran and India.

# AUSTRALIA

Australia, the only continent that is also a country, measures 2,978,000 square miles. It is in the Southern Hemisphere and holds .5% of the world's population.

# AFRICA

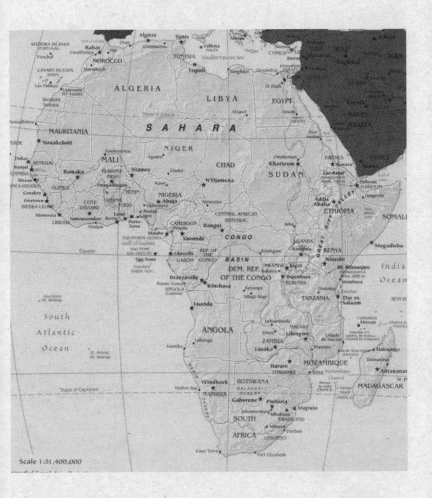

Africa measures 11,657,000 square miles and holds 12.7% of the world's population. The equator goes right through the middle of Africa.

# NORTH AMERICA

North America measures 9,348,000 square miles. The United States, Canada and Mexico are the major countries in North America which holds 7.9% of the world's population.

# SOUTH AMERICA

South America measures 6,885,000 square miles and is in the Southern Hemisphere.  South America contains 5.9% of the world's population.

# ANTARCTICA

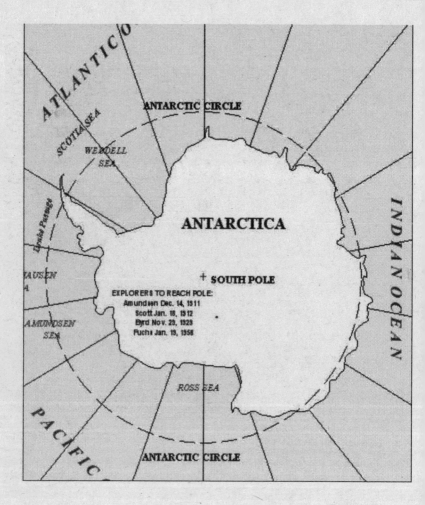

Located south of the Antarctic Circle, Antarctica is 5,404,000 square miles. Antarctica the coldest and windiest place on earth, there are no indigenous inhabitants, but there are seasonally staffed research stations. The Antarctic Treaty governs the continent of Antarctica.

# EUROPE

Europe is 4,051,000 square miles and holds 12% of the world's population. Many countries make up the continent of Europe including France, Italy and Germany.

# FACTS ABOUT COUNTRIES

*The information gathered here is derived from*

<u>*The World Factbook 2006*</u> *compiled by the Central Intelligence Agency.*

### AFGHANISTAN
**Location:** Southern Asia, north and west of Pakistan, east of Iran
**Area:** 250,000 sq mi (647,500 sq km)
**Area —comparative:** slightly smaller than Texas
**Population:** 31,056,997
**Population growth rate:** 2.67%
**Nationality:** noun: Afghan(s), adjective: Afghan
**Ethnic groups:** Pashtun 42%, Tajik 27%, Hazara 9%, Uzbek 9%, others 13%
**Religions:** Sunni Muslim 80%, Shi`a Muslim 19%, other 1%
**Languages:** Pashtu 35%, Afghan Persian (Dari) 50%, Turkic languages 11%, 30 minor languages 4%
**Government type:** Islamic republic
**Capital:** Kabul
**Budget:** revenues: $269 million, expenditures: $602 million          **Currency:** afghani (AFA)

### ALBANIA
**Location:** Southeastern Europe, bordering the Adriatic Sea and Ionian Sea, between Greece and Serbia and Montenegro
**Area:** 11,099 sq mi (28,748 sq km)
**Area —comparative:** slightly smaller than Maryland
**Population:** 3,581,655
**Population growth rate:** 0.52%
**Nationality:** noun: Albanian(s), adjective: Albanian
**Ethnic groups:** Albanian 95%, Greeks 3%, other 2%
**Languages:** Albanian (official- derived form Tosk dialect), Greek, Vlach, Romani, Slavic dialects
**Religions:** Muslim 70%, Albanian Orthodox 20%, Roman Catholic 10%
**Government type:** emerging democracy
**Capital:** Tirana
**Budget:** revenues: $1.96 billion, expenditures: $ 2.377 billion, including capital of $500 million
**Currency:** lek (ALL)

### ALGERIA
**Location:** Northern Africa, bordering the Mediterranean Sea, between Morocco and Tunisia
**Area:** 919,590 sq mi (2,381,740 sq km)
**Area- comparative:** slightly less than 3.5 times the size of Texas
**Population:** 32,930,091
**Population growth rate:** 1.22%
**Nationality:** noun: Algerian(s), adjective: Algerian
**Ethnic groups:** Arab-Berber 99%, European less than 1%
**Languages:** Arabic (official), French, Berber dialects
**Religions:** Sunni Muslim (state religion) 99%, Christian and Jewish 1%
**Government type:** republic
**Capital:** Algiers

**Budget:** revenues: $42.05 billion, expenditures: $30.75 billion, including capital expenditures of $5.8 billion
**Currency:** Algerian dinar (DZD)

*AMERICAN SAMOA*
**Location:** Oceania, group of islands in the South Pacific Ocean approximately half way between Hawaii and New Zealand
**Area:** 77 sq mi (199 sq km)
**Area-comparative:** slightly larger than Washington, DC
**Population:** 57,794
**Population growth rate:** -0.19%
**Nationality:** noun: American Samoan(s), adjective: American Samoan
**Ethnic groups:** Samoan (Polynesian) 89%, Caucasian 2%, Tongan 4%, and other 5%
**Language:** Samoan (closely related to Hawaiian and other Polynesian languages), English
**Religion:** Christian Congressionalist 50%, Roman Catholic 20%, Protestant and other 30%
**Government:** NA
**Capital:** Pago Pago
**Budget:** revenues $121 million (37%-local, 63% US Grants) expenditures:$127 million, capital $NA
**Currency:** US dollar (USD)

*ANDORRA*
**Location:** Southwestern Europe, between France and Spain
**Area:** 180 sq mi (468 sq km)
**Area –comparative:** 2.5 times the size of Washington, DC
**Population:** 71.201
**Population growth rate:** 0.89%
**Nationality:** noun: Andorran(s), adjective: Andorran
**Ethnic groups:** Spanish 43%, Andorran 33%, Portuguese 11%, French 7%, other 6%
**Languages:** Catalan (official), French, Castilian, Portuguese
**Religion:** Roman Catholic (predominant)
**Government type:** parliamentary democracy
**Capital:** Andorra la Vella
**Budget:** revenues: $373.5 million, expenditures: $373.5 million          **Currency:** euro (EUR)

*ANGOLA*
**Location:** Southern Africa, bordering the South Atlantic Ocean, between Namibia and Democratic Republic of the Congo
**Area:** 481,351 sq mi (1,246,700 sq km)
**Area-comparative:** slightly less than twice the size of Texas
**Population:** 12,127,071
**Population growth rate:** 2.45%
**Nationality:** noun: Angolan(s), adjective: Angolan
**Ethnic groups:** Ovimbundu 37%, Kimbundu 25%, Bakongo 13%, Mestico 2%, European 1%, other 22%
**Languages:** Portuguese (official), Bantu and other African languages
**Religions:** indigenous beliefs 47%, Roman Catholic 38%, Protestant 15%
**Government:** Republic, nominally a multiparty democracy with a strong presidential system
**Capital:** Luanda
**Budget:** revenues: $8.5 billion; expenditures: $10 billion, including capital of $963 million
**Currency:** kwanza (AOA)

*ANGUILLA* (overseas territory of the UK)
**Location:** islands between the Caribbean Sea and the North Atlantic Ocean, east of Puerto Rico

**Area:** 39 sq mi (102 sq km)
**Area-comparative:** about one half the size of Washington, DC
**Population:** 13,477
**Population growth rate:** 1.57%
**Nationality:** noun: Anguillan(s), adjective: Anguillan
**Ethnic groups:** black (predominant), mulatto, white
**Religions:** Anglican 40%, Methodist 33%, other 12%, Seventh-Day Adventist 7%, Baptist 5% Catholic 3%
**Languages:** English (official)
**Government:** NA (overseas territory of the UK)
**Capital:** The Valley
**Budget:** revenues: $22.8 million, expenditures: $22.5 million   **Currency:** East Caribbean dollar (XCD)

## ANTIGUA AND BARBUDA
**Location:** islands between the Caribbean Sea and North Atlantic Ocean, east-southeast of Puerto-Rico
**Area:** 171 sq mi (total 443 sq km)
**Area-comparative:** 2.5 times the size of Washington, DC
**Population:** 69,108
**Population growth rate:** 0.55%
**Nationality:** noun: Antiguan(s), Barbudan(s), adjective: Antiguan, Barbudan
**Ethnic groups:** black, British, Portuguese, Lebanese, Syrian
**Languages:** English (official), local dialects
**Religions:** Christian, (predominantly Anglican with other Protestant and some Roman Catholic)
**Government type:** constitutional monarchy with UK-style parliament
**Capital:** Saint John`s
**Budget:** revenues: $123.7 million, expenditures: $145.9 million
**Currency:** East Caribbean dollar (XCD)

## ARGENTINA
**Location:** Southern South America, bordering the South Atlantic Ocean, between Chile and Uruguay
**Area:** 1,068,297 sq mi (2,766,890 sq km)
**Area-comparative:** slightly less than three tenths the size of the US
**Population:** 39,921,833
**Population growth rate:** 0.96%
**Nationality:** noun: Argentine(s), adjective: Argentine
**Ethnic groups:** white (mostly Spanish and Italian) 97%, mestizo, or other nonwhite groups 3%
**Languages:** Spanish (official), English, Italian, German, French
**Religions:** Roman Catholic 92%, Protestant 2%, Jewish 2%, other 4%
**Government type:** republic
**Capital:** Buenos Aires
**Budget:** revenues: $42.63 billion, expenditures $39.98 billion, including capital of $NA
**Currency:** Argentine peso (ARS)

## ARMENIA
**Location:** Southwestern Asia, east of Turkey
**Area:** 11,505 sq mi (29,800 sq km)
**Area-comparative:** slightly smaller than Maryland
**Population:** 2,976,372
**Population growth rate:** -0.19%
**Nationality:** noun: Armenian(s), adjective: Armenian
**Ethnic groups:** Armenian 93%, Azeri 1%, Russian 2%, other (including Kurd) 4%
**Languages:** Armenian 96%, Russian 2%, other 2%
**Religions:** Armenian Apostolic 94%, other Christian 4%, Yezidi 2%

**Government type:** republic
**Capital:** Yerevan
**Budget:** revenues: $786.1 million, expenditures: $930.7 million      **Currency:** dram (AMD)

*ARUBA* (part of the Kingdom of the Netherlands)
**Location:** Caribbean, island in the Caribbean Sea, north of Venezuela
**Area:** 74.5 sq mi (193 sq km)
**Area-comparative:** slightly larger than Washington, DC .
**Population:** 71,891
**Population growth rate:** 0.44%
**Nationality:** noun: Aruban(s), adjective: Aruban: Dutch
**Ethnic groups:** mixed white/ Caribbean Amerindian 80%
**Languages:** Dutch (official), Papiamento (a dialect) English, Spanish
**Religions:** Roman Catholic 82%, Protestant 8%, Hindu, Muslim, Confucian, Jewish
**Government type:** parliamentary democracy
**Capital:** Oranjestad
**Budget:** revenues: $135.8 million, expenditures: $ 147 million    **Currency:** Aruban guilder/florin (AWG)

*AUSTRALIA*
**Location:** Oceania, continent between the Indian Ocean and the South Pacific Ocean
**Area:** 2,967,895 sq mi (7,686,850 sq km)
**Area-comparative:** slightly smaller than the US contiguous 48 states
**Population:** 20,264,082
**Population growth rate:** 0.85%
**Nationality:** noun: Australian(s), adjective: Australian
**Ethnic groups:** Caucasian 92%, Asian 7%, other (including Aboriginal) 1%
**Languages:** English (official), native languages
**Religions:** Roman Catholic 26%, Anglican 26.1%, other Christian 24.3%, non-Christian 11%, other 12.6%
**Government type:** democratic, federal-state system, recognizing British monarch as sovereign
**Capital:** Canberra
**Budget:** revenues: $249.8 billion, expenditures: $ 240.2 billion    **Currency:** Australian dollar (AUD)

*AUSTRIA*
**Location:** Central Europe, north of Italy and Slovenia
**Area:** 32,377 sq mi (83,858 sq km)
**Area-comparative:** slightly smaller than Maine
**Population:** 8,192,880
**Population growth rate:** 0.09%
**Nationality:** noun: Austrian(s), adjective: Austrian
**Ethnic groups:** German 88.5%, indigenous minorities 1.5%, recent immigrant groups 10%
**Language:** German (official)
**Religions:** Roman Catholic 73.6%, Protestant 4.7%, Muslim 4.2%, other 0.1%, none 17.4%
**Government type:** federal republic
**Capital:** Vienna
**Budget:** revenues: $148.6 billion, expenditures: $154.5 billion, including capital of $NA
**Currency:** euro (EUR)

*AZERBAIJAN*
**Location:** Southwestern Asia, bordering the Caspian Sea, between Iran and Russia
**Area:** 33,436 sq mi (86,600 sq km)
**Area-comparative:** slightly smaller than Maine
**Population:** 7,961,619
**Population growth rate:** 0.66%

**Nationality:** noun: Azerbaijani(s), adjective: Azerbaijani
**Ethnic groups:** Azeri 90%, Dagestani 3.2%, Russian 2.5%, Armenian 2% , other 2.3%
**Languages:** Azerbaijani (Azeri) 89%, Russian 3%, Armenian 2%, other 6%
**Religions:** Muslim 93.4%, Armenian Orthodox 2.3%, Russian Orthodox 2.5%, other 1.8%
**Government type:** republic
**Capital:** Baku (Baki)
**Budget:** revenues: $3.18 billion, expenditures: $2.986 billion          **Currency:** Azerbaijani manta (AZM)

## THE BAHAMAS
**Location:** Caribbean, chain of islands in the North Atlantic Ocean, northeast of Cuba
**Area:** 5,382 sq mi (13,940 sq km)
**Area-comparative:** slightly smaller than Connecticut
**Population:** 303,770
**Population growth rate:** 0.64%
**Nationality:** noun: Bahamian(s), adjective: Bahamian
**Ethnic groups:** black 85%, white 12%, Asian and Hispanic 3%
**Languages:** English (official), Creole
**Religions:** Baptist 32%, Anglican 20%, Roman Catholic 19%, Methodist 6%, Church of God 6%,
            Protestant 12%, other 5%
**Government type:** constitutional parliamentary democracy
**Capital:** Nassau
**Budget:** revenues: $1.03 billion, expenditures: $1.03 billion, & capital expenditures of $130 million
**Currency:** Bahamian dollar (BSD)

## BAHRAIN
**Location:** Middle East, east of Saudi Arabia
**Area:** 257 sq mi (665 sq km)
**Area-comparative:** 3.5 times the size of Washington, DC
**Population:** 689,585
**Population growth rate:** 1.45%
**Nationality:** noun: Bahraini(s), adjective: Bahraini
**Ethnic groups:** Bahraini 63%, Asian 19%, other Arab 10%, Iranian 8%
**Languages:** Arabic (official), English, Farsi, Urdu
**Religions:** Shi'a Muslim 70%, Sunni Muslim 30%
**Government type:** constitutional hereditary monarchy
**Capital:** Manama
**Budget:** revenues: $4.662 billion, expenditures: $3.447 billion; capital expenditures of $700 million
**Currency:** Bahraini dinar (BHD)

## BANGLADESH
**Location:** Southern Asia, bordering the Bay of Bengal, between Burma and India
**Area:** 55,598 sq mi (144,000 sq km)
**Area-comparative:** slightly smaller than Iowa
**Population:** 147,365,352
**Population growth rate:** 2.09%
**Nationality:** noun: Bangladeshi(s), adjective: Bangladeshi
**Ethnic groups:** Bengali 98%, other 2%
**Languages:** Bangla (official), English
**Religions:** Muslim 83%, Hindu 16%, other 1%
**Government type:** parliamentary democracy
**Capital:** Dhaka
**Budget:** revenues: $5.993 billion, expenditures: $8.598 billion
**Currency:** taka (BDT)

### BARBADOS

**Location:** Caribbean, island in the North Atlantic Ocean, northeast of Venezuela
**Area:** 166 sq mi (430 sq km)
**Area-comparative:** 2.5 times the size of Washington, DC
**Population:** 279,912
**Population growth rate:** 0.37%
**Nationality:** noun: Barbadian(s) or Bajan, adjective: Barbadian or Bajan
**Ethnic groups:** black 90%, white 4%, Asian and mixed 6%
**Languages:** English (official)
**Religions:** Protestant 67%, Roman Catholic 4%, none 17%, other 12%
**Government type:** parliamentary democracy
**Capital:** Bridgetown
**Budget:** revenues: $847 million, expenditures: $886 million          **Currency:** Barbadian dollar (BBD)

### BELARUS

**Location:** Eastern Europe, east of Poland
**Area:** 80,154 sq mi (207,600 sq km)
**Area-comparative:** slightly smaller than Kansas
**Population:** 10,293,011
**Population growth rate:** -0.06%
**Nationality:** noun: Belarusian(s), adjective: Belarusian
**Ethnic groups:** Belarusian 81.2%, Russian, 11.4%, Polish, Ukrainian, and other 7.4%
**Languages:** Belarusian (official), Russian (official); other
**Religions:** Eastern Orthodox 80%, other (including Roman Catholic, Protestant, Jewish and Muslim) 20%
**Government type:** republic in name, although in fact a dictatorship
**Capital:** Minsk
**Budget:** revenues: $5.903 billion, expenditures: $ 6.343 billion, including capital of $180 million
**Currency:** Belarusian ruble (BYB/BYR)

### BELGIUM

**Location:** Western Europe, bordering the North Sea, between France and Netherlands
**Area:** 11,779 sq mi (30,510 sq km)
**Area-comparative:** about the size of Maryland
**Population:** 10,379,067
**Population growth rate:** 0.13%
**Nationality:** noun: Belgian(s), adjective: Belgian
**Ethnic groups:** Fleming 58%, Walloon 31%, mixed and other 11%
**Languages:** Dutch 60%, French 40%
**Religions:** Roman Catholic 75%, other (including Protestant) 25%
**Government type:** federal parliamentary democracy under a constitutional monarch
**Capital:** Brussels
**Budget:** revenues: $180.4 billion, expenditures: $180.5 billion, including capital of $1.56 billion
**Currency:** euro (EUR)

### BELIZE

**Location:** Middle America, bordering the Caribbean Sea, between Guatemala and Mexico
**Area:** 8,867 sq mi (22,966 sq km)
**Area-comparative:** slightly smaller than Massachusetts
**Population:** 287,730
**Population growth rate:** 2.31%
**Nationality:** noun: Belizean(s), adjective: Belizean
**Ethnic groups:** Mestizo 49%, Creole 25%, Maya 11%, Garifuna 6%, other 9%

**Languages:** English (official), Spanish, Mayan, Garifuna, Creole
**Religions:** Roman Catholic 50%, Protestant 27%, other/nonreligious 23%
**Government type:** parliamentary democracy
**Capital:** Belmopan
**Budget:** revenues: $262 million, expenditures: $329 million, including capital of $70 million
**Currency:** Belizean dollar (BZD)


## BENIN

**Location:** Western Africa, bordering the Bight of Benin, between Nigeria and Togo
**Area:** 43,482 sq mi (112,620 sq km)
**Area-comparative:** slightly smaller than Pennsylvania
**Population:** 7,862,944
**Population growth rate:** 2.73%
**Nationality:** noun: Beninese (singular and plural), adjective: Beninese
**Ethnic groups:** African 99% (42 ethnic groups, including Fon, Adja, Yoruba, and Bariba), Europeans 1%
**Languages:** French (official), Fon and Yoruba, tribal languages (at least six major ones in north)
**Religions:** indigenous beliefs 50%, Christian 30%, Muslim 20%
**Government type:** republic under multiparty democratic rule
**Capital:** Porto-Novo(official capital) ; Cotonou is the seat of government
**Budget:** revenues: $766.8 million, expenditures: $1.017 billion
**Currency:** Communaute Financiere Africaine franc (XOF)


## BERMUDA *(overseas territory of the UK)*

**Location:** North America, group of islands in the North Atlantic Ocean, east of North Carolina (US)
**Area:** 20.5 sq mi (53.3 sq km)
**Area-comparative:** about one third the size of Washington, DC
**Population:** 65,773
**Population growth rate:** 0.61%
**Nationality**: *noun*, Bermudian(s); *adjective*, Bermudian
**Ethnic groups:** black 58%, white 36%, other 6%
**Languages:** English (official), Portuguese
**Religions:** non-Anglican Protestant 39%, Anglican 27%, Roman Catholic 15%, other 19%
**Government type:** parliamentary British overseas territory with internal self-government
**Capital:** Hamilton
**Budget:** revenues: $738 million, expenditures: $665 million
**Currency:** Bermudian dollar (BMD)


## BHUTAN

**Location:** Southern Asia, between China and India
**Area:** 18,146 sq mi (47,000 sq km)
**Area-comparative**: about half the size of Indiana
**Population:** 2,279,723
**Population growth rate:** 2.1%
**Nationality: noun:** Bhutanese (singular and plural), adjective: Bhutanese
**Ethnic groups:** Bhote 50%, ethnic Nepalese 35%, indigenous or migrant tribes 15%
**Languages:** Dzongkha (official), Tibetan, Nepalese dialects
**Religions:** Lamaistic Buddhism 75%, Indian- and Nepalese-influenced Hinduism 25%
**Government type:** monarchy, special treaty relationship with India
**Capital:** Thimphu
**Budget:** revenues: $146 million, expenditures: $152 million
**Currency:** ngultrum; Indian rupee (BTN,INR)

## BOLIVIA

**Location:** Central South America, southwest of Brazil
**Area:** 424,162 sq mi (1,098,580 sq km)
**Area-comparative:** slightly less than three times the size of Montana
**Population:** 8,989,046
**Population growth rate:** 1.45%
**Nationality:** noun: Bolivian(s), adjective: Bolivian
**Ethnic groups:** Ouechua 30%, Mestizo 30%, Aymara 25%, white 15%
**Languages:** Spanish (official), Ouechua (official), Aymara (official)
**Religions:** Roman Catholic 95%, other 5%
**Government type:** republic
**Capital:** La Paz (seat of government); Sucre (legal capital and seat of judiciary)
**Budget:** revenues: $2.848 billion, expenditures: $3.189 billion, including capital of $741 million
**Currency:** boliviano (BOB)

## BOSNIA AND HERZEGOVINA

**Location:** Southeastern Europe, bordering the Adriatic Sea and Croatia
**Area:** 19,740 sq mi (51,129 sq km)
**Area-comparative:** slightly smaller than West Virginia
**Population:** 4,498,976
**Population growth rate:** 1.35%
**Nationality:** noun: Bosnian(s), Herzegovinian(s); adjective: Bosnian, Herzegovinian
**Ethnic groups:** Serb 37%, Bosniak 48%, Croat 14%, other 1%
**Languages:** Croatian, Serbian, Bosnian
**Religions:** Muslim 40%, Orthodox 31%, Roman Catholic 15%, other 14%
**Government type:** emerging federal democratic republic
**Capital:** Sarajevo
**Budget:** revenues: $4.373 billion; expenditures: $4.401 billion          **Currency:** marka (BAM)

## BOTSWANA

**Location:** Southern Africa, north of South Africa
**Area:** 231,803 sq mi (600,370 sq km)
**Area-comparative:** slightly smaller than Texas
**Population:** 1,639,833
**Population growth rate:** -0.04%
**Nationality:** noun: Motswana (singular); Batswana (plural); adjective: Motswana; Batswana
**Ethnic groups:** Tswana 79%, Kalanga 11%, Basarwa 3% and other 7%
**Languages:** English (official), Setswana
**Religions:** indigenous beliefs 85%, Christian 15%
**Government type:** parliamentary republic
**Capital:** Gaborone
**Budget: revenues:** $3.766 billion; expenditures: $3.767 billion          **Currency:** pula (BWP)

## BRAZIL

**Location:** Eastern South America, bordering the Atlantic Ocean
**Area:** 3,285,618 sq mi (8,511,965 sq km)
**Area-comparative:** slightly smaller than the US
**Population:** 188,078,227
**Population rate growth:** 1.04%
**Nationality:** noun: Brazilian(s), adjective: Brazilian
**Ethnic groups:** white (including Portuguese, German, and Italian) 55%, mixed 38%, black 6%, other 1%
**Languages:** Portuguese (official), Spanish, English, French

461

**Religions:** Roman Catholic 80%, other 20%
**Government type:** federative republic
**Capital:** Brasilia
**Budget:** revenues: $140.6 billion; expenditures: $172.4 billion       **Currency:** real (BRL)


*BRITISH VIRGIN ISLANDS* (overseas territory of the UK)
**Location:** Caribbean, between the Caribbean Sea and the North Atlantic Ocean, east of Puerto Rico
**Area:** 59 sq mi (153 sq km)
**Area-comparative:** about 0.9 times the size of Washington, DC
**Population:** 23,098
**Population growth rate:** 1.97%
**Nationality:** noun: British Virgin Islander(s); adjective: British Virgin Islander
**Ethnic groups:** black 83%, white, Indian, Asian and mixed
**Language:** English (official)
**Religions:** Protestant 86%, Catholic 10%, other 4%
**Government type:** NA (overseas territory of the UK)
**Capital:** Road Town
**Budget:** revenues: $121.5 million; expenditures: $115.5 million       **Currency:** US dollar (USD)


*BRUNEI*
**Location:** Southeastern Asia, bordering the South China Sea and Malaysia
**Area:** 2,227 sq mi (5,770 sq km)
**Area-comparative:** slightly smaller than Delaware
**Population:** 379,444
**Population growth rate:** 1.87%
**Nationality:** noun: Bruneian(s); adjective: Bruneian
**Ethnic groups:** Malay 67%, Chinese 15%, indigenous 6%, other 12%
**Languages:** Malay (official), English, Chinese
**Religions:** Muslim (official) 67%, Buddhist 13%, Christian 10%, indigenous beliefs and other 10%
**Government type:** constitutional sultanate
**Capital:** Bandar Seri Begawan
**Budget:** revenues: $3.765 billion; expenditures: $ 4.815 billion       **Currency:** Bruneian dollar (BND)


*BULGARIA*
**Location:** Southeastern Europe, bordering the Black Sea, between Romania and Turkey
**Area:** 42,811 sq mi (110,910 sq km)
**Area-comparative:** slightly larger than Tennessee
**Population:** 7,385,367
**Population growth rate:** -0.86%
**Nationality:** noun: Bulgarian(s); adjective: Bulgarian
**Ethnic groups:** Bulgarian 83.9%, Turk 9.4%, Roma 4.7%, other 2%
**Languages:** Bulgarian (official), secondary languages closely correspond to ethic breakdown
**Religions:** Bulgarian Orthodox 82.6%, Muslim 12.2%, Roman Catholic 1.7%, Jewish 0.1%, Protestant,
        Georgian-Armenian, and other 3.4%
**Government type:** parliamentary democracy
**Capital:** Sofia
**Budget:** revenues: $11.18 billion; expenditures: $10.9 billion, including capital of $NA
**Currency:** lev (BGN)


*BURKINA FASO*
**Location:** Western Africa, north of Ghana
**Area:** 105,841 sq mi (274,200 sq km)

**Area-comparative:** slightly larger than Colorado
**Population:** 13,902,972
**Population growth rate:** 3%
**Nationality:** noun: Burkinabe (singular and plural); adjective: Burkinabe
**Ethnic groups:** Mossi over 40%, Gurunsi, Senufo, Lobi, Bobo, Mande, Fulani
**Languages:** French (official), Sudanic tribal languages spoken by 90%
**Religions:** Muslim 50%, indigenous beliefs 40%, Christian (mainly Roman Catholic) 10%
**Government type:** parliamentary republic
**Capital:** Ouagadougou
**Budget:** revenues: $1.033 billion; expenditures: $1.382 billion
**Currency:** Communaute Financiere Africaine franc (XOF)

### BURMA

**Location:** Southeastern Asia, bordering the Andaman Sea and the Bay of Bengal
**Area:** 261,901 sq mi (678,500 sq km)
**Area-comparative:** slightly smaller than Texas
**Population:** 47,382,633
**Population growth rate:** 0.81%
**Nationality:** noun: Burmese (singular and plural); adjective: Burmese
**Ethnic groups:** Burman 68%, Shan 9%, Karen 7%, Rakhine 4%, Chinese 3%, Indian 2%, Mon 2%,
    other 5%
**Languages:** Burmese, minority ethnic groups have their own languages
**Religions:** Buddhist 89%, Christian 4%, Muslim 4%, animist 1%, other 2%
**Government type:** military junta
**Capital:** Rangoon
**Budget:** revenues: $473.3 million; expenditures: $716.6 million       **Currency:** kyat (MMK)

### BURUNDI

**Location:** Central Africa, east of Democratic Republic of the Congo
**Area:** 10,742 sq mi (27,830 sq km)
**Area-comparative:** slightly smaller than Maryland
**Population:** 8,090,068
**Population growth rate:** 3.7%
**Nationality:** noun: Burundian(s); adjective: Burundian
**Ethnic groups:** Hutu (Bantu) 85%, Tutsi 14%, Twa 1%, other 1%
**Languages:** Kirundi (official), French (official), Swahili
**Religions:** Roman Catholic 62%, indigenous beliefs 23%, Protestant 5%, Muslim 10%
**Government type:** republic
**Capital:** Bujumbura
**Budget:** revenues: $215.4 million; expenditures: $278 million       **Currency:** Burundi franc (BIF)

### CAMBODIA

**Location:** Southeastern Asia, bordering the Gulf of Thailand, between Thailand, Vietnam, and Laos
**Area:** 69,881 sq mi (181,040 sq km)
**Area-comparative:** slightly smaller than Oklahoma
**Population:** 13,881,427
**Population growth rate:** 1.78%
**Nationality:** noun: Cambodian(s); adjective: Cambodian
**Ethnic groups:** Khmer 90%, Vietnamese 5%, Chinese 1%, other 4%
**Languages:** Khmer (official) 95%, French, English
**Religions:** Theravada Buddhism 95%, other 5%
**Government type:** multiparty democracy under a constitutional monarchy

**Capital:** Phnom Penh
**Budget:** revenues: $559.4 million; expenditures: $772 million; capital expenditures of $291 million
**Currency:** riel (KHR)

## CAMEROON

**Location:** Western Africa, bordering the Bight of Biafra, between Equatorial Guinea and Nigeria
**Area:** 183,519 sq mi (475,440 sq km)
**Area-comparative:** slightly larger than California
**Population:** 17,340,702
**Population growth rate:** 2.04%
**Nationality:** noun: Cameroonian(s); adjective: Cameroonian
**Ethnic groups:** Cameroon Highlanders 31%, Equatorial Bantu 19%, Kirdi 11%, Fulani 10%, Northwestern Bantu 8%, Eastern Nigritic 7%, other African 13%, non-African less than 1%
**Languages:** 24 major African language groups, English (official), French (official)
**Religions:** indigenous beliefs 40%, Christian 40%, Muslim 20%
**Government type:** unitary republic; multiparty presidential regime
**Capital:** Yaounde
**Budget:** revenues: $3.263 billion; expenditures: $ 2.705 billion
**Currency:** Communaute Financiere Africaine franc (XAF)

## CANADA

**Location:** Northern North America, bordering the North Atlantic Ocean, Arctic Ocean and North Pacific Ocean, north of the 48 mainland states of the U.S.
**Area:** 3,850,790 sq mi (9,984,670 sq km)
**Area-comparative:** somewhat larger than the US
**Population:** 33,098,932
**Population growth rate:** 0.88%
**Nationality:** noun: Canadian(s), adjective: Canadian
**Ethnic groups:** British Isles origin 28%, French origin 23%, other European 15%, other (primarily Asian) 6%, Amerindian 2%, mixed background 26%
**Languages:** English (official), French (official)
**Religions:** Roman Catholic 46%, Protestant 36%, other 18%
**Government type:** confederation with parliamentary democracy
**Capital:** Ottawa
**Budget:** revenues: $159.6 billion; expenditures: $152.6 billion
**Currency:** Canadian dollar (CAD)

## CAPE VERDE

**Location:** Western Africa, group of islands in the North Atlantic Ocean, west of Senegal
**Area:** 1,556 sq mi (4,033 sq km)
**Area-comparative:** slightly larger than Rhode Island
**Population:** 420,979
**Population growth rate:** 0.64%
**Nationality:** noun: Cape Verdean(s); adjective: Cape Verdean
**Ethnic groups:** Creole 71%, African 28%, European 1%
**Language:** Portuguese (official), Crioulo (a blend of Portuguese and West African words)
**Religion:** Roman Catholic (infused with indigenous beliefs), Protestants
**Government type:** republic
**Capital:** Praia
**Budget:** revenues: $328.1 million; expenditures: $393.1 million
**Currency:** Cape Verdean escudo

**CAYMAN ISLANDS** (overseas territory of the UK)
**Location:** Caribbean, island group in Caribbean Sea, nearly one half of the way from Cuba to Honduras
**Area:** 101 sq mi (262 sq km)
**Area-comparative:** 1.5 times the size of Washington, DC
**Population:** 45,436
**Population growth rate:** 2.56%
**Nationality:** noun: Caymanian(s); adjective: Caymanian
**Ethnic groups:** mixed 40%, white 20%, black 20%, various other 20%
**Language:** English
**Religions:** United Church (Presbyterian and Congregational), Anglican, Baptist, Church of God, Protestant, Roman Catholic
**Government type:** British crown colony
**Capital:** George Town
**Budget:** revenues: $ 265.2 million, expenditures: $248.9 million
**Currency:** Caymanian dollar (KYD)

**CENTRAL AFRICAN REPUBLIC**
**Location:** Central Africa, north of Democratic Republic of the Congo
**Area:** 240,471 sq mi (622,984 sq km)
**Area-comparative:** slightly smaller than Texas
**Population:** 4,303,356
**Population growth rate:** 1.53%
**Nationality:** noun: Central African(s); adjective: Central African
**Ethnic groups:** Baya 33%, Banda 27%, Mandjia 13%, Sara 10%, Mboum 7%, M'Baka 4%, Yakoma 4%, other 2%
**Language:** French (official), Sangho (lingua franca and national language), tribal languages
**Religion:** indigenous beliefs 35%, Protestant 25%, Catholic 25%, Muslim 15%
**Government type:** republic
**Capital:** Bangui
**Budget: revenues:** $NA; expenditures: $NA    **Currency:** Communaute Financiere Africaine franc (XAF)

**CHAD**
**Location:** Central Africa, south of Libya
**Area:** 495,624 sq mi (1,284,000 sq km)
**Area-comparative:** slightly more than 3 times the size of California
**Population:** 9,944,201
**Population growth rate:** 2.93%
**Nationality:** noun: Chadian(s); adjective: Chadian
**Ethnic groups:** Sara, Sudanic Arab, Mayo-Kebbi peoples, Kanem-Bornu peoples, Ouaddaï peoples, Hadjeray, Tangale peoples, Gorane peoples, Fitri-Batha peoples, Fulan , 200 distinct groups, other
**Languages:** French (official), Arabic (official), Sara, over 120 different languages and dialects
**Religions:** Muslim 51%, Christian 35%, animist 7%, other 7%
**Government type:** republic
**Capital:** N`Djamena
**Budget:** revenues: $765.2 million; expenditures: $653.3 million; capital expenditures of $146 million
**Currency:** Communaute Financiere Africaine franc (XAF)

**CHILE**
**Location:** Southern South America, bordering the South Atlantic Ocean and South Pacific Ocean, between Argentina and Peru
**Area:** 292,182 sq mi (756,950 sq km)

**Area-comparative:** slightly smaller than twice the size of Montana
**Population:** 16,134,219
**Population growth rate:** 0.94%
**Nationality: noun:** Chilean(s); adjective: Chilean
**Ethnic groups:** white and white-Amerindian 95%, Amerindian 3%, other 2%
**Language:** Spanish (official)
**Religions:** Roman Catholic 89%, Protestant 11%
**Government type:** republic
**Capital:** Santiago
**Budget:** revenues: $29.2 billion; expenditures: $24.75 billion, including capital of $3.33 billion
**Currency:** Chilean peso (CLP)

## CHINA

**Location:** Eastern Asia, bordering the East China Sea, Korea Bay, Yellow Sea, and South China Sea, between North Korea and Vietnam
**Area:** 3,704,426 sq mi (9,596,960 sq km)
**Area-comparative:** slightly smaller than the US
**Population:** 1,313,973,713
**Population growth rate:** 0.59%
**Nationality: noun:** Chinese (singular and plural); adjective: Chinese
**Ethnic groups:** Han Chinese 92%, Zhuang, Uyger, Hui, Yi, Tibetan, Miao, Manchu, Mongol, Buyi, Korean, and other nationalities 8%
**Languages:** Standard Chinese or Mandarin (official), Yue, Wu, Minbei, Minnan, Xiang, Gan, Hakka dialects, minority languages
**Religions:** officially Atheist, Daoist (Taoist), Buddhist, Muslim 1%-2%, Christian 3%- 4%
**Government type:** Communist state
**Capital:** Beijing
**Budget:** revenues: $392.1 billion; expenditures: $424.3 billion          **Currency:** yuan (CŃY)

## COLOMBIA

**Location:** Northern South America, bordering the Caribbean Sea, between Panama and Venezuela, bordering the North Pacific Ocean, between Ecuador and Panama
**Area:** 439,619 sq mi (1,138,910 sq km)
**Area-comparative:** slightly less than 3 times the size of Montana
**Population:** 45,593,035
**Population growth rate:** 1.46%
**Nationality: noun:** Colombian(s); adjective: Colombian
**Ethnic groups:** mestizo 58%, white 20%, mulatto 14%, black 4%, mixed black- Amerindian 3%, Amerindian 1%
**Language:** Spanish (official)
**Religions:** Roman Catholic 90%, other 10%
**Government type:** republic, executive branch dominates government structure
**Capital:** Bogota
**Budget:** revenues: $46.82 billion; expenditures: $ 48.77 billion
**Currency:** Colombian peso (COP)

## COMOROS

**Location:** Southern Africa, group of islands in the Mozambique Channel, about two-thirds of the way between northern Madagascar and northern Mozambique
**Area:** 838 sq mi (2,170 sq km)
**Area-comparative:** slightly more than 12 times the size of Washington, DC
**Population:** 690,948

**Population growth rate:** 2.87%
**Nationality:** noun: Comoran(s); adjective: Comoran
**Ethnic groups:** Antalote, Cafre, Makoa, Oimatsaha, Sakalava
**Languages:** Arabic (official), French (official), Shikomoro (a blend of Swahili and Arabic)
**Religions:** Sunni Muslim 98%, Roman Catholic 2%
**Government type:** independent republic
**Capital:** Moroni
**Budget:** revenues: $27.6 million; expenditures: $NA          **Currency:** Comoran franc (KMF)

## CONGO, DEMOCRATIC REPUBLIC OF THE (ZAIRE)
**Location:** Central Africa, northeast of Angola
**Area:** 905,328 sq mi (2,345,410 sq km)
**Area-comparative:** slightly less than one-fourth the size of the US
**Population:** 62,660,551
**Population growth rate:** 3.07%
**Nationality:** noun: Congolese (singular and plural); adjective: Congolese or Congo
**Ethnic groups:** Over 200 African ethnic groups the majority are Bantu, the four largest tribes-Mongo, Luba, Kongo, and the Mangbetu-Azande- make up about 45% of the population
**Languages:** French (official), Lingala, Kingwana (a dialect of Kiswahili or Swahili), Kikongo, Tshiluba
**Religions:** Roman Catholic 50%, Protestant 20%, Kimbanguist 10%, Muslim 10%, other 10%
**Government type:** dictatorship; presumably undergoing a transition to representative government
**Capital:** Kinshasa
**Budget:** revenues: $700 million; expenditures: $750 million, including capital expenditures of $24 million
**Currency:** Congolese franc (KMF)

## CONGO, REPUBLIC OF THE
**Location:** Western Africa, bordering the South Atlantic Ocean, between Angola and Gabon
**Area:** 132,012 sq mi (342,000 sq km)
**Area-comparative:** slightly smaller than Montana
**Population:** 3,702,314
**Population growth rate:** 2.6%
**Nationality:** noun: Congolese (singular or plural); adjective: Congolese or Congo
**Ethnic groups:** Kongo 48%, Sangha 20%, Teke 17%, M'Bochi 12%, other 3%
**Languages:** French (official), Lingala and Monokutuba, many local languages and dialects
**Religions:** Christian 50%, animist 48%, Muslim 2%
**Government type:** republic
**Capital:** Brazzaville
**Budget:** revenues: $1.328 billion; expenditures: $1.065 billion
**Currency:** Communaute Financiere Africaine franc (XAF)

## COSTA RICA
**Location:** Central America, bordering both the Caribbean Sea and the North Pacific Ocean, between Nicaragua and Panama
**Area:** 19,724 sq mi (51,100 sq km)
**Area-comparative:** slightly smaller than West Virginia
**Population:** 4,075,261
**Population growth rate:** 1.45%
**Nationality:** noun: Costa Rican(s); adjective: Costa Rican
**Ethnic groups:** white and mestizo 94%, Black 3%, Amerindian 1%, Chinese 1%, other 1%
**Language:** Spanish (official) , English
**Religions:** Roman Catholic 76%, Evangelical 13%, other 11%
**Government type:** democratic republic

**Capital:** San Jose
**Budget:** revenues: $ 2.722 billion; expenditures $ 3.195 billion, including capital $NA
**Currency:** Costa Rican colon (CRC)


## COTE d'IVOIRE

**Location:** Western Africa, bordering the North Atlantic Ocean, between Ghana and Liberia
**Area:** 124,469 sq mi (322,460 sq km)
**Area-comparative:** slightly larger than New Mexico
**Population:** 17,654,843
**Population growth rate:** 2.03%
**Nationality:** noun: Ivorian(s); adjective: Ivorian
**Ethnic groups:** Akan 42.1%, Voltaiques or Gur 17.6%, Northern Mandes 16.5%, Krous 11%, Southern Mandes 10%, other 2.8%
**Languages:** French (official), 60 native dialects with Dioula the most widely spoken
**Religions:** Muslim 35-40%, Christian 20-30%, indigenous 25-40%
**Government type:** republic; multiparty presidential regime
**Capital:** Yamoussoukro (official); Abidjan remains the commercial and administrative center
**Budget:** revenues: $2.434 billion; expenditures: $2.83 billion; capital expenditures of $420 million
**Currency:** Communaute Financiere Africaine franc (XOF)


## CROATIA

**Location:** Southeastern Europe, bordering the Adriatic Sea, between Bosnia, Herzegovina, and Slovenia
**Area:** 21,824 sq mi (56,542 sq km)
**Area-comparative:** slightly smaller than West Virginia
**Population:** 4,494,749
**Population growth rate:** -0.03%
**Nationality:** noun: Croat(s), Croatian(s); adjective: Croatian
**Ethnic groups:** Croat 89.6%, Serb 4.5%, Bosniak 0.5%, Hungarian 0.4%, Slovene 0.3%, Czech 0.2%, Roma 0.2%, Albanian 0.1%, Montenegrin 0.1%, other 4.1%
**Languages:** Croatian 96%, other 4%
**Religions:** Catholic 87.8%, Orthodox 4.4%, Muslim 1.3%, Protestant 0.3%, others and unknown 6.2%
**Government type:** presidential/parliamentary democracy
**Capital:** Zagreb
**Budget:** revenues: $17.69 billion; expenditures: $19.35 billion       **Currency:** Croatian kuna (HRK)


## CUBA

**Location:** Caribbean, island between the Caribbean Sea and the North Atlantic Ocean, south of Florida
**Area:** 42,791 sq mi (110,860 sq km)
**Area-comparative:** slightly smaller than Pennsylvania
**Population:** 11,382,820
**Population growth rate:** 0.31%
**Nationality:** noun: Cuban(s); adjective: Cuban
**Ethnic groups:** mulatto 51%, white 37%, black 11%, Chinese 1%
**Language:** Spanish (official)
**Religions:** nominally 85% Roman Catholic prior to Castro assuming power; Protestants, Jehovah`s Witnesses, Jews and Santeria are represented
**Government type:** Communist state
**Capital:** Havana
**Budget:** revenues: $22.11 billion; expenditures: $23.65 billion       **Currency:** Cuban peso (CUP)


## CYPRUS

**Location:** Middle East, island in the Mediterranean Sea, south of Turkey
**Area:** 3,571 sq mi (9,250 sq km)

**Area-comparative:** about 0.6 times the size of Connecticut
**Population:** 784,301
**Population growth rate:** 0.53%
**Nationality:** noun: Cypriot(s); adjective: Cypriot
**Ethnic groups:** Greek 77%, Turkish 18%, other 5%
**Languages:** Greek, Turkish, English
**Religions:** Greek Orthodox 78%, Muslim 18%, other (including Maronite and Armenian Apostolic) 4%
**Government type:** republic
**Capital:** Nicosia
**Budget:** revenues: Greek Cypriot area-$6.698 billion, Turkish Cypriot area $231.3 million
　　　　　expenditures: Greek Cypriot area $7.122 billion, Turkish Cypriot area $432.8 million
**Currency:** Greek Cypriot area: Cypriot pound, Turkish Cypriot area: Turkish lira (CYP: TRL)

## CZECH REPUBLIC
**Location:** Central Europe, southeast of Germany
**Area:** 30,403 sq mi (78,866 sq km)
**Area-comparative:** slightly smaller than South Carolina
**Population:** 10,235,455
**Population growth rate:** -0.06%
**Nationality:** noun: Czech(s); adjective: Czech
**Ethnic groups:** Czech 81%, Moravian 13%, Slovak 3%, Polish , German and other 3%
**Language:** Czech (official)
**Religions:** Roman Catholic 39.2%, Protestant 4.6%, Orthodox 3%, other 13.4%, atheist 39.8%
**Government type:** parliamentary democracy
**Capital:** Prague
**Budget:** revenues: $48.16 billion; expenditures: $53.04 billion　　　**Currency:** Czech koruna (CZK)

## DENMARK
**Location:** Northern Europe, bordering the Baltic Sea and the North Sea, on a peninsula north of Germany
**Area:** 16,634 sq mi (43,094 sq km)
**Area-comparative:** slightly less than twice the size of Massachusetts
**Population:** 5,450,661
**Population growth rate:** 0.33%
**Nationality:** noun: Dane(s); adjective: Danish
**Ethnic groups:** Scandinavian, Inuit, Faroese, German, Turkish, Iranian, Somali
**Languages:** Danish (official), Faroese, Greenlandic, German
**Religions:** Evangelical Lutheran 95%, other Protestant and Roman Catholic 3%, Muslim 2%
**Government type:** constitutional monarchy
**Capital:** Copenhagen
**Budget:** revenues: $144 billion; expenditures: $139.6 billion
**Currency:** Danish krone (DKK)

## DJIBOUTI
**Location:** Eastern Africa, bordering the Gulf of Aden and the Red Sea, between Eritrea and Somalia
**Area:** 8,878 sq mi (23,000 sq km)
**Area-comparative:** slightly smaller than Massachusetts
**Population:** 486,530
**Population growth rate:** 2.02%
**Nationality:** noun: Djiboutian(s); adjective: Djiboutian
**Ethnic groups:** Somali 60%, Afar 35%, French, Arab, and Ethiopian and Italian 5%
**Languages:** French (official), Arabic (official), Somali, Afar
**Religions:** Muslim 94%, Christian 6%
**Government type:** republic

**Capital:** Djibouti
**Budget:** revenues: $135 million; expenditures: $182 million
**Currency:** Djiboutian franc (DJF)

## DOMINICA
**Location:** Caribbean, island between the Caribbean Sea and the North Atlantic Ocean, about one-half of the way from Puerto Rico to Trinidad and Tobago
**Area:** 290 sq mi (754 sq km)
**Area-comparative:** slightly more than 4 times the size of Washington, DC
**Population:** 68,910
**Population growth rate:** -0.08%
**Nationality:** noun: Dominican(s); adjective: Dominican
**Ethnic groups:** black, mixed black and European, European, Syrian, Carib Amerindian
**Languages:** English (official), French patois
**Religions:** Roman Catholic 77%, Protestant 15%, other/nonreligious 8%
**Government type:** parliamentary democracy; republic within the Commonwealth
**Capital:** Roseau
**Budget:** revenues: $73.9 million; expenditures: $84.4 million
**Currency:** East Caribbean dollar (XCD)

## DOMINICAN REPUBLIC
**Location:** Caribbean, eastern two-thirds of the island of Hispaniola, between the Caribbean Sea and the North Atlantic Ocean, east of Haiti
**Area:** 18,810 sq mi (48,730 sq km)
**Area-comparative:** slightly more than twice the size of New Hampshire
**Population:** 9,183,984
**Population growth rate:** 1.47%
**Nationality:** noun: Dominican(s); adjective: Dominican
**Ethnic groups:** Multiracial (black and white) 73%, white16%, black 11%
**Language:** Spanish (official)
**Religions:** Roman Catholic 95%, other 5%
**Government type:** representative democracy
**Capital:** Santo Domingo
**Budget:** revenues: $5.322 billion; expenditures: $6.585 billion
**Currency:** Dominican peso (DOP)

## ECUADOR
**Location:** Western South America, bordering the Pacific Ocean at the Equator
**Area:** 109,454 sq mi (283,560 sq km)
**Area-comparative:** slightly smaller than Nevada
**Population:** 13,547,510
**Population growth rate:** 1.5%
**Nationality:** noun: Ecuadorian(s): adjective: Ecuadorian
**Ethnic groups:** mestizo 65%, Amerindian 25%, Spanish and others 7%, black 3%
**Languages:** Spanish (official), Amerindian languages (particularly Quechua)
**Religions:** Roman Catholic 95%, other 5%
**Government type:** republic
**Capital:** Quito
**Budget:** revenues: $8.822 billion; expenditures: planned $9.753 billion
**Currency:** US dollar (USD)

## EGYPT

**Location:** Northern Africa, bordering the Mediterranean Sea, between Libya and the Gaza Strip
**Area:** 386,560 sq mi (1,001,450 sq km)
**Area-comparative:** slightly more than three times the size of New Mexico
**Population:** 78,887,007
**Population growth rate:** 1.75%
**Nationality:** noun: Egyptian(s); adjective: Egyptian
**Ethnic groups:** Egyptians, Bedouins, and Berbers 99%, other including Greek, Nubian, and Armenian 1%
**Languages:** Arabic (official), English, French
**Religions:** Muslim (primarily Sunni) 94%, other (including Coptic Christian) 6%
**Government type:** republic
**Capital:** Cairo
**Budget:** revenues: $20.29 billion; expenditures: $27.68 billion; capital expenditures of $2.7 billion
**Currency:** Egyptian pound (EGP)

## EL SALVADOR

**Location:** Central America, bordering the North Pacific Ocean, between Guatemala and Honduras
**Area:** 8,121 sq mi (21,040 sq km)
**Area-comparative:** slightly smaller than Massachusetts
**Population:** 6,822,378
**Population growth rate:** 1.72%
**Nationality:** noun: Salvadoran(s); adjective: Salvadoran
**Ethnic groups:** mestizo 90%, Amerindian 1%, white 9%
**Languages:** Spanish (official), Nahua
**Religions:** Roman Catholic 83%, Protestant and other 17%
**Government type:** republic
**Capital:** San Salvador
**Budget:** revenues: $2.84 billion; expenditures: $3.167 billion
**Currency:** US dollar (USD)

## EQUATORIAL GUINEA

**Location:** Western Africa, bordering the Bight of Biafra, between Cameroon and Gabon
**Area:** 10,827 sq mi (28,051 sq km)
**Area-comparative:** slightly smaller than Maryland
**Population:** 540,109
**Population growth rate:** 2.05%
**Nationality:** noun: Equatorial Guinean(s) or Equatoguinean(s)
**Ethnic groups:** Bioko (primarily Bubi, some Fernandinos), Rio Muni (primarily Fang), Europeans
**Languages:** Spanish (official), French (official), pidgin English, Fang, Bubi , Ibo
**Religions:** nominally Christian and predominantly Roman Catholic, pagan practices
**Government type:** republic
**Capital:** Malabo
**Budget:** revenues: $1.973 billion; expenditures: $711.5 million
**Currency:** Communaute Financiere Africaine franc (XAF)

## ERITREA

**Location:** Eastern Africa, bordering the Red Sea, between Djibouti and Sudan
**Area:** 46,830 sq mi (121,320 sq km)
**Area-comparative:** slightly larger than Pennsylvania
**Population:** 4,786,994
**Population growth rate:** 2.47%
**Nationality:** noun: Eritrean(s); adjective: Eritrean
**Ethnic groups:** ethnic Tigrinya 50%, Tigre and Kunama 40%, Afar 4%, Saho 3%, other 3%

**Languages:** Afar, Arabic, Tigre and Kunama, Tigrinya, other Cushitic languages
**Religions:** Muslim, Coptic Christian, Roman Catholic, Protestant
**Government type:** transitional government
**Capital:** Asmara
**Budget:** revenues: $248.8 million; expenditures: $409.4 million
**Currency:** nakfa (ERN)

## ESTONIA

**Location:** Eastern Europe, bordering the Baltic Sea and Gulf of Finland, between Latvia and Russia
**Area:** 17,457 sq mi (45,226 sq km)
**Area-comparative:** slightly smaller than New Hampshire and Vermont combined
**Population:** 1,324,333
**Population growth rate:** -0.64%
**Nationality:** noun: Estonian(s) adjective: Estonian
**Ethnic groups:** Estonian 65.3%, Russian 28.1%, Ukrainian 2.5%, Belarusian 1.5%, Finn 1% other 1.6%
**Languages:** Estonian (official), Russian, Ukrainian, Finnish, other
**Religions:** Evangelical Lutheran, Russian Orthodox, Estonian Orthodox, Baptist, Methodist, Seventh-Day Adventist, Roman Catholic, Pentecostal, Word of Life, Jewish
**Government type:** parliamentary republic
**Capital:** Tallinn
**Budget:** revenues: $5.126 billion; expenditures: $5.017 billion, including capital of $NA
**Currency:** Estonian kroon (EEK)

## ETHIOPIA

**Location:** Eastern Africa, west of Somalia
**Area:** 435,071 sq mi (1,127,127 sq km)
**Area-comparative:** slightly less than twice the size of Texas
**Population:** 74,777,981
**Population growth rate:** 2.31%
**Nationality:** noun: Ethiopian(s); adjective: Ethiopian
**Ethnic groups:** Oromo 40%, Amhara and Tigre 32%, Sidamo 9%, Shankella 6%, Somali 6%, Afar 4%, Gurage 2%, other 1%
**Languages:** Amharic (official), Tigrinya, Orominga, Guaragigna, Somali, Arabic, other local languages
**Religions:** Muslim 45%-50%, Ethiopian Orthodox 35%-40%; animist 12%, other 3%-8%
**Government type:** federal republic
**Capital:** Addis Ababa
**Budget:** revenues: $2.338 billion; expenditures: $2.388 billion; capital expenditures of $788 million
**Currency:** birr (ETB)

## FIJI

**Location:** Oceania, island group in the South Pacific Ocean, 2/3's of the way from Hawaii to New Zealand
**Area:** 7,052 sq mi (18,270 sq km)
**Area-comparative:** slightly smaller than New Jersey
**Population:** 905,949
**Population growth rate:** 1.4%
**Nationality:** noun: Fijian(s); adjective: Fijian
**Ethnic groups:** Fijian 51%, Indian 44%, Europeans, Pacific Islanders, and overseas Chinese 5%
**Language:** English (official), Fijian, Hindustani
**Religion:** Christian 52%, Hindu 38%, Muslim 8%, other 2%
**Government type:** republic
**Capital:** Suva
**Budget:** revenues: $427.9 million; expenditures: $531.4 million          **Currency:** Fijian dollar (FJD)

## FINLAND
**Location:** Northern Europe, bordering the Baltic Sea, Gulf of Bothnia, and Gulf of Finland
**Area:** 130,094 sq mi (337,030 sq km)
**Area-comparative:** slightly smaller than Montana
**Population:** 5,231,372
**Population growth rate:** 0.14%
**Nationality:** noun: Finn(s); adjective: Finnish
**Ethnic groups:** Finn 93%, Swede 6%, other 1%
**Languages:** Finnish 93.4% (official), Swedish 5.9% (official), small Sami- and Russian-speaking minorities
**Religions:** Evangelical Lutheran 89%, Russian Orthodox 1%, none 9%, other 1%
**Government type:** republic
**Capital:** Helsinki
**Budget:** revenues: $99.61 billion; expenditures: $97.14 billion
**Currency:** euro (EUR)

## FRANCE
**Location:** Western Europe, bordering the Bay of Biscay and English Channel, between Belgium and Spain, southeast of the UK; bordering the Mediterranean Sea, between Italy and Spain
**Area:** 211,153 sq mi (547,030 sq km)
**Area-comparative:** slightly less than twice the size of Colorado
**Population:** 60,876,136
**Population growth rate:** 0.35%
**Nationality:** noun: Frenchman (men), Frenchwoman (women); adjective: French
**Ethnic groups:** Celtic and Latin with Teutonic Slavic, North African, Indochinese, Basque
**Language:** French (official)
**Religions:** Roman Catholic 83%-88%, Muslim 5%-10%, Protestant 2%, Jewish 1%, unaffiliated 4%
**Government type:** republic
**Capital:** Paris
**Budget:** revenues: $1.06 trillion; expenditures: $1.144 trillion, including capital expenditures of $ 23 billion
**Currency:** euro (EUR)

## GABON
**Location:** Western Africa, bordering the Atlantic Ocean at the Equator, between Republic of the Congo and Equatorial Guinea
**Area:** 103,319 sq mi (267,667 sq km)
**Area-comparative:** slightly smaller than Colorado
**Population:** 1,424,906
**Population growth rate:** 2.13%
**Nationality:** noun: Gabonese (singular and plural); adjective: Gabonese
**Ethnic groups:** Bantu tribes including four major tribal groups; Fang, Bapounou, Nzebi and Obamba, other Africans and Europeans
**Languages:** French (official), Fang, Myene, Nzebi, Bapounou/Eschira, Bandjabi
**Religions:** Christian 55%-75%, animist, Muslim 1%
**Government type:** republic, multiparty presidential regime
**Capital:** Libreville
**Budget:** revenues: $2.463 billion; expenditures: $1.618 billion; capital expenditures of $325 million .
**Currency:** Communaute Financiere Africaine franc (XAF)

## GAMBIA
**Location:** Western Africa, bordering the North Atlantic Ocean and Senegal
**Area:** 4,362 sq mi (11,300 sq km)
**Area-comparative:** slightly less than twice the size of Delaware

**Population:** 1,641,564
**Population growth rate:** 2.84%
**Nationality:** noun: Gambian(s); adjective: Gambian
**Ethnic groups:** African (including Mandinka, Fula, and Wolof) 99%, non-African 1%
**Languages:** English (official), Mandinka, Wolof, Fula
**Religions:** Muslim 90%, Christian 9%, indigenous beliefs 1%
**Government type:** republic under multiparty democratic rule
**Capital:** Banjul
**Budget:** revenues: $46.63 million; expenditures: $66.76 million          **Currency:** dalasi (GMD)

## GEORGIA
**Location:** Southwestern Asia, bordering the Black Sea, between Turkey and Russia
**Area:** 26,904 sq mi (69,700 sq km)
**Area-comparative:** slightly smaller than South Carolina
**Population:** 4,661,473
**Population growth rate:** -0.34%
**Nationality:** noun: Georgian(s); adjective: Georgian
**Ethnic groups:** Georgian 70%, Armenian 8%, Russian 6%, Azeri 6%, Ossetian 3%, Abkhaz 2%, other 5%
**Languages:** Georgian 71% (official), Russian 9%, Armenian 7%, Azeri 6%, other 7%
**Religions:** Georgian Orthodox 65%, Russian Orthodox 10%, Muslim 11%, Armenian Apostolic 8%, other
**Government type:** republic
**Capital:** T`bilisi
**Budget:** revenues: $1.43 billion; expenditures: $1.56 billion
**Currency:** lari (GEL)

## GERMANY
**Location:** Central Europe, bordering the Baltic Sea and North Sea, between the Netherlands and Poland
**Area:** 137,810 sq mi (357,021 sq km)
**Area-comparative:** slightly smaller than Montana
**Population:** 82,422,299
**Population growth rate:** -0.02%
**Nationality:** noun: German(s); adjective: German
**Ethnic groups:** German 92%,Turkish 2%, other 6%
**Language:** German (official)
**Religion:** Protestant 34%, Roman Catholic 34%, Muslim 4%, unaffiliated or other 28%
**Government type:** federal republic
**Capital:** Berlin
**Budget:** revenues: $1.249 trillion; expenditures: $1.362 trillion
**Currency:** euro (EUR)

## GHANA
**Location:** Western Africa, bordering the Gulf of Guinea, between Cote d'Ivoire and Togo
**Area:** 92,431 sq mi (239,460 sq km)
**Area-comparative:** slightly smaller than Oregon
**Population:** 22,409,572
**Population growth rate:** 2.07%
**Nationality:** noun: Ghanaian(s); adjective: Ghanaian
**Ethnic groups:** black African 98.5%, (major tribes- Akan 44%, Moshi-Dagomba 16%, Ewe 13%, Ga 8%), European and other 1.5%
**Language:** English (official), African languages (including Akan, Moshi-Dagomba, Ewe and Ga)
**Religion:** indigenous beliefs 21%, Muslim 16%, Christian 63%
**Government type:** constitutional democracy

474

**Capital:** Accra
**Budget:** revenues: $3.216 billion; expenditures: $2.506 billion
**Currency:** cedi (GHC)

*GREECE*
**Location:** Southern Europe, bordering the Aegean Sea, Ionian Sea, and the Mediterranean Sea
**Area:** 50,929 sq mi (131,940 sq km)
**Area-comparative:** slightly smaller than Alabama
**Population:** 10,688,058
**Population growth rate:** 0.18%
**Nationality:** noun: Greek(s); adjective: Greek
**Ethnic groups:** Greek 98%, other 2%
**Languages:** Greek (official), English, French
**Religions:** Greek Orthodox 98%, Muslim 1.3%, other 0.7%
**Government type:** parliamentary republic
**Capital:** Athens
**Budget:** revenues: $94.13 billion; expenditures: $103.4 billion
**Currency:** euro (EUR)

*GRENADA*
**Location:** Caribbean island between the Caribbean Sea and Atlantic Ocean, north of Trinidad and Tobago
**Area:** 133 sq mi (344 sq km)
**Area-comparative:** twice the size of Washington, DC
**Population:** 89,703
**Population growth rate:** 0.26%
**Nationality:** noun: Grenadian(s); adjective: Grenadian
**Ethnic groups:** black 82%, mixed black and European 13%, European and East Indian 5%, and trace of Arawak/Carib Amerindian
**Language:** English (official), French patois
**Religion:** Roman Catholic 53%, Anglican 13.8%, other Protestant 33.2%
**Government type:** constitutional monarchy with Westminster-style parliament
**Capital:** Saint George`s
**Budget:** revenues: $85.8 million; expenditures: $102.1 million, also, capital expenditures of $28 million
**Currency:** East Caribbean dollar (XCD)

*GUATEMALA*
**Location:** Central America, bordering the North Pacific Ocean, between El Salvador and Mexico, and bordering the Gulf of Honduras (Caribbean Sea) between Honduras and Belize
**Area:** 42,031 sq mi (108,890 sq km)
**Area-comparative:** slightly smaller than Tennessee
**Population:** 12,293,545
**Population growth rate:** 2.27%
**Nationality:** noun: Guatemalan(s); adjective: Guatemalan
**Ethnic groups:** Mestizo 55%, Amerindian or predominantly Amerindian 43%, whites and others 2%
**Languages:** Spanish, Amerindian languages
**Religions:** Roman Catholic, Protestant, traditional Mayan beliefs
**Government type:** constitutional democratic republic
**Capital:** Guatemala
**Budget:** revenues: $3.374 billion; expenditures: $4.041 billion; capital expenditures of $750 million
**Currency:** quetzal (GTQ) US dollar (USD), others allowed

*GUINEA*
**Location:** Western Africa, bordering the North Atlantic Ocean, between Guinea-Bissau and Sierra Leone
**Area:** 94,901 sq mi (245,857 sq km)
**Area-comparative:** slightly smaller than Oregon
**Population:** 9,690,222
**Population growth rate:** 2.63%
**Nationality:** noun: Guinean(s); adjective; Guinean
**Ethnic groups:** Peuhl 40%, Malinke 30%, Soussou 20%, other tribes 10%
**Language:** French (official), tribal languages
**Religion:** Muslim 85%, Christian 8%, indigenous beliefs 7%
**Government type:** republic
**Capital:** Conakry
**Budget:** revenues: $305.6 million; expenditures: $590.4 million      **Currency:** Guinean franc (GNF)

*GUINEA-BISSAU*
**Location:** Western Africa, bordering the North Atlantic Ocean, between Guinea and Senegal
**Area:** 13,942 sq mi (36,120 sq km)
**Area-comparative:** slightly less than three times the size of Connecticut
**Population:** 1,442,029
**Population growth rate:** 2.07%
**Nationality:** noun: Guinean(sh); adjective Guinean(s)
**Ethnic groups:** Balanta 30%, Fula 20%, other 17%, Majaca 12%, Mandinga 13%, Papel 7%, European and mulatto less than 1%
**Languages:** Portuguese (official), Crioulo, African languages
**Religion:** indigenous beliefs 50%, Muslim 45%, Christian 5%
**Government type:** republic, multiparty since mid-1991
**Capital:** Bissau
**Budget:** revenues: $NA; expenditures: $NA
**Currency:** Communaute Financiere Africaine franc (XOF);(GWP)

*GUYANA*
**Location:** Northern South America, bordering North Atlantic Ocean, between Suriname and Venezuela
**Area:** 82,978 sq mi (214,970 sq km)
**Area-comparative:** slightly smaller than Idaho
**Population:** 767,245
**Population growth rate:** 0.25%
**Nationality:** noun: Guyanese (singular and plural); adjective: Guyanese
**Ethnic groups:** East Indian 50%, black 36%, Amerindian 7%, white, Chinese, and mixed 7%
**Languages:** English, Amerindian dialects, Creole, Hindi, Urdu
**Religions:** Christian 50%, Hindu 35%, Muslim 10%, other 5%
**Government type:** republic within the Commonwealth
**Capital:** Georgetown
**Budget:** revenues $320.1 million; expenditures: $362.6 million; capital expenditures of $93.4 million
**Currency:** Guyanese dollar (GYD)

*HAITI*
**Location:** Caribbean, western one-third of the island of Hispaniola, west of the Dominican Republic
**Area:** 10,711 sq mi (27,750 sq km)
**Area-comparative:** slightly smaller than Maryland
**Population:** 8,308,504
**Population growth rate:** 2.3%
**Nationality:** noun: Haitian(s); adjective: Haitian

476

**Ethnic groups:** black 95%, mulatto and white 5%
**Languages:** French (official), Creole (official)
**Religions:** Roman Catholic 80%, Protestant 16%, none 1%, other 3%
**Government type:** elected government
**Capital:** Port-au-Prince
**Budget:** revenues: $400 million; expenditures: $600.8 million          **Currency:** gourde (HTG)

## HONDURAS
**Location:** Central America, bordering the Caribbean Sea, between El Salvador and Nicaragua
**Area:** 43,267 sq mi (112,090 sq km)
**Area-comparative:** slightly larger than Tennessee
**Population:** 7,326,496
**Population growth rate:** 2.16%
**Nationality:** noun: Honduran(s); adjective: Honduran
**Ethnic groups:** mestizo (mixed Amerindian and European) 90%, Amerindian 7%, black 2%, white 1%
**Languages:** Spanish (official), Amerindian dialects
**Religions:** Roman Catholic 97%, other 3%
**Government type:** democratic constitutional republic
**Capital:** Tegucigalpa
**Budget:** revenues: $1.693 billion; expenditures: $1.938 billion; capital expenditures of $106 million
**Currency:** lempira (HNL)

## HUNGARY
**Location:** Central Europe, northwest of Romania
**Area:** 35,910 sq mi (93,030 sq km)
**Area-comparative:** slightly smaller than Indiana
**Population:** 9,981,334
**Population growth rate:** - 0.25%
**Nationality:** noun: Hungarian(s); adjective: Hungarian
**Ethnic groups:** Hungarian 89.9%, Roma 4%, German 2.6%, Serb 2%, Slovak 0.8%, Romanian 0.7%
**Languages:** Hungarian 98.2%, other 1.8%
**Religion:** Roman Catholic 67.5%, Calvinist 20%, Lutheran 5%, atheist and other 7.5%
**Government type:** parliamentary democracy
**Capital:** Budapest
**Budget:** revenues $51.4 billion; expenditures: $58.34 billion, including capital of $NA
**Currency:** forint (HUF)

## ICELAND
**Location:** Northern Europe, island between the Greenland Sea and the North Atlantic Ocean
**Area:** 39,758 sq mi (103,000 sq km)
**Area-comparative:** slightly smaller than Kentucky
**Population:** 299,388
**Population growth rate:** 0.87%
**Nationality:** noun, Icelanders(s); adjective, Icelandic
**Ethnic groups:** a mixture of descendents of Norse and Celts 94%, population of foreign origin 6%
**Languages:** Icelandic, English, Nordic languages, German widely spoken
**Religions:** Evangelical Lutheran 87.1%, other Protestant 4.1%, Roman Catholic 1.7%, other 7.1%
**Government type:** constitutional republic
**Capital:** Reykjavik
**Budget:** revenues: $6.995 billion, expenditures: $6.761billion; capital expenditures of $467 million
**Currency:** Icelandic krona (ISK)

## INDIA

**Location:** Southern Asia, bordering the Arabian Sea and the Bay of Bengal, between Burma and Pakistan
**Area:** 1,269,009 sq mi (3,287,590 sq km)
**Area-comparative:** slightly more than one-third the size of the United States
**Population:** 1,095,351,995
**Population growth-rate:** 1.38%
**Nationality:** noun, Indian(s); adjective: Indian
**Ethnic groups:** Indo-Aryan 72%, Dravidian 25%, Mongoloid and other 3%
**Language:** Hindi (official), English and 14 other official regional languages
**Religions:** Hindu 81.3%, Muslim 12%, Christian 2.3%, Sikh 1.9%, Buddhist, Jain, Parsi 2.5%
**Government type:** federal republic
**Capital:** New Delhi
**Budget:** revenues: $111.2 billion; expenditures: $135.8 billion, including capital expenditures of $15 billion
**Currency:** Indian rupee (INR)

## INDONESIA

**Location:** Southeastern Asia, group of islands between the Indian Ocean and the Pacific Ocean
**Area:** 740,904 sq mi (1,919,440 sq km)
**Area-comparative:** slightly less than three times the size of Texas
**Population:** 245,452,739
**Population growth rate:** 1.41%
**Nationality:** noun: Indonesian(s); adjective: Indonesian
**Ethnic groups:** Javanese 45%, Sundanese 14%, Madurese 7.5%, Coastal Maylays 7.5%, other 26%
**Languages:** Bahasa Indonesia (official modified form of Malay), English, Dutch, Javanese, local dialects
**Religions:** Muslim 88%, Protestant 5%, Roman Catholic 3%, Hindu 2%, Buddhist 1%, other 1%
**Government:** republic
**Capital:** Jakarta
**Budget:** revenues: $54.3 billion; expenditures: $57.7 billion, including capital of $NA
**Currency:** Indonesian rupiah (IDR)

## IRAN

**Location:** Middle East, bordering the Gulf of Oman, the Persian Gulf, and the Caspian Sea, between Iraq and Pakistan
**Area:** 636,128 sq mi (1,648,000 sq km)
**Area-comparative:** slightly larger than Alaska
**Population:** 68,688,433
**Population growth rate:** 1.1%
**Nationality:** noun: Iranian(s), adjective: Iranian
**Ethnic groups:** Persian 51%, Azeri 24%, Gilaki and Mazandarani 8%, Kurd 7%, Arab 3%, Lur 2%, Baloch 2%, Turkmen 2%, other 1%
**Languages:** Persian and Persian dialects 58%, Turkic and Turkic dialects 26%, Kurdish 9%, Luri 2%, Balochi 1%, Arabic 1%, Turkish 1%, other 2%
**Religions:** Shi'a Muslim 89%, Sunni Muslim 9%, Zoroastrian, Jewish, Christian, and Baha'i 2%
**Government type:** theocratic republic
**Capital:** Tehran
**Budget:** revenues: $42.82 billion; expenditures: $60.4 billion, including capital of $7.6
**Currency:** Iranian rial (IRR)

## IRAQ

**Location:** Middle East, bordering the Persian Gulf, between Iran and Kuwait
**Area:** 168,710 sq mi (437,072 sq km)
**Area-comparative:** slightly more than twice the size of Idaho

**Population:** 26,783,383
**Population growth rate:** 2.66%
**Nationality:** noun, Iraqi(s); adjective: Iraqi
**Ethnic groups:** Arab 75%-80%, Kurdish 15%-20%, Turkoman, Assyrian or other 5%
**Languages:** Arabic, Kurdish (official in Kurdish regions), Assyrian, Armenian
**Religions:** Muslim 97% (Shi'a 60% - 65%, Sunni 32% - 37%), Christian or other 3%
**Government type:** transitional democracy
**Capital:** Baghdad
**Budget:** revenues: $19.3 billion; expenditures: $24 billion, including capital of $5 billion
**Currency:** Iraqi dinar (NID)

## IRELAND

**Location:** Western Europe, island in the North Atlantic Ocean, west of Great Britain
**Area:** 27,128 sq mi (70,280 sq km)
**Area-comparative:** slightly larger than West Virginia
**Population:** 4,062,235
**Population growth rate:** 1.15%
**Nationality:** noun: Irishman(men), Irishwoman(women), Irish (collective plural); adjective: Irish
**Ethnic groups:** Celtic, English
**Languages:** English (official), Irish (official)
**Religions:** Roman Catholic 92%, Church of Ireland 3%, other 5%
**Government type:** parliamentary democracy
**Capital:** Dublin
**Budget:** revenues: $70.46 billion; expenditures: $64.9 billion; capital expenditures of $5.5 billion
**Currency:** euro (EUR)

## ISRAEL

**Location:** Middle East, bordering the Mediterranean Sea, between Egypt and Lebanon
**Area:** 8,017 sq mi (20,770 sq km)
**Area-comparative:** slightly smaller than New Jersey
**Population:** 6,352,117
**Population growth rate:** 1.18%
**Nationality:** noun: Israeli(s); adjective: Israeli
**Ethnic groups:** Jewish (including European/American-born, Israeli-born, and African-born) 80.1%, non-Jewish 19.9% (primarily Arab)
**Languages:** Hebrew (official), Arabic, English
**Religions:** Jewish 80.1%, Muslim 14.6%, Christian 2.1%, other 3.2%
**Government type:** parliamentary democracy
**Capital:** Jerusalem
**Budget:** revenues: $43.82 billion: expenditures: $58.04 billion          **Currency:** new Israeli shekel (ILS)

## ITALY

**Location:** Southern Europe, peninsula extending into the central Mediterranean Sea, northeast of Tunisia
**Area:** 116,275 sq mi (301,230 sq km)
**Area-comparative:** slightly larger than Arizona
**Population:** 58,133,509
**Population growth rate:** 0.04%
**Nationality:** noun: Italian(s); adjective: Italian
**Ethnic groups:** Italian, small clusters of German, French, Slovene, and Albanian
**Languages:** Italian (official), German, French, Slovene
**Religions:** predominately Roman Catholic with mature Protestant and Jewish communities and a growing Muslim immigrant community

**Government type:** republic
**Capital:** Rome
**Budget:** revenues: $785.7 billion; expenditures: $861.5 billion       **Currency:** euro (EUR)

## *JAMAICA*
**Location:** Caribbean, island in the Caribbean Sea, south of Cuba
**Area:** 4,242 sq mi (10,991 sq km)
**Area-comparative:** slightly smaller than Connecticut
**Population:** 2,758,124
**Population growth rate:** 0.8%
**Nationality:** noun: Jamaican(s); adjective: Jamaican
**Ethnic groups:** black 90.9%, Multiracial (black and white) 7.3%, white 0.2%, Chinese 0.2%, other 0.1%, East Indian 1.3%
**Language:** English (official), patois English
**Religion:** Protestant 61%, other (including indigenous beliefs) 35%, Roman Catholic 4%
**Government type:** constitutional parliamentary democracy
**Capital:** Kingston
**Budget:** revenues: $ 2.8 billion: expenditures: $3.2 billion; capital expenditures of $180.4 million
**Currency:** Jamaican dollar (JMD)

## *JAPAN*
**Location:** Eastern Asia, island chain between the North Pacific Ocean and the Sea of Japan, east of the Korean Peninsula
**Area:** 145,844 sq mi (377,835 sq km)
**Area-comparative:** slightly smaller than California
**Population:** 127,463,611
**Population growth rate:** 0.02%
**Nationality:** noun: Japanese (singular and plural); adjective: Japanese
**Ethnic groups:** Japanese 99%, other 1%
**Language:** Japanese (official)
**Religion:** observe both Shinto and Buddhist 84%, other 16% (including Christian 0.7%)
**Government type:** constitutional monarchy with a parliamentary government
**Capital:** Tokyo
**Budget:** revenues: $1.43 trillion; expenditures: $1.77 trillion, including capital of about $71 billion
**Currency:** yen (JPY)

## *JORDAN*
*Location:* Southwestern Asia, northwest of Saudi Arabia
**Area:** 35,628 sq mi (92,300 sq km)
**Area-comparative:** slightly smaller than Indiana
**Population:** 5,906,760
**Population growth rate:** 2.49%
**Nationality:** noun: Jordanian(s); adjective: Jordanian
**Ethnic groups:** Arab 98%, Circassian 1%, Armenian 1%
**Languages:** Arabic (official), English
**Religions:** Sunni Muslim 92%, Christian 6%, other 2% (several small Shi'a Muslim and Druze populations)
**Government type:** constitutional monarchy
**Capital:** `Amman
**Budget:** revenues: $2.8 billion; expenditures: $4.68 billion; capital expenditures of $1.09 billion
**Currency:** Jordanian dinar (JOD)

## *KAZAKHSTAN*
**Location:** Central Asia, northwest of China

**Area:** 1,048,877 sq mi (2,717,300 sq km)
**Area-comparative:** slightly less than four times the size of Texas
**Population:** 15,233,244
**Population growth rate:** 0.33%
**Nationality:** noun: Kazakhstani(s); adjective: Kazakhstani
**Ethnic groups:** Kazakh (Qazaq) 53.4%, Russian 30%, Ukrainian 3.7%, German 2.4%, Uzbek 2.5%, Uygur 1.4%, other 6.6%
**Language:** Russian 95% (official), Kazakh (official) 5%
**Religion:** Muslim 47%, Russian Orthodox 44%, Protestant 2%, other 7%
**Government type:** republic; authoritarian presidential rule, with little power outside the executive branch
**Capital:** Astana
**Budget:** revenues: $12.19 billion; expenditures: $12.44 billion          **Currency:** tenge (KZT)

## *KENYA*
**Location:** Eastern Africa, bordering the Indian Ocean, between Somalia and Tanzania
**Area:** 224,903 sq mi (582,650 sq km)
**Area-comparative:** slightly more than twice the size of Nevada
**Population:** 34,707,817
**Population growth rate:** 2.57%
**Nationality:** Kenyan(s); adjective: Kenyan
**Ethnic groups:** Kikuyu 22%, Luhya/ Luo 27%, Kalenjin 12%, Kamba 11%, Kisii 6%, Meru 6%, other African 16%, non-African 1%
**Language:** English (official), Kiswahili (official), numerous indigenous languages
**Religion:** Protestant 45%, Roman Catholic 33%, indigenous beliefs 10%, Muslim 10%, other 2%
**Government type:** republic
**Capital:** Nairobi
**Budget:** revenues: $3.71 billion; expenditures: $3.88 billion          **Currency:** Kenyan shilling (KES)

## *KIRIBATI*
**Location:** a group of islands in the Pacific Ocean, about one-half of the way from Hawaii to Australia
**Area:** 313 sq mi (811 sq km)
**Area-comparative:** four times the size of Washington, DC
**Population:** 105,432
**Population growth rate:** 2.24%
**Nationality:** noun: I-Kiribati (singular and plural); adjective: I-Kiribati
**Ethnic groups:** predominantly Micronesian with some Polynesian
**Language:** I-Kiribati, English (official)
**Religion:** Roman Catholic 52%, Protestant 40%, Seventh-Day Adventist, Baha'i, Latter-day Saints and Church of God 6%
**Government type:** republic
**Capital:** Tarawa
**Budget:** revenues: $28.4 million; expenditures: $ 37.2 million          **Currency:** Australian dollar (AUD)

## *KOREA, NORTH*
**Location:** Eastern Asia, northern half of the Korean Peninsula bordering the Korea Bay and the Sea of Japan, between China and South Korea
**Area:** 46,541 sq mi (120,540 sq km)
**Area-comparative:** slightly smaller than Mississippi
**Population:** 23,113,019
**Population growth rate:** 0.84%
**Nationality:** noun: Korean(s); adjective: Korean
**Ethnic groups:** racially homogeneous; there is a small Chinese community and a few ethnic Japanese

**Language:** Korean (official)
**Religion:** traditional Buddhist and Confucianist, some Christians and syncretic Chondogyo
**Government type:** Communist state one-man dictatorship
**Capital:** Pyongyang
**Budget:** revenues: $NA; expenditures: $NA     **Currency:** North Korean won (KPW)

## KOREA, SOUTH
**Location:** Eastern Asia, southern half of the Korean Peninsula bordering Yellow Sea and Sea of Japan
**Area:** 38,013 sq mi (98,480 sq km)
**Area-comparative:** slightly larger than Indiana
**Population:** 48,846,823
**Population growth rate:** 0.42%
**Nationality:** noun: Korean; adjective: Korean
**Ethnic groups:** homogeneous (except for about 20,000 Chinese)
**Languages:** Korean, English widely taught in junior high and high school
**Religions:** no affiliation 46%, Christian 26%, Buddhist 26%, Confucianist 1%, other 1%
**Government type:** republic
**Capital:** Seoul
**Budget: revenues:** $195 billion; expenditures: $189 billion; capital expenditures of $NA billion
**Currency:** South Korean won (KRW)

## KUWAIT
**Location:** Southwestern Asia, the Middle East, bordering the Persian Gulf, between Iraq and Saudi Arabia
**Area:** 6,878 sq mi (17,820 sq km)
**Area-comparative:** slightly smaller than New Jersey
**Population:** 2,418,393
**Population growth rate:** 3.52%
**Nationality:** noun: Kuwaiti(s); adjective: Kuwaiti
**Ethnic groups:** Kuwaiti 45%, other Arab 35%, South Asian 9%, Iranian 4%, other 7%
**Languages:** Arabic (official), English widely spoken
**Religions:** Muslim 85% (Shi'a 30%, Sunni 70%), Christian, Hindu, Parsi, and other 15%
**Government type:** nominal constitutional monarchy
**Capital:** Kuwait
**Budget: revenues:** $47.21 billion; expenditures: $20.77 billion
**Currency:** Kuwaiti dinar

## KYRGYZSTAN
**Location:** Central Asia, west of China
**Area:** 76,621 sq mi (198,500 sq km)
**Area-comparative:** slightly smaller than South Dakota
**Population:** 5,213,898
**Population growth rate:** 1.32%
**Nationality:** noun: Kyrgyzstani(s); adjective: Kyrgyzstani
**Ethnic groups:** Kyrgyz 64.9%, Russian 12.5%, Uzbek 13.8%, other 5.7%, Ukrainian 1%, Dungan 1.1%, Uygur 15%
**Languages:** Kyrgyz (official), Russian (official)
**Religions:** Muslim 75%, Russian Orthodox 20%, other 5%
**Government type:** republic
**Capital:** Bishkek
**Budget: revenues:** $516.3 million; expenditures: $539.9 million
**Currency:** Kyrgyzstani som (KGS)

## LAOS

**Location:** Southeastern Asia, northeast of Thailand, west of Vietnam
**Area:** 91,405 sq mi (236,800 sq km)
**Area-comparative:** slightly larger than Utah
**Population:** 6,368,481
**Population growth rate:** 2.39%
**Nationality:** noun: Lao(s) or Laotian(s); adjective: Lao or Laotian
**Ethnic groups:** Lao Loum 68%, Lao Theung 22%, Lao Soung 9%, ethnic Vietnamese/Chinese 1%
**Languages:** Lao (official), French, English and various other ethnic languages
**Religions:** Buddhist 60%, animist and other 40%
**Government type:** Communist state
**Capital:** Vientiane
**Budget:** revenues: $319.3 million; expenditures: $434.6 million     **Currency:** kip (LAK)

## LATVIA

**Location:** Eastern Europe, bordering the Baltic Sea, between Estonia and Lithuania
**Area:** 24,931 sq mi (64,589 sq km)
**Area-comparative:** slightly larger than West Virginia
**Population:** 2,274,735
**Population growth rate:** -0.67%
**Nationality:** noun: Latvian(s); adjective: Latvian
**Ethnic groups:** Latvian 57.7%, Russian 29.6%, Belarusian 4.1%, Ukrainian 2.7%, Polish 2.5%, Lithuanian 1.4%, other 2%
**Languages:** Latvian (official), Lithuanian, Russian
**Religions:** Lutheran, Roman Catholic, Russian Orthodox
**Government type:** parliamentary democracy
**Capital:** Riga
**Budget:** revenues: $5.65 billion; expenditures: $5.89 billion     **Currency:** Latvian lat (LVL)

## LEBANON

**Location:** Middle East, bordering the Mediterranean Sea, between Israel and Syria
**Area:** 4,015 sq mi (10,400 sq km)
**Area-comparative:** about 0.7 times the size of Connecticut
**Population:** 3,874,050
**Population growth rate:** 1.23%
**Nationality:** noun: Lebanese (singular and plural); adjective: Lebanese
**Ethnic groups:** Arab 95%, Armenian 4%, other 1%
**Languages:** Arabic (official), French, English, Armenian
**Religions:** Muslim 59.7%, Christian 39%, other 1.3%
**Government type:** republic
**Capital:** Beirut
**Budget:** revenues: $4.95 billion; expenditures: $6.59 billion, including capital of $NA
**Currency:** Lebanese pound (LBP)

## LESOTHO

**Location:** Southern Africa, an enclave of South Africa
**Area:** 11,717 sq mi (30,355 sq km)
**Area-comparative:** slightly smaller than Maryland
**Population:** 2,022,331
**Population growth rate:** - 0.46%
**Nationality:** noun: Mosotho (singular), Basotho (plural); adjective: Basotho
**Ethnic groups:** Sotho 99.7%, Europeans, Asians and other 0.3%

**Languages:** Sesotho (official), English (official), Zulu, Xhosa
**Religions:** Christian 80%, indigenous beliefs 20%
**Government type:** parliamentary constitutional monarchy
**Capital:** Maseru
**Budget:** revenues: $738.5 million; expenditures: $792.1 million; capital expenditures of $15 million
**Currency:** loti; South African rand (LSL; ZAR)

### LIBERIA
**Location:** Western Africa, bordering the North Atlantic Ocean, between Cote d'Ivorie and Sierra Leone
**Area:** 42,989 sq mi (111,370 sq km)
**Area-comparative:** slightly larger than Tennessee
**Population:** 3,042,004
**Population growth rate:** 4.91%
**Nationality:** noun: Liberian(s); adjective: Liberian
**Ethnic groups:** indigenous African tribes 95%, Americo-Liberians 2.5%, Congo people 2.5%
**Languages:** English 20% (official), some 20 tribal languages
**Religions:** indigenous beliefs 40%, Christian 40%, Muslim 20%
**Government type:** republic
**Capital:** Monrovia
**Budget:** revenues: $85.4 million; expenditures: $90.5 million
**Currency:** Liberian dollar (LRD)

### LIBYA
**Location:** Northern Africa, bordering the Mediterranean Sea, between Egypt and Tunisia
**Area:** 679,182 sq mi (1,759,540 sq km)
**Area-comparative:** slightly larger than Alaska
**Population:** 5,900,754
**Population growth rate:** 2.3%
**Nationality:** noun: Libyan(s); adjective: Libyan
**Ethnic groups:** Arab-Berber 97%, Greeks, Turks, Maltese, Italians, Egyptians, Pakistanis, Indians, and Tunisians 3%
**Languages:** Arabic, Italian, English
**Religions:** Sunni Muslim 97%, other 3%
**Government type:** Jamahiriya (a state of the masses)
**Capital:** Tripoli
**Budget:** revenues: $25.34 billion; expenditures: $21 billion
**Currency:** Libyan dinar (LYD)

### LIECHTENSTEIN
**Location:** Central Europe, between Austria and Switzerland
**Area:** 62 sq mi (160 sq km)
**Area-comparative:** about 0.9 times the size of Washington D.C.
**Population:** 33,987
**Population growth rate:** 0.78%
**Nationality:** noun: Liechtensteiner(s); adjective: Liechtenstein
**Ethnic groups:** Alemannic 86%, Italian, Turkish and other 14%
**Languages:** German (official), Alemannic dialect
**Religions:** Roman Catholic 76.2%, Protestant 7%, unknown 10.6%, other 6.2%
**Government type:** hereditary constitutional monarchy on a democratic and parliamentary basis
**Capital:** Vaduz
**Budget:** revenues: $424.2 million; expenditures:$ 414.1 million
**Currency:** Swiss franc (CHF)

## LITHUANIA

**Location:** Eastern Europe, bordering the Baltic Sea, between Latvia and Russia
**Area:** 25,167 sq mi (65,200 sq km)
**Area-comparative:** slightly larger than West Virginia
**Population:** 3,585,906
**Population growth rate:** -0.3%
**Nationality:** noun: Lithuanian(s); adjective: Lithuanian
**Ethnic groups:** Lithuanian 80.6%, Russian 8.7%, Polish 7%, other 2.1%, Belarusian 1.6%
**Languages:** Lithuanian (official), Polish, Russian
**Religions:** Roman Catholic, Russian Orthodox, Lutheran, Protestant, Christian, Baptist, Muslim, Jewish
**Government:** parliamentary democracy
**Capital:** Vilnius
**Budget:** revenues: $8.429 billion; expenditures: $9.103 billion
**Currency:** litas (LTL)

## LUXEMBOURG

**Location:** Western Europe, between France and Germany
**Area:** 998 sq mi (2,586 sq km)
**Area-comparative:** slightly smaller than Rhode Island
**Population:** 474,413
**Population growth rate:** 1.23%
**Nationality:** noun: Luxembourger(s); adjective: Luxembourg
**Ethnic groups:** Celtic base (with French and German blend), Portuguese, Italian, Slavs, and Europeans
**Languages:** Luxembourgish, German, French
**Religions:** Roman Catholic 87%, Protestant 13%, Jews and Muslims
**Government type:** constitutional monarchy
**Capital:** Luxembourg
**Budget:** revenues: $9.20 billion; expenditures: $9.57 billion; capital expenditures of $975.5 million
**Currency:** euro (EUR)

## MACEDONIA

**Location:** Southeastern Europe, north of Greece
**Area:** 9,778 sq mi (25,333 sq km)
**Area-comparative:** slightly larger than Vermont
**Population:** 2,050,554
**Population growth rate:** 0.26%
**Nationality:** noun: Macedonian(s); adjective: Macedonian
**Ethnic groups:** Macedonian 64.2%, Albanian 25.2%, Turkish 3.8%, Roma 2.7%, Serb 1.8%, other 2.3%
**Languages:** Macedonian 68%, Albanian 25%, Turkish 3%, Serb- Croatian 2%, other 2%
**Religions:** Macedonian Orthodox 70%, Muslim 29%, other 1%
**Government type:** parliamentary democracy
**Capital:** Skopje
**Budget: revenues:** $2.105 billion; expenditures: $2.15 billion, including capital of $114 million $NA
**Currency:** Macedonian denar (MKD)

## MADAGASCAR

**Location:** Southern Africa, island in the Indian Ocean, east of Mozambique
**Area:** 226,597 sq mi (587,040 sq km)
**Area-comparative:** slightly less than twice the size of Arizona
**Population:** 18,595,469
**Population growth rate:** 3.03%
**Nationality:** noun: Malagasy (singular and plural); adjective: Malagasy
**Ethnic groups:** Malayo-Indonesian, Cotiers, French, Indian, Creole, Comoran

**Languages:** French (official), Malagasy (official)
**Religions:** indigenous beliefs 52%, Christian 41%, Muslim 7%
**Government type:** republic
**Capital:** Antananarivo
**Budget:** revenues: $703.6 million; expenditures: $853 million, including capital of $331 million
**Currency:** Malagasy franc (MGF)

## *MALAWI*

**Location:** Southern Africa, east of Zambia
**Area:** 45,733 sq mi (118,480 sq km)
**Area-comparative:** slightly smaller than Pennsylvania
**Population:** 13,013,926
**Population growth rate:** 2.38%
**Nationality:** noun: Malawian(s); adjective: Malawian
**Ethnic groups:** Chewa, Nyanja, Tumbuko, Yao, Lomwe, Sena, Tonga, Ngoni, Ngonde, Asian, European
**Languages:** English (official), Chichewa (official)
**Religions:** Protestant 55%, Roman Catholic 20%, Muslim 20%, other 2%, indigenous beliefs 3%
**Government type:** multiparty democracy
**Capital:** Lilongwe
**Budget:** revenues: $844.6 million; expenditures: $913.9 million
**Currency:** Malawian kwacha (MWK)

## *MALAYSIA*

**Location:** Southeastern Asia, peninsula and northern one-third of the island of Borneo, south of Vietnam
**Area:** 127,283 sq mi (329,750 sq km)
**Area-comparative:** slightly larger than New Mexico
**Population:** 24,385,858
**Population growth rate:** 1.78%
**Nationality:** noun: Malaysian(s); adjective: Malaysian
**Ethnic groups:** Malay and other indigenous 58%, Chinese 24%, other 10%, Indian 8%,
**Languages:** Bahasa Melayu (official), English, Chinese dialects, Indian languages, Thai
**Religions:** Muslim, Buddhist, Hindu, Daoist, Sikh, and Christian
**Government type:** constitutional monarchy
**Capital:** Kuala Lumpur
**Budget:** revenues: $30.57 billion; expenditures: $34.62 billion, including capital of $9.4 billion
**Currency:** ringgit (MYR)

## *MALDIVES*

*Location:* Southern Asia, group of atolls in the Indian Ocean, south-southwest of India
**Area:** 116 sq mi (300 sq km)
**Area-comparative:** about 1.7 times the size of Washington D.C.
**Population:** 359,008
**Population growth rate:** 2.78%
**Nationality:** noun: Maldivian(s); adjective: Maldivian
**Ethnic groups:** South Indians, Sinhalese, Arabs
**Languages:** Maldivian Divehi (official), English
**Religion:** Sunni Muslim 100%
**Government:** republic
**Capital:** Male
**Budget:** revenues: $265 million; expenditures: $262 million, including capital expenditures of $80 million
**Currency:** rufiyaa (MVR)

## MALI

**Location:** Western Africa, southwest of Algeria
**Area:** 478,640 sq mi (1,240,000 sq km)
**Area-comparative:** slightly less than twice the size of Texas
**Population:** 11,716,829
**Population growth rate:** 2.63%
**Nationality:** noun: Malian(s); adjective: Malian
**Ethnic groups:** Mande (including Bambara, Malinke, and Sarakole) 50%, Peul 17%, Voltaic 12%, Tuareg and Moor 10%, Songhai 6%, other 5%
**Languages:** French (official), Bambara 80%, numerous African languages
**Religions:** Muslim 90%, indigenous beliefs 9%, Christian 1%
**Government type:** republic
**Capital:** Bamako
**Budget: revenues:** $764 million; expenditures: $828 million
**Currency:** Communaute Financiere Africaine franc (XOF)

## MALTA

**Location:** Southern Europe, islands in the Mediterranean Sea, south of Italy
**Area:** 122 sq mi (316 sq km)
**Area-comparative:** slightly less than twice the size of Washington, DC
**Population:** 400,214
**Population growth rate:** 0.42%
**Nationality:** noun: Maltese (singular and plural); adjective: Maltese
**Ethnic groups:** Maltese
**Languages:** Maltese (official), English (official)
**Religions:** Roman Catholic 98%, other 2%
**Government type:** republic
**Capital:** Valletta
**Budget: revenues:** $2.503 billion; expenditures: $2.703 billion          **Currency:** Maltese lira (MTL)

## MARSHALL ISLANDS

**Location:** Oceania, group of atolls and reefs in the North Pacific Ocean, about one-half of the way from Hawaii to Australia
**Area:** 70 sq mi (181.3 sq km)
**Area-comparative:** about the size of Washington D.C.
**Population:** 60,442
**Population growth rate:** 2.25%
**Nationality:** noun: Marshallese (singular and plural); adjective: Marshallese
**Ethnic groups:** Micronesian
**Languages:** English and Marshallese are both official languages, 2 major Marshallese dialects, Japanese
**Religions:** Christian (mostly Protestant)
**Government type:** constitutional government in free association with the United States
**Capital:** Majuro
**Budget: revenues:** $42 million; expenditures: $40 million          **Currency:** United States dollar (USD)

## MAURITANIA

**Location:** Northern Africa, bordering the North Atlantic Ocean, between Senegal and Western Sahara
**Area:** 397,850 sq mi (1,030,700 sq km)
**Area-comparative:** slightly larger than three times the size of New Mexico
**Population:** 3,177,388
**Population growth rate:** 2.88%
**Nationality:** noun, Mauritanian(s); adjective: Mauritanian

**Ethnic groups:** multiracial Maur and Black 40%, Maur 30%, Black 30%
**Languages:** Arabic (official), Pulaar, Soninke, Wolof, French, Hassaniya
**Religion:** Muslim 100%
**Government type:** republic
**Capital:** Nouakchott
**Budget:** revenues: $421 million; expenditures: $378 million including capital expenditures of $154 million
**Currency:** ouguiya (MRO)

## MAURITIUS
**Location:** Southern Africa, island in the Indian Ocean, east of Madagascar
**Area:** 787 sq mi (2,040 sq km)
**Area-comparative:** almost 11 times the size of Washington D.C.
**Population:** 1,240,827
**Population growth rate:** 0.82%
**Nationality:** noun: Mauritian(s); adjective: Mauritian
**Ethnic groups:** Indo-Mauritian 68%, Creole 27%, Sino-Mauritian 3%, Franco-Mauritian 2%
**Languages:** English (official), Creole, French (official), Hindi, Urdu, Hakka, Bhojpuri
**Religions:** Hindu 52%, Roman Catholic 26%, Muslim 16.6%, other 3.1%, Protestant 2.3%
**Government type:** parliamentary democracy
**Capital:** Port Louis
**Budget:** revenues: $1.377 billion; expenditures: $1.77 billion
**Currency:** Mauritian rupee (MUR)

## *MEXICO*
**Location:** located in the southern part of North America, bordering the Caribbean Sea and the Gulf of Mexico, between Guatemala and the United States
**Area:** 761,404 sq mi (1,972,550 sq km)
**Area-comparative:** slightly less than three times the size of Texas
**Population:** 107,449,525
**Population growth rate:** 1.16%
**Nationality:** noun: Mexican(s); adjective: Mexican
**Ethnic groups:** Mestizo 60%, Amerindian or predominantly Amerindian 30%, Caucasian 9%, other 1%
**Languages:** Spanish (official), Mayan and Nahuatl dialects
**Religions:** Roman Catholic 89%, Protestant 6%, other 5%
**Government type:** federal republic
**Capital:** Mexico (Distrito Federal)
**Budget:** revenues: $181 billion; expenditures: $184 billion, including capital of $NA
**Currency:** Mexican peso (MXN)

## *MICRONESIA*
**Location:** Federated state of Oceania, island group in the North Pacific Ocean, about three-quarters of the way from Hawaii to Indonesia
**Area:** 271 sq mi (702 sq km)
**Area-comparative:** four times the size of Washington D.C.
**Population:** 108,004
**Population growth rate:** -0.11%
**Nationality:** noun:Micronesian(s); adjective: Micronesian; Chuukese, Kosraen(s), Pohnpein(s), Yapese
**Ethnic groups:** nine ethnic Micronesian and Polynesian groups
**Languages:** English (official), Trukese, Pohnpeian, Yapese, Kosrean, Ulithian, Woleaian, Nukuoro, Kapingamarangi
**Religions:** Roman Catholic 50%, Protestant 47%, other 3%
**Government type:** constitutional government in the association with the United States
**Capital:** Palikir

**Budget:** revenues: $161 million ($69 million less grants); expenditures: $160 million
**Currency:** United States dollar (USD)

## *MOLDOVA*
**Location:** Eastern Europe, northeast of Romania
**Area:** 13,060 sq mi (33,843 sq km)
**Area-comparative:** slightly larger than Maryland
**Population:** 4,466,706
**Population growth rate:** 0.28%
**Nationality:** noun: Moldovan(s); adjective: Moldovan
**Ethnic groups:** Moldavian and Romanian 64.5%, Ukrainian 13.8%, Russian 13%, Jewish 1.5%,
  Bulgarian 2% Gagauz and other 5.2%
**Languages:** Moldovan (official), Russian, Gagauz
**Religions:** Eastern Orthodox 98%, Jewish 1.5%, Baptist and other 0.5%
**Government type:** republic
**Capital:** Chisinau
**Budget:** revenues: $1.069 billion; expenditures: $1.065 billion      **Currency:** Moldovan leu (MDL)

## *MONACO*
**Location:** Western Europe, bordering the Mediterranean Sea, on the southern coast of France, near the
  border with Italy
**Area:** .75 sq mi (1.95 sq km)
**Area-comparative:** about 3 times the size of The Mall in Washington, DC
**Population:** 32,543
**Population growth rate:** 0.4%
**Nationality:** noun: Monegasque(s); adjective: Monegasque or Monacan
**Ethnic groups:** French 47%, Monegasque 16%, Italian 16%, other 21%
**Languages:** French (official), English, Italian, Monegasque
**Religions:** Roman Catholic 90%
**Government type:** constitutional monarchy
**Capital:** Monaco
**Budget:** revenues: $518 million; expenditures: $531 million      **Currency:** euro (EUR)

## *MONGOLIA*
**Location:** Northern Asia, between China and Russia
**Area:** 604,090 sq mi (1,565,000 sq km)
**Area-comparative:** slightly smaller than Alaska
**Population:** 2,832,224
**Population growth rate:** 1.46%
**Nationality:** noun: Mongolian(s); adjective: Mongolian
**Ethnic groups:** Mongol 94.9%, Turkic 5%, other 0.1%
**Languages:** Khalkha Mongol 90%, Turkic, Russian
**Religions:** Tibetan Buddhist Lamaisian 50%, none 40%, Muslim 4%, Shamanism and Christian 6%
**Government type:** mixed parliamentary/presidential
**Capital:** Ulaanbaatar
**Budget:** revenues: $702 million; expenditures: $651 million, including capital of $NA
**Currency:** togrog / tughrik (MNT)

## *MOROCCO*
**Location:** Northern Africa, bordering the North Atlantic Ocean and the Mediterranean Sea, between
  Algeria and Western Sahara
**Area:** 172,368 sq mi (446,550 sq km)

**Area-comparative:** slightly larger than California
**Population:** 33,241,259
**Population growth rate:** 1.55%
**Nationality:** noun: Moroccan(s); adjective: Moroccan
**Ethnic groups:** Arab-Berber 99.1%, other 0.7% , Jewish 0.2%
**Languages:** Arabic (official), Berber dialects, French
**Religions:** Muslim 98.7%, Christian 1.1%, Jewish 0.2%
**Government:** constitutional monarchy
**Capital:** Rabat
**Budget: revenues:** $12.94 billion; expenditures: $16.77 billion; capital expenditures of $2.19 billion
**Currency:** Moroccan dirham (MAD)

## *MOZAMBIQUE*

**Location:** South-eastern Africa, bordering the Mozambique Channel, between South Africa and Tanzania
**Area:** 309,414 sq mi (801,590 sq km)
**Area-comparative:** slightly less than twice the size of California
**Population:** 19,686,505
**Population growth rate:** 1.38%
**Nationality:** noun: Mozambican(s); adjective: Mozambican
**Ethnic groups:** indigenous tribal groups 99.66%, Europeans 0.06%, Euro-Africans 0.2%, Indians 0.08%
**Languages:** Portuguese (official), indigenous dialects
**Religions:** indigenous beliefs 50%, Christian 30%, Muslim 20%
**Government type:** republic
**Capital:** Maputo
**Budget:** revenues: $1.03 billion; expenditures: $1.93 billion
**Currency:** metical (MZM)

## *NAMIBIA*

**Location:** Southern Africa, bordering the South Atlantic Ocean, between Angola and South Africa
**Area:** 318,611 sq mi (825,418 sq km)
**Area-comparative:** slightly more than half the size of Alaska
**Population:** 2,044,147
**Population growth rate:** 0.59%
**Nationality:** noun: Namibian(s); adjective: Namibian
**Ethnic groups:** black 87.5%, white 6%, mixed 6.5%,
**Languages:** German 32%, English 7% (official), Afrikaans 60%,indigenous languages:
Oshivambo, Herero, Nama
**Religions:** Christian (at least 50% Lutheran) 80-90%, indigenous beliefs 10-20%
**Government type:** republic
**Capital:** Windhoek
**Budget:** revenues: $1.945 billion; expenditures: $2.04 billion
**Currency:** Namibian dollar; South African rand (NAD; ZAR)

## *NAURU*

**Location:** Oceania, island in the South Pacific Ocean, south of the Marshall Islands
**Area:** 8 sq mi (21 sq km)
**Area-comparative:** about 0.1 times the size of Washington D.C.
**Population:** 13,287
**Population growth rate:** 1.81%
**Nationality:** noun: Nauruan(s); adjective: Nauruan
**Ethnic groups:** Nauruan 58%, other Pacific Islander 26%, Chinese 8%, European 8%
**Languages:** Nauruan (official), English

**Religions:** Protestant 67%, Roman Catholic 33%
**Government type:** republic
**Capital:** government offices in Yaren District
**Budget:** revenues: $13.5 million; expenditures: $13.5 million
**Currency:** Australian dollar (AUD)


*NEPAL*
**Location:** Southern Asia, between China and India
**Area:** 54,349 sq mi (140,800 sq km)
**Area-comparative:** slightly larger than Arkansas
**Population:** 28,287,147
**Population growth rate:** 2.17%
**Nationality:** noun: Nepalese (singular and plural); adjective: Nepalese
**Ethnic groups:** Brahman, Chetri, Newar, Gurung, Magar, Tamang, Rai, Limbu, Sherpa, Tharu, and others
**Languages:** Nepali (official, spoken by 90% of the population), 12 other languages and 30 dialects
**Religions:** Hindu 86.2%, Buddhism 7.8%, Islam 3.8%, other 2.2%
**Government type:** parliamentary democracy and constitutional monarchy
**Capital:** Kathmandu
**Budget:** revenues: $1.153 billion; expenditures: $1.789 billion
**Currency:** Nepalese rupee (NPR)


*NETHERLANDS*
**Location:** Western Europe, bordering the North Sea, between Belgium and Germany
**Area:** 16,029 sq mi (41,526 sq km)
**Area-comparative:** slightly less than twice the size of New Jersey
**Population:** 16,491,461
**Population growth rate:** 0.49%
**Nationality:** noun: Dutchman (men), Dutchwoman (women); adjective: Dutch
**Ethnic groups:** Dutch 83%, other 17%
**Languages:** Dutch (official), Frisian (official)
**Religions:** Roman Catholic 31%, Protestant 21%, Muslim 4.4%, other 3.6%, unaffiliated 40%
**Government type:** constitutional monarchy
**Capital:** Amsterdam, The Hague is the seat of government
**Budget:** revenues: $291.8 billion; expenditures: $303.7 billion
**Currency:** euro (EUR)


*NEW ZEALAND*
**Location:** Oceania, islands in the South Pacific Ocean, southeast of Australia
**Area:** 103,710 sq mi (268,680 sq km)
**Area-comparative:** about the size of Colorado
**Population:** 4,076,140
**Population growth rate:** .99%
**Nationality:** noun: New Zealander(s); adjective: New Zealand
**Ethnic groups:** New Zealand European 74.5%, Maori 9.7%, Asian and others 7.4%, European 4.6%, Pacific Islander 3.8%
**Languages:** English (official), Maori (official)
**Religions:** Anglican 24%, Presbyterian 18%, Roman Catholic 15%, Methodist 5%, Baptist 2%, Protestant 3%, unspecified or none 33%
**Government type:** parliamentary democracy
**Capital:** Wellington
**Budget:** revenues: $43.1 billion; expenditures: $37.57 billion
**Currency:** New Zealand dollar (NZD)

### NICARAGUA

**Location:** Central America, bordering both the Caribbean Sea and the North Pacific Ocean, between Costa Rica and Honduras
**Area:** 49,985 sq mi (129,494 sq km)
**Area-comparative:** slightly smaller than the state of New York
**Population:** 5,570,129
**Population growth rate:** 1.89%
**Nationality:** noun: Nicaraguan(s); adjective: Nicaraguan
**Ethnic groups:** mestizo 69%, white 17%, black 9%, Amerindian 5%
**Language:** Spanish (official)
**Religion:** Roman Catholic 85%, Protestant 15%
**Government type:** republic
**Capital:** Managua
**Budget:** revenues: $1.134 billion; expenditures: $1.358 billion
**Currency:** gold cordoba (NIO)

### NIGER

**Location:** Western Africa, southeast of Algeria
**Area:** 489,062 sq mi (1,267,000 sq km)
**Area-comparative:** slightly less than twice the size of Texas
**Population:** 12,525,094
**Population growth rate:** 2.92%
**Nationality:** noun: Nigerien(s); adjective: Nigerien
**Ethnic groups:** Hausa 56%, Djerma 22%, Fula 8.5%, Tuareg 8%, Beri Beri 4.3%, Arab, Toubou, and Gourmantche 1.2%
**Languages:** French (official), Hausa, Djerma
**Religions:** Muslim 80%, remainder indigenous beliefs and Christian
**Government type:** republic
**Capital:** Niamey
**Budget:** revenues: $320 million; expenditures: $320 million, including capital expenditures of $178 million
**Currency:** Communaute Financiere Africaine franc (XOF)

### NIGERIA

**Location:** Western Africa, bordering the Gulf of Guinea, between Benin and Cameroon
**Area:** 356,574 sq mi (923,768 sq km)
**Area-comparative:** slightly more than twice the size of California
**Population:** 131,859,731
**Population growth rate:** 2.38%
**Nationality:** noun: Nigerian; adjective: Nigerian
**Ethnic groups:** Hausa, Fulani 29%, Yoruba 21%, Igbo 18%, Ijaw 10%, Kanuri 4%, Ibibio 3.5%, Tiv 2.5%
**Languages:** English (official), Hausa, Yoruba, Igbo, Fulani
**Religions:** Muslim 50%, Christian 40%, indigenous beliefs 10%
**Government type:** federal republic
**Capital:** Abuja
**Budget:** revenues: $12.86 billion; expenditures: $13.54 billion
**Currency:** naira (NGN)

### NORWAY

**Location:** Northern Europe, bordering the North Sea and the North Atlantic Ocean, west of Sweden
**Area:** 125,149 sq mi (324,220 sq km)
**Area-comparative:** slightly larger than New Mexico
**Population:** 4,610,820

**Population growth rate:** 0.38%
**Nationality:** noun: Norwegian(s); adjective: Norwegian
**Ethnic groups:** Norwegian, Sami 20,000
**Language:** Norwegian (official), small Sami- and Finnish-speaking minorities
**Religions:** Evangelical Lutheran 86%, other Protestant and Roman Catholic 3%, other/nonreligious 11%
**Government type:** constitutional monarchy
**Capital:** Oslo
**Budget:** revenues: $176.1 billion; expenditures: $131.3 billion
**Currency:** Norwegian krone (NOK)

## *OMAN*

**Location:** Middle East, bordering the Arabian Sea, Gulf of Oman, and the Persian Gulf, between
    Yemen and United Arab Emirates
**Area:** 82,010 sq mi (212,460 sq km)
**Area-comparative:** slightly smaller than Kansas
**Population:** 3,102,229
**Population growth rate:** 3.28%
**Nationality:** noun: Omani(s); adjective: Omani
**Ethnic groups:** Arab, Baluchi, Indian, Pakistani, Sri Lankan, Bangladeshi, African
**Languages:** Arabic (official), English, Baluchi, Urdu, Indian dialects
**Religions:** Ibadhi Muslim 75%, other including Sunni Muslim, Shi'a Muslim, Hindu 25%
**Government type:** monarchy
**Capital:** Muscat
**Budget:** revenues: $14.36 billion; expenditures: $10.61 billion
**Currency:** Omani rial (OMR)

## *PAKISTAN*

**Location:** Southern Asia, bordering the Arabian Sea, between India on the east and Iran and Afghanistan
    on the west and China in the north
**Area:** 310, 321 sq mi (803,940 sq km)
**Area-comparative:** slightly less than twice the size of California
**Population:** 165,803,560
**Population growth rate:** 2.09%
**Nationality:** noun: Pakistani(s); adjective: Pakistani
**Ethnic groups:** Punjabi, Sindhi, Pashtun, Baloch, Muhajir
**Languages:** Punjabi 48%, Sindhi 12%, Siraiki 10%, Pashtu 8%, Urdu (official) 8%, Balochi 3%,
    Hindko 2%, Brahui 1%, English, Burushaski, and other 8%
**Religions:** Sunni Muslim 77%, Shi'a Muslim 20%, other (including Christian and Hindu) 3%
**Government type:** federal republic
**Capital:** Islamabad
**Budget:** revenues: $15.45 billion; expenditures: $20.07 billion, including capital of $NA
**Currency:** Pakistani rupee (PKR)

## *PALAU*

**Location:** Oceania, group of islands in the North Pacific Ocean, southeast of the Philippines
**Area:** 177 sq mi (458 sq km)
**Area-comparative:** slightly more than 2.5 times the size of Washington, DC
**Population:** 20,579
**Population growth rate:** 1.31%
**Nationality:** noun: Palauan(s); adjective: Palauan
**Ethnic groups:** Palauan 70%, Asian 28%, white 2%
**Languages:** English, Palauan, Sonsorolese, Angaur, Japanese, and Tobi (all official within certain states)
**Religions:** Roman Catholic 49%, Protestant religions 18%, Modekngei,(religion indigenous to Palau) 33%

**Government type:** constitutional government in free association with the U.S.
**Capital:** Koror
**Budget:** revenues: $57.7 million; expenditures: $80.8 million and capital expenditures of $17.1 million
**Currency:** United States dollar (USD)

## PANAMA

**Location:** Central America, bordering both the Caribbean Sea and the North Pacific Ocean, between Colombia and Costa Rica
**Area:** 30,185 sq mi (78,200 sq km)
**Area-comparative:** slightly smaller than South Carolina
**Population:** 3,191,319
**Population growth rate:** 1.6%
**Nationality:** noun: Panamanian(s); adjective: Panamanian
**Ethnic groups:** mestizo 70%, Amerindian and Multiracial (West Indian) 14%, white 10%, Amerindian 6%
**Languages:** Spanish (official), English 14%
**Religions:** Roman Catholic 85%, Protestant 15%
**Government type:** constitutional democracy
**Capital:** Panama
**Budget:** revenues: $3.426 billion: expenditures: $3.959 billion; capital expenditures of $471 million
**Currency:** balboa; United States dollar (PAB; USD)

## PAPUA NEW GUINEA

**Location:** Oceania, group of islands including the eastern half of the island of New Guinea, east of Indonesia
**Area:** 178,656 sq mi (462,840 sq km)
**Area-comparative:** slightly larger than California
**Population:** 5,670,544
**Population growth rate:** 2.21%
**Nationality:** noun: Papua New Guinean(s); adjective: Papua New Guinean
**Ethnic groups:** Melanesian, Papuan, Negrito, Micronesian, Polynesian
**Languages:** English spoken by 1-2%, pidgin English widespread, Motu
**Religions:** indigenous beliefs 34%, Roman Catholic 22%, Lutheran 16%, other Protestant 10%, Anglican 5%, Evangelical Alliance 4%, Seventh Day Adventist 1%
**Government type:** constitutional monarchy with parliamentary democracy
**Capital:** Port Moresby
**Budget:** revenues: $1.368 billion; expenditures: $1.354 billion; capital expenditures of $344 million
**Currency:** kina (PGK)

## PARAGUAY

**Location:** Central South America, northeast of Argentina
**Area:** 157,005 sq mi (406,750 sq km)
**Area-comparative:** slightly smaller than California
**Population:** 6,506,464
**Population growth rate:** 2.45%
**Nationality:** noun: Paraguayan(s); adjective: Paraguayan
**Ethnic groups:** mestizo (Mixed Spanish and Amerindian) 95%, other 5%
**Languages:** Spanish (official), Guarani
**Religions:** Roman Catholic 90%, Mennonite and other Protestant 10%
**Government type:** constitutional republic
**Capital:** Asuncion
**Budget:** revenues: $1.334 billion; expenditures: $1.37 billion; capital expenditures of $700 million
**Currency:** guarani (PYG)

## PERU

**Location:** Western South America, bordering the South Pacific Ocean, between Chile and Ecuador
**Area:** 496,094 sq mi (1,285,220 sq km)
**Area-comparative:** slightly smaller than Alaska
**Population:** 28,302,603
**Population growth rate:** 1.32%
**Nationality:** noun: Peruvian(s); adjective: Peruvian
**Ethnic groups:** Amerindian 45%, mestizo 37%, white 15%, black, Japanese, Chinese, and other 3%
**Languages:** Spanish (official), Quechua (official), Aymara, minor Amazonian languages
**Religions:** Roman Catholic 90%, other 10%
**Government type:** constitutional republic
**Capital:** Lima
**Budget:** revenues: $21.87 billion; expenditures: $22.47 billion
**Currency:** nuevo sol (PEN)

## PHILIPPINES

**Location:** Southeastern Asia, group of islands between the Philippine Sea and the South China Sea, east of Vietnam
**Area:** 115,800 sq mi (300,000 sq km)
**Area-comparative:** slightly larger than Arizona
**Population:** 89,468,677
**Population growth rate:** 1.8%
**Nationality:** noun: Filipino(s); adjective: Philippine
**Ethnic groups:** Christian Malay 91.5%, Muslim Malay 4%, other 3%, Chinese 1.5%
**Languages:** Filipino (based on Tagalog) and English are official languages; eight major dialects
**Religions:** Roman Catholic 83%, Protestant 9%, Muslim 5%, Buddhist and other 3%
**Government type:** republic
**Capital:** Manila
**Budget:** revenues: $12.38 billion: expenditures: $15.77 billion
**Currency:** Philippine peso (PHP)

## POLAND

**Location:** Central Europe, east of Germany
**Area:** 120,696 sq mi (312,685 sq km)
**Area-comparative:** slightly smaller than New Mexico
**Population:** 38,536,869
**Population growth rate:** -0.05%
**Nationality:** noun: Pole(s); adjective: Polish
**Ethnic groups:** Polish 96.7%, German 0.4%, Ukrainian 0.1%, Belarusian 0.1% , other 2.7%
**Language:** Polish (official)
**Religions:** Roman Catholic 95%, other (including Eastern Orthodox and Protestant) 5%
**Government type:** republic
**Capital:** Warsaw
**Budget:** revenues: $52.73 billion; expenditures: $63.22 billion
**Currency:** zloty (PLN)

## PORTUGAL

**Location:** Southwestern Europe, bordering the North Atlantic Ocean, west of Spain
**Area:** 35,663 sq mi (92,391 sq km)
**Area-comparative:** slightly smaller than Indiana
**Population:** 10,605,870
**Population growth rate:** 0.36%

**Nationality:** noun: Portuguese (singular and plural); adjective: Portuguese
**Ethnic groups:** homogeneous Mediterranean stock, African
**Language:** Portuguese (official), Mirandese (official-but locally used)
**Religions:** Roman Catholic 94%, Protestant
**Government:** parliamentary democracy
**Capital:** Lisbon
**Budget:** revenues: $78.84 billion; expenditures: $90.27 billion
**Currency:** euro (EUR)

*PUERTO RICO* (commonwealth associated with the US)
**Location:** Caribbean, island between the Caribbean Sea and the North Atlantic Ocean, east of the Dominican Republic
**Area:** 3514 sq mi (9,104 sq km)
**Area-comparative:** slightly less than three times the size of Rhode Island
**Population:** 3,927,188
**Population growth rate:** 0.4%
**Nationality:** noun: Puerto Rican(s) (United States citizens); adjective: Puerto Rican
**Ethnic groups:** white 80%, black 8%, mixed and other 10.9%, Amerindian 0.4%, Asian 0.2%
**Languages:** Spanish, English
**Religions:** Roman Catholic 85%, Protestant and other 15%
**Government type:** commonwealth
**Capital:** San Juan
**Budget:** revenues: $6.7 billion; expenditures: $9.6 billion
**Currency:** United States dollar (USD)

*QATAR*
**Location:** Middle East, peninsula bordering the Persian Gulf and Saudi Arabia
**Area:** 4,415 sq mi (11,437 sq km)
**Area-comparative:** slightly smaller than Connecticut
**Population:** 885,359
**Population growth rate:** 2.5%
**Nationality:** noun: Qatari(s); adjective: Qatari
**Ethnic groups:** Arab 40%, Pakistani 18%, Indian 18%, other 14%, Iranian 10%
**Languages:** Arabic (official), English
**Religions:** Muslim 95%
**Government type:** traditional monarchy
**Capital:** Doha
**Budget:** revenues: $17.31 billion; expenditures: $11.31 billion, including capital of $2.2 billion
**Currency:** Qatari rial (QAR)

*ROMANIA*
**Location:** Southeastern Europe, bordering the Black Sea, between Bulgaria and Ukraine
**Area:** 91,675 sq mi (237,500 sq km)
**Area-comparative:** slightly smaller than Oregon
**Population:** 22,303,552
**Population growth rate:** -0.12%
**Nationality:** noun: Romanian(s); adjective: Romanian
**Ethnic groups:** Romanian 89.5%, Hungarian 6.6%, Roma 2.5%, Ukrainian 0.3%, German 0.3%, Russian 0.2%, Turkish 0.2%, other 0.4%
**Languages:** Romanian (official), Hungarian, German
**Religions:** Eastern Orthodox 87%, Protestant 6.8%, Catholic 5.6%, other, mostly Muslim 0.4%
**Government type:** republic

**Capital:** Bucharest
**Budget:** revenues:$29.97 billion; expenditures: $31.37 billion, including capital of $2.2 billion
**Currency:** leu (ROL)

## RUSSIA
**Location:** bordering the Arctic Ocean, between Europe and the North Pacific Ocean to the east, Europe is generally divided from Asia by the water which is divided by the Ural mountains, the Ural River and by the Caspian Sea.
**Area:** 6,591,027sq mi (17,075,200 sq km)
**Area-comparative:** approximately 1.8 times the size of the United States
**Population:** 142,893,540
**Population growth rate:** -0.37%
**Nationality:** noun: Russian(s); adjective: Russian
**Ethnic groups:** Russian 81.5%, Tatar 3.8%, Ukrainian 3%, Chuvash 1.2%, Bashkir 0.9%, Belarusian 0.8%, Moldavian 0.7% , other 8.1%
**Languages:** Russian (official), many others
**Religions:** Russian Orthodox, Muslim, other
**Government type:** federation
**Capital:** Moscow
**Budget:** revenues: $176.7 billion; expenditures: $125.6 billion
**Currency:** Russian ruble (RUR)

## RWANDA
**Location:** Central Africa, east of Democratic Republic of the Congo
**Area:** 10,166 sq mi (26,338 sq km)
**Area-comparative:** slightly smaller than Maryland
**Population:** 8,648,248
**Population growth rate:** 2.43%
**Nationality:** noun: Rwandan(s); adjective: Rwandan
**Ethnic groups:** Hutu 84%, Tutsi 15%, Twa 1%
**Languages:** Kinyarwanda (official), French (official), English (official), Kiswhahilli
**Religions:** Roman Catholic 56.5%, Protestant 26%, Adventist 11.1%, Muslim 4.6%, indigenous beliefs 0.1%, none 1.7%
**Government type:** republic, presidential, multiparty system
**Capital:** Kigali
**Budget:** revenues: $509.9 million; expenditures: $584.6 million      **Currency:** Rwandan franc (RWF)

## SAINT KITTS AND NEVIS
**Location:** Caribbean, islands in the Caribbean Sea, about one-third of the way from Puerto Rico to Trinidad and Tobago
**Area:** 101 sq mi (261 sq km)
**Area-comparative:** 1.5 times the size of Washington, D C
**Population:** 39,129
**Population growth rate:** 0.5%
**Nationality:** noun: Kittitian(s), Nevisian(s); adjective: Kittitian, Nevisian
**Ethnic groups:** predominately black, some British, Portuguese, and Lebanese
**Language:** English (official)
**Religions:** Anglican, other Protestant, Roman Catholic
**Government type:** constitutional monarchy with Westminster-style parliament
**Capital:** Basseterre
**Budget:** revenues: 89.7 million; expenditures: $128.2 million and capital expenditures of $19.5 million
**Currency:** East Caribbean dollar (XCD)

### SAINT LUCIA

**Location:** island between the Caribbean Sea and North Atlantic Ocean, north of Trinidad and Tobago
**Area:** 238 sq mi (616 sq km)
**Area-comparative:** 3.5 times the size of Washington, D C
**Population:** 168,458
**Population growth rate:** 1.29%
**Nationality:** noun: Saint Lucian(s); adjective: Saint Lucian
**Ethnic groups:** black 90%, mixed 6%, East Indian 3%, white 1%
**Languages:** English (official), French patois
**Religions:** Roman Catholic 90%, Anglican 3%, other Protestant 7%
**Government type:** Westminster-style parliamentary democracy
**Capital:** Castries
**Budget:** revenues: $141.2 million; expenditures: $146.7 million; capital expenditures of $25.1 million
**Currency:** East Caribbean dollar (XCD)

### SAINT VINCENT AND THE GRENADINES

**Location:** Caribbean, islands in the Caribbean Sea, north of Trinidad and Tobago
**Area:** 150 sq mi (389 sq km)
**Area-comparative:** twice the size of Washington D.C.
**Population:** 117,848
**Population growth rate:** 0.26%
**Nationality:** noun: Saint Vincentian(s) or Vincentians(s); adjective: Saint Vincentian or Vincentian
**Ethnic groups:** black 66%, mixed 19%, East Indian 6%, Carib Amerindian 2%, other 7%
**Languages:** English, French patois
**Religions:** Anglican 47%, Methodist 28%, Roman Catholic 13%, Hindu, Seventh-Day Adventist, other, Protestant 12%
**Government type:** parliamentary democracy; independent sovereign state within the Commonwealth
**Capital:** Kingstown
**Budget:** revenues: $94.6 million; expenditures: $85.8 million
**Currency:** East Caribbean dollar (XCD)

### SAMOA

**Location:** Oceania, group of islands in the South Pacific Ocean, about one-half of the way from Hawaii to New Zealand
**Area:** 1,136 sq mi (2,944 sq km)
**Area-comparative:** slightly smaller than Rhode Island
**Population:** 176,908
**Population growth rate:** -0.2%
**Nationality:** noun: Samoan(s); adjective: Samoan
**Ethnic groups:** Samoan 92.6%, Euronesians 7%, Europeans 0.4%
**Languages:** Samoan (official), English
**Religions:** Christian 99.7%, other 0.3%
**Government type:** mix of parliamentary democracy and constitutional monarchy
**Capital:** Apia
**Budget:** revenues: $105 million; expenditures: $119 million
**Currency:** tala (SAT)

### SAN MARINO

**Location:** Southern Europe, an enclave in central Italy
**Area:** 24 sq mi (61 sq km)
**Area-comparative:** about 0.3 times the size of Washington, DC
**Population:** 29,251

**Population growth rate:** 1.26%
**Nationality:** noun: Sammarinese (singular and plural); adjective: Sammarinese
**Ethnic groups:** Sammarinese, Italian
**Language:** Italian (official)
**Religion:** Roman Catholic
**Government type:** Independent republic
**Capital:** San Marino
**Budget:** revenues: $400 million; expenditures: $400 million
**Currency:** euro (EUR)

## SAO TOME AND PRINCIPE
**Location:** Western Africa, islands straddling the Equator in the Gulf of Guinea, west of Gabon
**Area:** 386 sq mi (1,001 sq km)
**Area-comparative:** more than 5 times the size of Washington, DC
**Population:** 193,413
**Population growth rate:** 3.15%
**Nationality:** Sao Tomean(s); adjective: Sao Tomean
**Ethnic groups:** mestico, angolares, forros, servicais, tongas, Europeans
**Language:** Portuguese (official)
**Religions:** Christian 80%, including Roman Catholic, Evangelical Protestant, Seventh Day Adventist
**Government type:** republic
**Capital:** Sao Tome
**Budget:** revenues: $26.39 million; expenditures: $59.48 million; capital expenditures of $54 million
**Currency:** dobra (STD)

## SAUDI ARABIA
**Location:** Middle East, bordering the Persian Gulf and the Red Sea, north of Yemen
**Area:** 756,785 sq mi (1,960,582 sq km)
**Area-comparative:** slightly more than one-fifth the size of the US
**Population:** 27,019,731
**Population growth rate:** 2.18%
**Nationality:** noun: Saudi(s); adjective: Saudi or Saudi Arabian
**Ethnic groups:** Arab 90%, Afro-Asian 10%
**Language:** Arabic (official)
**Religion:** Muslim 100%
**Government type:** monarchy
**Capital:** Riyadh
**Budget:** revenues: $143.7 billion; expenditures: $89.65 billion, including capital of $NA
**Currency:** Saudi riyal (SAR)

## SENEGAL
**Location:** Western Africa, bordering the North Atlantic Ocean, between Guinea-Bissau and Mauritania
**Area:** 75,729 sq mi (196,190 sq km)
**Area-comparative:** slightly smaller than South Dakota
**Population:** 11,987,121
**Population rate growth:** 2.34%
**Nationality:** noun: Senegalese (singular and plural); adjective: Senegalese
**Ethnic groups:** Wolof 43.3%, Pular 23.8%, Serer 14.7%, Jola 3.7%, Mandinka 3%, Soninke 1.1%, European and Lebanese 1%, other 9.4%
**Languages:** French (official), Wolof, Pulaar, Jola, Mandinka
**Religions:** Muslim 94%, indigenous beliefs 1%, Christian (primarily Roman Catholic) 5%
**Government type:** republic under multiparty democratic rule

**Capital:** Dakar
**Budget:** revenues: $1.657 billion; expenditures: $1.926 billion; capital expenditures of $357million
**Currency:** Communaute Financiere Africaine franc (XOF)

## *SEYCHELLES*

**Location:** Eastern Africa, group of islands in the Indian Ocean, northeast of Madagascar
**Area:** 176 sq mi (455 sq km)
**Area-comparative:** 2.5 times the size of Washington, DC
**Population:** 89,541
**Population growth rate:** 0.43%
**Nationality:** noun: Seychellois (singular and plural); adjective: Seychellois
**Ethnic groups:** mixed French, African, Indian, Chinese, and Arab
**Languages:** English (official), French (official), Creole
**Religions:** Roman Catholic 86.6%, Anglican 6.8%, other 4.1%, Christian 2.5%
**Government type:** republic
**Capital:** Victoria
**Budget:** revenues: $343.3 million; expenditures: $332.2 million
**Currency:** Seychelles rupee (SCR)

## *SIERRA LEONE*

**Location:** Western Africa, bordering the North Atlantic Ocean, between Guinea and Liberia
**Area:** 27,692 sq mi (71,740 sq km)
**Area-comparative:** slightly smaller than South Carolina
**Population:** 6,005,250
**Population growth rate:** 2.3%
**Nationality:** noun: Sierra Leonean(s); adjective: Sierra Leonean
**Ethnic groups:** 20 native African tribes 90%, Creole 10%, refugees from Liberia, small numbers of Europeans, Pakistanis, Lebanese and Indian
**Languages:** English (official), Mende, Temne, Krio
**Religions:** Muslim 60%, indigenous beliefs 30%, Christian 10%
**Government type:** constitutional democracy
**Capital:** Freetown
**Budget:** revenues: $96 million; expenditures: $351 million        **Currency:** leone (SLL)

## *SINGAPORE*

**Location:** Southeastern Asia, islands between Malaysia and Indonesia
**Area:** 267 sq mi (692.7 sq km)
**Area-comparative:** slightly more than 3.5 times the size of Washington, DC
**Population:** 4,492,150
**Population growth rate:** 1.42%
**Nationality:** noun: Singaporean(s); adjective: Singapore
**Ethnic groups:** Chinese 76.7%, Malay 14%, Indian 7.9%, other 1.4%
**Languages:** Chinese, Malay, Tamil, English
**Religions:** Buddhist, Muslim, Christian, Hindu, Sikh, Taoist, Confucianist
**Government type:** parliamentary republic
**Capital:** Singapore
**Budget:** revenues: $18.67 billion; expenditures: $18.21 billion, including capital of $5.1 billion
**Currency:** Singapore dollar (SGD)

## *SLOVAKIA*

**Location:** Central Europe, south of Poland
**Area:** 18,854 sq mi (48,845 sq km)

**Area-comparative:** about twice the size of New Hampshire
**Population:** 5,439,448
**Population growth rate:** 0.15%
**Nationality:** noun: Slovak(s); adjective: Slovak
**Ethnic groups:** Slovak 85.7%, Hungarian 10.6%, Roma 1.6%, Czech, Moravian, Silesian 1.1%, Ruthenian and Ukrainian 0.6%, German 0.1%, Polish 0.1%, and other 0.2%
**Languages:** Slovak (official), Hungarian
**Religions:** Roman Catholic 60.3%, atheist 9.7%, Protestant 8.4%, Orthodox 4.1% , other 17.5%
**Government type:** parliamentary democracy
**Capital:** Bratislava
**Budget:** revenues: $22.7 billion; expenditures: $23.2 billion       **Currency:** Slovak koruna (SKK)

## SLOVENIA
**Location:** Central Europe, eastern Alps bordering the Adriatic Sea, between Austria and Croatia
**Area:** 7,825 sq mi (20,273 sq km)
**Area-comparative:** slightly smaller than New Jersey
**Population:** 2,010,347
**Population growth rate:** -0.05%
**Nationality:** noun: Slovene(s); adjective: Slovenian
**Ethnic groups:** Slovene 92%, Croat 1%, Serb 0.5%, Bosniak 0.3% , Hungarian 0.4%, other 5.8%
**Languages:** Slovenian 92%, Serbo-Croatian 6.2%, other 1.8%
**Religions:** Roman Catholic 70.8%, Lutheran 1%, Muslim 1%, atheist 4.3%, other 22.9%
**Government type:** parliamentary democratic republic
**Capital:** Ljubljana
**Budget:** revenues: $16.02 billion; expenditures: $16.73 billion, including capital of $NA
**Currency:** tolar (SIT)

## SOLOMON ISLANDS
**Location:** Oceania, group of islands in the South Pacific Ocean, east of Papua New Guinea
**Area:** 10,981 sq mi (28,450 sq km)
**Area-comparative:** slightly smaller than Maryland
**Population:** 552,438
**Population growth rate:** 2.61%
**Nationality:** noun: Solomon Islander(s); adjective: Solomon Islander
**Ethnic groups:** Melanesian 93%, Polynesian 4%, Micronesian 1.5%, European 0.8%, Chinese 0.3%, other 0.4%
**Languages:** Melanesian, Polynesian, 120 indigenous languages, English is official but spoken by 1-2% of the population
**Religions:** Anglican 45%, Roman Catholic 18%, United (Methodist/Presbyterian) 12%, Baptist 9%, Seventh-Day Adventist 7%, other Protestant 5%, indigenous beliefs 4%
**Government type:** parliamentary democracy
**Capital:** Honiara
**Budget:** revenues: $49.7 million; expenditures: $75.1       **Currency:** Solomon Islands dollar (SBD)

## SOMALIA
**Location:** Eastern Africa, bordering the Gulf of Aden and the Indian Ocean, east of Ethiopia
**Area:** 246,135 sq mi (637,657 sq km)
**Area-comparative:** slightly smaller than Texas
**Population:** 8,863,338
**Population growth rate:** 2.85%
**Nationality:** noun: Somali(s); adjective: Somali
**Ethnic groups:** Somali 85%, Bantu and other non-Somali 15%
**Languages:** Somali (official), Arabic, Italian, English

**Religion:** Sunni Muslim 100%
**Government type:** no permanent national government; transitional, parliamentary national government
**Capital:** Mogadishu
**Budget:** revenues: $NA; expenditures: $NA
**Currency:** Somali shilling(SOS)

## SOUTH AFRICA

**Location:** Southern Africa, at the southern tip of the continent of Africa
**Area:** 470,886 sq mi (1,219,912 sq km)
**Area-comparative:** slightly less than twice the size of Texas
**Population:** 44,187,637
**Population growth rate:** -0.4%
**Nationality:** noun: South African(s); adjective: South African
**Ethnic groups:** black 75.2%, white 13.6%, Multiracial (black and white) 8.6%, Indian 2.6%
**Languages:** 11 official languages, including Afrikaans, English, Ndebele, Pedi, Sotho, Swazi, Tsonga, Tswana, Venda, Xhosa, Zulu
**Religions:** Christian 68%, indigenous beliefs and animist 28.5%, Muslim 2%, Hindu 1.5%
**Government type:** republic
**Capital:** Pretoria (administrative), Cape Town (legislative center), Bloemfontein (judicial center)
**Budget:** revenues: $65.91 billion; expenditures: $70.62 billion
**Currency:** rand (ZAR)

## SPAIN

**Location:** Southwestern Europe, bordering the Bay of Biscay, Mediterranean Sea, North Atlantic Ocean, and Pyrenees Mountains, southwest of France
**Area:** 194,846 sq mi (504,782 sq km)
**Area-comparative:** slightly more than twice the size of Oregon
**Population:** 40,397,842
**Population growth rate:** 0.13%
**Nationality:** noun: Spaniard(s); adjective: Spanish
**Ethnic groups:** composite of Mediterranean and Nordic stock
**Languages:** Castilian Spanish 74% (official), Catalan 17%, Galician 7%, Basque 2%
**Religions:** Roman Catholic 94%, other 6%
**Government type:** parliamentary democracy
**Capital:** Madrid
**Budget:** revenues: $440.9 billion; expenditures: $448.4 billion; capital expenditures of $12.8 billion
**Currency:** euro (EUR)

## SRI LANKA

**Location:** Southern Asia, island in the Indian Ocean, south of India
**Area:** 25,325 sq mi (65,610 sq km)
**Area-comparative:** slightly larger than West Virginia
**Population:** 20,222,240
**Population growth rate:** 0.78%
**Nationality:** noun: Sri Lankan(s); adjective: Sri Lankan
**Ethnic groups:** Sinhalese 74%, Tamil 18%, Moor 7%, Burgher, Malay, and Vedda 1%
**Languages:** Sinhala 74%, Tamil 18%, other 8%
**Religions:** Buddhist 70%, Hindu 15%, Christian 8%, Muslim 7%
**Government type:** republic
**Capital:** Colombo; note- Sri Jayewardenepura Kotte is the legislative capital
**Budget:** revenues: $3.804 billion; expenditures: $5.469 billion
**Currency:** Sri Lankan rupee (LKR)

## SUDAN

**Location:** Northern Africa, bordering the Red Sea, between Egypt and Eritrea
**Area:** 967,242 sq mi (2,505,810 sq km)
**Area-comparative:** slightly more than one-quarter the size of the US
**Population:** 41,236,378
**Population growth rate:** 2.55%
**Nationality:** noun: Sudanese (singular and plural); adjective: Sudanese
**Ethnic groups:** black 52%, Arab 39%, Beja 6%, foreigners 2%, other 1%
**Languages:** Arabic (official), Nubian, Ta Bedawie, diverse dialects of Nilotic, English
**Religions:** Sunni Muslim 70%, indigenous beliefs 25%, Christian 5%
**Government type:** authoritarian regime-ruling military junta took power in 1989, government is run by an alliance of the military and the National Congress Party (NCP)
**Capital:** Khartoum
**Budget:** revenues: $6.182 billion; expenditures: $5.753 billion, capital of $304 million
**Currency:** Sudanese dinar (SDD)

## SURINAME

**Location:** Northern South America, bordering the North Atlantic Ocean, between French Guiana and Guyana
**Area:** 63,022 sq mi (163,270 sq km)
**Area-comparative:** slightly larger than Georgia
**Population:** 439,117
**Population growth rate:** 0.2%
**Nationality:** noun: Surinamer(s); adjective: Surinamese
**Ethnic groups:** Hindustani 37%, Creole 31%, Javanese 15%, Maroons 10%, Amerindian 2%, Chinese 2%, other 2%, white 1%
**Languages:** Dutch (official), English, Sranang Tongo, Hindustani, Javanese
**Religions:** Hindu 27.4%, Protestant 25.2%, Roman Catholic 22.8%, Muslim 19.6%, indigenous beliefs 5%
**Government type:** constitutional democracy
**Capital:** Paramaribo
**Budget:** revenues: $392.6 million; expenditures: $425.9 million
**Currency:** Surinamese guilder (SRG)

## SWAZILAND

**Location:** Southern Africa, between Mozambique and South Africa
**Area:** 6,702 sq mi (17,363 sq km)
**Area-comparative:** slightly smaller than New Jersey
**Population:** 1,136,334
**Population growth rate:** 0.23%
**Nationality:** noun: Swazi(s); adjective: Swazi
**Ethnic groups:** African 97%, European 3%
**Languages:** English, siSwati
**Religions:** Zionist 40%, Roman Catholic 20%, Muslim 10%, Anglican, Bahai, Methodist, Mormon, Jewish and other 30%
**Government type:** monarchy, independent member of Commonwealth
**Capital:** Mbabane; Lobamba is the royal and legislative capital
**Budget:** revenues: $805.6 million: expenditures: $957.1 million; capital expenditures of $147 million
**Currency:** lilangeni (SZL)

## SWEDEN

**Location:** Northern Europe, bordering the Baltic Sea, Gulf of Bothnia, Kattegat, and Skagerrak, between Finland and Norway

**Area:** 173,686 sq mi (449,964 sq km)
**Area-comparative:** slightly larger than California
**Population:** 9,016,596
**Population growth rate:** 0.16%
**Nationality:** noun: Swede(s); adjective: Swedish
**Ethnic groups:** Swedes and Finnish and Sami minorities; Finns, Yugoslavs, Danes, Norwegians, Greeks
**Languages:** Swedish (official); small Sami-and Finnish-speaking minorities
**Religions:** Lutheran 87%, Roman Catholic. Orthodox, Baptist, Muslim, Jewish, Buddhist
**Government:** constitutional monarchy
**Capital:** Stockholm
**Budget:** revenues: $210.5 billion; expenditures: $205.9 billion
**Currency:** Swedish krona (SEK)

### *SWITZERLAND*

**Location:** Central Europe, east of France, north of Italy
**Area:** 15,938 sq mi (41,290 sq km)
**Area-comparative:** slightly less than twice the size of New Jersey
**Population:** 7,523,934
**Population growth rate:** 0.43%
**Nationality:** noun: Swiss (singular and plural); adjective: Swiss
**Ethnic groups:** German 65%, French 18%, Italian 10%, other %, Romansch 1%
**Languages:** German (official) 63.7%, French 19.2%, other 8.9%, Italian 7.6%, Romansch 0.6%
**Religions:** Roman Catholic 46.1%, Protestant 40%, none 8.9%, other 5%
**Government type:** federal republic
**Capital:** Bern
**Budget: revenues:** $138.1 billion; expenditures: $143.6 billion
**Currency:** Swiss franc (CHF)

### *SYRIA*

**Location:** Middle East, bordering the Mediterranean Sea, between Lebanon and Turkey
**Area:** 71,479 sq mi (185,180 sq km)
**Area comparative:** slightly larger than North Dakota
**Population:** 18,881,361
**Population growth rate:** 2.3%
**Nationality:** noun: Syrian(s); adjective: Syrian
**Ethnic groups:** Arab 90.3%, Kurds, Armenians, and other 9.7%
**Languages:** Arabic (official), Kurdish, Armenian, Aramaic, Circassian, French, English
**Religions:** Sunni Muslim 74%, Alawite, Druze, and other Muslim sects 16%, Christian (various sects) 10%
**Government type:** republic under military regime since March 1963
**Capital:** Damascus
**Budget:** revenues: $6.392 billion: expenditures: $7.613 billion; capital expenditures of $3.23 billion
**Currency:** Syrian pound (SYP)

### *TAJIKISTAN*

**Location:** Central Asia, west of China
**Area:** 55,237 sq mi (143,100 sq km)
**Area-comparative:** slightly smaller than Wisconsin
**Population:** 7,320,815
**Population growth rate:** 2.19%
**Nationality:** noun: Tajikstani(s); adjective: Tajikstani
**Ethnic groups:** Tajik 64.9%, Uzbek 25%, other 6.6%, Russian 3.5%
**Languages:** Tajik (official), Russian

**Religions:** Sunni Muslim 85%, Shi'a Muslim 5% other (including Russian Orthodox) 10%,
**Government type:** republic
**Capital:** Dushanbe
**Budget:** revenues: $442.3 million; expenditures: $542.6 million; capital expenditures of $86 million
**Currency:** somoni (TJS)

## TANZANIA
**Location:** Eastern Africa, bordering the Indian Ocean, between Kenya and Mozambique
**Area:** 364,804 sq mi (945,087 sq km)
**Area-comparative:** slightly larger than twice the size of California
**Population:** 37,445,392
**Population growth rate:** 1.83%
**Nationality:** noun: Tanzanian(s); adjective: Tanzanian
**Ethnic groups:** African 99%, other 1%
**Languages:** Kiswahili or Swahili (official), English, Arabic, many local languages
**Religions:** Muslim 35%, indigenous beliefs 35%, Christian 30%; Zanzibar more than 99% Muslim
**Government type:** republic
**Capital:** Dares Salaam (administrative); Dodoma (legislative)
**Budget:** revenues: $2.235 billion; expenditures: $2.669 billion, including capital of NA
**Currency:** Tanzanian shilling (TZS)

## THAILAND
**Location:** Southeastern Asia, bordering the Andaman Sea and the Gulf of Thailand, southeast of
          Myanmar
**Area:** 198,404 sq mi (514,000 sq km)
**Area-comparative:** slightly more than twice the size of Wyoming
**Population:** 64,631,595
**Population growth rate:** 0.68%
**Nationality:** noun: Thai (singular and plural); adjective: Thai
**Ethnic groups:** Thai 75%, Chinese 14%, other 11%
**Languages:** Thai (official), English, regional dialects
**Religions:** Buddhism 94.6%, Muslim 4.6%, other 0.1%, Christianity 0.7%
**Government type:** constitutional monarchy
**Capital:** Bangkok
**Budget:** revenues: $30.64 billion; expenditures: $31.76 billion, including capital of $5 billion
**Currency:** baht (THB)

## TOGO
**Location:** Western Africa, bordering the Bight of Benin, between Benin and Ghana
**Area:** 21,919 sq mi (56,785 sq km)
**Area-comparative:** slightly smaller than West Virginia
**Population:** 5,548,702
**Population growth rate:** 2.72%
**Nationality:** noun: Togolise; adjective: Togolese
**Ethnic groups:** native African (37 tribes, largest are Ewe, Mina, and Kabre) 99%, European and Syrian-
          Lebanese less than 1%
**Languages:** French (official), Ewe, Mina, Kabye, Dagomba
**Religions:** indigenous beliefs 51%, Christian 29%, Muslim 20%
**Government type:** republic under transition to multiparty democratic rule
**Capital:** Lome
**Budget:** revenues: $251.3 million; expenditures: $292.9 million
**Currency:** Communaute Financiere Africaine franc(XOF)

### TONGA

**Location:** Oceania, group of islands in the South Pacific Ocean, about two-thirds of the way from Hawaii to New Zealand

**Area:** 289 sq mi (748 sq km)

**Area-comparative:** four times the size of Washington, DC

**Population:** 114,689

**Population growth rate:** 2.01%

**Nationality:** noun: Tongan(s); adjective: Tongan

**Ethnic groups:** Polynesian, Europeans (about 300)

**Languages:** Tongan (official), English

**Religions:** Christian (Free Wesleyan church claims 30,000 adherents)

**Government type:** hereditary constitutional monarchy

**Capital:** Nuku'alofa

**Budget:** revenues: $39.9 million; expenditures: $52.4 million, including capital expenditures of $1.9 million

**Currency:** pa'anga(TOP)


### TRINIDAD AND TOBAGO

**Location:** Caribbean, islands between the Caribbean Sea and the North Atlantic Ocean, northeast of Venezuela

**Area:** 1,979 sq mi (5,128 sq km)

**Area-comparative:** slightly smaller than Delaware

**Population:** 1,065,842

**Population growth rate:** -0.87%

**Nationality:** noun: Trinidadian(s), Tobagonian(s); adjective: Trinidadian, Tobagonian

**Ethnic groups:** Indian (South Asian) 40%, African 37.5%, mixed 20.5%, other 2%

**Languages:** English (official), Hindi, French, Spanish, Chinese

**Religions:** Roman Catholic 26%, other 10.8%, Hindu 22.5%, Anglican 7.8%, Baptist 7.2%, Pentecostal 6.8%, other Christian 5.8%, Muslim 5.8%, Seventh Day Adventist 4%, unspecified 1.4%, none 1.9%

**Government type:** parliamentary democracy

**Capital:** Port-of-Spain

**Budget:** revenues: $4.5 billion; expenditures: $4.06 billion; capital expenditures of $117.3 million

**Currency:** Trinidad and Tobago dollar (TTD)


### TUNISIA

**Location:** Northern Africa, bordering the Mediterranean Sea, between Algeria and Libya

**Area:** 63,153 sq mi (163,610 sq km)

**Area-comparative:** slightly larger than Georgia

**Population:** 10,175,014

**Population growth rate:** 0.99%

**Nationality:** noun: Tunisian(s); adjective: Tunisian

**Ethnic groups:** Arab 98%, European 1%, Jewish and other 1%

**Languages:** Arabic (official), French

**Religions:** Muslim 98%, Christian 1%, Jewish and other 1%

**Government type:** republic

**Capital:** Tunis

**Budget:** revenues: $7.322 billion; expenditures: $8.304 billion; capital expenditures of $1.6 billion

**Currency:** Tunisian dinar (TND)


### TURKEY

**Location:** Southeastern Europe, Southwestern Asia, bordering the Black Sea, between Bulgaria and Georgia, between Greece and Syria

**Area:** 301,304 sq mi (780,580 sq km)

**Area-comparative:** slightly larger than Texas

**Population:** 70,413,958
**Population growth rate:** 1.06%
**Nationality:** noun: Turk(s); adjective: Turkish
**Ethnic groups:** Turkish 80%, Kurdish 20%
**Languages:** Turkish (official), Kurdish, Arabic, Armenian, Greek
**Religions:** Muslim 99.8% (primarily Sunni); Christians and Jews 0.2%
**Government type:** republican parliamentary democracy
**Capital:** Ankara
**Budget:** revenues: $93.58 billion; expenditures: $115.3 billion          **Currency:** Turkish lira (TRL)

## *TURKMENISTAN*
**Location:** Central Asia, bordering the Caspian Sea, between Iran and Kazakhstan
**Area:** 188,406 sq mi (488,100 sq km)
**Area-comparative:** slightly larger than California
**Population:** 5,042,920
**Population growth rate:** 1.83%
**Nationality:** noun: Turmen(s); adjective: Turkmen
**Ethnic groups:** Turkmen 85%, Uzbek 5%, Russian 4%, other 6%
**Languages:** Turkmen 72% (official), Russian 12%, Uzbek 9%, other 7%
**Religions:** Muslim 89%, Eastern Orthodox 9%, unknown 2%
**Government type:** republic; authoritarian presidential rule, with little power outside the executive branch
**Capital:** Ashgabat
**Budget:** revenues: $1.401 billion; expenditures: $1.542 billion          **Currency:** Turkmen manta (TMM)

## *UGANDA*
**Location:** Eastern Africa, west of Kenya
**Area:** 91,111 sq mi (236,040 sq km)
**Area-comparative:** slightly smaller than Oregon
**Population:** 28,195,754
**Population growth rate:** 3.37%
**Nationality:** noun: Ugandan(s); adjective: Ugandan
**Ethnic groups:** Baganda 17%, Ankole 8%, Basogo 8%, Iteso 8%,Bakiga 7%, Langi 6%,
                  Rwanda 6%, Bagisu 5%, Acholi 4%, Lugbara 4%, Bunyoro 3%, Batoro 3%, Alur 2%,
                  Bagwere 2%, Bakonjo 2%, Jopodhola 2%, Karamojong 2%, Rundi 2%, non-African
                  (European, Asian, Arab) 1%, other 8%
**Languages:** English (official), Ganda, Luganda, Swahili, Nilo-Saharan languages, Arabic
**Religions:** Roman Catholic 33%, Protestant 33%, indigenous beliefs 18%, Muslim 16%
**Government type:** republic
**Capital:** Kampala
**Budget:** revenues: $1.845 billion; expenditures: $1.904 billion          **Currency:** Ugandan shilling (UGX)

## *UKRAINE*
**Location:** Eastern Europe, bordering the Black Sea, between Poland and Russia
**Area:** 233,028 sq mi (603,700 sq km)
**Area-comparative:** slightly smaller than Texas
**Population:** 46,710,816
**Population growth rate:** -0.6%
**Nationality:** noun: Ukrainian(s); adjective: Ukrainian
**Ethnic groups:** Ukrainian 77.8%, Russian 17.3%, other 1.8 %, Belarusian 0.6%, Moldovan 0.5%,
                  Crimean Tatar 0.5%, Bulgarian 0.4%, Hungarian 0.3%, Romanian 0.3%, Polish 0.3%,
                  Jewish 0.2%
**Languages:** Ukrainian 67% (official), Russian 24%, Romanian, Polish, Hungarian

507

**Religions:** Ukrainian Orthodox 19%, Ukrainian Greek Catholic 6%, Orthodox 16%, Protestant, Jewish and none 38%, Ukrainian Autocephalous Orthodox 1.7%

**Government type:** republic

**Capital:** Kiev (Kyyiv)

**Budget:** revenues: $23..59 billion; expenditures: $22.98 billion

**Currency:** hryvnia (UAH)

## UNITED ARAB EMIRATES

**Location:** Middle East, bordering the Gulf of Oman and the Persian Gulf, between Oman and Saudi Arabia

**Area:** 31,992 sq mi (82,880 sq km)

**Area-comparative:** slightly smaller than Maine

**Population:** 2,602,713

**Population growth rate:** 1.52%

**Nationality:** noun: Emirati(s); adjective: Emirati

**Ethnic groups:** South Asian 50%, Arab and Iranian 23%, Emirati 19%, other (including Westerners and East Asians) 8%

**Languages:** Arabic (official), Persian, English, Hindi, Urdu

**Religions:** Muslim 96% (Shi'a 16%), other (including Christian and Hindu) 4%

**Government type:** federation with specified powers delegated to the UAE federal government and other powers reserved to member emirates

**Capital:** Abu Dhabi

**Budget:** revenues: $34.93 billion; expenditures: $29.4 billion, including capital of $3.4 billion

**Currency:** Emiriati dirham(AED)

## UNITED KINGDOM

**Location:** Western Europe, between the North Atlantic Ocean and the North Sea, northwest of France

**Area:** 94,500 sq mi (244,820 sq km)

**Area-comparative:** slightly smaller than Oregon

**Population:** 60,609,153

**Population growth rate:** 0.28%

**Nationality:** noun: Briton(s), British (collective plural); adjective: British

**Ethnic groups:** English 83.6%, Scottish 8.6%, West Indian and Indian 1.8%, Pakistani 1.3%, Irish 2.9%, Welsh 4.9%, black 2%, other 1.6%, mixed 1.2%

**Religions:** Christian (Anglican, Roman Catholic, Presbyterian, Methodist) 71.6%, Muslim 2.7%, Hindu 1%, other 1.6%, unspecified or none 23.1%

**Languages:** English, Welsh, Scottish form of Gaelic

**Government type:** constitutional monarchy

**Capital:** London

**Budget:** revenues: $881.4 billion; expenditures: $951 billion

**Currency:** British pound (GBP)

## UNITED STATES OF AMERICA

**Location:** North America, bordering both the North Atlantic Ocean and the North Pacific Ocean, between Canada and Mexico

**Area:** 3,716,829 sq mi (9,631,418 sq km)

**Area-comparative:** about half the size of Russia; about three-tenths the size of Africa; about half the size of South America( or slightly larger than Brazil); slightly larger than China; about two and half times the size of western Europe

**Population:** 298,444,215

**Population growth rate:** 0.91%

**Nationality:** noun: American(s); adjective: American

**Ethnic groups:** white 81.7%, black 12.9%, Asian 4.2%, other 4%, Amerindian and Alaska native 1%, native Hawaiian and other Pacific Islander 0.2%

**Languages:** English (official), Spanish

**Religions:** Protestant 52%, Roman Catholic 24%, Mormon 2%, Jewish 1%, Muslim 1%, nonreligious 10%, other 10%

**Government type:** Constitution-based federal republic; strong democratic tradition

**Capital:** Washington, DC

**Budget:** revenues: $2.119 trillion; expenditures: $2.466 trillion

**Currency:** United States dollar (USD)


## URUGUAY

**Location:** Southern South America, bordering the South Atlantic Ocean, between Argentina and Brazil

**Area:** 68,021 sq mi (176,220 sq km)

**Area-comparative:** slightly smaller than the state of Washington

**Population:** 3,431,932

**Population growth rate:** 0.46%

**Nationality:** noun: Uruguayan(s); adjective: Uruguayan

**Ethnic groups:** white 88%, mestizo 8%, black 4%

**Languages:** Spanish, Portunol, or Brazilero

**Religions:** Roman Catholic 66%, other or not religious 31%, Protestant 2%, Jewish 1%

**Government type:** constitutional republic

**Capital:** Montevideo

**Budget:** revenues: $4.68 billion; expenditures: $4.845billion; capital expenditures of $193 million

**Currency:** Uruguayan peso (UYU)


## UZBEKISTAN

**Location:** Central Asia, north of Afghanistan

**Area:** 172,696 sq mi (447,400 sq km)

**Area-comparative:** slightly larger than California

**Population:** 27,307,134

**Population growth rate:** 1.7%

**Nationality:** noun: Uzbekistani; adjective: Uzbekistani

**Ethnic groups:** Uzbek 80%, Russian 5.5%, Tajik 5%, Kazakh 3%, Karakalpak 2.5%, Tartar 1.5%, other 2.5%

**Languages:** Uzbek 74.3%, Russian 14.2%, other 7.1%, Tajik 4.4%

**Religions:** Muslim 88% (primarily Sunni), Eastern Orthodox 9%, other 3%

**Government type:** republic; authoritarian presidential rule, with little power outside the executive branch

**Capital:** Tashkent

**Budget:** revenues: $2.815 billion; expenditures: $2.917 billion, including capital of $NA

**Currency:** Uzbekistani sum (UZS)


## VANUATU

**Location:** Oceania, group of islands in the South Pacific Ocean, about three-quarters of the way from Hawaii to Australia

**Area:** 4,709 sq mi (12,200 sq km)

**Area-comparative:** slightly larger than Connecticut

**Population:** 208,869

**Population growth rate:** 1.49%

**Nationality:** noun: Ni-Vanuatu (singular and plural); adjective: Ni-Vanuatu

**Ethnic groups:** indigenous Melanesian 98%, French, Vietnamese, Chinese, other Pacific Islanders

**Languages:** English, French, Bislama, and more than 100 local languages

**Religions:** Presbyterian 31.4%, other Christian 13.8%, Anglican 13.4%, Catholic 13.1%, Seventh-Day

Adventist 10.8%, indigenous beliefs 5.6%, other 9.6%, Church of Christ 3.8%, none 1%, unspecified 1.3%
**Government type:** parliamentary republic
**Capital:** Port-Vila (Efate)
**Budget:** revenues: $52.6 million; expenditures: $54.3 million; capital expenditures of $700,000
**Currency:** vatu (VUV)

## *VENEZUELA*
**Location:** Northern South America, bordering the Caribbean Sea and the North Atlantic Ocean, between Colombia and Guyana
**Area:** 352,051 sq mi (912,050 sq km)
**Area-comparative:** slightly more than twice the size of California
**Population:** 25,730,435
**Population growth rate:** 1.38%
**Nationality:** noun: Venezuelan(s); adjective: Venezuelan
**Ethnic groups:** Spanish, Italian, Portuguese, Arab, German, African, indigenous people
**Languages:** Spanish (official), numerous indigenous dialects
**Religions:** Roman Catholic 96%, Protestant 2%, other 2%
**Government type:** federal republic
**Capital:** Caracas
**Budget:** revenues: $39.63 billion; expenditures: $41.27 billion, including capital of $2.6 billion
**Currency:** bolivar (VEB)

## *VIETNAM*
**Location:** Southeastern Asia, bordering the Gulf of Thailand, Gulf of Tonkin, and South China Sea, alongside China, Laos, and Cambodia
**Area:** 127,210 sq mi (329,560 sq km)
**Area-comparative:** slightly larger than New Mexico
**Population:** 84,402,966
**Population growth rate:** 1.02%
**Nationality:** noun: Vietnamese (singular and plural); adjective: Vietnamese
**Ethnic groups:** Kinh (Viet) 86.2%, Tay 1.9%, Thai 1.7%, Muong 1.5%, Khome 1.4%, Hoa 1.1%, Nun 1.1%, Hmong 1%, others 4.1%,
**Languages:** Vietnamese (official), Chinese, English, (increasingly favored as 2nd language), French, Khmer, tribal languages
**Religions:** none 80.8%, Buddhist 9.3%, Hoa Hao 1.5%, Cao Dai 1.1%, Roman Catholic 6.7%, Muslim 0.1%, Protestant 0.5%
**Government type:** Communist state
**Capital:** Hanoi
**Budget:** revenues: $11.64 billion; expenditures: $12.95 billion; capital expenditures of $1.8 billion
**Currency:** dong (VND)

## *VIRGIN ISLANDS*
**Location:** islands between the Caribbean Sea and the North Atlantic Ocean, east of Puerto Rico
**Area:** 136 sq mi (352 sq km)
**Area-comparative:** twice the size of Washington, DC
**Population:** 108,605
**Population growth rate:** -0.12%
**Nationality:** noun: Virgin Islander(s); adjective; Virgin Islander
**Ethnic groups:** West Indian 81%, US mainland 13%, Puerto Rican 4%, other 2%
**Languages:** English (official), Spanish, Creole
**Religions:** Baptist 42%, Roman Catholic 34%, Episcopalian 17%, other 7%
**Government type:** NA

**Capital:** Charlotte Amalie
**Budget:** revenues: $NA; expenditures: $NA
**Currency:** U S dollar (USD)

## *YEMEN*

**Location:** Middle East, bordering the Arabian Sea, Gulf of Aden, and Red Sea, between Oman and Saudi Arabia
**Area:** 203,796 sq mi (527,970 sq km)
**Area-comparative:** slightly larger than twice the size of Wyoming
**Population:** 21,456,188
**Population growth rate:** 3.46%
**Nationality:** noun: Yemeni(s); adjective: Yemeni
**Ethnic groups:** predominantly Arab, some Afro-Arab, South Asians, Europeans
**Language:** Arabic
**Religions:** Muslim including Shafi'i and Shi'a, small numbers of Jewish, Christian, and Hindu
**Government type:** republic
**Capital:** Sanaa
**Budget:** revenues: $5.616 billion; expenditures: $5.719 billion, including capital of $NA
**Currency:** Yemeni rial (YER)

## *ZAMBIA*

**Location:** Southern Africa, east of Angola
**Area:** 290,509 sq mi (752,614 sq km)
**Area-comparative:** slightly larger than Texas
**Population:** 11,502,010
**Population growth rate:** 2.11%
**Nationality:** noun: Zambian(s); adjective: Zambian
**Ethnic groups:** African 98.7%, European 1.1%, other 0.2%
**Languages:** English (official), Bemba, Kaonda, Lozi, Lunda, Luvale, Nyanja, 70 indigenous languages
**Religions:** Christian 50%-75%, Muslim and Hindu 24%-49%, indigenous beliefs 1%
**Government type:** republic
**Capital:** Lusaka
**Budget:** revenues: $1.688 billion; expenditures: $1.866 billion
**Currency:** Zambian kwacha (ZMK)

## *ZIMBABWE*

**Location:** Southern Africa, between South Africia and Zambia
**Area:** 150,764 sq mi (390,580 sq km)
**Area-comparative:** slightly larger than Montana
**Population:** 12,236,805
**Population growth rate:** 0.62%
**Nationality:** noun: Zimbabwean(s); adjective: Zimbabwean
**Ethnic groups:** Shona 82%, Ndebele 14%, other 2%, mixed and Asian 1%, white less than 1%
**Languages:** English (official), Shona, Sindebele, and numerous other tribal dialects
**Religions:** syncretic 50%, Christian 25%, indigenous beliefs 24%, Muslim and other 1%
**Government type:** parliamentary democracy
**Capital:** Harare
**Budget:** revenues: $1.409 billion; expenditures: $1.905 billion, including capital of $NA
**Currency:** Zimbabwean dollar (ZWD)

# The World

**Area:** 510.072 million sq km;
*land*: 148.94 million sq km;
*water*: 361.132 million sq km.
*Note*: 70.8% of the world's surface is *water*,
29.2% is *land*.

## Area-comparative:
land area about 16 times the size of the US
**Population:** 6,525,170,264
**Population growth rate:** 1.14%

**Languages:** Chinese Mandarin 13.69%; Hindi
2.82%; English 4.84%; Spanish 5.05%,
Bengali 2.68%, Portuguese 2.77%, Russian
2.27%, Japanese 1.99%, German 1.49%,
Wu Chinese 1.21%

**Religions**: Christians 32.84%; (of which Roman
Catholics 17.34%, Protestants 5.78%, Orthodox
3.44%, Anglicans 1.27%), Muslims 19.9%,
Hindus 13.29%, Buddhists 5.92%, Sikhs o.39%,
Jews 0.23%, other religions 12.63%,
non-religious 12.44%, atheists 2.63%.

# 2007 Calendar with Islamic dates in North America
## ISLAMIC DATES BEGIN AT SUNSET THE PRECEDING EVENING

| NY=<br>NewYear | Aa=<br>Aashurah | MN=<br>Miladun-Nabi | IM=<br>Isra/Me'raj | NS=<br>NisfuSha'ban | RM=<br>Ramadan | LQ=<br>Lailatul-Qadr | EF=<br>Eidul-Fitr | YA=<br>Yaumu-Arafah | EA=<br>Eidul-Adha |
|---|---|---|---|---|---|---|---|---|---|

### January
#### ZHJ 1427/MHM 1428

| S | M | T | W | T | F | S |
|---|---|---|---|---|---|---|
| | 1 | 2 | 3 | 4 | 5 | 6 |
| | *11* | *12* | *13* | *14* | *15* | *16* |
| 7 | 8 | 9 | 10 | 11 | 12 | 13 |
| *17* | *18* | *19* | *20* | *21* | *22* | *23* |
| 14 | 15 | 16 | 17 | 18 | 19 | 20 |
| *24* | *25* | *26* | *27* | *28* | *29* | NY |
| 21 | 22 | 23 | 24 | 25 | 26 | 27 |
| *2* | *3* | *4* | *5* | *6* | *7* | *8* |
| 28 | 29 | 30 | 31 | | | |
| *9* | Aa | *11* | *12* | | | |

### February
#### Muharram/Safar

| S | M | T | W | T | F | S |
|---|---|---|---|---|---|---|
| | | | | 1 | 2 | 3 |
| | | | | *13* | *14* | *15* |
| 4 | 5 | 6 | 7 | 8 | 9 | 10 |
| *16* | *17* | *18* | *19* | *20* | *21* | *22* |
| 11 | 12 | 13 | 14 | 15 | 16 | 17 |
| *23* | *24* | *25* | *26* | *27* | *28* | *29* |
| 18 | 19 | 20 | 21 | 22 | 23 | 24 |
| *30* | SF | *2* | *3* | *4* | *5* | *6* |
| 25 | 26 | 27 | 28 | | | |
| *7* | *8* | *9* | *10* | | | |

### March
#### Safar/Rabi-I

| S | M | T | W | T | F | S |
|---|---|---|---|---|---|---|
| | | | | 1 | 2 | 3 |
| | | | | *11* | *12* | *13* |
| 4 | 5 | 6 | 7 | 8 | 9 | 10 |
| *14* | *15* | *16* | *17* | *18* | *19* | *20* |
| 11 | 12 | 13 | 14 | 15 | 16 | 17 |
| *21* | *22* | *23* | *24* | *25* | *26* | *27* |
| 18 | 19 | 20 | 21 | 22 | 23 | 24 |
| *28* | *29* | RA | *2* | *3* | *4* | *5* |
| 25 | 26 | 27 | 28 | 29 | 30 | 31 |
| *6* | *7* | *8* | *9* | *10* | *11* | MN |

### April
#### Rabi-I/Rabi-II

| S | M | T | W | T | F | S |
|---|---|---|---|---|---|---|
| 1 | 2 | 3 | 4 | 5 | 6 | 7 |
| *13* | *14* | *15* | *16* | *17* | *18* | *19* |
| 8 | 9 | 10 | 11 | 12 | 13 | 14 |
| *20* | *21* | *22* | *23* | *24* | *25* | *26* |
| 15 | 16 | 17 | 18 | 19 | 20 | 21 |
| *27* | *28* | *29* | ?? | RT | *2* | *3* |
| 22 | 23 | 24 | 25 | 26 | 27 | 28 |
| *4* | *5* | *6* | *7* | *8* | *9* | *10* |
| 29 | 30 | | | | | |
| *11* | *12* | | | | | |

### May
#### Rabi-II/Jumada-I

| S | M | T | W | T | F | S |
|---|---|---|---|---|---|---|
| | | 1 | 2 | 3 | 4 | 5 |
| | | *13* | *14* | *15* | *16* | *17* |
| 6 | 7 | 8 | 9 | 10 | 11 | 12 |
| *18* | *19* | *20* | *21* | *22* | *23* | *24* |
| 13 | 14 | 15 | 16 | 17 | 18 | 19 |
| *25* | *26* | *27* | *28* | *29* | JA | *2* |
| 20 | 21 | 22 | 23 | 24 | 25 | 26 |
| *3* | *4* | *5* | *6* | *7* | *8* | *9* |
| 27 | 28 | 29 | 30 | 31 | | |
| *10* | *11* | *12* | *13* | *14* | | |

### June
#### Jumada-I/Jumada-II

| S | M | T | W | T | F | S |
|---|---|---|---|---|---|---|
| | | | | | 1 | 2 |
| | | | | | *15* | *16* |
| 3 | 4 | 5 | 6 | 7 | 8 | 9 |
| *17* | *18* | *19* | *20* | *21* | *22* | *23* |
| 10 | 11 | 12 | 13 | 14 | 15 | 16 |
| *24* | *25* | *26* | *27* | *28* | *29* | JT |
| 17 | 18 | 19 | 20 | 21 | 22 | 23 |
| *2* | *3* | *4* | *5* | *6* | *7* | *8* |
| 24 | 25 | 26 | 27 | 28 | 29 | 30 |
| *9* | *10* | *11* | *12* | *13* | *14* | *15* |

### July
#### Jumada-II/Rajab

| S | M | T | W | T | F | S |
|---|---|---|---|---|---|---|
| 1 | 2 | 3 | 4 | 5 | 6 | 7 |
| *16* | *17* | *18* | *19* | *20* | *21* | *22* |
| 8 | 9 | 10 | 11 | 12 | 13 | 14 |
| *23* | *24* | *25* | *26* | *27* | *28* | *29* |
| 15 | 16 | 17 | 18 | 19 | 20 | 21 |
| *30* | RJ | *2* | *3* | *4* | *5* | *6* |
| 22 | 23 | 24 | 25 | 26 | 27 | 28 |
| *7* | *8* | *9* | *10* | *11* | *12* | *13* |
| 29 | 30 | 31 | | | | |
| *14* | *15* | *16* | | | | |

### August
#### Rajab/Sha'ban

| S | M | T | W | T | F | S |
|---|---|---|---|---|---|---|
| | | | 1 | 2 | 3 | 4 |
| | | | *17* | *18* | *19* | *20* |
| 5 | 6 | 7 | 8 | 9 | 10 | 11 |
| *21* | *22* | *23* | *24* | *25* | IM | *27* |
| 12 | 13 | 14 | 15 | 16 | 17 | 18 |
| *28* | *29* | ?? | SB | *2* | *3* | *4* |
| 19 | 20 | 21 | 22 | 23 | 24 | 25 |
| *5* | *6* | *7* | *8* | *9* | *10* | *11* |
| 26 | 27 | 28 | 29 | 30 | 31 | |
| *12* | *13* | *14* | NS | *16* | *17* | |

### September
#### Sha'ban/Ramadan

| S | M | T | W | T | F | S |
|---|---|---|---|---|---|---|
| | | | | | | 1 |
| | | | | | | *18* |
| 2 | 3 | 4 | 5 | 6 | 7 | 8 |
| *19* | *20* | *21* | *22* | *23* | *24* | *25* |
| 9 | 10 | 11 | 12 | 13 | 14 | 15 |
| *26* | *27* | *28* | *29* | RM | *2* | *3* |
| 16 | 17 | 18 | 19 | 20 | 21 | 22 |
| *4* | *5* | *6* | *7* | *8* | *9* | *10* |
| 23 | 24 | 25 | 26 | 27 | 28 | 29 |
| *11* | *12* | *13* | *14* | *15* | *16* | *17* |
| 30 | | | | | | |
| *18* | | | | | | |

### October
#### Ramadan/Shawwal

| S | M | T | W | T | F | S |
|---|---|---|---|---|---|---|
| | 1 | 2 | 3 | 4 | 5 | 6 |
| | *19* | *20* | *21* | *22* | *23* | *24* |
| 7 | 8 | 9 | 10 | 11 | 12 | 13 |
| *25* | LQ | *27* | *28* | *29* | *30* | EF |
| 14 | 15 | 16 | 17 | 18 | 19 | 20 |
| *2* | *3* | *4* | *5* | *6* | *7* | *8* |
| 21 | 22 | 23 | 24 | 25 | 26 | 27 |
| *9* | *10* | *11* | *12* | *13* | *14* | *15* |
| 28 | 29 | 30 | 31 | | | |
| *16* | *17* | *18* | *19* | | | |

### November
#### Shawwal/Zul-Qa'dah

| S | M | T | W | T | F | S |
|---|---|---|---|---|---|---|
| | | | | 1 | 2 | 3 |
| | | | | *20* | *21* | *22* |
| 4 | 5 | 6 | 7 | 8 | 9 | 10 |
| *23* | *24* | *25* | *26* | *27* | *28* | *29* |
| 11 | 12 | 13 | 14 | 15 | 16 | 17 |
| *30* | ZQ | *2* | *3* | *4* | *5* | *6* |
| 18 | 19 | 20 | 21 | 22 | 23 | 24 |
| *7* | *8* | *9* | *10* | *11* | *12* | *13* |
| 25 | 26 | 27 | 28 | 29 | 30 | |
| *14* | *15* | *16* | *17* | *18* | *19* | |

### December
#### Zul-Qa'dah/Zul-Hijjah

| S | M | T | W | T | F | S |
|---|---|---|---|---|---|---|
| | | | | | | 1 |
| | | | | | | *20* |
| 2 | 3 | 4 | 5 | 6 | 7 | 8 |
| *21* | *22* | *23* | *24* | *25* | *26* | *27* |
| 9 | 10 | 11 | 12 | 13 | 14 | 15 |
| *28* | *29* | ZH | *2* | *3* | *4* | *5* |
| 16 | 17 | 18 | 19 | 20 | 21 | 22 |
| *6* | *7* | *8* | YA | EA | *11* | *12* |
| 23 | 24 | 25 | 26 | 27 | 28 | 29 |
| *13* | *14* | *15* | *16* | *17* | *18* | *19* |
| 30 | 31 | | | | | |
| *20* | *21* | | | | | |

?? Very slight chance, month may start on this day.

# Calendar for year 2007 (United States)

### January 2007

| Su | Mo | Tu | We | Th | Fr | Sa |
|----|----|----|----|----|----|----|
|    | 1  | 2  | 3  | 4  | 5  | 6  |
| 7  | 8  | 9  | 10 | 11 | 12 | 13 |
| 14 | 15 | 16 | 17 | 18 | 19 | 20 |
| 21 | 22 | 23 | 24 | 25 | 26 | 27 |
| 28 | 29 | 30 | 31 |    |    |    |

### February 2007

| Su | Mo | Tu | We | Th | Fr | Sa |
|----|----|----|----|----|----|----|
|    |    |    |    | 1  | 2  | 3  |
| 4  | 5  | 6  | 7  | 8  | 9  | 10 |
| 11 | 12 | 13 | 14 | 15 | 16 | 17 |
| 18 | 19 | 20 | 21 | 22 | 23 | 24 |
| 25 | 26 | 27 | 28 |    |    |    |

### March 2007

| Su | Mo | Tu | We | Th | Fr | Sa |
|----|----|----|----|----|----|----|
|    |    |    |    | 1  | 2  | 3  |
| 4  | 5  | 6  | 7  | 8  | 9  | 10 |
| 11 | 12 | 13 | 14 | 15 | 16 | 17 |
| 18 | 19 | 20 | 21 | 22 | 23 | 24 |
| 25 | 26 | 27 | 28 | 29 | 30 | 31 |

### April 2007

| Su | Mo | Tu | We | Th | Fr | Sa |
|----|----|----|----|----|----|----|
| 1  | 2  | 3  | 4  | 5  | 6  | 7  |
| 8  | 9  | 10 | 11 | 12 | 13 | 14 |
| 15 | 16 | 17 | 18 | 19 | 20 | 21 |
| 22 | 23 | 24 | 25 | 26 | 27 | 28 |
| 29 | 30 |    |    |    |    |    |

### May 2007

| Su | Mo | Tu | We | Th | Fr | Sa |
|----|----|----|----|----|----|----|
|    |    | 1  | 2  | 3  | 4  | 5  |
| 6  | 7  | 8  | 9  | 10 | 11 | 12 |
| 13 | 14 | 15 | 16 | 17 | 18 | 19 |
| 20 | 21 | 22 | 23 | 24 | 25 | 26 |
| 27 | 28 | 29 | 30 | 31 |    |    |

### June 2007

| Su | Mo | Tu | We | Th | Fr | Sa |
|----|----|----|----|----|----|----|
|    |    |    |    |    | 1  | 2  |
| 3  | 4  | 5  | 6  | 7  | 8  | 9  |
| 10 | 11 | 12 | 13 | 14 | 15 | 16 |
| 17 | 18 | 19 | 20 | 21 | 22 | 23 |
| 24 | 25 | 26 | 27 | 28 | 29 | 30 |

### July 2007

| Su | Mo | Tu | We | Th | Fr | Sa |
|----|----|----|----|----|----|----|
| 1  | 2  | 3  | 4  | 5  | 6  | 7  |
| 8  | 9  | 10 | 11 | 12 | 13 | 14 |
| 15 | 16 | 17 | 18 | 19 | 20 | 21 |
| 22 | 23 | 24 | 25 | 26 | 27 | 28 |
| 29 | 30 | 31 |    |    |    |    |

### August 2007

| Su | Mo | Tu | We | Th | Fr | Sa |
|----|----|----|----|----|----|----|
|    |    |    | 1  | 2  | 3  | 4  |
| 5  | 6  | 7  | 8  | 9  | 10 | 11 |
| 12 | 13 | 14 | 15 | 16 | 17 | 18 |
| 19 | 20 | 21 | 22 | 23 | 24 | 25 |
| 26 | 27 | 28 | 29 | 30 | 31 |    |

### September 2007

| Su | Mo | Tu | We | Th | Fr | Sa |
|----|----|----|----|----|----|----|
|    |    |    |    |    |    | 1  |
| 2  | 3  | 4  | 5  | 6  | 7  | 8  |
| 9  | 10 | 11 | 12 | 13 | 14 | 15 |
| 16 | 17 | 18 | 19 | 20 | 21 | 22 |
| 23 | 24 | 25 | 26 | 27 | 28 | 29 |
| 30 |    |    |    |    |    |    |

### October 2007

| Su | Mo | Tu | We | Th | Fr | Sa |
|----|----|----|----|----|----|----|
|    | 1  | 2  | 3  | 4  | 5  | 6  |
| 7  | 8  | 9  | 10 | 11 | 12 | 13 |
| 14 | 15 | 16 | 17 | 18 | 19 | 20 |
| 21 | 22 | 23 | 24 | 25 | 26 | 27 |
| 28 | 29 | 30 | 31 |    |    |    |

### November 2007

| Su | Mo | Tu | We | Th | Fr | Sa |
|----|----|----|----|----|----|----|
|    |    |    |    | 1  | 2  | 3  |
| 4  | 5  | 6  | 7  | 8  | 9  | 10 |
| 11 | 12 | 13 | 14 | 15 | 16 | 17 |
| 18 | 19 | 20 | 21 | 22 | 23 | 24 |
| 25 | 26 | 27 | 28 | 29 | 30 |    |

### December 2007

| Su | Mo | Tu | We | Th | Fr | Sa |
|----|----|----|----|----|----|----|
|    |    |    |    |    |    | 1  |
| 2  | 3  | 4  | 5  | 6  | 7  | 8  |
| 9  | 10 | 11 | 12 | 13 | 14 | 15 |
| 16 | 17 | 18 | 19 | 20 | 21 | 22 |
| 23 | 24 | 25 | 26 | 27 | 28 | 29 |
| 30 | 31 |    |    |    |    |    |

## Holidays and Observances

| | | |
|---|---|---|
| Jan 1 New Year's Day | Jul 4 Independence Day | Nov 12 'Veterans Day' observed |
| Jan 15 Martin Luther King Day | Sep 3 Labor Day | Nov 22 Thanksgiving Day |
| Feb 14 Valentine's Day | Oct 8 Columbus Day | Dec 25 Christmas Day |
| Feb 19 Washington's Birthday | Oct 31 Halloween | |
| May 28 Memorial Day | Nov 11 Veterans Day | |

# Calendar for year 2007 (Israel)

### January 2007

| Su | Mo | Tu | We | Th | Fr | Sa |
|----|----|----|----|----|----|----|
|    | 1  | 2  | 3  | 4  | 5  | 6  |
| 7  | 8  | 9  | 10 | 11 | 12 | 13 |
| 14 | 15 | 16 | 17 | 18 | 19 | 20 |
| 21 | 22 | 23 | 24 | 25 | 26 | 27 |
| 28 | 29 | 30 | 31 |    |    |    |

### February 2007

| Su | Mo | Tu | We | Th | Fr | Sa |
|----|----|----|----|----|----|----|
|    |    |    |    | 1  | 2  | 3  |
| 4  | 5  | 6  | 7  | 8  | 9  | 10 |
| 11 | 12 | 13 | 14 | 15 | 16 | 17 |
| 18 | 19 | 20 | 21 | 22 | 23 | 24 |
| 25 | 26 | 27 | 28 |    |    |    |

### March 2007

| Su | Mo | Tu | We | Th | Fr | Sa |
|----|----|----|----|----|----|----|
|    |    |    |    | 1  | 2  | 3  |
| 4  | 5  | 6  | 7  | 8  | 9  | 10 |
| 11 | 12 | 13 | 14 | 15 | 16 | 17 |
| 18 | 19 | 20 | 21 | 22 | 23 | 24 |
| 25 | 26 | 27 | 28 | 29 | 30 | 31 |

### April 2007

| Su | Mo | Tu | We | Th | Fr | Sa |
|----|----|----|----|----|----|----|
| 1  | 2  | 3  | 4  | 5  | 6  | 7  |
| 8  | 9  | 10 | 11 | 12 | 13 | 14 |
| 15 | 16 | 17 | 18 | 19 | 20 | 21 |
| 22 | 23 | 24 | 25 | 26 | 27 | 28 |
| 29 | 30 |    |    |    |    |    |

### May 2007

| Su | Mo | Tu | We | Th | Fr | Sa |
|----|----|----|----|----|----|----|
|    |    | 1  | 2  | 3  | 4  | 5  |
| 6  | 7  | 8  | 9  | 10 | 11 | 12 |
| 13 | 14 | 15 | 16 | 17 | 18 | 19 |
| 20 | 21 | 22 | 23 | 24 | 25 | 26 |
| 27 | 28 | 29 | 30 | 31 |    |    |

### June 2007

| Su | Mo | Tu | We | Th | Fr | Sa |
|----|----|----|----|----|----|----|
|    |    |    |    |    | 1  | 2  |
| 3  | 4  | 5  | 6  | 7  | 8  | 9  |
| 10 | 11 | 12 | 13 | 14 | 15 | 16 |
| 17 | 18 | 19 | 20 | 21 | 22 | 23 |
| 24 | 25 | 26 | 27 | 28 | 29 | 30 |

### July 2007

| Su | Mo | Tu | We | Th | Fr | Sa |
|----|----|----|----|----|----|----|
| 1  | 2  | 3  | 4  | 5  | 6  | 7  |
| 8  | 9  | 10 | 11 | 12 | 13 | 14 |
| 15 | 16 | 17 | 18 | 19 | 20 | 21 |
| 22 | 23 | 24 | 25 | 26 | 27 | 28 |
| 29 | 30 | 31 |    |    |    |    |

### August 2007

| Su | Mo | Tu | We | Th | Fr | Sa |
|----|----|----|----|----|----|----|
|    |    |    | 1  | 2  | 3  | 4  |
| 5  | 6  | 7  | 8  | 9  | 10 | 11 |
| 12 | 13 | 14 | 15 | 16 | 17 | 18 |
| 19 | 20 | 21 | 22 | 23 | 24 | 25 |
| 26 | 27 | 28 | 29 | 30 | 31 |    |

### September 2007

| Su | Mo | Tu | We | Th | Fr | Sa |
|----|----|----|----|----|----|----|
|    |    |    |    |    |    | 1  |
| 2  | 3  | 4  | 5  | 6  | 7  | 8  |
| 9  | 10 | 11 | 12 | 13 | 14 | 15 |
| 16 | 17 | 18 | 19 | 20 | 21 | 22 |
| 23 | 24 | 25 | 26 | 27 | 28 | 29 |
| 30 |    |    |    |    |    |    |

### October 2007

| Su | Mo | Tu | We | Th | Fr | Sa |
|----|----|----|----|----|----|----|
|    | 1  | 2  | 3  | 4  | 5  | 6  |
| 7  | 8  | 9  | 10 | 11 | 12 | 13 |
| 14 | 15 | 16 | 17 | 18 | 19 | 20 |
| 21 | 22 | 23 | 24 | 25 | 26 | 27 |
| 28 | 29 | 30 | 31 |    |    |    |

### November 2007

| Su | Mo | Tu | We | Th | Fr | Sa |
|----|----|----|----|----|----|----|
|    |    |    |    | 1  | 2  | 3  |
| 4  | 5  | 6  | 7  | 8  | 9  | 10 |
| 11 | 12 | 13 | 14 | 15 | 16 | 17 |
| 18 | 19 | 20 | 21 | 22 | 23 | 24 |
| 25 | 26 | 27 | 28 | 29 | 30 |    |

### December 2007

| Su | Mo | Tu | We | Th | Fr | Sa |
|----|----|----|----|----|----|----|
|    |    |    |    |    |    | 1  |
| 2  | 3  | 4  | 5  | 6  | 7  | 8  |
| 9  | 10 | 11 | 12 | 13 | 14 | 15 |
| 16 | 17 | 18 | 19 | 20 | 21 | 22 |
| 23 | 24 | 25 | 26 | 27 | 28 | 29 |
| 30 | 31 |    |    |    |    |    |

## Holidays and Observances

| Date | Hebrew Date | Observance |
|------|------|------|
| Feb 3  | Shevat 15 | Tu B'Shevat (Arbor Day) |
| Mar 1  | Adar 11   | Ta'anit Esther (Fast of Esther) |
| Mar 4  | Adar 14   | Purim (Deliverance of the Jews) |
| Mar 5  | Adar 15   | Shushan Purim |
| Apr 3  | Nisan 15  | Pesach I (First day of Passover) |
| Apr 4  | Nisan 16  | Pesach II (Passover) |
| Apr 5  | Nisan 17  | Pesach III (Passover) |
| Apr 6  | Nisan 18  | Pesach IV (Passover) |
| Apr 7  | Nisan 19  | Pesach V (Passover) |
| Apr 8  | Nisan 20  | Pesach VI (Passover) |
| Apr 9  | Nisan 21  | Pesach VII (Last day of Passover) |
| Apr 15 | Nisan 27  | Yom HaShoah (Holocaust memorial) |
| Apr 23 | Iyar 5    | Yom HaZikaron (Memorial Day) |
| Apr 24 | Iyar 6    | Yom HaAtzmaut (Independence Day) |
| May 6  | Iyar 18   | Lag B'Omer |
| May 16 | Iyar 28   | Yom Yerushalayim (Jerusalem Day) |
| May 23 | Sivan 6   | Shavuot (Pentecost) |
| Jul 3  | Tammuz 17 | Fast of Shiva Asar B'Tammuz |
| Jul 24 | Av 9      | Tisha B'Av |
| Sep 13 | Tishri 1  | Rosh Hashana (New Year) |
| Sep 14 | Tishri 2  | Rosh Hashana II (New Year day 2) |
| Sep 16 | Tishri 4  | Tzom Gedaliah |
| Sep 22 | Tishri 10 | Yom Kippur |
| Sep 27 | Tishri 15 | Sukkot I |
| Sep 28 | Tishri 16 | Sukkot II |
| Sep 29 | Tishri 17 | Sukkot III |
| Sep 30 | Tishri 18 | Sukkot IV |
| Oct 1  | Tishri 19 | Sukkot V |
| Oct 2  | Tishri 20 | Sukkot VI |
| Oct 3  | Tishri 21 | Sukkot VII/Hoshanah Rabah |
| Oct 4  | Tishri 22 | Shmini Atzeret/Simchat Torah |
| Dec 5  | Kislev 25 | Chanukah I (Holiday of lights) |
| Dec 6  | Kislev 26 | Chanukah II |
| Dec 7  | Kislev 27 | Chanukah III |
| Dec 8  | Kislev 28 | Chanukah IV |
| Dec 9  | Kislev 29 | Chanukah V |
| Dec 10 | Tevet 1   | Chanukah VI/Rosh Chodesh Tevet |
| Dec 11 | Tevet 2   | Chanukah VII |
| Dec 12 | Tevet 3   | Chanukah VIII |
| Dec 19 | Tevet 10  | Asarah B'Tevet |

# THE PLANETS

## THE PLANETS - SUMMARY

| | Distance From Sun (000 km) | Radius (km) | Planet Mass $E=mc^2$ |
|---|---|---|---|
| Mercury | 57,910 | 2439 3.30 | e23 |
| Venus | 108,200 | 6052 4.87 | e24 |
| Earth | 149,600 | 6378 5.98 | e24 |
| Mars | 227,940 | 3397 6.42 | e23 |
| Jupiter | 778,330 | 71492 1.90 | e27 |
| Saturn | 1,426,940 | 60268 5.69 | e26 |
| Uranus | 2,870,990 | 25559 8.69 | e25 |
| Neptune | 4,497,070 | 24764 1.02 | e26 |
| Pluto | 5,913,520 | 1160 1.31 | e22 |

Energy equals Mass times the speed of light squared.

$E=mc^2 = 0.111 \times 300,000,000 \times 300,000,000 =$ **10,000,000,000,000,000 Joules**

There are nine planets that revolve around the sun in our solar system. A planet is a celestial body that is in orbit around the sun, has enough mass to be nearly round, and dominates its orbit. Each planet is the largest body of matter in its neighborhood that shines by reflected light. Like Earth, the other planets do not give off light of their own. When you see a planet shining brightly in the night sky, it is giving off the sun's light. These planets travel around the sun in fixed paths called orbits. A planet's gravitational pull depends on two things: size and density. The term *density* refers to the amount of matter contained in a given space. A block of iron and a block of ice that are equal in size are not equal in weight; the block of iron weighs more than the block of ice. A scientist would say that the iron is more *dense*; the block of iron has more matter in it.

The sun is by far the largest object in the solar system. It is about 4.5 billion years old. Since its birth it has used up about half of the hydrogen in its core. It will continue to radiate for another 5 billion years, but eventually it will run out of hydrogen fuel. The sun contains more than 99.8% of the total mass of the solar system (Jupiter contains most of the rest). The sun is composed of 75% hydrogen and 25% helium. The diameter of the sun is 864,000 miles— more than 100 time's Earth's diameter.

Every star in the night sky is the sun of another solar system. Therefore, our sun would look like a small twinkle if you saw it from the planet of another solar system.

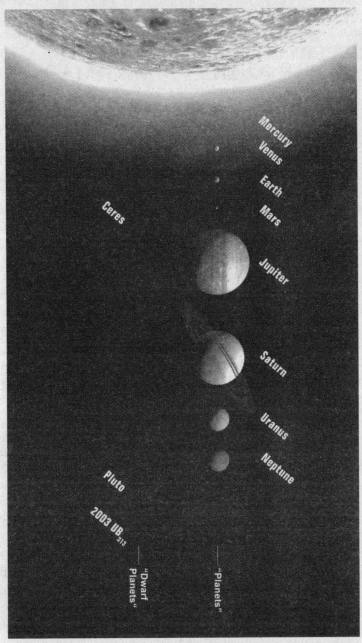

Mercury
Venus
Earth
Mars
Ceres
Jupiter
Saturn
Uranus
Neptune
Pluto
2003 UB₃₁₃
"Dwarf Planets"
"Planets"

We would like to thank NASA for providing the images of the planets in our solar system.

517

**MERCURY** is the planet closest to the sun and the eighth largest. It was named for Mercury, who in Greek myths was the speedy messenger of the gods. Mercury revolves around the sun in 88 days, faster than any other planet. Its orbit has the shape of an ellipse—a sort of flattened circle. Because of its irregular shape, sometimes it is only about 28,550,000 miles away from the sun, while at other times it is about 43,350,000 miles away. Its diameter is approximately the same as the width of the Atlantic Ocean. Mercury has a surface temperature of about − 9.6 degrees Fahrenheit on its dark side. The planet is surrounded by a thin atmosphere of carbon dioxide. Mercury's pull of gravity is much weaker than Earth's. A man weighing 140 pounds on Earth would weigh about 50 pounds on Mercury. He would be able to jump over an elephant.

**VENUS** is the second planet from the sun and the sixth largest. It is named the Evening Star because it shines brighter than any other planet or star. Venus travels around the sun in a circular orbit. It revolves around the sun in 225 days. It is almost the same size as the Earth, its diameter is 7,600 miles. Venus' pull of gravity is also nearly the same as the Earth's. A man who weighed 150 pounds on Earth would weigh about 135 pounds on Venus. Venus is the planet closest to the Earth, surrounded by a layer of white clouds composed of sulfuric acid. These clouds completely obscure our view of the surface. A glowing halo of hydrogen surrounds Venus, about 1,800 miles above its surface. The atmosphere of Venus is made up chiefly of carbon dioxide gas. The surface temperature of the planet is about 536 degrees (hot enough to melt lead).

**EARTH** is the third planet from the sun, about 93 million miles from the sun. It is the fifth largest planet and the densest major body in the solar system. Simply put, the Earth is a ball of rock and metal that is about 4.5 to 4.6 billion years old. The estimated weight of our planet is 6,580,000,000,000,000,000,000 tons.

Three-fourths of Earth's surface is water. One-fifth of the land surface is mountains. Earth travels around the sun in a circular orbit. It takes about 365 days to make one orbit of the sun. It takes almost 24 hours to rotate once on its axis. It is surrounded by a thin atmosphere of nitrogen and oxygen. The oxygen in Earth's atmosphere is produced and maintained by biological processes. Without life there would be no free oxygen. Earth's diameter is 7,913 miles. Everything falls to the ground, since there is a strong pull of gravity. The hottest recorded temperature on Earth is 58 degrees Celsius in Lybia which is 136.4 degrees Fahrenheit, and the coldest was -89 degrees Celsius (-128.2 degrees Fahrenheit) in Vostok, Antarctica where nobody lives. The lowest recorded temperature in an inhabited region is -72 degrees Celsius (-97.6 degrees Fahrenheit) in the Siberian Village of Oymyakon, Russia. The temperature of the Earth's core is believed to be 4,000 degrees Celsius.

**MARS** is the fourth planet from the sun, about 142 million miles away. It is the seventh largest planet; it takes 687 days to revolve around the sun. Its orbit is an ellipse. Mars is called the Red Planet because it shines in the sky with a reddish color. At its closest, it is 128,500,000 miles from the sun, at its farthest it is 154,500,000 miles. Mars is a small, rocky world that measures 4,200 miles in diameter. It contains the largest volcano in the solar system, Olympus Mons, which is 15 miles high, almost three times higher than Mount Everest, the highest mountain on Earth. Spirit and Opportunity are Rovers sent to Mars to see if life did exist on the planet. The Martian atmosphere is made up mainly of carbon dioxide, there is little if any oxygen. A man weighing 150 pounds on Earth would weigh 57 pounds on Mars. The hottest temperature on Mars is about 70 degrees Fahrenheit on a hot day at the equator, at the poles which are covered with ice in the winter, the temperatures drop to 150 degrees below zero.

**JUPITER** is the fifth planet from the sun, about 484 million miles away. It is the largest planet; its diameter is almost 11 times the size of the earth. Jupiter takes 11.9 years to revolve around the sun. The planet spins very quickly, it takes less than 10 hours to rotate once. Jupiter radiates more energy into space than it receives from the Sun. It is surrounded by clouds that are thousands of miles deep, composed of 90% hydrogen and 10% helium. The temperature at the top of the cloud layers is about 202 degrees below zero. The gases surrounding the planet are moving at different speeds, creating bands of colors in the cloud layers. The pull of gravity is about two and a half times stronger than Earth's. A man weighing 150 pounds on Earth would weigh about 397 pounds on Jupiter.

**SATURN** is the sixth planet from the sun, about 888 million miles away. It was the first known planet. Galileo was the first to observe it with a telescope in 1610, since it is a very large planet. It takes nearly 29 years to make one trip around the sun. Saturn is not quite as large as Jupiter. Its diameter is about nine times that of Earth. Saturn rotates very quickly. The planet takes only 10 hours and two minutes to turn once on its axis. Saturn's atmosphere is surrounded by 75% hydrogen and 25% helium. The winds on Saturn blow at about 900 miles an hour—about six times stronger than hurricane-force winds on Earth. Its gravitational pull is a little less than the pull of Earth. Saturn can be distinguished by the flat rings that circle its equator that seem to be composed primarily of water and ice, but they may also include rocky particles with icy coatings.

**URANUS** is the seventh planet from the sun, about 1.8 billion miles away. It is the third largest, about four times larger than Earth. A year on Uranus, or the time it takes to revolve around the sun, is 84 years on Earth. It spins on its side; its axis is tilted nearly 98 degrees. Observed through a telescope, Uranus appears to be slightly blue, the result of absorption of red light by methane in the upper atmosphere, surrounded by 11 rings that appear as a broad band of a silvery color around its equator. Uranus is composed primarily of rock and various ices. The gravitational pull is a little more than Earth's. A man weighing 150 pounds on Earth would weigh 162 pounds on Uranus.

**NEPTUNE** is the eighth planet from the sun, about 2.8 billion miles away from it. Pluto's orbit is so eccentric, it sometimes crosses the orbit of Neptune making Neptune the most distant planet from the sun. Its diameter is 30,603 miles, and it takes 165 years to revolve around the sun. Neptune has rapid winds confined to bands of latitude, Neptune's winds are the fastest in the solar system, reaching 2000 km/hour. Like Jupiter and Saturn, Neptune has an internal heat source— it radiates more than twice as much energy as it receives from the sun. Neptune looks like a twin of Uranus. It has almost the same diameter and it also appears as a dim blue-green object with a few bands of color around it. Scientists believe that the surface of the planet is very hot. A man weighing 150 pounds on Earth would weigh about 165 pounds on Neptune.

**PLUTO** was considered a planet until 2006, when it was reclassified as a dwarf planet by the International Astronomy Union. It was discovered by Clyde Tombaugh at Lowell Observatory in 1930. Pluto is approximately 3.6 billion miles away from the sun. Any atmosphere surrounding Pluto must be frozen. The temperatures probably never rise beyond 348 degrees below zero. Pluto has not been visited by a spacecraft. Its diameter is half the width of the earth. Pluto's orbit is a long ellipse. It rotates in the opposite direction from most of the other eight planets. Pluto is about 35,000,000 miles closer to the sun than Neptune. Pluto's journey around the sun takes about 248.4 earth years.

# Sign Language

## The American Manual Alphabet

Drawings show a side view. In actual practice the letters should face the persons with whom you are communicating.

# BRAILLE

*The numeral symbol indicates that the letters A–J are being used as digits.*

*"There is a wonder in reading Braille that the sighted will never know: to touch words and have them touch you back."*
Jack Fiebig

# *The Longest Word*
## *in the English Language*

Methionylglutaminylarginyltyrosylglutamylserylleucylphenylalanylalanyl-
glutaminylleucyllysylglutamylarginyllysylglutamylglysylalanylphenylalanylvalyl-
Prolylphenylalanylyalylthreonylleucylglcycylaspartylprolylglicylisoleucy-
glutamylglutaminlserylleucyllysylisoleucylaspartylthreonylleucylisoleu-
cylglutamylalanylglyclyalanylaspartylalanylleucyglutamylleucylgluycyliso-
leucylproluylphenylalanyserylaspartyprolylleucelalanylaspartylglycylprolylthreo-
Nylisolleucyglutaminylasparaginylalanythreonylleucylarginylalanylphenylalany-
Lalanylalanylglycylvalylthreonylprolylalanylglutaminylcysteinylphenylalanyl-
Glglutamylmethionylleucyalanylleucylisoleucylarginylglutaminyllysylhistidyl-
Prolyuthreonylisoleucylprolylisoleucylglycyllleucyllleucylmethionyltyrosylalany-
Lasbaraginylleucylvalylphenylalanylsparaginyyllysylglycylisoleucylaspartyl-
Glutamylphenylalanylyltyrosylalanylglutaminylcysteinylglutamyllysylvalyl-
Glycylvalylspartylserylvalylleucylvallalanylaspartylvalylprolylvalvlglutaminyl-
Glutamylserylalanylprolylphenylalalrginylglutaminylalanylalanylleucylarginyl-
Histidylasparaginylvalylalalprolylisoleucylphenylalanylisoleucylcysteinylproly-
Prolylaspartylalanylaspartylaspartyspartyleucylleucylarginylglutaminylisoleucy-
Lalanylseryltyroslglycylarginylglycyltyrosylthreonyltyrosylleucylleucylsery-
larginlalanylglycylvalylthreonylglycylalanylglutamylasparaginylarginyla-
nylalanylleucylprolylleucylaspaaginylhistidylleucylvalylalanyllysylleucylly-
sylglutamyltyrosylasparagimylalanylalanyprolylprolylleucylglutaminylglycyl-
phenlalanylglycylisoleyucylserylalanylprolylaspartylglutaminylvalyllysylalany-
lalanylisoleucylalspartylalanylglycylalanylalanylglycylalanylasoleucylse-
rylglycylserylalanylisoleucylbalyllysylisoleucylisoleucylglutamylglutaminyl-
histidylasparaginylisoleucylglutamylpronylglu-0-tamyllysylmethionylluecy-
lalanylalanyoeucyllysylvalylphenylalanylvalylglutamilylprolylmethionylly-
sylalanylalanylthreonylarginylserine.

This word consists of 1,909 letters. It is the term for the formula
$C1289H2051N343O375S8$. A Tryptophan synthetase A protein,
an enzyme that has 267 amino acids.